# A WANDERER ALL MY DAYS

Written with the patience of a true scholar and the pleasure of an aficionado, J. Parker Huber's *A Wanderer All My Days: John Muir in New England* is a delightful and deeply informative book. Huber is steeped in the lore of Muir's life and travels. As a result, he has uncovered and delineated the vast network of Muir's associations with the literary and naturalist luminaries of America's early era of conservation, including many highly accomplished women. For the modern pilgrim, Huber's book offers the added bonus of maps and geographical commentary. From years of assiduously tracking Muir's footsteps throughout New England—much of it hallowed ground—the author preserves Muir's intriguing trail from vanishing into the ever-diminishing past. Richly detailed and informative, composed out of Huber's hard-earned intimacy with its subject, *A Wanderer All My Days* illuminates as never before John Muir's connection to the New England landscape.

> —Robert J. Begiebing, Professor of English and Director of Creative Writing at Southern New Hampshire University, and author of many books, most recently *Rebecca Wentworth's Distraction*

John Muir will always be primarily associated with the sublime wilderness of the Sierra Nevada and Alaska. But Parker Huber now offers an engrossing account of Muir's five pilgrimages to New England, over the two decades starting in 1893. *A Wanderer All My Days* skillfully incorporates the landscape and culture of the East into the larger map of Muir's achievement in a way that is thoroughly enjoyable.

> —John Elder, Professor of English and Environmental Studies at Middlebury College, and author of many books including *Imagining the Earth: Poetry and the Vision of Nature* and *Reading the Mountains of Home*

A luminous contribution to Muir scholarship, *A Wanderer All My Days* artfully reconstructs the Great Man's five trips to New England between 1893 and 1912. But this is so much more than a simple chronicle; J. Parker Huber effortlessly places us in the culture of that time in America, acts as our guide in retracing Muir's steps, and most helpfully, includes a series of wonderful maps (lovingly rendered by Jennifer Irion) that light the way for those of us eager to recreate one or more of Muir's sojourns. Muir is revered on the west coast as the founder of the Sierra Club, and students of environmental history will be familiar with his famous oratory battles in Washington, D.C. with Gifford Pinchot over the flooding of the Hetch Hetchy valley in Yosemite National Park. What is less well known, and what ultimately makes *A Wanderer All My Days* such a welcome addition to the Muir canon, is the sense of Muir as a private citizen, indulging his passion for relaxed travel. In placing us beside Muir in his saunters through the New England towns and countryside of turn-of-the-century America, Huber reminds us, as Muir would have wanted, that if we take the time to experience the land, we will learn much from it.

—Robert M. Abbott, founder of Abbott Strategies, and editor of *Uncommon Cents: Henry David Thoreau and the Nature of Business*, published by Green Frigate Books

J. Parker Huber's absorbing and prodigiously researched narrative of John Muir's five trips to New England will fascinate those who admire Muir and want to know more about the scores of people and places he encountered. This many-layered book conveys Muir's love of nature and his "passionate caring" about everything he saw. Along the way, Huber takes note of the overlapping paths followed by others like Thoreau and Emerson, and carries the reader with him as he follows in Muir's footsteps.

—Rita K. Gollin, distinguished Professor of English, Emerita and SUNY Geneseo, and author of many books including *Portraits of Nathaniel Hawthorne: An Iconography* and *Annie Adams Fields: Woman of Letters*

A rich banquet for anyone interested in John Muir or New England. Parker Huber shows that the two subjects, not often linked, belong together. Though usually identified with California's Yosemite Valley and Sierra Nevada, Muir was first published in Boston, and most of his major intellectual enthusiasms and connections were New Englanders. Huber's stupendous research and passionate engagement with his subject have produced an implicit re-visioning of Muir's ties to the human world. The book also tracks the living connections between Muir's New England and today's, bringing the past forward to the present. When we go into nature, Muir liked to say, the clock stops and experience becomes timeless. After fifteen years of scholarly love and well-steeped devotion, Huber has absorbed Muir's New England essence and brought him back alive.

—Stephen Fox, writer and author of many books including *John Muir and His Legacy: The American Conservation Movement*

John Muir has been described as a "wilderness saint," and the commentary devoted to him often seems to have extracted every possible meaning from his life and work. J. Parker Huber nevertheless illuminates an essential and underappreciated dimension of Muir's personality and intellect. Muir's many cultural and personal connections to New England are assiduously researched. Huber allows us to make the same journeys, see the same places, and meet the many eastern cultural figures that Muir knew well. The author demonstrates, with amazing detail, how both the landscapes and the cultural life of New England were indeed "part of Muir's soul."

—Ethan Carr, Assistant Professor of Landscape Architecture at the University of Massachusetts, Amherst, Visiting Professor, Bard Graduate Center and author of *Wilderness by Design: Landscape Architecture and the National Park Service*

J. Parker Huber's book, *A Wanderer All My Days*, is truly humbling in its degree of scholarship displayed. At the same time, the reader is happily drawn into the world of New England letters and landscapes with an intimacy so detailed that it almost feels as if one is a voyeur looking over John Muir's shoulder as he saunters along with his characteristic curiosity about all that he encounters. We tend to delineate our world into elements that are either of "nature" or of "culture." In contrast, this important book clearly demonstrates that at least for Muir, the master integrator, such a dichotomization is a false way in which to view our cultural landscapes.

—Robert France, Associate Professor of Landscape Ecology at Harvard University, and author or editor of many books including *Deep Immersion: The Experience of Water* and *Profitably Soaked: Thoreau's Engagement With Water*, both published by Green Frigate Books

# A Wanderer All My Days

## OTHER BOOKS BY J. PARKER HUBER

*The Wildest Country: A Guide to Thoreau's Maine*
*Elevating Ourselves: Thoreau on Mountains*

## OTHER GREEN FRIGATE BOOKS

### Published Titles

*Deep Immersion: The Experience of Water*—Robert Lawrence France

*Liquid Gold: The Lore and Logic of Using Urine to Grow Plants*—Carol Steinfeld

*Profitably Soaked: Thoreau's Engagement With Water*—Robert Lawrence France

### Forthcoming Titles

*Uncommon Cents: Thoreau and the Nature of Business*—Robert M. Abbott

*Wetlands of Mass Destruction: Ancient Presage for Contemporary Ecocide in Southern Iraq*—Robert Lawrence France

*Where We Live: Chasing the Dream of Urban Sustainability*—Robert M. Abbott and Mark Holland

*Ultreia! Onward! Progress of the Pilgrim*—Robert Lawrence France

# A Wanderer All My Days

### John Muir in New England

## J. Parker Huber

**Green Frigate Books**

**Sheffield, Vermont**

**2006**

First Edition

Printed in Canada

Huber, J. Parker
>A Wanderer All My Days: John Muir in New England
>Foreword by Michael P. Branch
>LCCN: 2005936017
>ISBN: 0-9717468-4-2
>ISBN13: 978-0-9717468-4-8
>1.John Muir. 2. New England. 3. Travel. 4. American letters.
>5. Landscapes. 6. Huber, J. Parker.

Sections previously occurred in *The Concord Saunterer* (Fall 1995: 104-118, Fall 1997:132-154, 2000:102-125, and 2003:38-49)

Cover by Jennifer Irion. It includes Jerome B. Thompson (American: 1814-1886), *The Belated Party on Mansfield Mountain*, 1858, Oil on canvas: 38 x 63 1/8 in. (96.5 x 160.3 cm): "The Metropolitan Museum, Purchase, Rogers Fund, 1969 (69.182) Photograph copyright 1983 The Metropolitan Museum of Art," and John Muir's letter and photograph from the Holt-Atherton Special Collections, University of the Pacific Libraries, Stockton, California, Copyright 1984 Muir-Hanna Trust, all of which are used with permission.

Printing this book on 100% recycled stock has saved:
>13.1 trees (40' tall and 6-8" diameter); 5,554 gallons of water;
>2,234 kilowatt hours of electricity, 612 pounds of solid waste;
>1,203 pounds of greenhouse gases.

# For
# Jennifer

"the Love which moves the sun and the other stars."

—Longfellow's translation of the final words of Dante's *Paradiso*

Dec 3 [1999]

Yesterday to Boston. It was all so lovely. We are in that place of deep connection where every little moment becomes illuminated—elevated—so that we are alive to one another in the most delicious way. We walk through Beacon Hill. I am deeply moved by the presence of a most exquisite flower shop. It calls to me—Why?

Jennifer's Journal

# CONTENTS

# MAPS BY JENNIFER IRION

An asterisk in the legend indicates that the building is no longer there.

# FOREWORD

*A Rambling Life*

"Every excursion I have made in all my rambling life has been fruitful and delightful," wrote John Muir, "from the smallest indefinite saunter an hour or two in length to the noblest summer's flight with steady aim like a crusader bound for the Holy Land or a bird to its northern home following the flight of the seasons." And while many think of Muir's "Holy Land" as the Sierra Nevada, the celebrated mountain wilderness he famously called "the Range of Light," Muir certainly did lead a rambling life. He was a saunterer in the Thoreauvian sense, and the inspired crusades of his many fine walks took him far beyond the deep shadows of Yosemite Valley's Half Dome and El Capitan.

In addition to walking, climbing, and exploring much of the American West—from the flaming redrock depths of the Grand Canyon to the snow-capped volcanic heights of the Cascades—Muir also made many trips to the wild country of Alaska, and he botanized in Canada for seven months during 1864. In 1893 he traveled throughout Europe, and in 1903-1904 he made a year-long journey around the world, visiting places as far-flung as western Europe, Siberia, Manchuria, China, India, Egypt, Australia, New Zealand, Malasia, and Japan. Even into this seventies Muir was an indefatigable traveler, and in 1911-1912 he made an eight-month, 40,000-mile journey through South America and Africa. By the time John Muir died on Christmas Eve, 1914, he had in fact sauntered all over the globe. When in his later years, Muir was asked about his occupation, he often gave a simple reply: "Tramp." John Muir was, as Parker Huber's title reminds us, a wanderer all his days; and he was, as Muir himself insisted, "good at it."

Between John Muir's journeys in the American West and his journeys around the world, however, another body of Muir's travels has remained largely unexamined. These travels, so richly chronicled in *A Wanderer All My Days*, are Muir's five trips to New England, made in 1893, 1896, 1898, 1903, and 1911-1912. And what remarkable trips these were! Thanks to Parker Huber's meticulous literary detective work, we can at last read the fascinating New England chapter in Muir's lifelong book of travels. Although Muir is rarely associated with eastern landscapes, he experienced many of them during this clutch of rewarding trips to New England. Here we see John O' Mountains not in the Sierra or Cascades, but in the White Mountains of New

Hampshire and the Green Mountains of Vermont—along the rocky coast of Maine rather than among the glacially-polished rocks of California, on the shores of Cape Cod instead of the sands of the Mojave, training north past Lake George and the Adirondacks rather than paddling into an Alaskan fiord. As we learn here, Muir's eastern journeys, though centered in New England, actually took him from Montreal to Key West, and many points between. But Muir was Muir wherever he went, and so we see in the story of eastern travels a man whose sensibility was keenly attuned to the beauty of nature in all places and all seasons. Muir's scientific, aesthetic, and spiritual appreciation of the natural world remain tightly braided, and he brings to his experiences of New England landscapes both the understanding of the scientist and the enthusiasm and curiosity of the *amateur*—a word that grew from the *love* at its etymological root.

Much of the charm and interest of John Muir's New England travels comes from his visits to landscapes of great cultural and literary significance. Among my favorites is his pilgrimage to Concord, Massachusetts, the hub of American Transcendentalism, during his first visit to the region in 1893. Accompanied by his friend, *Century* editor Robert Underwood Johnson, Muir rambled the maple-lined dirt roads of the famous village. He visited the "Old Manse," the house built by Ralph Waldo Emerson's grandfather and celebrated by Nathaniel Hawthorne, who lived in the home with his new bride, Sophia, as he wrote many of the stories included in *Mosses from an Old Manse*—published in 1846, the year that Concord neighbor Henry David Thoreau was living and writing at Walden Pond. Nearby the Manse, Muir visited the old North Bridge over the lovely Concord River, where, as Emerson famously put it in verse, embattled farmers fired "the shot heard round the world" in the opening skirmishes of the American Revolution. Muir also visited the final resting places of Emerson and Thoreau, on a wooded ridge in Sleepy Hollow Cemetery, where he laid flowers on the Transcendentalists' graves and declared Sleepy Hollow "the most beautiful graveyard I ever saw." And Muir paid respects to perhaps his greatest literary predecessor at Walden Pond, where he enthusiastically celebrated the beauty of the place itself. Walden is "fairly embosomed like a bright dark eye in wooded hills," Muir wrote. "No wonder Thoreau lived here two years. I could have enjoyed living here two hundred years or two thousand."

Also fascinating are Muir's visits to major American cultural landscapes and landmarks with which he has never before been associated. In 1896, for example, he traveled to Cambridge to receive an honorary degree from the institution at which he had adamantly refused to teach: Harvard. Two years later he visited Washington, D.C. and marveled at both the autumnal glory of eastern oaks and the grandeur of the Library of Congress. And, despite its being only a fifth of the height of the sheer rock face of Yosemite's El Capitan, Muir was deeply impressed as he stood at the foot of the 555-foot marble cliff that is the Washington Monument. Muir's eastern journeys were also regularly punctuated by visits to a variety of interesting cultural events: the World's Fair in Chicago in 1893; the celebration of the centennial of Emerson's birth in Boston in 1903; a Yale baseball game in New Haven in 1911; John Burroughs's seventy-fifth birthday party in New York in 1912.

When readers often picture Muir alone, scrambling through the high Sierra with only a blanket and a bit of bread and tea, he was in fact a public figure with extensive and often treasured connections to many of the major figures of his day. Parker Huber's account of Muir's New England journeys is thus replete with Muir's meetings with scientists, writers, artists, politicians, and environmentalists. How many of us know that John Muir met and talked with Sarah Orne Jewett, author of the New England classic *The Country of the Pointed Firs* (1896)? Or that he knew Charles Dudley Warner, the writer, who, along with his friend Mark Twain, gave the "Gilded Age" its name? In *A Wanderer All My Days* we have the pleasure of seeing Muir's reaction after being introduced to Gifford Pinchot, with whom he would later differ so strongly on issues of forest preservation. We learn of Muir's friendships with such leading scientists as ichthyologist David Starr Jordan, botanist Charles Sprague Sargent, and paleontologist Henry Fairfield Osborn. Indeed, Parker Huber tells us the stories of Muir's encounters with everyone from fellow nature writers, like Bradford Torrey and John Burroughs, to U.S. Presidents including Theodore Roosevelt and William Howard Taft. But these human connections don't end with Muir's meetings, for *A Wanderer All My Days* also tells the stories of figures Muir did not meet, but who were important to him or to the places he visited. For example, Parker Huber's rich treatment of the landscape through which Muir traveled includes discussion not only of the Transcendentalists, but also of Nathaniel Hawthorne, Henry Adams, Emily Dickinson, James Russell Lowell, Henry Wadsworth Longfellow, Richard Henry Dana, William Dean Howells, Mark Twain, William James, and many others.

In order to tell the compelling story of Muir's New England travels, Parker

Huber has had to make a journey of his own—one that has included patient research, wide-ranging fieldwork, and a rich imagination firmly guided by a sensitivity to the natural landscapes of New England and a deep understanding of the complex field of cultural currents and contacts through which Muir moved. It has been said that Henry James is the novelist whose work best exemplifies the use of third-person omniscient narration, for in a James novel the narrator even knows what the dogs are thinking. Parker Huber's command of the cultural context of Muir's New England travels is nearly as extensive and penetrating. He has used every source available, from Muir's unpublished journals and correspondence, to period newspapers, to his own rambles in Muir's footsteps, in order to reconstruct Muir's eastern journeys. Rather than simply relate the few known facts of Muir's rambles in Concord, for example, Parker Huber also tells us what the weather was like when Muir stepped off the train from Boston at just after noon on Thursday, June 8, 1893. We learn whose houses Muir walked past, and who was home that day. We hear stories of the lives and work of those neighbors, and are offered surprising and interesting connections among them and between them and Muir—and Muir's own friends, neighbors, and influences. We're told what sorts of books were in the village's public library in the summer of 1893, and which of them Muir had read to his daughters in California. Indeed, Parker Huber's ability to reveal layer upon layer of natural and cultural interconnections in the New England of Muir's day makes *A Wanderer All My Days* a world of its own—an animated, interesting, nuanced world that we, too, want to ramble through. This book is not, ultimately, just a story about what John Muir did on his summer (and fall, winter, and spring) vacations back east. Instead, it is a richly detailed study, *in situ*, of the constellation of people and events, natural landscapes and cultural sites, within which Muir experienced late nineteenth and early twentieth-century New England. In this book we not only see Muir, we also see him seeing, and we see what he saw.

In the flyleaf of his very first travel journal, begun as he prepared to walk 1,000 miles from Indianapolis to the Gulf of Mexico in 1867, John Muir penned a now-famous inscription to identify the journal as his own and simultaneously to locate himself in the cosmos: "John Muir, Earth-planet, Universe." Thanks to Parker Huber's *A Wanderer All My Days*, we now understand the important place of New England in the rich universe of John Muir's travels.

Michael P. Branch

29 April 2005

Michael P. Branch is Professor of Literature and Environment at the University of Nevada, Reno, and editor of *John Muir's Last Journey* (Island Press, 2001) and *Reading the Roots: American Nature Writing before Walden* (The University of Georgia Press, 2004).

# I HAVE NO DOUBT I'LL BE
## A WANDERER ALL MY DAYS

—John Muir
*Riverside Daily Press*
21 January 1911

# PROLOGUE: CONNECTIONS

*I cannot rest from travel…*
*I am a part of all that I have met.*
—Tennyson, "Ulysses"

## MAY 1869

In May 1869, two Americans, who had been born four days apart in March 1834, came to leadership positions. In the East, the MIT chemistry professor Charles William Eliot was elected president of Harvard College, a succession opposed by the eminent geologist Louis Agassiz. In the West, the one-armed Civil War veteran John Wesley Powell left Green River Station, Wyoming, in a fleet of four specially made oak and pine boats to begin exploring the Green and Colorado rivers; three months later, he would emerge triumphantly from the Grand Canyon. Seventeen years later, in early November 1886, at the celebration of Harvard's 250th anniversary, President Eliot would confer one of forty-two honorary degrees on a Washington bureaucrat—the head of the U.S. Geological Survey and the Bureau of Ethnology—John Wesley Powell.[1] During his forty years as Harvard president, Eliot would transform education by adopting an elective curriculum and overseeing the founding of Radcliffe College. He would retire in 1909, seven years after the death of Powell in 1902 in Haven, Maine—a hamlet separated by lovely Blue Hill Bay from Eliot's retreat in Northeast Harbor, on Mount Desert Island.

That May thirty-one-year-old John Muir prepared to tend flocks of sheep in the Sierra Nevada. Muir had arrived in San Francisco by sea from New York the previous spring (on 28 March 1868), a part of the mythmaking North American westward migration.[2] His arrival had coincided with an especially snowy season that compounded the work of the Central Pacific Railroad. The CP chose to cross the Sierra Nevada through the 7,135-foot-high Donner Pass, north of Lake Tahoe—for years the way west of migrants—where forty-seven of eighty-seven pioneers under George Donner had perished while snowbound in autumn 1846. In October 1874, at the campground of the Donner party, Muir would reflect, "They were not good mountaineers or they would not have suffered. The whole winter could have been spent delightfully in so beautiful a spot." Marveling at the geology, he would praise the railroad's engineers for selecting a route that he observed lay along the moraines of glaciers which here had made their deepest cut.[3]

In that March of 1868, more than fifteen feet of snow had buried the CP's track and its roadbed. Early April's warm weather and melting snow had encouraged completion of the summit transit. Then, on the 10th, four feet of fresh snow had fallen on the summit and sent two avalanches over the line. Several thousand Chinese workers had shoveled and shoveled eleven hours a day for two months, to clear the path. Finally, in mid-June, after a twenty-four-hour period of snow and rain, the passage had been finished.[4]

Mark Twain had made this mountain crossing that spring. Arriving in San Francisco via steamer from Panama late in the afternoon of 2 April 1868, five days after Muir, he had given his first San Francisco lecture on 14 April. Two days later he had taken a steamer to Sacramento, where he had lectured again on the night of the 17th. "I have had the *hardest* trip over the Sierras," Twain had written his mother from Virginia City, Nevada. "Steamboat to Sacramento (balmy summer weather & the peaches & roses all in bloom)—railway to the summit (snow thirty feet deep on level ground & 100 in the drifts)—6-horse sleighs to Donner Lake—mail coaches to Coburn's—railway to Hunter's—stage-coaches to Virginia—all in the space of 24 hours." Twain had found tiresome "the shift from cars to stages and back again every now and then in the mountains." He had recalled his earlier passage in the spring of 1864: "We used to rattle across all the way by stage, and never mind it at all, save that we had to ride thirty hours without stopping." After lecturing in Virginia City and Carson City, Twain had returned to San Francisco on 5 May via the same pass. There he had worked furiously each night on *The Innocents Abroad*. In July he had traveled back to New York.[5]

That May of 1869, Annie Adams Fields and her husband, the publisher James Fields of Boston toured about London. The most famous writer in the world, Charles Dickens, was their host. They had embraced Dickens when he came to Boston in November 1867 for his second American tour, which had lasted five months. Henry Wadsworth Longfellow still hoped to see the Fieldses while they were abroad: "We find it hard to get out of Italy, or any other country," he explained their inertia to Annie later in the month from Cadenabbia, on the western shore of Lake Como. "There never was a family that dragged along like this. Every town seems a quicksand, in which we sink to the knees."[6]

On the clear Monday of 10 May 1869, the iron railroads of the Central Pacific and the Union Pacific—ten spikes to a rail, four hundred rails to a mile—converged at Promontory Summit, Utah. The strokes of the hammer on the last spike, telegraphed to New York and San Francisco, excited jubilation. Mark Twain heard them repeated on the great fire bell in Hartford, Connecticut, while he read page proofs of *The Innocents Abroad*, the first copies of which came out two months later, on 20 July. That May day he also wrote his agent James Redpath in Boston about possible California lectures, since the railroad's completion had focused "so much attention in that direction." Instead of going west that fall, however, Twain toured New England. On 10 November, he spoke for the first time in Boston, at the Music Hall, before "4,000 critics" (actually the hall seated only about 2,600), on "Our Fellow Savages of the Sandwich Islands." It was Mark Twain and Charles Dudley Warner who designated this period the Gilded Age.[7]

The press quickly alerted others to the momentous Western event. "The Pacific Railroad—Open: How to Go:What to See" by Samuel Bowles, editor of the Springfield, Massachusetts, *Republican*, began running in the *Atlantic* for April 1869. In May and June, the *Atlantic* reader had a glimpse of urban and wild California—respectively, San Francisco and the Yosemite and Hetch Hetchy valleys, the Big Trees of the Mariposa and Calaveras groves and the High Sierra—forests and mountains that Muir would zealously adopt, study, describe, and worship. Bowles recommended that "a full purse, Professor Whitney's new and model guide-book and maps…and a camping suit, with duster and overcoat" accompany the tourist.[8]

Also featured in the May 1869 *Atlantic* was "Spring in Washington," written during his free time while counting currency at the Treasury by a thirty-two-year-old federal employee, John Burroughs. Weekends Burroughs spent with nature. Four years earlier, on Saturday, 4 March 1865, Burroughs had "thought it more desirable to see Spring inaugurated than President Lincoln." Though he greatly admired the president, he had rambled nearby woods that day, finding bluets blooming.[9]

Rapidly, railroads became the primary means of crossing North America. Overland travel from coast to coast was reduced from months to days. Railroad would facilitate Muir's connection with people and places. He would meet President Eliot of Harvard, Annie Fields, John Burroughs, Mark Twain, Charles Dudley Warner, and others in the East, even visit Longfellow's home in Cambridge after the poet's death, and be introduced to the Washington of John Wesley Powell.

Mail no longer required two to three weeks to travel between San Francisco and New York. There were delays, of course: In January 1895, when sending a photograph of the Muir Glacier to the Century Company in New York to accompany his article on "The Discovery of Glacier Bay," Muir would report: "It is now snowing gloriously on the Sierra & has been for a week, all trains stalled. Ten to twenty feet on the level. Heavens how I should enjoy a week[']s snowshoeing." His letter would take ten days to reach its destination.[10]

## THE WANDERER

Travel was Muir's passion; roving was a state of his being. He discovered glaciers in the Sierra Nevada of California and along the Alaskan coast. He went to great depths to see the strata of the Grand Canyon and climbed to great heights to sleep under sugar pines. In his sixties and seventies, he joined Sierra Club Outings with one to two hundred other ecstatic campers. Like a bear, he could roam anywhere.

In *River-Horse: The Logbook of a Boat across America*, William Least Heat-Moon has admitted that he has "never been as interested in where I am as in what it was like to get there."[11] Muir was awake to the value of both processes. He liked moving and being in place. He was a seeker and a dweller. Muir had a sense of belonging that was both domestic and wild. Once landing in California at age thirty, Muir made that state his home for the rest of his life. From his marriage to Louie Strentzel, on 14 April 1880, until his death in 1914, thirty-four years later, Martinez was his residence. Yet his attachment to Yosemite and the Sierra Nevada never diminished. Nor could even the second largest state in the Union contain him.

Quartered for too long, Muir became frustrated. In 1894, the year after his first New England and European trip, which kept him away for five months, Muir settled into his study to read proofs for his first book, *The Mountains of California*. Eventually, the time turned fallow. "Not a single glacier in it," he wailed to a friend, "or piece of wild woods or garden." Still he heard "the hum of bees in the bryanthus beds on top of the Alaska mountains" and "the winds in the woods & the boom & crash & roar of avalanches & icebergs on the slopes of the peaks & at the heads of the icy fiords....This summer has been Saharaly hot[.] I have been hibernating—living on the fat of better times like a bear in its den."[12] The tension between motion and stillness animated his entire life.

His correspondence from afar reflected this dialogue. His longing to be with his family back on the ranch was expressed continually along with his enthusiasm for where and with whom he was. He filled his wife and daughters Helen and Wanda with descriptions of the wonders he saw. For the most part, this was happily received. Yet there were cautions: "O John why do you keep rushing along from place to place without resting," Louie asked the vagabond. She wanted him "to take better care of yourself for the sake of all who love you. We have all hoped that this grand journey will wonderfully strengthen and refresh you in every way and so thinking, we are contented to stay quietly at home."[13] That is to say, she was at peace with staying put with the family as long as his travels were salubrious. Wellness was an important reason for Muir's wanderings.

No sooner was he back from a year's circuit of the planet on 27 May 1904 than he was off again. Eight days later, on Saturday night, 4 June, he and his two daughters and their friend William Keith boarded a train for a ten-day excursion to Arizona. From the south rim of the Grand Canyon, Wanda Muir wrote her mother, who stayed behind, of their ecstatic witness of a thunderstorm that morning. "Papa keeps finding people that he knows," she added, "and the circle around our campfire keeps steadily growing." On to the Petrified Forest they went, before returning to Martinez on 14 June.[14]

Muir's mobility signifies something deeper. He did crave constant contact with the landscape; he searched far and wide to know its features, forests, flora. And too much of the sedentary life did make him ill. Yet sometimes sickness beset him while on the go as well. His cross-country trip to Massachu-setts in 1898 caused indigestion, for example, and recovery did not come until he was high in the southern Appalachians.  After being in New York and Boston, London and Edinburgh in 1893, he confessed, "it seemed very hard work to travel in a civilized tourist way & I got very tired of it."[15] His preference was to be outside afoot, not inside machines or residences. That kind of natural travel nourished him most. Wilderness restored his wholeness. Had he found there, as Sarah Orne Jewett advised Willa Cather to find, his "own quiet centre of life"? Or was he seeking something in the external world that would quell an inner restlessness? Equipoise dominated his character at home and afield; that balance enabled him to touch lovingly many places and people.[16]

"You know I never like to travel," he revealed to his daughter Helen before his last great odyssey, "and somehow I feel less and less inclined to leave home than ever." Having made this confession, though, he cast away again. Like the great Japanese poet Bashō, Muir's desire to wander was strong.[17]

## NEW ENGLAND

Less well known than Muir's wild track are his excursions to the Eastern Seaboard and its urban areas. Like tundra swans migrating from the Alaskan Arctic to the Atlantic Coast, Muir came east five times by train for reasons mainly social, literary, and arboreal. He returned to California four times by train, once by ship.

New England was part of Muir's soul. He imbibed it from various sources. His direct association with the region spanned two decades. In all he spent about five weeks there at the end of the nineteenth and the beginning of the twentieth centuries. He came first to eastern Massachusetts—Concord, Cambridge, Brookline, Boston, Cape Ann—for five days of June 1893. On his second and shortest trip, he returned to Cambridge for Harvard's commencement on 24 June 1896. His longest visit—in both duration and itinerary—took in the familiar Brookline, Boston. and Cambridge, and added Vermont, New Hampshire, and Maine, as well as Cape Cod, Wellesley, and the Berkshires of Massachusetts. His fourth trip brought him back to Boston and Brookline for four days in May 1903. Boston and New Haven were his final destinations, in May and June 1911, respectively.[18] His last day in New England was spent in Boston in April 1912.

Both public and private places accommodated Muir. He slept two nights aboard trains moving through Maine and New Hampshire, a third while coming to Vermont via Albany and Montreal. Two of his hotels, the Green Mountain Inn in Stowe, Vermont, and the Bellevue in Boston, remain. Sadly, his primary New England residence, Holm Lea, the grand manor of Charles Sprague Sargent and Mary Robeson Sargent in Brookline, was demolished. Their summer cottage on Cape Cod, however, where he stayed one night, still looks seaward. He also enjoyed three other stays in places that survive: three days each at Four Brooks Farm in Tyringham, Massachusetts, with Richard Watson and Helena de Kay Gilder and at the home of William and Annabel Phelps in New Haven, and an overnight with Walter and Alice Page in Cambridge. Other homes that he visited for part of a day, such as Thunderbolt Hill on Cape Ann and Hunnewell's in Wellesley, serve their contemporary owners.

These peregrinations show Muir's gift to be with a variety of places and people and in different situations. While in New York in the spring of 1911, for example, he interspersed stays with the Harrimans in Manhattan and at their Catskill Mountains cottage and with the Osborns at Castle Rock in Garrison-on-the-Hudson with trips to Washington, D.C.; Rochester, Boston, and New Haven.

Over time it seemed Muir knew everyone, and vice versa. Moreover, he kept in touch. He was a superb conversationalist. He wrote articles, books, some sixty journals, and countless letters. He was a bibliophile. "Reading is being," to paraphrase Rilke, aptly characterized him. This endeavor was for him a way of listening. In his quiet hours, relationships were formed with writers and ideas.[19]

Muir "traveled" a great deal more in New England than his wanderings indicate. He also came to know the country through Yankees whose love of their land and its literature ran deep. Their writings and conversations expanded his horizons. Two in particular, became close friends: Jeanne Carr and Charles Sprague Sargent, natives of Vermont and Massachusetts respectively, provided him entrée to this landscape and its inhabitants.

Had Muir lingered on the East Coast in 1868—in Florida or Cuba or New York, for instance—there is the strong possibility that he would have come to New England then, a quarter century before he actually did. In May 1868, Jeanne Carr wrote Muir from Madison, Wisconsin, where they had met, inviting him to her birthplace, Castleton, Vermont, where she planned to spend the summer. By then, however, Muir was on the other side of the continent, and the chances of his returning were slim. Besides, as Muir wrote her at the end of July from near Snelling, California, he had not received any letters from her or anyone else.[20]

Jeanne Carr introduced Muir to Ralph Waldo Emerson, who visited Muir in Yosemite in 1871, and most likely to the writings of Henry David Thoreau, too. Often Muir's New England itinerary duplicated that of his mentors Thoreau and Emerson. His first days in Massachusetts brought him to their childhood city, Boston; their college, Harvard; and the town they became synonymous with, Concord. His 1898 solitary tour of the north woods, ostensibly to acquaint himself with this magnificent autumnal forest, also joined him with them. He rode up Mt. Mansfield in Vermont, where Emerson had slept; gazed upon Mt. Washington in New Hampshire, which Thoreau and Emerson had climbed; and touched Moosehead Lake in Maine, where Thoreau had canoed.

And there were others who acquainted Muir with this region. Two artists, Elizabeth and William Keith, who have not been mentioned in this role, steeped Muir in New England culture. The trio shared the same birth year of

1838. Elizabeth, a fourth cousin of Ralph Waldo Emerson and native of Thomaston, Maine, and William, who like Muir came from Scotland, were married in San Francisco in 1864. In the fall of 1869, the Keiths traveled by the new transcontinental railway to New England, where they stayed with her aunts, Jane Emerson and Margaret Emerson Hutchins, in Newcastle, Maine. This quiet village nestled next to the Damariscotta River, still tidal some fifteen miles from the sea. With great blue herons flying over deep green water, kingfishers chattering from riverside pines, cormorants fishing from wet rocks, alewives charging upstream another two miles to Damariscotta Lake to spawn each May, the scene provided much artistic inspiration for the Keiths. In February 1870, the couple sailed to Europe for further art education in Düsseldorf, Germany. Most of 1871 they spent in Maine, before going for the winter to Boston, where they worked in a studio in the Lawrence Building. The following year, in October 1872, William met Muir in Yosemite, thus beginning a lifelong friendship that included Elizabeth until her death in 1882.[21]

Vicariously, too, Muir went about New England with Thoreau. Unlike the earlier writer, whose *The Maine Woods* and *Cape Cod* exposed his excursions in detail, Muir left no rich narrative of his New England travels. This landscape was not a focus for Muir's literary energy, as it was for Thoreau's. Instead, Muir's experience was captured spontaneously, hastily, in journals and letters that as a result of their rapid execution left many spaces. These absences—of conversations, reading matter, menus, and what poet Philip Booth in "Seventy" called "the deep old dark"—arouse much curiosity.

Muir made his five transcontinental journeys alone. His wife, Louie, and their two daughters, Wanda and Helen, ages twelve and seven respectively at the time of the first trip, did not accompany him. Louie, besides was caring for her invalid mother until her death in 1897. A great benefit of their staying behind, however, is the track of his travels made in his handwritten letters home.

All of his five northeast passages were the beginnings of wider reaches. In 1893, Muir continued on to his native Scotland, as well as to Norway, Switzerland, and England. Three years later, after being in Cambridge, he toured the West with Charles Sprague Sargent and others of the Forestry Commission. In 1898, he joined Sargent and William Canby for another exploration of the Southern Appalachian forests, his first one having been on foot thirty-one-years earlier, in 1867. In 1903, he circled the planet for a year, part of the way with Sargent and his son Andrew. In 1911 he departed for the "hot continents" of South America and Africa, not returning home until a year later, shortly after his seventy-fourth birthday, having had "the most fruitful time of my life."[22]

In the last year of his long life, 1914, he remained relatively stationary. Insufferable grippe kept the venerable traveler housebound. He pecked away at his Alaska book. Two late summer sojourns to the Shasta forests uplifted his spirits. In December he packed his bags once more, and on the 17th entrained south to see Helen. A week later, on Christmas Eve, he died at the California Hospital in Los Angeles, "hopeful and cheerful to the very last," as his daughter Wanda divulged to Robert Underwood Johnson.[23]

As close as Muir was to people and places—and he had true love for many of both—his greatest connection was with what was beyond them. This invisible dimension suffused all his relationships. "Heaven guides us more than we know," he reflected on his life in a nine-page handwritten letter to an old Sierran friend, "& our fate none of us can forsee. Mine has been to wander in all wild places as a lover of nature[,] botanist, geologist, naturalist."[24]

# Concord

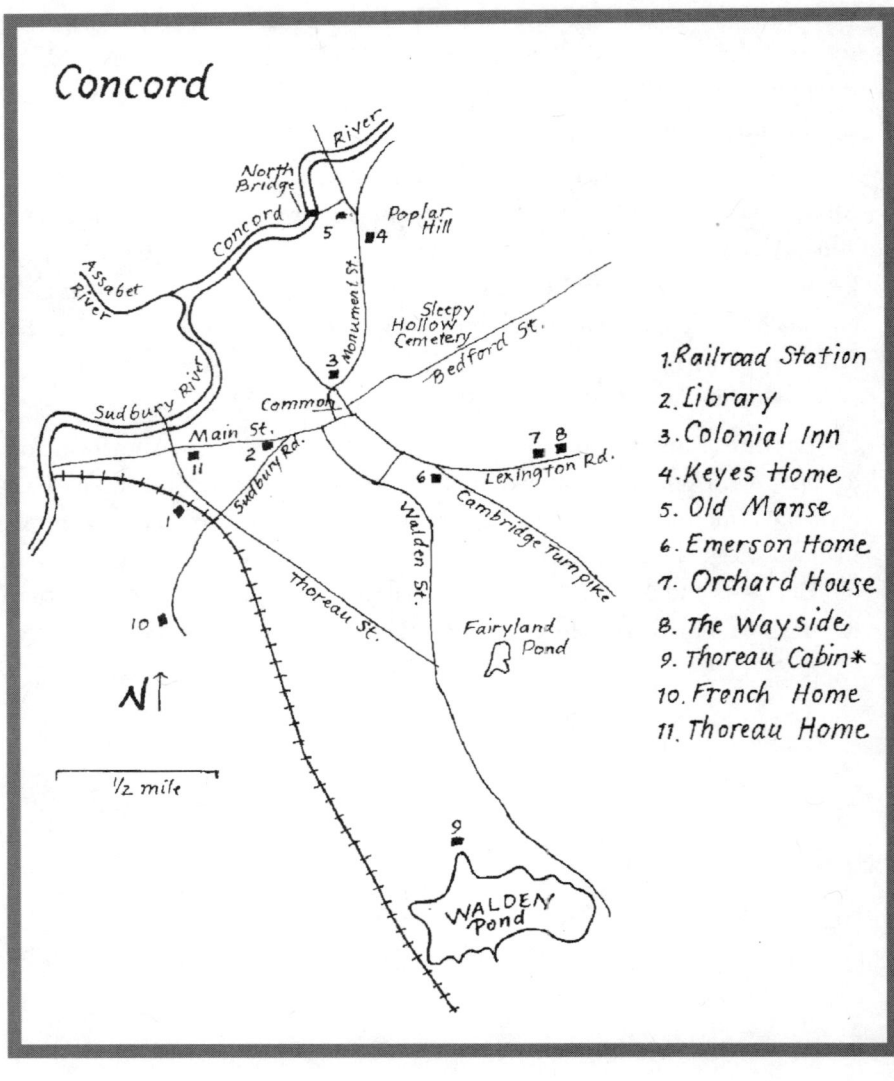

North Bridge
Concord River
River
Poplar Hill
Assabet River
Monument St.
Sleepy Hollow Cemetery
Bedford St.
Sudbury River
Common
Main St.
Sudbury Rd.
Lexington Rd.
Cambridge Turnpike
Walden St.
Thoreau St.
Fairyland Pond
N
½ mile
WALDEN Pond

1. Railroad Station
2. Library
3. Colonial Inn
4. Keyes Home
5. Old Manse
6. Emerson Home
7. Orchard House
8. The Wayside
9. Thoreau Cabin*
10. French Home
11. Thoreau Home

# 1. Concord

*No wonder Thoreau lived here two years. I could have*
*enjoyed living here two hundred years or two thousand.*
Muir to Louie Muir, 13 June 1893

## Thursday, 8 June 1893

On the train from Boston to Concord rode Robert Underwood Johnson, the forty-year-old associate editor of the New York monthly *Century*, and John Muir, fifteen years his senior, the first president of the Sierra Club of San Francisco, elected at the organization's inception the year before. The two men had met four years ago in June at the Palace Hotel in San Francisco. From there Muir had escorted Johnson to the "Holy of Holies," Yosemite Valley, and then through the Sierra Nevada to Tuolumne Meadows, where they had camped for five days, planned the protection of this paradise, and formed a lasting friendship that would have great impact on the course of American conservation.[1]

This spring they had left Johnson's home in New York City, taking a steamer at five last evening, passing through Long Island Sound, sleeping in a cabin berth or stateroom, and arriving at dawn in Fall River, Massachusetts, from where they were whisked cross-country on an Old Colony train, arriving in Boston by breakfast time.

As they approached Concord, Walden Pond appeared through the trees eastward. "The cars never pause to look at it," its foremost resident, Henry Thoreau, who lived there when the railroad first came by, had pondered, "yet I fancy that the engineers and firemen and brakemen, and those passengers who have a season ticket and see it often, are better men for the sight."[2] During summer, "Lake Walden" was a train stop. On the opposite side of the track from Walden, the Fitchburg Railroad had just completed another track; this one, composed of cinders in a straight line for 120 yards and in a circle for 220 yards, was used for foot and bicycle races. It is still visible in the woods today.[3] Moments later their train was at the station. It was just after noon on Thursday, 8 June 1893.[4]

On his way east from California, Muir had visited the World's Fair in

Chicago, which had opened the first of May, the month coincidentally that the stock market began a decline that would lead to its collapse on 27 June. The day before that, the 26th, Muir would sail from New York to begin an odyssey through England, Scotland (his boyhood home), Ireland, Norway, Switzerland, and Italy, before returning from Liverpool on 16 September.

Motivated by the World's Fair, the German house of Baedeker had produced its first *Handbook for Travellers* in the United States. It recommended a tour of Concord that began from the depot: "We proceed to the right along *Thoreau Street* to *Sudbury Street*, which we follow to the left. To the left, where Sudbury St. joins *Main Street*, stands the *Free Public Library*, containing many interesting autographs. Following Main St. to the right, we cross the *Mill Brook* and reach a square whence several streets radiate."[5]

I presume that Muir and Johnson walked this way—a fifteen-minute stroll past homes and stores to Monument Square, the green center of this community of 4,427 people (now 17,076). You are invited to follow them on foot. You can still take the train—the MBTA—from Boston to Concord.

Concord's dirt roads could be muddy and dusty in turn. The roots of large trees raised parts of the sidewalk. Muir admired the elms and maples that shaded the streets. Horses and carriages trotted by. The week's heat, 91 degrees two days earlier, had silenced the steam heaters of the public library, though this morning started crisply at 46 degrees. The library, open every day except Sundays and holidays, closed for two hours between noon and two, thus precluding a call by Muir and Johnson. In the Mill Dam, the business section, they passed the post office, recently moved from Whitcomb's store. Imagine the astonishing quality of words transferred through here: in early July 1855 Ralph Waldo Emerson had found *Leaves of Grass* in his mail, for example. Two apothecaries, Friend's and Richardson's, faced each other at the head of Walden Street. The latter's new bay window, soda fountain, and tile floor might have enticed them in for cherry phosphates or Hires' Root Beers.

At the common's north end stood the Thoreau House Hotel, where in 1800 John Thoreau had moved with his son John, who became Henry's father in 1817. Muir and Johnson could have spent the night there for $2.50. Rooms were not always available, however, for Concord received applications for board from all over the country, and last year could not accommodate everyone. As it was the noon hour, the proprietress, Mrs. P.A. Gillespie, might have been glimpsed on her daily tricycle ride. In July, she would vacation in Nova Scotia.[6] Now, as the Colonial Inn, the hotel lodges guests from $155 upward (1999), serves meals for special functions in the Thoreau Room, and still provides a convivial oasis.

At the opposite end of the common, the historic, refurbished Wright Tavern had reopened, providing meals and rooms for the tourists, who were already arriving in the village by train, carriage, and bicycle—the safety bicycle having been invented five years earlier, in 1888; the automobile did not come until the next century. Today the Wright Tavern serves as offices for realtors, the Chamber of Commerce, the Center for Spiritual Renewal, The Mortgage Connection, and furniture and antique stores.

## BULLET HOLE HOUSE

Past the Thoreau House Hotel, they continued northeast on Monument Street for a half mile to the Bullet Hole House, its name taken from the result of a British shot on 19 April 1775—now the home of the superintendent of Minuteman National Historical Park.

"Are you Judge Keyes?" Johnson introduced himself to an old man sitting on the porch. Receiving no response, Johnson presented his companion, whereupon the Judge ignited, "John Muir!" He "seized me as if I were a long-lost son," Muir related in a long, effusive letter home. "He declared he had known me always, and that my name was a household word."[7]

John Shepard Keyes, born on 19 September 1821 in Concord, was almost seventy-two. He had been judge of the Middlesex District Court since 1874. He introduced his wife, Martha Lawrence Prescott, three years his senior, who at age eighteen had declared in her diary "that the woods, the fields, are God's fittest temples." She was "a charming old-fashioned lady," Muir wrote, "who also took me for a son." They had been married on Keyes's twenty-third birthday in 1844, and his birthday present to her in 1863 had been this house. Three of their children were married: Annie and Florence both had their own children, while Prescott and his wife Alice Reynolds, who customarily saw her husband off each morning on the Fitchburg Railroad for his Boston law office at 42 Court Street, never did. Alicia, whose thirty-eighth birthday was in five days, stayed single all her life.[8]

"[R]efreshments, cider, etc." were provided, Muir said. Apparently, not Concord grapes or juice, though they grew abundantly this year. Apparently, not lunch either. Were they not famished? "I put them on their way," Keyes noted, keeping this visit brief.[9]

## OLD MANSE

The tourists went sightseeing; Johnson was the guide. "It was only by having been at the Boston station betimes that we got places in the train," Johnson reported on his excursion of 19 April 1875 to Concord's Centennial.[10] (William Dean Howells and Mark Twain could not find seats and had missed the celebration.) In Concord, Johnson had listened to Ralph Waldo Emerson, James Russell Lowell, George William Curtis, watched the dedication of a lone, harried, bronze soldier by a young—he would be twenty-five the next day—local sculptor, Daniel Chester French, who was now living in Florence, Italy, having moved there the year before, and mingled with the crowd, which Judge Keyes, the event's organizer, had estimated was between 3,500 and 5,000. Most likely, Johnson had met the Keyeses at their open house that went on all day until the evening ball at the Cattle Show Hall. Now he wanted Muir to meet them and one of their sons-in-law, Edward Emerson, son of Ralph Waldo Emerson, of whom we shall hear later.

From the Keyes home, Johnson and Muir walked across Monument Street to the Old Manse, a gambrel-roofed, Georgian clapboard, built by Ralph Waldo Emerson's grandfather in 1769-1770. "A moss grown parsonage," this was to Nathaniel Hawthorne, who had brought his bride, Sophia Amelia Peabody, there for their wedding night, 9 July 1842. The newlyweds had spent three blissful years there before returning to Salem. She sewed. He wrote. He split wood. She served tea. They skated and boated on the Concord River, at their back door, Thoreau having sold them his boat. They harvested string beans, summer squash, musk and water melons, corn, beets, and carrots, Thoreau having planted their garden. They savored cherries, currants, peaches, pears and apples from their orchard. They walked to the village and Walden. They created their first child Una.

## NORTH BRIDGE AND THE MINUTE MAN MONUMENT

From the Old Manse, Johnson and Muir strolled across a broad meadow to the North Bridge over the Concord River, which would be protected as a Wild and Scenic River in 1999. On the north side of this "rude bridge" they admired the weathered *Minute Man* by Daniel Chester French. Muir was familiar with French at least from his statue *The Republic*, which at sixty-five feet tall could not be missed at the World's Fair. A drawing of it had also appeared in the May issue of *Century*.

According to the *Concord Enterprise* of 8 June 1893, a three-cent weekly that Muir and Johnson may have seen, Mr. and Mrs. French (he married his cousin Mary Adams French in 1888 and they settled in New York, where he kept a studio until his death in 1931) had arrived in Concord last week. Their daughter, Margaret, four in August, was not mentioned. Twenty-eight years later, on 10 January 1921, at the Monastery of Santa Caterina in Taormina, Sicily, Johnson, then U.S. ambassador to Italy, would witness, with the Frenches Margaret's wedding to William Penn Cresson.[11]

Daniel Chester French had lived in Concord from 1867 to 1874, on a large farm on Sudbury Road, a five-minute walk south from the depot. Here he had made a three-foot tall model of the *Minute Man*. Needing more space for the statue, he had rented a room on the third floor of the Studio Building in Boston, at Tremont and Bromfield streets; then he had finished the plaster cast in their Concord barn. When he first saw his statue in place, on Sunday, 6 August 1876, he was escorted by his father and John Keyes and John's brother George; two days later there was a picnic in celebration of Dan.[12]

Apparently, Dan worked summers in his Concord studio, though the previous summer, 1892, he and Mary had gone to Cornish, New Hampshire, to be part of an art colony centered around the sculptor Augustus Saint-Gaudens. They would return there again in summer 1894. This year, however, he had been working in Chicago on his World's Fair statues; he and Mary would go there in July.[13]

When I stopped by 342 Sudbury Road (1 June 1999), the refurbished French house was empty. It was for sale: the price, $1,950,000. Dan's studio, the first in Concord according to Margaret Cresson, the next house north, was a private home.

In 1891, Dan French's Cambridge-boyhood, bird-collecting friend William Brewster (Dan had given Will his first taxidermy lesson on New Year's Day 1862), had purchased Ball's Hill on the Concord River, a mile and a half east of North Bridge. He called his domain, eventually 300 acres, October Farm. Brewster missed serendipitously meeting Muir, Johnson, and French, for at this moment he and two companions were walking the cedar and kalmia swamps of Saybrook, Connecticut, looking for birds, and taking their lunch beside a spring, serenaded by wood thrush and warblers. Brewster would not return to Concord until 26 June.[14]

## SLEEPY HOLLOW

Turning around, Muir and Johnson faced Poplar Hill, where Thoreau had sat one "warm Indian summerish afternoon" in "perfect autumn" watching "a hundred smokes arising through the yellow elm tops in the village—where the villagers are preparing for tea."[15] A road now curls up this rise, today thick with trees and houses.

He had passed the Keyeses' home again, and "Went through lovely, ferny, flowery woods and meadows to the hill cemetery," Muir wrote his wife.

This is still possible. Before Bartlett Hill Road, turn left (east) on a woodland trail and proceed a quarter mile (seven minutes). This, the former bed of the Boston and Maine Railroad, the tracks of which Muir crossed on Monument Road, the cars of which on 20 October 1875 had demolished Judge Keyes's buggy and killed a passenger, continues east past the Great Meadows of the Concord River. The former site of its depot, half a mile west almost at Lowell Street (a block north of the common), is now a lovely stroll through Mill Brook Way conservation land. After a quarter mile of the woodland trail, follow the path to the right (south), which shortly comes to Sleepy Hollow just west of its small pond, from where a trail leads up to Authors' Ridge.

Muir and Johnson "laid flowers on Thoreau's and Emerson's graves. I think it is the most beautiful graveyard I ever saw." Muir, deeply moved by Sleepy Hollow, contemplated eventually residing here himself. Instead he would choose a small family cemetery near his Martinez, California, home. Taking this same walk one day, Hawthorne had found Margaret Fuller alone here reading and meditating. They talked until a voice "still hidden among the trees" called to Margaret. Then Emerson "emerged from the green shade," announcing to them "that there were Muses in the woods to-day!"[16]

## EMERSON HOUSE

Next Muir and Johnson descended Authors' Ridge to Bedford Street, which they took west to the common again, and from there continued east on Lexington Road. Crossing directly between Bedford and Lexington streets to come to Ralph Waldo Emerson's home on Cambridge Turnpike would have involved trespassing. Today residences packing this area discourage any such linear passage.

The walkers apparently missed the Antiquarian Society on Lexington

Road, open daily on summer afternoons. Thoreau's desk, bed, chair, and table—all used at Walden—still reside there. Now called the Concord Museum, it is located opposite Emerson's home.[17]

From Sleepy Hollow's Prichard Gate to the Emerson House is a three-quarter-mile, fifteen-minute walk.

Emerson had died at home on 27 April 1882. Church bells tolled his age, seventy-nine; snow fell that night. His wife of forty-six years, Lidian, had died here also, at the age of ninety, in the fall before the Muir-Johnson visit. Their younger daughter, Ellen, who had cared for them both, Baedeker informed travelers, "still occupied" the house in 1893.

Probably, Johnson here recalled for Muir his pacing before Bush, as the Emerson home was known, that spring day of 1875 when other celebrants of Concord's Centennial flowed in and out of the gate. Ellen Emerson, who was "prepared for 18 by night and 150 by day", had had "only thirteen to spend the nights and forty or fifty in the day."[18] Johnson had longed to go in, but was "too timid to make an advance to so great a man."[19]

Muir appreciated his reticence. When Emerson had come to Yosemite Valley in May 1871, Muir, too shy to approach him directly, had left a note at his hotel, inviting him to join him for "a month[']s worship with Nature in the high temples of the great Sierra. . . ."[20] Their meeting, shorter and flatter, was nonetheless meaningful. Afterwards, they had corresponded. Emerson read Muir's letters to his family (his daughter Edith and her husband William H. Forbes were the only family to accompany him in the West) and told his friends, surely the Keyeses among them, of his happiness in finding Muir. He sent Muir his *Collected Essays*. He wanted Muir in New England. Muir's pilgrimage, thus, belatedly fulfilled one of Emerson's wishes.

Returning from California, Emerson had found Bush under quarantine due to Edward's illness and had had to lodge at the Old Manse temporarily. On the morning of 24 July 1872, with Ellen at Beverly Farms, Edward in England, and Edith with her family somewhere on the Atlantic Ocean returning from England, Emerson had awoken to Bush's burning. He had raised Lidian and then the neighbors. The First Parish bell had sounded the alarm. Judge Keyes had raced to the scene. With others Keyes had rescued furniture, books, manuscripts. He had brought Lidian and Emerson home for breakfast and dinner and then settled them again at the Old Manse before returning to the salvage work. Later, he had overseen the restoration of Bush.[21]

Johnson and Muir entered Bush "and were shown through the house. It is just as he left it, his study, books, chair, bed," Muir wrote his wife, "and all the paintings and engravings gathered in his foreign travels." Who was their cicerone? Ellen, who lived there until her death in 1909, would have been ideal.

"Why, Mr. Muir," Ellen ushered them in. "O, I wish I could have been with Father when he visited you in Yosemite…. When his memory failed and he could not think of your name he referred to you as 'that bearded young man in California.'

"This is the bust of Father that Dan French did in 1879," she said as she took them about in her high-necked, long-skirted dress. "My sister Edith has one, too, in her home in Milton."

They entered the parlor. "Edith's wedding to William Forbes happened in this room. Her dress was white muslin." Ellen restrained herself from describing the "crowning festivity of my life." Muir recalled meeting them and Will's parents in Yosemite.

"This is the eruption of Mount Vesuvius," she continued, pointing to a painting in the hall. "A favorite of Father's. He rode up it on a donkey sixty years ago." In August Muir would be sailing on Lake Como in northern Italy. "Father and I visited Pompeii twenty years ago," she continued. Father gave me a donkey, Graciosa, whom you must meet before you leave."

Two duotone photographs on the north wall of the dining room needed no introduction: *Mt. Shasta* and the *Cathedral Spires of Yosemite Valley*, by Carleton Watkins. "These were a gift to Father in memory of his western trip," Ellen anticipated their question. Probably they were from John and Sarah Forbes, the parents of Edith's husband.

When Edward Emerson had gone overland to California to regain his health, leaving on 12 May 1862, he had met with his father's friend the Reverend Thomas Starr King, then the pastor of the First Unitarian Church in San Francisco, who had given Edward two of Watkins's photographs of the sequoia *Grizzly Giant* for his father. Edward had missed seeing Yosemite and the Mariposa Grove, however. He had returned via sea and Panama on 6 October, in time to reenter Harvard; his father there sent him a barrel of apples from his orchard.[22]

We must imagine the Muir-Watkins relationship. Watkins had first photographed Yosemite in 1861. By 1878, when he went there for the summer, he was "a legendary figure in the valley," according to his biographer Peter E.

Palmquist. Though that summer Muir was with the Coast and Geodetic Survey in Utah and Nevada, they both had been in Yosemite in 1872, likely when Asa Gray came in July, for Watkins was documenting flora for the botanist. Though Muir was subject to a wash of imagery at the Chicago World's Fair, the masterpieces of Watkins were not represented, his declining health and income having prevented his participation.[23] Muir had a collection of his photographs, however: one of Shasta, which Watkins climbed with Clarence King on 11 September 1870; another of the Calaveras Mammoth Trees—which he may have purchased from his San Francisco studio. When Watkins was nearly blind and destitute, their mutual friend William Keith wrote Muir suggesting that he send money to him. The 1906 San Francisco earthquake destroyed Watkins's studio and inventory. Four years later he was committed to an insane asylum, where he died in 1916.

Each room at Bush had a fireplace. They burned twenty-five cords of wood a year. "Thoreau parched popcorn over this fire," Ellen said. "I was two when he first came to stay. He helped in the garden and orchard. That year, 1841, Edith was born. He danced with baby Edie in his arms. For years he never called Father by his first name."

"This is the red room." They stood in the northeast corner of the first floor. "Margaret Fuller stayed here," Ellen did not elaborate on their friendship. "Father contributed to a biography of her." Johnson mentioned the article on her in April's *Century*. Muir had not read her books—*Summer on the Lakes* (1844), *Woman in the Nineteenth Century* (1845), and *Papers on Literature and Art* (1846).

"Yes, I'd be happy to join you later at the Keyes'…. Edward will be thrilled to meet you." She might even have brought pie or cake.

Unfortunately for Muir and Johnson, this scenario did not unfold. Ellen had left that April for England, with her sister and younger nephew, for a much-needed respite after her devoted care of her dying mother. Ellen would not return until October 1894. In fact, today's newspaper had reported her in Venice. In her absence, Helen A. Legate, then thirty-five, was boarding at Bush. Since she was the head teacher of the Emerson School at the corner of Stow and Hubbard streets, four blocks away, and since school was still in session, until 16 June, it is likely she was not at home this afternoon. Yet, as Muir's letter reveals an informed introduction to Bush, she may have been there.[24]

They walked about the gardens and perhaps petted Graciosa before taking, to the left of the old barn, Emerson's path to Walden, now, in mid-August 1999, filled with ferns, goldenrod, and jewelweed.

## ORCHARD HOUSE

The "other home near Emerson's" that Muir and Johnson saw, but neither identified nor entered, was Orchard House, which faces Lexington Avenue a quarter mile east of Bush. The Alcotts—Abigail and Bronson and their daughters, Anna, May, Louisa, and Elizabeth—who had lived here from 1858 to 1877 (the sisters' tenures varied), had named their home for its enfolding apple orchard. Affectionately, they called it Apple Slump. Before renovations were completed and the family moved in in July 1858, Elizabeth had died. Here on 23 May 1860 Anna married John Bridge Pratt. The guests danced around the married couple on the lawn. Emerson kissed the bride. Louisa described Anna's wedding and their family life in *Little Women*, which Roberts Brothers of Boston published on 1 October 1868, during Muir's first California autumn. Royalties enabled Louisa and May to go to France in April 1870 and on to Italy and England; Louisa returned the following June, while May stayed to study art until November. In spring 1873, May was in London pursuing art for another year, thanks to Louisa. In September 1876 she settled in Paris; she had a still life accepted for the Salon of 1877, married the next year, and died the next, soon after their daughter's birth. A "pale & tearful" Emerson brought the news of May's death to Orchard House at the end of December 1879. The "hard moment was made bearable by the presence of this our best & tenderest friend," Louisa wrote in her journal that day.[25]

One wonders if Muir read *Little Women*. No Alcott books are found in his extant library. If Muir was not familiar with it, Johnson may have enlightened him then.[26]

At this time, the Concord Free Public Library acquired *A. Bronson Alcott: His Life and Philosophy* (Boston: Roberts Brothers, 1893), authored by two Concordians, Frank B. Sanborn and William T. Harris, which the *New York Times* had reviewed while Muir was in New York.[27]

In June 1884, Louisa had sold Orchard House to one of the authors of her father's biography, the philosopher William Torrey Harris (1835-1909), who had come to establish the Concord School of Philosophy. He lived here with his wife, Sarah T. Bugbee, and their daughter, Edith, when Muir and Johnson passed, though Harris, serving as U.S. Commissioner of Education from 1889 to 1906, may have been in Washington that day. *The Concord Enterprise* of 15 June 1893 reported that he would be spending the summer in Concord. "Hardly any American philosopher was more widely acclaimed in his own time," the *Dictionary of American Biography* states, "hardly any so little read today." Harris was also chief editor of the Appletons' School Readers, one of which, *The Second Reader* (1878), is in Muir's library, and which he may have read with his daughters.

## THE WAYSIDE

Outside Orchard House, Johnson and Muir were close enough to glimpse The Wayside eastward along Lexington Avenue, an architectural amalgam influenced by prior dwellers, the Alcotts and Hawthornes. Had Muir and Johnson knocked at the door, they might have met Harriett Lothrop (known to readers as Margaret Sidney), who had lived here since 1883 with her husband Daniel Lothrop, whom she had married 4 October 1881. He had commuted to work at his Boston publishing house (except winters when they stayed in a nearby hotel), while she wrote children's books, being already famous for *Five Little Peppers and How They Grew* (1881), which was serialized first in *Wide Awake*, a juvenile periodical her husband founded.[28]

A year ago in March, Daniel Lothrop had died (Walt Whitman died later that month, too), leaving Harriett and their almost nine-year-old daughter Margaret in residence. Since her husband's death, Harriet Lothrop had devoted herself to his publishing business. On 8 October 1892, she had attended the memorial service in Haverhill, Massachusetts, for their friend the poet, John Greenleaf Whittier, who had died on 7 September. She had written and dedicated to her husband, *Whittier with the Children*, which had just been released from D. Lothrop Company. In July she and her daughter would go to Chicago for the World's Fair, where she would deliver an address, "The Companionship of Mother and Child" to the literary congress at the Art Institute on the 13th, and, five days later, would show an enthusiastic young audience in the Children's Building how to make a World's Fair scrapbook.[29]

The next year, 1894, Harriett Lothrop would purchase the home of Ephraim Wales Bull, the Concord grape propagator, located next door to her, and restore his "Grapevine Cottage," still there, though now a house stands between them. She also would revive the DAR Chapter House on Monument Square, which Muir and Johnson had passed earlier, as well as

Orchard House, buying it from William Torrey Harris in 1900. Her intention was not to live there, but to create a museum, which eventually opened in 1911. She coveted the School of Philosophy enough to have it moved to her property, where she would move it about every now and then. Not until 1976 would it be returned to its original place.

Did Muir read *Five Little Peppers, Five Little Peppers Grown Up* (1892), *Five Little Peppers Midway* (1893) to his daughters? Possibily he did, for these books held such a prominent place in the culture then.[30] Clearly, though, Helen and Wanda preferred their father's own tales: "During meals at home my little girls make me tell stories," he wrote, "many of them very long, continued from day to day, for a month or two."[31] He transported them with Proverbs, Milton, Wordsworth, his Alaskan adventures, and his favorite Scottish bard, Bobbie Burns:

> *Gie me ae spark o' Nature's fire,*
> *That's a' the learning I desire.*

Mostly Muir wanted "wild knowledge" for his children. "Go to Nature's school," he advised, "the one true University."[32]

## WALDEN

Now Muir and Johnson participated in the common recreation of Emerson, Thoreau, Hawthorne, and the Alcotts. They "walked through the woods to Walden Pond," he said, most likely from Emerson's on his path, which went through what is now the Town Forest, over Brister's Hill. and across Walden Road, now bisected by four lanes of insufferable traffic.

Muir found this distance of a mile and a half to be "a mere saunter." "It is a beautiful lake about half a mile long," he wrote home, "fairly embosomed like a bright dark eye in wooded hills of smooth moraine gravel and sand, and with a rich leafy undergrowth of huckleberry, willow, and young oak bushes, etc., and grass and flowers in rich variety. No wonder Thoreau lived here two years. I could have enjoyed living here two hundred years or two thousand."

Muir was already familiar with Walden from *Walden*. In the spring of 1872, a year after Emerson's visit to Yosemite Valley, Muir had received from Abba G. Woolson of Boston a copy of the second edition, published by Ticknor and Fields of Boston on 21 March 1862 (see chapter 10). In this book, which is still in his library, he made his presence felt. In "The Ponds" chapter occurs this repartee:

Thoreau: "I have said that Walden has no visible inlet nor outlet,..." (194)[33]

Muir: "Walden is a Moraine pond wh[ich] dates back to the close of the last glacial period when the general New England ice sheet was reeding[sic—receding] & is fed by currents wh[ich] ooze thro[ugh] beds of drift." (210)

Thoreau: "Some have been puzzled to tell how the shore became so regularly paved." (182)

Muir: "By the expansion of the ice in the winter." (198)

Thoreau also pondered why "The pond rises and falls. . . ." (180)

Muir: "caused by differences in general rain-fall & evaporation" (196)

In the first page of the "Baker Farm" chapter, Muir changed Thoreau's "red-alder berry" (201) of the swamps to elder-berry by striking a line through the "a" and putting an "e" in the margin (217). Thoreau referred to common winterberry, *Ilex verticillata*, which has red berries and grows in wet places. The common elder, *Sambucus canadensis*, of wines and jellies, which Thoreau also knew well, likes swamps but has purple-black berries. The red-berried elder, *Sambucus pubens*, which is not native to or naturalized in Concord, Thoreau became acquainted with on Mount Monadnock in 1858 and 1860, where it inhabits the higher ground it prefers.

Muir did not restrict his comments to the landscape. In the "Former Inhabitants; and Winter Visitors" chapter is this:

Thoreau: "I should not forget that during my last winter at the pond there was another welcome visitor,...One of the last of the philosophers,—Connecticut gave him to the world, . . ." (268)

Muir, correctly puts: "Alcott?" (288)

Evidently, then, Muir was informed of Bronson Alcott (born in Wolcott, Connecticut, in 1799) and of his friendship with Thoreau, perhaps by his professors at the University of Wisconsin or by Emerson himself, or by their mutual friend Jeanne Carr, if not by all of them.

Muir also guessed "Emerson?" (287) as the "poet", "who came from farthest to my lodge, through deepest snows and most dismal tempests. . . ." (267-68) Walter Harding, however, identified this guest as William Ellery Channing of Concord, who had lived on Ponkawtasset Hill north of the

Concord River, about a mile and a half beyond Keyes's, farther in that direction than Muir went. Another "who looked in upon me from time to time," Thoreau related in the chapter's next-to-last paragraph, was Emerson, according to Harding.[34] Muir did not recognize Emerson here, or at least made no indication that he knew this visitor.

In "The Bean-field" chapter, Thoreau related, "I felt as if I could spit a Mexican with a good relish,—for why should we always stand for trifles?—and looked round for a woodchuck or a skunk to exercise my chivalry upon." (161)

Muir commented, "rather silly" (174)

Harding explained: "The United States was at war with Mexico during T's stay at Walden. Need it be pointed out that T is using irony here?" (156, n10)

Besides his natural history, Muir appreciated Thoreau's philosophy. In the "Conclusion" chapter, he underlined this entire sentence: "In proportion as he simplifies his life, the laws of the universe will appear less complex, and solitude will not be solitude, nor poverty poverty, nor weakness weakness." (324)

I like to believe that Johnson and Muir walked around Walden, thereby performing a ritual carried out by many pilgrims before and after them that has ancient roots in the Tibetan *kora* and the Hindu *pradakshina*.[35] Muir picked wildflowers and sent them home to his younger daughter Helen; he did not say which ones.[36] According to Thoreau, he had many choices. On this date in 1851, Thoreau had gathered the first strawberries of the season; the next day, twinflowers. "The lupine is now in its glory," Thoreau had observed three days earlier in 1852, "of such a pleasing variety of colors, purple-pink or lilac-and white. . . It paints a whole hill side with its blue. . . ." At Walden, it was blossoming time for high and low blueberries, high blackberries, and huckleberries, and their sweet scents filled the air, as Thoreau knew. "The Mt Laurel will begin to bloom tomorrow," he had noted 10 June 1853.[38] "Find the great fringed orchis out," Thoreau wrote on 9 June 1854: "A large spike of peculiarly delicate pale-purple flowers."[39] And so on.

## THOREAU HOUSE

At some point in their afternoon idyll, Johnson and Muir visited "Thoreau's village residence." This is the Yellow House at 73 Main Street, where Thoreau lived from 1850 to his death in 1862. Unfavorable circumstances, to which Keyes probably alerted them, prohibited their entrance. Louisa May Alcott had bought the Yellow House on 28 May 1877 for $4,500 for her widowed sister, Anna Alcott Pratt, and her two boys Frederick and John, who moved there that July, followed by Bronson, Abigail, and Louisa. Abigail had died shortly thereafter (25 November 1877). On 10 October 1885, Bronson, Louisa, Anna and her sons had departed for Boston's Beacon Hill. On 4 and 6 March 1888, Bronson and Louisa had died, respectively. On 8 February 1888, Frederick Alcott Pratt had married Jessica Lilian Cate. They and their first two children had resided with his mother Anna at 5 Chestnut Street in Boston until they all returned to Concord in spring 1893. When they did, Anna was ill. Further exhausted from the move, she made her last journal entry 20 May and died 17 July. Her edition, with her foreword, of *Comic Tragedies*, the adolescent plays she and Louisa had composed and performed with their sisters, appeared that year from Roberts Brothers. The Pratts continued to live at the Thoreau House.[40]

## BULLET HOLE HOUSE REDUX

They returned to the Keyes home, Muir said, "at six o'clock"; Keyes recalled, "to tea and to meet Edward who came at 5. . . ."[41]

Edward Waldo Emerson, forty-nine in July 1893, was the son of Ralph Waldo and Lidian Emerson. He had also been nurtured by Thoreau, who came to live in his home when he was three for seven months, while his father was in England. Thoreau had taken him boating on Walden and berrying, and introduced him to wildflowers. Thoreau had celebrated Edward's fifth birthday with onion and squash pipes and rhubarb whistles; in late August 1861, Thoreau had consoled an anxious Edward before his entrance into Harvard, from which he had graduated in 1866, having taken leave to recover from typhoid fever. After finishing Harvard's medical school, Edward had married Annie Shepard Keyes, on 19 September 1874, after a three-year engagement, right here in this house, before one hundred guests. At four that afternoon they had left for a honeymoon with Mount Monadnock in southwestern New Hampshire.[42]

The forty-six-year-old Annie did not accompany her husband to meet Muir. Presumably she was with their four children, Ellen, Florence, William Forbes, and Raymond, ages thirteen, ten, nine, and six, respectively, at their home at 452 Lowell Road, which still stands a mile west of Keyes's place. It seems more likely, however, that she was in Fitzwilliam, New Hampshire, with Florence and Raymond, awaiting Edward 's arrival the next day with Ellen and William. The family had been staying at the home of Edward's sister and brother-in-law in Milton, while she and her family were abroad with Ellen Emerson.[43]

Edward had practiced medicine in Concord until the death of his father. Since then, he had pursued a life of writing and painting. In 1888, he had written *Emerson in Concord* for the town's all-male "Social Circle"; it had appeared as a book in 1889 from Houghton Mifflin. This profile mentioned Ralph Waldo Emerson's California trip, but did not refer to Muir. Edward devoted himself to editing his father's works, which were published in 1903-1904 in twelve volumes, and then his journals, which were released between 1909 and 1914 in ten volumes. After Muir's death in 1914, Houghton Mifflin published Edward's *Henry Thoreau as Remembered by a Young Friend* (1917).

Muir found Edward "very like his father—rather tall, slender, and with his father's sweet perennial smile. Nothing could be more cordial and loving than his reception of me."

These engaging personalities must have had a lively time. How much was Muir-Emerson dialogue? How much was Keyes-Johnson? What role did Martha play? Did she sit silently and let the men go on? What did they make of and for each other? Sadly, there is no record of their conversation. The common interests they shared— Thoreau and Emerson, nature and horticulture, writing and books—must have been addressed.

Perhaps they traded mountain stories, Edward telling of his beloved Monadnock, a solitary 3,165-foot eminence in southwestern New Hampshire, visible from Concord. Thoreau, who was intimate with it, had inspired Edward's first ascent, in July 1861. Edward often camped on the mountain with his sister Ellen. A late June 1866 expedition was especially memorable, for their father had come with Annie Keyes, with William Ellery Channing—who had accompanied Thoreau there in August 1860—and with Una Hawthorne and three others. "[T]he thunder shook the mountain," Ralph Waldo Emerson wrote, "& much of the time was continuous cannonade." The elder Emerson with four women and a young man had retreated to the Mountain House for the night, leaving Edward and Ellery and another with plenty of room in their tent. Returning to the scene the next morning, they had witnessed a glorious clearing and later "haloes, rainbows, and little pendulums of cloud," and spent a cold, clear night outside.[44]

Alicia Keyes enjoyed Monadnock too. Like Edward, she painted it. This summer she was engaged with making an oil of it, situating herself south of her subject atop Gap Mountain. Eventually, she would give this picture to the Concord Free Public Library. At the end of this year, 1893, she would exhibit her sketches, one of which was titled, *Monadnock from Fitzwilliam*, at the Court House.[45]

Though Muir was never to climb Monadnock, he saw it from afar and had visited it vicariously through Thoreau's journal of his 1858 and 1860 excursions. Of the former account, Muir indexed, "Tourists names on Mtns. Yo[semite] g[ood]", which refers to Thoreau's chastisement of the graffiti makers, and Muir's consideration of this for his book, *The Yosemite* (1912), which he would dedicate to Robert Underwood Johnson, who for a decade had urged Muir to write it. He also marked in the margin "gl." for glaciation in the margin opposite Thoreau's description of a smooth and rounded profile of rocks. Regarding the 1860 visit, Muir made one index for "Thoreau's outfit for Monadnock," Thoreau's list of some thirty items, followed by his provisions.[46]

Now Edward had to excuse himself in order to go home to pack for tomorrow's train trip to Fitzwilliam, New Hampshire, where the family summered. Four years later, in 1897, he would build a beautiful home between Fitzwilliam and Monadnock, which still stands on New Hampshire Route 124.

Muir recorded no supper menu. What board was spread—pies, biscuits, chocolates, ices—must be imagined.

I presume that the Keyeses shared with their guests some of their four-month-long California journey of the last year. Crossing the Continental Divide just after midnight on 22 January 1892, their westbound train had collided with another coming east. Six were killed and "6 or 8 badly wounded," Keyes wrote, "our baggage car over turned & set on fire, trunks smashed & pulled out. fire put out. and we laid there till daylight...an awful night but we got breakfast in dining car all right after it was cleared."[47]

In Los Angeles, they had experienced an earthquake. In San Francisco, they had stayed at the Palace Hotel, where Muir and Johnson had first met in June 1889, and where Muir in his new suit would come to meet President Teddy Roosevelt in May 1903.[48] In April, they were riding in Yosemite Valley to Mirror Lake, as Emerson had done, walking the trail to Nevada Falls (but not up it) and playing whist and dancing in the evenings at their hotel. Afterwards they had gone to see Thomas Hill's studio in Wawona. Hill, who was born in England in 1829, worked here from 1884 until his death in 1908. Muir had commissioned him to paint the Muir Glacier in Glacier Bay, Alaska, in 1887, and had paid him $500.[49] As editor and illustrator, Muir and Hill had collaborated on *Picturesque California* (1888).[50] The previous summer, 1892, Hill had been in New Hampshire painting the White Mountains with his brother Edward.[51] The Keyeses had also seen the Big Trees of the Mariposa Grove, as Muir and Emerson had done twenty-one years before them. They had returned to Concord on 21 May.

Thomas Hill went to Chicago for the World's Fair, where five of his landscapes were displayed in the Art Gallery of the California Building, among them *Muir Glacier, Alaska*.[52] Hill's work in Chicago, however, did not impress Muir, "four by Hill, not his best," he wrote his wife.[53] He did admire "a good small one by Yelland."

This was Raymond Dabb Yelland (1848-1900), then the director of the San Francisco School of Design (Hill had briefly been its director, before going to Alaska), which in 1893 moved into the Mark Hopkins mansion on Nob Hill. Yelland had his studio at 430 Pine Street, the home of the San Francisco Art Association of which he, Hill, and William Keith were members, and lived in Oakland. He had two paintings in Chicago: *Moonrise on the Bay of Monterey* and *Scene in San Mateo, California*.[54]

It is likely that Muir spoke at the Keyses' of the World's Fair, for he was the only one of the party to have been there, and it was the major cultural event of the year. It is surprising how many people visited it between 1 May and 31 October 1893—27.5 million. It had an elevated electric railroad, movable sidewalk, elevators, and waterways with a variety of craft. The vast fairgrounds, The White City as it was called, were designed and planted with thousands of trees by Frederick Law Olmsted, who had selected the site next to Lake Michigan. Admission was fifty cents. "There never has been an occasion in the world's history," the *New York Times* boasted, "when so much was given for so small a price."[55] The May *Century* had featured an article on the Fair by Mrs. Schuyler van Rensselaer, and a poem by its editor Richard Watson Gilder, who on 10 July addressed the opening of its Congress on Literature, as well as a profile of John Muir by his friend John Swett.

"I most enjoyed the art galleries," Muir wrote home. "There are about eighteen acres of paintings by every nation under the sun, and I *wandered* and *gazed* until I was ready to fall down with utter exhaustion." It was in fact the largest collection of paintings that had ever been assembled.

Muir's second visit to the Fair was with Johnson. On his way back to California at the end of September, he would stop in Washington D.C. to lobby for forests before going on to Chicago with Johnson, who stayed five days before returning to New York. Muir continued west. Crossing Arizona his train also hit another, leaving him "shaken up & scared" but, amazingly, uninjured. After five months of travel, he would arrive home on 16 October.[56]

Judge Keyes took Muir and Johnson to the depot for their 8 p.m. train.[57] As daylight dissolved, they passed Walden again. "Lakes of Light," Thoreau had called Walden and White Pond, while Muir referred to the Sierra Nevada as the "Range of Light."[58] Fittingly, Muir's first New England day was spent at the shrine of his mentors, for whom, in Mary Oliver's view, "life itself was light."[59]

Were there promises of return? Muir never saw Concord again. Nor did he see his hosts. Martha Keyes died in 1895, her husband in 1910, Annie and Edward Emerson in 1928 and 1930, respectively. Had Muir met Ellen Emerson, the inveterate letter writer, they might have corresponded until her death in January 1909, thereby keeping "that bearded young man in California" in the Concord circle.[60] But it was twenty-one years later, in 1914, that he received a note from her namesake and niece, Ellen Tucker Emerson, daughter of Edward and Annie. "Your wonderful country certainly appeals to all our family," she wrote him from Merced Lake, while on a Sierra Club Outing, "now in the third generation. I've so often heard of my grandfather's trip with you."[61]

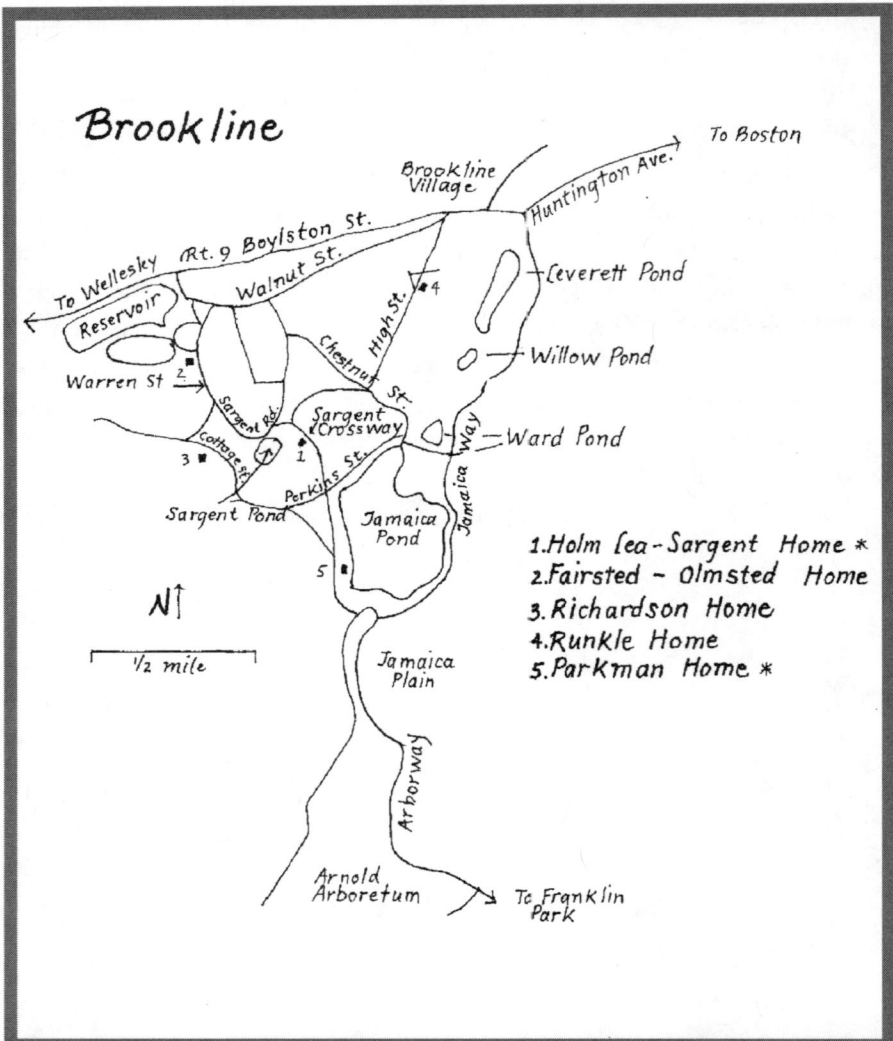

**Brookline**

To Boston

Brookline Village

Huntington Ave.

To Wellesley

Rt. 9 Boylston St.

Walnut St.

Leverett Pond

Reservoir

High St.

4

Willow Pond

Warren St. 2

Chestnut St.

Sargent Rd.

Sargent Crossway

Ward Pond

3

Cottage St.

1

Jamaica Way

Perkins St.

Sargent Pond

Jamaica Pond

5

Jamaica Plain

N↑

½ mile

1. Holm Lea - Sargent Home *
2. Fairsted - Olmsted Home
3. Richardson Home
4. Runkle Home
5. Parkman Home *

Arborway

Arnold Arboretum

To Franklin Park

# 2: Brookline

*I am most anxious to have the benefit of your society.*
—Charles Sprague Sargent to John Muir, 28 October 1895

*I urge you to hunt for beauty in commonplace and pleasant conditions....*
—Frederick Law Olmsted to William Platt, 1 February 1892

*My business is to look on and wonder at everything on the earth and off it.*
—Henry Adams to Lucy Baxter, 18 October 1893

## FRIDAY, 9 JUNE 1893

The morning after their day in Concord, Muir and Johnson awoke in their Boston hotel—presumably the Thorndike, at 240 Boylston Street, overlooking the Public Gardens. (Its rooms from $1.00 were competitive with other hotels on the European Plan in the city.) Soon they went off to Brookline, four miles west, for breakfast with Charles and Mary Sargent. Charles Sargent, now fifty-two, three years younger than Muir, had been a resident of Brookline since he was twelve, when his family moved there from his birthplace on Boston's Beacon Hill. Charles and Mary's large country estate, Holm Lea, conjoined by Charles's father in a series of purchases between 1845 and 1872, was Sargent's primary school for horticulture.[1]

Holm Lea totally captivated Muir. "This is the finest mansion and grounds I ever saw," he enthused to Louie. "The house is about two hundred feet long with immense verandas trimmed with huge flowers and vines, standing in the midst of fifty acres of lawns, groves, wild woods of pine, hemlock, maple, beech, hickory, etc., and all kinds of underbrush and wild flowers and cultivated flowers—acres of rhododendrons twelve feet high in full bloom, and a pond covered with lilies, etc., all the ground waving, hill and dale, and clad in the full summer dress of the region, trimmed with exquisite taste."[2]

His description was not hyperbole. "The most beautiful suburban country place that I know," wrote critic Mariana Griswold Van Rensselaer in the *Century*, confirming Muir's impression. "The charm of the artistically composed landscapes at Holm Lea is greatly enhanced by the variety of the trees and shrubs and flowers which compose them." Here azaleas and rhododendrons flourished in June, she noted. Garden, meadow, tree plantations, and wilderness enhanced each other. Landscape gardening attained the status of art and reigned over architecture. "A sense of unthreatened peace, of intimacy with unthreatened nature" predominated.[3]

Sauntering about house and grounds on this late spring day, 9 June, Muir felt immediately at one with his surroundings. Mary Sargent had a gift for making people feel at home. She was also a talented artist. When time permitted, she painted, making realistic watercolors of Holm Lea wildflowers.[4]

Today I circle counterclockwise on the roads—Walnut, Warren, Cottage, Perkins, Chestnut—that surround where Holm Lea once stood: it is a two-mile circuit. Sargent Road now divides the old grounds. Since it is posted "No Trespassing" and "Private Property," I am reluctant to enter until I ask two suburban strollers, who inform me that they are trespassers. Just south of this road's southernmost point lies Sargent Pond, named for its creator, blessedly protected by historic easement. The rhododendrons that once embraced its edges have disappeared. Its still surface without water lilies is ringed with tall yellow iris and cattails. A narrow dirt path bridges the outflow, which expands into a wide, open, wet green that runs to residences along Perkins Street. Across Perkins sits the larger Jamaica Pond, which a part of the Sargent estate touched.

The manse, which stood northeast of Sargent Pond, was damaged by fire in December 1896. "The contents, however, are fortunately all safe and practically uninjured," Sargent would report to Muir, "so by spring I hope we shall be as good as new." A resurrected Holm Lea would be home to Muir on his return visits. Soon after Charles Sargent's death on 22 March 1927 (Mary had died in 1919), the estate would be redesigned to accommodate private residences. Alice Sargent would occupy her parents' home until her death in 1946, after which it was so altered as to lose all semblance to the original. When and why it was finally removed, I have not discovered. Van Rensselaer's *Century* article with Harry Fenn's drawings preserve at least in part this sadly vanished sanctuary where Muir stayed.[5]

## GOOD NEIGHBORS

While at Holm Lea in June 1893, and in other years ahead, Muir saw a good deal of the neighborhood.

West across Warren Street from the Sargents lived Frederick Law Olmsted. In 1881, he and his wife Mary had moved with their family to Brookline; two years later they had bought an 1810 farmhouse, which he named Fairstead, now a

National Historic Site. He and Sargent had been engaged in designing the Arnold Arboretum and securing its inclusion in Boston's park system. Of his own two acres, Olmsted made an inviting mini park. His mantra directed his scheme: "Less wildness and disorder I object to." The American elm, known as the Olmsted elm, that he planted in the center of his south lawn still stands, as well as his Canadian hemlock in the center of the carriage turn. In the rock garden at the southeast corner is a large cucumber magnolia. Olmsted's presence is still felt in the ambiance of serenity and beauty created here.

Like Muir, Olmsted had "wandering habits."[6] A sampling of his travels illustrates his nomadic life. Three days before his twenty-first birthday, he sailed from New York as an apprentice seaman on a merchant ship bound for the Orient. Almost a year later, on 16 April 1844, he returned, having suffered from a variety of sicknesses and having seen little of China. Six years later, in the spring of 1850, when he was twenty-eight, he traveled through England, from Liverpool to London, mostly on foot, delighting in the scenery of the countryside and the urban public parks. His *Walks and Talks of an American Farmer in England*, written from his diary and letters home and published in two parts by George P. Putnam in 1852, showed his powers of perception.[7] Six years later, he was abroad again, this time for nine months. He visited London on his firm's business—the publishing house Dix and Edwards, to whom Putnam had sold his literary magazine—though his free time was spent strolling the city's parks. For pleasure he toured the Continent with his two half sisters and their friend. "I was born for a traveler," he wrote his father from Italy: "I do enjoy it exceedingly."[8]

He also saw much of his own country. Between his two transatlantic trips he made two epic journeys through the South, reporting on slavery and culture for the *New-York Daily Times* and the *New-York Daily Tribune*. The first, of four months duration, from 11 December 1852 to 6 April 1853, was made alone; the second and longer, from 10 November 1853 to 2 August 1854, with his brother John. Olmsted produced three books recording these ventures: *A Journey in the Seaboard Slave States* (Dix & Edwards, 1856), *A Journey through Texas* (Dix & Edwards, 1857) with John's great contribution, and *A Journey in the Back Country* (Mason Brothers, 1860).[9]

Omsted was also familiar with Muir's sacred turf. Three years before Muir arrived, he had spent two years (1863-1865) in California. He had lived primarily in the Sierra Nevada foothills, directing the Mariposa gold-mining company that owned the estate of John C. Frémont, but he also resided in San Francisco. In July and August of 1864, the Olmsted family took a vacation. From Clark's Station (now Wawona) on the South Fork of the Merced River, they made excursions to see the sequoias of Mariposa and Fresno. After a fortnight's absence to attend to work, Olmsted returned, and with his family, on 12 August, moved northward from Clark's to Yosemite Valley, where they camped opposite the Yosemite Falls into early September. For six of those days, 28 August to 2 September, Olmsted, his eleven-year-old son John Charles, and William Brewer of the California Geological Survey, plus a guide, crossed the Sierra from Yosemite to Mono Pass and back. The party made the first ascent—young John and Brewer afoot, Olmsted on horse-back—of a 12,764-foot peak, which Olmsted named Mount Gibbs for Harvard chemist Oliver Wolcott Gibbs, with whom he had served on the U.S. Sanitary Commission.[10]

Shortly after Olmsted's return to Mariposa, the governor of California, Frederick F. Low, had on 28 September 1864 appointed the Yosemite Park Commission, with Olmsted as head. Almost a year later, on 9 August 1865, Olmsted had made his report to the commissioners, who were gathered with other dignitaries in Yosemite Valley. With prescient psychological insight, he detailed the benefits of the enjoyment of scenery for the body and mind, noting the connection between the two, and how this entertainment was real-ly a form of meditation—though he did not use that word—for it focused one's attention on the present moment. The total effect of this practice ren-dered "refreshing rest and reinvigoration to the whole system." He called for "the preservation and maintenance" of this land where the "union of the deepest sublimity with the deepest beauty of nature" occurred, and for improved access via roads to and a "double trail" around the valley, as well as to the Mariposa Grove and around the Big Trees, for fire prevention. He even wanted five cabins constructed in Yosemite, one room of each to be open for a "free resting place for visitors." His ideas were not presented to the California legislature, however—his biographer Laura Wood Roper says that J. D. Whitney suppressed the report for fear it would receive funding at the expense of his own Geological Survey. They were publicized nonethe-less. Samuel Bowles, for one, who was in the company listening to Olmsted read his report, sent letters describing his Western journey to the *Republican*, his Springfield, Massachusetts, newpaper, and collected these into a best-seller, *Across the Continent*.[11]

The next week, on 13 June 1893, Frederick and Mary Olmsted celebrated their thirty-fourth wedding anniversary. (They had been married on the Great Hill of New York's Central Park.) On 28 June Olmsted was in

Cambridge to receive an honorary Doctor of Letters from Harvard. In October the *Century* featured Mariana Griswold van Rensselaer's article on Olmsted, "the most comprehensive" biography on him and his work to date, according to Laura Wood Roper. That month, also, the fifth volume of Sargent's *Silva of North America* appeared, with its dedication to Olmsted: "the great artist whose love of nature has been a priceless benefit to his fellow-countrymen."[12]

Often Olmsted rode or walked five minutes south down Warren Street alongside Holm Lea to Cottage Street, where in an 1803 West Indian country home he visited architect H. H. Richardson, who had lived here since 1874. During the summer of 1875, Richardson had vacationed with Olmsted and their wives. At Cottage Street, he and Olmsted discussed a variety of projects, from railroad stations to North Easton's Town Hall, on which Richardson was particularly pleased to have his neighbor's advice. On Monday nights, they socialized with apprentices and former students. Once a month, they joined with other men of the Saturday Club for dinner at the Parker House in Boston. All this conviviality had ended though, in March 1886, when Richardson died of Bright's disease at age forty-seven.[13]

About a fifteen-minute walk east from the Sargent estate was the home of John Daniel Runkle, his wife Catherine Robbins Bird, and their family. This brick Victorian with a steep slate roof, tall chimneys, and corner turret still occupies 84 High Street, on Pill Hill above Brookline Village. On one of their trips in and out of Boston, I imagine Sargent pointed out this place to Muir, perhaps even stopped, though no mention is made of this. Runkle had been with Muir in Yosemite Valley for five days during the first week of September 1871. Runkle had been impressed with Muir, enough so as to invite him to join the faculty of the Boston Institute of Technology (later the Massachusetts Institute of Technology), of which he had been president from 1870 to 1878, and where he was now (1893) teaching mathematics. Muir had never accepted his offer, however. In 1897, the Runkles moved to Cambridge.[14]

From Pill Hill, Muir could look east to Boston, and southward two miles to Sargent's workplace, the Arnold Arboretum in Jamaica Plain, where on occasion Muir accompanied the director (see chapter 7).

## MARIANA GRISWOLD VAN RENSSELAER

Five and a half years later, in New York City, Muir would meet Mariana Griswold Van Rensselaer, the author of art and architectural commentary on Holm Lea, Frederick Law Olmsted, and Henry Hobson Richardson. It was Tuesday, 7 November 1898: Election Day in New York, and at the end of it Theodore Roosevelt would be the state's new governor. Johnson would invite Van Rensselaer to luncheon to meet Muir along with Richard Watson Gilder, who was her mentor, and his wife Helena de Kay, as well as Richmond P. Hobson (the latter three will appear more fully in chapter 13). Where they would dine is not known—perhaps the Players Club at 16 Gramercy Park, their previous day's meeting place. In 1898, Van Rensselaer was forty-seven and an independent writer. Her *Art Out-of-Doors: Hints on Good Taste in Gardening* had just been published and reviewed. She wore a black dress in honor of her husband of eleven years, Schuyler Van Rensselaer, who had died in 1884. Her apparel could equally commemorate their only child, George Griswold, who after completing his first year at Harvard, 1892-1893, had gone west with his mother to restore his health, only to succumb to tuberculosis in April 1894 in Colorado Springs, at age nineteen.[15]

Van Rensselaer took Muir on a postprandial tour of Manhattan. They went "from top of World building & cab thro[ugh]Wall St," he jotted in his journal. The World, or Pulitzer, Building—the home of Joseph Pulitzer's famous newspaper the *New York World*—stood at 61 Park Row, between Frankfort Street and Tryon Row, in a cluster of skyscapers surrounding City Hall Park. (It has since been demolished.) When it had been erected in 1889-1890, no office building anywhere exceeded its 309-foot height, a contemporary guidebook reported. From its twentieth-sixth floor, Van Rensselaer pointed out the landmarks of her city to Muir. A half mile south of the World, Wall Street sat in the heart of a Financial District filled with trust companies. They probably also passed the Renaissance facade of the New York Stock Exchange, which faced Broad around the corner from Wall Street.[16]

"Many of its [New York's] down-town streets now look less like streets than like cañons cut by patient rivers between stupendous cliffs fretted and carved by a hand as vigorous and ingenious, though hardly as artistic, as the hand of Nature herself," Van Rensselaer found. "These, I think, are our [New York's] most characteristic, our most typical places."[17]

From the southern end of Manhattan, they returned northward, pausing, no doubt, here and there. Washington Square Park and environs was Van

Rensselaer's most familiar ground. She had been born and raised a half mile north on Fifth Avenue. Her paternal and maternal grandparents resided in the square as well. She may have pointed out to Muir the James residence, a three-story brick house at 21 Washington Place, between the park and Broadway, where Thoreau, while living on Staten Island, had called over a month before Henry James Jr. was born on 15 April 1843. William James, who had arrived fifteen months earlier at the Astor Hotel, had been in residence too, when Thoreau visited. Thoreau had enjoyed "three hours' solid talk" with Mr. James. An older Henry James Jr. would set his novel *Washington Square* (1880) at number 18 (demolished) on the north side of the park, the home of his mother Mary Walsh and grandmother Elizabeth Robertson Walsh. Even later, in May 1905, Henry would revisit "the great face of New York" only to find it sadly changed—his birthplace and adjacent dwellings replaced by a gray New York University building.[18]

The icon of Washington Square, the Washington Arch, Henry James found "lamentable"—"lamentable because of its poor and lonely and unsupported and unaffiliated state." The classically formed marble monument, the design of architect Stanford White, commemorated the centennial of Washington's inauguration as the nation's first president on 30 April 1789, in the then national capital, New York; it had been dedicated six years later, on 4 May 1895. It was the inspiration of William Rhinelander Stewart, who with Richard Watson Gilder, treasurer and secretary of the Arch Committee, respectively, and others raised the funds for its erection.[19] On their stroll, Muir and Van Rensselaer no doubt passed the Washington Arch, in the center of the north edge of the park.

At Washington Square, Fifth Avenue began and ran in a straight line north 2.5 miles to Central Park, she had written. They went up Fifth Avenue for two blocks and around the corner of West Ninth Street, where they stopped at number 9, Van Rensselaer's home since 1884, and for the rest of her life. (But not for ours, alas, though a number of other Greek Revival homes of that period survive to convey the *fin de siècle* atmosphere.) Here they had tea and talked with her unidentified friend and probably her mother, who would live there until her death in 1908. Muir told his Alaskan dog tale (see chapter 4). He departed favorably impressed by her, though he gave no specifics.[20]

As Van Rensselaer's *Art Out-of-Doors: Hints on Good Taste in Gardening* had been published just before Muir's arrival at Holm Lea in June 1893, and was receiving critical attention, it is possible that Sargent and Muir discussed her and her work.[21]

Sustained by their mutual devotion to forests and leavened with banter, the friendship of Muir and Sargent was lifelong. Their companionship nourished them—up to a point, that is. After over three months traveling with Sargent across the Atlantic, Europe, and Russia, Muir would be only too happy to part company with him on 10 September 1903 in Shanghai, and go his own way. "I am at last free," he would note in his journal.[22]

One of them was always inviting the other to come east or west, as the case might be, or to accompany him here or there. "Of course my summer's outing is still in embryo," Sargent would write Muir in the fall of 1895. "When it takes shape you shall be the first to know as I am most anxious to have the benefit of your society." Deprived of his desire, Sargent's disposition could sour. When Muir was too busy writing to join him in Texas in the spring of 1901, for example, an upset Sargent accused him of quitting. Using logic and humor, Muir replied, "how can a fellow quit what he has never found. To explain this would require the wry wisdom of a Jamaica Plain transcendentalist." He continued, "What has bothered you this winter to so completely abolish your calm Boston temper? Judging by your letters you are as stinging & prickly as a cockspur Crataegus [the hawthorn family that Sargent was researching]." In closing, he added, "May the balmy south woods sweeten you."[23]

Despite their differences, Muir and Sargent touched each other deeply. The book whose work prevented Muir's leaving his desk would be released on 9 November 1901 as *Our National Parks*, and was dedicated to Sargent. The tribute surprised and delighted Sargent, who wrote, "I do not know that anything which has happened to me has given me so much real pleasure as this evidence of your good feeling."[24]

When not together physically, they communicated by mail. "Your letters always cheer and inspire me," Sargent revealed, "and I wish I could get more of them." He continued to prod Muir with admiration: "the sight of you would do more to rejuvinate [sic] me than anything I can think of." And with whim: "Perhaps by next spring you will have developed sense enough to come east and see the opening of the eastern spring flowers."[25]

## APPRENTICE BEATRIX JONES

It seems that no one of import missed the World's Fair. Some even went twice— inveterate travelers Henry Adams and John Muir included. The fifty-five-year-old Adams—the same age as Muir—had arrived from the nation's capital on Saturday, 20 May, in a private railroad car, along with his Lafayette Square neighbors Senator J. Donald Cameron of Pennsylvania and Elizabeth Sherman, his beautiful brunette wife, twenty-four years younger, whom Adams loved. That night Adams had witnessed the White City illuminated with electric lights for the first time. Sunday it was closed, and early Monday morning he had left. Though there "hardly enough to take it in," he had returned to Washington, "a wiser and gladder man." Three days after Adams had gone, Muir's train pulled into Chicago, at 3:00 p.m. on Thursday, 25 May.

Their second rounds coincided. Astounded by his one spring evening at the Columbian Exposition, more so than by Niagara Falls or the Yellowstone geysers, Adams—the newly elected president of the American Historical Association, meeting in Chicago, though ostensibly retired from his profession—would return for the first two weeks of October. Besides the art and architecture, he enjoyed the pleasures of the Ferris wheel by day and the gondolas by night. Later, he reflected on his experience in *The Education of Henry Adams*. Muir, in addition to his May visit, stopped again in Chicago the second of October for "about a week," he wrote Johnson. Unfortunately, he would leave no record of his second impressions of the Fair.[26]

As the Columbian Exposition was also a desired destination for the Sargents, they were glad to have a personal preview from Muir. Their visit would have to wait, however, until the Fair's final weeks. On or about 17 October, the day after Muir had returned to California, they left Boston by train for the windy southern shores of Lake Michigan.

Accompanying the Sargents would be twenty-one-year-old Beatrix Jones, fresh from her mother's summer home on Mount Desert Island, Maine. Mary Cadwalader Rawle of Philadelphia had married Freddy Jones of New York on 24 March 1870. Their love of Mount Desert had inspired them to build a cottage there. Reef Point, completed in 1883, lay between the shore of Frenchman Bay and Main Street of Bar Harbor. When after a dozen years their marriage dissolved, he had deeded the land to her. Mary Jones had asked her good friend Mary Sargent if her husband would be willing to educate her daughter in the art of landscape gardening. He had agreed.[27]

Considering the magnitude of the World's Fair, Jones's journal observations are meager. They pale in comparison, for instance, with the attention she had given to Oldfarm, the estate of Mary Gray Ward Dorr on Compass Harbor south of Bar Harbor, just before coming to Chicago. At the Fair, she confined her remarks to the landscaping at three pavilions, especially to the names and use of shrubs and trees. Only two of her drawings augment her written record: one of the wooden fence surrounding the Massachusetts State Building; the other of a blossom of *Aralia lieboldi*.[28]

The incomparable resources of Holm Lea, the grand Sargent library, and the Arnold Arboretum were at Beatrix Jones's disposal. So were Sargent himself, and his devoted gardeners at both places—Charles Sander and Jackson Thornton Dawson, respectively, both of whom Muir must have met too.[29] Her education was also enriched by travel. In February 1894, she would go to the Biltmore Estate in Asheville, North Carolina, with her mother, the Sargents, Frederick Law Olmsted, and others. The following year's six-and-a-half-month Grand Tour with her mother exposed her to Italian, French, German, and English gardens, as well as to the virtuosos Gertrude Jekyll of Munstead Wood in Surrey and William Robinson of Gravetye Manor in Sussex, both of whom influenced her greatly. Upon returning, the young Beatrix would begin her practice.

Much of her early work would be done on her beloved island, Mount Desert; in fact, her biographer, Jane Brown has pointed out that a quarter of her 202 lifetime commissions were executed here. Jones and her husband Max Farrand, a Yale history professor, whom she married in 1913, would work together to make her Reef Point gardens an educational center. After his death in 1945, she would carry on for a decade before deciding to dismantle Reef Point. Her best work can be seen in The Eyrie Garden for Abby Aldrich Rockefeller, at Seal Harbor. Her other celebrated creation, now owned by Harvard University, is Dumbarton Oaks in Washington, D.C., which Brown ranks "with the greatest gardens in the world." Both of these gems are open to the public. In addition, there are eight campuses, including Yale, Princeton, and Chicago, and five smaller colleges, and schools that she contributed to and that can be admired today. The "greatest honour" of her professional life she reserved for her role as consulting landscape architect to the Arnold Arboretum—a project that allowed her to honor her mentor Sargent.[30]

Though Muir never saw the famous landscape gardener, he would meet her prime clients, the Blisses, who bought Dumbarton Oaks in 1920 and engaged Jones in the consummate expression of its gardens. On 28 November 1911, in Buenos Aires, Argentina, Muir would be introduced to the secretary of the American Legation, Robert Woods Bliss, a graduate of Harvard (Class of 1900), and perhaps also to Bliss's wife of three years, Mildred Barnes. Regrettably, Muir would have to decline the latter's luncheon invitation on the following day.[31]

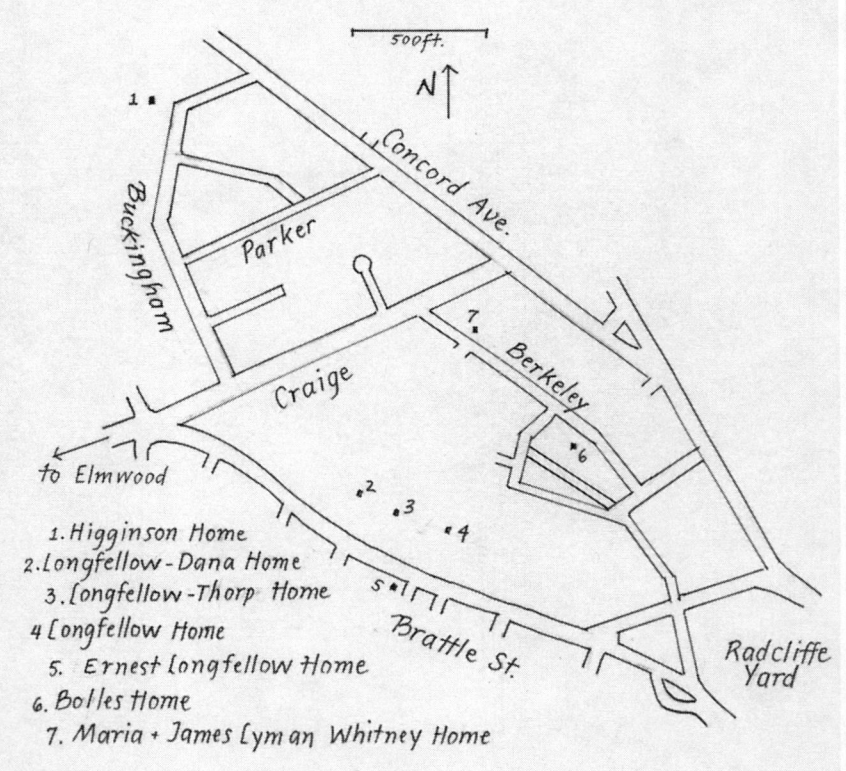

# Cambridge 1893
## West of Radcliffe Yard

500ft.

N↑

1.

Buckingham

Parker

Concord Ave.

Craige

Berkeley

7.

6

to Elmwood

.2

.3

.4

s .

Brattle St.

Radcliffe Yard

1. Higginson Home
2. Longfellow-Dana Home
3. Longfellow-Thorp Home
4. Longfellow Home
5. Ernest Longfellow Home
6. Bolles Home
7. Maria + James Lyman Whitney Home

# 3: Cambridge

*Stay, stay at home, my heart, and rest;*
*Home-keeping hearts are happiest,*
*For those that wander they know not where*
*Are full of trouble and full of care;*
*To stay at home is best.*
—Henry Wadsworth Longfellow, "Song" (1877), first stanza

## Saturday, 10 June 1893

From Brookline on Saturday afternoon, the 10th, Muir and Johnson went to Cambridge. At the door of 29 Buckingham Street a tall, slender, dignified man greeted them. Thomas Wentworth Higginson, who would be seventy in December, was still known as the Colonel from his command of the Union's first black regiment in the Civil War. A Harvard classmate of Judge John Keyes of Concord, he had graduated from Harvard's Divinity School as well. While minister of the Unitarian Church of Newburyport, he had heard Thoreau lecture on "An Excursion to Cape Cod" on 6 December 1850, and had had him for a house guest that night. He had been married for fourteen years to Mary Thacher, who, twenty-three years younger than he, was a grandniece of Henry Wadsworth Longfellow, and a writer; their daughter Margaret would be twelve this July 25th.[1]

During the morning, Higginson had been working in his study, arranging thirty-four letters that he had received from Emily Dickinson. Already, Higginson had commented on some of Dickinson's letters in the *Atlantic* of October 1891, which Muir may have seen. Higginson had put Dickinson's manuscript and printed letters in an envelope, added a note, and sent them to Mabel Loomis Todd in Amherst. These letters would appear along with others that Mabel Todd had collected in November 1894, the month after the Century Company put out Muir's *The Mountains of California*, a copy of which Muir instructed Johnson send to Higginson.[2] Higginson had collaborated with Todd—at her request, in person, on 6 November 1889—in bringing to light Dickinson's *Poems* (Boston: Roberts Brothers). This collection had appeared on 12 November 1890, with Higginson's introduction, followed by another selection from the same publisher a year later, on 9 November 1891, with Todd's preface.

Though Todd had lived close to Emily Dickinson and been frequently in her house, she never had seen the reclusive poet. When Higginson had visited the Dickinson Homestead, an elegant ocher brick cupolated Federal at 280 Main Street in Amherst, on 16 August 1870, she had greeted him in "white piquè with a blue net worsted shawl," looking "quaint and nun-like," and handed him two daylilies, saying, "These are my introduction." When Emerson had lectured on "The Beautiful in Rural Life" to the Amherst community on 16 December 1857, Emily Dickinson had heard him. Emily's brother Austin and his wife Susan had entertained Emerson for the night at their Italianate villa, the Evergreens, next door to Dickinson's. Both residences, near to the railroad station (c.1853), are open to the public today.[3]

Todd and Higginson would miss meeting in June 1893. Todd worked on Emily's correspondence on an "Excessively almost intolerably hot" Sunday, 11 June, and the next day. On the solstice, the Colonel asked her, "Where are you to be this summer?" Evidently she had not told him of her plans. The day after the 29 June commencement of Amherst College—where Mabel had danced to 3:30 a.m., then slept four hours—she, with her husband David P. Todd, a professor of astronomy at the college, and their thirteen-year-old daughter, Millicent, took the train to Washington, D.C. and on to Chicago, where they stayed with her widowed cousin, Lydia Coonley, for a fortnight. Most days found them at the World's Fair, visiting the Amherst College alcove, turning in the Ferris Wheel, or riding the "intramural railway" about the grounds, or a launch on the lagoon. Even on the "excessively hot" days, they were at the Fair. On the 9th, Austin Dickinson arrived and stayed until the 16th. Mabel and Austin toured many of the buildings of the Fair, even watching one burn.[4]

Reluctantly, the Todds departed Chicago on Monday afternoon, 17 June, traveling by train for two days to Colorado Springs. In this relatively new (1858) town of 11,040 souls (1890 census), they were the guests of Frank and Mabel Louds—he was professor of mathematics and astronomy at Colorado College and an 1873 graduate of Amherst College—at their home at 1203 North Tejon. Their lack of sociability did not appeal to the gregarious Mabel. David gave five lectures on various topics—the corona, the 1889 African solar eclipse expedition, the planets and their satellites, the universe of stars, and mountain observations—in the Colorado Summer School of Science, Philosophy, and Languages held at Colorado College. At the end of its second decade in 1893, the college was under the leadership of William F. Slocum—a Congregationalist minister from Massachusetts and a graduate of

Amherst College (1874) and Andover Theological Seminary (1878). Its faculty of seventeen professors and instructors plus five lecturers and campus of five buildings on an open prairie nurtured a graduating class of five.[5]

On Saturday, 22 July, the Todds participated in a summer school excursion. Taking the 8:10 a.m. train from Colorado Springs twelve miles west to Cascade, David and Mabel joined six others, who included two Wellesley College professors: Katharine Coman (Economics) and her lover Katharine Lee Bates (English). At Cascade the entourage boarded four carriages for a trip "over a mountain road of seventeen miles, with six hours of magnificent views, and a sufficiently gradual ascent into the region of thin air," Mabel related. After luncheon—Professor Todd warned them against eating above the clouds—and a change of horses at the halfway house, they continued to the 14,110-foot summit of Pikes Peak.[6]

"It was then and there," Katharine Bates remembered, that "the opening lines of the hymn floated into my mind":

> O beautiful for halcyon skies,
> For amber waves of grain,
> For purple mountain majesties
> Above the enameled plain!

"But our stay was brief," Bates recalled, "barely half an hour." Owing to the altitude, "Professor Todd himself fainted and we were all unceremoniously bundled into the big wagon." That night at the Antlers Hotel (1883-1898, destroyed by fire) at 4 South Cascade in Colorado Springs, Bates completed "America the Beautiful."[7]

Though Muir never topped Pikes Peak, he was, in Lawrence Buell's conception, "the most charismatic celebrator of purple mountain majesty." The entire Colorado Rockies, in fact, eluded his one-step-after-another engagement. He crossed them by train on his transcontinental travels. He learned about them from friends Helen Hunt Jackson, Enos Mills (the creator of Rocky Mountain National Park), Charles F. Lummis, and others. He read about them in William Cullen Bryant's *Picturesque America*. But he was never drawn to their summits.[8]

"But even here was no desolation," Mabel wrote of Pikes Peak, "equal to Fuji's lonely peak in Japan."[9] Six years earlier, she and David had traveled to Japan to join a solar eclipse expedition. They had ascended the 12,389-foot Fujiyama on foot—for scientific purposes, Mabel stressed, not religious. With the moon setting behind Fuji's volcanic peak at four a.m. on Saturday, 3 September 1887, they had departed their small inn in the village of Subashiri at the base of the holy mountain and walked ever upward, sustained by chocolate, through mist and wind, even a cloud ("there was no snow on the mountain, except in protected gorges...of the crater. . . ."). At the 8th Station, they had spent the night in "the absence of all comfort and convenience." Mabel wrote "Reach top in an hour in heavy mist" in her next morning's diary. From midnight—with the sky crystal clear, the temperature below freezing, and the west wind brisk— astronomical observations were made until the following noon. She descended that day, her husband following later.[10]

At thirty-one Mabel Todd was the first Western woman to climb Mt. Fuji. Even Muir did not attain that summit, though he may have had that pilgrimage in mind on the afternoon of 9 May 1904, when he saw her majesty from ship's deck in the harbor of Yokahama.[11] Todd's accounts—one written while en route appeared in three articles in the *Nation*; another was subsequently created for the *Century* of August 1892— presented the opportunity for Muir to know of her accomplishment, even before his meeting with Higginson.[12]

Two days after ascending Pikes Peak, with David fully restored, Mabel met with William S. Jackson in Colorado Springs. She asked the "charming cordial" Jackson about Emily Dickinson's letters to his former wife Helen Hunt Jackson. Jackson assured her that they had not been destroyed and that he would search for them, Todd reported to Higginson. None were found, however, as his new wife Helen Banfield related to Todd in mid-September.[13]

Like Muir, Mabel Loomis Todd loved nature. Her drives in the Amherst countryside, especially with Austin Dickinson, delighted her. Her attention focused on the weather and on the hills in the east, as these excerpts from her autumn 1893 journal reveal:

> Is anything so dear to me as the days when leaves are falling, and the remembered spaces get light and open to the sky? (23 October 1893)

> My ideal November day—cold, windy, brown leaves whirling, grey & white clouds, rifts of startling blue, a snow-flake now & then, purple shadows & brilliant sunshine on the Pelham hills. (16 November 1893)

When I first wake, a gentle snow storm in progress—The meadow quite white. But it soon stopped, and the grass is green again, and an uncertain sunshine glinting over the hills. (19 November 1893)[14]

The Pelham Hills meant so much to her that she arranged the preservation of a section of them that included 957-foot Mt. Orient. Later, in 1908, when she and David discovered tree choppers assailing Hog Island in Muscongus Bay, Down East, she and a friend would buy all but the north end of the island. On the east side, she would build a rustic cottage, which still stands (though sadly in need of repair when I saw it in May 2002), and would go there for summers. Here she would complete a revised edition of *The Letters of Emily Dickinson* that was published in 1931. A year later, on 14 October 1932, while preparing to leave for the season, she would suffer a cerebral hemorrhage and die. Inheriting Hog Island, her daughter Millicent would interest the Audubon Society in it. The Audubon summer camp, started there in 1936, continues to this day.[15]

During their Cambridge meeting, Emily Dickinson and Mabel Loomis Todd may have been a topic of conversation among Higginson, Johnson, and Muir. Higginson had also mentored Dickinson's Amherst childhood neighbor, Helen Hunt Jackson, who was born on 14 October 1830, two months before Dickinson. Jackson's Greek Revival home at 249 South Pleasant Street (c.1830) stood next to Amherst College, where her father Nathan Fiske, an ordained Congregational minister, taught Greek and Latin languages, Greek literature, and moral philosophy. Helen's home was a half mile from either of Emily's dwellings—a salubrious stroll north over the town common, then east on Main Street; or, after 1840, north on North Pleasant Street, where the poet lived until returning to the Homestead in 1855. To accommodate her mother's poor health—she suffered from tuberculosis—however, Jackson often stayed with friends out of town. On 19 February 1844, when Helen was thirteen and away at boarding school, her mother had died. The loss of her father three years later, in May 1847, set off a life of movement from one place to another. Not until her marriage to William S. Jackson in October 1875 did she have a home of her own.[16]

In fact, it was Higginson who had "made them aware of each other's poetry," according to Kate Phillips. But it was Helen Hunt Jackson, the acclaimed poet of her day, who saw the greatness in Dickinson's poems, accepted them as they were, and encouraged her to publish.[17]

Although Muir's extant library reveals no trace of Emily Dickinson, there is a good chance that he knew her work. Dickinson's *Poems* sold briskly: six editions in six months, Higginson said. Possibly, Helen Hunt Jackson introduced Muir to her poetry.

Dickinson and Muir held mutual sympathies. They both loved botany, the Bible, and Shakespeare. "I am from the fields," she declared, "at home with the Dandelion." Mountains were the subject of twenty-three of her poems, Judith Farr states. She, however, was the paragon of non-travelers: "To shut our eyes is Travel." She had a "wondering hand;" he, a wandering foot. Their errands into the wilderness differed. Hers was interior: "Within is so wild a place." Her life was private: "How dreary—to be— Somebody!"[18]

Though Muir would never come to Amherst, in one way at least he eventually found himself there. In May 1901, a thirty-one-year-old editor for *McClure's Magazine*, Ray Stannard Baker, met the sixty-three-year-old Muir in Martinez, California—their April birthdays were four days apart. "We took long tramps: we talked early and late," Baker wrote in his memoir. Baker left with great admiration for the naturalist (placing him "side-by-side with Thoreau"), and with Muir's autographed "portrait" in hand. During the next two years, 1902 and 1903, Baker's writings about the Southwest and Northwest appeared in the *Century*, as did Muir's "The Grand Cañon of the Colorado."[19] The *Outlook* of 6 June 1903—the day when Muir arrived in Liverpool at the start of his world journey—carried Baker's biographical article on him. This set forth the legendary image of Muir, now a commonplace, as explorer of mountians, discoverer of glaciers, and lover of nature.[20]

In late August 1910, Baker would move his family from Michigan to Massachusetts, settling in the quiet village of Amherst, where he would live until his death in 1945. Here he would prepare his eight-volume *Woodrow Wilson: Life and Letters*, a Pulitzer Prize winner in 1940. He also would continue to describe his adventures in nature, begun in 1906, under the nom de plume David Grayson. Through all these years of composing, Muir's portrait, hanging on Baker's study wall, would bless him. His home of brick, stucco, and slate still stands at 118 Sunset Avenue, now (August 2002) woefully neglected by University of Massachusetts fraternity brothers. Gone are

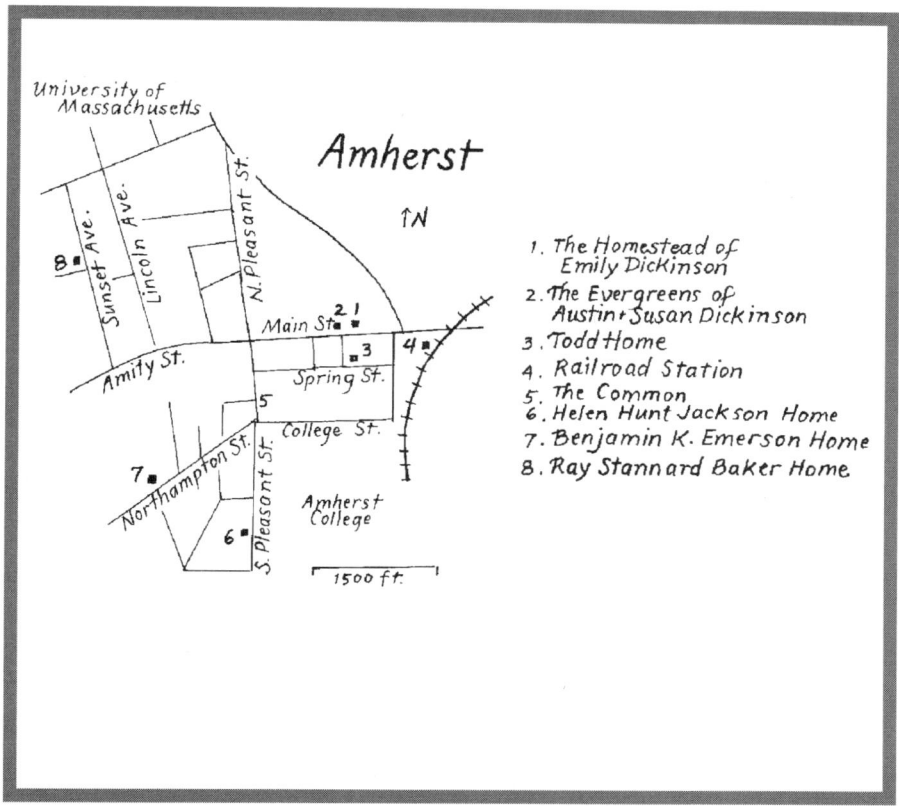

University of Massachusetts

Amherst

↑N

1. The Homestead of Emily Dickinson
2. The Evergreens of Austin + Susan Dickinson
3. Todd Home
4. Railroad Station
5. The Common
6. Helen Hunt Jackson Home
7. Benjamin K. Emerson Home
8. Ray Stannard Baker Home

Baker's gracious gardens, orchards, and beehives on the west side of the house that overlooked a large expanse of the Connecticut River Valley. Still to be enjoyed, however, is the venerable Grayson elm that before Sunset Avenue was created stood in Baker's front yard. An immense trunk lifts skyward; thick branches arcade over the street. "A grand tree," Muir would have exclaimed. *Under My Elm* (1942) was Grayson's last book.[21]

Another Amherst resident, Benjamin K. Emerson, would meet Muir aboard the steamship *Elder* along the Alaska coast in 1899. When they met, Emerson, fifty-six and with a long, flowing white beard, was professor of mineralogy and geology at Amherst College (as well as at Smith College). He had graduated from Amherst in 1865 and had been teaching there since 1870. He lived at 21 Northampton Road, close to the College. Two years earlier, in the summer of 1897, his wife of twenty-four years, Mary Annette Hopkins—they had six children—had died. (In 1901, he remarried.) Emerson authored the "General Geology" section of the Harriman Alaska Expedition, as well as other books on the geology of his surrounds.[22]

After their initial conversation, Higginson took his guests on a walking tour of Cambridge, a city (since 1846) with some 80,000 residents in 1893.

They stopped at the homes of James Russell Lowell at 33 Elmwood and Henry Wadsworth Longfellow at 105 Brattle Street. "Both of these are just as they were when their famous owners were living in them," Muir wrote his daughter Wanda; "Mr. Higginson knew them & made our visit very interesting." To Wanda, Muir identified his guide as "the man who wrote the pretty out-door book I gave to Lou[ie]", her mother. He referred to *Out-door Papers* (Ticknor and Fields, 1863)—a copy of which Higginson had spied in Emily Dickinson's library when he visited her (Dickinson read all of Higginson), and a book that Helen Hunt Jackson regarded as exemplary for composition. All fourteen essays in this collection had appeared in the *Atlantic*. Higginson's nature studies, "Water-Lilies," "The Life of Birds," "The Procession of the Flowers," and "Snow" would have attracted Muir.[23]

A former Appalachian Mountain Club president in 1885, Higginson had lived a life outdoors as well as in. A devout tramper, he had done considerable wandering himself. He was the first to describe Carter Notch in the White Mountains, the result of his 23 September 1853 journey there with guides and artists. His ascents of Katahdin in Maine—he had escorted five women to its summit in September 1855 (and even after his 1859 trip to the Adirondacks, where he did no mountain climbing, held Katahdin superior)—and the Grands Mulets 10,113 feet up on the north side of Mont Blanc in France, in 1878, would have intrigued Muir, who in two months himself would look upon Mont Blanc and five years later pass close to Katahdin (see chapter 10), though without the pleasure of sauntering on these eminences.[24]

They walked west along Brattle Street, past the colonial residences of Tory Row, Higginson pointing out who lived where. Number 145 was the home of William Brewster. Five-eighths of a mile brought them to Elmwood, Lowell's residence. This was familiar to Johnson, who, with Higginson, had called on Lowell before. "Lowell's letters are perhaps the finest body of epistolary writing by an American," Johnson believed. "He knew everything that had been written worth knowing except, perhaps, the work of his contemporaries."[25] Higginson's esteem for Lowell was no less than Johnson's. Lowell, who had held the chair of modern literature at Harvard after Longfellow, had died two years earlier, in August 1891. Elmwood, now without elms, is the home for Harvard's presidents. On its west side is Lowell Park, bifurcated by Fresh Pond Parkway, and beyond that the great greensward, Mt. Auburn Cemetery.

Muir appreciated Lowell, too. He owned his *Poems* (1896-1898; 4 vols.), *Literary and Political Addresses* (1896), *Political Essays* (1898), *Literary Essays* (1898-1899; 4 vols.), and *Latest Literary Essays and Addresses* (1899), all published by Houghton Mifflin. In the first volume of *Literary Essays*, Muir had learned of Lowell's sense of this academic town in 1824, of Emerson and Thoreau, and of Lowell's August 1853 steamboat passage on Moosehead Lake in Maine for a mid-lake stay at Mount Kineo, a month before Thoreau passed the same way, through an area familiar to Muir from Thoreau's *The Maine Woods*. What did Muir make of Lowell's scathing criticism of Thoreau? Certainly, it did not dissuade him from pursuing the naturalist.[26]

They returned along Brattle Street for three-quarters of a mile, to number 105. Here Longfellow had lived until his death in 1882. The colonial mansion, now a National Historical Park, reopened after renovations in 2002. Its gardens, still in progress, are even more conducive, sans tourists, to contemplation. A huge American linden filling the east lawn is about two-hundred years old, dating to 1800-1810, the guide told me. It may have been planted by

Andrew Craigie, who bought the home in 1791. His widow sold the property to Nathan Appleton, who made it a wedding gift in 1843 for his daughter, Fanny, and her husband, Henry Wadsworth Longfellow. Their home was "the centre of a generous hospitality," Higginson remarked. "[O]ur dinner hour being half past two," Longfellow had invited friends to come if they were near. On 23 November 1848, Hawthorne brought Thoreau here to dine. Five years later, on 14 June 1853, Emerson attended Longfellow's farewell dinner for the Liverpool-bound Hawthorne, a Bowdoin College classmate of Longfellow's. The next August, the day after its publication, Longfellow bought a copy of *Walden*. On a hot summer day, 9 July 1861, Fanny Longfellow went up in flame when hot sealing wax ignited her dress. Her grief-stricken husband never remarried. Emerson included six of Longfellow's poems in his anthology, *Parnassus* (1874), which Muir owned and read.[27]

In residence now was Henry and Fanny's forty-three-year-old daughter Alice. Though she lived here all her life (22 September 1850 to 7 December 1928), she, like Muir, relished travel. At eighteen she had made a Grand Tour of Europe. And now, at this moment when Muir and the others stopped by, she had like many Cantabrigians this year, gone to Chicago for the World's Fair, not to return until Wednesday, 14 June. Her excursion came after being confined in the house with illness and sorrow: Her brother Charles Appleton Longfellow of Boston, who wintered with her, had succumbed to pneumonia on 12 April, at the age of forty-eight. Her uncle the Reverend Samuel Longfellow, who had produced a biography of her father, had died the previous fall, on 3 October 1892, in Portland, Maine, at seventy-three. Alice herself had not been well that spring.[28]

She had the comfort of family close by, however. Her younger sisters—Edith, married in 1878 to Richard Henry Dana III, the son of the author of *Two Years Before the Mast*, and Annie Allegra, married to Joseph G. Thorp in 1885—were her west side neighbors, at 113 and 115 Brattle Street, respectively, while her older brother Ernest, an artist, and his wife, her childhood playmate, Harriet Spelman, lived across the street at number 108, a house they had built in 1870, two years after their marriage. Apparently, Edith, her husband, and their two oldest boys, Richard Henry Dana IV and Henry ("Harry") Wadsworth Longfellow Dana, were also at the Columbian Exposition at this time, though afterwards the couple left all six children to travel through Ireland, England, Switzerland, Austria, and France. As soon as Alice was back, she was busy preparing Edith's two oldest sons for Camp Asquam, in Holderness, New Hampshire.[29]

An early advocate for women's education, Alice, who preferred to be single, was now engaged in creating Radcliffe College, which she would serve as a trustee until her death. Her home was an oasis for students. The red-brick neo-Georgian Longfellow Hall (1930) along the Appian Way side of Radcliffe Yard honors her.[30] The next day Muir would meet two of her friends, Annie Fields and Sarah Orne Jewett, in Manchester-by-the-Sea.

Henry Wadsworth Longfellow had loved to walk. "To the River Charles," which flowed 150 yards south of his front gate, to consort with this "generous giver."[31] To the center of Boston and back the bard went, seven miles round-trip via what is now the Longfellow Bridge. About the Boston Common he paced. Mostly he was spied ambling down and up his own street in his dark frock coat, kid gloves, and stovepipe hat. "Walked before breakfast to inhale the air from the cherry blossoms, and drink the first foam of the spring," he wrote in his journal on 10 May 1860. Strolling the quiet streets of old Cambridge is still a delight. The surprises of spring especially enhance this pastime. A variety of flora flourishes in many small gardens. Fresh soft lemon and lime leaves emerge in April. Huge creamy white blossoms of magnolias light up front yards; lilacs scent the air. A tall weeping cherry graces the corner of Ash Street and Ash Place. A small patch of fritillaria begins a path between Ash Place and Hilliard Street. Pear trees whiten the south yard of an 1846 Greek Revival house at 221 Norfolk Street, recalling Gustav Klimt's 1903 oil, *Pear Tree*. Even some old elms have survived the scourge: one stands tall at 65 Langdon Street, another at 16 Traill Street.

Muir, Johnson, and Higginson next stopped at 56 Brattle Street, the still-surviving 1808 home of Dexter Pratt, "The Village Blacksmith" of Longfellow's poem, whose "spreading chestnut-tree" would have been in bloom this fine June day had it not been removed to accommodate an expanded roadway. Now, a terrace before the Pratt House, whose current occupants are the Cambridge Adult Education administrators and the High Rise Bread Company, fills in season with conviviality.

A block east of the smithy put them in Harvard Square. Lyceum Hall on the west side evoked memories for Higginson. There as a youth he had first heard Ralph Waldo Emerson speak. Though Higginson did not understand Emerson then, the seer's presence had stirred him. At Harvard Higginson read and reread Emerson's books. Currently the Harvard Co-operative Society, founded in 1882, is in residence in Lyceum Hall, which "The Coop" (its common name) purchased in 1903 and rebuilt in 1924-1925. When Muir came The Coop was in Dane Hall (1832), across the square. Dane Hall, which had housed the Law School before 1883, burned in 1918.[32]

Two years ago, in 1891, the Higginsons had built a summer home in Dublin, New Hampshire. Six days later, on Friday, 16 June 1893, they would go there. On the south shore of Dublin Lake, with Mt. Monadnock in view to the south, Higginson had "felt for the first time that conscious happiness wh[ich] Thoreau describes." The family marveled at nature and socialized with their community, though apparently not with Annie and Edward Emerson, who stayed on the other side of the mountain. At the end of August, they drove around the mountain and up the toll road a mile, from where they proceeded on foot, he and Mary coming "close to top," their daughter and others "nearly." On Thursday, 14 September, he left for Chicago, arriving two days later. That Sunday, he visited the World's Fair. Monday and Thursday, he spoke to the Parliament of Religions. Thursday afternoon, he departed for Dublin, arriving home on Saturday, 23 September. Thursday morning, 5 October, the Higginsons returned by train to Cambridge. They did not light their furnace until the 16th.[33]

At some point, probably at Harvard Yard, along the east side of Harvard Square—though we do not know where and when and why—Muir and Johnson's escort left them and was replaced by another.

## JOSIAH ROYCE

Now Josiah Royce—a short, stout, freckle-faced redhead—"guided us," Muir wrote to his wife. Royce, who would be thirty-eight in November, had come to Harvard in 1882 as an instructor, to replace William James while he was on leave, and stayed. The year before his encounter with Muir, he had been promoted to the position of professor of the History of Philosophy. Like Muir, he was an entertaining conversationalist.

They had several touchstones. Royce was born and raised in California. A gold mining town, Grass Valley at 2690 feet, fifty miles northeast of Sacramento, was his birthplace; later his family resided in San Francisco. From late April to late October 1849, his parents, Sarah and Josiah, had made the arduous trek from Iowa to Weaverville, a mining town at the north end of California's Sacramento Valley. Guides helped them across the snowy Sierra Nevada—they reached the summit on the 19th of October—supplying two mules to replace their oxen, who could not make the grade with their possession-loaded wagons.[34]

At the University of California, which moved from Oakland to Berkeley in

1873, Royce had been inspired by Professor Joseph LeConte. He took all LeConte's courses—botany, zoology, geology—before graduating in 1875. Muir met LeConte in Yosemite on 5 August 1870; the two had been alerted to each other by their mutual friend Jeanne Carr, whose husband was at the university, and who had herself visited Yosemite in the summer of 1869, though she missed Muir. Muir traveled with LeConte and his party for five days, from Yosemite to Tuolumne Meadows to Mono Lake. En route, he heard three LeConte campfire lectures, on glaciers, carbonate springs, and salt and alkaline lakes. Leaving their horses to feed in the "rich grass" at tree-line on Mt. Dana, they made their own ways. When the forty-seven-year-old LeConte reached the 13,053-foot-summit named for the century's leading geologist, James Dwight Dana of Yale, the fifteen-year-younger Muir had greeted him. LeConte found much nourishment in Yosemite and the High Sierra, returning often over the next thirty years. On 15 August 1872, he and Muir climbed Illilouette Fall. Twelve days after Muir's Cambridge visit, in fact, on 22 June 1893, LeConte left home again for Yosemite. He was also in Yosemite, on the first annual Sierra Club excursion, when he died on 6 July 1901. Subsequently, Muir and Royce both wrote tributes to their friend.[35]

LeConte and his daughter Caroline would be guests of the Royces in November 1896. LeConte lectured on "The Relation of Biology to Philosophy" and met with friends Elizabeth Cary Agassiz and Jane Loring Gray, whose professor spouses he had studied with in Cambridge in 1850-1851. Later, at Royce's arrangement, the LeContes went to visit his friend Molly Dorr at Oldfarm, her summer home in Bar Harbor, Maine, where Royce had just been, before the fall term began. Mrs. Dorr encouraged Caroline with her book *The Statue in the Air*, publication of which Royce arranged for with MacMillan the next year. This short piece of mythology— in which Love overwhelms Chaos; in which the valley and its people are saved by a prophet who sends a herdsman to bring a statue over the mountain while avoiding the all-devouring Troglodyte Abyss—had certain resonances with Muir.[36]

The *Century* of September 1890 had continued a focus on California with Muir's "Features of the Proposed Yosemite National Park" (his "The Treasures of the Yosemite" had been the lead article of the August issue) and Royce's "Light on the Seizure of California," an extract from his book *California from the Conquest in 1846 to the Second Vigilance Committee in San Francisco* (1886).[37] In March 1891, Royce also contributed "Montgomery and Frémont: New Documents on the Bear Flag Affair." He contended that John

Charles Frémont had exceeded his orders in conquering California. The length of the California controversy eventually tired readers and the publisher, and Johnson had to give it up.

Since September 1889, Royce and his wife Katherine Head and their three boys—Christopher, eleven, Edward, seven this Christmas, and Stephen, four—had lived at 103 Irving Street, a section of an estate called Norton's Woods Royce had purchased in April 1889 from another Harvard professor, Charles Eliot Norton. Their commodious three-story house (with parlor, dining room, kitchen, and library on the first floor; four bedrooms and a nursery on the second) had enough space to accommodate Muir and Johnson overnight, had the Royces proffered an invitation. Students also came to their home. Royce was teaching a Tuesday evening class at home this October, and was available for consultation there on Mondays from 4:00 to 6:00 p.m.

Surely Royce pointed out the capacious dwelling two doors south of his at 95 Irving Street as the home of his colleague William James, who was spending his leave from Harvard (June 1892 to September 1893) in Europe with his wife, Alice, and their four children, ages seventeen months to thirteen; otherwise, he would have introduced them. They had been neighbors since 1889, when the James house was built, and would be until James's death in 1910. Both places still survive.

Five blocks south, Royce, Muir, and Johnson returned to Harvard Yard. The term was almost over: Senior Class Day was 23 June; Commencement the 28th. Royce pointed out where he taught at University Hall, a Charles Bulfinch creation of white granite dating to 1815, where on the second floor Longfellow had instructed Higginson, who later wrote a biography of his teacher that Houghton Mifflin published in 1902. As Royce was preparing to go to Chicago later this month to help with the planning of the Philosophical Congress in August, he was eager to learn of Muir's impressions of the World's Fair.[38]

Twenty years later both Muir and Royce would be invited to Johnson's Testimonial Dinner, marking the end of his editorship of the *Century*, which occurred in New York on 11 December 1913. Though neither could attend, they sent their respects.[39]

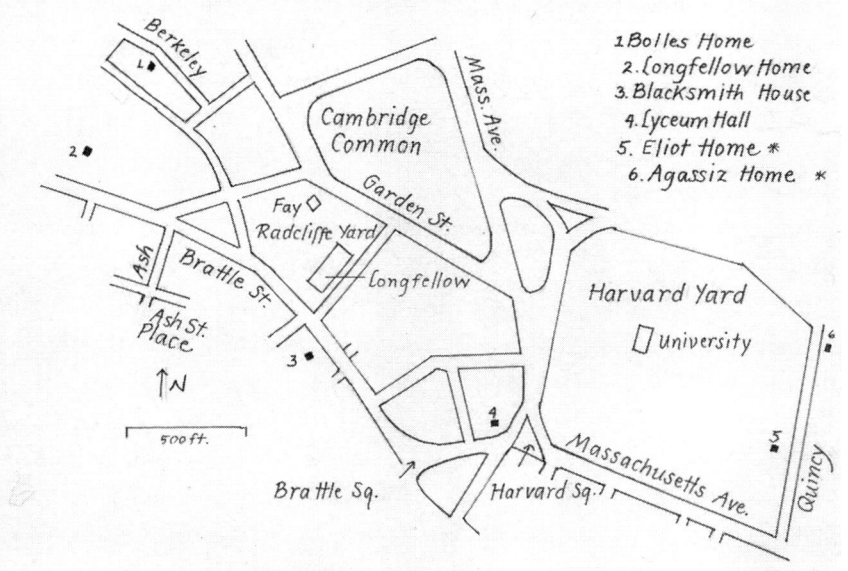

Cambridge 1893
Harvard and Radcliffe Yards and West

1. Bolles Home
2. Longfellow Home
3. Blacksmith House
4. Lyceum Hall
5. Eliot Home *
6. Agassiz Home *

Berkeley

Cambridge Common

Mass. Ave.

Garden St.

Fay
Radcliffe Yard

Ash

Brattle St.

Longfellow

Ash St. Place

↑N

500 ft.

Brattle Sq.

Harvard Yard

University

Quincy

Massachusetts Ave.

Harvard Sq.

## FRANCIS PARKMAN

While they were on campus, the strollers met Francis Parkman. "A Harvard Overseer," Professor Simon Schama has characterized him, "the first President of the St. Botolph; a gentleman scholar, rose-grower and anti-feminist; a man whose whole life had been consumed by the historical vocation; in short, one of nature's aristocrats."[40] Parkman, who suffered from arthritis, rheumatism, and failing sight, was ensconced at his summer home on Jamaica Pond, north of the Arnold Arboretum, and close to Sargent's Holm Lea. (He wintered at 50 Chestnut Street, on Beacon Hill in Boston.) One of the century's foremost historians in the romantic mode, Parkman was also a famous gardener. He especially loved lilies—one of his hybrids was named for him—and roses that he explicated in *The Book of Roses* (1866). Five months later Parkman would die at Jamaica Pond; he was seventy. Muir certainly read one of the many tributes paid to him.[41]

Among others, they also "saw Porter," Muir wrote his wife, as if she would recognize this man without further identification. Three Porters, all medical doctors, were teaching at Harvard in 1893: fifty-three-year-old Charles Burnham Porter and his twenty-seven-year-old son Charles Allen Porter, both of whom had received their M.D. degrees from Harvard, in 1865 and 1892, respectively; and thirty-one-year-old William Townsend Porter, who had graduated from St. Louis Medical College in 1885. Charles Burnham was professor of Clinical Surgery, and lived at 5 Arlington Street in Boston. From his age, I deduce that he is the Porter Muir refers to. Other than this, however, there does not appear to be any connection between them.[42]

## ELIZABETH CARY AGASSIZ

Bordering the east side of Harvard Yard, Quincy Street was home to Harvard professors and its president. At the northeast end, at 36 Quincy Street, Mrs. Elizabeth Cary Agassiz lived in a big mansard, which she and her husband Louis had built in 1854, four years after their marriage. Their home, wherein she conducted a school for women, burned in 1919 (a marker identifies the place). Since 1927 the Fogg Art Museum, the inspiration of its director, Emerson's grandson Edward W. Forbes, stood here. In 1879 Elizabeth Agassiz, Alice Longfellow, and others provided for the "Private Collegiate Instruction for Women," which became the Harvard Annex, with Elizabeth Agassiz its president. The transformation of the Annex into Radcliffe College under Elizabeth Agassiz's guidance happened in this year of 1893, and Radcliffe was officially chartered in 1894. At this time it had no campus, dormitories, or faculty of its own; male Harvard professors, Josiah Royce among them, taught the women. Classes were held in Fay House, at 10 Garden Street, which had been restored through the generosity of Alice Longfellow and redesigned by her cousin Alexander Wadsworth Longfellow Jr. Here President Agassiz, always in a black dress with white widow's cap, held her midweekly afternoon teas for students, faculty, and friends.[43]

Curiously, twenty years later, Muir was to receive a letter from 10 Garden Street. The sender was Florence Willard, who attended Radcliffe in 1913-1914. While reading Muir's *Mountains of California*, she had discovered that her classmates were impressed that she knew the author. She "wanted to tell you [Muir] how very much beloved you are here." Muir greatly admired her father, Charles Dwight Willard, for his progressive reform work in Los Angeles. When the Willard house burned, Muir would send Florence money to replace her lost books. Florence Ryerson (she married Harold Ryerson in September 1914) became a playwright. Later, with her second husband Colin Clements (they married in 1927), she wrote plays for theater and screen, as well as novels.[44]

At home this Saturday, 10 June, Elizabeth Agassiz was busy packing to go to Nahant, a peninsula in Massachusetts Bay ten miles northeast of Cambridge, which she had loved since childhood; her maternal grandfather, Thomas H. Perkins, had built the first summer stone cottage there in 1820. Earlier in the month, she had returned from an eleven-day trip to Chicago to see the World's Fair. Some of her late May days at the Fair coincided with Muir's. Though apparently neither was aware of the other's presence, they were part of the same crowd in that immense space. She and her husband had not seen Muir while they were in San Francisco in 1872, though they had corresponded. Muir would twice relish *A Journey in Brazil*, an account of their expedition into the Amazon region of Brazil in 1865-1866, which she had coauthored with her husband. Now, she missed Muir again. At five o'clock, she arrived at Nahant. She returned to Cambridge only when needed: on the 16th for an Annex committee meeting and again on the 26th for the Annex commencement.[45]

The previous year, 1892, Lizzie Agassiz had spent an entire season away from Cambridge. On 10 March she departed for the West. On Friday morning, 18 March, while her train passed through the world's largest forest of ponderosa pines, in northern Arizona, the San Francisco Peaks traveled with her. Happily, she noted in her small diary the highest of them, Humphrey

(12,633 feet), and its companions Humboldt and Agassiz, surely snow-capped, though she does not give this detail. After visiting family and friends in Los Angeles and Santa Barbara, she headed north. Friday afternoon, 27 May, she spent with the colossal sequoias of the Mariposa Grove. The next day, Saturday the 28th, while Muir was meeting at 101 Sansome Street in San Francisco to launch the Sierra Club, she had entered Yosemite. She would have been pleased to find women among the Sierra Club's charter members, including Muir's daughter Wanda. In the afternoon while sitting quietly on her porch (she didn't say which one), she was "happy to let in such a presence as this valley gives on every side." Sunday, she walked to Yosemite Falls; Monday she rode up the trail to Vernal and Nevada falls, finding the precipices scary. On Wednesday, 1 June, she departed the "enchanted valley" for Palo Alto. On 11 June, she began her return, which took her through Portland, Seattle, and the Canadian Rockies, to Montreal and Cambridge, arriving just in time to speak and present diplomas at the Annex commencement.[46]

Elizabeth Agassiz served as president of Radcliffe until her retirement in 1901. In celebration of her seventy-ninth birthday that December, the president of Wellesley College, Caroline Hazard, would conclude a poem to her:

> *All women owe a loving debt to you,*
> *You opened doors to let new light shine through*
> *On countless lives in our beloved land.*[47]

She died six years later, on 27 June 1907, in her eighty-fifth year.

Fay House now holds administrative offices for Radcliffe, which has become part of Harvard University. Gone is the charming library on the third floor. Looking through the glass front wall of the second-floor reception area of the dean's office, over a polished desk with a clear glass bowlful of oranges, and through the office's open door, one sees the Common white with snow, gray with sky, and black with trees and coats of passerbys, the framing enhancing this 10 February 2000 scene reminiscent of a Childe Hassam urban portrait.

## PRESIDENT CHARLES WILLIAM ELIOT

Down Quincy Street from the Agassiz residence, number 16 had held the James family from 1868 to 1882, the sign says, though their home has not survived. In 1869, the young William James had watched his new neighbors move in across the street at number 17.[48]

They were the president of Harvard, Charles W. Eliot, and his wife since 1877, Grace Mellen Hopkinson. Two sons, Charles and Samuel, thirty-four and thirty-one respectively, from his first marriage, with Ellen Derby Peabody, who had died in 1869, had graduated from Harvard, married, and had their own families. Currently, in 1893, Samuel was minister of the Unitarian Church in Brooklyn, while Charles had helped his old teacher Frederick Law Olmsted complete his World's Fair design and had joined his firm. He would meet Muir tonight at the Sargents'.[49] The 1860 mansard with curved slate roof that Eliot occupied for the duration of his forty-year presidency ( the national average for college presidents is now seven years!) was replaced by his successor president, A. Lawrence Lowell, in 1912 with a three-story brick mansion.[50] This is now designated the Office of the Governing Boards and Secretary. A bell may be rung to enter.

Muir had met the Eliots while they were in California in March 1892. The previous spring, 1891, the Eliots had been west as far as Colorado, where they saw son Samuel, then pastor of Denver's Unitarian Church.[51] The occasion for their coming to California was the Charter Day exercises at the University of California in Berkeley, where on Wednesday morning, 23 March, Eliot addressed a packed gymnasium. The evening before, the Harvard Club had honored him with a dinner at the Palace Hotel in San Francisco. Though he had declined to speak, Muir had joined the distinguished guests, evidently all men, at the table set for one hundred. Monday morning Grace Eliot had "received the many ladies—wives, daughters and sisters of former students under her husband," while that evening Muir had attended another fraternal reception for President Eliot, at the University Club on Sutter Street.[52]

While the young John Muir explored the Sierra Nevada, the young Eliot had become familiar with the Maine coast. Mount Desert Island, which he first saw aboard his sloop *Jessie* in 1871, captivated him. Here he returned each summer, building a cottage in Northeast Harbor in 1881, on a site along the eastern entrance of the harbor that son Charles recommended. President and Mrs. Eliot would be there this summer of 1893. Charles would join them for a short vacation, 5-13 August, before leaving for Chicago, Kansas City, and Louisville. In autumn 1889, Charles had written advocating the public ownership of the scenery of the Maine coast. In August 1901, President Eliot actually would become the first to put his son's idea into practice by creating a commission to acquire and keep reservations unspoiled on Mount Desert island. Thus began the creation of Acadia National Park.[53]

Both Muir and Eliot had described their paradises in essays that appeared in the August 1890 issue of the *Century*. "The Treasures of the Yosemite" was the lead article. Fifty-six pages later came "The Forgotten Millions: A Study of the Common American Mode of Life." The latter dwelt on the people of Mount Desert, a town of one small village Somesville, with about 280 houses, that was little affected by summer visitors, though about a dozen families had taken in boarders, some even enlarging their homes to accommodate more, others selling portions of their farms. Even before Muir and Eliot met, they thus knew of each other's love of nature and zeal to protect it.

When Johnson and Muir called, the Eliots were not at their Quincy Street home. A walk with President Eliot would have to wait for three years, their next time in Cambridge together. The next year, 1894, marked the twenty-fifth anniversary of Eliot's leadership, but a celebration Muir would miss.

## FRANK BOLLES

One of the "etc etc" whom Muir told his wife he saw at "the classic old shades of learning" may have been Frank Bolles, the secretary of Harvard. Bolles had earned a second law degree from Harvard in 1882—his first had been from The George Washington University (in Washington, D.C., then Columbian University) in June 1879—and while a student there had been a founding member of the Harvard Co-operative Society for one year. His office now was in University Hall in the center of the Yard, where Royce taught and Eliot presided. From there, crossing the Yard and Massachusetts Avenue, Bolles, at the end of each work day, had walked westward along Garden Street, past the Common on the right with its famous elm, where George Washington took command of the Continental Army, turning left and then right on Berkeley Street, and down that two doors on the south side to number 6 (a former residence of William Dean Howells; see chapter 4). Inside this handsome three-story, slate-roofed Greek Revival house, he had joined his wife of almost nine years, Elizabeth Quincy Swan ("Lily") and their four daughters, Elizabeth Quincy and Katherine Dix, who were eight and six, respectively, in 1893; Evelyn, who was four on 22 April, the day after Muir's fifty-fifth birthday; and infant Elinor.[54]

At twenty-seven, Frank Bolles had been three years younger than Lily when they were married on 1 October 1884 in Cambridge. Their honeymoon entailed a stay at the Chocorua Inn in the village of Tamworth Iron Works (from 1890, Chocorua), New Hampshire, within the town of Tamworth

(1,025 souls in 1890). The previous September, they had climbed for the first time the landscape's most distinctive feature, Mt. Chocorua (3,500 feet) in the Sandwich Range of the White Mountains. Chocorua's bald pyramidal top, tilting east, without hotels or embellishments, contrasted with Washington's crowded summit to the north. The scene drew hundreds of painters in the nineteenth century, according to art historian Robert McGrath, and the peak was the most frequently depicted one in New Hampshire.[55]

The newlyweds had rowed their boat northward over Chocorua Lake, to a white sand beach in the northwest corner. There they inspected the old Doe farm—"a red-roofed cottage in the midst of an ancient orchard" and to its north a "lonely lake among the dingles." Two years later, Lily's mother had bought this 1830 farmhouse with approximately 230 acres for her daughter. The Bolleses named it Crowlands. (The house is still a private residence, while the land was the gift in 1969 of "Bolles' daughter, Evelyn Phenix, in her father's name to the Nature Conservancy," Stephen Ells says.) If not for President Eliot's offer of employment that same year, 1886, this might have been the Bolleses' only address, for according to Ells, he had abandoned his editorial post with the *Boston Daily Advertiser* with the set intention of being a freelance writer, living simply in the woods. Instead, these highlands became the sanctuary of his heart, the respite from his toils at Harvard. They also excited the literary imagination of Bolles the naturalist.[56]

Two years before Muir's Cambridge visit, in the fall of 1891, Bolles's *Land of the Lingering Snow: Chronicles of a Stroller in New England from January to June* had been published. All of his rambles had taken place in eastern Massachusetts, in, near or within an easy train ride of Cambridge—the farthest being at Highland Light on the outer banks of Cape Cod, prompted no doubt by Thoreau's visits there. The fecund month of May, however—the focus of eight of the book's twenty-six essays—Bolles began and ended at Crowlands. There once he listened to the "voices of May day": "Song, field, chipping, vesper, white-throats, and juncos" in an air "superlatively pure, sparkling, full of that which makes deep breathing a pleasure." Though penetrated by peace, he also felt "a thrill of life was trembling in earth and air and water"—the emergence of spring. The next morning he returned to Cambridge full of "the mocking laughter of loons and the sweet song of the hermit thrush." He had kept track of the birds of Crowlands since their first summer there, and Lily, the plants. In December 1887 he had been elected into the all-male Nuttall Ornithological Club in Cambridge, to whom he spoke on occasion about his avifauna.[57]

Bolles's *At the North of Bearcamp Water: Chronicles of a Stroller in New England from July to December*, had appeared earlier this year, in February 1893, and had been reviewed favorably in this month's (June 1893) *Atlantic*, which Muir may well have seen.[58] Unlike its predecessor, this collection of twenty-one essays took as its territory Crowlands and environs, in the second half of the year of 1892. Like Muir, Bolles enjoyed his elevations. On 10 August, he walked the Hammond path, which started a mile north of his cottage, and proceeded almost four miles to the summit of Chocorua. There he spent the night in expectation of viewing the Perseids, which had been so spectacular the year before—when from his meadow some 3,000 feet below he had "counted two hundred and fifty meteors between sunset and eleven o'clock p.m." This time storminess interfered until after two o'clock, when one large meteor shot across the sky, followed by several smaller ones. Three months later, in November, Bolles had ascended Bald Mountain (2,140 feet), which the Hammond path reached in about two miles. Though it had occurred in December of the previous year and was north of the Sandwich Mountains, he also told of his snowy climb of Bear Mountain (3,220 feet).[59]

Bolles's Cambridge neighbor and Harvard colleague, William James, also was attracted to Chocorua. Both had acquired their farms in 1886. (Even Henry James considered being a Chocorua landowner, but never assumed that role.[60]) They would arrive at the West Ossipee train station from Cambridge, and from there take an open wagon four miles north to Chocorua. Their homes, only three-quarters of a mile apart, were separated by Lake Chocorua. One early April day in 1887, they had walked together from east to west, from James's to Bolles's, across the frozen lake, the ice two feet thick. In warmer weather they would swim and bathe in the lake. They might meet at the post office, coming down the road by buggy or down the lake by boat and walking up the hill to the village. In 1888, they had collaborated on the creation of the Chocorua Public Library, now one of the few remaining privately sustained public libraries. Bolles was the prime mover, soliciting funds and books from James and others, and serving as a trustee. He shared this post with John Henry Nickerson, who with his wife Clarinda ran an inn, where James stayed for five spring days on his first visit. The library was in the village post office until the completion of Runnells Hall, wherein it occupied a first-floor room. Professor James spoke at the dedication of Runnells Hall on Saturday, 28 August 1897. Even with Chocorua in his life, though, James continued to retreat to Keene Valley in the Adirondacks, confiding to Alice that that place felt the most intimate to him.[61]

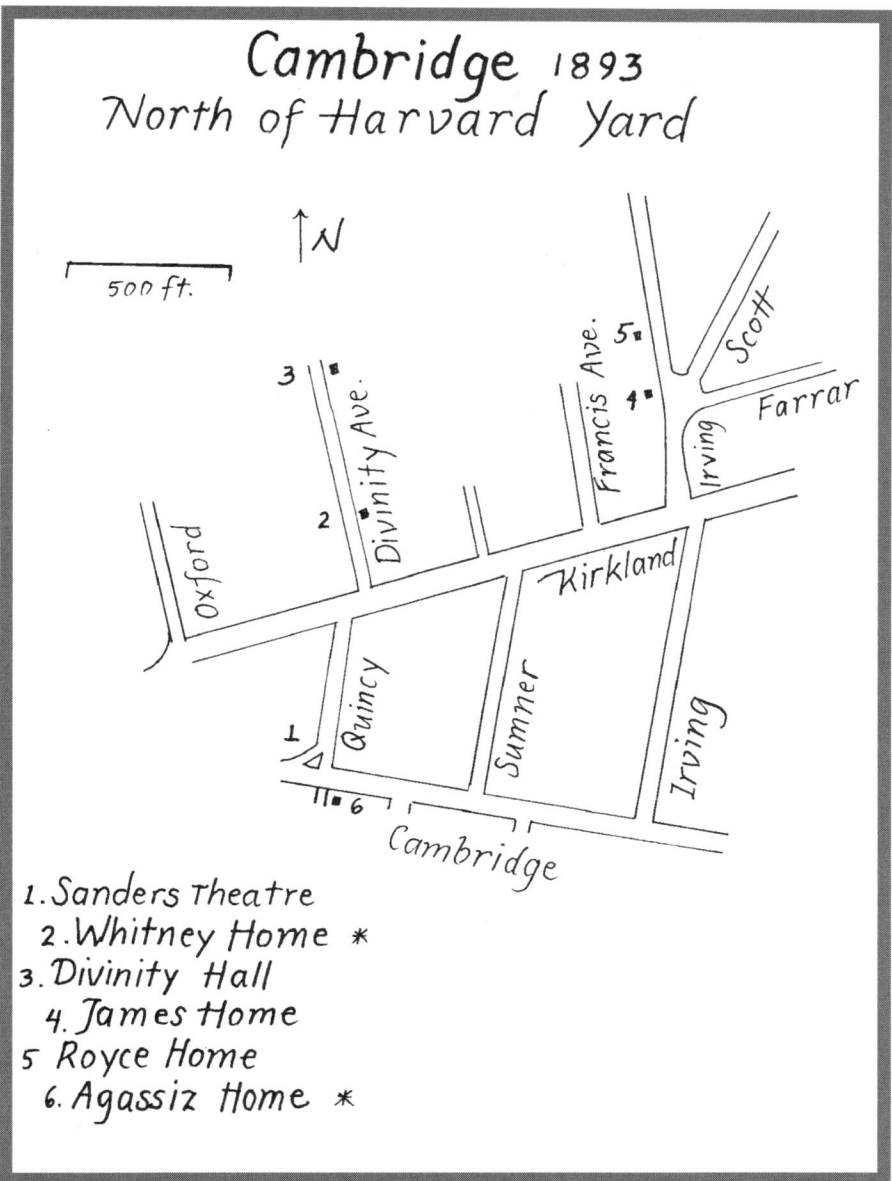

# Cambridge 1893
## North of Harvard Yard

500 ft.

1. Sanders Theatre
2. Whitney Home *
3. Divinity Hall
4. James Home
5 Royce Home
6. Agassiz Home *

Later in June 1893, on Wednesday the 28th, at Harvard's commencement, President Eliot would present Bolles with an honorary A.M. degree in company with Frederick Law Olmsted, Hollis Horatio Hunnewell (see chapter 11), and others. The next month, Frank and Lily Bolles would sail from Boston for a month in Nova Scotia. They traversed the maritime province from Yarmouth in the south to Ingonish in the north, mostly by train, though also by horse-drawn wagon, steamboat, and shanks' mare. Two headlands bounded the narrative of their journey: Blomidon of Minas Basin, and Smoky of South Bay Ingonish in the Cape Breton Highlands, 670 and 1,200 feet respectively—both of which they ascended, the former by carriage, the latter on foot; both are now provincial parks. Smoky gave them their most beautiful view: "Bays [Bolles wrote], headlands, islands, sandy beaches, lighthouses, cosy villages, passing ships, sailing ravens, and sparkling waves shone on the right, while on the left mountain after mountain, all heavily wooded, though showing many a bare cliff or sculptured summit, filed away from foreground to distance in mighty ranks."[62]

It was to be the couple's last summer together, and his final autumn at Harvard. He had reduced his work in order to write more. "I take twice as much exercise as last year and see twice as much of my family," he would write his mother in early November. Before Christmas, cold or grippe confined him to home. There was no holiday vacation at Chocorua. In early winter, on 10 January 1894, Bolles died of pneumonia in Cambridge. He would have been thirty-eight in October. The first of his four Nova Scotia essays began in *Atlantic* in May 1894. Later that year, in October, these pieces, combined with others, were published as *From Blomidon to Smoky and Other Papers*, thanks to Lily Bolles. If not for his early death, presumably Bolles would have read Muir's *The Mountains of California*, which appeared in the same month as *From Blomidon to Smoky*, and would have been present with Muir at Harvard's 1896 commencement.[63]

## JOSIAH WHITNEY

Walking along Kirkland Street, Muir and Johnson passed Divinity Avenue, opposite Quincy Street, named for the Divinity School, where Emerson had been a student in 1825-1827.[64] The first house on the east side, number 2 Divinity, was the home of Josiah Dwight Whitney—later it was replaced by the Harvard-Yenching Institute (1930), now under the modern skyscraper to its south, William James Hall (1963). Whitney had been born in Northampton, Massachusetts, in 1819, the oldest of eight children of Josiah

Dwight and Sarah Williston Whitney; he would be seventy-four years old in November. He was approaching the eleventh anniversary of the greatest tragedy of his life: the deaths on 13 June 1882 of his wife of twenty-eight-years, Louisa Goddard Howe, and several hours later of their twenty-five-year-old daughter and only child—"Nora," who had married the year before, Thomas Allen, an artist, and was living with him and their infant daughter near Paris. Since 1865, Whitney himself had been the Sturgis Hooper Professor of Geology at Harvard. Regularly, he walked across Divinity Avenue to his second-floor office in the Agassiz Museum, now the Peabody Museum of Archaeology and Ethnology (11 Divinity Avenue), and through the Yard to Harvard Square for groceries.[65]

Living nearby at 21 Berkeley Street was Whitney's sister Maria. She had been a friend of Emily Dickinson and Samuel Bowles, and a teacher of modern languages at Smith College in its initial years. Sixteen years later, in 1909, she would send Muir $25 to support his effort to save the Hetch Hetchy Valley, and would offer her help in "the good cause." With her letter she would enclose a copy of *The Life and Letters of Josiah Dwight Whitney*, having heard of Muir's interest in it through her grandniece Marian Hooker. Muir would read of her brother with interest, being especially attentive to his California years. He would note that Whitney had climbed Mt. Shasta (14,162 feet) and had measured its height within 300 feet of its true elevation.[66]

Residing with Maria at the same Berkeley Street address was Whitney's bachelor half brother, James Lyman Whitney, head of the catalog department of the Boston Public Library, of which he would later become director. Josiah Whitney also corresponded with his younger brother, William Dwight, professor of Sanskrit at Yale since 1854. In less than a year, on 7 June 1894, William would be dead, and on 19 August 1896, Whitney himself died.[67]

If Muir thought of Whitney while in Cambridge, he kept it to himself. He might have recalled their differences over the origins of Yosemite Valley, Muir believing in glaciers, not in the loss of the valley's bottom in a cataclysmic upheaval, as Whitney claimed in his *Yosemite Guide-book*. "He took Whitney on at many turns," historian Dennis Williams asserted, in *The Mountains of California*, "but he never mentioned him outright." Even in the White Mountains of New Hampshire, Whitney found no evidence for their being covered by an ice sheet, only some "local glaciation, and not much of that."[68]

Whitney had begun his geological explorations in New Hampshire in 1840. As an unpaid field assistant to Dr. Charles T. Jackson, the state's geologist, in whose Boston chemistry laboratory he worked, Whitney with Moses B.

Williams had inventoried parts of the Granite State's natural resources. In the process, they had made several ascents: Red Hill (2,029 feet) north of Lake Winnipesaukee; Rump Mountain (3,647 feet) on the northern New Hampshire-Maine border, where they camped on the summit (actually in Maine); and Mount Lafayette (5,260 feet). They had been the first to ride horses on the Crawford Path to the top of Mount Washington. Back in Boston that winter, Whitney had prepared six lithographs and with Williams four sectional reports for Jackson.[69]

As California's state geologist from 1860 to 1874, Whitney had been all over that state. His exploration of the Yosemite Valley, though, seems to have been limited to seven days in June 1863, with botanist William Henry Brewer, who, like Whitney, was a Yale alumnus. Whitney had also served on the Yosemite Park Commission, appointed by the governor in 1864, with Frederick Law Olmsted, Galen Clark, and five others. Whitney actually had been in San Francisco when Muir had arrived on 28 March 1868, but he had departed for the East at the end of April. He had returned again and again, however; in one year, 1870, he had crossed the continent four times.[70]

Muir might also have been transported to Mount Whitney in the southern Sierra—the highest point (14,495 feet) in the conterminous United States—which Clarence King and Richard Cotter of the Whitney Geological Survey had named in July 1864. At 8:00 a.m. on 21 October 1873, Muir had reached the summit. Then "sketch etc gain glorious views & descend to foot of range," he noted briefly in his journal. Though the first ascent of Mt. Whitney had occurred only two months before Muir's, on 18 August, Muir's was the first via the east side.[71] Two years later, on 20-21 July 1875, Muir returned to Whitney, this time with two companions. This approach was "by the quick direct route discovered by me two years ago," he wrote. After sleeping at 11,500 feet, they made their way, from dawn to ten o'clock the next morning, to the top. By sunset they were back in the Owens Valley. On 11 August 1902, Muir, in his sixty-fourth year, made his last ascent of Whitney. This time he came from the west, out of the Kern River Valley, accompanied by Marian Hooker, a grandniece of Whitney's.[72]

After a full afternoon of continuous company and conversation with Cantabrigians, Johnson and Muir returned to the Sargents and Holm Lea for the night. Such was the pace of their engagements that Muir did not write home until after his New England experience was over.

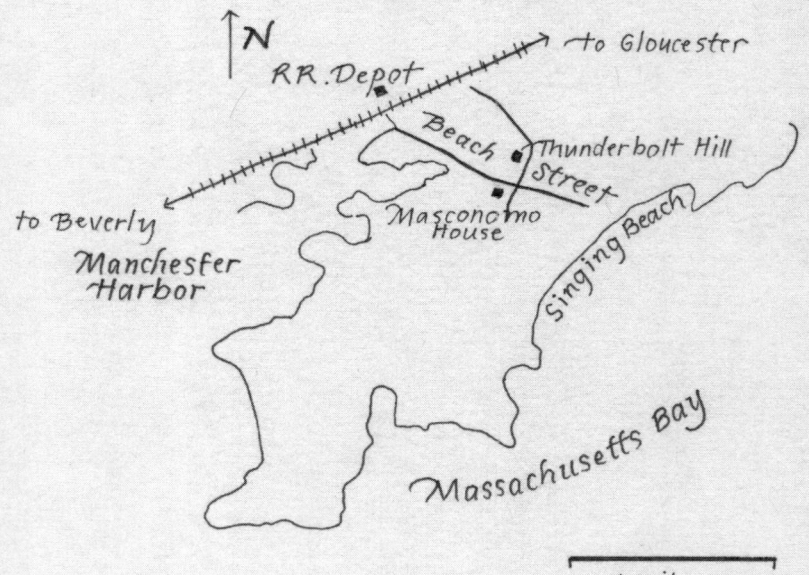

# 4. MANCHESTER-BY-THE-SEA

*Cape Ann, from Beverly round to Squam, is bristling with little capes, projecting from the main one and similar to it.*
—Henry D. Thoreau, *Journal*, 24 September 1858

*Indeed the day should be sacred to giving rather than receiving....*
—Sarah Wyman Whitman to Minna Timmins, 5 December [no year]

*People wonder why I go so much.*
*Well, I go partly for my health, partly to familiarize myself with the road.*
—Mark Twain, luncheon speech
Cramp's Shipyard, Philadelphia, 25 March 1895

## SUNDAY, 11 JUNE 1893

Johnson had one more Massachusetts excursion for the itinerant Californian. The next day after being in Cambridge, they took the train from Boston along the North Shore to Manchester-by-the-Sea on Cape Ann, passing through the communities of Lynn, Swampscott, Marblehead, Salem, and Beverly, through varied landscapes of rivers, salt marshes, and sand beaches with generous ocean vistas—all territory new to Muir—a twenty-five-mile ride you can still enjoy courtesy of the Massachusetts Bay Transportation Authority (MBTA).

Soon their train stopped at Lynn, a shoe manufacturing center with some 55,000 people. From here they could see a long beach with fishing shacks and lobster traps, and a slender strand stretching two miles south to join an otherwise small island to the mainland. Such a formation is called a tombolo, and this particular land-tied island, according to geologist Sherman Clebnik, is a classic example. Named Nahant, the island was frequented by a number of Muir's peers—they had included Emerson, who had walked from Nahant to Lynn after having tea with the Longfellows and William and Emelyn Story on Sunday, 31 August 1851.[1] The Longfellows had stayed at Nahant every summer since 1850 (except in 1868 and 1869, when they traveled abroad). In the early years, the family had moved to Nahant via Malden and Lynn by carriage and "a pair of dapple-grey horses."[2]

In 1860, Longfellow and his brother-in-law Thomas Gold Appleton bought the Wetmore Cottage on Nahant's south shore, north of Bass Rock, where Longfellow had first stayed in 1858. Their families shared this comfortable, commodious, light-filled space furnished with bamboo chairs and carpeted floors, enjoying views of the sea from the dining room and the back terrace. Here, on 29 July 1865, the bard composed "The Bells of Lynn," which was included in the Longfellow collection owned by Muir. They all had fun sailing aboard Tom's yacht *Alice*, sometimes as far Down East as Mt. Desert. When not quite a teenager, Alice Longfellow sailed with her Uncle Tom along the North Shore to Pigeon Cove at the tip of Cape Ann.[3]

Nahant had also been Thoreau's destination on the Thursday forenoon of 14 January 1858, after his lecture in Lynn the previous evening. And Elizabeth Agassiz owned a home there on the north side. She had, in fact, arrived the day before Muir and Johnson passed through Lynn.[4]

By now Muir had most likely heard of Charles Fletcher Lummis, who was born in Lynn on 1 March 1859. Educated at home by his father, the Reverend Henry Lummis, and at Harvard (he left his senior year without finishing his degree, which would finally be awarded in 1906), Lummis spent his college summers in the White Mountains. There he climbed and worked in the print shop of the Profile House, where he self-published his first of many books, *Birch Bark Poems* (1879). On 12 September 1884 he began walking west from Cincinnati—climbing Pikes Peak, encountering "a fierce snow-squall" atop Middle Creek Pass in the Sangre de Cristo mountains south of La Veta Pass (9,382 feet), stopping in Santa Fe and at the hacienda of Amado Chaves near San Mateo, New Mexico, descending to the Colorado River at the western end of the Grand Canyon north of Peach Springs, and crossing the Mojave Desert and Cajon Pass (4,257 feet) between the San Gabriel and San Bernardino mountains into a "paradise" of "orchards of peach, pear, apricot and English walnut," Cucamonga wine, and orange groves, before arriving in Los Angeles on 1 February 1885, having covered a distance of 3,507 miles—a kind of Muir walk to the third power. En route he wrote dispatches to the *Chillicothe* [Ohio] *Leader* and to his future employer, the *Los Angeles Times*. Later, in 1892, his book, *A Tramp Across the Continent*, had been published.[5]

*The Mountains of California* excited Lummis to have Muir in his new periodical *Land of Sunshine*. "I wish I could write as quickly & easily as most writers[,] then you would surely get more from me than you want," Muir responded, "But I am slow & awkward & write but little, still I'll try to give you something ere long." Though Muir never appeared in *Land of Sunshine* (which became *Out West* in January 1902), Mary Austin, Robinson Jeffers, Jack London, Joaquin Miller, Charles and Louise (illustrations) Keeler, David Starr Jordan, and other eminent writers did. Later, Muir visited Lummis and his family in their home El Alisal (Place of the Sycamore) at 200 East Avenue 43, Los Angeles, an eclectic place of Arroyo Seco stones, cement floors, and redwood ceilings that Lummis built (1898-1904) and where the Historical Society of Southern California now resides. Muir received Lummis's support for conservation, corresponded, and kept the friendship until the end of his life.[6]

In less than an hour from Lynn, the train carrying Muir and Johnson passed along the north side of Manchester Harbor and soon stopped at Manchester-by-the-Sea, a pastoral village of some 1,789 residents that swelled in population during the summers of the 1890s. Their destination being less than half a mile from the station, they probably walked the three short blocks south on Beach Street to Masconomo Street, named for the Sagamore chief who greeted the Puritans in 1630. On the southwest corner of this intersection stood the Masconomo House (1878), presiding over twelve acres of lawn that rolled to Singing Beach. They went northward on Masconomo Street, up to the top of a granite rise that was almost bare of vegetation.

Annie Adams Fields—"small, delicate, extremely refined and sensitive" in Johnson's words—welcomed them to her summer home, Thunderbolt Hill. Her permanent residence, a Beacon Hill townhouse at 148 Charles Street in Boston (sadly, no longer existent), was a haven for notable writers and intellectuals. Her husband, James T. Fields, had died in 1881 at sixty-four. The head of the distinguished publishing house Ticknor and Fields and editor of *The Atlantic Monthly* through the Civil War decade (before retiring in 1871), he had married Annie in 1854, when she was twenty and he thirty-seven.[7] The Fieldses had been summer boarders in Manchester and elsewhere—Campton, in the Pemigewasset Valley of New Hampshire, with its extraordinary view of the White Mountains that Starr King so admired, charmed them—before buying this land in 1873; then construction persisted for two years until they could entertain guests.

Wherever they were they always invited dear Longfellow to come.[8] Though he had Nahant, he also occasionally enjoyed Thunderbolt Hill. His three-day visit in August 1878 had included a jaunt to Gloucester to see Elizabeth Stuart Phelps, author of *The Gates Ajar* and other novels, at her summer abode at Eastern Point, The Sea Shell. Longfellow regretted that fog prevented his sighting of Norman's Woe, for "I have never seen those fatal rocks." He referred to the exposed reef two miles west across the entrance of Gloucester Harbor from Eastern Point. Here the Sunday night storm of 15 December 1839 had thrashed the schooner *Hesperus* and provoked his poem "The Wreck of the Hesperus," which Muir knew.[9] Longfellow's memory of Manchester "will gladden me for the rest of the year," he wrote James Fields.[10] He returned the following August (1879) for last time.[11] The Fieldses could not have enough of Longfellow. "So many years of my life have been made beautiful by the music you have translated into it," Annie wrote him, "that I praise God for such singing as I do for the air and trees and the great blue heaven."[12]

Muir and Johnson paused on the porch of Annie Fields's shingled, gambrel-roofed, three-story house, also called Gambrel Cottage. Muir stood straight, his hands clasped behind his back, his blue eyes relaxed, smiling, admiring the view of Singing Beach and Massachusetts Bay. It is an idyll now mostly obscured by mature trees, while the cottage still serves as a private residence.[13]

"One of its special features," Baedeker proclaimed of Manchester, "is the *Singing Beach*, the white sand of which emits a musical sound when stirred." Thoreau had walked along this beach, when on two fair-weather days of September 1858 he went to Rockport and back—a one-way distance of thirty-five miles. He set out with his companion botanist John Lewis Russell from Russell's home in Salem. When they passed Singing Beach, Thoreau likened its music to "the sound made in waxing a table." From there, "travelling partly across lots till we fell into a road" five and a half miles later, they came "in the dark at mid-evening" to Gloucester, where they lodged. From their chamber window, they "saw the moonlight reflected from the smooth harbor and lighting up the fishing vessels, as if it had been the harbor of Venice." Night overtook the adventurers, who felt "every where at home."[14] Later, Muir, who did not have an opportunity to make this walking excursion of Cape Ann, participated vicariously by reading Thoreau's *Journal* account of his wanderings. On Singing Beach, Annie Fields had walked in grief after her husband's death, conversed with flowers, butterflies, and the sea, and written poetry.

On Tuesday, 6 June 1893, Annie Fields had celebrated her fifty-ninth birthday. Three days later, on Friday 9 June, she honored the twenty-third anniversary of the death of her beloved Charles Dickens at the age of fifty-eight. Two days after his arrival in Boston for his second American tour, on 21 November 1867, the Fieldses had hosted a dinner for the great Victorian novelist at their Charles Street home that included Emerson, Longfellow, and Agassiz. The next evening Longfellow had invited him for supper at his Cambridge home. Dickens stayed at Boston's Parker House, rehearsing his readings in his room and sallying forth for long afternoon walks—"the most magnificently attired pedestrian," one observer remarked. Dickens called often at 148 Charles Street, too. Then came his first public performance. On 2 December at the completely filled Tremont Temple, he entertained an enthusiastic audience that included Annie and James Fields, Emerson, and Longfellow, with his *A Christmas Carol*. Annie collaborated with her husband on a memorial essay that appeared in the *Atlantic* in August 1870, "the first of her many memoirs of celebrated writers," English professor Rita Gollin says.[15]

## SARAH ORNE JEWETT

On this late spring day of 11 June 1893, Annie Fields introduced Muir to her companion since the autumn after her husband's death, Sarah Orne Jewett. Sarah had made her first visit to Thunderbolt Hill in August 1880. When not with Annie, Sarah resided at her home in Berwick, Maine, her birthplace forty-four years ago in September. The previous year, on 27 February 1892, Annie and Sarah had sailed with Robert Johnson and his wife Katherine—a trip inspired to aid Sarah's recovery from rheumatism, an affliction relieved periodically by water cures, and from caring for her mother, who had died recently (Johnson himself was recovering from a ten-week bout with typhoid fever). They traveled on the steamer *Werra* for the Mediterranean, an excursion that kept the two women away in Italy, France, and England for seven months; the Johnsons returned earlier. On Annie's birthday, after a sumptuous ride south from Martigny, Switzerland, over the Tête Noire Pass, they arrived in Chamonix, France, at nightfall. Mont Blanc, Europe's highest peak (15,771 feet), in full moonlight startled them. In just over two months, on 15 August 1893, Muir himself would repeat their drive by diligence from Martigny to Chamonix. "Mt. B[lanc] is not as fine looking a m[oun]t[ai]n as Rosa from Chamonix," he felt. (Two days before Monte Rosa [15,217 feet] had been a presence on his ascent of the Gornergrat [10,283 feet] from Zermatt.) Compared to the glaciers he had seen, Blanc's largest, the Mer de

Glace, was a small one. The next day he spent strolling "at moderate heights for general views. A fine hot flowery walk." Only blistered feet and lack of time kept him from being drawn higher.[16]

Perhaps Annie took Muir along the path that ran down the hill behind her house, to show him her two decades of landscaping with plants and shrubs. At some point, they all settled in the parlor or on the piazza. Though their conversation was not recorded, the four had much in common. At some point, we know that Muir entertained everyone with his dog story, "Stickeen." He set the scene: encampment, head of Taylor Bay, Alaska, summer 1880. Muir, sans breakfast and with only a piece of bread in his pocket, had sauntered about an unexplored glacier all of a stormy day with a small, black mutt. He gave details of his discoveries. Then he came to the climax as dog and naturalist returned to shore over this "grand crystal prairie." They groped their way through a densely crevassed area with darkness descending and snow "flying thick and fast," Muir told his attentive listeners. "I now began to feel anxious about finding a way in the blurring storm. Stickeen showed no trace of fear." Then an uncrossable crevasse stopped them. He described their situation. A thin ice bridge was the only way forward. With his ice ax, he cut steps down the wall, inched his way along the sliver over the "tremendous abyss," then cut his way up the cliff on the other side. He was safe, only the "beastie" was not. He had not followed. So Muir encouraged his four-legged companion step by step over the same arduous course he had just endured. When Stickeen reached him, the dog broke into "uncontrollable joy. He flashed and darted hither and thither as if fairly demented, screaming and shouting, swirling round and round in giddy loops and circles like a leaf in a whirlwind, lying down, and rolling over and over, sidewise and heels over head, and pouring forth a tumultuous flood of hysterical cries and sobs and gasping mutterings." It might have been a mime of his master's wilderness ecstasy. The shore was still miles away. "We reached camp about ten o'clock," Muir concluded, "and found a big fire and a big supper." "During the rest of the trip," Muir may have added, "he always lay by my side.…At night, when all was quiet about the camp-fire, he would come to me and rest his head on my knee with a look of devotion as if I were his god. And often as he caught my eye he seemed to be trying to say, 'Wasn't that an awful time we had together on the glacier?'"[17]

Jewett may have acquainted Muir with some of the places in Maine that she knew intimately. In July of 1887, Sarah and her younger sister Carrie had discovered Mouse Island, a mile and a half to sea off Boothbay Harbor and a quarter mile east of Juniper Point, Maine. The Eastern Steamship

Company served the island, where the Samoset House (1877-1913) provided accommodations. This sanctuary captivated Jewett. The next summer Alice Longfellow joined her here, and they went back the following season.[18] Sarah had known Alice's father, and her involvement with the benefit for the Longfellow Memorial that had occurred at the Boston Museum on 31 March 1887—she had invited Thomas Wentworth Higginson, Julia Ward Howe, Mark Twain, and others to read—brought her close to Alice. Today, Mouse Island is privately owned, and there are no inns for the public.[19]

## WILLIAM DEAN HOWELLS

Jewett was also familiar with Cambridge, where Muir and Johnson had just been. She had visited her cousin Mrs. John Nichols at Brattle Street, Lowell at Elmwood, and William Dean Howells, who four years after his 1862 marriage to Elinor Mead of Brattleboro, Vermont, had come to Cambridge in May 1866. Howells loved "the elmy quiet of the dear old Cambridge streets," his long walks with Henry James, often to Fresh Pond, and his Wednesday night meetings of the Dante Club at Longfellow's. The Howellses changed residences frequently. Howells was "the most addressless man" Henry James knew.[20] In 1872, they built a home at 37 Concord Avenue, which paralleled Brattle Street a quarter mile north. Higginson may have mentioned their address to Muir. In 1878, they moved to the neighboring country village of Belmont. This time Elinor's younger brother, the architect William Rutherford Mead, designed their Queen Anne cottage with California redwood shingles, Redtop. In 1881 they boarded at 7 Garden Street in Cambridge before renting 16 Louisburg Square on Beacon Hill. Returning from Europe, they again leased in Louisburg Square, this time at number 4. In 1884 they bought another house, at 302 Beacon Street. In late 1891, they moved to Manhattan. Summers, they left town for the country, most often to a different place. Their brilliant daughter Winny died suddenly on 3 March 1889, at twenty-five, while undergoing force-feeding treatment for anorexia, whereupon Elinor, whose health was never strong, became an invalid for the rest of her life. Elinor would die in 1910, ten years before her husband. Their other children, John Mead and Mildred, distinguished themselves in architecture and art, respectively.[21]

After an apprenticeship under James Fields, Howells succeeded him as editor of the *Atlantic*. In this capacity for a decade, 1871-1881, he nurtured talent like Henry James and Mark Twain, Annie Fields and Sarah Orne Jewett. He published five of Annie's articles. He accepted Sarah's first story, "Mr.

Bruce," which appeared in the December *Atlantic* of 1869, and six more about small-town Maine, and encouraged her to collect these into her first book, *Deephaven* (James R. Osgood, 1877). When Sarah's *Strangers and Wayfarers*—which combined three of her *Atlantic* stories—appeared in 1890, Howells was moved by her "precious gift" to write, "We all have a tender pleasure in your work, which there is no name for but love. I think no one has shown finer art in a way, than you, and that something which is so much better than art, besides. Your voice is like a thrush's in the din of all the literary noises that stun us so."[22]

As Howells was a major force in literary America in the 1890s, there is no doubt that Muir was aware of him. If Higginson did not talk about him to Muir, Johnson surely did. Johnson admired Howells's "princely courtesy" and the "flexibility, freshness, suavity, humanity and graceful strength of his work"; he put Howells "among the first of American writers." In 1884-1885, Johnson and Howells had worked together on Howells's *The Rise of Silas Lapham* for its run in the *Century* magazine before it came out as a book in late summer of 1885. This became Howells's best-known novel, "an outstanding example of late nineteenth century realistic fiction."[23]

The very day that Muir and Johnson were in Concord, 8 June 1893, the Howellses had come to Boston. They stayed in Auburndale, a ten-minute train ride west of Boston, at the Woodland Park Hotel, a grand Queen Anne set on six acres at the corner of Woodland and Washington streets, which they had enjoyed before (the hotel is now gone). From here Howells and Mildred went by train to Chicago to see the World's Fair, arriving 19 September, when Muir was crossing the Atlantic Ocean to New York. Their first night the Howellses took a launch across the lagoon by moonlight. They stayed at least until 2 October, the day Muir arrived in Chicago to see the Fair again. "It is the greatest thing that ever came into my life," Howells enthused to the press upon his return to New York. The "atmosphere of true courtesy and politeness everywhere" impressed him greatly.[24]

In May 1894, *Harper's* would begin the serialization of Howells's "My first Visit to New England," which continued in the next three issues. Herein Muir could read of Howells's meetings with Lowell in Cambridge—Longfellow was at Nahant, though Howells's shyness might have inhibited his calling without proper introduction even if the bard had been at home—with Hawthorne, Thoreau, and Emerson in Concord, and with Oliver Wendell Holmes and the Fieldses in Boston, all in August 1860. With the magazine articles, Muir could also see illustrations of James T. Fields, of the

Fieldses' Charles Street dining room, and of their view of the Charles River. Six years after its *Harper's* debut, in 1900, this essay appreared as the first chapter in Howells's *Literary Friends and Acquaintance*, which biographer Kenneth S. Lynn has called "one of the indispensable books in the history of American culture." Unlike Muir, Howells had been moved enough by his initial exposure to the New England literary environment to write about it, though some thirty years later. Their work even appeared together in the same magazine. The December 1898 issue of the *Atlantic* featured Howells's account of his summers at York Harbor, Maine, "Confessions of a Summer Colonist," followed by Muir's "Among the Birds of the Yosemite."[25]

Later, in 1902, Howells bought a home on the Maine coast. Here, at 36 Pepperrell Road in Kittery Point, five miles southwest of York Harbor, over-looking Pepperrell Cove, he "retreated each year between May and November." Daily he would stroll the half mile east past Fort McClary to the post office—mail was delivered four times a day then—stop at the grocery (1828), which is still in the same family and still serving customers, and talk with craftsman John Haley Bellamy at his home across the road from the market—all this closely gathered together just above the town wharf. Back home, he would write. They would entertain. When Mark Twain and his wife summered in York Harbor in 1902, they drove over to see the Howellses. And Howells and Twain read their manuscripts to each other on the veranda of Twain's "wide, low cottage in a pine grove overlooking York River." "[W]e saw each other often," Howells remembered. Before leaving for England on 4 July 1905, Henry James came to say good-bye in late June. Despite the heat, the trolley eased their fourteen-mile trip north to South Berwick, Maine, to see Sarah Orne Jewett.[26]

## SARAH WYMAN WHITMAN

Next to Annie Fields, Sarah's closest friend was Sarah Wyman Whitman. Whitman, fifty-one in 1893, married and childless, had resided on Boston's Beacon Hill since 1867, on Chestnut and Mount Vernon streets, close to Annie Fields on Charles Street, whose companionship she cultivated. An artist in several media, Whitman had created the stained glass panes that adorned Fields's Charles Street home. The Lily Glass Works, her studio at 184 Boylston Street (near today's Four Seasons Hotel), was close enough to the Common that Muir must have passed it. Since 1880, she had summered at The Old Place in Beverly Farms, which was only six miles west from Thunderbolt Hill, and was the stop before Manchester for Muir's train. Close to Beverly Farms station—a half mile south and then east on West Road— The Old Place looked out to sea over West Beach. Since being with her on the North Shore in July 1890, her confidant William James had longed to return.[27]

Whitman was also the leading book cover designer for Houghton Mifflin; in fact, she was one of the best in the country. Her impressive oeuvre showcased most of the covers for Jewett's novels (*Strangers and Wayfarers*, 1890, is dedicated to Whitman), as well as that of *An Island Garden* by Celia Thaxter (1894), illuminated with Childe Hassam's art (see chapter 12) and the 1896 edition of Thoreau's *Cape Cod*, whose pages were graced with Amelia Watson's delicate illustrations. Had Houghton Mifflin instead of the Century Company published Muir's *The Mountains of California* in 1894, it is likely it would have been embellished by Whitman. Her declining health in the late 1890s eclipsed her prolific career and excluded her from any chance of work on Muir's *Our National Parks* (Houghton Mifflin, 1901). She died in Boston on 25 June 1904.[28] William James was one of her eight pallbearers.[29] After Whitman's death, Jewett produced a brief preface to a collection of her letters.[30]

Like Muir, Jewett and Fields had attended the World's Fair in Chicago in May. Surely, this recent commonality entered into their Thunderbolt Hill discourse. Among the many attractions, Jewett had seen her own portrait (artist unknown) hanging in the State of Maine Building. If Muir had seen it too, he did not say.[31] The Houghton Mifflin pavilion in the building for Manufactures and the Liberal Arts reflected the ingenuity of Sarah Wyman Whitman. For them, she had made a suitably contemplative space: an oak-paneled library with stained-glass windows. A circular writing desk and chairs stood before a large tiled fireplace surrounded by the products of the pens of some whose busts sat atop the cases—Emerson, Longfellow, and Harriet Beecher Stowe among them, though not Jewett or Thoreau.[32]

The Fine Arts Building also displayed two of Whitman's oil paintings: a portrait of Oliver Wendell Holmes and the vibrantly white *Niagara*. Niagara Falls was a place of spiritual renewal for Whitman. A "supreme sight...an altar" that "must be painted," she wrote Jewett of her thirty-six hours with the cataract in July 1891. After the dedication of her stained glass windows in Memorial Hall at Harvard's commencement on 29 June 1898—at which Thomas Wentworth Higginson would receive an honorary degree —she fled west to the great waterworks for "forty-eight hours of silence and solitude," she wrote Jewett, and "studied and sketched and wondered every minute."[33]

## RICHARD HENRY DANA JR.

From Thunderbolt Hill, Muir could see the home of Manchester's first summer resident, the poet Richard Henry Dana, Longfellow's friend and Cambridge neighbor.[34] On 9 April 1845, his attorney son, Richard Henry Dana Jr. (1815-1882) had procured the deed to thirty acres to the east of Singing Beach and Eagle Head. Dana Jr. had interrupted his Harvard education for one of another kind. As a common seaman, he had sailed from Boston on 14 August 1834 on the brig *Pilgrim*, bound for California. Upon his return he joined the Harvard Class of 1837, graduating with Thoreau. He then became a student of law and later teacher of elocution at Harvard. Even while studying and lecturing, Dana managed to turn his journal and notes of his voyage into a chronicle that was published in 1840 as *Two Years Before the Mast*.[35]

"Good as Robinson Crusoe," Emerson told his brother about *Two Years Before the Mast* in October of 1840, "& all true. He was my scholar once, but he never learned this of me: more's the pity."[36] The same month Emerson's review appeared in *The Dial*, a review that Thoreau probably saw.

Muir's reception of *Two Years Before the Mast* appears to have been more reserved than Emerson's. In his copy, his usual marginalia are missing. His index contains only fourteen items from 27 pages of the entire text, and leaves a gap of 132 pages, indicating that he skipped or at least skimmed this portion.[37] The bulk of Dana's narrative (60 per cent) concerns his being off or on the coast of California, then a sparsely populated Mexican province, where in fact he had spent some fifteen and a half months of the twenty-five-month journey. He refers to the nascent ports of Monterey and San Francisco, where wood and water were brought aboard, where deer abounded on the hills and islands; Pueblo de los Angeles, "the largest town in California"; San Pedro, where they discharged cargo and took on hides (They needed to fill their ship—with 40,000 hides—before returning to Boston); and San Diego, where Dana lived on the beach for four months curing hides. Dana's gift is to show the nearly pristine condition of what has become the endangered shoreline of the most populous state of the nation (California became a state in 1850). This glorious country, however, did not impress the sailors, who labored from sunup to sundown and longed to be home.

With the happy prospect of returning to Boston earlier—delaying another year, he felt, would be detrimental to his career—Dana switched ships to the larger and newer *Alert*. The voyage home lasted over four months, from

8 May to 19 September 1836. The lone passenger, who boarded in San Diego, was the fifty-year-old naturalist Thomas Nuttall, a Yorkshireman who had lived in America since 1808. He had been curator of the Botanical Garden at Harvard, where he also taught natural history and botany, before leaving to join the Nathaniel J. Wyeth expedition to the Pacific Northwest coast in 1834, the same year the second and last volume—*Water Birds* (*Land Birds* [1832] was the first)—of his *A Manual of the Ornithology of the United States and Canada* was published. Crossing the Rockies at South Pass in the Wind River Range of Wyoming, Nuttall discovered a whip-poor-will (now called a poor-will), which his friend Audubon—they had met in Boston in August 1832—later named for him. Though Dana knew Nuttall from college, he "saw little of him" at sea. Besides, ship's rules prohibited conversation between passengers and crew.[38]

The homebound passage tested the *Alert*'s crew to the utmost. Their greatest challenge was rounding Cape Horn. Winter weather lambasted them. Gales altered their course. Thick fog obscured it. Snow covered the decks. Sleet drove them below. Ice encased the rigging, masts, and yards. A constant lookout searched for floating ice and icebergs. For a week Dana suffered in his berth in the forecastle, his face swollen from the wet and cold nights on deck, too sick to eat or sleep.[39]

Amazingly, they survived. Except for this one illness, Dana and the other sailors stayed healthy. A diet of salt beef and hard bread, a quart of tea morning and night, and on Sundays duff, a pudding of boiled water and flour with molasses, sustained them. On their outward voyage of 135 days they ate no fruit, yet remained free of scurvy. Only in the last month of their return to Boston did this disease beset them, and it was cured by eating fresh raw onions and potatoes, received from a passing ship south of the Bermudas.[40]

Muir, too, had been in the Atlantic and Pacific oceans. Sailing on a schooner in March 1868 from Cuba to New York, he ate salt mackerel, plum duff, and copious oranges, the latter being the ship's main cargo. The captain's husky Newfoundland gobbled flying fish that landed amidst the oranges. From New York, Muir had also sailed—this time in steerage, quite a change from the orangery—to Aspinwall (Colón since 1890), Panama, where he took a train across the Isthmus "with cruel speed through this gorgeous Eden of vines & palms, & I could only gaze from the car platform, & weep, & pray that the Lord would someday give me strength to see it better." Northbound through the Pacific Ocean, he had proceeded to San Francisco.[41]

Almost a quarter century after his famous trip, Dana would return to

California—this time via steamers and the Isthmus of Panama. "On my birthday cross a Continent," he declared of his three-hour, interoceanic train trip. In contrast to Muir, Dana was repelled by Panama: "Dismal place," he groaned; "all full of miasma." After arriving in San Francisco on 13 August 1859, he found that "every American in California" had read his book. This time he saw the hinterland—Clark's Camp, the Mariposa Grove of sequoias, and "a stupendous miracle of nature," Yosemite Valley—though evidently not the High Country. Leaving California on 10 September—he hoped, for the last time—he had his round-the-world journey aborted by a disastrous ship fire that sent him back to California for a month. His long odyssey, which resumed on 11 January, took him to China, Japan, Penang, India, Egypt, Italy, Switzerland—where he observed, "Nothing in America is to be compared with the Alps"—and England. On Saturday, 29 September 1860, he was back in Cambridge, dining in style and telling stories at Longfellow's.[42]

Engagement in rugged outdoor pursuits was a balm for Dana. Exhausted from his cerebral law practice and public life, he sought wilderness for renewal of his health and spirits. When his body expressed symptoms of fatigue, his doctor prescribed "a journey to the mountains." Taking this medical advice acquainted Dana with the great North Woods of the Northeast.

In June 1849, the thirty-four-year-old Dana, with Theodore Metcalf, "an experienced traveler," had journeyed to the Adirondacks. At Westport, New York, Villeroy S. Aikens joined them as guide. Early in the morning of 23 June they stopped at a log cabin in North Elba, south of Lake Placid, for breakfast. This was the home of the abolitionist John Brown, his wife Mary, and their large family (Brown had seven children with his first wife and thirteen with his second). After "corn cakes, poor tea, good butter & eggs, & unlimited supply of the best milk," they set off—with the addition of a local farmer to show the way—walking seventeen miles southward through Indian Pass to the Adirondack Iron Works, situated between Henderson and Sanford lakes. From there on the 25th they went up Mt. Marcy, thick underbrush making it "probably the most difficult ascent in America," Dana wrote in his journal. Early on the 26th they reached the Adirondack Iron Works, and from there, after a two-hour rest, left to retrace their steps northward, this time without the aid of their native companion, who stayed behind. After Indian Pass, they lost the trail and were forced to bivouac for the night, foodless except for one trout caught and split three ways. The next morning, finding their way, they went back to the door of the hospitable Browns, who again nourished them. Three days later, Dana—with another guide and without the lame Metcalf—

went up and down Whiteface (4,867 feet) from Lake Placid.[43]

Two years later, in August 1851, Dana was in the Maine woods. He sailed up Moosehead Lake, the largest lake in New England. Thoreau would transit Moosehead in 1853 and 1857, and Muir would behold it in 1898 (see chapter 10). Dana stayed at the Kineo House on the peninsula in the lake's center and climbed Mt. Kineo twice, six years before Thoreau's ascent. He hunted for moose, shooting one before upsetting the birchbark canoe from which he fired. He rationalized his kill by "the truth of Scripture & of reason." He ate meals of tea, boiled pork, and hard bread. Touring the lake in a sloop—where he used his nautical skill at the helm and slept aboard two nights —recalled his "old sea life." "I make it a rule never to read or study when I am away on these excursions," he entrusted to his notebook, "Except this journal, wh.[ich] I always write in daily."[44]

In 1853, Dana made a walking tour of the White Mountains that included a night (1 September) atop Mt. Washington in one of the two "stone cabins called hotels"—the Summit and Tip-Top houses had just been completed that summer. (When on Washington earlier, on 21 August 1844, he had ridden up on the Crawford Path and come down the same day, giving his horse to a tired walker and continuing on foot for the last three miles to Tom Crawford's Notch House.) After sleeping atop, on Friday, 2 September 1853, he descended in three hours to the Glen House. The next day he strolled south to Samuel W. Thompson's Tavern in North Conway, a distance of seventeen miles, where he lodged with ten artists, among them the Boston painter Benjamin Champney, who was responsible for attracting artists here to work and who had bought a farmhouse in town that year, 1853. On Tuesday, 6 September, Dana and William F. Channing, whose local farm he visited, walked up Mt. Kearsarge (3,268 feet), munching on blueberries along the way. Dana proclaimed the view from the top "the best of all." On Wednesday and Thursday, Dana progressed afoot northward through Crawford Notch to "Gibb's"— Joseph L. Gibb was the first manager of the Crawford House—from where, on Friday, he rode in an open wagon to the train depot in Littleton. The next year, in the afternoon of 13 July 1854, he and his wife Sarah Watson (they were married on 25 August 1841 and had six children) surmounted Washington— she rode while he walked—and slept in the thin air. The next morning they both walked down to the Glen House in six hours.[45]

More tranquil and shorter in duration, though still pleasantly restorative, were Dana's frequent sojourns in bucolic Manchester-by-the-Sea. There he reveled in the beauty, sauntered in the woods, fished in the harbor, watched the shimmering sea, and bathed in the surf before breakfast.[46]

Curiously, eye troubles had precipitated both Muir's and Dana's passages to California. While recovering from a work accident in Indianapolis—adjusting a machine belt, his file slipped, piercing his right eye—that left him blind for four weeks, Muir had decided to trade his life with machines for one with nature. Dana's painful eyes, so strained by measles that he could not read, had caused his withdrawal from Harvard in his junior year. Until this point in their lives, they had not seen their higher callings. Divinity in the form of eye injury intervened to clear their vision and to steer them to their destinies. Muir's was to study and preserve wilderness; Dana's, to call attention to the plight of the seamen and to protect them from the tyranny of their captains.

## CHARLES DUDLEY WARNER

In three months—after his trip abroad—Muir would be introduced to another mutual friend of Annie Fields and Sarah Orne Jewett. Charles Dudley Warner had celebrated his sixty-fourth birthday fifteen days before meeting Muir. A native of Plainfield, Massachusetts, a community adjacent to William Cullen Bryant's birthplace in Cummington, Warner lived there for eight years. He moved with his mother and brother in 1837 to Charlemont, Massachusetts, and from there in 1841 to Cazenovia, New York. In 1860, he came to Hartford, Connecticut, at the behest of his friend Joseph R. Hawley, whom he had met at Hamilton College. Hawley wanted Warner to help him with his newspaper, the *Evening Press*. In 1867, when the *Evening Press* consolidated with the *Hartford Courant*, the country's oldest newspaper in terms of continuous publication, Warner became its editor—a position he still held when he met Muir more than a quarter century later.[47]

Daily, in all weathers, Warner walked about a mile east to work at 66 State Street, Hartford. He and his wife of thirty-seven years, Susan Lee, now lived in a "commodious Queen Anne 'cottage'" on Forest Street (later replaced by the football field of Hartford Public High School) in the Nook Farm neighborhood, which Warner's brother George had built in 1873 and lived in until 1884. The Warners had no children. Their neighbors were Mark Twain and Harriet Beecher Stowe, both of whose homes are open to the public today. Susan Warner's piano music and gracious hospitality enriched their home. In 1899 she became a founding patron of the Hartford Philharmonic Orchestra, and she served as its vice president until her death in 1920. Besides her informal Wednesday evening recitals at home, she performed at the Hartford School of Music, and once at New York's Carnegie Hall.[48]

Warner's first book, *My Summer in a Garden* (1871), told of their former residence's three acres on Hawthorn Street, which joined Forest Street. Susan nurtured the flowers and Charles cared for fruits—Concord grapes, pears, fifteen varieties of strawberries—and vegetables—lettuce was "the best society;" but onion, cabbage, carrot, parsnip, were not grown—all the while contending with the vagaries of nature. For Warner, ultimate gardening was not the raising of crops, but "the philosophical occupation of contact with the earth, and companionship with gently growing things and patient processes; that exercise which soothes the spirit, and developes the deltoid muscles." The great green space was his teacher of moral lessons, of "the higher virtues."[49]

"With Warner I had a long talk on Yosemite & forest affairs last evening," Muir would write his wife from New York on 28 September 1893. All of their conversation that Muir shares is this: "He promised to do all he could to help us, & seemed surprised to learn the methods of the Yo[semite] Commissioners."[50] Warner knew whereof he spoke. He had seen Yosemite Valley and the Mariposa Grove, even described them in a book, though without mention of Muir or Galen Clark or of any time spent in the High Country. He had also inspected the Grand Canyon from its South Rim—coming there from Flagstaff over the roughest road imaginable, camping along the way—and related his experience, though without reference to a descent.[51]

Warner was most intimate with the Adirondacks, however. There he and his wife summered with their Hartford friends, the Rev. Joseph H. Twichell, pastor of the Asylum Hill Congregational Church, and his wife, the former Julia Harmony Cushman of Orange, New Jersey, and their ever-expanding family (they had nine children) in Keene Valley—a hamlet Warner described in 1866, their first summer together there, as situated "along a sandy road strung with farm houses and a post office with mail twice a week. Also a school house, which serves for itinerant preachers occasionally." Warner's many adventures—including ascents of the high peaks Marcy (5,344 feet)—called Mercy by their guide Orson Phelps—Nipple Top (4,620 feet), and its lower, western neighbor, Colvin (4,057 feet)—were published in the *Atlantic* in 1878 and in a book that same year.[52]

Warner had been in the Southern Appalachians, too. Departing from Abington, Virginia, on 22 July 1884, he and a companion referred to as the Professor—actually, Thomas R. Lounsbury of Yale—traveled by horseback through western North Carolina and eastern Tennessee. In Banner's Elk (now simply Banner Elk), North Carolina, they talked with Shepherd M. Dugger, author of *The Balsam Groves of the Grandfather Mountain*, a book given to Muir when he was in these mountains in 1898 (see chapter 12). Though the Professor expressed an outright hostility to elevations, they did ride up three mountains on their journey. First, following the Doe River, "a pretty brook shaded with laurel and rhododendron," from Roan Station, Tennessee, for six miles and then a carriage road "through splendid forests, specially of fine chestnuts and hemlocks," they reached the summit of Roan Mountain (6,285 feet)—a total distance of twelve miles, Warner said, though "probably nearer fourteen"—"our horses were five hours in walking it." They spent the night atop in the forerunner of the Cloudland Hotel (1885), where Muir stayed, as we shall see. Next, in North Carolina with Big Tom Wilson as guide, they surmounted, over a neglected bridle path, and preceded by a "huge bear," Mount Mitchell (6,684 feet). Caught in a thunderstorm on the highest ground in the East, which even Big Tom feared, they hastened down, "passing over Clingman, Gibbs, Holdback." From north to south, these are Hallback (6,300 feet), Gibbes (6,571 feet), and Clingmans Peak (6,560 feet), riding twelve miles in five and a half hours to their night's lodging. The next day they came to the most civilized stop of their wanderings. "It was the leisure hour of an August afternoon," Warner wrote, "and Asheville was in all its watering-place gayety, as we reined up at the Swannanoa hotel." From Asheville they made several sojourns. Their last climb was "a gentle ascent" of Paint Mountain, its 2,320-foot summit in southern Tennessee, two miles north of the border with North Carolina. "The open forest road, with the murmur of the stream below, was delightfully exhilarating, and as we rose the prospect opened," Warner wrote. By the end of August, they were back in Abington.[53]

Warner edited the *Library of the World's Best Literature*, which appeared from 1896 to 1898, in thirty-one volumes. Billed as "a household companion for any mood and any hour," it featured Muir's sketch of Linnaeus—"he found biology a chaos and left it a cosmos," Muir said—as well as his "A Wind Storm in the Forest" from *The Mountains of California*. It seems unlikely that Warner wrote the biographical introduction to the latter, as it was flawed with errors, such as those concerning the years of the author's birth and marriage. Selections from Sarah Orne Jewett's *The King of Folly Island and Other People* (1888) and *Deephaven* (1877) were also included in Warner's Library. Both Muir and Jewett appeared in the "Biographical Dictionary of Authors," volume 29 of the set, along with Annie and James Fields.[54]

Earlier in September 1893—before Muir met Warner in New York—Warner had visited Annie Fields and Sarah Orne Jewett at Manchester-by-the-Sea. During his three-day stay, they had luncheon with Oliver Wendell Holmes, who rode over in an open carriage from his summer cottage at 868 Hale Street in Beverly Farms, two and a half miles west of Thunderbolt Hill. Also present were William Dean Howells with his daughter Mildred from neighboring Magnolia—where Fields and Holmes had driven their last time together, on 25 August—and the pianist Jessie Cochrane of Louisville, Kentucky, who was also staying with Annie. This occasion, on Sunday, 3 September, was in effect a celebration of Holmes, whose eighty-fourth birthday had been five days earlier, on 29 August. Annie diligently recorded the conversation that Holmes, once fully engaged—he'd arrived depressed about his nephew's death, though Annie believed the reason for his despondency lay in the lack of stimulating intellectual company—directed and delighted in. Howells, who never forgot this moment, remembered that Holmes "said a thousand witty and brilliant things that day." Especially memorable was Holmes's recitation of what he thought were his two deepest lines:

*Till naught remains, the saddening tale to tell,*
*Save home's last wrecks—the cellar and the well!* [55]

Fields, Jewett, Holmes, and Howells had all been together before, to celebrate the birthday of the creator of "The Breakfast Table" essays, that time his seventieth. At noon on Wednesday, 3 December 1879, in Boston's Hotel Brunswick on the corner of Boylston and Clarendon streets, they had convened with a hundred other eminent guests, among them Harriet Beecher Stowe, Ralph Waldo Emerson, President Eliot of Harvard, Thomas Wentworth Higginson, and Mark Twain. Longfellow was sick and could not come. Warner expressed his "profound gratitude to one of the noblest doctors in any literature, for the cheer and delight I owe him all along in life, ever since I could read." Warner then read a poetic tribute by Helen Hunt Jackson, who sat at his left, along with Dr. Holmes, at the head table. "She refused to speak in public," shunning the public eye, her biographer Kate Phillips has disclosed.[56]

On his train ride back from Manchester-by-the-Sea to Hartford, Warner read "The Hiltons' Holiday" in September's *Century*. In this short story, Sarah Orne Jewett told of John Hilton's spring excursion by horse and carriage with his two daughters Susan Ellen and Katy—Mrs. Hilton (her first name is not given) stayed at home—to Topham, seventeen miles distant, a rare vacation from school and farm chores. "The greatest triumph" of their "whole day of pleasure," except their delightful meeting with John's acquaintance Judge Masterson, was having their picture taken. They returned at nightfall, without the trip's incentives of hoe and turnip seed, "tired out and happy." Moved to tears by "The Hiltons' Holiday," Warner wrote Annie of his emotions in a letter that contained his "warmest love" for "the dear sweet writer."[57]

## MARK TWAIN

Before talking with Warner, Muir had met Warner's former Nook Farm neighbor, Mark Twain. Both Muir and Twain had crossed the Atlantic and landed in New York in September 1893. Twain arrived first, on Thursday, 7 September—he and his family had left Hartford in June 1891 to live in Europe—and stayed with his friend Dr. Clarence C. Rice at 123 East 19th Street. Twain's business life was at a nadir, his publishing house and his investments in the Paige typesetter failing. He talked with Gilder and Johnson at the *Century* about his story *Pudd'nhead Wilson*, and was busy proofreading it. On Friday, 22 September, the *Campania* from Liverpool docked, letting Muir ashore. Muir stayed at the Holland House on Fifth Avenue at the corner of 30th Street, "another magnificent hotel," Baedeker advertised. Twain was three years Muir's senior. When they met, they talked at the Century Club or at the magazine's editorial offices, or at the Players'—all familiar places to them—most likely on Monday the 25th or Tuesday the 26th. What they said to each other was not recorded by either party. On Friday, 29 September, Twain moved to an economy room at the Players' Club at 16 Gramercy Park, while Muir and Johnson took the train for Washington, D.C.[58]

How much Muir and Twain knew about each other is unclear. Like Muir, Twain had a lot of geography stowed in him. Twain had gone West himself, as a youth of twenty-six, in July 1861, seven years before Muir, and stayed five and a half years, until December 1866. He spent almost three years in Nevada—and engaged in various pursuits, one of them journalism, for the first time—before going to California at the end of May 1864. In San Francisco, he continued writing for newspapers and produced his "Jumping Frog" story, which—reprinted in the press throughout the country and published as *The Celebrated Jumping Frog of Calaveras County, and Other Sketches* (1867)—made him famous. His second major book, *Roughing It*, which was published in February 1872, told about his Western experience.[59]

If Muir had read this book, he would have learned of Twain's adventures in California. Twain was enthralled with his four-day camp in mid-September

1861 at Lake Tahoe (then Lake Bigler). His descriptions of the lake as "a noble sheet of blue water lifted six thousand three hundred feet above the level of the sea," of the air as "very pure and fine, bracing and delicious" and of camping— "There is no end of wholesome medicine in such an experience"—anticipated Muir. Twain's campfire escaped, however, burning everything in sight. Farther south, on the other side of the Sierra Nevada from Yosemite, both men had also camped at Mono Lake: Twain in August 1862 with Calvin Higbie (to whom he dedicated *Roughing It*), Muir in June 1875 with William Keith, John Swett, and J. B. McChesney. Both parties had gone by rowboat to the larger of the lake's two volcanic islands. Twain and Higbie searched futilely for a spring to quench their thirst. Muir inspected "cone basalt, lavas, hot springs, and vegetation." Both encountered windstorms on their return to the mainland. The severity of the tempest forced Muir back to the island for the night. After midnight, when the wind "slightly abated," his hungry and unblanketed companions persuaded Muir to set out again. Muir "sat with shoes unlaced, ready to swim." Despite raging wind, water coming over the sides of the boat, and constant bailing, they reached shore near dawn. Twain and Higbie might have gone back too; yet dreading upsetting in the process of turning around, they pressed on. Higbie rowed all the way, while Twain steered, Twain fearing that the changing of positions would capsize them. "Just as the darkness shut down we came booming into port, head on," wrote Twain. In August, Twain went higher from Mono to fish in Trumbull Lake (probably) under Castle Peak (since 1878 Dunderberg Peak).

In general, Twain thought that the mountains and forests were best appreciated from a distance. The climate, though luscious, was too monotonous for him. "The idea of a man falling into raptures over grave and sombre California"—exactly what Muir did—he could not understand, particularly if he had witnessed the variety of weather and seasons of New England—Muir had not, yet. "Change is the handmaiden Nature requires to do her miracles with," Twain declared in *Roughing It*. But Muir stayed on the Pacific coast even after his exposure to the Atlantic seaboard.[60]

Years later, in summer 1878, when Twain toured Switzerland with his and Warner's, Hartford walking companion, Joseph H. Twichell, Twain's engagement with mountains provoked a very different response, one that even surprised him. Their itinerary at a glance looked like this. On 15 August Twain and Twichell stolled up the Rigi (5,906 feet) and descended by the cog railway. From 23-27 August, they went, partly on foot, from Kandersteg (3,839/3,937 feet) over the Gemmi Pass (7,640 feet) to Leukerbad (4,629 feet), and from there via Visp to Zermatt, where they stayed three days. They observed the Matterhorn. Walking from the Riffelberg to the Gornergrat, Twain noted "we climbed up on end of Gorner glacier." Later, on 6 September, in Chamonix, France, they climbed the Montanvert, "[c]rossed the Mer de Glace & ascended the confounded moraine" before descending through the Mauvais Pas, "a villainous place." Reflecting on this experience later, Twain wrote Twichell, "Those mountains had a soul...And, Lord, how pervading were the repose and peace and blessedness that poured out of the heart of the invisible Great Spirit of the Mountains! Now, what is it? There are mountains and mountains and mountains in this world—but only *these* take you by the heart-strings. I wonder what the secret of it is? Well, time and time again it has seemed to me that I *must* drop everything and flee to Switzerland once more. It is a *longing*, a deep, strong, tugging *longing*—that is the word. We must go again." Muir and Twain could have talked and talked about the Alps.[61]

## FAREWELL

After a "grand time" in Manchester-by-the-Sea with Fields and Jewett, Muir and Johnson returned to Brookline for the night. The next day, Monday, 12 June, the Mayor of Boston, Nathan Matthews Jr., called for them with carriages and "drove us through the public parks and the most intriguing streets of Boston" before taking them to the station. They departed that evening on the 6:00 or 7:00 p.m. train—he did not say which—to Fall River, and from there by overnight boat to New York City, arriving at 7:00 a.m. on Tuesday morning, 13 June. From the wharf, they hastened to the *Century* offices at Union Square, where Muir's eager expectation to hear from home was fulfilled. Muir then began a long letter to tell his wife what had been happening. Later he traveled up Broadway to 27th Street, where he checked into the Coleman again—he had stayed here when he first arrived in New York, on 30 May, until coming to New England—for the duration, until his sailing for Liverpool on 26 June.[62]

Despite bright sunshine the east wind off the ocean made Friday, 16 June, feel chilly. It was cold enough for Annie Fields to wear her medium overcoat when Dr. Holmes called at Thunderbolt Hill. On their ride he told her of his penchant for naming most of their neighborhood trees. She may have remarked of another tree-lover who had just visited her.[63]

Late the next year, 1894, after the publication of *The Mountains of*

*California*, Muir would ask Johnson to send copies to Annie Fields, Sarah Orne Jewett, Thomas Wentworth Higginson, and Mary Sargent in appreciation of their hospitality in June 1893. Annie conveyed to Muir her delight with his book, and invited him to come again. But though she made a fine art of making and keeping relationships, as did Muir, this was apparently their last communication.[64]

# Cambridge
## Harvard Yard

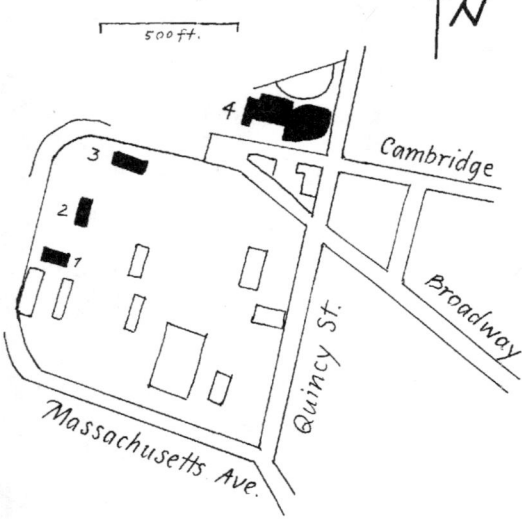

1. Massachusetts Hall
2. Hollis Hall
3. Holworthy Hall
4. Sanders Theatre

# 5. CAMBRIDGE

*I have had the grippe—several coughs & colds that require icy excursions
rather than exciting ceremonies, therefore I'm run down & nervous.
However, I'll face the fine music & look to you to see me through.*
—Muir to Robert Underwood Johnson, 3 June 1896

*Go back to the dear country of the* Pointed Firs,
come *back to the palpable present-*intimate *that throbs responsive…*
—Henry James to Sarah Orne Jewett, 5 October 1901

## JUNE 1896

Three years later, Muir was back in Cambridge. He almost did not go. While
in Martinez, California, in the spring of 1896, he had the premonition that
his eighty-three-year-old mother, Ann, was dying and that this would be his
last chance to see her. Immediately, he took the train east. When he arrived
at Ann Muir's home in Portage, Wisconsin, early in the afternoon of 10 June,
feeling "sleepy & benumbed after so much carbonic acid in the sleeping car,"
he found his mother "sick and low." Beside her were his sisters Sarah and
Anna, who exclaimed, "God has sent you."[1] Muir's presence lifted their spirits and shifted the atmosphere. Soon he was spinning Scots yarns and everyone was laughing.

His mother's revival allowed Muir to leave for the East on 17 June. Two days
later he arrived in New York at 6:40 p.m. Johnson came to his hotel, Holland
House, where Muir had stayed in 1893, and they had supper. The next day,
Muir bought a new hat and pair of shoes.[2] Then they traveled north to the
country home of Henry Fairfield Osborn, a paleontologist at Columbia
University and the American Museum of Natural History, and his wife
Lucretia Thatcher Perry, in Garrison, New York. Called Wing-on-Wing from
its various additions, the house had been built by Osborn's father on a hill
above the east bank of the Hudson River, and is now on the National Historic
Register.[3] Here Muir rested happily for a day. On Monday the 22nd, he and
Johnson continued north, crossing the Hudson River to West Park in order to
confer with John Burroughs at his writing cabin, Slabsides. A telegram awaited their return to New York that evening, informing Muir of his mother's
death at six o'clock that night. Her last words: "It's all right. It's all well."[4]

The next day, Tuesday the 23rd, Muir and Johnson went to Cambridge. Though they did not disclose where they spent the night, it was most likely with the Sargents, who had invited them to their residence, Holm Lea, again. The purpose of their abbreviated visit was for Muir to receive the "Harvard baptism" that Johnson had prepared for him. Had he wished, Muir might have been on the Harvard faculty, but he would not consider "leaving God's big show for a mere profship."[5]

Early on Wednesday morning, the 24th, the Massachusetts National Lancers, a special cavalry troop established in 1836, escorted Acting Governor Roger Wolcott in his carriage from Boston to Cambridge.[6] At ten o'clock, before Harvard's Massachusetts Hall, President Eliot and the overseers, having just finished appointing the university preachers and awarding the degrees, received the governor, himself a graduate of Harvard and its law school. Joined by faculty, honorary degree candidates, and invited guests— Josiah Royce, John Muir, and Robert Underwood Johnson among them— they all marched across Harvard Yard. Along the way they collected the graduates to lead the procession in front of Hollis Hall, which had been the undergraduate residence of Emerson for three of his four years (1817-1821) and of Thoreau (1833-1837). They passed Holworthy Hall before crossing Cambridge Street to the old Sanders Theater. From start to finish, the processional covered about a quarter mile, one of Muir's shortest walks.

The honorary degrees were awarded last in the ceremony. President Eliot spoke of Muir in Latin: "*Johannem Muir, locorum incognitorum exploratorem insignem; fluminum qui sunt in Alaska serratisque montibus conglaciatorum studiosum; diligentem silvarum et rerum agrestium ferarumque indagatoreum, artium magistrum* (distinguished explorer of places unseen: devotedly engaged among rivers which are in Alaska and among glaciers in ragged mountains: keenly perceptive in forest and field: and of wildlife a searcher, of mechanical arts a master)."[7] Muir shared the masters of arts with "Wilberforce Eames, the bibliographer; Gordon McKay, the inventor of shoe machinery; Thomas Bailey Aldrich, the author; Booker T. Washington, the colored president of Tuskeegee [sic] university," the *Boston Daily Globe* reported. Another Scot, Alexander Graham Bell, received a LL.D.[8] Muir knew Aldrich, who had been editor of the *Atlantic Monthly* from February 1881 to March 1890, from their meeting in New York in June 1893.[9] Washington, the most famous black man in America, was surely known to Muir. Five years later he would be welcomed to the White House by Teddy Roosevelt, the first of his race to be entertained there by a president.[10] Applauding in the large audience were Charles Eliot and Elizabeth Cary Agassiz; the latter found the event "extremely interesting."[11]

After the Commencement exercises there was an alumni dinner at which Muir spoke of the "Harvard men…God's nobles. Emerson, Agassiz, Gray— these men influenced me more than any others. These men were the first to find me and hail me as a brother. First of all, and greatest of all, came Emerson." He continued to tell of their meeting in Yosemite Valley twenty-five years earlier.[12]

Thomas Wentworth Higginson missed all this. He and his family were happily ensconced in their summer home in Dublin, New Hampshire. This time (on 6 June) he had had to travel there in a reclining carriage, "the most expensive way but comfortable," he said in his journal, owing to his not having fully recovered from the illness that since last October had kept him in bed and on a milk diet. This affliction also prevented his attending the 17 June commencement of Western Reserve College in Cleveland, Ohio, which notwithstanding awarded him an honorary doctor of laws.[13]

William James was also absent. Finishing his Harvard duties on 19 June, he forsook Cambridge for a vacation with his family in Chatham on Cape Cod's southeast shore, where they arrived on the 23rd. He most likely skipped commencement in order to lengthen his holiday, for he had to be back to lecture to the summer school in early July. Following that he was on the move. First he traveled to Buffalo and on to Chautauqua, New York, to lecture, then back home across New York, Vermont (staying at the Van Ness House, where Muir would come in 1898; see chapter 8), and New Hampshire.[14]

Muir did not linger in Cambridge. "I…caught a fast train," he wrote home, "and got back to Portage in time for the funeral," of his mother on Friday noon, 26 June.[15]

That Friday Sarah Wyman Whitman wrote a letter to her "beloved" friend Sarah Orne Jewett. She expressed her gratitude for her new novel *The Country of the Pointed Firs*, whose "last chapters" she had indulged in the night before. As the book did not appear until November, Whitman must have been reading a proof copy given her by the publisher, Houghton Mifflin.[16] The front green cloth cover of *The Country of the Pointed Firs* — with three mayflowers at the top, two alongside the title and one below the author's name in distinctive sans serif lettering, each of their long stems connected to hearts along the bottom—was the gift of Sarah Whitman.[17]

A year later in August, William James climbed Chocorua, a 3,500-foot eminence in New Hampshire near his summer home (see chapter 3). So delicious was the day atop that he lay about for three hours dozing and reading *The Country of the Pointed Firs*. So delightful was the book that he wrote the author a thank-you that day. The next day he recommended it to his brother Henry in England "to recall the very taste & fragrance of your native seaside air." Henry took William's advice. He even had the chance to tell the author directly how much he appreciated her novel when she and Annie Fields arrived in Rye on Sunday, 11 September 1898—while John Muir was making a "Long Tedious [train] ride all day over grassy plains mixed with short sage in dryest places"—heading back to New England for the third time.[18]

South West Cape Cod

↑N

Woods Hole

To Falmouth →

Great
Harbor

RR Depot

Little Harbor

• Sargent House

Nonamesset Island

Vineyard Sound

½ mile

# 6. Cape Cod

*But this shore will never be more attractive than it is now.*
—Thoreau, *Cape Cod*

*Nothing remarkable done in prosaic mood*
—from Muir's index to Thoreau's *Cape Cod*, 1906 edition

## SATURDAY, 17 SEPTEMBER 1898

John Muir arrived in Boston at 10:00 a.m. on Saturday, 17 September 1898, completing a ten-day transcontinental trip.

He had taken the northern route: from San Francisco to Portland, Oregon, to Spokane, Washington, then east over the Rocky Mountains via the Great Northern Railway, across the Great Plains, where one engine was replaced by another and another and another. From St. Paul, Minnesota, he had caught a night train to Duluth in time for "the last steamer of the season" through the Great Lakes—Superior, Huron, Erie—in three nights to Buffalo, New York, where he boarded the 7:10 p.m. train for New England, emerging at daylight from the Hoosac Mountain tunnel of northwestern Massachusetts. (Fifty-four years earlier, in July 1844, Thoreau had walked over Hoosac Mountain in the opposite direction, on his way west to ascend Saddleback Mountain [now Greylock], which he saw from the 2,018-foot West Summit of Hoosac Mountain, six miles west.) Muir's train continued south through Connecticut and Rhode Island, then north to Boston.[1]

En route, new landscapes and people levitated him. His eyes absorbed natural wonders: "goldenrod all across the continent. great is goldenrod."[2] This image with others jotted ever so briefly in his journal and letters home, despite "the swaying jolting jumbling car," captured his connection to the natural world.[3] He may have worked more on his essays on the animals and birds of Yosemite for the *Atlantic*. He tried "to keep restingly quiet." Mostly, he dished out delectable anecdotes: "I have picked up quite a lot of companions to whom I preach daily. some of them preachers."[4] Until Buffalo, where he left, "feeling very weak & sick."[5]

Dyspepsia was his diagnosis. "The horrible food and eternal jolting and carbonic acid upset my stomach."[6] Dining car menus of the era show the influence of the region transited. Typically, dinners of soup, fish or roast beef, lettuce salad; a choice of vegetables—potatoes (mashed or boiled), French peas, string beans, succotash; for dessert, ice cream, cake, or pie. All for one dollar.[7] At the Spaulding Hotel in Duluth, Muir had a "beefsteak breakfast."[8] Aboard ship, boiled Lake Superior trout, corned beef and cabbage, pork and beans.[9] Always, his elixir of life, tea.

From the Boston and Providence Railroad Depot on Park Square, Muir went directly to the Adams House at 553 Washington Street, four blocks east, presumably by livery. There he took a room for one dollar, bathed, changed clothes, and read a message from Charles Sprague Sargent.[10]

Sargent himself was soon knocking on Muir's hotel-room door. He had invited Muir and William M. Canby of Wilmington, Delaware, to see the southern Appalachian forests. The previous summer, the trio had traveled to British Columbia and Alaska to witness Western trees. Sargent dedicated to Canby his just completed volume 12 of *The Silva of North America* (1891-1902).[11] He had bestowed the same honor on Muir for the previous volume, which appeared earlier in 1898. "[I]t made my heart jump with joy as no other honor I have received ever did," Muir responded.[12] Sargent affirmed his gift in a letter: "For if there is any man who loves and knows trees, and knows how to write about them better than anybody else, you are the Fellow."[13]

Shortly after his Boston arrival, at one o'clock, a weary and still woozy Muir was moving again. Their destination, in Sargent's words: "a spot where you will find a great many things to interest you."[14] Sargent had enticed Muir to "pass a few days on the end of Cape Cod where my family goes for a few weeks every summer."[15] Their means of transportation, though undisclosed, was assuredly train, the Old Colony Line.[16] Their route on Saturday, 17 September 1898, was from Boston south through Middleboro to Buzzards Bay, then east over the Monument River (now the Cape Cod Canal), and south along Cape Cod's west coast, a moraine of pitch pines and scrub oaks, cranberry bogs, strawberries in sandy soil, and small villages with glimpses of water. A stretch of the last four miles from Falmouth ran between ocean with cormorants and eiders on one side and ponds with cattails and reeds, saltspray rose, and bittersweet on the other. Muir noted it in his journal: "Fine woods all the way perhaps 90 m[ile]s. Many fine residences of rich people seeking summer coolness. Magnificent Asters & goldenrods[.] deep glacial bays. heavy drift[.] Extreme end of Cape sandy."

Two-and-a-half hours and seventy-two miles from Boston they pulled into Woods Hole, whose depot is now replaced by a ferry terminal for the islands of Martha's Vineyard and Nantucket. Sargent's home was not far: a mile east past the north end of Little Harbor, then south three-quarters of a mile down Church Street, which passed over the railroad, now a bicycle path from Falmouth. The two men, laden with baggage, likely went by carriage, though Muir had inadvertently lightened his load in New York: "Lost small grip by mistake of a gentleman who left his in exchange."[17]

From Church Street a long drive descended to the back of a gracious home that incorporated the oldest dwelling in the village, once an inn.[18] A veranda extended across the south and west faces of the house. On the south side, the main door opened into a reception area with dining room to the right and parlor to the left, both with shallow brick fireplaces. Beyond the dining room, a commodious kitchen and pantry; beyond the parlor, another entryway, this one with stairs to the second-floor bedrooms. They arrived in time for tea.

"Met Mrs. Sargent & the fine girls & manly boys just getting ready for Harvard," Muir commented in his journal. Some twenty-five years earlier, on 26 November 1873, at Emmanuel Church in Boston, Charles Sargent, thirty-two, had married Mary Allen Robeson, twenty, a woman of refinement, wealth, and—like Muir—Scottish ancestry. Asa Gray of Harvard, who the previous summer had been botanizing in Yosemite Valley with Muir, had attended their wedding. Surely he had told them about Muir.[19]

At the time of Muir's 1898 visit, the Sargents had five children: three daughters and two sons. The oldest, Henrietta, twenty-four, was not present. Though Sargent had not written Muir about her marriage to architect Guy Lowell on 17 May, he undoubtedly noted that event now to explain her absence. So Muir greeted Molly (Mary) and Alice, ages twenty and sixteen. On 25 January 1908, Molly would marry Dr. Nathaniel Bowditch Potter of Columbia University and thereafter reside in New York. Alice, staying single, would remain at home in Brookline until her death in 1946. When Alice came west, in October 1901, Muir escorted her up Mt. Tamalpais (2,604 feet), north of San Francisco. Andrew, twenty-two that December, and Charles, four years younger, would graduate Harvard in 1900 and 1902 (as their father had in 1862), pursuing careers in landscape architecture and finance, respectively.[20]

After graduation, Andrew, or "Bobo," as he was called, worked in the Boston office of his brother-in-law, Guy Lowell. Of the children, Muir came to know him best. Five years after Muir's Cape Cod visit, Muir and Sargent, with Andrew, would travel part way around the world. From May to December 1903, from Boston to Shanghai, they explored gardens and forests, collecting a trove of seeds, before going their separate ways. The Sargents returned home, where Andrew reported to the press the "incalculable value" of their study.[21] Muir went on to India, Egypt, Australia, and New Zealand before coming back to California in May 1904. Andrew would die of pneumonia in 1918, at age forty-two. In his short life, he designed superb private gardens on Cape Cod, the Massachusetts North Shore, Islesboro (Maine), and Long Island.[22]

On the day of Muir's arrival at the Sargents' summer home, he closed his diary, "Still sick unable to eat the fine dinner prepared for me—a miserable trip." The persistent rearrangement of his insides precluded any leisurely feast enlivened by storytelling, any strolls along the shore, any engagement with the environment, spirited or otherwise.

The next day, Sunday, 18 September 1898, Muir was still healing. His diary contains only twenty words. As there is nothing about Cape Cod, he must have stayed put. Presumably, he at least did not miss the view from Sargent's of Little Harbor, of spritsails and ferries crossing Vineyard Sound, of Martha's Vineyard and the Elizabeth Islands—the closest being Nonamesset, two miles distant; almost touching it was the largest in the chain, Naushon.

On one of those Elizabeth Islands, Penikese (which Muir could not see), a co-educational summer school of natural history had been created in 1873 by Harvard professor Louis Agassiz, whose glacial theories informed Muir's.[23] The August before this, 1872, Agassiz's illness had prevented him from meeting Muir in California and seeing the Sierra Nevada. In 1893, Muir had made a pilgrimage to Agassiz's homeland, Switzerland. In Neuchâtel, at whose university Agassiz had been professor of natural history from 1832 until his coming to America in 1846, Muir observed: "another beautiful & quaint old town on the shore of a lovely lake more than 20 miles long."[24] Here Agassiz, in a stone shelter dubbed "Hôtel des Neuchâtelois," on the great medial moraine of Aar glacier, had monitored the motion of the ice.

Two of the students attending Agassiz's lectures that summer of 1873 on Penikese had been David Starr Jordan, an 1872 graduate of Cornell University, and Susan Bowen, a teacher at Mount Holyoke Female Seminary. They returned the next year. Even though Agassiz had died in December of 1873, his only son, Alexander, managed the school for its second season, after which it closed forever. Jordan and Bowen were married on 10 March 1875. They lived in Indiana, where he taught at what is now Butler University until becoming president of Indiana University in January 1885. In November of that year, Bowen died of pneumonia at age forty-one.[25]

When David Starr Jordan had come to California in 1891 as president of the new Leland Stanford University, he knew about Muir both from Muir's essay on water ouzels and from their mutual friend Catharine Merrill, in Indiana.[26] In California, they became friends, charter members of the Sierra Club, and collaborators on behalf of forest conservation. In a 1903 letter to Muir, Jordan expressed regret over not visiting him at Martinez: "One trouble is that we have such absolute confidence in your soundness and sweetness that we do not need to watch you all the time as we might some poet of whose personality we were less sure."[27]

On that Sunday in September 1898, Muir and Sargent returned to Boston by late afternoon train, while the family stayed in Woods Hole. The boys did not have to be at Harvard until later in September; the girls were not in school. Molly Sargent would soon be bound for Europe to join her older sister, Henrietta, in Paris. On 26 October, Sargent and Muir would escort her to New York. They would stay at the Albermarle Hotel at Madison Square West, "a small but expensive [two dollars a night!] & convenient house" where they would enjoy a "[f]ine champagne supper" including Molly's suitor, a Mr. Jay, with whom they would have some fun with the next day: "Sargent teases him by inviting me to ship to see Molly off taking his [Mr. Jay's] place in carriage. Amusing half earnest talk with Jay advising him to run away & leave all—ropes would not hold me I said."[28]

Meanwhile, back in Boston from Cape Cod on 18 September, Muir had a "fine drive in Sargen[t]'s cab thro park to Brookline." Their route—four miles westward—to Holm Lea, Sargent's home, probably followed the Back Bay Fens and Muddy River greenway created by Frederick Law Olmsted. Since 1883 Olmsted had lived at 99 Warren Street, across the street from Sargent, as we have seen in chapter 2. Though Muir and Olmsted had much in common, and it would have been convenient for them to meet here, they did not do so. Failing memory had forced Olmsted's retirement in 1895, at age seventy-three. For some time he had been secluded on Deer Island, Maine, until this very month of September 1898 when his wife, Mary, committed him to McLean Asylum in Waverly (Belmont), Massachusetts, where he would die on 28 August 1903. Muir wrote of his arrival at Sargent's home, "Eat toast & to bed."[29]

The next day, Monday, 19 September, Muir recuperated at Sargent's— "sleeping sauntering reading still sick." Their only visitor was Walter H. Page, whom they telegraphed to come for lunch. Page, forty-three, had just assumed the editorship of the *Atlantic* in August. Three years earlier, he had come to the magazine as assistant to the editor, Horace E. Scudder.

Serendipity had brought Page and Sargent together in February 1897. The editor wanted forest articles; the arborphile knew the perfect person; they both wrote John Muir asking for his words.[30] Muir granted their wish, though not immediately. He had a commitment to *Harper's Weekly* for "The National Parks and Forest Reservations," which appeared in June. August's *Atlantic*, though, carried Muir's "The American Forests," to the great joy of Page and Sargent.[31] From then on, Muir was welcome at that prestigious magazine. "Wild Parks and Forest Reservations of the West" followed in January 1898, and "Yellowstone National Park" in April.

Page liked Muir's "bird and beast articles," and published them in the *Atlantic* in November and December.[32] The next year, 1899, Page published another Muir park piece, then two more the next year, and the next. Eventually, these ten essays became *Our National Parks*, published by Houghton Mifflin in 1901. "To you and Sargent," Muir thanked Page, "it owes its existence; for before I got your urgent and encouraging letters I never dreamed of writing such a book."[33]

During the two-hour conversation at Sargent's house the day after their return from Cape Cod, Muir and his host probably outlined their upcoming Southern journey for Page, who was a native of North Carolina. Muir summed up their meeting: "had good chat. Smart fellow." Page and Muir would meet again, later in the next month (see chapter 12).[34]

At 10:00 a.m. the next day, Tuesday, 20 September, Muir and Sargent headed south by train for two days. It was not until the 24th, when walking among the rhododendrons atop Roan Mountain on the Tennessee-North Carolina border, that Muir felt well for the first time since leaving home more than two weeks before.[35]

## THOREAU'S CAPE COD

In 1849, the same year that Muir had come to America from Scotland and settled on Fountain Lake Farm in Wisconsin, Thoreau made his first of five trips to Cape Cod. Thoreau's destination four times was the lower Cape, the Great Beach, that twenty-seven-mile stretch of sand between Provincetown in the north and Orleans in the south, between the Atlantic Ocean and Cape Cod Bay, much of which is fortunately now National Seashore. He reached this region from Concord in October 1849 via Boston by train to Sandwich and from there by stagecoach to Orleans; in June 1850 and again in July 1855 by steamer from Boston to Provincetown; and in June 1857 from Manomet on foot to Scusset and by cars to Sandwich and then on foot diagonally across the Cape to Friends Village, then northward to Orleans, Wellfleet, Highland Light, and Provincetown, from where he steamed to Boston. His winter excursion of December 1854 took him only to mid-Cape: by train via New Bedford to Hyannis, and from there by ferry to Nantucket Island, where he lectured.[36]

Though Thoreau never entered the village of Woods Hole, where Muir stayed, he did observe Woods Hole from aboard the New Bedford steamer *Eagle's Wing* on 27 June 1856. That summer day, Thoreau also saw all the Elizabeth Islands, and for two-and-a-half hours delighted in walking amid beech, oaks, and tupelo on the largest of these, Naushon.[37]

Thoreau presented his impressions of Cape Cod to the world. He gave several lectures in 1850 and 1851.[38] Then, the summer 1855 issues of *Putnam's Monthly* carried what would become four chapters of his book. At last, ten years later and three years after Thoreau's death, *Cape Cod*, a book of ten chapters, was published by Ticknor and Fields of Boston; it has been in print ever since.[39] Modern editions feature introductions by Henry Beston (1951), Robert Finch (1984), Paul Theroux (1987), and Robert Pinsky (2004).

Muir's immersion in *Cape Cod* was considerably more thorough than his exposure to Cape Cod itself. Here he received the essence of this place. First, he read volume 4 of the Riverside Edition of *The Writings of Henry David Thoreau*, published by Houghton Mifflin from 1896 to 1898. As usual, he marked passages in pencil in the margins: thirty-one vertical lines and one horizontal line. And, on a blank page at the back of the book, he created his own index: twenty-one items with twenty-five page references.[40]

Muir considered *Cape Cod* worthy of further reflection. In 1906 Houghton Mifflin published *The Writings of Henry David Thoreau* in twenty volumes. Muir acquired this set in 1908. Volume 4 is titled, *Cape Cod and Miscellanies*. This time his pencil was busier in the margins: sixty-six vertical lines and nine horizontal lines. As there are no marks in the first three chapters, he presumably ignored these. His markings begin with Thoreau's powerful metaphors in the first two paragraphs of chapter four, "The Beach." Muir's own index appeared at the back and identified twenty items on thirty pages (the last reference is to multiple pages).[41]

# 7. Boston Parks and Others

*A grand blessing for Boston*
—John Muir, Journal

*Boston is immortal*
—Henry Adams

*[C]reation of designs that are in keeping with the natural scenery
and topography; respect for, and full utilization of, the genius of the place.*
—Frederick Law Olmsted, *Six Principles of Landscape Design*

## October-November 1898

At 8:30 on Friday night, 14 October 1898, the two weary travelers Muir and Sargent stepped off the train in Boston. Their first priority was for the ailing Sargent to see his doctor. His illness, which Muir described in his journal as "thirst, fever, headache, sore bones etc," had set in two days ago when they were in Delaware. That accomplished, they went on to Holm Lea in Brookline, where they entered into a much-needed sleep. After twenty-five days their Southern Appalachian sojourn was over. It was Muir's last real communion with those mountains.

## Jamaica Park

The next day, Saturday the 15th, was cold and cloudy. Muir rested, reflected on the pleasures of their trip, and wrote "a little." He did not say in his journal what he was composing— perhaps some of his journal—for it does not appear that he wrote any letters this day. Apparently, Sargent had recovered enough to escort Muir to his other domain.

Though Muir had toured the Boston parks by carriage once before, on 12 June 1893, with Nathan Matthews Jr., then the mayor of Boston, now he had an opportunity for a closer look.[1] The three he saw—Jamaica Park, the Arnold Arboretum, and Franklin Park—formed the southernmost extension of Olmsted's "emerald necklace"—a greenway running west through the Boston Common and Garden and the center of Commonwealth Avenue, then south along the Back Bay Fens and Muddy River through Olmsted Park with its three small ponds. (These were, from south to north, Ward and Willow, and the largest of the lot, the quarter-mile-long, lenticular Leverett.) Finally, the greenway ran around Jamaica Pond to the Arnold Arboretum, and from there east to Franklin Park—a total distance of seven and a half miles.

On the way to the Arnold Arboretum, Sargent must have made Muir aware of his friend Francis Parkman's house and garden on the west shore of Jamaica Pond, ensconced in a bevy of fine trees that one biographer described thus: "There was a tall, wide-spreading beech, elms sixty feet high, a big chestnut, a tulip, a plane-tree, two white oaks, a sassafras, Scottish maples and scarlet maples, lindens, willows, pines, and hemlocks...a Kentucky coffee-tree, a gingko, the magnolia acuminata, and the Parkman crab...." Having read Parkman and met him in Cambridge on 10 June 1893, Muir would have been especially gratified to see his country home.[2]

Four years earlier, Sargent had done similarly for his protégée Beatrix Jones (see chapter 2). On Sunday, 10 June 1894, they had taken in Jamaica Pond and the Arnold Arboretum. Upon inspection Jones had pronounced the Parkman property "awfully dreary." "The house is being torn down" and the gardens "look as if they had been deserted for years," she noted in her journal. She was gladdened to see "Bruno's Lily, *Anthericum* [blank space] in bloom & its white-pendent bells were very pretty. Azalea calendulacea was still fine Too, & a splendid specimen of *Magnolia macrophylla*."[3]

The Park Commission's plan for Jamaica Pond, however, did not impress Jones. In December 1892, the Olmsted firm had completed a design to encompass Jamaica Pond, which was already part of the Boston park system. Construction began in 1894. Jones objected to the lack of plantings along the borders of paths and walkways and to the use of retaining walls. Sargent protested about the Park Commission's proposed road in a particularly beautiful area of the littoral.[4] As is the case today, a busy highway separated the lake from the surrounding land, thereby virtually isolating the Francis Parkman property from the wayfarer. A grove of black walnuts with a lone yellow poplar now stands before the former homesite. In the center of an exedra, a sculpture of an Iroquois emerging from a vertical shaft of granite, executed by Daniel Chester French from 1897 to 1906, honors the writer whose subject was the Native Americans.[5] French's clay portrait relief of the historian/horticulturist has been vandalized. Behind the Parkman Memorial, the rustic, quiet Prince Road still conveys the aura of the author's era. On any pleasant warm weekend the paved circumference of Jamaica Pond fills with strollers, joggers, bicyclists, and sitters-on-benches—of all girths. Parkman enjoyed boating on the pond until the end of his life, a pastime not permitted today, except for those participants in the sailing program. No swimming or skating, either.

## ARNOLD ARBORETUM

Olmsted's vision of the Boston greenway is best retained in the landscape of the Arnold Arboretum. Apparently, upon arrival Sargent and Muir occupied themselves inside.[6] They compared specimens of a Texas elm they had seen a week ago, on 8 October, in Huntsville, Alabama, with those in the herbarium, and learned that they had discovered a new species. They talked of the esteemed naturalist/artist/writer William Bartram, whose four-year journey through the Southeast started in April 1773 when he sailed from Philadelphia to Charleston. Though Bartram's itinerary differed from Muir's and Sargent's, there was enough resonance to make it relevant at this time; besides, Muir was returning to California via the South in November, as we shall see. Sargent gave Muir a copy of Bartram's *Travels* (1791), which he began the next day.[7] At the Arboretum, Muir was also involved in planning his trip to New England's North Country with botanical illustrator Charles Edward Faxon (1846-1918) and with reading François André Michaux's *The North American Silva* (1810-1813) in the library.[8]

Strange is the silence of Muir about the many trees in this sanctuary. Perhaps it was the weather? Fatigue? Their having been so focused on the dendrology of the South? Even upon his return to the arboretum ten days later, though, Muir simply mentioned the fact of his presence there. For whatever reason(s), he left no description of the Arnold Arboretum, though he may have known of the one that had just appeared in April's *Century*.[9] For the evening they were back at Holm Lea.

## FRANKLIN PARK

The next day, Sunday, 16 October, Muir wrote in his journal: "Mr Stratton & Mr Pelligrew [sic. Muir forgot to cross the *t*s of his surname.] chairman of park commissioners took me thro[ugh] the park. grand view towards Blue hills, picturesque - fine colors[.] features of landscape small but many & richly combined[.] part of park still wild woods[.] a grand blessing for Boston[.]"[10] Though Muir did not name the place, his description makes clear that he referred to Franklin Park, which Olmsted had designed in 1885 and which had been finished ten years later, in 1895.

He was ably guided by Charles E. Stratton and John A. Pettigrew. At fifty-two, Stratton was younger than both Muir and Sargent. A distinguished man—his black hair, parted in the middle, pressed close to his head, full mustache turned at the ends, bushy eyebrows over perceptive eyes—he had graduated from Harvard in 1866 and from its law school two years later. Since 1869, he had practiced law in Boston, where he also lived, at 68 Devonshire Street in the city's center. His one foray into politics, as the Democratic candidate for lieutenant governor in 1894, ended in defeat. In May 1896 he joined the board of the Boston Parks Commission, and he became its chairman in August 1897. Stratton and Muir undoubtedly talked parks and plantings; perhaps their conversation included a bit about a Harvard classmate of Stratton's, Edward Emerson.[11]

John A. Pettigrew, fifty-four, with short hair, mustache, goatee, and wire-rimmed glasses, had come to Boston in January 1897 to be the head of the city's park department. Sargent had recommended his appointment. Since his arrival from his homeland, England, in the mid-1860s, Pettigrew had had extensive experience with America's parks. He had been superintendent of Chicago's parks, where he beautified Lincoln Park and the shoreline boulevard, from April 1889 to August 1894, when he had gone to the same post in Milwaukee. There he served until 1 March 1896, when he departed to take charge of Brooklyn's parks. But not for long: on 7 November, he had showed Prospect Park to Sargent, Stratton, and Boston Mayor Josiah T. Quincy, who were impressed enough by him to impress upon him that his destiny lay in Boston. Pettigrew and his wife and their three daughters and son resided in Franklin Park, where he enjoyed bowling on the green or curling on the ice of Scarboro Pond.[12]

Such companions assured Muir's enhanced pleasure in Franklin Park. Certainly they pointed out the two prospects that Olmsted had made to enable walkers to feel connected to a vaster expanse of nature. One sightline traveled the mile and a half westward between Refectory Hill and Bussey Hill in the Arnold Arboretum. The other extended a greater distance—six miles—from the Playstead south across the Country Park and Forest Hills Cemetery to the Blue Hills. This east-west trending range, forming the southern boundary of the Boston Basin with its 635-foot granite dome, the high point of New England's southern coast, was visible also from Muir's trains going to and from Boston.[13]

Schoolmaster Hill, south of the Playstead, offers the best view of the undulating Country Park. Olmsted planned this space for "quietness; quietness both to the eye and the ear." He wanted "A grateful serenity" to be enjoyed by all. Here Olmsted's injunction "nothing shall be built, nothing set up, nothing planted" has been mostly obeyed. Encircling woods still keep the surrounding civilization out of view. The central meadow remains open, though kept so not by the grazing sheep of its early days, but for its current clutches of golfers. Even in 1898, Muir may have witnessed golf in the Country Park—three years earlier, in 1895, the first U.S. Open had occurred in Newport, Rhode Island, with eleven competitors—tennis on the grass courts in the Ellicott Dale section (now a baseball field), and "picnic and basket" parties, to use Olmsted's phrase, scattered about the lawn and at the tables under the vined trellises of the terrace just below Schoolmaster Hill's crest.[14]

At Schoolmaster Hill, Muir again crossed paths Ralph Waldo Emerson had walked. Muir's guides may have alerted him to Emerson's country residency for two years (1823-1825; the place is now commemorated on the map marker at the road). Emerson's first full day in the rented farmhouse on Canterbury Lane in Roxbury was his twentieth birthday. From this rural domain, he had walked four miles east to Federal Street in Boston, where he taught in his brother William's school for girls. Though unfulfilled in the classroom, Emerson delighted in his woodland surrounds.[15]

Franklin Park honors Benjamin Franklin, who lived in Boston from his birth in 1706 until his move to Philadelphia in 1723. Franklin returned to Boston often, however, says historian Edmund S. Morgan. Having been away only seven months, in fact, he came back to see his family and friends. Later, after both his parents were dead, his postal inspection tour of New England, for another instance, kept Franklin in Boston for almost three months, from 20 July to 12 October 1763.[16]

An urbanite all his life, Franklin nonetheless had his hinterland moments when duty called. To defend Pennsylvania's southeastern frontier, he led the militia from Bethlehem on a four-day—one of those rainy days was his fiftieth birthday (17 January 1756)—twenty-five-mile winter march to present-day Weissport (471 feet), where they erected Fort Allen. Along the Lehigh River, they passed through the Blue Mountains—"Hills like Alps on each Side and a long narrow Defile where the Road scarcely admitted a single Waggon at the Bottom of it a rapid Creek," observed one ensign. His wife Deborah provided nourishment with shipments of roast beef, apples, and minced pies, for which he was most thankful.[17]

In regard to wilderness, Franklin adhered to the conventions of his day. He was "as oblivious to conservation as his contemporaries," Morgan writes.

"He would have liked to limit immigration to the British, but not from any sense of the value of open space."[18] His outstanding trait, Morgan cites, was his service to his country. Though his gift of diplomacy and peacemaking was exhibited in England and France, he also did much to improve the quality of life where he lived. All Philadelphia greatly benefited from his creation of a small discussion club (which he called the Junto), library (still thriving), hospital, academy (the future University of Pennsylvania), and fire companies. Unlike Muir, he was a joiner.

Franklin's *Autobiography*, begun in Twyford, England, in 1771, and unfinished at the time of his death in 1790, was widely read in the nineteenth century. Emerson and Thoreau partook of the wise man's life. Its great spell even fell on Muir. Muir owned a slender volume in red cloth cover, priced at thirty cents, *Little Masterpieces: Benjamin Franklin*, which contained selections from his *Autobiography*, *Poor Richard's Almanac*, essays, and letters made by Bliss Perry, whom Muir met in May 1903 in Boston (see chapter 14). Perry praised Franklin's prose in general, and his *Autobiography* in particular for "Its ease and originality, its humor, its combination of shrewd worldliness and overflowing benevolence." Muir's indulgence being confined to the first fifty-five pages, the "Early Life" section as Perry divided it—he made eight marginal lines in the text and indexed one item at the back referring to page 48 ("'Sotting with brandy' & dramming")—was indicative of Muir's interest in these years for the writing of his own autobiography. While Muir learned little about early-eighteenth-century Boston in the first fifty-five pages of the *Autobiography*, he did gain insight into Franklin's English heritage, his experiment with a vegetable diet and his reason for eating fish (his thirteen virtues and precepts beginning with temperance of food and drink are found on pages 87-89), his Boston-to-Philadelphia journey—by sea to [Perth] Amboy, overland across New Jersey to Burlington, and from there down the Delaware River—and his entry into the city "fatigued with travelling, rowing and want of rest," passing his future wife at her door, and falling asleep in "the great meeting-house of the Quakers."[19]

## MORE PARKS

As Muir's attention continued to be focused on the human-created, open landscapes in urban and suburban environments, we continue to follow him outside of New England as he inspects these places.

On Wednesday, 9 November, three and a half weeks after being in Franklin

Park, Muir, on his way to Florida with Sargent, rendezvoused with Stratton and Pettigrew in Wilmington, Delaware. William Canby toured them about his hometown and through a park along Brandywine Creek. Along this very creek, 121 years earlier, in September 1777, Washington had tried unsuccessfully to stop the British, who two weeks after the battle had marched into Philadelphia. Muir had "magnificent views of the Chesapeake Bay." "Many fine wild oak woods" enthralled him, "scarlet oak gloriously vivid blending with purple & bronze & brown of white & black oaks[.] Yel[low] of maples. red oak always yel[low] & brown—only wood red." At five o'clock, Canby put them on the train for Baltimore, seventy miles southwest.[20]

That night they stayed in the center of Baltimore, a seaport of half a million souls on the Patapsco River estuary. Muir remarked of their accommodations, at the Mount Vernon House at 105 West Monument Street: "quiet rich old fashioned house" with "queer rooms. too hot. Fat fussy Irish steward most effusively recommends different dishes. Dinner only so so. The fat oysters stale. No good." Afterwards, Muir and Stratton took an evening stroll "thro[ugh] poorly lighted street" in the rain. In the center of Mount Vernon Square, just east of their hotel, they saw the "fine, nobly simple round shaft" of the Washington Monument. "Then took 2d walk with Sargent."

The next morning's weather continued inclement. They drove in a closed carriage through Druid Hill Park (1860) on the northwest edge of town, about two and a quarter miles from the Washington Monument. This 745-acre park, the design of Howard Daniels, contained a large forest called "The Wilderness." Again Muir was thrilled by the "Noble Oaks gloriously purple most excitingly beautiful. mostly white large in majestic groups[.] never imagined oaks could color so supremely fine. Deer in park. innumerable roads too much cut up & the underbrush too closely cleared away. Large reservoir called lake." He made no mention of the park's architecture, for example, the arched gateway, boathouse, and railway stations.[21]

In search of more nourishing cuisine, they "ate lunch at another hotel." In doing so they missed a luncheon invitation that Harry Fielding Reid left at the Mount Vernon House. A native of Baltimore, Reid lived with his wife Edith Gittings— their fifteenth wedding anniversary was to be celebrated on 22 November—and their two children, Francis and Doris, at 608 Cathedral Street, in the same block as Muir's hotel. (The house, divided into apartments, survives.) At thirty-nine, Reid was a geology professor at Johns Hopkins University, from where he received his B.A. in 1880 (that summer he climbed Monte Rosa, Aiguille du Goûter, Dent du Midi in Alps) and his

Ph.D. in 1885. Muir had first met him in Alaska on 1 July 1890, when Reid with five assistants and their equipage landed at Muir's camp in Glacier Bay. "We have now a village," Muir had wryly observed. During his stay until mid-September, Reid explored and mapped the Muir Glacier and Inlet. Although Reid did not accompany Muir on his eleven-day sled trip late in July— made with a "sack of hardtack, a little tea and sugar, and a sleeping-bag"— over the Muir Glacier, which completely cured his three-month cough, the two men did inspect several other large glaciers together, noting changes in their behavior since Muir had first seen them in October 1879. They also witnessed a spectacular display of northern lights, "one span five miles wide," with "boundless admiration."[22]

Though the focus of Muir's party was parks, they would have been entertained by Reid and his Johns Hopkins University. Its urban campus, bounded by Centre, Eutaw, Monument and Howard streets, was just two blocks due west of Reid's home. Then in the fall term of its twenty-second year, which had begun October lst, with 128 faculty and 649 students, 187 of whom were undergraduates, Johns Hopkins was still under the leadership of its first president, Daniel Coit Gilman. Before coming to Baltimore, Gilman, who was born in Norwich, Connecticut, on 6 July 1831, and educated at Yale, Class of 1852, had presided over the University of California for over two years, from November 1872 to March 1875—the period of its move from Oakland to Berkeley. One of Johns Hopkins's first doctorates, granted on 13 June 1878, went to the blue-eyed twenty-two-year-old whom Gilman had nurtured at California and provided a fellowship to study at Johns Hopkins, Josiah Royce. William James lectured there, 11-22 February 1878, and explored with Gilman the possibility of his joining the faculty. Graduate students contemporary with Reid included John Dewey and Woodrow Wilson, who in 1884 debated each other on the issue of federal funding of Southern black children's education. After the Raker Bill, which allowed the damming of California's Hetch Hetchy Valley, passed the U.S. House and Senate, Muir's fervent prayer would be that the president of the United States, Woodrow Wilson, would veto it. To Muir's great grief Wilson, on 19 December 1913, made it the law of the land.[23]

Instead of spending the afternoon with Reid at Johns Hopkins University, Muir and company "went off to view another Park." This one, Clifton Park, was located on the same longitude as Druid Park, two and a quarter miles to its east, and at the same distance from city center as Druid Park. Therein, Muir wrote, they "Saw the old Johns Hopkins home—fine meadows—noble taxodium [bald cypress] like Sequoia[.] Here also oak is King[,] the glory of this park & woods in general."[24] This estate, the summer home of Johns Hopkins—he wintered in town at 18 West Saratoga Street—from 1841 until his death in 1873, he had transformed from a farm into "one of the most elaborate places in this country" with "a fine and costly house...diversified and extensive grounds...varieties of trees, shrubs, walks, lawns, large pieces of ornamental water, containing numerous islands planted with masses of rhododendrons and evergreen shrubs, and connected by appropriate and tasteful bridges," according to horticulturist Henry Winthrop Sargent. Parterre gardens, orchards and greenhouses filled with grapes, oranges and tropical plants were also present. From the main entrance—there were six—on Hartford Road, signified by a gatehouse, the one Muir most likely used, a curvaceous drive adorned with statuary led to the mansion that was hidden from the road. Hopkins bequeathed this property to the university he founded, expecting it to be used for the main campus. The trustees, however, never located the academy there, and finally in 1895, needing cash and preferring to remain situated downtown, sold Clifton to the city for use as a public park. Like Boston's Franklin Park, Clifton Park today accommodates a public golf course.[25]

Afterwards Muir and associates went three miles northwest to visit the "Garrett mansion" at 4545 North Charles Street. Now called Evergreen House, it is owned (since 1942) by Johns Hopkins University and is open to the public. Again, Muir was more impressed with the surrounds than with the four Corinthian columns at the entrance of the 1858 Italianate structure: "plain buildings in very fine oak woods natural save from a little trimming of lower limbs & cutting out of underbrush. Seems to have been sown with grass - lawn-like. a few dogwood, maples or young oaks would make it the finest bit of oak woods in the region where oak is King."[26] A couple of white oaks that were near a century and half old in 2003 still stand.

At five o'clock, they departed Baltimore, and an hour later arrived in Washington, D.C., thirty-five miles southwest. They stayed at the Arlington, at the intersection of Vermont Avenue and H Street, two long blocks north of the White House—"good room, with bath at $6. per day. exclusion of meals," Muir put in his journal. The next day, 11 November, they took a cold, windy carriage ride to look at Soldiers' Home (now the U.S. Soldiers' and Airmen's Home) at 3700 North Capitol Street NW, about two miles north of their hotel, and separated from Howard University by the McMillan Reservoir. "Charming oak woods," Muir found, "scarlet oak vivid red hot every leaf." Still autumnal, "No trees are more gloriously colored in all the American forests than these eastern oaks," he wrote his daughter Helen. Then they drove through nascent Rock Creek Park, which Congress had created in 1890—going two and a quarter miles west of the Arlington to its Connecticut Avenue entrance—where roads were being built, a favorite place of John Burroughs before it was a park and the capital was "such a vast spread of wild, wooded, or semi-cultivated country," and later of Theodore Roosevelt, when he lived at the White House. The park—some 1,754 acres of sylvan valley—encompassed the National Zoo, with buffalo, elk, kangaroo, llama, sheep, deer, antelope, and a variety of birds "pelican, swan, geese etc"—all of which Muir reported seeing. In the afternoon, they saw the new Library of Congress (1897), now the Thomas Jefferson Building. To its west, they looked approvingly on the Capitol within its Olmstedian setting, where a ginkgo "peculiar pale pure pleasant tulip [?] yellow" captivated Muir. Of all the buildings the 555-foot Maryland marble shaft of the Washington Monument most impressed him. They did not see the president or his chief forester, Gifford Pinchot. At 3:46 p.m., Muir entrained for Jacksonville, Florida, with Sargent "seated in front of me trying to sleep." They spent the night on the train coming down the Atlantic coast.[27]

## FLORIDA

Sargent and Muir were together in Florida for nine days. Their train took them to St. Augustine for the first night, Miami for the next two nights. From there they went by boat to Key West. On Wednesday morning, 16 November, after a night at the Key West Hotel, they "charted sloop & sailed at 8.15 for Marquesas Keys for palms," Muir noted in his journal. "A succession of keys mostly small the largest 1 to 2 m[ile]s long with shallow water between extend to Marquesas group 18 to 20 m[ile]s from K[ey].W[est]. All of these densely covered with vegetation & prescribing smooth outline 20 to 30 or 40 f[ee]t ab[ove] sea. top of forest gently irregular with bosses of densely bared branches of Mangrove 2 sp[ecie]s & with the crowns of 2 sp[ecie]s of palms. Mangrove most ab[undant] & characteristic of all." Though they started back to Key West at two o'clock, tacking against a headwind made their 10:30 arrival "too late to catch steamer for Tampa."[28]

The next day, the 17th, they had time to drive around. Though not impressed with the town of Key West—"a miserable place of squalid shanties mostly with sickly cats, dogs & pale weak looking Cuban cigar makers"—Muir did delight in "a wonderful ficus or banyan tree at Barracks."[29]

After boarding the *Miami* at 9:00 p.m., they sailed at one o'clock northward along Florida's Gulf coast to Tampa, arriving about four on the next afternoon, and were on the train all the 19th traveling northeastward to Palatka on the St. Johns River. The next morning, Sunday the 20th, they saw along the river "the most magnificent magnolias, some four feet in diameter and one hundred feet high, also the largest and most beautiful hickories and oaks," Muir wrote his wife. At 11:30 a.m., their train left Palatka and crossed the state through Gainesville to Cedar Key off the west coast. They arrived at 7:00 p.m. and stayed in the Dutch Hotel. The next day Muir inquired about the Hodgson family, who had cared for him when he suffered from malaria from late October 1867 for "about three months." He learned that Richard W. B. Hodgson and his eldest son were dead, "but Mrs. [Sarah A.] Hodgson & the rest of the family—two boys and three girls are alive and well & I saw them all today except one of the boys," Muir excitedly wrote Louie that night. They "talked over old times in grand style." Sarah Hodgson knew that the Muir Glacier had been named for him. Their happy reunion, which covered four hours and included dinner, occurred in Archer, about forty miles inland—back the way they had come.[30]

Later that same day, at the railroad station in the hamlet of Archer, Muir and Sargent parted ways. Immediately, Muir was "lonely," he wrote Louie from the "dreary" Hotel Ethel in Live Oak, Florida, where he had to spend the night to await the New Orleans train at noon the next day. Yet he was ever so happy "to be at last facing westward. It seems years & years since I left home. Im quite well but my eyes are a little sore with gazing out of the car windows with eager botanical discrimination, especially at the forests of the Longleafed pine of which I can never see enough—big, little & babies. A single tassel contains nearly 2000 needles a foot long."[31]

Sargent went directly to Boston. Muir made stops in Mobile, Alabama, to drive through "a grand forest of Magnolia & liquid ambar [sweet gum]" with botanist Charles T. Mohr, "Asa Gray's friend" with whom he and Sargent had spent a day earlier, 5 October, in Tuscaloosa, Alabama, and in New Orleans on Thanksgiving to see on the following day another botanist, J.H. Mellichamp, friend of Sargent and Canby, who was staying with his daughter.[32] Then he took a night train out of New Orleans across Texas to California, coming home 30 November.[33]

## MELLICHAMP REDUX

On 5 June 1903, Mellichamp would arrive in San Francisco. He had come to fulfill his dream—to see the sequoias before he died—and he wanted Muir to go with him. From the Hotel St. Denis at 24 Turk Street, he wrote Muir requesting directions to the Big Trees of Calaveras. Apparently Muir was not free to accompany him, but he sent him a letter of introduction to James M. Hutchings. "Surely the finest & most glorious sight for my decaying eyes that I ever had," Mellichamp wrote Muir upon his return to San Francisco. Among the many kindnesses Hutchings gave him were sequoia seeds that he intended to plant in Charleston or nearby James Island, or farther south in South Carolina at his old home in Bluffton. Earlier, in January, Mellichamp had told Muir that his "happiest days" had been on the Sea Islands of South Carolina.[34]

In the afternoon of 9 August 1903, Mellichamp returned to Bluffton, coming from his brother's in Charleston, he told Muir in a letter written that same day. He thanked Muir for sending Joseph LeConte's *Autobiography*, which he relished. He said nothing about planting any sequoia seeds, however. That same August 9th Muir was in Irkutsk, Russia, on his way east to the Pacific. On 3 October 1903, while visiting a friend on James Island, Mellichamp died. That day Muir was in Darjeeling, India, feasting his eyes on the Himalayas. Mellichamp's home on Calhoun Street, between Green and Bridge streets, is gone. No sequoias grow in Bluffton.[35]

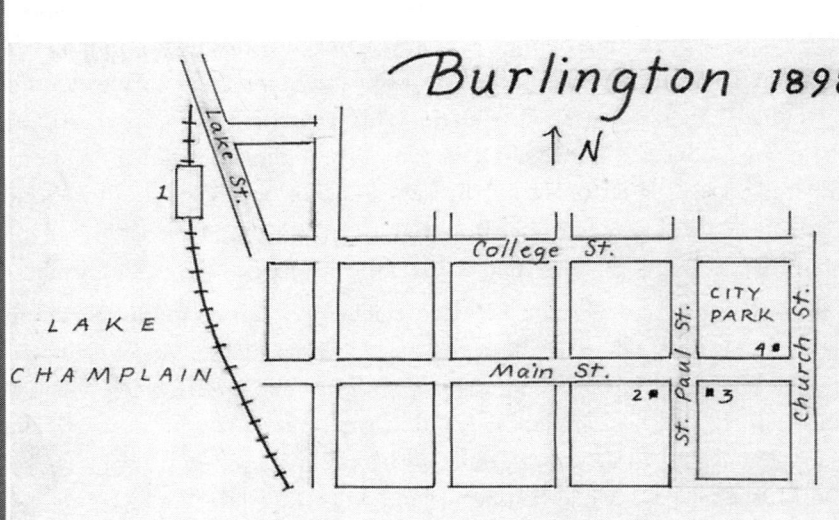

Burlington 1898

↑ N

Lake St.

College St.

LAKE
CHAMPLAIN

Main St.

St. Paul St.

CITY
PARK

4 ■

Church St.

2 ■

■ 3

1

1. Railroad Station
2. Van Ness House *
3. American House
4. City Hall

250 ft.

# 8. VERMONT

*I like driving in our own carriage thro the woods so much better than the cars.*
—Muir to Helen Muir, 26 September [1898]

*Give this good reason to yourself for having gone over the mountains, for mankind is ever going over a mountain.*
—Thoreau to H.G.O. Blake, 16 November 1857

## OCTOBER 1898

The North Woods tour was not vintage Muir. Charles E. Faxon, a botanical illustrator at the Arnold Arboretum, who knew the mountains of northern New England intimately, had shaped the itinerary: an abbreviated, spontaneous journey to fill time while Charles Sprague Sargent recuperated. Muir wished to witness the trees in autumn, thereby joining the performers of this seasonal ritual that has since become a cliché. Instead of focusing on one area in depth, Muir preferred to take in as broad a swath as possible. He was compelled to travel by train—bound to its space, speed, and schedules. His passions to converse with plants, to camp in the wilds, to listen to birds, to climb the mountains and "get their good tidings," all had to be sacrificed for the grand view. His meditation on landscape was from the perspective of movement by machine.

Early Monday morning, 17 October 1898, Sargent's youngest daughter, Alice, took Muir to the station "& saw me fairly off." From Boston, his train crossed Massachusetts to Albany, New York, where he arrived at 2:30 p.m. He walked to Stanwix Hall, a nearby hotel on Broadway, from where he wrote letters to his wife and Johnson, telling them of his plans and of his lonesomeness.[1] Already he missed his traveling companions. Then he entrained for Lake George. The every-other-day schedule of the Lake George steamer thwarted his desire to proceed that way north. Instead he decided to go to Montreal. He waited for the 11:00 p.m. train, on which he went to bed after midnight in "a confounded stuffy jiggling bunk at the top of a sleeping or sleepless car."[2] Apparently, only an upper berth was available.

Muir arrived in Montreal at 7:30 a.m. In the hour and a half available to him, he had breakfast and a "good gen[eral] view" of the city. He said nothing of walking up Mount Royal (763 feet). "The river 2 m[ile]s wide with many islands" was what he wrote. "A glorious flood clear pure northland water. Still looks wild." At 9:00 a.m., he left for Burlington. His car window offered good views of Lake Champlain. "Woods in fine color, " he noted in his journal, "vivid red hot & all shades of yel[low] brown & purple & red. Here & there mixed with pines & hemlocks wh[ich] help to show forth the burning trees & bushes[.] Maples ashes elms oaks poplar vaccinium [blueberry] dogwood etc. Sometimes a clump of colored maples is seen surrounded by dark hemlocks or pines, looking like a richly colored bouquet with an outside rim of grass lvs [leaves] or oaks. glacial traces everywhere. Many huge sand beds, as well as ordinary gravelly bowldery drift. Many gl[acial] bosses & mouto[n]nee rocks."[3]

## BURLINGTON

Shortly after noon, Muir stepped onto Burlington's platform. The old station is gone and Union Station (1915), one block south of its predecessor, is closed to travelers. Its sheltered platform benches were deserted, plants greening the uprights, iron rails stretching south to a yard of freight cars, when I first saw it in June 1993.

"[T]his day was so crisp & bright & delightful, so full of lovely & wild scenery it might awaken the dead & do away with sleep altogether," a resurrected Muir observed. From the depot he walked one block south to Main Street and three uphill blocks east to St. Paul Street, where he entered "a fine clean commodious hotel" on the southwest corner.[4] A solid, four-story brick with porches, balconies, chimneys, flat roof, the Van Ness House looked eternal to me in photographs. Such is not the case, however; the Howard Bank has replaced it.

The Van Ness, attractively situated on the hillside, afforded Muir an eyeful of topography. In the west, Lake Champlain and the Adirondack Mountains. Across St. Paul Street stood Burlington's leading hotel, The American House, where Muir might have stayed had it been open other seasons than summer. Then his name might appear on the current plaque of the apartment building that American House has become, along with presidents and generals who slept here. Diagonally across Main Street from the Van Ness was City Park with City Hall, the Fletcher Free Library, and YMCA, all in the same block. While the Fletcher Free Library and the YMCA have relocated to College Street, a new City Hall resides in the same place as the old one. On Saturdays, from May to October, the Farmer's Market now enlivens the park, whose trees are too young to have known John Muir.

After "a nice dinner" at the hotel—he does not say of what his midday meal consisted—Muir toured the city of 18,640 in a buggy. He went east to the top of the hill, passing "many fine school buildings & residences," commenting that "The State University buildings of red brick look well."

## THE UNIVERSITY OF VERMONT

The fall term of the University of Vermont (1791), called UVM from *Universitas Viridium Montium*, Latin for University of the Green Mountains, was in full swing. It had begun 28 September with 292 male and female undergraduates, preparing in the classics (82), literary-scientific fields (77), engineering (70), chemistry (35), agriculture (24), and unclassified (4), plus 210 medical and 52 dairy students—all guided by 42 professors and 17 instructors.[5]

Of the eight English courses, American literature, an elective offered every other year, encapsulated "The greatest writers of the country and century.... Lectures, reports, and collateral reading. Text-book, Beers' 'Outline Sketch of American Literature.'"[6] This text, published in 1887, a companion to that in English Literature issued the year before, is a small, slim volume of 287 pages. Its author, Henry Augustin Beers, was that autumn teaching English at his alma mater, Yale College, as he had done since 1871 and would continue to do until 1916. While attending the Concord School of Philosophy in the summer of 1879, he had paid his respects to the graves of Thoreau and Hawthorne in Sleepy Hollow, met Bronson and Louisa May Alcott at Orchard House, listened to Emerson in his library, and boated the Concord River with Thoreau's friend Edward Hoar. "I was often a truant to the discussions of the School," he confessed later, preferring to wander "off through the woods for a bath in Walden."[7]

UVM students found Emerson the main attraction, in Beers's chapter on "The Concord Authors," while Thoreau was covered in six pages. Later, Beers admitted that he was "reading Thoreau more and Emerson less."[8] "No one has lived so close to nature," Beers said of Thoreau, "and written of it so intimately." "His life was a lesson in economy and a sermon on Emerson's text, 'lessen your denominator.' He wished to reduce existence to the simplest terms....He had a passion for the wild." Thoreau's legacy: "He has had

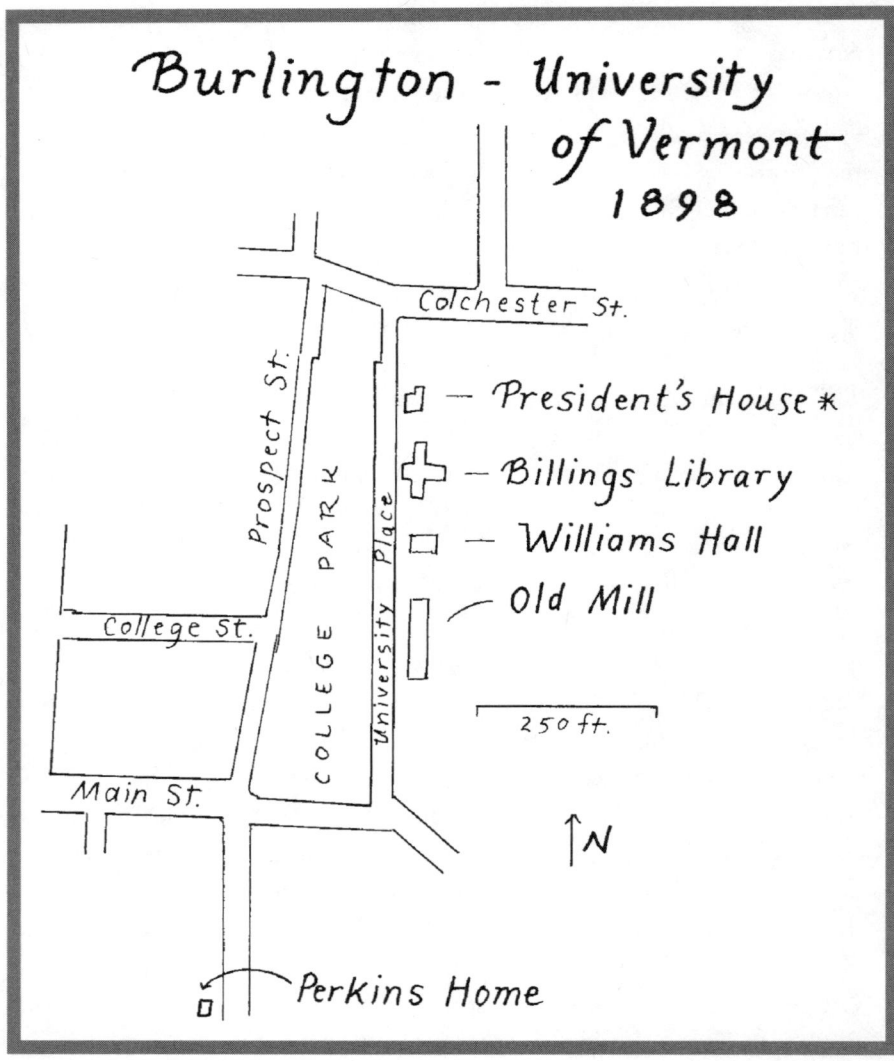

Burlington - University of Vermont 1898

Colchester St.

Prospect St.

COLLEGE PARK

University Place

College St.

Main St.

◻ — President's House *

✚ — Billings Library

▢ — Williams Hall

⌐ Old Mill

⌐ 250 ft. ⌐

↑ N

Perkins Home

many followers, who have produced much pleasant literature on out-door life. But in none of them is there that unique combination of the poet, the naturalist and the mystic which gives his page its wild original flavor."[9] Beers's "Sketch" did not include Muir, whose essays had by 1887 been in national magazines, but not in books. Either Beers had not read Muir or had found him not textbook material.

Thoreau, however, had entered the academy at least as early as 1886. That spring a Wellesley College student from Terre Haute, Indiana, Emma Condit, wrote under "Naturalists" in her "American Literature" notebook:

> Henry D. Thoreau 1817-1862
>
> Rare—close—observer.
>
> "Walden" "Week on Concord & Merrimack Rivers"

Louise Manning Hodgkins, Professor of English Literature at Wellesley from 1877 to 1891, taught the course. Her *A Guide to the Study of Nineteenth Century Authors* (1888; D.C. Heath & Co., 1895), however, covering eighteen (two of whom were female) English and eight American authors, did not include Thoreau or Muir.[10]

In the fall of 1898, at Princeton University, Professor Theodore Whitefield Hunt taught American Literature, as he had since 1894 and would until 1903. His syllabus, sans Muir, included Thoreau under "Minor Authors," concluding:

> As a Writer underrated.
>
> ...
>
> Not a genius, but—out of sympathy with the age.
>
> Had a place and left an impress.

Later, at Princeton, Professor J. Duncan Spaeth offered "Literary History of American Ideals." "The collateral reading is an essential part of the course," his 1921 syllabus stated. "Each student is expected to read ten books on the list. At least one book must be chosen from each of the five groups." Group III, "Travel, Adventure, Outdoor Life, and Nature Study" featured Thoreau and Muir with Theodore Roosevelt, Francis Parkman, Joshua Slocum, Richard H. Dana, and seven other men. The reading for Thoreau was *A Week on the Concord and Merrimack Rivers*, *The Maine Woods*, *Cape Cod*, and *Walden*; for Muir, *A Thousand-Mile Walk to the Gulf* and *Travels in Alaska*. A "long term essay" on one of the five groups or periods was required, too.[11]

At UVM, Muir saw a smaller campus than today's. College Park, a ten-acre common with walks, benches, statues, lawns, and fountain, retains much of its nineteenth-century flavor, though most of its trees, three white pines excepted, are twentieth-century commemorations: pin, red, and white oaks; ginkgo, red and Scotch pine, horse chestnut, lilac, tulip, silver maple, Serbian and Colorado spruce, ash, crabapple, Douglas fir, Sargent Cherry—the last honoring Muir's friend Charles Sprague Sargent.

East of the common, across University Place, the college stood boldy before Muir. An impressive row of four edifices faced westward, lakeward. From south to north stood Old Mill, Williams Hall, Billings Library, and the President's House.[12]

Old Mill had been rebuilt after an 1824 fire and remodeled in 1882 through the gift of John Purple Howard, whose wealth came from the Exchange and Irving hotels in New York. His bust—weathered forehead and crown, serious eyes, generous ears, bulbous nose, lush beard hiding a bow tie, lapelled shoulders squared back to almost bursting four vest buttons—looks out from an ivied recess of Old Mill into today's western sun.

"O.O. Howard lives here," Muir noted in his journal, "his bust in nitch [sic; niche] of University University building." Muir confused the identity of the benefactor. No bust of O. O. Howard existed on campus. True, Oliver Otis Howard lived in Burlington from 1894 until his death in 1909. Most likely, he was at his home at 26 Summit Street or in his office at 156 College Street that day. Muir's relationship with Howard was not strong enough to elicit a call.

It is curious that Muir should mention him, though, given the differences between their lives. Howard was born in Leeds, Maine (1830), and graduated from Bowdoin College (1850) and West Point (1854). Muir never earned a degree. Howard served in the Civil War, losing his right arm at Fair Oaks and marching with General Sherman to the sea. Muir avoided the conflict by moving to Canada. In 1872, Howard concluded peace with the Apaches by "giving" them what they worshiped, the Chiricahua Mountains of Arizona. Five years later he was in the Northwest with orders to evacuate Chief Joseph and his Nez Perces from the Wallowa Valley to the Lapwai reservation. The Nez Perces out-maneuvered "One-Armed Soldier Chief, General Howard," for 1,300 miles. They would have escaped to Canada had not they run into General Sherman vacationing in Yellowstone, a national park since 1872. Sherman called in reinforcements, to whom Chief Joseph surrendered. Muir visited Yellowstone in 1885, but never fought Indians.[13]

As by 1898 Howard had written numerous magazine and newspaper articles along with four books, the first of which was *Nez Perce Joseph* (1881), Muir may have read him. More likely he had heard of Howard's finest hour. Appointed commissioner of the Bureau of Refugees, Freedmen and

Abandoned Lands, better known as the Freedmen's Bureau, in 1865, Howard became involved in black education. This led in 1867 to the creation of a university in Washington, D.C., of which he served as first president, from 5 April 1869 to 30 November 1873, the Yosemite years of Muir. On 11 November 1898, Muir may have passed Howard University (see chapter 8).[14]

After the Old Mill came Williams Science Hall, the gift of alumnus Dr. Edward H. Williams of Philadelphia in 1896, an imposing facade with arched windows and reliefs of three American scientists—Alexander Agassiz, Samuel F.B. Morse, and Joseph Henry. To Williams Hall in June 1902, Cyrus Pringle brought a gift from his home in East Charlotte, eleven miles south of Burlington: some 50,000 preserved plants from New England, the Southwest, and Mexico. By his death in 1911, he had augmented his collection three-fold. His legacy, the Pringle Herbarium, now ensconced in Torrey Hall (1862; Torrey Hall was moved in 1895 to its present location to make way for Williams Hall), is the third best in New England after Harvard's and Yale's.[15]

In many respects Pringle was Muir's spiritual twin. Born under the same sun sign, Taurus, of the same year, 1838, Pringle was fifteen days younger than Muir. They were conscientious objectors during the Civil War. They ate sparely. (Pringle avoided even tea, although Muir imbibed unlimited quantities.) Pringle married, separated, and divorced before Muir married. Pringle had one daughter; Muir, two. They shared a passion for plants and robust rambles. Returning from Ontario on the first day of the year 1898, Pringle walked "from the station in a blizzard," reaching home at 1:00 a.m. Six days later, he walked "7 or 8 miles in all and in the rain" to catch a train at Bellows Falls, Vermont. "The train did not stop at Charlotte, so I got off at Shelburne and walked home before day light came"—about six miles. On 25 October 1898, he walked two-thirds of the way to Lincoln, or about twenty miles.[16]

It is strange that they never met. Almost any leading botanist could have introduced them. They both collected plants for Asa Gray. They might have met in California in 1882. That year, Charles Sargent employed Pringle to comb California for wood for the Morris K. Jesup Collection of the American Museum of Natural History. When in late September Pringle took a break in San Francisco from his abhorrent labors of killing live trees, chopping them into logs and shipping them East, Sargent rankled him with back-to-work commands, to the point of his resignation.[17] "I am home again and sooner by a month or two than I expected," Pringle wrote George E. Davenport, "Thanks to Mr. Sargent's outrageous treatment."[18] Davenport responded with full support for his friend.[19]

What a conversation could have ensued between Pringle and Muir on that day in 1898. Pringle was at home. He had departed an alder-blooming, bud-swelling Vermont on 30 March on the 4:00 p.m. train for Montreal, Chicago, and Santa Fe, making his fourteenth excursion to Mexico. Returning by August's end, Pringle had busied himself with his new plants. His diary recorded laconically his 1898 autumn activities:

16 September    I go to Burlington, draw money from bank and pay bill for
                mounting paper.

20 September    I begin mounting plants into my herbarium….

11 October      I work about the farm….

17 October      I mount some plants. Then after a late dinner take Mr.
                Baker to Mt. Philo. [F.A. Baker had come to visit him
                on the 15th.]

18 October      [Muir is in Burlington] I carry Mr. Baker to Thompson's
                Point and on our return we call on Fred Horsford [a cousin
                in the seed nursery business].

19 October      I poison and mount plants.

It is the same thing for the next three days. On the 23rd Pringle walked nine miles south to Ferrisburgh to visit friends, returning the following day.

Muir could also have engaged in fruitful exchanges with UVM faculty. George Henry Perkins had come to UVM in 1870 with his wife Mary and a Yale Ph.D. in zoology. In May 1877, they had their first and only child, Henry Farnham Perkins, who graduated from UVM in the year of Muir's visit. The senior Perkins was then (1898) Howard Professor of Geology (John Purple Howard's endowment in 1881) and dean of the Department of Natural Sciences. They lived at 205 South Prospect Street, a long block from College Park. Ten years earlier he had published *Flora of Vermont* (1888) with Pringle and Ezra Brainerd, the president of Middlebury College, as editors.[20] During the decade of the 1880s, he served as state entomologist. A year before Muir's Burlington visit, in 1897, he had been appointed state geologist, a position he would hold until his death in 1933. Three days before Muir's visit, he had submitted his important "Report on the Marble, Slate and Granite Industries of Vermont."[21]

The Perkinses were planning to travel to British Columbia and Alaska to collect for the museum the next summer. They were eager to see the Muir Glacier. Gladly, Muir would have given them earfuls: Told them of his first trip to Alaska in 1879, when he explored Glacier Bay and therein discovered the great white mass that is named for him.[22] Told them that "the Muir looks like a broad undulating prairie streaked with medial moraines and gashed with crevasses, surrounded by numberless mountains from which flow its many tributary glaciers."[23]

The Perkinses would go to Muir Glacier. Departing from Victoria, British Columbia, on 29 July 1899, they steamed northward via the Inland Passage.[24] Ironically, that same morning Muir arrived in Seattle, completing two months of investigations with the Harriman Alaska Expedition, during which he saw his glacier for the last time. Thus they passed in the night, and here, too, missed an opportunity to converse.[25]

The Perkinses waited at the mouth of Glacier Bay for the fog of 4 August to lift. Once rowed ashore, they walked the beaches and climbed the moraines. Mary described the Muir to her son: "the great cerulean wall, columned, crumpled, seamed, and scarred, each angle catching and reflecting the light in a different degree, giving the most ineffable display of turquoise, beryl, sapphire, amethyst, lapis-lazuli." Even though it was a smaller version of what Muir first witnessed due to melting, they savored every moment of their "day never to be forgotten." Their timing was propitious, for the next month, a resounding earthquake packed so much ice into Glacier Bay that no tourists could enter for nine years.[26]

Mary Perkins recommended that their son read "Scidmore's 'Journey In Alaska' which will describe all our trip better than I can do." She referred to Eliza Ruhamah Scidmore (1856-1928) and her *Alaska Its Southern Coast and the Sitkan Archipelago*, on whose top cover is embossed "Journeys in Alaska." In July 1883, Scidmore, not quite twenty-seven, had steamed into Glacier Bay aboard the *Idaho*. "The great Muir glacier" left her speechless: "Words and dry figures can give one little idea of the grandeur of this glacial torrent flowing steadily and solidly into the sea, and the beauty of the fantastic ice front, shimmering with all the prismatic hues, is beyond imagery or description."[27]

Likely, Muir would have suggested the same book to the Perkinses. Scidmore sent him an autographed copy at the end of the year of its publication, 1885. He read it with delight, listing in its back what he wanted to recall:

Haidas

Ind[ians]

Klawak

Aurora

Totems

(The Trip)

the Narrow channels

Canneries

Forests Color

Ind[ian] furniture

Chilcat [sic] Blankets

Shamans

Wrangell Narrows & Taku

smallpox

Chilcats [sic], Davidson's visits 1867 & 1869

Head of Stickeen [Stikine is her spelling.]

Mission bells of Cal[ifornia]. Cast in Sitka

Potlaches

Devil fish

Fort Ross in Cal[ifornia]

Alaska Purchase in 1867

The census of SE Al[aska] tribes & Missions

Alutian [sic] Island & seals.

Muir would also have read therein that General O.O. Howard had made a trip to Alaska.[28]

Throughout her book, Scidmore referred to "Professor Muir." She read his letters in the San Francisco *Daily Evening Bulletin* and consulted him.[29] They had mutual friends such as Jeanne Carr and William Keith. She traveled around the world, and wrote books on Java, Japan, China, and India. She served the National Geographic Society as a member of the Board of Managers (1892-1896)—the first woman to do so—and as corresponding secretary (1892-1898), foreign secretary (1899-1907), and associate editor (1896-1903). Once, while visiting the Muirs in Martinez, California, she told

John that the great glacier had been named for him. "Which one of the glaciers do they call mine?" he responded.[30]

Back on the UVM campus this October 1898 day, Muir next passed the Billings Library, with landscaping by Frederick Law Olmsted—"a pity he was not commissioned to design the whole campus," historian T. D. Seymour Bassett commented. A Class of 1844 alumnus, Frederick Billings (1823-1890) had donated the building, a H.H. Richardson Romanesque design completed in 1885. Billings was an attorney, the first to open an office in San Francisco in 1849, where he and his partners created a prestigious law firm and the Montgomery Block. While in California Billings visited Yosemite several times. In 1863, he and his wife Julia Parmly (they were married 31 March 1862) returned to the East to reside in New York and Woodstock, Vermont, where the Billings family had moved in 1835 when Frederick was twelve. In various capacities including its president, Billings oversaw the completion of the Northern Pacific Railway in August 1883. The year before, in 1882, Billings, Montana, on the Yellowstone River had been named for him, a town on the Northern Pacific's line that Muir had just passed through.[31]

Had Muir entered the Billings Library, he would have encountered the library of George Perkins Marsh (1801-1882), some 12,479 titles, which Billings bought from him and gave to UVM in 1887, along with funds to build an annex. Billings was influenced by Marsh and Muir. Though he never met Muir, he read his work.[32] Muir knew Marsh's *Man and Nature*, which within a decade of its May 1864 publication, according to biographer David Lowenthal, became "an international classic." Sargent, who credited *Man and Nature* for his devotion to forests and their preservation, surely discussed Marsh's ideas with Muir.[33]

Like Muir, Marsh wished to know the mountains of the world. He grew up in Woodstock, Vermont, with 1,359-foot Mount Tom on his property. Later he went to greater heights in the Green and White Mountains. Going no farther west than St. Louis, however, Marsh never saw the Rockies or the Sierra. The Alps of Europe, however, brought him ecstacy. While serving as U.S. envoy to Italy for two decades, from 1861 to his death, he went to the Alps for nourishment. In the Piedmontese capital of Turin, Marsh looked north to Mount Blanc, the Matterhorn, and Monte Rosa. In August 1861 he crossed 10,883-foot Théodule Pass on the southeast side of the Matterhorn, descending to Zermatt, Switzerland. In the Bernese Alps, he ascended Schilthorn (9,744 feet) and Faulhorn (8,796 feet), but not the Jungfrau above them. In Northwest Italy, he climbed the Pic di None and the Col de la

Traversette north of Monte Viso. Marsh explored glaciers, too, monitoring their movements, though not publishing his observations. His "love of the Alps never waned," Lowenthal wrote. "Nothing in nature gave him more pleasure." He died in his post at the Italian Forestry School on Mt. Vallombrosa on 23 July 1882.[34]

In 1963, when the Billings Library was transformed into the Billings Student Center, Marsh's collection was moved to the Guy W. Bailey Library, a five-minute walk away. The Student Center is magnificent with pine paneling, enormous fireplaces, and long study tables. Outside, a student in shorts and sneakers clings with bare hands to the red Longmeadow, Massachusetts, sandstone several feet above the ground and moves slowly southward from the entrance arch. Puzzled, I ask his purpose. Hearing that he intends to walk around the building on this perch, I wonder if he has done that before. "Not yet," he replies, still gripping the facade. "This is only my second try."

The last in the row—28 University Place—was the President's House. A grand Victorian with Mansard roof and porch, it was built in 1870 as an inducement to keep President James B. Angell from going to the University of Michigan. Angell went to Ann Arbor anyway, serving an unprecedented thirty-eight years as its chief executive.[35] His successor at UVM in August 1871, Matthew Henry Buckham, exceeded even Angell's long tenure. A Scottish minister's son, UVM alumnus and classics professor, Buckham was still at the helm when Muir came and would remain there until his death on 29 November 1910! Sadly, this residence was razed for space for the Ira Allen Chapel (1925).

At the north end of University Place, Muir turned onto Colchester Avenue. In 1972 a memorial was placed here to a UVM student of the Class of 1879, John Dewey, who was born in Burlington in 1859 and became a famous educational philosopher.

## ENVIRONS

Muir went east on Colchester Avenue to Green Mountain Cemetery. There he saw the statue of Ethan Allen that still stands in the graveyard. "[A] swaggering and blustery giant," one historian pictured Allen, "who spoke with awe and terror and whose strength made him invincible."[36] He and his brother Ira were revered for wresting Fort Ticonderoga from the British in 1775 and for bringing the state of Vermont into existence.

Muir then swung into the "hills south of city," where he savored "grand views" of the Green Mountains to the east, in particular Mt. Mansfield and Camels Hump, and "the glorious Lake & rich folds ridging of Adirondacks to W[est]. all timbered all colored[.] lake islands also colored."

Most prominent of a number of hills south of Burlington is Mt. Philo. Though just under a thousand feet, it offers the spectacle Muir envisioned. Philo, an island in Glacial Lake Vermont 13,500 years ago, is composed of red, buff Monkton quartzite and black Stony Point shales, as are other area hills. The lowland shows its glaciation in till, kames, beach gravels, and Lake Vermont sediments.[37] Pringle, Philo's neighbor and intimate, would have been the perfect escort for Muir.

Though a road runs to its summit, it is unlikely that Muir took it. Philo is in another town, too far south (fifteen miles) from Burlington. Besides, Muir does not mention it. More likely, he rode out Spear Street about three miles to what is now called Overlook Park. Though not much over three hundred feet, this stone-walled lay-by with grass slope, bicycle path, and two picnic tables gives ample scope to all Muir beheld. My guide, historian Kevin Dann, called it "a profane place" due to its development. The view west was over a sea of condominium roofs into the second-floor bedrooms of a nondescript new home. Poet Mona Van Duyn has made another observation that also applies here:

> I have never enjoyed those roadside overlooks from which
> you can see the mountains of two states. The view keeps
>     generating
> a kind of pure, meaningless exaltation
> that I can't find a use for. It drifts away from things.[38]

Muir returned to Burlington, perhaps via Queen City and Redrocks parks. Back at the Van Ness House, he may have glanced at the headlines of the *Burlington Free Press*:

Amusements/OPERA HOUSE/TO-NIGHT/DANIEL R. RYAN/ in/JIM THE PENMAN.

SNOWSTORM./Worst Early Storm on Rec/ord Visited Kansas City/Yesterday.

HIS CREED./Col. Roosevelt Would Make/Rigid Honesty the Stand-/ard of Service.

The latter article informed Muir of Theodore Roosevelt's campaign for governor of New York. On 17 October, Roosevelt went by private train up the Hudson River Valley to Glens Falls for the night. The next day, while Muir was in Burlington, the candidate was on the opposite side of Lake Champlain, headed to Plattsburgh and then Ogdensburg, where he arrived at 7:00 p.m. The hero of the Spanish-American War, who led his Rough Riders to victory at Kettle Hill on 1 July, Roosevelt also won this political contest: he was elected governor on 8 November. Somehow, he also managed to write about his exploits; *The Rough Riders* appeared in May of the following year.[39] Though they were only a lake apart at this moment, Roosevelt and Muir would have to wait four and a half years to meet. Then, President Roosevelt would camp with Muir in Yosemite Valley of California (see chapter 14).

The next day, Wednesday, the *Burlington Free Press* in its "Personal Mention" column, which featured such comings and goings as "George Atkins of Montpelier was a visitor in this city yesterday" and "C.N. Mosley left for Boston last night," reported

> John Muir of Martinez, Cal., was
> registered at the Van Ness last night.

If Pringle or the Perkinses read this, they probably realized what an opportunity had been missed.

Friday's paper—Muir was in Maine then—announced that Captain Joshua Slocum would give "two of his illustrated talks one in the Williams Science Building and one in the Y.M.C.A. Hall, November 1st and 2d. proximo."

Slocum did just that. On 27 June 1898, he had arrived in Newport, Rhode Island, having hailed from East Boston three years, two months and two days earlier aboard a 36-foot, 9-inch-sloop, *Spray*, a derelict, old oysterman he had restored in thirteen months. A tornado off Fire Island had prevented his landing in New York two days earlier. Though he had circled the globe five times, this was his premier navigation of "the world around" alone. He was fifty-four. Slocum did not stay at the Van Ness House. Pringle, who was working at home selecting plants for various herbariums, does not mention hearing him. Undoubtedly, the Perkinses would have attended this event.[40]

Muir dined again at the Van Ness. Wanting a solid sleep after last night's debacle, he did not go to the opera, nor tell his famous dog story "Stickeen," nor walk along the lake. Instead, he wrote about his travels to his family, recommending that they "read or reread" Parkman for his "charming descriptions of this region."[41]

## FRANCIS PARKMAN

Francis Parkman had been on Muir's mind this trip. "Think of the wild adventurous times drawn so well by Parkman," he jotted in his journal, while moving eastward past Lake Erie on 16 September 1898. Perhaps Muir had been reading Parkman before he came away, or en route, though he does not mention having the histories with him.

Muir devoted considerable energy to Parkman. His library contained Parkman's oeuvre. Ten of twelve volumes of the 1902 edition published by Little, Brown and Company of Boston were all indexed by Muir for reference; the exception was the two-volume *Conspiracy of Pontiac*. The subjects Muir most noted are Indians, animals (buffalo, wolves, moose, elk, squirrels, etc.), trees, places (Yellowstone, Lake George, Alaska), morals, people (Montcalm, Wolfe, Pitt, Champlain, Jesuits), and the author's style.

Muir learned from a biography of Francis Parkman by Charles H. Farnham that young Parkman lived "on his grandfather's farm at Medford [Massachusetts], where he developed his love of nature by roaming the woods of the Middlesex Fells," and that his diaries give the details of his college-years trips to New England's wilds.[42]

In 1842, after his sophomore year, Parkman, like Muir, traveled by train from Boston to Albany, there lodging at the Eagle Hotel. Then, by stage and train, he proceeded north to Lake Champlain, crossing by steamer to Burlington for the night of 27 July. Unlike Muir, Parkman was not impressed with UVM: "It was term time and the students were lounging about the ugly buildings or making abortive attempts at revelry in their rooms. The air was full of their diabolical attempts at song. We decided that they were all green, and went back, drawing comparisons by the way between the University of Vermont and old Harvard."[43] The next day, he began walking across Vermont. The next summer, 1843, Parkman followed lakes George and Champlain and the Richelieu River north to Montreal before returning to the White Mountains, planning "his journeys precisely to recover as far as he could the direct, physical experience of those whose lives he would one day write," Simon Schama says.[44]

Again, Muir made his own index of Farnham, some twenty-one items. He was most interested in Parkman's "character," "education," "hardihood," "walking," and "death;" his views on "women," "female suffrage" (Parkman opposed it), "government," "religion," "Thoreau," and "Wordsworth." In reference to the latter, Farnham wrote of Parkman: "Two of his strongest characteristics were love of the real and aversion to the visionary and spiritual.... He loved nature, but not as a lover who sits down quietly for intimate communion. He could not abide Wordsworth and his followers. Although admitting that Thoreau was a notable man, he had little sympathy with him; he felt repelled by what he considered Thoreau's eccentricities, transcendentalism, self-consciousness, and affectation of being natural."[45]

Muir's love of nature was broader than Parkman's. Muir's was "visionary and spiritual." Like Thoreau, Muir celebrated the divinity in nature, reveling in quiet, intimate communion with the natural world. He lived to experience wilderness directly, freshly, fully, ecstatically; while Parkman, Schama says, lived to write the drama enacted there with "the forest as its principal character." The West that Parkman encountered in 1846 left him disenchanted. His wilderness journeys ended with his youth. They awaited his mature talents to be transformed into art.

Yet parts of Parkman resonated with Muir. "He took great pleasure in what is vast, powerful, savage," Farnham related, "often noting the effects of light and atmosphere over a landscape, breathing most freely on a mountain top surrounded by limitless plains, responding best to the roaring life and irrepressible activity of cataracts, to the wild energy of a storm sweeping over the prairie or the ocean."[46]

## THOREAU

Thoreau, who had been here ever so briefly, never really experienced Vermont under foot, except for long walks in Brattleboro during four days in September 1856. Traveling to and from Montreal and Quebec within a week's time at midcentury, Thoreau told little of this place; he did not express the particularity of the landscape. Arriving in Burlington by train from Concord, Massachusetts, at 6:00 p.m. on 25 September 1850, "too late to see the lake," he went directly to the wharf and boarded a steamer. "We got our first fair view of the lake at dawn, just before reaching Plattsburg [sic], and saw blue ranges of mountains on either hand, in New York and in Vermont, the former especially grand." Later, he disclosed that he had spent "half a night in Burlington," which would agree with a dawn arrival in Plattsburgh, for the ferry required about two hours.[47] His return was equally swift. Departing Montreal late in the afternoon of 2 October, he reached Burlington early the next morning, and home that evening.

Thoreau's narrative of his excursion, "A Yankee in Canada", is mostly concerned with his travels in Canada, not his passage through New England. "It concerns me but little," its author confessed when only half of it was serialized in *Putnam's* in 1853, "and probably is not worth the time it took to tell it."[48]

If Muir was not familiar with "A Yankee in Canada" by October 1898, he certainly was later. His copy of *Excursions and Poems* of which "A Yankee in Canada" is the first essay attests to that: thirteen passages/sentences of the text are marked in the margin; and his index contains this list:

Names

Baggage

Montmorenci Fall

Cold weather

St. Lawrence River

St. Anne Row brothers row[49]

In four days from this October Tuesday in Burlington, Muir would be in Quebec, witnessing the St. Lawrence River and Montmorenci Falls for himself. Parkman's scene of the British-French clash there in 1759 may have come to mind:

> The position of the hostile forces was a remarkable one. They were separated by the vast gorge that opens upon the St. Lawrence; an amphitheatre of lofty precipices, their brows crested with forests, and their steep brown sides scantily feathered with stunted birch and fir. Into this abyss leaps the Montmorenci with one headlong plunge of nearly two hundred and fifty feet, a living column of snowy white, with its spray, its foam, its mists, and its rainbows; then spreads itself in broad thin sheets over a floor of rock and gravel, and creeps tamely to the St. Lawrence.[50]

Muir was equally awed. "View of Montmorenci Falls glorious even at dist[ance] of 5 or 6 m[ile]s," he put in his journal, "Never saw more imposing fall save Niagara." Had he forgotten that he considered Yosemite Falls "perhaps the most wonderful of its kind in the world"?[51]

## WEDNESDAY, 19 OCTOBER: STOWE

Leaving Burlington at 7:30 a.m., crossing the Champlain lowlands, changing trains in fifteen minutes, following the Winooski River valley east through the Green Mountains, Muir observed, "fine rich scenery by the way[.] streams in rocky gorges[.] hills & dales in rich combinations[.] small farms. Many little quiet villages."

This is an ancient, beautiful passage, taken by water and snow geese. Returning to their Quebec homes from their raid on the small frontier settlement of Deerfield, Massachusetts (March 1704), some two hundred fifty Canadians and Indians —Abenakis and Caughnawagas—along with their English captives, among them the Reverend John Williams, his wife, and five remaining children (two had been killed in the attack; one was away from home) had snowshoed the Connecticut and White River valleys, "crossing the snowy backs of the Green Mountains," Parkman related, "they struck the headwaters of the stream then called French River, now the Winooski, or Onion," which they followed to Burlington."[52]

Twenty-five miles later Muir was in Waterbury. From there he sat in a nine-window-long car of the year-old Mount Mansfield Electric Railroad, "riding up grand mtn val [mountain valley]" ten miles to Stowe.

Stowe still satisfies the soul. Highway 100 has displaced the train track. The valley road bisects the 1836 May Farm, now the home of the Green Mountain Club, which was founded at the Van Ness House in Burlington on 11 March 1910. Muir would be happy at the Club's, and his staying place's, service to conservation. The Club's supreme gift to Vermont was the creation of a footpath—the Long Trail—that spans the length of this tall state, passing just west of this way.[53] Walking Stowe's unpaved byways during an August thunder/lightning/rain storm, I watched mist rising from fields of goldenrod over copses and barns and up forested slopes east and west, embracing mountaintops, conversing with clouds.

At 10:00 a.m., Muir's electric train pulled into a building on Stowe's Main Street. This 1897 depot now hosts "A Community of Shops"—Stowe Mercantile on the first floor; Bear Pond Books, Thompson's Flour Shop, and Vermont Furniture Works on the second.

The depot is joined to the Green Mountain Inn by an elevated walkway over an alley. The inn, begun as a private residence in 1833, became part of the huge Mt. Mansfield Hotel, survived its 1889 burning, was refurbished for its 150th birthday, and now holds fifty-four rooms and suites. "In the four suites you find," its brochure indicates, "VCRs, wetbars, and jacuzzis in pleasing combination with antique furnishings." Both depot and inn are painted red over clapboard or brick with green shutters and white window trim. Both are on the National Register of Historic Places.

Muir must have lodged here.[54] Now he would be lucky to get in. In 1993, on the ninety-fifth anniversary of his visit, the inn overflowed with tourists from all over North America. They had come to watch the changing of the seasons. At ten in the morning there were still rooms available for $79. In 1972 I had spent a magical winter week here at half that nightly price. Arriving at dark with snow falling through the inn's lights onto empty sidewalks, I had been transported to an earlier era. This silent, snowy village had expressed the virtues of being small and beautiful.

Contemporary autumn swells Stowe's population. Congestion contributes to its sense of compactness. From three directions automobiles, even a trolley, converge at the Green Mountain Inn. The curious disperse into gift shops—"Is there only one in town?" asks one visitor—into the Stowe Area Association for travel/lodging information; into the Helen Day Library and Art Center, which has only one Muir book, *Steep Trails*; into Lackey's Variety Store, with drugs, sundries, period postcards; into Stafford's, a pharmacy since 1872, and into the many beds of sixty-five inns, motels, and resorts, not to mention those in second homes and condominiums. Aside from these modern lodgings, they see much the same architecture that Muir did, for Stowe's core is blessedly well preserved.

From the livery behind the Green Mountain Inn, Muir paid four dollars for a horse and buggy and driver for the day. The buggy took him northwest for seven miles along the Mountain Road, now Route 8, to the Toll Road, which they ascended four and a half miles to the elysium of Vermont's *ne plus ultra*, Mount Mansfield.

On 1 October 1993, I followed Muir by bicycle over Stowe's Recreation Path. Joined by walkers, joggers, rollerbladers, I passed McDonald's, disguised as a blue-green home, and the Shed restaurant, where in January 1990 artist Elaine Dixon of Putney, Vermont, and I had talked about greenways with Anne Lusk, who created this one.[55] Elegant bridges elevated me ten times over a slalom of West Branch rocks and water. Leaves danced in October's light. The lodestone Mansfield radiated over a red farm house with black and white cows and green pasture. When the path ended at Brook Street, I was forced to flow with Mountain Road traffic for 1.5 miles, passing inns and B&Bs, gaining altitude, until I reached the Toll Road entrance. There stands a sign that prohibits bicycles. My heart sank. "There are exceptions," a cheerful gatekeeper resuscitated me, "for a fee of $7."

For three dollars more you can drive your car up this road—until 11 October, that is. Or soar up by gondola for $8.50. If you wait for snow, you can buy a lift ticket for $42 and ski down the Toll Road, a tradition inaugurated by Dartmouth librarian Nathaniel Goodrich in 1914, the year of Muir's death.[56] Horses and carriages are no longer allowed. The first day of autumn in this year, 1993, thick fog closed the road. Three days later torrential rain kept everyone at the base. The road opens 22 May, if the snow melts.

The Toll Road, completed in 1870, winds narrowly, vertically westward. After a quarter mile of pavement, it becomes brown earth. Ski trails open lines of vision through dense forest to Stowe Valley and Smuggler's Notch. Cars descend the one lane cautiously, pulling over to allow those coming up to pass. Baked brakes smelled and irritated my lungs. After two hours of mostly walking my bicycle, I came to a saddle between the highest peaks: the 4,062-foot Nose is a short, supergrade south; a mile-plus tundra trek north culminates on the Chin, at 4,393 feet. Nestled on this ridge was the Summit House, which served guests for a century of summers, 1858 to 1958. To this hostel came John Muir in his carriage.

"A grand ride," Muir exulted. "How the wind sang & the rain & streams." He embraced a "Forest of oak maples white, red, black birch large trees white pine spruce Abies [*Abies balsamea*, balsam fir] at top. hemlock. Mtn [Mountain] ash with red berries v[ery] ab[undant] to top Clubmoss ab[undant] v[ery] fine. Elm Buckeye." All in a riot of "greens, golds, reds. fresh & lovely."

The varieties of weather notwithstanding: "Rain snow mist wind v[ery] cold." Although bundled in "2 overcoats[,] one of them huge buffalo coat borrowed from landlord...arctic overshoes & heavy goat robe & blanket over knees," Muir was still cold. Did his younger enthusiasms revisit him? "I must borrow a big coat and mingle in the storm and make some studies," he had told Jeanne Carr in 1875.[57]

"Wind roaring…. Got horses into stable & fed them. ate our lunch in stable. & took short walk. a fresh mansion in the sky." By "mansion," apparently Muir meant an abode, a dwelling place.

Most likely, he rambled afoot northward a bit over what is now the Long Trail. He beheld a "fine arctic scene[.] abies bent with snow - every needle cased in ice from frozen rain. Crags at summit marvellous [sic] beautiful with snow & ice white 1/2 white etc. Some stones margined with crystalized [sic] snow as on Rocks at Cape Prince of Wales."

The latter is Alaskan. Seventeen years earlier, in July 1881, the *Corwin* had anchored off this promontory pointing into the Bering Strait toward Siberia with all North America behind it. Ashore, Muir discovered seven plants; two of them also grace Mt. Mansfield: mountain cranberry (*Vaccinium Vitis-Idaea*) and alpine azalea (*Loiseleuria procumbens*).[58] Muir, however, did not see these two plants on Mansfield. In fact, botanizing was impossible on this

October day, for as Muir observed, "Snow 2 ft deep,"

With global warming, it is now unusual to have that amount of snow that early in the season. Though snow had fallen 29 September 1993—or rather "graupel", as a meteorologist put it (that is, soft hail or snow pellets)—it did not remain. This 19 October 1993, hoarfrost bearded the Chin's west side, where ravens play. It spread north to cover the Adam's Apple and downward almost to the Lake of the Clouds. It imitated in white the green balsam fir needle along one edge. This white-evergreen pattern repeated ad infinitum across the mountain. Plants and rocks were bare to the beaks of juncos. Clouds let in sun intermittently. A couple from near Stuttgart, Germany, closed their three-week New England holiday on top. A young lad with a big backpack camped in solitude on his birthday.

Though Thoreau recommended journeying over the Green Mountains in autumn for the variety of colors displayed, and passed Mansfield on his way to and from Burlington, he never climbed it.

Ralph Waldo Emerson was here thirty years before Muir. He came in high summer, from the west. On Thursday morning, 13 August 1868, the sixty-five-year-old philosopher and his twenty-nine-year-old daughter, Ellen, walked from Prouty's Hotel in Underhill Center four miles to the Summit House atop Mansfield with "clouds gradually rising & passing from the summit." "Cold & a little wet," they reached their destination, "but found the house warm with stoves." After dinner, leaving Ellen on a settee by the hearth, the author took "a rough & grand walk" to the Chin. "A perpetual illusion…a piece of yellow sky," Lake Champlain appeared to him, "until careful examination of the islands in it, & the Adirondac summits beyond brought it to the earth for a moment." A gay evening awaited his return. Troubadour George Bartlett "amused us mightily with charades of violent fun." Before breakfast, father and daughter climbed the Nose. At 9:30, they departed, walking back to the their hotel. From there they boarded a wagon for Stowe, probably stopping at the Green Mountain Inn for the stage to Essex Junction, from where they went by train to Burlington for the night.[59]

Obviously, Emerson was still a hearty walker. Three years later, in May 1871, he would meet Muir in Yosemite Valley. Likely, Emerson then told Muir of his days with Mansfield and other New England mountains.[60]

"Rain most of way down," Muir headed back, "arrived at Stowe at 4.15." About the same time I did, in 1993, when innkeepers were busy filling the Green Mountain Inn for the night. Requests for reservations for the Christmas holiday were having to be declined.

Muir's evening at the Green Mountain Inn has to be imagined, since he wrote nothing about it. Warming by the fire in the common room, reading the newspaper, sipping tea, talking and dining with others, Muir passed the time. His quiet autumn evening contrasts with Emerson's social summer one at the Summit House. Granted, the unpleasant weather and the lessened light of that season limited Muir's options. Or was it less a difference of lifestyle than of what Muir penciled out of himself onto 3 1/2" x 6" cross-section pages of his maroon leather journal? His wordwork done quickly in situ or on the go—"It's awfully trying to write on the quivering jiggling train"—reduced the amount of details he might have conveyed.[61] Emerson's, though, flowed in the leisured luxury of his Concord library two days after the event.

What more might Muir have told us about that evening? His journal indicates no private encounters for this day, until in the back appears his scrolled reminder:

D R Smith

Stowe Vt

Send book

Dow R. Smith of the Green Mountain Inn Livery was twenty-four that May, young enough to be Muir's son. He was born in Vermont, as were his parents, William and Alma. A year after Muir's visit, on 23 October 1899, Smith would wed Mary Vearen, who was four years his senior. They had no children. He became a teamster, delivering mail, and a farmer "working out" for wages. Mary became a clerk at the General Store. He lived to be eighty, dying on 23 May 1954.[62]

Taking the long way home via Florida, Muir did not reach Martinez, California, until the end of November 1898 (see chapter 7). Soon after his arrival, he honored his promise by sending *The Mountains of California* (1894) to D. R. Smith. Six days before Christmas, Smith expressed his gratitude to Muir for the gift in flowing black ink. Apparently he had not read the book yet, since he did not comment on its contents. "We were the Last ones on the Mt this Fall," he informed Muir, "until they went up there to make their ice about a week ago." They reported four feet of snow, double the amount Muir had stepped through two months earlier. "We have about two feet of snow," in Stowe "and the weather is about 10° below zero." An invitation to Mansfield in the summer was extended. "I am still in the livery business," he said, and signed off with supper waiting and a hope of seeing Muir again.

"PS Many thanks for the Book."[63]

On that night of 19 October 1898, Muir sent no messages home. His family would have to wait nine days until he was comfortably ensconced in the Albermarle Hotel of Madison Square West in New York City before he let them into his life:

> I've been trying to tell you the course of my wanderings since I left home partly that I might thus help to keep track of myself. I've been going so fast & have made so many turns & doubles far & near in so many states north & south—enjoyed so much & been bothered & fussed so much—mixed day & night so much in cars, hotels, friends homes steamboats shanties etc it is no easy matter to keep anything like a clear record.
>
> I think I wrote last from Burlington, Vermont....[64]

## THURSDAY, 20 OCTOBER: SMUGGLER'S NOTCH

The next day, 20 October, Muir crossed northern New England to the Atlantic coast, 130 air miles in fourteen rail hours with a two-hour, forty-five minute stop in St. Johnsbury, Vermont.

Rising before the sun, he left Stowe at 6:30 a.m. Again he was back in a buggy with "a pleasant young driver," though not D. R. Smith, heading north on the Mountain Road. Beyond the Toll Road, a four-year-old dirt track led through the Green Mountains at Smuggler's Notch, 1,400 feet above Stowe, and not negotiable in winter.

"[M]ostly rough & hilly. road very wet[.] still raining at 8 & dark," Muir recorded. Yet, "fine views of mtn clds [mountain clouds]," rewarded him, "rising make Mansfield look huge & high & impressive flaked with snow as if 15000 ft high. the colors freshened by the rain. Still bright hereabouts." He inventoried: "Trees in notch large. Spruce pine birch 3 sp[ecies of birch] 2 ab.[undant] some 3 ft dia[meter] ground ferny. huge earthquake bowlders." One of these birch, probably a yellow or white one, for they appear more often, blocked their way. They "had hard job lifting buggy over it." Muir did not say how many it took to accomplish that feat.

A lower, surfaced, improved gradient still thrills the modern traveler. One lane crosses the watershed. Here I feel as though I have left the highway and merged with the landscape. I feel that I am part of these giant boulders sprouting moss and birch; part of the gray cliffs from which no escape seems possible; part of the various shades of green in moss, fern, conifer; part of the flowing water from a big spring; part of the copper-bronze jewelry of beech trees; part of an occasional yellowing of birch. Though this 20 October (1993) features more leafless trees than Muir saw, the reply to my query about winter passage is still the same as it was for him, "O, my, no." Yet, Vermont historian Tom Bassett told me of having crossed it on snowshoes.

Ferny, indeed. Muir needed time to explore these woods with Pringle, who had been here on 23 August 1876. He had slept at the Summit House, then "descended the mountain side through the trackless forest. As the masses of broken rock covering the slope were half hidden beneath the shrubs and mosses, the first half of our descent was not without its peril." Once in Smuggler's Notch, he had followed a trail, searching the surroundings. "A hasty survey" revealed "the best botanizing ground in Vermont." Midafternoon, he had begun an arduous ascent to the summit hotel. "On all my subsequent visits," Pringle made clear, "I never felt a desire to follow the wild course of that first weary day."[65]

Though a trail now marks the climb that Pringle made from the Notch to Lake of the Clouds and beyond, it is no less steep. It was at Lake of the Clouds that Horace Mann Jr. (1844-1868) discovered a new quillwort, *Isoetes echinospora*, Pringle reported. Most likely Mann found this after he had traveled with Thoreau to Minnesota in 1861. Mann's coming to Mansfield thus brings Thoreau here by association.[66]

By mid-September 1876 Pringle was back. This time he camped at the Old Notch House, which Muir passed. He found many plants in his daily rambles. The next year, he botanized Mansfield with Charles Faxon, who, we recall, had designed this trip for Muir earlier at the Arnold Arboretum. Faxon was so impressed with Mansfield that he recommended it to Muir. Why then didn't he provide Muir with a letter of introduction to Pringle?

"[A]scent & descent steep"; Muir came down into the Lamoille River valley, which he followed for eight miles to Jeffersonville, arriving at nine o'clock. Here he boarded the train.

## ST. JOHNSBURY

Three hours elapsed while Muir traversed fifty miles of Vermont to St. Johnsbury. His train, following what is now Route 15, stopped in a gazetteer of hamlets—Johnson, Hyde Park, Morrisville (the Lamoille Valley Railroad still makes summer excursions from here), Wolcott, Hardwick, Greensboro,

Walden, Danville—about which Muir's penciling is nil. Though Parkman walked this country, he also is silent about its impact.[67]

Becalmed for 165 minutes in "a brisk pretty town" of 6,567 people, Muir improvised. Leaving the railroad station (1883), a luxurious, three-storied, slate-roofed Queen Anne that now houses the welcome center and the chamber of commerce, Muir crossed Railroad Street on the diagonal to a "good hotel" for dinner. The New Avenue House filled 160 feet of Eastern Avenue five floors high and 180 feet of Railroad Street three floors high. It had a center tower of one million bricks. It exceeded its predecessor, which was the largest building in town, complete with stores, a hoop-skirt manufacturer, and a barber shop with hot and cold baths, until its burning in 1896. The New Avenue House was ten months old when Muir stepped silently on its rubber-tiled floors. It had elevators and telephones.[68] Muir might have called home, for there was a phone on the other end, but there were no wires between them. Transcontinental service was not available until 1915. Besides, Muir preferred to write; phones he thought were only good for "a shouting match."[69] Today, the edifice is transformed into a warren of apartments.

After dinner, Muir strolled up Eastern Avenue to Main Street, which spans a long, level sandbank called the Plain. This landform is actually "the largest and most continuous esker in the region," running twenty-four miles south to north. Eskers—gravel-filled ridges formed by glacial stream deposition—are common, if imperiled, New England residents. Though Muir was familiar with them from Wisconsin, it is not clear whether he recognized this particular one or not.[70]

The weather changed: rain ceased, skies cleared, and temperatures rose into the low fifties. Muir could see "residences & business blocks on hillside. Colored woods on mtn [mountain] ridge opposite." As he meandered the Plain, he witnessed homes of a prosperous community, a Fairbanks legacy. The brothers Erastus and Thaddeus founded an iron company in 1824, called E. & T. Fairbanks. When Thaddeus invented the platform scales in 1830, they began manufacturing them. When Muir came they were being shipped worldwide for weighing everything from letters to humans. They are still being produced.[71] I thought Muir might have had one in his home, but apparently he did not.[72]

The Fairbanks Museum (1890), another H. H. Richardson Romanesque brownstone like UVM's Billings Center, was the largest of Franklin Fairbanks. Under its barrel-vaulted oak ceiling, Muir could have seen Fairbanks's fine bird collection, though he would have preferred them alive and in the wild, not stuffed and faded in an exhibit. There is also an assortment of animals. A Nova Scotia moose was shot the year Muir came; muskrats in summer and winter homes recalled those at his Fountain Lake, in Wisconsin. A planetarium is upstairs; the Northern New England Weather Center, with more than a century of weather reports, is in the basement.

At the south end of Main Street, the St. Johnsbury Academy flourishes. It was started by Thaddeus Fairbanks in the Ephraim Paddock House (1820), a Federal mansion modeled on Charles Bulfinch's in Boston and located at the other end of the street.[73]

Muir could not have missed the Athenaeum; from its perch atop Main Street it peers down Eastern Avenue. This was the gift of Horace Fairbanks in 1871. Two years later, he made an addition to accommodate a new acquisition. Had Muir entered Fairbanks's art gallery, he would have been transported home. Occupying the entire back wall under natural light is a grand oil (9'8"x15') of Muir's heartland, *The Domes of the Yosemite*. On the left, Yosemite Falls hangs like a sash cord, spilling its water into the Merced River, which winds through a massive rock-walled meadow. Center-left, the seal head of North Dome exhales clouds that drift upon snowy peaks. On the right, Half Dome like Buddha blesses all creation. Evoking our contemporary poet Emily Hiestand's lines "there is something appealing about a gigantic vision," the painting transfixes one in its grandeur.[74]

The artist is Albert Bierstadt. Though rendered in his Irvington, New York, studio, *The Domes* is the inspiration of his camping and sketching in Yosemite Valley in the summer of 1863, six years before Muir's first Sierra summer. Exhibited in spring 1867, it then went to the Norwalk, Connecticut, mansion of Le Grand Lockwood. After his death in 1872, his wife auctioned it to the highest bidder, who in turn sold it to Horace Fairbanks.[75]

Both Muir and Bierstadt were in Yosemite Valley in 1872. Though no evidence has emerged, it is likely they met then.[76] Bierstadt came in March to see the Sierra in snow, returned for a summer of painting, and went into the Kings River country with geologist Clarence King in the autumn. All the while, Muir was in and out of the valley on various excursions. In late July he botanized with Asa Gray. In October, he began a lifelong friendship with artist William Keith, who was to paint many of Muir's favorite landscapes. Surely Keith, who was influenced by Bierstadt, would have discussed the Easterner with Muir. A San Francisco exhibit in May 1873 of Bierstadt's *Autumn in the Sierras* would have excited much conversation between them. Ah, for Muir's impressions of the great Romantic luminist's representation.

Apparently, Bierstadt came to St. Johnsbury to restore *The Domes of the Yosemite*.[77] Serendipity would fancy Muir stopping at the Athenaeum at the moment when Bierstadt was brushing up Half Dome's paunch. Instead, Muir returned to the depot in time to catch his 2:45 p.m. train. Soon he crossed the Connecticut River into New Hampshire.

# 9. New Hampshire

*Hawthorne says that steam spiritualizes travel,*
*but I think that it squarely degrades and materializes travel.*
—Muir to Jeanne Carr, 4 November 1870

## Thursday, 20 October 1898

Crossing New Hampshire by train on Thursday afternoon, 20 October 1898, John Muir had his first view of the White Mountains: "The White Mtns make fine show as I saw them draped lightly here & there with after storm mist cl[ou]ds."

From the village of Whitefield eastward to Hazen's Pond, a sumptuous panorama prevailed in the east. He gazed across a forest of black spruce and tamarack surrounding a heath bog with Cherry and Little Cherry ponds, now the Pondicherry National Wildlife Refuge, to Cherry Mountain, with the peaks of Jefferson and Adams of the Northern Presidentials beyond and the Twin Mountains in the south.[1]

Muir as ever appreciated trees.

> Saw a good many tamaracs today lol [between] Johnsbury [Vermont] & White Mtns. some good size standing alone all handsome all colored yel[low] brownish delicate branches showing dark thru mellow yel[low] foliage - ground boggy like Muirs of Scotland.[2]

Now his train trended southward. "Magnificent broad open valleys at base of White Mtns huge moraines sand & gravel," he noted in his journal. A brief stop at Fabyan House, thirteen miles south of Whitefield in Carroll, at 4:40 p.m. and, minutes later, at the Mount Pleasant Hotel, presented opportunities for Muir to look up at New England's most extensive alpine region, which had had its first snow of the season a month ago, on 19 September.

> Mt Washington not very imposing m[oun]t[ai]n. gray with snow. lightly sculptured by residual gls.[glaciers] No massive priapus here or in celebrated Notch tho magnif[icent] in simple [undeciphered word] slopes mostly densely feathered with birch & maple & aspen[.] Colors dull brown lvs [leaves] frost killed. Many trees naked specially [?] aspen & birch limbs & trunks white & gray. many hotels.

The Bretton Woods Motor Inn has replaced the Mt. Pleasant Hotel. The railroad does not stop there anymore. Across the road, the forest is gone, cleared for a golf course and the state's largest wooden structure, the Mt. Washington Hotel, which opened its 600-guest accommodations on 28 July 1902, four years after Muir's visit . On Sunday, 16 October 1994, it is a bee-hive. Its white Spanish Renaissance Revival facade and red tower roofs gleam in autumn light. Four Conway Greyline buses, motors idling, seats empty, doors open, block the porte cochere. Passengers parade the piazza. From its south end guides point out Crawford Notch, and from its front, Mt. Washington, before which a congenial coterie, all badged "Humphreys Fellowship Program—B.U.," are photographed. Inside, conferees register at white linen tables; guests relax before a huge fieldstone fireplace; tourists shop and eat downstairs. This convivial ambiance belies the fact that this is the last evening of their 1994 season.

"Meant to ascend Washington," Muir jotted his intention in his journal, but "weather too doubtful head now clear now muffled. saw buildings on top distinct from Fabyans."

How did Muir anticipate doing this? The day before, in Vermont, he had been fulfilled with a horse and buggy ride up snow-covered Mount Mansfield (4,395 feet). Now he was at the place from which a side train went four miles to the Base Station, from where the cog railway chugged upward 3,719 feet, three miles in ninety minutes, to the summit of Mount Washington. This technological marvel impressed Muir. Surely, he had it in mind four years later when he wrote of the ease of travel for tourists, who "go almost every-where in smooth comfort, cross oceans and deserts scarce accessible to fish-es and birds, and, dragged by steel horses, go up high mountains, riding glo-riously beneath starry showers of sparks, ascending like Elijah in a whirlwind and chariot of fire."[3]

Since it was too late in the day to attempt a Mount Washington climb, Muir would have had to spend a night somewhere nearby and set out the next day. But the nearby Mount Pleasant Hotel and the Fabyan House were likely closed that late in the season.[4]

Muir did not mention what guidebooks and maps informed his choices. He was familiar with *Picturesque America*, edited by William Cullen Bryant and published in two volumes in 1872 and 1874, respectively, which served as a travel guide for many. Volume I contains Susan N. Carter's essay on the White Mountains, which Harry Fenn illustrated. *Picturesque America* was a model for *Picturesque California: The Rocky Mountains and the Pacific Slope* (The J. Dewing Company, 1888), which Muir edited and contributed to. The distinguished Dartmouth College professor Charles Henry Hitchcock, whose *Geology of New Hampshire* included descriptions of the White Mountains in words and images, also acquainted Muir with this land.[5]

He had planned this trip just five days earlier, on 15 October, at the Arnold Arboretum in Jamaica Plain, outside Boston, with Charles Edward Faxon, who had been in charge of its library and herbarium since 1882. Faxon was a botanical illustrator par excellence, publishing some 1,925 drawings. Being intimate with the Green and White mountains, he undoubtedly urged Muir to see them. Alpine bluets, found in the United States only on the White Mountains, are named in Latin in honor of Faxon and his older brother Edwin.[6]

Besides the Mount Pleasant Hotel and Fabyan House, the Crawford House, ten minutes south by rail and under the proprietorship of C.H. Merrill (1840-1908) from 1872 until his death, was another possible resting place. Here again the inn may have closed—the last guests were on 2 October—and Merrill may have gone home to Shelburne Falls, Massachusetts, soon thereafter.[7] Had Muir stayed here he might have walked the Crawford Path eight miles to the top of Washington. Had Muir attained the 6,288-foot summit of Mt. Washington, that would have been his highest elevation in the East—three feet above Roan Mountain on the North Carolina-Tennessee border, where he had stood the month before, on 24 September 1898 (see chapter 12).

Muir would have taken interest in the artist's studio adjacent to the Crawford House, which still serves as part of the new Highland Center of the Appalachian Mountain Club, which opened in September 2003—especially in its summer artist in residence from 1877 through 1893, Frank Henry Shapleigh, whom Jeanne Carr had directed to Muir in Yosemite Valley. In June and July of 1870, Shapleigh spent six weeks painting landscapes of the Yosemite and Hetch Hetchy, two of which he exhibited in his rooms at the Studio Building in Boston in May 1871. Anna Cabot Lowell Quincy and her husband the Rev. Robert Cassie Waterston, also Carr friends, accompanied him. Anna's passion for novelist Jane Austen may have been inflicted on Muir. She selected a Shapleigh sketch of Sentinel Rock for their home at 71 Chester Square, Boston. After their return, in February 1871, Rev. Waterston gave a series of lectures for the Lowell Institute in Boston on the Sierra Nevada and the Rocky Mountains. On 15 January 1873, he read a letter from

Galen Clark, about Clark's and Muir's exploration of the Tuolumne River canyon, to the Boston Society of Natural History.[8]

In the fall, after returning from California, Shapleigh had married Mary A. Studley of Cohasset, Massachusetts. Their twenty-eighth wedding anniversary was 19 October 1898. That summer was their first in their new cottage, "Maple Knoll," in the village of Jackson Falls, on the east side of the Presidential Range, twenty-three miles by road from the Crawford House and three miles north of Glen, through which Muir's train would soon pass. In mid-August Shapleigh was atop Mount Washington with his niece, Louise S. Wright of Milton, Massachusetts; he had first been there forty years earlier, in 1858.[9]

None of these scenarios unfolded, however. Instead, Muir had to be content with a visual appreciation of the White Mountains aboard his eastbound train, as he descended through Crawford Notch and "on down derry down to Portland Maine."[10]

## HENRY DAVID THOREAU

Reading and conversation also taught Muir about these ancient peaks. He had several prominent New Englanders to teach him.

If Muir had chosen the Crawford Path up Mt. Washington, he would have followed the 10 September 1839 footsteps of Henry David Thoreau and his brother, John, who started from Thomas J. Crawford's Inn, to which they had walked two days earlier from Franconia.[11] Thoreau entered his itinerary in his *Journal* and mentioned his being on the summit of Agiocochook (the Indian name for Mt. Washington) in *A Week on the Concord and Merrimack Rivers*. Muir read both these accounts, but made no notes in text or his index. Ascending these mountains, at least at his time of reading, appears not to have been his priority.[12]

Thoreau did not return to the White Mountains until July 1858, this time with Edward Hoar in a private carriage. This extended visit allowed Thoreau time to climb Mt. Washington from the Glen House of Pinkham Notch via the road, and to descend westward through fog into Tuckerman's Ravine, where he camped four nights (8-11 July) before returning to the road. They then rode northward to Jefferson, where, from a hillside, he attained "the grandest mountain view I ever got." This hill, I presume, is Mt. Starr King (3,907 feet), which is named for Boston Unitarian preacher Thomas Starr King (1824-1864), as is the (9,092-foot) Sierra Nevada peak near Yosemite

Valley. King went to San Francisco in 1860, the year his *The White Hills* was published. I suspect that Muir knew King's popular guidebook, but can find no evidence that he did.[13] From Jefferson, Thoreau proceeded south through Whitefield and Bethlehem to Franconia Notch, where he climbed Mt. Lafayette (5,260 feet, on 14-15 July), before returning home.

Muir also read Thoreau's account in his *Journal* of his 1858 White Mountains journey. Within these sixty-two pages, Muir marks only one passage: the first two lines of Thoreau's meditation on the advantages of foot travel. This also is Muir's only marked index item for Thoreau's entire trip. In general, judging by the paucity of his annotations throughout this whole volume of Thoreau's *Journal*, Muir found little he wanted to remember.[14]

## RALPH WALDO EMERSON

Ralph Waldo Emerson went to the White Mountains several times. In August 1829, at age twenty-six, he drove there in a chaise with his frail fiancée, Ellen Tucker, from her home in Concord, New Hampshire, while her mother followed behind them in a coach with their baggage. From Conway they passed through Crawford Notch and spent a night at Crawford's.[15] Their marriage, extended into the last day of the next month, ended with Ellen's death, in February 1831, at age nineteen.

Emerson returned to the White Mountains on 13 July 1832. This time he was accompanied by his paternal maiden aunt, Mary Moody Emerson (1784-1863), an "original genius...visionary...prophet," according to Robert Richardson Jr.[16] They proceeded from her home, Vale Farm, in the village of South Waterford, Maine. They stayed at Ethan Allen Crawford's, close to Fabyan station, where Muir would stop, and four miles north of Thomas Crawford's.[17] "The good of going into the mountains is that life is reconsidered," Emerson noted, and indeed on this alpine journey he pondered his destiny and affirmed his resolve to leave the ministry. On the 16th of July he ascended Mt. Washington via the Crawford Path in four hours and fifteen minutes. Remaining atop for forty-three minutes, he then retraced his steps to the inn in under four hours for a five o'clock supper. He went alone, Mary deciding to head eastward toward home. The next day he took a wagon to Tom Crawford's for dinner and then a stage into Conway.[18]

Which Crawford Path was Emerson's? There were two possibilities. The first (CP1), laid out by Abel and his son Ethan Allen in 1819 from the Gate of the Notch (Tom Crawford's), is still used. This was Thoreau's route. The second (CP2), built in 1821 by Ethan Allen Crawford and Charles Jesse Stuart, went from Ethan Allen Crawford's to the base of Ammonoosuc Ravine, and from there up its west shoulder. The latter path, which left from Emerson's inn, was more convenient and more popular in this time, according to the Watermans. It was also longer, an estimated 9 miles one way, compared to the former's 8.2 miles. These trailheads (inns) were four miles apart, so that if Emerson climbed Washington via CP1, he would have required transport. He makes no mention of this, however, nor does his accounting reflect any expense for it—he does record a wagon fee to Tom Crawford's the next day—though this may have been complimentary, or included in his lodging bill. Nor was there sufficient time to go to and from CP1. He left Ethan Crawford's at 8:10 and reached the top at 12:25; his descent was equally swift: from 1:08 to 5:00 p.m. When I climbed CP1 in celebration of the 150th anniversary of Thoreau's ascent (10 September 1989), I took longer than Emerson: 5 hours 35 minutes up and 4 hours 15 minutes down. Granted that Emerson was twenty years younger than I, he still moved faster and covered an additional 1.6 miles. In 1846, however, Emerson recommended the road not taken "…the Notch House of Crawford the true place from which the ascent should be made; & not Fabyan's."[19] Having gone both ways, I agree with Emerson: CP1 offers a more spectacular alpine walk than CP2.

Seven years later, Emerson was back in the White Mountains. This time his companion was George P. Bradford, who had introduced him to Lydia Jackson, now his wife. Their trip spanned eleven days, from 23 August to 2 September 1839. Pausing a few days in Center Harbor, Emerson climbed Red Hill (2,029 feet) for a grand view of lakes Winnipesaukee and Squam. Their travels took them on to Conway for the night, through Crawford Notch to Fabyan's White Mountain Hotel for another night, then through Franconia Notch with its Profile Mountain and Flume. By the time they returned home via the Connecticut River valley (Haverhill, Walpole, Keene), the Thoreau brothers had embarked northward to see the White Mountains. From Concord, Emerson wrote Margaret Fuller to tell her about his excursion.[20]

Thirty-one years lapsed before Emerson saw the White Mountains again. Now a father, he brought his children. First he came with his son Edward in September 1870 from Waterford, Maine (Mary Moody Emerson had left in 1850, and died in 1863), where they climbed Bear Mountain, before going to Gorham and the Glen House of Pinkham Notch. From there, on 5 September, Edward at twenty-six climbed Mt. Washington, while his father rode to the top in an open carriage. They had dinner on the summit, then descended in different directions: Edward via the Crawford Path; Ralph Waldo on the cog railway. They joined at the Crawford House for the night.[21]

The following spring, May 1871, Emerson met Muir in Yosemite Valley. I speculate that some of their conversation was about New England's mountains.[22]

His last visit was with his younger daughter, Ellen, in the summer of 1875. From Plymouth, New Hampshire, where they "climbed the hills & gathered strawberries," they entered Franconia Notch, staying at the Flume House. "I had seen nothing of the local wonders for forty years," Emerson reflected: "they were far better than I remembered." Back to Fabyan's for a night and then Crawford's before leaving for Massachusetts.[23]

## NATHANIEL HAWTHORNE

In September 1832, the White Mountains welcomed Nathaniel Hawthorne, a twenty-eight-year-old bachelor from Salem, Massachusetts. He stayed two nights at Ethan Allen Crawford's, from where, at four on "a showery morning," he rode horseback with a guide and four other men "six miles to the foot of Mt. Washington"—the same approach Emerson had taken two months earlier. "The other particulars," he wrote his mother, "how I climbed three miles into the air, and how it snowed all the way, and how, when I got up the mountain on one side, the wind carried me a great distance off my feet and almost blew me down the other, and how the thermometer stood at twelve degrees below the freezing point, I shall have time enough to tell you when I return."[24]

This excursion inspired Hawthorne's imagination. His short stories "The Notch of the White Mountains" and "Our Evening Party among the Mountains," (included in "Sketches from Memory") were published in *New England Magazine* in November 1835 and collected in *Mosses from an Old Manse* (1846). The latter story seeded another, this one of adventurers seeking a radiant and precious gem, "The Great Carbuncle"; it appeared in 1837 in *The Token and Atlantic Souvenir* and in *Twice-Told Tales*. The latter collection also featured "The Ambitious Guest" (from the June 1835 *New England Magazine*), which recounted the death of the Willey family—father, mother, five children, hired hand, and a boy—who, on 28 August 1828, while running from their home in Crawford Notch to a shelter, were consumed by an avalanche that ironically left their house unharmed.[25] Hawthorne passed the Willey house en route to Ethan Allen Crawford's inn, presumably afoot, though "The Notch of the White Mountains" does not mention how he traveled.

Muir owned *The Complete Works of Nathaniel Hawthorne*, the 1884 Houghton Mifflin edition of twenty-four volumes.[26] He read "The Great Carbuncle," marking six passages with vertical lines in the margins, and in the last of those he underlined "thrillingly" ("cold water of the enchanted lake", p.189). His own index at the back of *Twice-Told Tales* (volume I) contained two items: "mountains" and "crystal," on pages 185 and 186, respectively. The first reference describes the ascent of Matthew and Hannah, the treasure seekers, through krummholz to the land above the trees, and the gradual disappearance of the summit in mist. The second, while not using "crystal" per se, tells "that a radiance was breaking through the mist," as they discovered the Great Carbuncle. "The Ambitious Guest" concerned Muir less, it appears, as he notes only this sentence: "Is not the kindred of a common fate a closer tie than that of birth?" While reading Hawthorne, Muir was writing his dog story, "Stickeen," professor Ronald Limbaugh has shown, and he responded to Hawthorne's ideas in his own handwriting as endnotes.[27]

Later Hawthorne wrote "The Great Stone Face," which was published in *The National Era* for 24 January 1850 and collected in *The Snow-Image, and Other Twice-Told Tales* (1852). Muir read this story, marking eight passages in as many pages of its 25-page length and indexing two items, as follows:

426

430 Great Stone Face   El Cap

(All good)  Life of Mtns

Though Muir does not specify why he selected page 426 for his index, he does mark with a broken vertical pencil line nine lines on that page, which describe Ernest at midlife, who "would always reach a blessing to his neighbor." On page 430 Muir is reminded of his beloved El Capitan, a spectacular 7,569-foot cliff of Yosemite Valley.

## JOHN SWETT

The north country recalled to Muir an old friend, now his neighbor in the Alhambra Valley. "I wonder if John Swett is still here-abouts," he wrote home on 18 October. "How he must have enjoyed his New Hampshire hills."[28] Some sixty-seven miles due south of Mt. Washington, on a farm, which ran a half-mile east to the Suncook River south of Pittsfield, New Hampshire, John Swett was born on 30 July 1830, the only child of Eben and Lucretia French Swett. Their three-story 1790s Federal home still stands on

Swett Road. Two and a half miles from here in the southeast Swett could see 1,378-foot Catamount Mountain, stretching north-south for almost two miles along the horizon. He climbed this mountain, even working there on a farm one summer. Beyond Catamount the Blue Hills rose in the east, with Parker Mountain (1,420 feet) in the south and Blue Job (1,356 feet) in the north. Swett was most drawn, however, to Mount Kearsarge (2,930 feet), visible twenty-eight miles due west, where once he walked—the only long tramp recorded in his autobiography—and "slept one cold night on its summit in the open air under a granite ledge." This Muir-style cold camping was part of an autumn excursion in 1850 that extended around Lake Winnipesaukee and the adjacent Ossipee Mountains (2,990 feet) to the northeast and the Belknap Range (2,382 feet) in the southwest—both alps in view from Pittsfield; neither of them did he ascend.[29]

At the age of seventeen, Swett began his lifelong career in education as a teacher in a small school near Pembroke in the Merrimack Valley, thirteen miles southwest of home, for "two winter terms of four months each." From there he went to another school in West Randolph, Massachusetts, south of Boston, where he also taught two winter sessions. While there, he heard Emerson lecture on "Power," after which he proceeded to read all of Emerson's essays as they were printed. Evidently, he had no exposure to Thoreau. Then he enrolled in the Normal Institute under William Russell— a formative influence on Swett—in Reed's Ferry, on the west bank of the Merrimack River, five miles south of Manchester, New Hampshire. After twenty-two years in New England, however, Swett decided to leave in the expectation that a more salubrious climate would strengthen his health and the poor eyesight that had prevented his pursuing college. On 15 September 1852, he sailed from Boston; rounding Cape Horn, he docked in San Francisco on 31 January 1853. After briefly mining for gold, he resumed his profession, serving as the principal of San Francisco's Rincon School for nine years (1853-1862); state superintendent of public instruction for five years, through 1867; principal of Denman Grammar School in San Francisco, and later of its Girls' High School, to 1889; and then city school superintendent, before retiring in 1896.[30]

Swett married Mary Tracy on 8 May 1862. They lived with their five children (one died in infancy, another in 1892), and both their mothers at 1419 Taylor Street on Russian Hill in San Francisco. (Their residence was consumed by the fire following the 1906 earthquake.) To their house, starting in February 1875 and continuing at intervals through the 1870s, Muir came to live and write. On the cusp of summer 1875, Muir took Swett into the Sierra Nevada. They were joined by artist William Keith and by J. B. McChesney, principal of Oakland High School, with whom Muir had stayed from December 1873 to September 1874. Both had traveled in the mountains with Muir before. Their excursion began in a mid-June snow and hail storm. All this meteorology excited Muir. He found creation in destruction, "a constant development toward higher and yet higher beauty." They passed on horseback north of Yosemite Valley, crossed Yosemite Creek, camped at Lake Tenaya and at Tuolumne Meadows, surmounted Mono Pass, and descended to Mono Lake before returning to Yosemite.[31]

Earlier this year, 1898, Swett had preceded Muir to New England. Crossing Canada by train in July, he was in Boston by mid-August. Coming to Pittsfield on 17 August, he climbed Catamount, and for six days "lingered around that mountain, recalling slumbering memories of the past." Then with his cousin, John C. French, he headed north to the White Mountains for a week. They stayed at the Deer Park Hotel (destroyed by fire in 1952) near the North Woodstock railroad station in the Pemigewasset Valley. From there they made day excursions: One to the summit of Mt. Washington on Wednesday, 7 September—he did not say how; likely by rail. Another by carriage through Franconia Notch that evoked Yosemite—"the most beautiful bit of woodland scenery" he had ever seen. By 19 October he was in New York, presenting his manuscript on American public schools to the American Book Company. He returned home via the Great Northern Railway.[32]

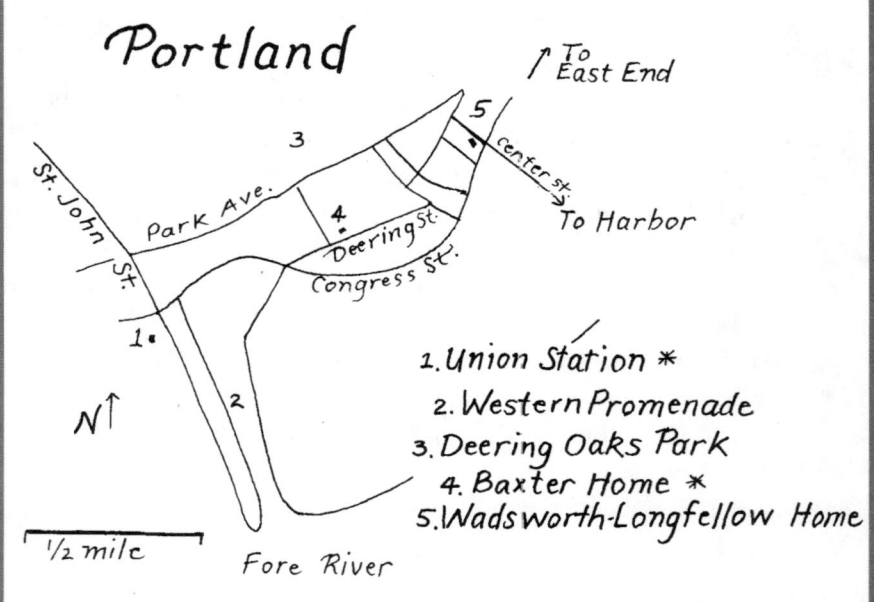

Back Cove

Portland

To East End

To Harbor

St. John St.

Park Ave.

Deering St.

Congress St.

Center St.

N ↑

½ mile

Fore River

1. Union Station *
2. Western Promenade
3. Deering Oaks Park
4. Baxter Home *
5. Wadsworth-Longfellow Home

# 10. Maine

*So we saunter toward the Holy Land, till one day the
sun shall shine more brightly than ever he has done,
shall perchance shine into our minds and hearts, and
light up our whole lives with a great awakening light,
as warm and serene and golden as on a bankside in
autumn.*
—Thoreau, "Walking"

## Thursday, 20 October 1898

From the White Mountains Muir proceeded seventy-five miles southeast to
Portland, Maine. His train came down the Saco River valley, through
Fryeburg, Hiram, and Steep Falls, where the Saco turned south; then went
east, along a scenic stretch of Sebago Lake, to South Windham, a borough
on the east bank of the Presumpscot River, two stops before Portland.

## Windham: Abba Woolson

Abba Louisa Goold Woolson was born in Windham, four miles north of the
depot, on 30 April 1838, nine days after Muir's birth. Her father, William
Goold, was a businessman, Maine state legislator, and later in life an historian; her mother, Nabby Tukey Clark, a caretaker of their eight children (one
died before he was three). Abba's home, which she purchased from her
father on 28 November 1870 for $250, still stands at 280 Windham Center
Road, and is on the National Register of Historic Places. Sundays she drove
horse and carriage to Quaker meeting along the same road—now Route
202—that she would have taken to meet Muir's train.[1]

In 1856, Abba Goold graduated from Portland High School for Girls, vale-
dictorian of her class. On 14 August of that year, she married the school's
principal, Moses Woolson, a native of Concord, New Hampshire, a graduate
of Colby College, and seventeen years her senior. After living in Portland, in
Cincinnati, and in Concord, New Hampshire, the couple came to Boston in
1868, he to be a master in the English High School for six years.[2]

On the evening of 21 March 1872, from her window at 64 Boylston Street,
Abba Woolson had watched spring's debut on Boston Common. Sitting with

Moses at a long table before a coal fire, she wrote John Muir to thank him for his invitation to spend a year in Yosemite Valley. Having visited Muir in Yosemite the previous summer (1871)—the connection between them made most likely by Jeanne Carr—and having viewed the High Sierra from Glacier Point, she yearned to return. "But how to get there," she pondered in her epistle to Muir, "and how to leave this reeling old world below, which I am struggling so hard to set right! Oh, wouldn't I be willing to live on bread and water, and to wear sackcloth and ashes for the next six months if I thought I could thereby be sure of looking up at Sentinel Rock and the South Dome from the meadow's edge beside the river. I shall come there some day, I am sure of that. The only question is—when." She also announced that "My 'Walden'" is to go to you at once by mail," adding, "it will give you infinite delight." Indeed, her copy of *Walden* nourished Muir to his core. "Just now I am the busiest woman on the globe," she closed, "and envy your calm, secure leisure. I am writing no newspaper articles at present."[3]

In a series of essays for the *Boston Journal*, published as *Woman in American Society* in 1873, Abba Woolson called women to awaken to their highest potential. She railed against the culture's unenlightened constraints. "[W]oman's sphere," she contended, was not necessarily in the home or the workplace, but "is wherever she is healthiest and happiest." She celebrated their finding pleasure in "out-of-door rambles." Abandon summer resorts, "the crowds at fashionable watering-places," she exhorted them, "for the freedom and wildness of Nature." Find the simple life in country towns. Exercise. "A free ramble through wood and dale, in search of flowers and minerals, or from a mere love of scenery and wide skies, might imbue them with a taste for sauntering; and it would, for the time at least, bring a glow to their cheeks and a freshness and variety to their daily life."

The next spring, March 1873, Muir's "Hetch Hetchy Valley" in the *Boston Weekly Transcript*, which she had just read, "made me homesick for the Yosemite," she wrote him. She sent Muir a copy of *Woman in American Society* with this admonishment, "I am sorry you are to read my little book, because you can never understand why it should be written; and such things as social reforms seem to you needless botherations." Yet she had not forgotten that "you told me once that I had convinced you of the right of woman suffrage. I still claim you as a convert." "Let us know what further books we can send you," she closed.[4]

Another of her gifts to him was Thoreau's *Excursions*, which contained the seminal essays "The Succession of Forest Trees" and "Walking." The latter

Thoreau began by explaining "the art of walking" by offering two derivations of the word sauntering. One suggested that it came from those Middle Agers, who roamed about asking for charity on the pretense they were making a pilgrimage to the Holy Land. "They who never go to the Holy Land in their walks, as they pretend, are indeed mere idlers and vagabonds; but they who do go there are saunterers in the good sense." This meaning Muir took to heart, making it his practice, preaching it to others. When on the Sierra Club Outing in July 1908 Albert W. Palmer, the twenty-nine-year-old pastor (1907-1917) of Plymouth Congregational Church in Oakland, heard from Muir his distaste for hiking and preference for sauntering, he made a parable of it: "How much better to 'saunter' along this trail of life, to measure it in terms of beauty and love and friendship!"[5]

Another writer Woolson admired was the English poet Jean Ingelow (1820-1897), who gained popularity in America. Emerson, too, enjoyed her: "She has a wonderful ear & lyric facility, an eye for the beauty & the significance of Nature....But the delicious melody of the verse could almost spare the other gifts." Woolson sent to Muir her copy of Ingelow's *Poems* (Boston: Roberts Brothers, 1865) and *The Monitions of the Unseen and Poems of Love and Childhood* (1871), from the same publisher. Since neither book shows evidence of Muir's reading, nor has his reply to Woolson been found, we cannot tell his reactions to Ingelow's poetry.[6]

It was not until the following fall, on 27 September 1874, that she wrote Muir again. By then the Woolsons were living in Concord, New Hampshire, where Moses was principal of the high school. She delighted in reading Muir's "By-Ways of Yosemite Travel. Bloody Cañon" in the September issue of the *Overland Monthly*. Still "homesick" for the Sierra, she "would sell all my belongings, and depart to spend all the year in the Yosemite." Instead, she was now "preaching the divinity of the body, and striving to lead women to respect their natural selves sufficiently to wear garments that do not pinch and burden and crucify their suffering frames." She had "devised such comfortable attire for myself that I think I could now skip over your slanting mountain trails like a bounding doe." In a month she expected her book "out on that theme." Her *Dress-Reform,* which appeared that year, contained five lectures, four by female physicians and one by Woolson, given before the New England Women's Club.[7]

Her next letter, of 28 February 1876, enclosed her photograph—"a good likeness," she remarked. Her piquant, slender face appeared above a lace collar rising out of a shallow V-necked, long-sleeved dress; her hair was parted in the middle, combed back on both sides, and braided in a coiffure. Nothing prepossessing about her clothes! She also gave him a picture of their life: "We, two Woolsons[,] live a very quiet happy life, caring little for the persons about us, though having many pleasant acquaintances in our immediate world." They had no children. "[B]ut," she continued, "living more really in the world of books, newspapers, and the letters of absent and beloved friends." She went to Boston often, she told him, "and breathe mental ozone while there. I work less in Reforms than I did,—though as 'strongminded' and radical as ever." She felt more content to "leave the Lord to take care of his own world; only I am sure he needs me to help him do it." She added, "I long to forget the human part of the world, and to see more of the divine," this being one reason she wanted "to sit down for months between Washington Column & the Half Dome, with Nevada thundering in my ears."[8]

Two letters from her husband followed. In the first, that of 19 October 1878, Moses told Muir that the third volume of Charles H. Hitchcock's *Geology of New Hampshire* was "nearly ready" and would be sent to Muir from the governor, Benjamin F. Prescott (see chapter 9). Moses had just read Muir's November *Harper's* article, "The New Sequoia Forests of California," to Abba. "God grant you may write your geology in as interesting a manner." He applauded Muir's "kind treatment of wild animals." Abba, he said, was "making much of her Yosemite lecture," and would deliver it in Newport, Rhode Island, "in a few weeks." In the second letter, of 14 February 1880, Moses thanked Muir for his two letters, commented at length about Charles H. Hitchcock, and commended Muir's Alaska writing.[9]

This was the last of their communication. One wonders if Muir's change of lifestyle in the 1880s—marriage, children, fruit farming in Martinez—had something to do with the demise of their correspondence, on both their accounts. With this transition Muir no longer held the image of the independent mountain man for Woolson. Or was there more written between them that has been lost? Nor did he see her on any of his five trips to New England; at least, there is no mention of her in his letters and diaries. Whether she returned to California and saw him again I would like to know. After the death of Moses in 1896, Abba Woolson spent her summers in Windham, where she enjoyed entertaining friends. Had she stayed this late in the season when Muir passed?

Her contribution to Muir's development is nonetheless significant. She was a source of personal and literary sustenance in his early California years. As noted, she sent him Thoreau's *Walden* and *Excursions* and Jean Ingelow's poetry, among other items we can surmise. She also increased his awareness about women and the need for reforms to ensure their equality, freedom, and self-realization.

## PORTLAND: THE BAXTERS

Nine and a half miles from South Windham, Muir arrived at Portland's Union Station at 8:10 p.m. He had supper and waited for his 11:00 p.m. train. He may have taken a gander at the latest edition of the *Portland Evening Express* (for two cents) and learned that this city of 50,000 still had an emphasis on daily life. In columns "About People You Know" and in the surrounding towns—Westbrook, Deering, and South Portland—he tasted the flavor of these residents' lives.

> Byron D. Verrill has returned from a hunting trip with a deer and 17 partridges.

> The wedding of Mr. Joshua Clement Libby and Miss Alice Maud, daughter of Mr. and Mrs. George Milliken, will occur this evening at the bride's home, 235 Brackett street. A reception will be held from 8:30 to 10 p.m.

> The Maine Farmer's Almanac for 1899 is published and is on sale by Loring, Short & Harmon.

> On account of the rain but nine of the members of the East End Whist club were present at the preliminary meeting....

The paper's forecast was for fair weather, freshened by northerly winds, tonight and tomorrow. Although it was already dark—the sun set before six—Muir, wanting to stretch his legs after a long day's journey that had begun at 6:30 a.m. in Stowe, Vermont, may have gone out to look around.[10]

Across the street, the Western Promenade presented just such an opportunity. Here Muir might profitably pursue a half-mile stroll from the Maine General Hospital in the north to the Western Cemetery in the south. The John Bundy Brown estate, "Bramhall," dominated this neighborhood of fashionable residences. To the south he might see the Fore River running east to become Portland's harbor before entering Casco Bay with its many islands. To the north, on a clear day he would be able to see the White Mountains, where he had been this afternoon.[11]

Or he might have walked a half mile north of Union Station into another park, Deering Oaks, the gift of James and Mary Deering to the town in March 1879. Portland's talented civil engineer William Goodwin had preserved its woodland character, adding a Mill Pond that skaters enjoyed and some architecture. Here young Longfellow had roamed and later in his heart's memory found "My Lost Youth."[12]

Four blocks south of the center of Deering Oaks, at 61 Deering Street, was the elegant home of James Phinney Baxter, his wife Hetty (Mehitabel Cummings Proctor Perkins; his first wife had died in 1872) and family. Sadly, the building was demolished in 1973 for a parking lot. James Baxter, sixty-seven in 1898, had been Portland's Republican mayor from 1893 to 1897. Four years earlier, in October 1894, Mayor Baxter had been shown Boston's park system by mayor Nathan Matthews, as Matthews had done for Muir the previous year, on 12 June 1893 (see chapter 4). Inspired by what he had seen, Baxter wished the same for his city: "Portland will be wise to follow her [Boston's] example," he wrote in *New England Magazine* in 1895. In 1896, the Olmsted firm presented a plan for Portland's Back Cove to be a "great public water park" with a "circuit shore drive" and promenade around it. Immediately, Baxter set about acquiring the necessary land. His defeat in the election of 1897 stalled progress. Regaining the mayoralty in 1904, through a campaign managed by his son Percival, he sought to connect the Back Cove boulevard with Deering Oaks and the Western and Eastern promenades, for which the Olmsted brothers again provided designs. But Baxter's defeat again, in 1905, denied Portlanders their boulevard until 1917.[13]

Baxter would gladly have entertained John Muir, shown him this enterprising seaport and its parks. He would have pointed out the White Mountains, where he had vacationed briefly in early June, and reminisced about his many good times there since he had first gone almost a half century ago, in 1849. He would have recalled other mountains, those seen with his family in France and Switzerland in 1885. On the morning of 5 September that year, he and Hetty, with eleven-year-old Emily and Percy, not quite nine, had left their hotel in Chamonix, at the base of the snowy peak of Mont Blanc, with "four mules and two guides." They had climbed 2,858 feet to the inn at Montanvert (6,303 feet)—slightly higher than Washington, but less elevation gain—with the Aiguille du Dru (12,516 feet) in full view—"the most striking object in the Range of Mont Blanc," according to Edward Whymper, who made the first ascent of the Matterhorn in 1865. After lunch the Baxters had crossed the Mer de Glace without difficulty, a ten-minute walk, then descended via

Mauvais Pass, a perspiring paterfamilias holding the handrail on one side, his guide on the other. After resting at the Chapeau, they were soon on their mules, "which had been sent around to meet us," and on the road to Chamonix. After dinner at their hotel, they had walked the town, "not being at all fatigued." The next day, Sunday, after attending the English church, they walked west through several hamlets to the Glacier of Bossons and its Grotto, which Whymper described as "a gallery excavated in the side of the glacier." Muir might have interjected here his Chamonix experience of August 1893 (see chapter 4). Nine days later, after visiting the shops of Lucerne, Switzerland, the Baxters had taken a steamer to Vitznau, from where they ascended, via cog railway—the first built in Europe, in 1871, two years after Mount Washington's was completed—the Rigi-Kulm (5,906 feet). Staying overnight, they had watched sunset and sunrise—the latter had disappointed Father Baxter, who preferred the unobstructed solar emergence seen from Washington. After breakfast, they had taken the train down, reaching Lucerne in mid-morning.[14]

The evening before Muir arrived in Portland, however, Baxter had been at the station to take the train to Boston, where he spent the night. The next morning, after breakfast with his son Percival, he conducted business at the New England Genealogical and Historical Society at 18 Somerset Street (It is now at 101 Newbury Street). Baxter was the society's vice president for Maine, and would be its president from 1901 until his death. Late in the afternoon, he took the train to Worcester, lodging at the Bay State Hotel. The evening Muir was in Portland, Baxter was attending a meeting of the American Antiquarian Society, of which he had been a member since 1887, at the home of Senator George Frisbie Hoar and his wife, Eliza Susan Morton, at 34 Oak Street in Worcester (their mansion was later razed), which included supper. Baxter did not return to Portland until the next night, Friday the 21st, on the day when *The Portland Evening Express* reported his election to the council of the American Antiquarian Society.[15]

Muir also missed seeing Percival Baxter. Four months earlier, on 23 June 1898, Percy had graduated from Bowdoin College in Brunswick—the commencement was attended by his father, who was an overseer of the College from 1894 until his death. On 28 September, he left home to live in Cambridge and study at the Harvard Law School, from where he would graduate in 1901. (That same September day his younger sister Madeleine traveled for her first college year to Wellesley College, a place Muir would visit in three days.) A week after Muir's departure from Portland, Percy would return home, on Thursday, 27 October. That night he would attend a meeting of the Maine Historical Society with his father, who was president of the organization. The next two days he would help him prepare their summer home on nearby Mackworth Island for winter, before returning to Cambridge on the Sunday afternoon train.

Like Muir, Percy was a lover of wilderness. After serving in the Maine House and Senate and as governor from 1921 to 1925, he purchased the state's highest mountain, Katahdin, in 1930, and made it a gift to the people of Maine. In subsequent years, he acquired adjacent lands, presenting these, too, to the public trust to be kept forever wild.[16]

A half-mile stroll east from the Baxters' on Deering Street brought one to 485 Congress Street. There, situated on high ground, stood the three-story brick Federal (1785) that had afforded young Longfellow a panoramic prospect of the surrounding country and water. Muir, his curiosity piqued by his visit to Longfellow's Cambridge home five years earlier, on 10 June 1893 (see chapter 2), might have come this way. If he had knocked on the door, the poet's sister, Anne Longfellow Pierce (1810-1901), who had lived here all her life except for her brief marriage to George Washington Pierce (who died in 1832), would have answered. She would have invited him into her parlor, served tea, told him the history of this place—the home of her mother's parents, Peleg and Elizabeth Wadsworth—even shown him her garden behind the house. Owing to her largesse, the Wadsworth-Longfellow House is owned by the Maine Historical Society today, and is open to the public.[17]

From Portland, at 11:00 p.m., Muir continued Down East on the Maine Central Railroad. Passing through Brunswick, Augusta (the capital of Maine), and Waterville in the night, he slept in his seat. Over five hours later, he arrived in Bangor, on the Penobscot River, at 4:15 a.m., 136 miles from Portland.

## GREENVILLE: THOREAU AND THEODORE ROOSEVELT

After a wait of two hours and forty-five minutes, Muir departed Bangor at

7:00 a.m. on Friday, 21 October, on the Aroostook Railroad for Greenville, 89 miles northwest. His train followed the Penobscot River to Oldtown, then inland to Milo, from where it turned west to Sangerville (the main line ran to Caribou, in northeast Maine) and Guilford and then proceeded north through Monson to its destination—a four-hour trip. The abundance and beauty of tamaracks delighted Muir, their "airy dainty branches ascending—often many delicate slim leaders on tip[,]not rigid." He "had forgotten it was so handsome a tree;" in fact, he thought it "the handsomest conifer in [the] woods."[18]

Greenville sat at the southern end of Moosehead Lake, New England's largest. A two-and-a-half hour wait here gave Muir time to commune with this "charming sheet of pure water 40 m[ile]s long full of picturesque islands," as he wrote home.[19] The lake, his journal added, was "forested to waters edge gloriously colored Maple birch ash Tamarac etc[.] [undeciphered word]. Lake inclosed in finely moudled[? moulded] basin moderately high hills & m[oun]t[ai]ns plain & gently sloped[.] water clear spruces & pines."[20]

In the 1850s, Thoreau had come to Greenville from Bangor twice, each time with Penobscot Indian guides. He came first by wagon, then by stage, since the first, wood-burning locomotive did not reach Greenville until July 1884. In 1853, Thoreau went the length of Moosehead Lake by steamer, and after canoeing the Penobscot West Branch to Lake Chesuncook and back, returned by the same means to Greenville. In 1857 he paddled a birchbark canoe to the north end of Moosehead, from where he continued as far north as Eagle Lake before turning southward via Webster Brook, the Penobscot East Branch, and the Penobscot River to Bangor. These two experiences, along with his earlier trip to Katahdin, he turned into lectures and essays— which in 1864, after his death, were published as *The Maine Woods*.[21]

While the spring of 1870 unfolded in Yosemite Valley, Muir had read Thoreau's *The Maine Woods* (1868)—the fourth edition from Ticknor and Fields of Boston, presumably a gift of Jeanne Carr.[22] The first essay, "Ktaadn," began: "On the 31st of August, 1846, I left Concord in Massachusetts for Bangor and the backwoods of Maine," and continued, "I proposed to make excursions to mount Ktaadn…and to some of the lakes of the Penobscot….The mountain may be approached more easily and directly on horseback and on foot from the north-east side."[23] Muir marked this last sentence with vertical pencil lines in the margin. If this indicated his desire to climb Katahdin, it was a wish not realized.

In reality, Thoreau had approached Katahdin from the south, walking in a direct line from Abol Stream off the Penobscot West Branch, on 7

September 1846. He ascended to the east of the Abol Slide, overnighted on the mountain's south side, and nearly gained its summit on the following morning, before returning to the river. In 1857 he intended to climb Katahdin again, this time from the Penobscot East Branch at William Hunt's farm, from where lumber roads and the Reverend Marcus R. Keep's path made the first trail to Katahdin. This opportunity was lost due to his companion's sore feet, which kept them in their canoe, ably steered by their guide, Joe Polis.[24]

By the late nineteenth century, the West Branch-Abol Slide route, marked by a rude trail and recommended in guidebooks, was in vogue. At Milo, Muir could have continued north on the main line of the Bangor and Aroostook Railroad instead of its Greenville branch, to Norcross on North Twin Lake, where he could have retraced Thoreau's 1846 water route to Abol Stream and from there gone on foot to the Abol Slide and up that to the top. Or he could have stayed on the train from Norcross to Stacyville, from where a road led six miles west through the forest to Hunt's farm. It is unfortunate that time did not permit Muir this excursion, thereby foreclosing any possibility that we might have his impressions of this wilderness that had so moved Thoreau.

When Muir met Theodore Roosevelt in May 1903 (see chapter 14), the then president of the United States could have told him about this country. While at Harvard, Roosevelt had made three trips into the Maine woods, all in the space of thirteen months. On his first journey, on 6 September 1878, the nineteen-year-old Teddy—he would be twenty at the end of the next month—stepped off the train at Mattawamkeag, Maine, at that time the end of the line. From there a buckboard transported him thirty-six miles north to Island Falls on the Mattawamkeag River, near its entry into the lake of the same name. He stayed with lumberman William Sewall, who was born in Island Falls in 1845. When not bossing the river log drives, Sewall ran his home as a hunting lodge with his nephew Wilmot Dow. Sewall and young Roosevelt canoed Mattawamkeag Lake, hunted, tramped the woods—one day, for thirty miles—and recited poetry to each other. Roosevelt returned to Island Falls the next year, 1879, in March, and again that August. It was on the latter visit that he made an eight-day excursion to Katahdin, visible thirty-two miles west in a beeline from Sewall's. Their route then was somewhat longer. The first day, Tuesday, 26 August, they traveled by wagon eighteen miles, probably south to Stacyville via Sherman. (It would have been two miles farther via Patten.) Then they went east six miles to Hunt's. (Roosevelt's diary says they drove twenty-three miles total.) After crossing the East

Branch, they tramped ten miles east, Roosevelt says, via rough lumber roads along Wassataquoik Stream to camp. Fording these waters, Teddy lost a shoe, and wore his moccasins thereafter.[25] The next day, the 27th, they hunted and progressed to the head of Katahdin Lake. On the 28th, they caught trout in Sandy Brook before losing their way, not reaching "a small water hole" until after dark, and seeing bear and caribou tracks. From there on Friday, 29 August, they ascended Katahdin, most likely via the Great Basin, the view Roosevelt found "beautiful," commenting later in a letter that he had been the sole person to gain the top. Returning they "followed a spotted trail which sometimes set at fault even the two skilled backwoodsman[sic]." At dark, soaked from rain, they came to their Katahdin Lake camp.[26]

Admittedly not a mountaineer in a class with Muir, Roosevelt nonetheless had seen his share of heights, both domestic and foreign; in fact, in his youth he had outdone Muir abroad. His first climbing was part of the family's year-long Grand Tour. On 6 August 1869, Teddy, eleven that October, with his father had topped an unidentified 8,000-foot mountain at Chamonix, France. The next day, when going up a glacier, they exceeded their previous day's elevation. On the 11th, they walked into Switzerland, across the Tête Noire Pass (9,830 feet), south of Finhaut (he noted the mileages of the various family members; his was nineteen). Atop the Eggishorn (9,625 feet), east of Visp and 6,165 feet above Fiesch, on 18 August, they encountered a snowstorm. On 8-9 September, father and son walked over the Splügen Pass (6,933 feet) into Italy.[27]

Two years later he was exposed to some of the Northeast's mountains. In the Adirondacks, on 12 August 1871, he summited Mount St. Regis (2,873 feet), after a 3.4- mile hike from Upper Saint Regis Lake. Later that August, in Franconia Notch of the White Mountains, he ascended Cannon (4,100 feet), on the 19th, Bald (2,340 feet) twice on the 21st, and Lafayette (5,260 feet) on the 23rd. The next day he traveled by stagecoach from the Profile House to the Crawford House for the night, and took a carriage to Mount Willard for the view. On the 25th, he went up Mount Washington by the cog railway, descending by stage on the east side. But due to its remoteness in 1879, Katahdin presented his greatest alpine challenge.[28]

More Swiss summits levened his 1881 summer honeymoon with Alice Lee, whom he married on his twenty-second birthday, 27 October 1880. Their prenuptial vacation on Mount Desert Island in Maine had given her a taste of his need for altitudes; on 3 August he had walked up Newport (now Champlain) Mountain (1,058 feet).[29] Now, back in Switzerland twelve years after his first visit, Roosevelt on 2 July 1881 warmed up with the 8,265-foot

Mount Muottas, 2,600 feet above Samaden in the broad Inn Valley with St. Moritz to its south, his wife coming along on horseback. Walking north from Alpnach and descending eastward to Hergiswil on 15 July, he crossed over Pilatus (6,964 feet), which overlooked lakes Lucerne and Zug and a sea of alps. Three days later, they ascended the Rigi-Kulm (5,906 feet)—perhaps via the cog railway, as the Baxters did four years later, though there is no comment on the means—and stayed atop to see the sun set and rise. Then, on 24-25 July, with guides, he successfully engaged the Jungfrau (13,642 feet), coming over the Mönchjoch, Jungfraufirn, and Roththal-Sattel to the peak, his diary noted. Four days later, on 29 July, as they proceeded to Visp via the Gemmi Pass (7,640 feet) and Leuk, Alice turned twenty. Though his diary said nothing of her birthday, earlier, on 25 May in Ireland, he had proclaimed her a superlative traveling companion, despite her seasickness on the Atlantic crossing. The next day, 30 July, a twenty-one-mile walk (Alice rode horseback) brought them from Visp to Zermatt, an elevation gain of 2,856 feet (he had walked this way in the reverse direction, thirteen miles downhill, on 16 August 1869). Monday, 1 August, they went up to the Gornergrat (10,290 feet), almost 5,000 feet above Zermatt—as Muir would do in August 1893, by foot and mule. Alice and Theodore stayed at the hotel Riffel, partway down. Again with guides and an overnight, on 3-4 August the incomparable Matterhorn (14,692 feet—almost two hundred feet higher than Whitney in the Sierra), which he had eyed nine years before, was attained. Coincidentally, other future friends of Muir's, David Starr Jordan and Melville B. Anderson (see chapters 6 and 12, respectively) also climbed the Matterhorn that same month, after Roosevelt. On 6 August, the honeymooners beheld Mont Blanc in moonlight, as Annie Fields and Sarah Orne Jewett did later (see chapter 4), but made no ascent. They departed Switzerland through Geneva and Basel, reaching Strasbourg on 11 August.[30]

Twenty years later, on Friday, 13 September 1901, back in the Adirondacks, Roosevelt stared into the fog atop Mount Marcy. As he started down, word reached him that William McKinley was dying in Buffalo, and that he was needed immediately at the president's bedside.[31]

Though Muir did not climb Katahdin nor even mention seeing it in his journal and letters, he did pay close attention to what Thoreau had written about it. As Thoreau ascended Katahdin, "A torrent...tumbling down in front, literally from out of the clouds" confronted him. Muir underlined "literally from" in text. He was also attracted to "roaring down, with a copious tide." "[C]ertainly the most treacherous and porous country I ever travelled," Thoreau remarked as he made his way upward. "Having slumped, scrambled, rolled, bounced, and walked, by turns, over this scraggy country, I arrived upon a side-hill, or rather side-mountain". Muir liked Thoreau's "m[oun]t[ai]n scrambling - Ex[cellent]." From "the summit of the ridge," Thoreau's observations appealed to Muir. "It was like sitting in a chimney and waiting for the smoke to blow away" and the last ten lines of that paragraph, beginning, "This ground is not prepared for you"; and the following paragraph beginning, "The tops of mountains are among the unfinished parts of the globe." Muir savored Thoreau's "Reflections—Soul & body etc in the wilderness" as he descended. In a long paragraph, Muir marked "It is difficult to conceive of a region uninhabited by man. We habitually presume his presence and influence everywhere....Nature was here something savage and awful, though beautiful....Here was no man's garden, but the unhandselled [Muir underlined the first two syllables] globe....but here not even the surface had been scarred by man, but it was a specimen of what God saw fit to make this world."[32]

A wonderful word, unhandselled means "unused, untested, untried," according to professor Lewis Hyde; it evidently impressed Muir, who used it in describing his first impressions of Hetch Hetchy Valley. Camping there in November 1871 beside the Tuolumne River "in the middle of a close group of cedars," he "was at home in this vast, unhandselled Yosemite." Returning from Hetch Hetchy to Yosemite, Muir weathered a snowstorm in a makeshift "hut...a sort of bear's nest," created from "laths" splinted from a fallen tree and "lined...with branchlets of fir." His delight in watching and hearing the tall firs' embrace of wind and snow provoked, "How perfectly would the pure soul of Thoreau have mingled with those glorious trees, and he would have been content with my log house."[33]

From Greenville at 1:30 p.m.—now aboard the Canadian Pacific Railroad, which had first come through here a decade earlier, in 1888—Muir proceeded close to the west shore of Moosehead Lake, where he could have viewed Katahdin, forty-five miles northeast, had it been clear. However, Muir noted in his journal, it was "cl[ou]dy." At the East Outlet of the Kennebec River, eleven miles from Greenville, his train turned west, along the southern ends of Brassua Lake and Long Pond, to the hamlet of Jackman. From there the CP track edged three ponds—Wood, Attean, and Holeb—before following the Moose River to the height of land and the Canadian border. Of this territory, his journal related: "rough m[ountai]ns & valley flats forests burned badly —few seedlings—desolation—pulp mills. only rocks boulders—3 deer brought on bord [sic] v[ery] ab[undant] here. A pretty summer resort on island of one of many lakes."[34] This was Attean Lake Lodge on Birch Island, which is still in operation.[35] It is a wonder that Muir did not report seeing any moose in this region where they were (and still are) plentiful and where his train often paralleled the water.[36]

When at 7:50 p.m., he arrived at Mégantic, on the north end of Lake Mégantic in Quebec Province—a total distance of eighty-four miles from Greenville—it was raining. For the first time since Stowe, Muir luxuriated in a hotel, "surrounded with spruces & aspens yel[low]" for the night. "Went to bed early."

## SATURDAY, 22 OCTOBER 1898

"[U]p at 5. Start…at 6:30." Heading north through "forests spruce, hemlock thuya [Northern white cedar or arborvitae, *Thuja occidentalis*] few white p[ine]. taller. Many mills using small stuff. No color hardly in woods on highest ground 2000 f[ee]t? until near Quebec[.] Magnif[icent] miles of larch bright yel[low] a grand show[.]" Soon after Tring Junction, the train came out of the woods into "lovely Chaudiere [River] val[ley] open - hundreds of farms on sandy drift—sloping smoothly—hills 200 f[ee]t h[igh] of gl[acial] sand." A ferry transported him across the St. Lawrence River to Quebec City, where he walked about the Plains of Abraham on the bluff and "had dinner in old fashioned French hotel"—the Château Frontenac? Then, at 2:30 p.m., he recrossed the river, and boarded a sleeper bound for Boston. "Rai[n]ing" still. He had supper at "Dudleys Junction," which is Dudswell Junction, 118 miles south of Quebec.

This is the last landmark Muir indicated until he awoke next morning "on bank of Merrimac[k] R[iver], beautiful stream oaks ash maple etc in Color[.] many mills neat villages." He arrived in Boston at 8:10 a.m. From Dudswell, it is likely he went directly south ninety-two miles to Lancaster, New

Hampshire, following the upper Connecticut River for the last half. From Lancaster southward, he passed through Whitefield again, then west, keeping the White Mountains to his east, to Woodsville and from there south through Plymouth, Concord, Nashua, and on into Boston.[37]

# Wellesley

Central St.

5  6

Wellesley College

3

↑N

4→

Lake Waban

2

Pond Rd.

Washington St.

1

1. Hunnewell Home
2. Durant Home
3. College Hall
4. Woodland Garden
5. Wellesley Station
6. Wellesley Town Hall

½ mile

# 11. Wellesley

*No occupation is so delightful to me as the culture of the earth,
and no culture comparable to that of the garden.*
—Thomas Jefferson to Charles Wilson Peale, 20 August 1811

*To put the best expression of any landscape into the consciousness
of one's day's work is more to be desired than much riches.*
—Liberty Hyde Bailey, *The Holy Earth*

## Sunday, 23 October 1898

No sooner had Muir returned from the North Country than he set out again, thankful that this trip was just for the day. After Sunday breakfast at Holm Lea on 23 October 1898, Sargent drove Muir in his carriage to Wellesley, Massachusetts, about ten miles west of Brookline. Sargent meandered a bit on back roads—Muir says they went twelve miles—to show off both Brookline's autumnal scenery and The Country Club, created by John Murray Forbes, whom Muir knew from his Yosemite visit with Emerson. (The club's now famous golf course had opened in 1893.) Eventually, they took Boylston Street directly to the Charles River at the Wellesley town line, whereupon it became Worcester Street, which they pursued to Wellesley Hills. Though a period map recommended this way for bicycling, this highway (Route 9) clotted with cars pinched between shopping malls, is wisely avoided on two wheels today.[1]

At Wellesley Hills, they turned south on Washington Street and passed through Wellesley, then a village of 4,229 people (estimated 1895 census), now expanded to 26,615 (1990 census). Both of these hamlets and a third one to the north, Wellesley Farms, offered railroad service—their stations and grounds designed by H. H. Richardson and Frederick Law Olmsted. As a member of the Board of the Boston & Albany Railroad, Sargent had urged Richardson's expertise for a number of stations. Instead of going to Boston to board the train, Muir and Sargent opted this time for private transportation. They did not miss in passing, nonetheless, the Wellesley Hills station (1885-1886), which now offers passengers a dank sheltered waiting area, and on the street side, a cleaner's and an antique dealer; the post office is next door. While the Wellesley depot (1887) was sadly demolished in 1961, the one at Wellesley Farms, (1890) with pond and bucolic byways, still retains the intended flavor of its designers.[2] The MBTA commuter rail system from Boston stops at these three places now.

Shortly after the shops and broughams and traps of town, Sargent and Muir turned off Washington Street. An entrance avenue led them through pine, magnolia, laurel, and rhododendrons to an Italian garden, from which they saw a lake in one direction and a manse in the other—the home of Horatio H. Hunnewell and Isabelle Pratt Welles. They had been married almost fifty-three years before her death ten years earlier, in 1888. They had had nine children—six boys and three girls, one of whom had died in infancy. Welles was related to Sargent, being a cousin of Henry Winthrop Sargent, the first cousin of Sargent's father, Ignatius. She had inherited the property from her father, John Welles; they had expanded it to 117 acres, and the Renaissance Revival mansion they built in 1851 they called Wellesley in her honor. It is still a private residence, its grand white facade seen over a trim lawn and circular drive from Washington Street.

Hunnewell and Sargent were old friends. Sargent had dedicated volume IV of his *Silva of North America* to Hunnewell, whose generosity was manifested in the Arnold Arboretum's administration building that is named for him. It was designed by Alexander Wadsworth Longfellow, a nephew of the poet, and houses library, herbarium, and museum as well. Sargent himself gave $10,000 for books, as well as his personal library of over ten thousand items. The building was completed in the autumn of 1892.[3]

Periodically the two men visited each other's estates. Hunnewell was enraptured over the Indian azaleas of Holm Lea; Sargent gushed about Wellesley's tall pines. One winter Hunnewell called at Holm Lea in an open sleigh. Annually, they would open their places to the public; occasionally, to the Garden Committee of the Massachusetts Horticultural Society, of which they both were members—Hunnewell for half a century, Sargent since 1870. When a busy Hunnewell had declined the society's presidency in November 1874, Francis Parkman had served for three years. Currently, Hunnewell was the chairman of the Finance Committee (he had been a member of this committee for thirty-two years), while Sargent was involved in the creation of the society's new home. Both contributed to its annual exhibitions. Its spring flower show is still held. In late June 2001 the MHS relocated to Wellesley, at the Elm Bank Reservation (900 Washington Street), a half-mile west of the Hunnewell estate; its marvelous library reopened on 14 September of that year.[4]

Hunnewell greeted his guests and showed them around. "[F]ine residence looking out over charming glacial Lake[.]," Muir noted the attractions in his journal. "Shore Moderately high. the nat[ural? native?] maple forest etc charming w[ith] [undeciphered word] & color. Planted every tree here since he was 45 yr. old. (now 85) except one—an oak—250 yrs. old."[5]

Actually, Hunnewell had turned eighty-eight on 27 July. He had celebrated his birthday in Bethlehem, 1,450 feet above the sea in the White Mountains of New Hampshire. The village of Bethlehem, "one of the foremost summer-resorts of America," according to Sweetser, was packed with places to stay. Previous summers Hunnewell had resided at the elaborate Maplewood resort, a mile east of Bethlehem. But with the completion of the cottages of William Murray Sayer Jr. in 1897 and two more the following year, he preferred these.[6] Situated on the west end of Main Street, they looked west over the Connecticut River valley to the Green Mountains of Vermont. The small community of over 1,200 year-round residents expanded in summer, yet offered as much society and solitude as he wanted. Generous alpine vistas, leisurely drives along the Gale River through Franconia, and botanical rambles about Strawberry Hill and Mt. Agassiz enriched his days.

His son John's presence had made this summer's mountain vacation a joy. Hunnewell felt that John resembled the boy's older brother Hollis, who had died in 1884. John, now fifty-eight and single, had graduated from Harvard, as had all his brothers except Hollis. Since the Civil War, except for periodic visits home, however, he had been living abroad, primarily in Paris, for which he departed on 5 September. Hunnewell stayed in Bethlehem for over six weeks, not returning home until the last day of August.

Muir knew the place where his host had been, for three days earlier his train had passed within eight miles of Bethlehem. Helen Hunt Jackson was partly responsible for Bethlehem's popularity—an ironic twist, as her biographer Kate Phillips points out, since she wished to preserve the peacefulness of this place. Jackson had first summered in Bethlehem in 1865, when she was thirty-four. Her first travel essay related that experience. The people she met, her hotel, the easy access to "all the chief points of interest in the mountains," the informality of attire, and the economy of it all, from the livery fees to the fact that "Board, very plain, but wholesome and good, is five dollars and six dollars a week"—all pleased her, so much so that she returned summer after summer and "wrote about the town again and again," Phillips says.[7]

Jackson even ascended Mount Washington. Her first approach, in July 1866, was from the east, along the Androscoggin River from Bethel, Maine, to Gorham, New Hampshire, from where she climbed Mount Hayes (2,555 feet), a three-mile walk to the north of the river. At the Glen House, she began the "tramp upward" onto Washington. "The day is marvelously clear," she wrote. On the summit this afforded her a view of the Atlantic Ocean, "110 miles away." She could also see Katahdin, "celebrated by both Winthrop and Thoreau," she wrote, "175 miles distant." This shows her familiarity with two books published by Ticknor and Fields of Boston in the early 1860s: Theodore Winthrop's *Life in the Open Air, and Other Papers* (1863) and Thoreau's *The Maine Woods* (28 May 1864).[8] After dinner in the Tip-Top House, she descended on horseback over the Crawford Path to Crawford's.[9]

Her next ascent, four years later in 1870, used a novel mode of alpine transport. The first train had reached the summit on 3 July 1869, less than two months after the first transcontinental railroad was completed (see Prologue). Jackson was in the vanguard of tourists who took advantage of this opportunity. From Bethlehem, she rode east seventeen miles, she said (actually eighteen) to Mount Washington station. She sat in an open car just above the steam engine—"that mysterious puffing creature which stood with its shoulders against our car, and slowly pushed us up, up, three miles up, on that road in air." Her focus shifted this time from the mountain to the cog railway. She even quoted "a minute description of the machinery." Her descent was more daring. Riding on the tender "between trunks and fuel" thrust her into the present moment. Her "astonished soul took note of every second of time, every current of air, every pulsation of the throbbing force." "All was space, space was all." Even after the thrill of the ride, she concluded, "It is hardly worth while to run up just to turn round at the Tip Top House on Mount Washington and come down."[10]

Undaunted, she returned the next year, 1871. This time, the time of the autumnal equinox, she came again by carriage from Bethlehem. Eight miles along, she passed the Twin Mountain House, where on a prior September Sunday she had heard the most famous preacher of the day, Henry Ward Beecher. From Twin Mountain to Fabyan her route and Muir's in 1898 would intersect. Boarding the cog railway at the depot and "riding on the tender," she surmounted the clouds into the sun-filled summit. The atmosphere, though a blend of "those two almost contradictory and inconsistent qualities of haze and clearness," as she described it, did not inhibit her view of Katahdin, this time only 150 miles away, and Portland Harbor—she didn't say how far.[11]

After returning from Bethlehem to Wellesley this summer, Hunnewell told Muir and Sargent that he had been "devoting all my time to the care of the shrubs and trees on the place." In September he had faced the sad task of taking down from the upper Entrance Avenue five of his largest, most loved white pines, due to disease. He had planted them in 1852. Later a big sugar maple had been removed from south of the house, providing a view of white pines and chestnuts, as well as space in which the magnolia that he planted in 1856 could flourish. Abundant summer rain gave his trees an unusual lushness of green foliage.[12]

A financier, Hunnewell had made himself into a horticulturist of considerable acumen. At Wellesley, he had first created a nursery of "Norway spruce, white pines, balsams, Austrian pines, Scotch firs, larch, beech, oaks, elms, maples, etc." and from that made selections for his grounds.[13] Like Thomas Jefferson at Monticello, Hunnewell recorded the purchase and source of his plants.[14]

"[E]very tree that can be made to grow & bush & flr[flower]," Muir continued to take in his surrounds. "Lovely orchids. Cedar of Leb[anon]. Douglas Sp[ruce] Sug[ar] pine not doing well. Did not know them. Colors charming there & all the way. Lovely maples yel[low] & red glowing in the spaces /o/ [between] lvs [leaves] & limbs. ineffably fine. Also white oak & scarlet bronze & purple & crimson. hickory pure lemon yel[low]. Some maples only yel[low] along viens[veins] some tipped & margined with crimson. Wonder to see such color on white oak."

They admired the lush azalea and rhododendron gardens. Taking a cue from London, Hunnewell had organized for the Massachusetts Horticultural Society a Rhododendron Exhibition on the Boston Common in June 1873, which was attended by some 40,000 spectators. Thus promoted, this shrub attained prominence for landscaping. Hunnewell believed that such use of nature would enhance society.[15]

They walked through a pinetum of over one hundred species. They peeked into his dozen glass houses for peaches, grapes, oranges, palms, and other tropical delights. They took in the Italian garden that rose from the lake in seven terraces to the house and held some two hundred trees—white pines, spruces, hemlocks, cedars, and arborvitae—all in topiary. They saw the boathouse with the gondola that Hunnewell had imported from Italy along with a gondolier, though they did not ride in it. This waterfront and garden, owned now by the Trustees of Reservations, expresses Hunnewell's ecological vision, which saw property as trust to be held in the public interest.[16]

## GARDEN AND FOREST

Nine years earlier Sargent had described "The Terrace Garden in Wellesley" in a new weekly magazine, *Garden and Forest: A Journal of Horticulture, Landscape Art and Forestry,* which he, Hunnewell, Olmsted, and others initiated, and to which Sargent made numerous contributions, some thirty in 1893 alone.[17] William Augustus Stiles of New York, who had helped engineer the Central Pacific's transcending of the Sierra Nevada in the 1860s, was the editor. The first issue, of 29 February 1888, paid tribute to Asa Gray, who had died the previous month.

The "new ethos of conservation," historian Char Miller has written (in 2000), "found its first sustained and vivid expression in *Garden and Forest.*" It featured editorials in behalf of the green world, such as "The Forests of the National Domain," by Sylvester Baxter, who authored and published the first *Boston Park Guide* in 1895. Luminaries Francis Parkman, Frederick Law Olmsted, Charles Eliot, and M. G. Van Rensselaer also contributed. C. G. Pringle, whom Muir had missed in Vermont, told of the forests of northern Mexico. Cornell University's Liberty Hyde Bailey reported weekly from Chicago on the horticulture—apples, azaleas, rhododendrons, roses, etc.—of the World's Fair. Of citrus fruits, he observed that the largest exhibit in the Horticultural Building was from Los Angeles County: a thirty-five-foot-tall monument covered with 13,873 oranges and some lemons. Gifford Pinchot advocated for the protection and management of forests.[18]

Hunnewell, too, was represented, with a rhododendron article and four short letters to the editor on the effects of winter on his rhododendrons. Varieties celebrating Charles Sprague Sargent, Mrs. Charles Sprague Sargent, and Frederick Law Olmsted "have not suffered in the least in the past winter," he wrote of the 1894-1895 season.[19] In recent years, his youngest child, Henry Sargent Hunnewell, forty-four in 1898, had commented in the magazine on the roses and red cedars of his estate, The Cedars, located next to his father's (they are separated by the still marvelously sylvan Pond Road), which Wellesley's superintendent for forty years, T.D. Hatfield, praised in another issue. An architect, Henry Hunnewell had designed a twenty-nine-room, white clapboard house, where he and his family moved on 21 February 1891. "Boston would be better off," Henry advocated in another piece, "if her parks were half as large and twice as well taken care of."[20]

Sargent's understudy, Beatrix Jones, also made her debut in *Garden and Forest,* in 1893. She elaborated on her understanding of the color, light, and relationships of the trees of the Maine coast at Bar Harbor. Three years later she was back again with "Bridge over the Kent at Levens Hall"—an Elizabethan mansion with parkland, which she had seen in Westmoreland, England, in August 1895. Though initially drawn there by its topiary gardens, she was ultimately charmed by the ivied span over the Kent River. Later she extracted the essence of "The Garden in Relation to the House," a paper given to the Royal Institute of British Architects on 15 February 1897 by Henry Ernest Milner, author of *The Art and Practice of Landscape Gardening* (London, 1890). She allowed that "the artists"—the architect and landscape gardener—should "work side by side and in sympathy from the outset"; such collaboration was her wish.[21]

Beatrix Jones was familiar with Wellesley. Mary Sargent had brought her there on Monday, 4 November 1895. Her horticultural knowledge and enthusiasm impressed Hunnewell. On Monday, 11 June 1900, she would return again, this time with both Sargents and others to see the spectacle of rhododendrons that Hunnewell thought "if possible, finer than ever!"[22]

On 6 October 1897, William Stiles, who three years earlier had himself visited Wellesley, died at age sixty. "[A] brilliant and successful editor of a technical journal", Sargent eulogized him, an inveigher against the enemies of urban parks, especially Central Park.[23] *Garden and Forest* had also expired the end of that year—Sargent unable to sustain it financially and literarily after his able editor's death. Its last issue, of 29 December 1897, contained part XIII of Sargent's "Notes on Cultivated Conifers" and a description of "The Botanic Garden of Smith College" by William F. Ganong.

Not among the *Garden and Forest* authors, Muir was a subject instead. His ascent of Mt. Rainier in August 1888 with William Keith and seven others was duly noted by editor Stiles and botanist Charles V. Piper. An advertisement also cited him as one of thirteen contributors to a symposium on "Prof. Sargent's Scheme of Forest Preservation by Military Control" in the *Century* of February 1895. Muir was also one of the journal's readers, thanks to Sargent, who likely introduced him to the publication and its editor. On Muir's first visit to Holm Lea in June 1893, Sargent had invited Stiles to dine with them, prompting discussion of the magazine in which Sargent's series on "Forest Flora of Japan" was currently running.[24]

## LIBERTY HYDE BAILEY

Two *Garden and Forest* contributors—Liberty Hyde Bailey and Gifford Pinchot—had especially high regard for Muir.

"For many years I have been one of your admirers," Bailey would write Muir in July 1901, while Bailey was teaching at the College of Agriculture of the University of California in Berkeley. He wanted an interview with Muir and a "contribution to a new Eastern high-class magazine," *Country Life in America*, of which he was the editor. He was available to come to Muir in Martinez or San Francisco until 7 August, though his weekends were "engaged for excursions." That July, Muir took his two daughters on the Sierra Club Outing, "their first mountaineering." As usual the elements were restorative. "My miserable cold has gone with the frost & wind," he wrote Louie from Tuolumne Meadows. "Every breath is pure pleasure. [William] Keith too is much better. God's ozone sparkles in every eye." Not returning home until Saturday, 10 August, Muir found his table "loaded with letters," among them the one from Bailey. It was too late for the naturalists to talk in person, so they corresponded. Bailey responded to Muir's of the 17th of August by clarifying his desire for an article on the "'Mountains of California,'" though shorter than Muir's piece on sequoias in September's *Atlantic*. "I want your best—one of your clear, ringing, soulful descriptions." Muir was too busy to oblige the new editor. He had to correct the proofs of his book on national parks, which was published on 9 November and dedicated to Sargent.

The first issue of *Country Life*, dated November, pleased Muir. The large quarto pages and fine black-and-white photographs enhanced the monthly. Bailey's lead essay on "The Abandoned Farms" was followed by another of his, "Ellerslie, An American Country Seat." There was advice on growing chrysanthemums, pruning, gardening, even a review of *Pertaining to Thoreau* (1901), a collection of Thoreau critics edited by Samuel Arthur Jones. After the issue appeared Bailey again encouraged Muir to contribute at any time. Apparently, Muir never did, nor did Bailey ask again. The California number of *Country Life*, for January 1902, featured "The Country Life in California" by A. J. Wells, "The Story of a Great California Estate" by Charles Howard Shinn, "Plant-Growing and Human Culture" by E. J. Wickson, "Women Who Win Their Living from the Land" by Emma Shaffer Howard, "Almond Culture in California" by Katharine A. Chandler, two poems by Anna Botsford Comstock, and more.[25]

Though the California issue appeared without Muir prose, he was not forgotten. There he sat on a rock, his hat beside him, long beard, vest, and long-sleeved shirt, staring into a mountain meadow—in a photograph by Helen Lukens Jones accompanying her article "The Sierra Club in Camp" in the December 1902 issue. "No doubt you will learn to write well," editor Muir had commented after reviewing two of her pieces the year before, for which she was most grateful.[26] For the March 1903 issue, Bailey's associate editor Wilhelm Miller, who earned his doctorate at Cornell in 1899, illuminated Holm Lea in prose with superb pictures of the homes and grounds, including Sargent's favorite shrub, *Pyrus floribunda*, in flame. Emerson's home, with two photographs by Herbert Gleason, was the attraction of the May 1904 issue of the magazine. Bailey Millard wrote a tribute to Muir for the March 1915 issue.

That year, 1915, Bailey's *The Holy Earth* was published by Scribner's in New York. This philosophical treatise begs us to stay connected to the earth, to honor it, and to use wisely its resources. To do this, Bailey advised, all of us must "recognize the holiness of the earth." Therein Bailey celebrated persons of independent spirit who were connected to nature; to illustrate, he showcased Muir: "He has left a personal impression and a remarkable literature that has been very little influenced by group psychology. He is the interpreter of mountains, forests, and glaciers." Bailey stressed the importance of these "separate souls." Some of Bailey's sentences could have been Muir's; for example, "In the wind and in the stars, in the forest and by the shore, there is spiritual refreshment."[27]

## GIFFORD PINCHOT

In early June, 1893, Muir had first met Gifford Pinchot.[28] He was the guest of Pinchot's parents, James and Mary Pinchot, at their elegant home at Two Gramercy Park, Manhattan. We dined in "grand style," Muir wrote his wife. At twenty-eight, Gifford Pinchot was about half Muir's age. A native of Connecticut, he had graduated from Yale (1889), and studied abroad, primarily at the National Forestry School in Nancy, France. Olmsted's recommendation of Pinchot to work on Biltmore, the Vanderbilt estate in Asheville, North Carolina, in January 1892 (see chapter 12), launched his career as a forester. In April 1894 Pinchot sent Muir a copy of his study, *Biltmore Forest*, which he had prepared for the 1893 Chicago World's Fair.[29]

Muir's reputation preceded him. Pinchot had heard of Muir when he made a two-and-a-half-month trip west in the spring of 1891. On 7 May, Pinchot arrived by stage at Wawona, where he stayed in the hotel and talked with artist Thomas Hill. The next day, he horsebacked into the Mariposa Grove and wandered about the trees with caretaker Stephen M. Cunningham. On Saturday, 9 May, from Inspiration Point, he beheld Yosemite Valley for the first time. He honored the Sabbath by walking twenty-five miles to Mirror Lake, "which is really wonderful in its clear reflection," to Glacier Point— "Splendid to stand on end of Point & look down 3200 feet almost straight below you."—and "to and under Yosemite Upper Fall…Completely soaked." On Monday he rode and talked with Galen Clark, who, Pinchot noted in his diary, "knows all there is to know," and surely talked about Muir. Tuesday, 12 May, Pinchot left Yosemite, spending two days, the 14th and 15th, in San Francisco before going north to Guerneville and Cazadero, taking in the redwoods on the way. After a few days at Shasta, he arrived in Portland, Oregon, on the 22nd.[30]

The May of Pinchot's California sojourn, Muir was in Martinez, beleaguered with farm work, estate settlement (his wife's father had died on 31 October 1890), and preparation of his King's Canyon essay for the *Century*, which Johnson wanted promptly. It was not until the afternoon of Wednesday, 27 May—while Pinchot was absorbed in the scenery of his passage to Vancouver and the pages of *Paradise Lost*—that Muir departed for "that glorious wilderness," he told Johnson, in order to refresh himself and his memory of his subject.[31]

Muir traveled with artist Charles D. Robinson, a New England native, who had come to San Francisco at age three with his mother in 1850. (His father had preceded them by two years.) In May 1861 Robinson had returned to New England, where he studied with artists, notably George Inness in Boston and Jasper F. Cropsey in Newport, Vermont. Wanting to live in California, Robinson left the East again in 1873. Enroute overland, he stopped in Clinton, Iowa, on the Mississippi River. There he worked for the photographic firm Hildreth and Young, and met Kathryn Evelyn Wright, whom he married on 24 September 1874. The following year, Robinson came back to San Francisco with his wife. Robinson's quarter-century artistic engagement with Yosemite Valley began in 1880.[32]

In fact, while Robinson and Muir traveled, Robinson's teacher George Inness and his wife Elizabeth Hart, with their granddaughter, were in San Francisco. While he was there, William Keith invited Inness to share his studio at 115 Kearny Street. Sketching and painting excursions took them to the

Monterey Peninsula in mid-March and to the Yosemite Valley the first week of May—leaving the valley at the time Pinchot was arriving. In the spring of 1891 their work was part of three exhibits. The first, at the San Francisco Art Association, opening Thursday, 7 May, showcased Inness's *Near Monterey* (*Sunset Near Monterey*). The second, of works from the collections of Irving Scott and Charles Crocker, featured Inness's *Monterey Oaks* (now *California*; The Oakland Museum), which Robinson in a contemporary review (June 1891) called "remarkable for the very boldness of its simplicity as for its extraordinary method of execution." The third, from Sunday, 7 June, at Rabjohn & Morcom's Galleries, 240 Post Street, in San Francisco, was a joint show of Keiths and Innesses. Since Inness was so close to Keith this spring, it is likely that Muir met him and saw his art. It is even possible to imagine Robinson there with them at the same time.[33]

By mid-June, 1891, Muir was back home. "Had a good trip," he reported to Johnson, "but a little hard. Had to walk in to the Yosemite from the Sequoia Park Rain sleet snow & flooded streams Slid 2 miles on dead avalanche. Mule with all our goods went down the river but was caught on a grand jam. Robinson growling & blaming the sun spots for all. etc etc etc. But we had a fine rich time for a' that." Two months later, on 15 August, Muir sent Johnson about 10,000 words that went into November's *Century* along with Robinson's pictures. Therein Muir argued for the Kings River being a national park, a status that would not be conferred until 1940.[34]

Pinchot's and Muir's most enjoyable and intimate times happened in the wilderness. Sargent appointed Pinchot to the six-person National Forest Commission, of which Muir was an ex officio member. In July 1896, Muir joined the team in Chicago; Pinchot, in Montana. "[A]t 5.35 AM. July 16," Muir jotted in his journal, "Meet Pinchot with delight[.] Went to his camp on the bank of Flathead River & had coffee." Pinchot was equally thrilled to be with the mountaineer in his habitat. So began their reconnaissance of northwestern trees.[35]

After an all-day train ride, they arrived on 20 July in Spokane, Washington. Muir, "weary and feverish," decided to go directly home in order to prepare for travel to Alaska with the Osborns, a trip he invited Pinchot to come along on. The next day, the party left at noon for Missoula, Montana; later, Muir boarded the 3:35 p.m. train for Martinez via Portland. On Thursday the 23rd in Missoula, Pinchot wrote Muir the "bad news." The Commission had decided that his service was still needed for exploration of the Bitterroot Range along the Idaho-Montana border, thereby preventing his going to Alaska.

Muir's Alaska interlude—it included revisiting the Muir Glacier—encompassed three weeks, from 2 to 21 August. Then, after six days at home, Muir left San Francisco on the eve of the 26th, arriving the next day in Ashland, Oregon, where he rejoined Sargent and commissioner Henry Abbott. He does not mention Pinchot until the party were at Crater Lake, on the 30th. From there they traveled southward through California, where after "a rapid run up & down the mountains through the Sequoia Park to the summit of the western axis of the Sierra. The rapidist mouintaineering I ever did"—Pinchot alone ascending Mt. Dana—they arrived in Los Angeles the morning of 21 September. On the evening of 28 September the commissioners arrived at the Grand Canyon in Arizona, where Muir had his "first memorable & overwhelming view in light & shade of setting sun." The next day, Muir and Pinchot hiked along the South Rim. Camping out, they talked until midnight, then dozed, while tending the fire of "cedar for incense to the gods." Rising at 4:30, they walked to the hotel for breakfast with the others. The next day, 30 September, Sargent and Pinchot went to Flagstaff, while Muir with Commission member and geologist Arnold Hague of Newport, Rhode Island, and his wife Mary Bruce Robins Howe walked or rode—he did not say which—to the bottom of the canyon. On the first of October, Muir traveled to Flagstaff, while Sargent and Pinchot drove up Agassiz Peak. The next day, Muir wrote his family from the Bank Hotel in Flagstaff, "I start for home this afternoon, will stay a day at Los Angeles & another at Pasadena[.] then straight for Helen & Wanda & Louie Muir. The rest of the party are starting for Colorado." Stopping in Colorado Springs on his way East, Pinchot rode up Pikes Peak in a stage.[36]

A year later, on Sunday afternoon, 5 September 1897, Pinchot and Muir saw each other again—this time, inside. The lobby of the Rainier Grand Hotel in Seattle, Washington, at 909-911 Front Street (later First Avenue) was the venue. According to biographer Linnie Marsh Wolfe, their conversation was acrimonious. Reading in the morning paper that Pinchot favored sheep grazing on the reserves, an upset Muir confronted his young friend on the issue. Learning that Pinchot's position had been reported correctly, Muir, according to one account, indicated he was finished with Pinchot. In his recent Pinchot biography, Char Miller revisits this incident with fresh insight and reveals that it may be apocryphal. From Pinchot's diary, Miller indicates that their Sunday meeting was in fact harmonious. Further, he shows that the newspaper with Pinchot's views on grazing did not appear until the following morning. By then, Muir had boarded a ship scheduled to sail at 8:00 a.m., and therefore could not have addressed Pinchot in person on the matter.[37]

Nonetheless, there is no indication that the two saw each other the next year, 1898, nor that they corresponded. Even during Muir's three-month tour of the East, which brought him to New York and Washington, where he might have visited with Pinchot and his parents, there was no contact between them. Undoubtedly Pinchot, assuming on 1 July 1898 the head of the Division of Forestry in the Department of Agriculture—a forerunner of the Forestry Service (1905)—and moving to Washington, was consumed with business in this period. Historian Char Miller, however, sees this year as pivotal in their relationship, their divergent philosophies about wilderness becoming more evident, Pinchot advocating wise use, and Muir preservation, of the forest reserves.[38]

If their close friendship was frayed in any way, it was not evident on their next wild sojourn, in the following year, 1899. Returning from the Harriman Alaska expedition of over two months' duration on 2 August, Muir six days later joined Pinchot and Dr. C. Hart Merriam in San Francisco for a five-day ramble, on 8-12 August 1899. They surely all had fun going to, through, and from the Calaveras Grove of sequoias that lay between Lake Tahoe and Yosemite Valley. "Merriam & Muir told stories all the way. Two wonderful men to travel with," Pinchot noted in his dairy. He, too, loved the Big Trees. "They are the grandest of living things." Returning to San Francisco on the 11th, they continued from there the next day north to Mill Valley and drove through Redwood Canyon, which later became the Muir Woods (see chapter 16).[39]

With this jaunt their happy days afield seem to have ended. Their different visions for the highest use of the forests and the Sierra's grand Hetch Hetchy Valley separated them forever. Pinchot supported the damming of the great valley within Yosemite National Park for San Francisco's water supply, while Muir opposed such action as blasphemy. Emblematic of this rift was the absence of Muir, even as president of the Sierra Club (of which Pinchot was elected an honorary vice president in 1905), and Sargent at the first National Governors' Conference on Conservation, held at the White House in May 1908. Surely one would have expected them to be present in this august body convened by Teddy Roosevelt; however, Pinchot's influence, as the chief forester of the United States, was paramount.[40]

## WELLESLEY COLLEGE

Strolling about Wellesley on Sunday, 23 October 1898, Hunnewell, Sargent, and Muir stopped at the Pavilion to take in their surrounds. Across Lake Waban, Muir could see Wellesley College. The imposing French Empire-style College Hall with mansard roof, towers, and spires dominated the shoreline, and was reflected in the still water. The Center of College Hall, where women assembled for announcements, contained a large court of tropical plants in a marble basin, nourished by sunlight pouring through the five-story-high ceiling. What took four years to build burned in less than four hours in the early morning of 17 March 1914. Though no one perished, the structure was gutted and 5,661 books were destroyed.[41]

Founded in 1875, Wellesley had begun its twenty-third academic year on Wednesday, 21 September 1898. That autumn, eighty-one faculty taught 657 students, 216 of whom were Massachusetts residents, none of whom came from as far as Muir's California. They lived in cottages on campus and in College Hall (it accommodated 300 students), while a few boarded in approved places in the village. As they did every day, this Sunday morning they attended chapel. By this hour, they were studying in the library or engaged in recreation: tennis, golf, bicycling, or possibly boating on the lake. Each class had a crew of eight, who rowed vigorously in blouses and bloomers. On Float Day in June, the crews in their shells would join the prows for singing.[42]

The college had been the creation of neighbors of the Hunnewells, Pauline and Henry Fowle Durant of Boston. When the Durants began spending their summers in Wellesley in 1855, they occupied the Homestead, a farmhouse at the Washington Street entrance to the campus, now the Women's Resource Library. After the death of their son in 1863, they moved next door to a grand home (1854) that overlooked Lake Waban. After Henry Durant died in 1881 at age fifty-nine, Pauline Durant continued to live there. A woman of few vacations, she devoted herself daily to the concerns of the college, even bringing flowers to students, faculty, and staff when they were sick. After her husband's death, she served as treasurer of the college until her resignation in March 1895. Mr. Durant had selected the first president, Ada L. Howard, and recommended the next one, Alice Freeman. Mrs. Durant had moved the appointment of the current president, Julia J. Irvine, a Hicksite Quaker and professor of Greek, and now was involved in the search for her successor. Caroline Hazard, the first president to come from outside the college community, assumed office in March 1899. Upon Mrs. Durant's death in 1917 at age eighty-four, her home went to the college. It has since been the residence for the presidents of Wellesley.[43]

It is likely that both Muir and Sargent were acquainted with "Undergraduate Life at Wellesley" through the *Scribner's Magazine* article that May. The author reported that "'distinguished visitors' depart from Wellesley as much delighted with that institution and the students, as the college and the young women are with them."[44] At this point, it is hard to believe that Muir and Sargent could resist at least driving into the campus, especially to admire its trees, even perchance to plant one; yet no mention is made of this.

They might have perambulated Lake Waban, a popular pastime of residents and students in any season, then and now. A wide path still makes the two-and-a-half mile circle close to the shore. Starting at the college boathouse at the north end and proceeding southward along the west shore, today you encounter *Woodland Garden* by artist Michael Singer and architect Michael McKinnell. This sculpture, set in a depression between two low hills through which the lake is visible, evokes contemplation. It is a good place to pause, observe, and meditate. Looking down from the higher ground to the south offers an inviting perspective. You see two low, flat-topped fieldstone walls, which intersect in a lying-down T position, veritable racetracks for squirrels and chipmunks. A break in the top of the T, which parallels the path to the left, leads to an open, recessed rectangle, less its lower right quadrant, with knee walls above ground. It is composed of stucco, schist, granite, and bronze. Within this is another sculpture of horizontal and vertical lines, along with two places open to the earth. All this rests in a wood of oaks, beech, birch, and pines. Over a hundred trees were planted for *Woodland Garden*, along with wild blueberry bushes, ferns, and mosses.[45] Leaves of scarlet and black oak and yellow birch filled this sanctuary as I saw it on 2 November 2000.

Across the lake from *Woodland Garden*, the former Hunnewell and Durant homes can be seen, with the topiary evergreens between them. Continuing around the lake, you pass a hemlock grove with mountain laurel, rhododendrons at the southwest end, a radiant hickory similar to the one Muir saw, a tamarack or two, and the balustraded *promenade plantée* through the Italian Garden, above which is the Pavilion, with Chinese tiles. From the president's house (the former Durant home) a stone bridge crosses Waban Brook, which flows to the Charles River. Below the college buildings, students read on benches of hemlock-shaded wooden decks cantilevered over the placid water.

## DENDROLOGISTS THREE

Amid all this autumn arboreal splendor, the interior of the Hunnewell home was not Muir's interest. The Green Room with its grand piano, French Empire furniture, and fireplace; the Blue Room with Hunnewell's desk where his diary, letters, and garden ledgers were written; and across the hall the library, with his exceptional botanical collection, went unmentioned. The third floor, for servants, was probably not even seen. Electricity would be installed the next year.

Muir, however, appreciated his host. On reflection he found "Hunnewell himself the best of all." "[A] most agreeable guest," Hunnewell assessed Muir, "very modest and unassuming but full of interesting information in regard to all the conifers & vegetation in that wonderful part of our Country." Hunnewell, who had relished Muir's descriptions of the sequoias and other conifers in *The Mountains of California,* now experienced them extemporaneously.[46] Muir brought the dendrology of the land between the Pacific Ocean and the Sierra peaks to Hunnewell, who had never been there himself.[47] And both celebrated Sargent's devotion to understanding and conserving forests and their individual species. For an idyllic moment at least, three of the greatest tree lovers anywhere had gathered here at Wellesley.

"[H]ad good Lunch," Muir concluded his short journal entry for this day. His later letter home, however, enhanced the meal's reputation to a "grand champagne dinner."[48] After eating, Muir and Sargent departed. Passing again Pauline Durant's home and Wellesley College, and then the Town Hall (1887), with library within and park provided by Hunnewell, they headed back to Brookline.

Two days after Thanksgiving, a snowstorm of ten to twelve inches, with drifts "five to six feet high" kept Hunnewell from his trees. So in early December he returned for the winter to his home at 130 Beacon Street, at the corner of Berkeley Street, a block west of Boston's Public Garden. (His brownstone residence is now part of Emerson College.) Hunnewell continued to savor Wellesley in spring—his gardeners were astonished at how much work he did—and Bethlehem in summers. "The dry bracing mountain air agrees with me decidedly better than the salt air and east wind of the sea-shore in my old age," he wrote. In July 1900, Charles and Minnie Sargent and others came to Bethlehem to celebrate Hunnewell's ninetieth birthday, "a most happy occasion" for which he was "most grateful, as well as for the great prosperity and happiness with which I have been favored during my prolonged life." The next summer's Bethlehem stay of two months was his last. He died on 20 March 1902, the year before Muir next returned to New England.[49]

Cambridge 1898
Northwest of Radcliffe Yard

Gray
Gray Gardens East
Gray Gardens West
Madison
Garden St.
Concord
Buckingham
Parker
Riedesel
Craige
N
500 ft.
Bratle St.

1. Longfellow Home
2. Page Home
3. Higginson Home
4. Gray Home

# 12. Boston and Cambridge

*The traveling spirit; the spirit that is always with us—*
*I understand, and I bow my heart to the good fortune*
*that such a spirit exists and is so full of presence.*
—Letter from Ansel Adams to Nancy Newhall,
18 November 1948, Yosemite National Park, in
*Ansel Adams: Letters and Images 1916-1984*

*For me change of scenery and life is a vital necessity*
*without which I go out like a fire that is n't poked.*
—Letter, William James to Elizabeth Cass Goddard,
22 August 1895, Chocorua New Hampshire
*The Correspondence of William James 8:74*

*Hillside architecture is landscape gardening around a few*
*rooms for use in case of rain.*
—From *The Hillside Club Bulletin*, Charles Keeler,
President 1903-1905, in Richard Sexton, *The Cottage Book* (1989)

*There is something old-fashioned about climbing. It lets in*
*emotions that one does not readily admit to any longer:*
*companionship, commitment, even love.*
—Simon Mawer, *The Fall*
(Boston: Little, Brown, 2002)

## 24-26 October 1898

On Monday morning, 24 October 1898, Muir went to Houghton Mifflin, at 4 Park Street in Boston. This was Muir's first visit to the house that helped shape his literary destiny. After his death, Houghton Mifflin would publish *The Writings of John Muir* in ten volumes from 1916 to 1924, thereby assuring his legacy. Muir met with the publisher George H. Mifflin (his partner Henry Oscar Houghton had died in 1895) and joined for dinner some of the firm's editors: Walter Page, Bradford Torrey, Francis H. Allen, and Herbert R. Gibbs. Aside from Page, to whom Sargent had introduced him the previous month, these were all new faces for Muir.

Of all his mealtime companions, Muir saw the least of the forty-eight-year-old Herbert Gibbs. A year after graduating Phi Beta Kappa from Williams College in 1871, Gibbs had entered the Riverside Press of Houghton Mifflin as a clerk and proofreader. For the last eight years he had been an editor, assisting Horace Elisha Scudder and Walter Page with the *Atlantic*. Married to Sarah M. Cabot for twenty-three years, he now lived in the Boston suburb of Newtonville with their two sons and daughter, aged twenty, sixteen, and thirteen, respectively. Except for a year of study at Yale for an M.A. in 1880-81, the loyal Gibbs stayed at Houghton Mifflin all his working life.[1]

## BRADFORD TORREY, CELIA THAXTER, INA COOLBRITH

Bradford Torrey, who had turned fifty-five on 9 October, was a celebrated literary naturalist with five books to his credit.[2] His latest, *A World of Green Hills*, had appeared in 1898 with a cheerful cover by Sarah Whitman: beside its title in green on white cloth stood three light green stems of white flowers with yellow centers.[3] *A World of Green Hills* chronicled Torrey's search for birds in the southern Appalachians. In Highlands, North Carolina, in May 1896, certain birds reminded Torrey of his friends William Brewster, who had explored North Carolina's mountains in the spring of 1885, and Celia Thaxter.

Thaxter had a passion for birds and flowers, and for the writings of Richard Jefferies, Shakespeare, Tennyson, and Bradford Torrey. She had published her poetry in the magazine *Youth's Companion*, to which Torrey was a contributor, and from 1886 to 1901, an editor.[4] She enjoyed writing to Torrey about the birds of Appledore, one of Maine's Isles of Shoals, where she summered. Here she drew about her a close circle of artists, poets, and writers—Childe Hassam and John Greenleaf Whittier, Annie Fields and Sarah Orne Jewett among them. Torrey was always welcome too. "Oh, dear," she wrote him, "I shall not die happy till I have had a bird talk with you!"[5] Apparently, he had not come before she died on 26 August 1894. Five months before her death, on 24 March, Houghton Mifflin published her *An Island Garden*, with Childe Hassam's illustrations, which Vera Norwood, professor of American Studies at the University of New Mexico, has called "The best garden autobiography of the late nineteenth century."[6]

Ina Coolbrith eulogized Celia Thaxter as "The Singer of the Sea" in an elegy that appeared in December 1894. The month before its publication, Coolbrith had read Muir's *The Mountains of California* and written to thank him for his "prose-poem on the 'Mountains of God.' As if <u>all</u> were not the Mountains of God!" They had known each other for over twenty years, first meeting in Oakland, California, in 1872, where she served as head of the city library from 1874 until the last day of 1892, when she resigned. In June 1915, she would be honored as the first poet laureate of California—in fact, "the first female laureate in the United States," as professor and poet Alison Hawthorne Deming has pointed out.[7]

Though a Californian from age ten, Coolbrith had Yankee roots. Her four grandparents were New Englanders. Her mother, Agnes Moulton Coolbrith, grew up along the marshes of the Dunston River in Scarborough, on the south coast of Maine near Portland, where her Scottish ancestors had settled in the mid-seventeenth century. Ina was born on the Illinois bank of the Mississippi River, from where she migrated west through Beckwourth Pass of the Sierra Nevada with the guide for whom it is named in autumn, 1851.[8]

As an adult, Ina Coolbrith returned to New England to pay homage to her ancestors. In 1884 she crossed the continent by train, experienced her first New England autumn, met her Scarborough cousins, stayed at the United States Hotel in Boston, and talked with Oliver Wendell Holmes. In late October, in Danvers, Massachusetts, east of Salem and Beverly—where Muir's 1893 North Shore train later stopped—she visited John Greenleaf Whittier. Whittier, with whom she had corresponded since his inclusion of her poems in *Songs of Three Centuries* (Osgood, 1875), encouraged her to stay. Had she accepted his invitation, Muir might have visited her there. Instead, she returned to California via New York. Her meeting with Edmund Clarence Stedman, probably in New York, though his summer place "Kelp Rock" was in Newcastle on the New Hampshire shore, began a nurturing friendship that lasted until his death in 1908. Stedman's *American Anthology, 1787-1900* (Houghton Mifflin, 1900) would feature four of her verses: "Fruitionless," "Helen Hunt Jackson," "The Mariposa Lily," and "Where the Grass Shall Cover Me." It was to Stedman that she dedicated *Songs from the Golden Gate*, which William Keith illustrated and Houghton Mifflin published in October 1895.[9]

Again in autumn, nine years later, Coolbrith went east. The catalyst was the World's Fair in Chicago. Here, in October 1893, she participated in the commemoration of the new statue of Queen Isabella in the California Building by reading a poem. She also wrote another, "The Captive of the White City," decrying the humiliation of Chief Rain-in-the-Face, who was put on guarded display on the Midway Plaisance, while throngs passed "In brotherly love and grace." Afterwards, she continued to the northeast. In Maine, "While the snow falls, still and white," she contrasted the bicoastal regions lyrically in "Midwinter East and West." This poem was featured in the *San Francisco Examiner* on Christmas Day. After a brief stay in Boston, Coolbrith traveled to New York, where she remained until March.[10]

Conversant with Thaxter and other writers, Bradford Torrey was also intimate with New England's preserves. He would have been an invaluable companion to Muir in his just completed North Country tour. He had a particular affection for the White Mountains of New Hampshire. His favorite residence there was the hamlet of Franconia. From there he strolled in all directions: west through Sugar Hill and the Landaff Valley; north to the top of Mt. Agassiz (2,369 feet); south to Franconia Notch, from where he ascended the mountains on the west side, Bald (2,340 feet) and Cannon (4,100 feet), and on the east side, Lafayette (5,260 feet). One day "thrush music"—the voices of veeries, hermits, olive-backs, gray-cheeks—accompanied his entire saunter from his Franconia hotel to the summit of Lafayette and back.[11]

Torrey made his first visit to Crawford Notch—which Muir had just traversed—in early June 1883. His approach was on a platform car up the Notch to the Crawford House, a "most enjoyable ride." Anticipating its official season, he was the only guest. He roamed the woods about the hotel, renewing acquaintance with its songsters. On the 17th of June—in the footsteps of Thoreau over the Crawford Path forty-four years earlier—Torrey ascended Mt. Washington. Above the trees, the alpine plants were blooming despite snow's presence. He greeted diapensia and Lapland rosebay for the first time, and took a sample of the rare dwarf cinquefoil that grew only here. After a modest meal with the crew of the Signal Service Station—the hotel being closed—he made his descent, chased by a storm that kept him indoors the next day.[12]

Torrey and Muir could have compared stories of their Mt. Mansfield experiences. "I went up the mountain from the village of Stowe in very ignoble fashion,—in a wagon,— and was three hours on the passage. One of the 'hands' at the Summit House occupied the front seat with the driver," began Torrey's chronicle of his "Five Days on Mount Mansfield." At the top he encountered inclement weather, as Muir had, though it being July, no snow fell. He stayed at the hotel where Muir had taken shelter. By the following noon it was clear enough for Torrey "to clamber up the rocky peak— the Nose" for a view of the Adirondacks and Lake Champlain, and to walk two miles to the Chin, the highest point. All in all he spent many "happy hours" sauntering about, all the while watching and listening to the birds. The "finest singer," he thought, was the hermit thrush, "distinguished by an exquisite liquidity....The hermit's note is aspiration rather than repose." It says "'Higher, higher!'" He also admired butterflies and the alpine flora.[13]

Muir would see Torrey again. In 1907, Torrey went to California and, "after wandering up and down the state," settled in Santa Barbara.[14] Beginning on 11 May 1909, he camped in Yosemite for eight weeks. After his six o'clock breakfast, he tramped about alone each day, to various destinations: Mirror Lake, Nevada Fall, Sentinel Dome, and Glacier Point, where he slept six nights to take in sunrises and sunsets. He met Galen Clark, then ninety-five, and Muir, who arrived 2 July to accompany the ninth annual Sierra Club Outing until the 25th.[15] Torrey told of his time in "On Foot in Yosemite," which appeared in the *Atlantic* of August 1910. John Burroughs, who found Torrey like "a bird with his bright eyes and shy ways and sensitiveness" when they met in Boston in 1892, appreciated his Yosemite piece.[16] Three years later, in 1912, Torrey and Muir were again in Yosemite in July, Muir stopping en route by automobile from Los Angeles to Martinez, where he arrived on 22 July. Torrey died on 7 October 1912 in Santa Barbara. Some weeks before his death he sent a batch of his essays cross-country to Boston. A saddened Herbert Gleason, who attended Torrey's funeral in his native South Weymouth, Massachusetts, on 20 October, with the Rev. John G. Taylor presiding, read this manuscript and provided five photographs to accompany its publication. The following January, Houghton Mifflin issued Torrey's last book, *Field-Days in California*, a copy of which traveled west for Muir.[17]

## FRANCIS ALLEN, OLIVE THORNE MILLER, IRENE GROSVENOR WHEELOCK

Another at Muir's dinner table of 24 October 1898, Francis Allen, took Muir in the afternoon to the Riverside Press in Cambridge. Though Muir crossed the Charles River between Boston and Cambridge several times—then and now the late autumn scene of sailboats and shells gracefully, silently skimming the water—he never remarked on it in his writings. Which bridge they used, Longfellow or Western Avenue, is not disclosed. The Riverside Press, as its name implied, overlooked the Charles, from the former almshouse east of Harvard between Western Avenue and River Street; it is no longer there.

Francis Henry Allen, who was born in Jamaica Plain in 1866, had been at the press since 1884; he would serve there until his retirement in 1934. Three Octobers earlier, in 1895, he had married Margaret Hewins of West Roxbury.

They lived at 7 Rutledge Street in West Roxbury with their son Robert, who would be two in January. Like Torrey and Muir he was a naturalist, as well as a writer. An avid birder, he had been a member of the Nuttall Ornithological Club for almost five years, since 18 December 1893, and earlier this year, on 2 May 1898, had been elected its vice president, a position he held until 2 December 1912. Torrey was also a member of the NOC from 1884 to 1886. "A man of solitary tastes, he could not endure a crowd," the club's historian characterized him. "Our gatherings of half a dozen or more oppressed him, and after a couple of years we saw him no more."[18]

Allen's year-old *Nature's Diary* from Houghton Mifflin provided daily inspirational quotations. Though mostly by Thoreau, they also featured John Burroughs, Emerson, Hawthorne, Lowell, and Torrey, but not Muir. The only female voice in the collection— even in an era when about half the nature essays in the *Atlantic* were by women—was Olive Thorne Miller of Brooklyn, New York. Four years earlier, in 1894, she had conveyed to Muir her appreciation of his *The Mountains of California*, especially his renderings of the Douglas squirrel and water-ouzel, and her intent to visit him the following year. Of her eleven bird books published by Houghton Mifflin, Muir owned one: *A Bird-Lover in the West* (1894). This she would inscribe to him in commemoration of her time in Martinez, on the "red-letter day" of 12 June 1902. Though she had not even brought a toothbrush with her, the Muirs insisted she stay overnight.[19]

At the time of Miller's 1902 visit, Muir was writing about the Grand Canyon. The month before, on 21 May, the ever hospitable Muirs had entertained Irene Grosvenor Wheelock of Evanston, Illinois. Her stay rated the same red-letter-day sentiment as Miller's, she wrote Muir. Wheelock was writing *Birds of California* and wished for a Muir introduction. She waited for his reply. Her book went to press without any introduction. Over a year after her initial request to Muir, she found her letter still in her "traveling writing case," never having been mailed! In September 1903 she sent it to Muir, with her apologies. It took another year to reach the globe-trotting Muir, who responded that her book has "beautiful plumage, is bright and stout and well able to make its way on its own wings."[20]

At the Riverside Press, Allen introduced Muir to Bruce Rogers, a twenty-eight-year-old bachelor, who worked in a cubbyhole as a book designer. Three years earlier, in 1895, B. R., as he was called, had come to Boston from Lafayette, Indiana, where in 1890 he had graduated from Purdue University, a three-mile walk from his home. George Mifflin had hired him that same year. In two years, in 1900, he would be put in charge of the newly created Department of Special Bookmaking. Here he would become known for his production of some sixty special edition books. These included a large paper edition, limited to 600 numbered copies, of the *Journals of Ralph Waldo Emerson* (1909-1914). That same year, 1900, on 20 June, Rogers would marry Annie Embree Baker, one of his teachers at Purdue University—she had graduated from Purdue in 1886, and since 1887 had taught wood carving and freehand drawing there. In the next year their only child, Elizabeth, was born. Rogers stayed with Houghton Mifflin for sixteen years, to 1911.[21]

Allen, leaving Muir with Rogers, departed. Allen found Muir "a thoroughly delightful man, both as a writer and in his social relations." He admired Muir's capacity to speak with a half-dozen strangers as friends. "His writings are delightful too. His enthusiasm is boundless, and he has a big heart, poetic sensibilities and keen perceptions."[22]

Rogers escorted Muir "home far as Chestnut St[reet]." From Chestnut Street Muir walked along the eastern side of Holm Lea, to rejoin the Sargents at their estate. In March 1909, Houghton Mifflin published Muir's *Stickeen*—a book that Rogers designed.[23]

## JANE LORING GRAY

The next afternoon, Tuesday, 25 October, Walter Page, editor of the *Atlantic Monthly*, escorted Muir from Boston to his home at 9 Riedesel Avenue in Cambridge. From there, Muir and Page's wife, Willia Alice Wilson, "Allie", called on Jane Loring Gray at 79 Garden Street, a lovely half-mile stroll away. They probably passed the Higginsons' on Buckingham Street, but there is no mention of their knocking on the door. The Higginsons had returned eleven days earlier. They had been in Dublin, New Hampshire, since late spring, save for his attending Radcliffe's commencement on 28 June to receive an honorary degree. Crossing Concord Avenue, Muir and Allie Page proceeded north on Madison to Garden, then east to the northwest corner of Linnaean and Garden. "The streets in fine color," Muir reported to his journal, "Now at best every st[reet] in mellow light. an avenue bordered with elm & maple. Mrs. Gray's residence with botanic garden about it." In the 1820s naturalist Thomas Nuttall had lived here, in the southeast rooms of the first and second floor, overlooking the botanic garden that is no longer. The Harvard University Press is now at 79 Garden Street. The 1810 Federal of the Grays has been moved across Garden Street to number 88, on the northeast corner of Madison, where its new owners are restoring it.[24]

This is still a charming neighborhood. Nearby is Gray Gardens West, a secluded, peaceful cul-de-sac with ivied brick homes, green lawns, yellow crab apples, sycamores, and Japanese maples, all radiant in autumn light. A short hedge and ivy-bordered brick walk, which features a tall ginkgo, connects to Madison Street. Stroll down Gray Gardens East, its brick sidewalks sprouting violets, to number 19, a Georgian-style brick with slate roof, which was built in 1927 by Arthur and Elizabeth Bancroft Schlesinger, benefactors of Radcliffe's Schlesinger Library. Their son Arthur Schlesinger Jr., ten years old when they moved here, later joined his father on the history faculty of Harvard. In the 1960s, when I first read his *The Age of Jackson* (1945), he became one of my heroes.[25]

Muir and Jane Gray were already acquainted. She and her husband Asa Gray had first met Muir in Yosemite Valley in the summer of 1872, then again in San Francisco in September 1877, when Muir guided them to Mt. Shasta. Now, over tea, they talked of their past together. Since her husband's death ten years earlier, in 1888, Jane Gray had compiled his letters, which were published in 1893, the year of Muir's first Cambridge visit. Curiously, however, there is no mention of Muir in them. Upon reading them in December, 1893, Muir, nonetheless, found them engaging, and praised the botanist in a letter to Sargent: "Gray was one of the brightest sweetest & most charitable of men."[26]

These beautiful late October days of 1898, Josiah Royce regretted that his writing labors kept him from being with Mary Dorr and her son George in Bar Harbor, Maine, as in past summers. "But duty demands me here," he wrote George from the confines of his home library, "and even now I have no time to do more than breathe and work, and sleep between times. My warm love and greetings to your dear Mother."[27] Hence, he did not see Muir, as he had in 1893 and 1896.

## WILLIAM JAMES

Tuesday, 25 October 1898, provided "heavenly" weather for Royce's colleague William James. He took a bike ride around Jamaica Pond, entertained guests—"Pretty table but wretched dinner"—and wrote to his wife Alice.[28]

He had been back from California a month, having returned on 22 September (after six "uneventful" days on the train), a week before Harvard's academic term started. Though James had stopped teaching at Radcliffe, he was plenty busy. That fall he wrote out the lectures he had given in California. They were published the next year, serially first, in the *Atlantic Monthly*, and then in April as the book *Talks to Teachers on Psychology*.[29]

These lecture invitations served James as "a means of crossing the Continent and seeing the Pacific Slope." The professor had trained across Canada and then down the coast to San Francisco, where he had arrived on 10 August. "The fare is very good," he wrote of his stay at the Occidental Hotel. Three days later he set out for the Sierra Nevada, "with a young Californian philosopher named Bakewell as companion." His rationale for this destination was that "On the whole I prefer the works of God to those of man." From the Wawona Hotel, they sauntered eight miles into the Mariposa Grove, and then three miles among the Big Trees; a stage brought them back by six o'clock. Yosemite Valley, choked in forest-fire smoke, caused him to seek higher ground. With their guide, John Sax, they went by foot, mule, and horse for five days as far east as Tuolumne Meadows and Tioga Pass and Tioga Lake. Only James's fear of heights kept him from attaining the summit of Clouds Rest, at 9,926 feet. They returned via Glacier Point, "12 miles riding, 10 walking, and 10 staging," to Wawona. "The trip has done me a world of good," James proclaimed to brother Henry in England in a letter written when he was almost home. It was, James told his Adirondack hiking companion Josephine Goldmark, "my completest union with my native land."[30]

Too bad that Muir had not been James's guide. As we have seen, Muir did not start east until 7 September, and he arrived on the 17th, five days ahead of James. Thus he had left California before James's lectures of 12-15 September, but not before that of 26 August at the University of California in Berkeley.

While in California, James met Muir's friends, University of California professor Joseph LeConte (see chapter 3) and David Starr Jordan, president of Stanford University (see Chapter 6). At the latter's invitation, James stopped in Palo Alto on Monday, 5 September, and in the afternoon, at the university chapel, he spoke on "What Makes Our Lives Significant." The next night, in the Hotel Del Monte in Monterey, he conveyed his impressions of the campus by mail to Alice, who had once lived nearby while her father was ranching: "The whole is as simple and visible at once as a thing on the stage of the opera, and the peace serenity and purity which it all breathes are wonderful."[31]

Little did James know that he would be in California again, and at the time of its greatest natural cataclysm in modern times. His reason for coming was to teach psychology at Stanford University for a semester. On New Year's Day 1906, the philosopher set out by train for the West Coast alone. At sunset on 2 January 1906, he stopped at the Grand Canyon for two nights stay at the El Tovar Hotel. The next day's near-zero weather foiled his intended descent into the canyon. Instead, he kept warm by the hotel's giant stone fireplace. Before sunrise on the 4th, he was off to Los Angeles, where he spent an enjoyable day with Muir's "dear, dear friends" the Hookers—John and Katharine and their daughter Marian—at their home at 325 West Adams Street. Their "beautiful villa" impressed James, as did the Hookers themselves, Katharine being the conversationalist and "a really 'superior' person in all respects." Four years later, in 1910, Muir would change places with James, coming at various times to write in the Hookers' garret. And in May of that year, Muir and John Hooker would make a six-day trip to the Grand Canyon, staying at the El Tovar. James arrived in Palo Alto on Monday, 8 January 1906.[32]

On several occasions during his stay, James rode the train for an hour and fifteen minutes north to San Francisco. There he lectured to the Harvard and Pacific Coast Unitarian clubs and took in Golden Gate Park and the Cliff House (2-6 February), met Alice, who had come to join him (13-16 February)—her fifty-seventh birthday was on 5 February—and attended the meeting of the Association of American Universities (13-17 March). Over spring recess (28 March-8 April), the Jameses traveled south, stopping in Los Angeles—the Hookers entertained them—Redlands, Santa Barbara, and Monterey. Ten days after their return, in the early morning of 18 April, an earthquake tossed them out of bed. As most of Stanford's sandstone, tile-roofed buildings collapsed—the wooden ones survived, though all chimneys crumbled—classes had to be canceled for the rest of the term. Later that day, James saw much greater devastation in San Francisco, where he escorted his colleague Lillien Martin on the only train running to the city, to see her sister. James was glad to be there, however, "for the spectacle was memorable," he wrote his brother Henry four days later, "of a whole population in the streets, with what baggage they could rescue from their houses about to burn, while the flames and the dynamiting were steadily advancing and making everyone move farther."[33]

The jolt reaching 8.2 on the Richter scale shattered windows, jars of fruit and vegetable preserves, two fireplaces and a chimney in the new home (1903) of Charles Hitchcock Adams and Olive Bray Adams, which stood on the dunes behind Baker Beach, west of the Golden Gate at 129 24th Avenue. But the walls and ceilings held. The Swiss chalet-style house still stands, in fact, and remains a private residence.[34] (In Washington, D.C., Charles Adams—whose parents were both from Thomaston, Maine, and whose father's first two names were William James—took the first train for San Francisco, arriving five days later.) Three hours later, a potent aftershock sent their young son Ansel, age four, the future conservationist and maker of iconic black-and-white images of the Sierra Nevada, tumbling into a brick garden wall that forever skewed the ridge of his prominent nose leftward.[35]

Ruptured gas mains set San Francisco ablaze. The heart of the city burned for three days. On 26 April, both Alice and William went to San Francisco, inspected the ruins, then crossed the bay—the ferry building and wharves had been spared—to Berkeley for the night with the philosopher George H. Howison and his wife Lois Thompson Caswell at their new Victorian home (1891; it is no longer) at 2731 Bancroft Way, opposite the University of California campus. The next morning they started cross-country for Cambridge, where they arrived a week later on Thursday, 3 May.

Eight days after their homecoming, James wrote an article about the earthquake, which was published in June. Two qualities impressed him most: "the rapidity of the improvisation of order out of chaos" and "the universal equanimity." As an example of the latter he cited the efforts of "two citizens, lovers of his work" (unidentified by James) who went all about in an effort to save as many as possible of the landscapes of William Keith and then conveyed the good news to the artist, who, thinking that all was lost, had started painting again in his studio. The following Thursday, 18 May, James lectured about the convulsion at the Graduate Club.[36]

Apparently, Keith came to his studio at 424 Pine Street the morning of the earthquake, only to be turned away by police and the fire, after which he returned across the bay to Berkeley, where in his home at 2207 Atherton Street (replaced by the University's Edwards Field and Stadium in 1931) he began painting, losing only ninety minutes of work in the process, he said. Even though a large part of of his oeuvre, some 2,000 canvases, was lost,

Keith did not look back. A mutual friend of Keith's and Muir's, Charles Keeler, who was part of the city's relief effort, wrote an account of the catastrophe in which he applauded the artist's indomitable spirit.[37]

Even though James was in Muir territory from January through April 1906, it is unlikely that the two met. On the birthday of Robert Burns, 26 January, Muir at home paused to reflect on the great bard's "inspiring genius derived from heaven."[38] Mostly, however, Muir was in Adamana—then (but no longer) a Santa Fe Railroad stop—in east-central Arizona, nurturing his daughters: Helen, who was suffering from pneumonia, and Wanda, who was watching over her sister. Here Muir delighted in the discoveries he and Helen made while roaming about the nearby petrified forest. He kept an eye out for golden eagles, too, for the previous August he had spied one of their nests atop an "inaccessible residual capped pinnacle," and commented, "This bird a good judge of nest sites."[39] After the earthquake, he returned to Martinez to assess domestic damage—fortunately, little. He then oversaw the repair of the crumbled chimneys. The library, bank and Bergamini buildings in Martinez were "badly wrecked," he reported.[40]

Muir spent much of May and June in Berkeley. He visited with William Keith at 2207 Atherton Street, on the southwestern edge of the University of California, and they took walks together into the hill country. Keith, Muir wrote his daughters, was "busy accomplishing another pile of painting equal in size to the 2000 ones he lost & better in quality." Sometimes Muir stayed with his poet friend Charles Keeler and his artist wife Louise Mapes Bunnell and their three children. They lived just north of campus on Ridge Road and Highland Place, in a rustic hillside cottage of redwood (1895), the first private commission of architect Bernard Maybeck, who also had designed their studio (1902) next door. Both structures reflect the Keelers' simple-life philosophy, which Charles put forth in *The Simple Home*. Both remain: the home has been converted to condominiums and the studio is a private residence. After a short walk (five minutes, Muir wrote) from Keelers' to the UC library—the earthquake had delayed construction of the new Doe Memorial Library—Muir studied from nine to five, with a pleasant interlude of an hour or so of conversation with UC and visiting professors over lunch at the Faculty Club (1899), also the work of Bernard Maybeck.[41] Its style is now classified as First Bay Tradition.

Muir was researching the ancient plants of the petrified forest about Adamana, particularly the genera *Sigillaria* and *Lepidodendron*, the tall treelike evergreens of the Carboniferous period. Six months after signing the Preservation of American Antiquities Act on 8 June 1906, President Roosevelt proclaimed the Petrified Forest inviolate.[42] In 1962 this became a National Park.

It was not until Saturday, 9 June, that Muir traveled to Palo Alto to use Stanford's library—long after James's departure. That day he also took a carriage ride about campus with Charles Keeler, dined with Henry Winchester Rolfe, professor of Greek, and visited with Melville Best Anderson, professor of English Literature, and his wife Charlena Van Vleck. Undoubtedly, Anderson told Muir about the Founder's Day celebration three months earlier—when William James had addressed the theme of "Stanford's Ideal Destiny"—and gave Muir his impressions of the pragmatist.[43] After Wanda's wedding to Thomas Hanna on Friday, 20 June, Muir started for Adamana with a box of oranges for Helen. The newlyweds took a Sierra honeymoon.[44]

Muir and James had in common a high regard for mountains. Though James was not a joiner of clubs—not a member of the Appalachian or Sierra or American Alpine clubs—he sought out his beloved Adirondack and White mountains with the devotion and regularity of a pilgrim going to Mecca. They provided relief from his academic life, and renewal for his spirits.[45]

James, familiar with the northern Appalachians, had experienced also their southern counterparts, from where Muir had returned on 14 October 1898. Their journeys are intriguingly parallel. After attending James Russell Lowell's funeral on Friday noon of 14 August 1891, James had headed south by train. Sunday evening he had booked into the Battery Park Hotel, which sat atop the highest hill in Asheville, North Carolina. (The hotel was razed in 1924, and the hill leveled.) From his bedroom and the piazzas, he exulted over the alpine panorama. "The tone of this house is charmingly quiet," he wrote his wife Monday night, after a ramble up an unidentified hill about three miles distant. Tuesday and Wednesday he was engaged in a trip to the apex of the Appalachians, Mount Mitchell (6,684 feet), about forty miles northeast of Asheville. "The walk up Mitchell's peak is the most beautiful forest walk (only five hours) I ever made," he reported glowingly to a newspaper. Friday he entrained for the Roan Mountain Station Hotel at 2,600 feet, arriving on the Johnson City and Cranberry Railroad—"perhaps the wildest and most romantic little narrow-gauge concern that the world contains." The next day, Saturday, 22 August, he ascended Roan Mountain (6,285 feet), which straddles the North Carolina-Tennessee border, and slept atop in the Cloudland Hotel (of which only a historic marker remains). A two-mule stage hauled him down on Sunday afternoon "in a shower of rain," and he continued by train east to Cranberry and from there south by stage to Linville, where he spent the night at the Esceola Inn. On Monday, 24 August, he climbed Grandfather Mountain (5,964 feet), with its manager, the mining engineer Hugh MacRae, who had come to Cranberry in July 1885, just after his graduation from MIT. Then east to Blowing Rock—James likened it to an "inland Mount Desert"—and from there to home.[46]

A month before this Cambridge visit, on 24 September 1898, Muir himself had been atop Roan Mountain, with Charles Sargent and William Canby. Canby wanted Muir to see the mountain he had loved for thirty years.[47] They had traveled west by surrey from Cranberry, North Carolina, "through the most beautiful deciduous forest I ever saw," Muir exclaimed, to Roan's summit (evidently not walking up)—a trip of eighteen miles in six and a half hours, Muir said. Like James before them, they too lodged in the Cloudland Hotel. After lunch, Muir relished exploring that high ridge, which was clotted with five-foot-tall rhododendrons. Northward, beyond Carver's Gap, Muir could see the beautiful balds—Round (5,826 feet), Jane (5,807 feet), and Grassy Ridge (6,189 feet)—their invitingly open, gently rounded meadow summits. "I can walk ten miles without great weariness," he wrote his wife, "this air has healed me" (He had become sick on his train ride east, on 16 September). Now, the highest elevation he ever attained in the eastern United States revived him.[48]

The next day, Sunday, 25 September, en route from Roan back eastward to Blowing Rock—a drive Muir acknowledged as "the finest in America of its kind"—the trio of naturalists stopped to climb Grandfather Mountain, 5,964 feet up in the bonny Blue Ridge of North Carolina.[49] In the elevated atmosphere, John Muir at sixty was in ecstasy. He jumped up and down, singing, and reveling in the autumn light, while the younger Charles Sargent stood still and mute.

"Why don't you let yourself out at a sight like that?" Muir chided.

"I don't wear my heart upon my sleeve," Sargent retorted.

"Who cares where you wear your little heart, man?" Muir cried. "There you stand in the face of all Heaven come down on earth like a critic of the universe, as if to say, Come, Nature, bring on the best you have: I'm from BOSTON!"[50]

After Grandfather Mountain, they continued eastward to the Blowing Rock Hotel (which is no longer) for the night. On Monday, 26 September, they turned south to Lenoir, from where they took the late night train. They arrived in Asheville at 1:30 a.m. the next day, and checked into the Battery Park Hotel, "a big showy concern." Like James, Muir delighted in the mountainscape: "Mt Pisgah the highest & most mtn-like — a cone [drawing]," he entered in his journal.[51]

Muir's only contact with Pisgah was visual. He did not climb it, nor Mt. Mitchell, which James had been up, nor any other eminences here—on what was to be his last opportunity to do so. Instead, after a few hours' sleep that Tuesday, the 27th, the naturalists went off in a carriage to explore Biltmore, the estate of George W. Vanderbilt, which had opened to guests on Christmas Eve, 1895. The Vanderbilts were not home, however, and that may be why Muir did not stay there. That June in Paris, Vanderbilt had married Edith Stuyvesant Dresser of Newport, Rhode Island. Their European honeymoon lasted four months! The Biltmore guest book (which Muir did not sign) announced their homecoming on October first. Muir's memory is honored in Vanderbilt's fine library with his *My First Summer in the Sierra, The Story of My Boyhood and Youth, Our National Parks,* and *Stickeen.*[52]

Twelve years after his first visit, James returned to Asheville. This time he met the Vanderbilts at dinner on 31 March 1903, and took an afternoon drive about their place then and others later. He found it too "artificially civilized", as Muir had. "As for Vanderbilt's magnificent chateau and drives," he wrote Louie, "I soon tired of them."[53]

## DEPARTURE

Returning from visiting Jane Gray, Muir spent a "pleasant evening" with Allie and Walter Page—evidently staying overnight at their Cambridge home. They stayed in touch. Seven years later, in the spring of 1905, the Pages would be guests of the Muirs in Martinez, California.[54]

The next day, Wednesday, 26 October, was wet. At noon Muir was off from Boston to New York with Sargent, his daughter Molly, and Charles E. Stratton. As their train moved west through Worcester and the lustrous foliage of Massachusetts and Connecticut, Muir became further acquainted with Molly and Stratton, who along with John A. Pettigrew had shown him Boston's Franklin Park ten days ago.

Though snow was predicted, only rain fell in New York. They arrived after dark and slept at the Albermarle Hotel at Broadway and 24th Street, adjoining Madison Square. The following day, 27 October, was fair enough for sightseeing. After lunch Muir, Sargent, and Stratton took the cars north to Central Park. A "fine wilderness for town," Muir observed of the giant greensward within the country's largest city (of over three million people), "heartily appreciated by rich & poor." When Muir had arrived first in New York from Scotland in April 1849, there had been no Central Park. Nineteen years later, in March 1868, he had returned to Manhattan. Though he wandered about, he did not go far beyond the harbor of his "little schooner home. I saw the name of Central Park on some of the street-cars and thought I would like to visit it, but, fearing that I might not be able to find my way back, I dared not make the adventure." This reaction from the man who had just walked through the wild, montane, Reconstruction South. When Johnson first showed Central Park to Muir, on the afternoon of 31 May 1893, Muir was astounded to find there "one of the grandest pages of glacial history I ever saw outside of the Sierra."[55]

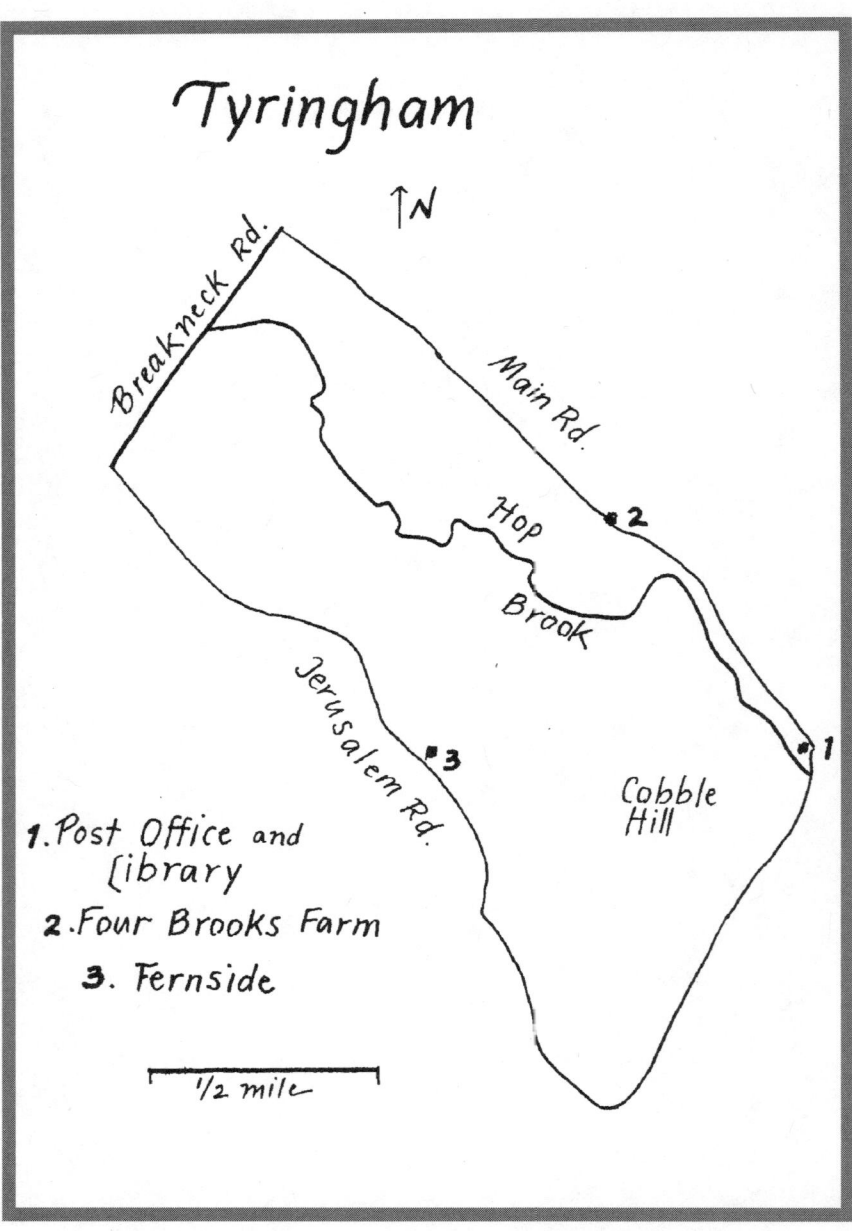

# Tyringham

↑N

Breakneck Rd.

Main Rd.

Hop

Brook

• 2

Jerusalem Rd.

• 3

• 1

Cobble
Hill

1. Post Office and
   Library
2. Four Brooks Farm
3. Fernside

½ mile

# 13. THE BERKSHIRES

*I wish I could be more moderate in my desires*
*but I cannot, & so there is no rest.*
—John Muir to Daniel Muir, 1 September 1867

*Never while I live will this mountain love die.*
—John Muir to Louie Muir, 12 August 1885

## SATURDAY, 29 OCTOBER 1898:
## LEE, MASSACHUSETTS

"Colors of foliage fading[,] yet grand in mass - brown red & good deal of yellow. all the hills feathered to top," John Muir wrote in his journal.[1] From his train window, he absorbed autumn in the Berkshire Hills of western Massachusetts for the first time.

Richard Watson Gilder rode with Muir. They had departed New York at nine this morning on the New York, New Haven & Hartford Railroad, bound for the Gilders' country home. Muir was sixty; Gilder, fifty-four. Neither had graduated from college, yet both held honorary degrees from Harvard and both appeared in the first edition of *Who's Who in America*, for 1899-1900.

"Charming," Muir had found Gilder when they first met five years ago in New York. A lean, handsome man with penetrating dark brown eyes and flowing reindeer lichen mustache, Gilder had been editor of *The Century Magazine* since 1881 and assistant editor of its predecessor, *Scribner's Monthly*, through the seventies. Both magazines had featured Muir, beginning in an 1878 issue of *Scribner's* with his evocation of his darling water ouzel and continuing to his oft-told dog story in the September 1897 number. Gilder had brought *The Century* to the pinnacle of periodicals in America. Its brilliant series on the Civil War through the eyes of the participants expanded its readers to a quarter million.[2]

At two that afternoon, their train stopped in Lee, Massachusetts, population 3,596. The 1893 railroad station has been the Sullivan Restaurant since 1981. When I entered, on 18 June 1989, Sunday brunch was being served in the former lobby. Daniel and Marilyn Sullivan had painstakingly restored the yellow pine wainscoting and walnut trim. A family ate around a table that sat atop the old bank safe of Western Union. Through the ticket booth, light-hearted banter emanated from the pub, where, even before noon, the six-teen-foot oak and mahogany bar was crowded. Rectangular rear windows framed the tracks and cars of the Berkshire Scenic Railway, which disap-pointingly was not operating, due to right-of-way and insurance issues. The closest active station is Pittsfield, nine miles north, served by Amtrak on its run between Springfield and Albany.[3]

Across the street a huge building sat on stilts. Two floors, eight windows, and boarded doors were visible from the front; a side profile revealed a third floor. This was St. Mary's School, built in 1885—donor, Jane Sedgewick of Stockbridge; architect, James Murphy of Springfield; teachers, Sisters of St. Joseph of Chambery, France. "There are still two nuns of that order," Joe Toole explained. His business, Lawrence Toole Insurance Company, resided next door in a mint-condition eclectic house—a mix of Colonial, Greek Revival, and Victorian styles—that dated to 1907. "I bought it [St. Mary's] for one dollar from the bishop," he told me. "I had it moved a month ago from behind the church for $50,000." He pointed across Main Street. "I hate to see old buildings torn down." He intended to restore and lease it.

Helena de Kay Gilder met her husband's train at Lee station. In 1872, the writer Helen Maria Fiske Hunt Jackson had introduced Helena de Kay, then a painting student at the Cooper Institute in New York, to Richard Gilder. Two years later, on 3 June 1874, they were married. Helen Hunt Jackson's wedding present was her sonnet "To Them That Do Rejoice." Gilder pub-lished Jackson's poetry and prose in *Scribner's* and the *Century*. Emerson car-ried her odes with him. A train conversation with Emerson inspired her hymn

*Midway in summer, face to face, a king
I met. No king so gentle and so wise.*[4]

Jackson longed to meet Muir, whom she knew through his writings and their mutual friend, Jeanne Carr, at whose Pasadena, California, home she had stayed. When in Yosemite Valley for eight days in late June of 1872, she had somehow missed him. Lodging at James M. Hutchings's cottage by the river, with Yosemite Falls framed in its back windows, she and Sarah Woolsey of Newport, Rhode Island, who at thirty-seven was four years younger than Jackson, made horseback excursions. Another Scotsman, John L. Murphy, guided them. They rode up beside Vernal and Nevada falls—whose native names of Pi-wy-ack ("white water" or "shower of shining crystals") and Yo-we-hi ("the twisting" or "the meandering"), she preferred for their veracity. Overnighting at "Mr. Snow's little inn" between the great cascades, which she described vividly, they proceeded to Little Yosemite Valley before returning. Another day, they went up to Glacier and Sentinel points. The next day, their last, Jackson and Murphy—Woolsey chose to go by the way they had previously come—left the valley via a new trail up Indian Canyon, which proved to be incomplete, then found the Mono Trail and headed west, reaching Gentry's in darkness, Jackson's esteem for Murphy reaching new heights.[5]

Like Muir, she had a penchant for places, domestic and foreign. Her admiration for Robert Burns, Muir's favorite poet, motivated her pilgrimage to the hilly lowlands of Scotland in 1880. She visited the places associated with Burns: the farmer's cottage where the poet was born on 25 January 1759, two miles south of Ayr on the Firth of Clyde; the farms in the parish of Tarbolton and Mossgiel, about three miles from the town of Tarbolton; and, a mile from Mossgiel, Mauchline, "the town of 'bonnie Jean.'" She even talked with two nieces of Burns. Finally, she drove through "the dingy, confused, and ugly streets of Dumfries," where the poet spent his last years, where he wrote "Auld Lang Syne" and "Ye Banks and Braes of Bonnie Doon." Though Muir was in Scotland for parts of July, August, and September 1893, even overnighted in Dumfries, he did not mention the bard, or going to other places associated with him, in letters home. Still, Muir must have been mindful of his presence as he crisscrossed the country.[6]

In June 1885 Jackson lay ill in San Francisco. Unable to walk, she wrote Muir requesting that he suggest an itinerary for a salutary sojourn for her spirit and her "cumbrous caravan" of eight horses, an ambulance, two camp wagons, phaeton, maid, doctor, and four servants. Aghast at her retinue, yet forever faithful to nature's healing power, Muir recommended that she circle Mt. Shasta, the acme of northern California's Cascade Range: "And think how glorious a center you would have!—so glorious and inspiring that I would gladly revolve there, weary, afoot, and alone for all eternity."[7]

"You are the only man in California who could tell me just what I needed to know," Jackson thanked Muir. But she never left San Francisco. Muir did come to see her. On Monday, 10 August, he rang the bell of 1600 Taylor Street. The blinds were drawn. There was no response. She died two days later, two months before her fifty-fifth birthday. That morning Muir honored Mt. Shasta for her: "Never while I live will this mountain love die."[8]

Jackson may have been remembered by Muir and the Gilders as they left Lee in 1898 in a phaeton. I followed them (18 June 1989) on foot from the railroad station down Main Street. So indelible was one of her poems from a grade school English class recitation that I sang out the first stanza:

*O suns and skies and clouds of June,*
*And flowers of June together,*
*Ye cannot rival for one hour*
*October's bright blue weather,*

## TYRINGHAM

"Let me welcome you," Helena Gilder said to Muir, as they entered Four Brooks Farm in Tyringham, five miles south of Lee. Helena was a skilled hostess, entertaining even Walt Whitman. She was a founding member of the Art Students League of New York in 1875 and had served as its women's vice president in 1879. Their New York residences—103 East 15th Street, a stable converted to a studio (sadly demolished) where the Society of American Artists was born in 1877; and (from 1888) 13 East 8th Street (also gone)—were veritable salons.[9]

The Gilders had first come to the Berkshires in 1893. They boarded at Riverside, two houses south of Four Brooks Farm, and at Hickory Farm, half a mile north. Four Brooks Farm, a two-and-half-story clapboard Federal dating to 1792, is now painted yellow. Its current owners are Gilder and Anne Palmer. Gilly, as he is commonly called, is a grandson of Richard Watson Gilder. They still refer to their home as the "Battle Place," after its original owner, Justus Battle.

My *WPA Guide* says that Gilder built Four Brooks Farm in 1898.[10] This is not correct. That year the Gilders bought the farm, and renovated it extensively—bathrooms installed, dormers and porch added, chimney and front attic stairs rebuilt. Evidently, it was completed sufficiently by mid-autumn to accommodate John Muir. Even so "1899 was our first full summer with guests at Four Brooks," Richard Gilder explained. "Mr. Cleveland being our first."[11]

Grover Cleveland, the 250-pound, forty-eight-year-old Democratic governor of New York, became the twenty-second president of the United States in 1885. That June a tall, attractive twenty-one-year-old, Frances Folsom, graduated from Wells College, in Aurora, New York. A year later, she married the president in the Blue Room of the White House. "The most charming woman seen in the Mansion since Dolly Madison," is one historian's assessment.[12] Mrs. Cleveland, elected a trustee of Wells College, returned for commencement on 22 June 1887. Richard Watson Gilder addressed the five happy graduates. Afterwards, Gilder escorted the First Lady to Washington, where he met the chief executive, thus beginning a friendship that lasted to Cleveland's death in June 1908.

The Gilders introduced the Clevelands to Marion, Massachusetts, on Buzzards Bay, where the Gilders recreated before discovering Tyringham. After staying two summers in Marion, the Clevelands purchased their own home, Gray Gables, on Marion's Monument Point, to which they came during the 1890s.

Gilly showed me a black and white photograph of Richard Watson Gilder and Grover Cleveland. It was probably taken in the summer of 1901, when the Clevelands stayed at Riverside in Tyringham. In the photograph, they are fishing in Goose Pond. Cleveland, facing center, is seated in the bow. He is wearing a pleated white linen shirt, bow tie, jacket, Swiss mountain hat, and placid expression. Nonchalantly, his fishing pole rests in his right hand, across his left thigh into starboard waters. In front of Cleveland, Gilder in striped shirt, suspenders, bow tie, and dress hat fishes the port side. They are two of the most composed, best attired fishermen you would ever see. "Mr. Cleveland was immoderate in only two things," Gilder wrote, "his desk-work and his fishing."[13]

Goose Pond is a mile-and-a-half walk north of Four Brooks Farm on George Cannon Road. The Appalachian Trail used to take this way past Four Brooks. Gilly, a former Colorado Outward Bound School instructor, always enjoyed meeting the hikers, who, I doubt, never suspected that one of America's foremost alpinists had slept here. Now the A.T. stays in the woods west of Four Brooks Farm—woods Muir explored, discovering "acres of Kalmia 2 to 6 ft high." Today lanes of mountain laurel, *Kalmia latifolia*, line the A.T., some of these evergreen shrubs over six feet. Their pink and white blossoms beautify the Berkshires between the 11th and 24th of June, 1989.

Muir, then, not Cleveland, holds the honor of being the first guest at Four Brooks Farm. The guest book Gilly showed me began on 27 May 1899 with Grover Cleveland, of Princeton, New Jersey (where the ex-president lived), and did not contain Muir's signature.[14] But a more significant legacy links the two men. Cleveland deserves the accolade for creating 21.4 million acres of forest reserve in the final days of his latter administration. This was the recommendation of the National Forestry Commission, headed by Charles Sargent, with consultation from John Muir.

During his 1898 Four Brooks weekend, Muir enjoyed not only the local countryside, but his hosts' family. "The two little girls make fine love stir," Muir commented in his journal. He referred to the youngest of the Gilder clan: Rosamond, seven, and Francesca, ten next month. Their eldest daughter, Dorothea, then sixteen, was in school in New York, studying geometry and Ovid. Their two sons were also absent. Rodman de Kay, at twenty-one, was completing his last year at Harvard. George de Kay, who would celebrate his thirteenth birthday in five days, was at Milton Academy, in Milton, Massachusetts. Their first-born, Marion, had died in her first year.[15]

Muir had no idea that Rosamond would become a renowned drama critic, editor of *Theatre Arts* and author of *Enter the Actress: First Women in the Theatre* (1931); that Francesca would marry Walter Walker Palmer, professor of Medicine at Columbia University, with whom she would raise Gilder Palmer, my host. Gilly's mother, along with his maternal grandparents, met John Muir.

After lunch, Muir and Gilder strolled along a stream banked with huge willows. It was "full of trout, many small rapids, birch, alder etc.," Muir reported to his journal. He found the "rather swift" stream "about 20 to 30 ft wide. 2 to 4 ft deep. current av[era]g[e] about 3 m[ile]s an hr. Fine meadow. wonderfull [sic] richness of grass. provides more wool & mutton, milk & beef than almost any other equal area I know of. Yet the country in gen[eral] is full of abandoned farms, some that a doz[en] or two y[ea]rs ago sold for $10,000 are now offered for 2000. Inhabitants going to towns to work in factories stores etc seeking fortunes they know not how. Look down on labor. Sweet hard independence bringing labor, health, manhood, all given away for the sake of something beyond their reach & wh[ich] even if attained would be found far less desirable by any sane person than the home farm life they despise."[16]

This is Hop Brook. I have slept well under a huge white pine, amid hemlocks, braided streams flowing into my dreams. In the early morning, I retrace the Appalachian Trail across Tyringham vale, which Hop Brook drains northward four miles into the Housatonic River, which flows south and east some hundred miles to Long Island Sound. This wetland, bibulous with June's copious rains, quickly soaks my feet. Haying will begin as soon as these fields are dry. Three dark blue silos penetrate fog. Horses graze a knoll. A white-tailed deer leaps through mist, curiously rocking to assure her footing among tussocks. Thrush melody floats from the woods. Redwings sound alarm at my trespass. Ovenbirds chide. Other voices I don't recognize, enrich the moment. Spider strings, spun during darkness, reflect dawn, dew, delight across my path. Large blue flag, *Iris versicolor*, blooms abundantly among green grasses. I go from flower to flower, drinking their delicate design, their purple passion. Why not beauty for breakfast? Though I have walked the entire Appalachian Trail in Massachusetts, nowhere have I been more nourished than here.

As I did not see any fish in Hop Brook, I suspected that there might be no native trout left. Perhaps Grover Cleveland caught them all? Anthony A. Gola, a game manager of the Massachusetts Division of Fisheries and Wildlife, which protects the north end of Hop Brook, confirmed my suspicion. The trout—rainbow, brown, and Eastern brook—must be stocked twice each April, he told me. Bridled minnow, black and longnosed dace, white sucker, common shiner, and slimy sculpin, however, are endemic.

"In Muir's day, the Cobble was covered with sheep," Gilly remarked, as we stared from his front yard across Main Road and Hop Brook at a low, rounded hill, rising four hundred feet above the valley (Muir estimated its height at five to six hundred feet). In 1963, Gilly's mother, Edward N. Perkins, and Dr. Rustin McIntosh gave this landform to the Trustees of Reservations for protection.[17] "I'll put sixty head of beef over there soon," Gilly asserted of the lowland beyond the road and in front of the Cobble. "They will keep things open," he said.

As we explored the Cobble, I noted that there was plenty for a herd of cattle to digest. Juniper, red clover, barberry, hawkweed, vetch, steeplebush, milkweed, thyme, buttercup, raspberry, meadowsweet, goldenrod, and ferns fill the slope. Among the birds, towhees are the most vocal, goldfinches the most active, and cedar waxwings the most startling—we saw a dozen at once. Gilly and Anne love Cobble birds and wildflowers, though he admitted, "She's a better birder than I am." To the summit ran stone walls and a forest of sugar maple, white pine, white birch, white ash, cherry, red oak, basswood, butternut, and Eastern hornbeam. The open east face offered a fine view of the hamlet and Four Brooks Farm.

Gilly told me about Cobble Runs. He has half a dozen T-shirts from them. This year's, the seventh annual, was canceled—preempted by Tyringham's 250th anniversary parade, scheduled to form at Four Brooks Farm on Saturday, 5 August 1989, as it had in 1939 for the town's bicentennial. "There are sixty-three entries." Gilly talked excitedly of the various moving displays and performances. "I don't know where we'll put them all." I sensed that the parade could not be in better hands.

Muir relished their Cobble communion. His educated eyes examined the landscape: "The hill trends in gen[eral] show that the ice sheet flowed S. Easterly[.] The sheer broken cliff-faces on the mountoneed [sic] rocks, tell this came & on the quartz veins weathered out to height of 2 or 3 inches a few spots are polished & striated & these stria also indicate the S. E[aster]ly flow of this portion of the bottom of the gl[acial] sheet[.]"[18]

Their Cobble consort inspired Gilder's merry muse:

> *Muir, of Alaska,*
> *Path-finder, cliff-basker,*
> *Known of bird, known of deer,*
> *(Grizzlies know him, won't harm,)*
> *John Muir has been here,*
> *And has hitched to the farm*
> *A great blanket glacier!*
> ...
> *"This giant of eld!*
> *See his path," said John Muir,—*
> *"Here it held*
> *North-west to south-east;*
> *Slow and sure,*
> *Like a king at a feast*
> *Eating down through the list;*
> *Inch by inch, crunch by crunch;*
> *Yonder hollow his lunch,*
> *Of this valley—one gobble,—*
> *Then he supped light on Cobble!...*[19]

Though "A Letter from the Farm" originated then, Gilder did not share it with Muir until a year later, having "added to it a bit since" he wrote. The recipient responded immediately, "Thanks for the rime of the ancient ice farmer. It is very funny, but you could and should write something better in dead glacial earnest."[20]

Gilly and I return to the farmhouse. Sitting on the divan in front of the coffee table and fireplace, Anne's grand piano behind us with music of Mozart, I look at a copy of Gilder's complete *Poems* that Gilly takes from the bookshelf. "A Letter from the Farm" appears here, with minor changes from the hand written copy sent Muir ninety-one years ago. According to *The Oxford Companion to American Literature*, the best of Gilder's sixteen volumes of poetry is his first, *The New Day* (1875), "a cycle of love sonnets," which Helena illustrated.[21] The *Century* is also here.

## CECILIA BEAUX

Above the mantel, Richard Watson Gilder looks down on us from an oil portrait painted by Cecilia Beaux in New York in 1902. Beaux was born in Philadelphia in 1855, and at the time of Muir's visit, was living there and teaching drawing and painting at the Pennsylvania Academy. In the second week of October 1898, she had been at Four Brooks Farm, painting a portrait of Dorothea Gilder, who took a week off from school to sit for her. Beaux, then, was an earlier visitor than Muir, though she had come to work. Had their stays coincided Muir might have been a Beaux subject. At the World's Fair in Chicago in 1893, Muir may have seen her portraits. Those on display at the Fair included the acclaimed *Les derniers jours d'enfance*, of Beaux's older sister Etta Drinker with her first-born, Harry, on her knee.[22]

Beaux was introduced to the Gilders in New York, where she attended their famous Friday evening salons, and even lived a winter in their house. "Richard was dynamic," she reflected; "Helena, contemplative." Together they were "phenomenal." Through them she made several significant friendships. Many mornings of her summer long visits at Four Brooks she walked the woods upon Mountain Hill. After the Gilders provided an old tobacco barn for her studio, adding a long, large window that opened onto an orchard, she wandered less. "Tyringham Valley is a realized version of the Twenty-Third Psalm," she felt.[23]

## FERNSIDE SHAKERS

Cecilia Beaux painted Gilder in a black Shaker cape, a common dress for him. Shaker furniture enriches this house. No doubt, Gilder pointed out to Muir the former Shaker community across Tyringham Valley—past his barns in the meadow, which Gilder removed in 1907 to improve the view. No Shakers were there then. The last ones had departed twenty-four years earlier, in

1874. Many went to Hancock, a twenty-mile journey to the northwest. The Tyringham settlement was purchased by Dr. Joseph Jones, who named it Fernside.

On the late Sunday afternoon of 18 June 1989, I walk from Four Brooks Farm to Fernside. Heading north on Main Road, I stop first at Hickory Farm, which is now owned by Gilly's brother, Walter de Kay Palmer, a financial consultant to small businesses, and formerly a vice president of Chase International Investment Corporation, New York. His daughter Helena greets me; her father is not at home. She is loading her car in preparation for returning to Cambridge tonight. She has Richard Watson Gilder's engaging dark eyes and Helena Gilder's pleasing hospitality. She welcomes me as family. A Harvard graduate in comparative literature in 1985, she now directs a home for mentally retarded adults in Lowell. Graciously, she gives me a tour of Hickory Farm. She shows me a painting of Four Brooks Farm by her father, a set of the *Century*, and a diary that reads: "From 1895 to 1922 Frederick M. Moore owned Hickory and Nellie Moore Fuller (1859-1941) lived there and ran a summer boarding house similar to her father's (L. B. Moore) at Riverside."

The diary is the gift of Cornelia Gilder, "who lives in the first red house on the left north of here," Helena explains, "with her husband George." She has clipped an article by him from the business section of today's *New York Times*, "Forget HDTV: It's Already Outmoded." "He's also written *Wealth and Poverty* and *Men and Marriage*," Helena explains.[24]

After passing the empty house of Cornelia and George Gilder, I turn left on Meadow Road, which Hop Brook crosses as it runs through this beautiful valley. At the next turn, I trend southward for over two miles to Fernside, the home of the Kramers, who are having a party. Virginia creeper on the front of their handsome brick Federal, once the Shaker elder's house, almost obscures the 1823 datestone above the open front door. Chatter and laughter animate the screen porch on the north side. Beyond, a guest strolls the lawn where once the Shaker Seed Company thrived. Here until 1874 beet, onion, parsnip, carrot, turnip, radish, tomato, asparagus, lettuce, cabbage, parsley, cucumber, squash, and muskmelon seeds were dried, packaged, labeled, and shipped throughout the Northeast, returning revenue and reputation to the Shakers.[25]

In early September 1854, tall, slender, sixteen-year-old Ellen Emerson visited the Tyringham Shakers with her classmates from Mrs. Charles Sedgwick's School for Girls in Lenox village. Their higher purpose seems to have been no less a delight than tasting the celebrated Shaker "sugar-nuts"—meats of shagbark hickories encrusted with maple syrup. The shop being sold out of sugar-nuts that day, they were placated by maple sugar, pears, candied flag-root and the charming Sister Desire— "about fifty," Ellen thought, "but still very pretty"—who graciously attended to the desires of her young partrons.[26]

Twelve years earlier, in September 1842, Ellen's father and his friend Nathaniel Hawthorne had visited the Shakers at Harvard, Massachusetts, walking from Concord and back. Emerson declined involvement in the utopian communities of his day; Hawthorne had lived with other Transcendentalists at Brook Farm for a year before deciding it was not for him. Thoreau was clear where he stood on the matter: "I think I had rather keep batchelor's hall in hell than go to board in heaven."[27] Muir never partic-ipated in such communities either, though his Martinez home sometimes appeared like one when it spilled over with family and friends.

South of the house stands the Shaker hay and cattle barn (c.1800), which still serves the same purpose. Across the road is the remainder of the village: the circa 1834 clapboard cobbler's cottage and two two-and-a-half-story Federals: the dwelling house that consisted of dormitory, dining room, and kitchen (1800) in front of the workshop (1833-1834). Finding these buildings still in use as residences, not museums, is gratifying.

## MARK TWAIN, IRMA CLARK, AND JEAN WEBSTER

On 7 June 1904, a bereft Mark Twain wrote the Gilders from Florence, Italy, for a favor. The *Century* had published portions of *Adventures of Huckleberry Finn* and *A Connecticut Yankee in King Arthur's Court* and serialized completely *Pudd'nhead Wilson*. The previous summer, the Gilders had chap-eroned the Twains' daughter Clara at Four Brooks Farm. Could he find "shelter near their summer home?"[28] Two days earlier his thirty-four-year marriage had ended with Livy's death.

After sailing home and burying Livy in her native Elmira, New York, Twain and his daughters Jean and Clara came to Tyringham on 14 July. They stayed at Glencote, next to the Gilders. Twain tried to write, but mostly sat on the piazza smoking his pipe and letting in the solace of the surrounding country to ease his grieving heart. Each morning Gilder and Twain, with Jean's St. Bernard, Prosper, walked to the post office.[29] In October the Twains departed for New York, where they resided at 21 Fifth Avenue, close that winter to the Gilders.

The post office then was located in the general store, a building that remains as a private residence. Now it is difficult to buy anything in Tyringham except stamps. There are no malls, gas stations, or fast-food franchises. Shopping happens in Lee.

The post office is now across the street from the former general store, in the southwest corner of the library, a 1902, field stone edifice with an ocher tile roof. It is the Tyringham meeting place—the common ground where villagers join spontaneously in the giving and receiving of words. Elsewhere coffeehouses and general stores fill this service. Here both letters and relationships are opened.

"I need a lift today and what's in my box won't do it," a patron groans. Another is happy: "O, my income tax return has arrived." "It was forty-four at my place this morning" [12 June 1989], reports postmistress Irma Clark to a customer. Someone tells her what the minister said in church. Another discloses their travel plans to her: "John will lecture in Finland. We'll take a side trip to Leningrad. Next year he'll be in Japan. We were in Australia; John loved New Zealand."

Irma Clark has lived in Tyringham forty-six years. Just before her eighteenth birthday, she moved here from Lee, where her father, Charles (Anglicized from Carlo) Laurenti still lives at ninety-six. When Muir came here, Laurenti was five years old and living in his native Italy. He did not come to the United States until his late teens. Irma's marriage to a logger and truck driver, Wilbur Clark Jr., brought her to Tyringham. Together they raised three children. Duffy, as everyone called him, who was born in Beartown Mountain in 1920, died of cancer in 1982.

"I'm not supposed to let anyone into the library through the post office," Irma Clark whispers, as she admits me. The library is only open Tuesday afternoons. Irma used to be the librarian; now her daughter-in-law holds that position. A large stone fireplace forms the common wall with the post office. *The Berkshire Cottages: A Vanishing Era*, by Carole Owens, lies on the reading table. Shelves of books, none by Muir, block the sunlight from the windows.

I look for Mark Twain. My *WPA Guide* informs me that he presented the library with a set of his complete works. They are not in the card catalogue. I try Samuel Clemens. Nothing. They are not in the stacks, either; nor in the lofts at both ends, which I search with my flashlight, discovering a carton full of *Tyringham: Old and New/Old Home Week Souvenir, August 7-13, 1905*. Someone must be collecting Twain.

Searching in the history room of the library, I find the works of a grandniece of Mark Twain, Jean Webster. In the fall of 1898, she was a sophomore at Vassar College in Poughkeepsie, New York, a small town about fifty-five miles southwest of here that Muir had passed two years ago on his Hudson River cruise to see John Burroughs (see chapter 5). When she came to Tyringham in the summer of 1911, she boarded at Orchard House, which still stands between the library and Four Brooks Farms. Here she wrote *Daddy-Long-Legs* (1912), a novel that made her famous. In Clarence White's black-and-white photographic portrait, her captivating gaze over her left shoulder is alert, refined, and soft, almost dreamy. She projects an aura of both introspection and presence in the world that simultaneously conceals and reveals her essence.[30]

Even Irma has not seen Mark Twain's books. "Edward Perkins might know," she suggests. When he comes for his mail, she introduces him—a retired New York attorney and owner of Glencote, where Twain stayed. When I ask him about the mystery of the missing volumes he responds excitedly: "Mark Twain gave his books, an autographed set no less, to Herbert Moore, Gilder's superintendent. I saw them in the bookcase at Glencote. As far as I know Moore didn't give them to the library. I'd love to know where they are." Clinton Elliott, director of the Tyringham Historical Commission, of which Irma is also a member, does not have any leads, either.

"There are a couple of hikers," Irma signals, pointing out the window at two men seated on the lawn alongside Hop Brook, beneath the shade of a huge willow. They are eating sandwiches. "I must get their signatures in the register." Irma exits through the screen door with a book that contains names from as early as July, 1980. They are walking the Appalachian Trail from Sheffield to Williamstown, about sixty-two miles in four days. Goose Pond tonight, Dalton tomorrow, then Greylock.

"You can leave it in the lobby," Irma instructs them. "I'm going to lunch." It's 11:06 a.m. Though the lobby remains open, the counter closes until four, when Irma returns for ninety minutes. "I take a long lunch hour," she smiles, turning to her car.

## SUNDAY, 30 OCTOBER 1898: STOCKBRIDGE

While Helena stayed with daughters Rosamond and Francesca, Gilder and Muir drove west through the countryside of the Housatonic River. Six miles later they came to Stockbridge, a hamlet of about two thousand persons with many maples and elms shading the streets. "The American elm I cannot prefer to the English," wrote British critic Matthew Arnold in July 1886, from Laurel Cottage, the Stockbridge home of his daughter Lucy and her husband Frederick Whitridge; "but still I admire it extremely."[31] Muir knew both species, which are virtually similar to the common eye. From his tours of Boston and Cambridge, where they were popular on thoroughfares, he became acquainted with the native variety. In the Royal Botanic Gardens in Kew, on 29 August 1893, he strolled along the flood plain of the River Thames with the garden director, Sir Joseph Dalton Hooker, in the shade of English elms.[32]

Stockbridge's 1893 depot survives as a restaurant. The Red Lion Inn, a landmark since 1773, had been rebuilt since fire devastated it in 1896. On its veranda guests relaxed, conversed, and perused the *New York Times*, as they still do today. Granted it was a thinner—twenty-four pages—and cheaper—five cents—Sunday *Times* than today's; yet it contained the very rationale for peace that became all too familiar through the next century: "if the mass of the people realized the immense amount of good things of life which could be bought with the $800,000,000 the armies of Europe cost every year, there would be an imperious popular demand for the stoppage of the military expense."[33]

From the Red Lion Inn, at the center of town, they turned north and climbed Prospect Hill for three quarters of a mile. They pulled up in front of a Norman-style gabled mansion with brick front, shingled back, and twenty-six rooms, the design of Stanford White in 1886. *Naumkeag*, meaning "Place of Rest," was the summer cottage of Joseph Hodges Choate and his wife Caroline Dutcher Sterling Choate. They had been married for thirty-seven years and had five children. The losses of their oldest son Ruluff in 1884 and of their first daughter Josephine in 1896 to death, and of their second son George to a sanitarium, left them bereft. Joseph Hodges Jr., now twenty-two, had followed his father to Harvard, from where he graduated in 1897, and to Harvard Law School, where he was in his second year. Mabel, at twenty-eight, lived at home. She had benefited greatly from her mother's summer art classes, and would put that experience to good use in the landscaping of this place. On the train ride the day before from New York, Muir had had a long talk, an hour or two, with the august attorney Joseph Choate.[34]

Again Muir's reputation had preceded him. Three years earlier, in October 1895, as part of a month's vacation in the Berkshires, Robert Underwood Johnson had spent a week at Naumkeag, his family having stayed in New York. On that occasion he had consulted the good lawyer about California's recession of Yosemite Valley to the federal government, and given the Choates a copy of Muir's *The Mountains of California*.[35]

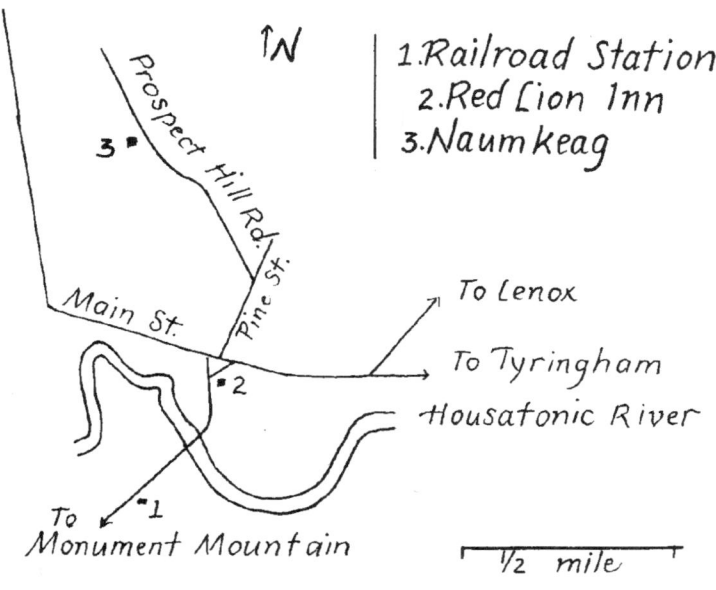

# Stockbridge

↑N

1. Railroad Station
2. Red Lion Inn
3. Naumkeag

Prospect Hill Rd.

3

Main St.

Pine St.

To Lenox

To Tyringham

Housatonic River

To
Monument Mountain

2

1

½ mile

After entering the manse, they walked through the hallway to the porch at the other end. From there they beheld the forty-nine-acre estate of gardens, fields, and woods, extending down Prospect Hill to Stockbridge's Main Street. The Taconic Mountains ennobled the western horizon; the isolated Monument Mountain (1,750 feet) lay three miles south. Its three-mile length, stretched north to south along the east side of the Housatonic River, is now covered with maples (striped, sugar, and red), pines (red, white, and pitch), witch hazel, oak, hemlock, paper birch, and mountain laurel. It had been celebrated in poetry by William Cullen Bryant in 1824, in literary history by the 5 August 1850 meeting of Herman Melville, Nathaniel Hawthorne, and Oliver Wendell Holmes, and in paintings by Asher B. Durand and others.[36] The next fall, on 19 October 1899, Rosalie Butler would give Monument Mountain to the Trustees of Reservations.

Sixty years later, in 1959, the Trustees of Reservations also received Naumkeag, from Mabel Choate. Since they have opened it to the public, you are now able to follow Muir's footsteps. What you see outside is largely Mabel Choate's vision and that of Boston landscape architect Fletcher Steele, whom she met in July 1926 when he lectured at the Lenox, Massachusetts, Garden Club. Together they created these pastoral surroundings pregnant with Japanese holly, white oak, birch, and ginkgo; it was a partnership that lasted until her death in 1958. "Naumkeag is now a work of art," she wrote Steele in 1950, "Thanks to you."[37] Muir and Gilder were toured about the grounds, through the arborvitae and linden allées, the latter laid out by Caroline Choate, and around the circular pool of the evergreen garden.

Later, they were escorted into Naumkeag's mahogany dining room, from where they could see the mountains. Warmed by a robust fire, they sat in Queen Anne chairs around a Queen Anne table spread with viands from Naumkeag's farm, dairy, and greenhouse, and served by butlers from the adjacent kitchen. Muir's talks on glaciers and forests were appreciated by Choate, a trustee of the American Museum of Natural History in New York. After dinner they adjourned to the library, where Muir's *Mountains of California* and other writings were discussed.

Though Naumkeag offered ten bedrooms, Muir and Gilder returned to Four Brooks Farm for the night. Thereby they forwent the customary breakfast in bed, an indulgence that Muir soon had elsewhere. After Tyringham, while staying at the country home of paleontologist Henry Fairfield Osborn, "Wing-and-Wing," at Garrison on the Hudson River, Muir experienced a bed "so soft and fine I like to lie awake to enjoy it, instead of sleeping. A servant brings in a cup of coffee before I rise."[38]

When Muir said good-bye to the Choates it was for the last time. On 22 February 1899, they sailed for England, Joseph Choate having been appointed ambassador to the Court of St. James's by President William McKinley. In May, Muir joined the Harriman Expedition to Alaska. In February 1900, Richard and Helena Gilder, while ensconced at Morley's Hotel, Trafalgar Square, London, visited Choate. On the eve of his world tour, 28 May 1903, Muir dined with the Gilders in New York. Later, in London, Muir walked through St. James's and Hyde parks and the Royal Botanic Gardens at Kew, and saw the Lady Wallace Gallery, British Museum and Library, Westminster Abbey, Zoo, but evidently not the Choates, who were in London until 1905.[39]

## MONDAY, 31 OCTOBER 1898: TYRINGHAM

The next morning, Muir and Gilder walked south on Main Road. They stopped at Marshall Steadman's shop alongside Hop Brook. The Steadmans had been producing rakes in Tyringham for seventy-two years. Their rakes with Berkshire white ash handles and shagbark hickory bows (made without steaming) and teeth—lathes shaped heads and tails, as the bows were called, while another machine tapered the teeth—were nonpareil.

"[I] could make rakes at 1/2 cost of those made here," Muir confided to his journal. His boast was not idle. He, too, had been a rake maker. In the employ of William H. Trout on Nottawasaga Bay in Meaford, Ontario, from 1864 to 1866, Muir, then in his late twenties, had made some six thousand rakes and thirty thousand broom handles. This achievement attested to his inventive genius, which led to machines "for making rake-teeth, and another for boring for them and driving them, and still another for making the bows, still another used in making the handles, still another for bending them." Soon after he wrote this, the factory was a smoldering ruin in a 1 March blizzard. By the spring of 1866 Muir had been among machines again, this time in Indianapolis.[40]

Unable to find Steadman's Shop, I asked Irma Clark. "It burned in 1978," she told me right off, "They were making only hockey sticks and ladder rungs then. The firehouse is there now."[41] Wanting to see how rakes are made, I was disappointed. "Are there any rakes in town?" I asked her. Fortunately, she had had the foresight to ask the workers to make two that she saved. These, with aluminum bows, stood tall in the corner of the library; as she proudly showed me.

After lunch, Muir and Gilder left Four Brooks Farm, likely provisioned with apples and cider. Fresh vegetables from Four Brooks Farm were shipped regularly by train to the Gilders' New York table. They returned to Lee by phaeton, and to New York by the 1:50 p.m. train, arriving at 7:00 p.m. Supper was at the Johnsons' at 327 Lexington Avenue, where presumably Muir lodged. There the twenty-eight-year-old Lieutenant Richmond Pearson Hobson of Alabama was writing of his heroic naval mission in the Spanish-American War. Attempting to close Cuba's Santiago harbor, Hobson and seven volunteers had steered the *Merrimack*, an old collier, into the port before dawn on 3 June 1898. Their explosives and the Spanish shore batteries ensured the ship's sinking. Though subsequently captured and imprisoned, they gained release. Next month, serialization in the *Century* would begin. There Hobson would appear youthful, clean-shaven except for an upturned mustache, his dark hair parted down the middle, as sketched on 13 August 1898 by Cecilia Beaux. "[A] quiet keen handsome fellow," he impressed Muir; "Firmness daring shown in face."[42]

After Gilder's death on 18 November 1909, Johnson succeeded him as editor of the *Century*. "I'm sad about Gilder," Muir wrote their mutual friend John Burroughs. "What a loss we have sustained and all the country. New York seems lonesome to me now he is gone."[43]

## CODA: SPRING 2001

A small footnote to my Tyringham adventures in 1989: After retiring from the post office in 1995, Irma Clark died on 28 November 1999 in Georgia, while visiting her son Gerald. Her father lived to be one hundred. Irma's close friend Marilyn Curtin is now the postmistress. Walter deKay Palmer died in 1995.[44]

Gilly and Anne Palmer are well and happy. They have perpetuated the Muir/Gilder conservation tradition by preserving Four Brooks Farm forever. About a third of their land has been given to the National Park Service for the Appalachian Trail. As selectman for the last three years and chair of the Board of Appeals, Gilly has worked to keep Tyringham a place that Muir and his grandfather Richard Watson Gilder would recognize. He is considering running for a second term as selectman this year. The Gilder papers in their attic have gone to the Lilly Library of Indiana University.

# 14. BOSTON

## MAY 1903

John Muir's association with New England continued into the early twentieth century. He made three short spring visits to Boston in as many years. The purpose of his first trip was to meet his partner in world travel Charles Sprague Sargent and to confer with his editors at Houghton Mifflin. The latter desire brought him back again eight years later. He was also motivated to come in order to make his plea in behalf of the lives of forests and to save the Hetch Hetchy Valley, a desire that also compelled his final Massachusetts day. In addition, he went to New Haven, Connecticut, for two days to receive an honorary degree from Yale.

Almost five years had lapsed since Muir's previous New England trip. His transcontinental journey this time comprised the first leg of a yearlong world tour. His 1903 departure was delayed, he explained to Sargent, because "An influential man from Washington wants to make a trip into the Sierra with me, and I might be able to *do some forest good* in freely talking around the campfire."[1]

From Friday, 15 May to Monday, 18 May, Muir escorted Theodore Roosevelt in the Sierra Nevada. First he showed the president the Mariposa Grove, which he had shared with Emerson thirty-two years ago, almost to the day. Unlike Emerson, the Rough Rider from the White House camped out with the naturalist and the sequoias. They both held trees in the deepest spiritual regard. The next night, they slept amid snow and silver firs at Glacier Point. After riding their horses along the rim, they went down to Yosemite Valley, where they spent their last evening together in the meadow before Bridalveil Fall.[2]

Muir accomplished "some forest good." Roosevelt extended protection for the trees from Yosemite Valley to Mt. Shasta. Later, he created five new national parks, sixteen national monuments (including the Grand Canyon, on Muir's advice), and fifty-three wildlife sanctuaries. He doubled the total area of national forests and expanded Yosemite National Park to encompass Yosemite Valley. On 13-15 May 1908, he hosted the first conservation conference at the White House. Conservation, biographer Edmund Morris believes, was Roosevelt's "single greatest achievement."[3]

Five days after leaving the president in California, Muir arrived in Boston. It was midnight of Saturday, 23 May, when he stepped off the train and "went to nearby hotel," as he wrote his wife. The Thorndike again? Sunday morning, Sargent, with his twenty-seven-year-old son Robeson, called for Muir and drove him to Holm Lea in Brookline. That evening, with "a large company at dinner," Muir was thankful to be de rigueur in his black suit, which had arrived ahead of him without a wrinkle in it. "I was glad for once to be inconspicuous," he revealed to Louie, "and shall, I suppose, have to wear suit clothes often on this trip."[4]

## RALPH WALDO EMERSON

Monday, 25 May, Muir awakened to quintessential spring. Bright blue sky prevailed in eastern Massachusetts. "Delightful day like all in this month," Thomas Wentworth Higginson entered in his journal, "70°". In fact, there had been no rain since 17 April. The fields, meadows, and plants were parched; forest fires prevalent; logs stranded high and dry along the rivers.

It was the hundredth anniversary of the birth of Ralph Waldo Emerson. He was born at home, two long blocks south of the Boston Common, still a community cow pasture then, in the parsonage of the First Church on Summer Street—a yellow wooden manse set on two to three acres amid gardens, orchard, elms, and Lombardy poplars. Since September 1799, his father had been minister of this, Boston's oldest church, where four days after Emerson's birth he baptized their fourth child. Neither landmark has survived. The parsonage was taken down in 1807 for the new First Church, which was demolished in 1868. The great fire of 9 November 1872 laid waste the heartland of Boston. The residents moved westward, leaving the center to commerce.[5]

On Emerson's centennial, the country was alive with celebration. "Every major city took note of Emerson's birthday," professor Len Gougeon has observed. Boston's commemoration had begun two days earlier, on Saturday, with the Free Religious Association (which Emerson and Bronson Alcott had helped to initiate in 1867) meeting in Parker Memorial Hall. Another founder, Edwin D. Mead, gave the opening address. Mead thought that "never in the world's history had there been so large an observance of a purely intellectual anniversary. It came as a special sacrament."[6]

Emerson was the focus of Sunday's sermons "in churches of all denominations in many parts of the country." At the Second Church in Boston, where Emerson had been pastor for almost four years (March 1829-December 1832), the Reverend Thomas Van Ness spoke on "Emerson as Preacher."[7]

Sunday night in Boston's Symphony Hall, while Muir dined with the Sargents and their guests, the Emerson centenary services unfolded. The Handel and Haydn Society sang, the Reverend Edward Everett Hale gave the opening prayer and the benediction, and Professor George Edward Woodberry of Columbia University read a poem. The centerpiece of the program, President Charles Eliot of Harvard, showed an audience of the American Unitarian Association Emerson's prophetic qualities in education, society, and religion. "Emerson insists again and again that true culture must open the sense of beauty," Eliot said. He liberally quoted Emerson: "We must be lovers, and at once the impossible becomes possible." His religious insights were the most advanced, Eliot thought. "He believed that revelation is natural and continuous, and that in all ages prophets are born....He sees in the deification of Jesus an evidence of lack of faith in the infinitude of the individual human soul." Eliot admitted that as a young man he had found Emerson's ideas "unattractive, and not seldom unintelligible. I was concerned with physical science, and with routine teaching and discipline." Later, when Eliot came to his "lifework for education," he had discovered in Emerson's poems and essays the rationale for reform.[8]

Periodicals praised Emerson. Eliot's talk illuminated June's *Atlantic*. In *Harper's*, Hamilton Wright Mabie attributed "the spiritual emancipation of the new nation" to Emerson. "He was a purely spiritual force," Mabie asserted. "Emerson affirmed the presence of the divine in every human being, the direct and personal relation between each man and the Infinite, the authority of individual insight, the dignity of the individual soul." Mabie also contributed "Concord and Emerson" to his own magazine *The Outlook*. Shorter than *Harper's*, the *Century's* anonymous editorial (presumably by either Robert Underwood Johnson or Richard Watson Gilder) found Emerson's works "of such transcendent value that they cannot imagine the literature of the world ever becoming so rich as to be able to dispense with them." His "highest artistic quality" had a "miraculously luminous effect." Thomas Wentworth Higginson held forth in various venues. In *The Outlook*, he assessed the sources of power of "our foremost literary man." Finding Emerson's maternal ancestry "imperfectly" examined, he found a key to this power in the lineage of the philosopher's mother and aunt. Other than giving the aunt's teaching her nephew the maxim, "Always do what you are afraid to do," Higginson did not elaborate on this theme. William Dean Howells, who had left Boston in 1891 for New York, gave *Harper's Weekly Magazine* his "Impressions of Emerson," whom he had met in Concord in 1860 along with Thoreau and Hawthorne, as well as at the Saturday Club.[9]

Concord predictably was seized with Emerson fervor. Schools, shops, and businesses closed—the holiday carefully planned by members of the Social Circle, which had included Emerson for forty-two years. On Monday morning, some six hundred students and teachers filled the Town Hall to hear addresses by their superintendent, William Lorenzo Eaton, and by Harvard professor LeBaron Russell Briggs. In the afternoon, at the First Parish meetinghouse, Cantabrigians Thomas Wentworth Higginson, William James, and Charles Eliot Norton and Concord's native sons Senator George Frisbie Hoar and Samuel Hoar spoke to an audience of eight hundred. Senator Hoar congratulated Higginson. "My address successful," Higginson jotted in his diary.

That evening John Shepard Keyes presided at a dinner in the First Parish vestry for 152 Social Circle members and their wives. After a meal of turbans of halibut, sliced cucumbers, lobster sauce, fillet of beef with potato croquettes, green peas, asparagus, lettuce and tomato salad, and dessert of ice cream and water ices, cakes, toasted crackers, frozen pudding, strawberries, and cheese, Judge Keyes introduced the first and only female orator of the day: Caroline Hazard, the president of Wellesley College since 1899. She was followed by attorney Moorfield Storey, Hugo Münsterberg, and Edward Waldo Emerson. A Harvard philosophy professor, Münsterberg, who on Monday, 18 May, had lectured there on "Emerson as a Philosopher," reported on the progress of his department's new home, Emerson Hall. He also read a letter from his colleague, Josiah Royce, who was on leave for the spring term in California. Before returning to Cambridge in mid-July, Royce visited Yosemite. All this preparation and excitement took its toll on the octogenarian Judge Keyes. The morning after, he slept late. Wednesday, he lay prostrate on the sofa. Thursday, he wrote thank-you letters. Friday, he revived and was back in court, thankful that Saturday was Memorial Day.[10]

One wonders why Muir was not in Concord. Granted, he had only four days before his departure from the United States for a year, and he had pressing matters to attend to. Granted, this time was the only respite from travel that he would have. Was it that his schedule simply would not allow any more? Was it that the Concord social program lacked appeal for him? Had he returned to Concord he would have met old friends— Mrs. William H. Forbes, from thirty-two years ago in Yosemite; Judge Keyes and Edward Emerson, from ten years ago in Concord (Edward and his wife Annie had been to California in the winter of 1902, but apparently not seen Muir); and Thomas Wentworth Higginson, from the same year, 1893, in Cambridge. He also would have been introduced, among others, to Ellen Emerson, Caroline Hazard, and William James.

Instead, Muir called at Houghton Mifflin in Boston. Number 4 Park Street still looks southwest over the Common and Public Garden, a seventy-three-acre green with wide paths across which Emerson and Whitman had strolled on the threshold of another spring, 17 March 1860, discussing *Leaves of Grass*—though Houghton Mifflin has moved a block west of the green to 222 Berkeley Street, where it resides today.[11]

Before entering the "round-arched doorway halfway up the street, between the Scotch suitings and the Book Room," Muir looked at two new books displayed in the window: *Nature, Addresses,* and *Lectures and Essays, First Series.* They were bound in green cloth with gilded top edges and the author's signature gold-stamped on the cover. They were the first to appear of The Centenary Edition of Emerson's *Works,* edited by Edward W. Emerson, who had provided a short biography of his father in the former. They cost $1.75 each. Did Muir purchase a set to be sent home?[12] Muir already knew their contents. It had all been in the first volume of *The Prose Works of Ralph Waldo Emerson* (Boston: Fields, Osgood, 1870), which Emerson had sent Muir, along with the second volume, in February 1872. Perhaps Muir paused long enough on the edge of the Boston Common to recall that Yosemite winter and spring when he read these gifts. Three years ago his account of meeting Emerson had appeared in the *Atlantic.*[13]

## BLISS PERRY

In his small third-floor study, Muir met for the first time the editor in chief of Houghton Mifflin's trade department, Bliss Perry, who was also editor of the *Atlantic Monthly*, having succeeded Walter Page in July, 1899. Perry had been teaching first at his alma mater, Williams College, in Williamstown, Massachusetts, where he was born, and then at Princeton University. He was forty-two (forty-three that November) and lived at 4 Mercer Circle in Cambridge, a couple of blocks from Thomas Wentworth Higginson, with Annie Bliss, his wife of fifteen years, and their three children, ages twelve to five. He indulged his love of fishing in Greensboro, Vermont, where he had summered since 1897. (Muir's train had passed through this village on 20 October 1898.) The Saturday Club, which he joined in 1903, and the Tavern Club (two years later) provided conversation and camaraderie.[14]

This spring, Perry had played a central role in the creation of a publishing milestone. Upon visiting E. Harlow Russell, the owner of Thoreau's journal, in Worcester, Perry had brought two volumes home. On 8 April 1903, he reported their "priceless value" to an editorial conference and urged their publication. The firm's head, George H. Mifflin, supported Perry, who negotiated the purchase of the publication rights from Russell. The contract was signed 29 April. Perry then secured the services of Bradford Torrey as general editor, with Francis Allen assistant, both of whom Muir had met five years ago. By 3 July they were at work on the project that would take them three years to complete. As early as January 1905, Perry featured in *Atlantic* Torrey's "Thoreau as Diarist," which became the introduction to the published *Journal* in fourteen volumes, along with extracts in this and subsequent *Atlantics*, to which Muir paid close attention.[15]

Perry also persuaded the firm to undertake the publication of Emerson's journals, which appeared in ten volumes between 1909 and 1914. Edward Emerson engaged his nephew, Waldo Emerson Forbes, who had graduated from Harvard in June 1902, as coeditor. They began work the first of July, 1903, at Edward's Monadnock home, and continued in Concord, as well at the Forbes family's Naushon Island. All was not literary, however, for in 1905 they vacationed in Greece, where Edward painted a great deal. Waldo Forbes's recollections of his paternal grandfather, who died when Forbes was three, were hazy. His "dignified and serene personality" being "in complete harmony with the spirit of his" study remained in his memory. Reading his writings, Forbes gained an appreciation of his wisdom.[16]

Later, Perry made the great philosopher more accessible with *The Heart of Emerson's Journals*, which Houghton Mifflin released in one volume in 1926, following it with *The Heart of Emerson's Essays* in 1933. In March 1931, in the Vanuxem Foundation lectures at Princeton University, Perry revealed his lifelong delight in reading Emerson and his esteem for this literary artist, whose essence he believed lay in his "personal force," his "spiritual energy."[17]

June's *Atlantic* was published the day Muir and Perry met. It was also available in the Book Room for thirty-five cents. Perry, proud that it contained President Eliot's previous night's talk on Emerson, showed Muir a copy. He and George Mifflin—who with twenty-six other men, including Higginson, attorney Richard H. Dana, historian Charles Francis Adams, and former *Atlantic* editor Thomas Bailey Aldrich, were involved on the Committee of Arrangements for the Emerson Centenary Services—had attended Eliot's lecture.[18] Perry would soon start writing a life of Whitman that was published in 1906.

As Muir had just completed his review of Sargent's *The Silva of North America*, they discussed this, along with Perry's plan for a California number of the *Atlantic*—more than half its circulation was now west of the Mississippi—that Perry insisted must contain Muir. Earlier in the year Muir had balked, pleading an overload of writing and travel. An ingenious solution surfaced. Muir's *Silva* piece became part of the California issue of July 1903. It came right after Herbert Bashford's lead, "The Literary Development of the Pacific Coast," which recognized Muir's contribution to the Sierra literature, and was followed by stories, essays, and poems by Mary Austin, Ethel Fountain Hussey, David Starr Jordan, Charles Keeler, Jack London, Bradford Torrey, and others. Muir's next appearance in the *Atlantic* would not come until 1911, two years after Perry had left the editorship and increased his teaching at Harvard from part- to full-time.[19]

## GEORGE MIFFLIN

That same day, while at Houghton Mifflin, Muir renewed his acquaintance with George Mifflin, whom Henry Houghton had hired in 1868. Fresh from Yosemite with Roosevelt, Muir told the publisher of their experience. Mifflin, a Republican and a fraternity brother of the president at Harvard's Porcellian Club (Mifflin graduated in 1865, at age twenty, fifteen years before

T.R.), listened attentively. Roosevelt had authored many books with several firms, including *Thomas Hart Benton* (1887) and *Gouverneur Morris* (1888) for the American Statesmen series of this house. Perhaps Mifflin even envisioned another entry by Roosevelt on Muir, or vice versa. At the chief executive's initiation, T.R. and Mifflin would meet at 4 Park Street on the cold winter morning of 23 February 1907.[20]

Likely, on 25 May 1903, while Muir was in Mifflin's office, Mifflin opened the morning's *Boston Globe* on his desk and pointed to the picture on page 9. There, at the big foot of a sequoia, stood an esteemed coterie of men in hats and suits. Front and center was President Roosevelt, with John Muir at his left shoulder.[21]

Before leaving, Muir also saw Francis H. Allen, with whom he had toured the Riverside Press on 24 October 1898. Muir talked about forests and glaciers to "a lot of other writers," who joined him for part of his time with Perry and Mifflin. His conversations were "even more wonderful than his writing," Perry exclaimed.[22] "They all want me to write, write, write," Muir told his wife later that day.[23] Too bad that no one sat him down right there with pen and paper to record his time with Roosevelt.

## THE FLANEUR

The next two days Muir rested, shopped, and prepared for further wayfaring. Imagine Muir perambulating the narrow streets of old Boston, giving himself over to the "spectacle of the moment," as the French dictionary Le Robert said in defining the *flâneur*—as Virginia Woolf did in London. Going into one store after another—Filene's and Jordan Marsh, both just a block southeast of the Common, S.S. Pierce & Company in the Tremont Building at the corner of Beacon and Tremont streets, the Quincy Market almost to the waterfront—were possibilities. Did he wear his black suit? Did he have company? Sargent? Did passerbys recognize him? Did he converse with any? What did he buy, or eat? Where did he take tea? Again our desire to know the ordinary aspects of his daily life is unfulfilled.

While Muir was sauntering about Boston, William James, after a busy day packing and dealing with affairs at his Cambridge home, left in the early morning of the 27th for his retreat at Chocorua Lake in New Hampshire, where he stayed until Harvard's commencement on Wednesday, 24 June. James's pleasure with the Concord celebration was evident in a letter to a friend: "the most harmoniously aesthetic or aesthetically harmonious thing!"

His preparation for his talk had given him a new appreciation of Emerson: "Reading the whole of him over again continuously has made me feel his real greatness as I never did before." And to his brother Henry, he added, "Emerson is exquisite!"[24]

After James departed Cambridge, Julia Ward Howe, at noon on Wednesday the 27th, went for a ride about Boston. It was the eighty-fourth birthday of the reformer and author of "The Battle Hymn of the Republic." Later that day, she celebrated in her second-floor room at 241 Beacon Street with all of her children, some of her grandchildren, and her first great-grandchild.[25]

On Thursday, 28 May, Muir traveled from Boston to New York, where he arrived at four in the afternoon. Johnson met him at the station and took him to the *Century* offices. Later, at the Hotel Netherland, at 783 Fifth Avenue, Muir visited with the fifty-five-year-old Edward H. Harriman, who was recovering from an appendectomy on the 20th. Scarlet fever inflicted his children, all five of whom had been part of their father's 1899 Alaska expedition. For John Muir, "the most exciting experience of the whole trip" had been the discovery of a fjord and glacier in Prince William Sound, both of which were named for E.H. Harriman. Their son Averell, then a boy of seven, recalled eighty years later talking with "long-bearded" Muir while walking the deck of the steamer. His stewardship of the earth he attributed to Muir's example. After Averell had been an ambassador for Franklin D. Roosevelt and John F. Kennedy, as well as governor of New York in his sixties, he reprinted Muir's tribute to his father of 1911. This he distributed to friends and acquaintances from his many travels. To Muir, E. H. Harriman was "one of the rare souls Heaven sends into the world once in centuries." He appreciated Harriman's kindness, "especially in his home, radiating a delightful, peaceful atmosphere, the finest domestic weather imaginable." He was indebted to the elder Harriman for "some of the most precious moments of my life."[26]

Having promised to dine with the Gilders, Muir had to decline Harriman's supper invitation. That may have agreed with Muir just fine. Three springs ago, on 9 April 1900, the Harrimans and their two boys, Averell and Roland, had been in Berkeley, California, for what Muir described as "a big dinner that I could not escape." He had "met a lot of famous folk & the table etc. was grand. but nothing compared to a crust of bread & champagne water in the silver-fir woods on the margin of a lily garden…"[27]

Sleep was at the Manhattan Hotel. Early the next morning, Muir, Sargent, and Robeson sailed out of the harbor aboard the *Celtic*, the Sandy Hook Light abeam, headed for Liverpool. A week later, on 6 June, they arrived— the day after Teddy Roosevelt returned to Washington from the West. Six days later, on 12 June, the president was regalling his dinner host, secretary of state John Hay, and the French ambassador and his wife with stories of his cross-country trip. So Washington and France learned of John Muir.[28]

# 15. BOSTON

*No Blossom stayed away*
—Emily Dickinson, c. 1862 [#348]

*All the world seems sweet in May*
—Allen Chamberlain,
*Boston Evening Transcript*, 12 May 1894, 15.

## MAY 1911

After eight years, Muir, now seventy-three, was back on the "crowded side of the continent." Again this stop was just one pause in a lengthy itinerary that included other continents and consumed a year of travel.[1] While in the East, he again entered New England, twice going to Boston and once to New Haven, Connecticut. Though the dates of his first arrival and departure from Boston in May 1911 are not known, he was likely there from about the 16th to the 22nd—in the fullness of spring.

While in Boston, Muir stayed at the Hotel Bellevue on 21 Beacon Street (converted to apartments in 1962), around the corner from Houghton Mifflin and the Boston Common. The Bellevue, where Louisa May Alcott lived and wrote for parts of four winters beginning in 1874, looked across Beacon Street to the Athenaeum, where Emerson filled Saturday mornings with reading pleasures.

In the Bellevue on Saturday afternoon, 20 May, a nattily attired Muir expounded for the press on his passion for forest preservation. This time his advocacy embraced the protection of the White Mountains of New Hampshire, which he had seen in October 1898. "He delayed his departure long enough," a reporter for *The Sunday Herald* stated, "to seize paper and pencil and sketch roughly some of the astonishing aspects of the Yosemite National Park." He also told them of his plans to search for the monkey puzzle tree in South America.[2]

Following the interview, Muir went a mile west on Beacon Street to the University Club, between Dartmouth and Exeter streets. There he had supper with "some fifteen gentlemen," largely members and past presidents of the thirty-five-year-old, 1,667-member Appalachian Mountain Club, assembled by Muir friend Allen Chamberlain, who loved May (see chapter 17).

Muir had been an honorary AMC member since his election in January 1899, and had been mentioned in their journal *Appalachia*.[3] This must have been a stag event, for women, who had been part of the AMC since its beginning in 1876, would normally be present at such a gathering.[4] At least one member and Muir acquaintance was absent: Just prior to Muir's Boston arrival, Thomas Wentworth Higginson had died, on Tuesday, 9 May, in his Cambridge home—where Muir had visited him eighteen years earlier. His funeral, on Friday the 12th at the First Parish Unitarian Church in Cambridge, attended by his wife and daughter and scores of friends including Edward Emerson, Charles W. Eliot, and George H. Mifflin, was front-page news.[5]

After the meal, at which there were no speeches, Muir entertained the group. He "discoursed for over an hour," according to the club's magazine, "now humorously, now eloquently, of many episodes of his eventful life, from his childhood in Scotland, his youth on the farm in Wisconsin, his college career, and the early days of his explorations in the Sierra Nevada." He also gave an "extended and earnest treatment of the Hetch Hetchy problem."[6] The issue was familiar to them. William F. Badè, a member of the Sierra Club (of which he would be president from 1919 to 1922) and a professor at the Pacific School of Religion in Berkeley, California, had addressed the Hetch Hetchy matter two years earlier, on 7 January 1909, in an AMC-sponsored lecture in Huntington Hall. The same month as Badè's talk, Muir's "The Endangered Valley. The Hetch Hetchy Valley in the Yosemite National Park" had appeared in the *Century*.[7]

Obviously, Muir's recent autobiographical writing was on his mind when he spoke to the AMC. He also discussed his memoir with his publishers. Though Houghton Mifflin wanted to bring out *The Story of My Boyhood and Youth* as soon as possible, Muir hesitated. He wished for its first appearance to be serial, in a major magazine, to ensure a greater readership. Though he did not have time to make these arrangements before sailing from Brooklyn for the southern hemisphere, Houghton Mifflin later consented. The *Atlantic Monthly* printed selections in four consecutive issues, starting in November 1912, before the book came out in March 1913.[8]

He was back in New York by Tuesday, 23 May, the opening day of the New York Public Library. Mary Averell Harriman was his hostess, her husband having died two years earlier. Their grand home at One East 69th Street over-looked Olmsted's Central Park, where Muir had driven with Sargent and Charles E. Stratton on 27 October 1898. John Muir & Company at 71 Broadway, specialists in odd lots and members of the New York Stock Exchange, would have amused him. Three days later he received a copy of his *My First Summer in the Sierra*, which Houghton Mifflin had just released, selections having appeared in the *Atlantic Monthly* during the first four months of the year.

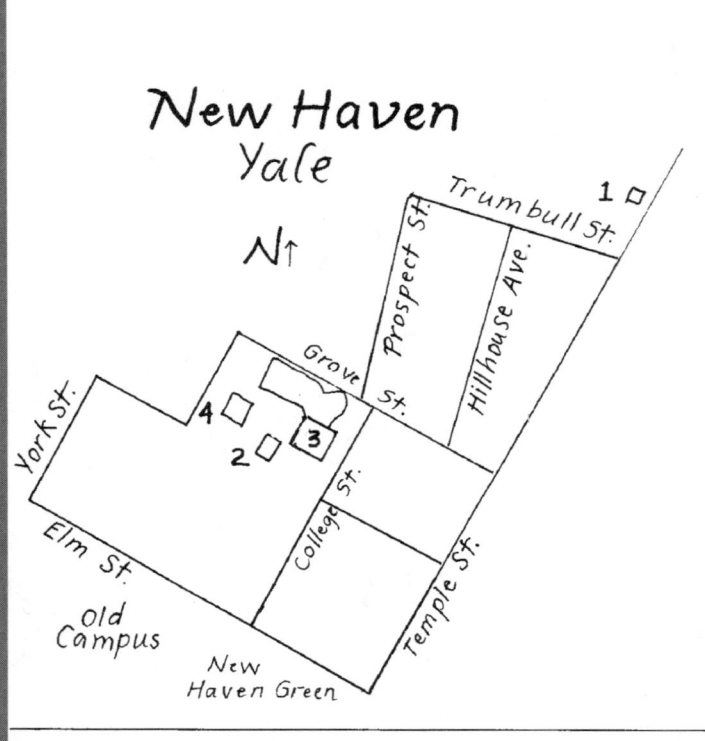

# New Haven
## Yale

N↑

Trumbull St.

1 □

Prospect St.

Hillhouse Ave.

Grove St.

York St.

4 □

2 □  3

College St.

Elm St.

Old Campus

Temple St.

New Haven Green

---

1. Phelps Home
2. Woodbridge Hall

3. Woolsey Hall
4. Beinecke Rare Book & Manuscript Library

¼ mile

# 16. New Haven, Connecticut

*I quickly caught the glow of the Yale enthusiasm.*
Muir to Katharine Hooker [26 June 1911]

## 20-22 June 1911

On Friday, 16 June, a 72-mile-per-hour gale hit New York City. Snow swirled around the Times Building for a short period in the afternoon. Trees and electric and telephone wires fell. Lights went out everywhere.

The next evening, Muir addressed the American Alpine Club at the Manhattan Hotel. He had been a member of the AAC since its formation in 1902, vice president for two years, and president from 1908 to 1910. Though predominantly male, the AAC—like the Sierra and Appalachian Mountain clubs—included women. Seventeen of its eighty members witnessed Muir's first and only appearance before the club. The current president, Harrington Putnam, a member since 1903, who had served as vice president under Muir, officiated. He held in common with Muir ascents of Shasta and Whitney in California. Now Putnam was sixty, a justice of the Supreme Court of New York, and very fit. In January 1912, he would walk from his Brooklyn home seventy-four miles east to Riverhead—essentially the length of Long Island. He and Muir undoubtedly had a good talk. After supper Muir spoke of his early career and his Sierra Nevada explorations. Gifford Pinchot, who was in New York, did not attend.[1]

On Tuesday morning, 20 June 1911, Muir took a train from New York to New Haven, Connecticut. William Lyon Phelps, the Lampson Professor of English at Yale, greeted him at the depot. Phelps had been teaching at Yale since September 1892, after earning his M.A. from Harvard and his Ph.D. from Yale, where he also had been an undergraduate.

In the afternoon they went to the first game of the annual Yale vs. Harvard baseball championship. The playing field was situated about a mile and a half west of the center of town, beyond where the West River ran through Edgewood Park. Phelps had played baseball from age five until last year. Since then, tennis and golf had become his twin passions. The previous afternoon he had played twenty-seven holes of golf, scoring forty for the last nine, his best so far for the season.[2]

Before this Muir had witnessed at least one other collegiate athletic contest. On Saturday, 5 November 1898, the Osborns had taken him from their home in Garrison, New York—either a short ferry ride across the Hudson River or a four-and-a-half-mile carriage ride south along the east side of the Hudson River to the Bear Mountain Bridge, across the Hudson River, and then six miles north—to the United States Military Academy in West Point, New York. There they had watched the cadets vie with Princeton on the football field. The "result a tie, five to five," Muir commented in his journal, "Tremendous excitement — a manly game but carried [?] on to extravagant lengths[.] many injured."[3]

In New Haven, "I quickly caught the glow of the Yale enthusiasm," Muir wrote a friend. "Never before have I seen or heard anything just like it. The alumni, assembled in classes from all the country, were arrayed in wildly colored uniforms, and the way they rejoiced and made merry, capered and danced, sang and yelled, marched and ran, doubled, quadrupled, octupled is utterly indescribable; autumn leaves in whirlwinds are staid and dignified in comparison."[4]

There were some 12,000 spectators, according to the press. From Muir's description of their hoopla, Yale's 8-to-2 loss was not apparent. The match upset Phelps: "stupidest I ever saw," he noted in his diary. The trustees, who two days earlier had voted for a new athletic stadium, may have had second thoughts about their decision.[5]

Muir spent the night at the Phelps home at 110 Whitney Avenue, a gracious Georgian manor, now filled with offices for attorneys, architects, financial advisors, and, in the brick carriage house. a psychiatrist. Next door, the New Haven Colony Historical Society has been ensconced since 1929. Annabel Hubbard, whom Phelps had met at the West Middle School in Hartford, Connecticut, in 1876 and married on 21 December 1892 at her family's home in Huron City, Michigan, made Muir welcome. The couple had no children. Muir himself was now a grandfather—Wanda with boys, two and four, and Helen with a son born on 2 February in California Hospital, Los Angeles, where Muir had visited them.[6]

The Phelpses had lived here a year and a half, moving in January 1910 from 44 High Street, the home his father had built in 1868, when Phelps was three. Now, for the first time, they had electric lights. Their first month in their new home saw the publication of his *Essays on Modern Novelists*. Many luminaries visited them. At the previous June's commencement, John Burroughs had stood before their front door wearing Phelps's cap and gown while Annabel Phelps took his picture. Now Muir, in a rented academic costume, posed in the same place.[7]

Usually the Phelpses summered in Huron City, Michigan, where the professor enjoyed writing each morning. At this moment, however, they were packing for a different destination: England and Europe, a trip made possible by his second Yale sabbatical, for which they would depart on 1 July.[8]

Three years earlier they had been in California. Crossing the country by train, they had stopped on 17 June in Los Angeles to see Phelps's brother Arthur before going to the University of California in Berkeley, where he taught through July. That same June, Muir had worked at home on a book version of his dog story "Stickeen." He left Martinez at the end of the month for a Sierra Club Outing in the Sierra Nevada, from which he did not return until 28 July— thereby preempting any serendipitous meeting with the guest lecturer.

Too bad Phelps was not a mountaineer, for then he might have run across Muir in his habitat. "I am a man of the city," he admitted, "and I like theatres, music, newspapers, and cultivated men and women."[9] On 18 July, though, the Phelpses did take the train up Mt. Tamalpais, north of San Francisco, the high point of Marin County at 2,604 feet. (That same day, Muir wrote Helen of his "fine trip all alone as of yore" far into the Kaweah Mountains— 13,802 feet—though not to any summits, while the others on the Sierra Club Outing climbed Mt. Whitney.[10])

On the lower slopes of Mt. Tam, the Phelpses paused to view a sanctuary of redwoods. Phelps's Yale classmate, William Kent, had preserved this grove and named it in honor of Muir—President Theodore Roosevelt had made Muir Woods a national monument in January 1908.[11] Their senior year, Phelps and Kent had been among the five chosen for the editorial board of the *Yale Literary Magazine*. Phelps praised Kent as "the best natural writer in college."[12] Muir was enormously grateful for Kent's generosity.[13] Kent encouraged Muir with his autobiography: "I should consider any help I might be in making this contribution to world literature as one of the most important things I can do."[14]

After his last Berkeley lecture, the Phelpses departed on the evening train on 31 July. From California, they went to Seattle, from where they took a steamer through the Inland Passage as far north as Skagway, a breathtaking route Muir knew well. Meanwhile, Muir went south to Theodore Van Dyke's ranch near Daggett, California, in the Mojave Desert, where Helen was regaining her health. There, on 12-13 August, he met the art historian John C. Van Dyke, author of *The Desert* (1901), who had come to see his brother.[15] Then Muir was off to the Harriman home, Pelican Lodge, in Klamath Falls, Oregon, where he dictated his memoirs to a stenographer.

"Then came memorable Wednesday," Muir wrote, after a good rest at the Phelpses' New Haven home, "when we donned our radiant academic robes and marched to the great hall where the degrees were conferred, shining like crow blackbirds." At 9.45 a.m, they gathered at Yale's Woodbridge Hall, a short walk from the Phelps home along quiet streets, under pleasant skies. Woodbridge Hall now holds the offices for commencements on the lower level, the president of the university on the first floor, and the secretary on the second. Yale's 210th commencement took place next door at Woolsey Hall, a Yale bicentennial building of Indiana limestone, erected in 1901-1902 with a vast, balconied auditorium in which a huge organ filled the wall behind the stage. " I was given perhaps the best seat on the platform, and when my name was called I arose with a grand air, shook my massive academic plumes into finest fluting folds, as became the occasion, stepped forward in awful majesty and stood rigid and solemn like an ancient sequoia while the orator poured praise on the honored wanderer's head...."[16] While a hood was put on his shoulders, President Arthur Twining Hadley gave Muir his diploma, Doctor of Letters of Yale.

Also honored, with a Doctor of Laws, was Josiah Royce, whom Muir remembered from his 1893 Cambridge visit. Royce stayed with Mrs. Eugene Bristol (née Julia Silliman Gilman), whose husband had died on 2 April 1910, and who had attended Royce's Yale lectures this year. As her home at 119 Whitney Avenue (which disappeared in 1960) was close to the Phelpses', there is a good possibility that Muir and Royce also saw each other outside the ceremonies, even that Muir talked with Mrs. Bristol about her famous uncles, the former president of Johns Hopkins University, Daniel C. Gilman (see chapter 7) and the geologist James Dwight Dana—namesake of Mt. Dana, on the eastern edge of Yosemite National Park, a red-brown 13,053-foot peak that Muir had climbed.[17]

Promised he would not have to speak at commencement or at the dinner following, Muir could relax.[18] President William Howard Taft, a Yale alumnus and trustee, held forth. He had arrived earlier this morning from New

York. His wife, Helen Herron, or "Nellie," remained in Washington. Three days earlier they had celebrated their silver wedding anniversary at the White House with 3,500 guests (she had invited 6,000). Today the president, who might have been in London for the coronation of King George V, instead came to Yale.

In early May Muir had been in Washington, among the Japanese cherry trees that Helen Taft had planted the year before. At that time Gifford Pinchot, whom Taft had removed from office in January 1910, was in The Hague and aboard the SS *Rotterdam*, which docked in New York on 13 May. Muir had discussed the preservation of Hetch Hetchy Valley with President Taft, a situation on which he had enlightened the chief executive earlier, when they were in Yosemite in October 1909. That autumn of 1909, the first of Taft's administration, the president had indulged his passion for riding the rails. This tour of the United States in his private car had begun on his fifty-second birthday, on 15 September, in Boston. It had kept the reluctant and unhappy president away from Washington and his wife for over two months. (He had just finished a five-week golfing vacation at their summer home in Beverly, Massachusetts.) William preferred the judicial life; Nellie wanted him in politics. In compensation Taft ate even more abundantly, his White House weight reaching its maximum of 355 pounds, and played golf almost every afternoon. Joining Taft and his party in San Francisco on Wednesday morning, 6 October 1909, Muir had traveled with them by train to El Portal. The next day, proceeding by stage, Taft had seen Yosemite Valley for the first time, from Inspiration and Artist points. (A nearby point is now named for him.) After spending the night at the Wawona Hotel, they had consorted with the big trees of the Mariposa Grove. Taft had welcomed Saturday's sunrise from the Glacier Point Hotel, then returned to bed until eight o'clock. After breakfast, they had walked the four-mile trail from Glacier Point to the valley floor, not an easy task for a man of Taft's august proportions, who blessedly did not have to go in the reverse direction. Muir had identified "every view, every tree, and flower on the way down", the *New York Times* reported, lectured on glaciation, and made clear that Yosemite and Hetch Hetchy were for prayer, not commerce. Yet Muir, equating increased public exposure with more advocacy for natural-resources conservation, had also proposed a system of roads that appealed to Taft. In hindsight, this plan was ecologically improvident, clotting Yosemite with people and automobiles. After Taft had rested in the Sentinel Hotel and his perspiration-soaked clothes dried, they had gone on to El Portal for the night. Taft relished Muir and Yosemite. Muir found Taft "the merriest man I ever saw." He would vote for Taft in November 1912.[19]

After his Yale talk, the president greeted 820 people at the reception. Then he took a nap in his car at the station. Oversleeping, he delayed another reception and supper. At 10:28, Taft left New Haven.[20] Just when in this full June day Muir had time to advocate again for Hetch Hetchy with Taft is not clear.

Nor did Muir see much more of the busy Phelps in New Haven. After proctoring entrance examinations all morning—apparently he could not even attend commencement—Phelps entrained at 3:15 p.m. for Springfield, Massachusetts, about an hour and a half ride by today's schedule. In the evening he addressed the graduates of Miss Porter's School. The next day he returned to New Haven on the 9 a.m. train, supervised exams again until three, then played golf in the rain.[21]

Muir himself traveled back to New York on Thursday, 22 June.[22] Since it was the first anniversary of the death of his sister Margaret Reid in Martinez, he must have been remembering those last days of Maggie, when, instead of coming to Yale for the honorary degree offered him a year earlier, he had held and comforted her.[23] On Friday, 23 June, Harvard again beat Yale, to win their annual competition in consecutive games. Muir found relief from New York's heat on the Osborns' hill up the Hudson River in Garrison, fifty miles north of the city. There he worked diligently on his Yosemite book. "Daily he rose at 4.30 o'clock, and after a simple cup of coffee labored incessantly on his two books, 'The Yosemite' and 'Boyhood and Youth,'" Osborn recalled, though the latter work was finished by then. "He loves the simplest English language," Osborn continued, "and admires most of all Carlyle, Emerson, and Thoreau." Muir's admiration of Thoreau initiated Osborn's reading of him.[24]

On 12 August Muir sailed from Brooklyn for Buenos Aires. In the spring of 1913, Taft would return to Yale, where he taught constitutional law until he was appointed chief justice of the Supreme Court in 1921. Phelps continued to teach at Yale until June 1933.

# Beacon Hill

↑N

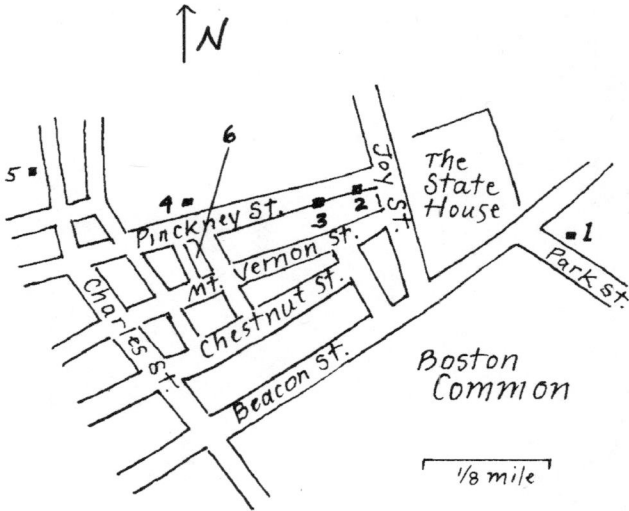

1. Houghton Mifflin
2. Thoreau Home in 1820s
3. Chamberlain Home
4. Gleason Home
5. Fields Home *
6. Louisburg Square

# 17. BOSTON

*Aye, my lassie, it is a blessed thing to go free in the light of*
*this beautiful world, to see God playing upon everything,*
*as a man would play on an instrument.*
—John Muir, quoted in *Sierra Club Bulletin* 12(1925): 204.

## THURSDAY, 11 APRIL 1912

Upon returning from the southern hemisphere on 27 March 1912, Muir again settled with the Osborns in their Manhattan home at 850 Madison Avenue. Proofreading *Yosemite* and his boyhood memoir and talking about his travels kept him busy.

On Thursday, 4 April, there he was on page 13 of the *New York Times*, dressed to the nines in a soft hat with banded crown and curved-up brim edges, a three-piece suit with watch fob and handkerchief in left front coat pocket, and an ascot below his beard. The occasion, the caption noted, was the seventy-fifty birthday the day before of John Burroughs, who stood equally fashionably attired beside Muir. That afternoon, Muir and Johnson made a thirty-minute commute from Grand Central Station to Woodby, at 424 Seventh Avenue in Pelham, New York, the home of Clara Barrus, who had invited them to the celebration. Evidently a reporter showed up too, and interviewed the septuagenarian. Burroughs, who attributed his good health to his simple lifestyle—"I gave up coffee and tea long ago"—would live to eighty-four.[1] In January 1921, three months before he died, emulating Emerson, he listed those men he most admired. In America, they were Emerson, Whitman, Thoreau, and "in a minor way" Muir.[2]

The next Thursday, 11 April, Muir was in Boston. He met with AMC members and friends Herbert Gleason and Allen Chamberlain. They discussed the Hetch Hetchy situation, possibly at one of their Beacon Hill homes, numbers 83 and 30 Pinckney Street, respectively. The Gleasons's— he and Lulie Wadsworth Rounds had been married for twenty-nine years this October—held the grander position. Situated atop the rise, his tall, granite-based brick facade looked southward to Mt. Vernon Street over Louisburg Square, a slim green surrounded with similar homes. Chamberlain's townhouse, a block east, which he shared with his wife, Grace M. Inman, and their son, Francis, was lower in elevation and north-facing. He was only a few doors away from number 4, where Thoreau had lived in the early 1820s, when he was four and five years old—a fact that Chamberlain would have noted had he been aware of it when he wrote about Beacon Hill a century after Thoreau was there.[3]

Gleason, a native of Malden, Massachusetts, five miles north of Boston, would be fifty-seven in June. Since 1899 he had been devoted to photographing Thoreau country. He had also played a role in keeping Muir up on Thoreau. In the summer of 1907, he had visited Muir in Martinez. No doubt he told Muir that his photographs graced the new Houghton Mifflin edition of *The Writings of Henry D. Thoreau* in tweny volumes (1906). Wanting a copy, Muir asked Gleason to place an order with the publisher. Gleason, however, did not return to Boston until late autumn, at which time he went to 4 Park Street to present Muir's request to George Mifflin, who said he would write Muir first to ask what kind of binding he wanted before shipping them (Muir's set with cloth with gold stamping cost $35). Then Gleason wrote Muir: "I guess you will think twice before you give me another verbal order for books! If you had written H. M. & Co. at the time you spoke to me, you might have had the books delivered and half read through by this time!"[4]

Gleason also had contributed his images to Muir's writings—the 1909 edition of *Our National Parks* and *My First Summer in the Sierra* (1911). In the summer of 1914, the Gleasons would travel to Alaska—Muir was not able to go—for photographs for his lectures and for Muir's book on Alaska. On their return, Gleason lectured on Alaska in Berkeley and San Francisco, on 9 and 16 October, respectively—Muir was unable to attend these. In November 1915—almost a year after Muir's death—Houghton Mifflin issued Muir's *Travels in Alaska* with Gleason's pictures. This was followed by the Gleason illustrated Sierra Edition of *The Writings of John Muir* from Houghton Mifflin.[5]

Chamberlain, born in Boston on 2 May 1867, was twelve years younger than Gleason. He had been a freelance writer since 1895. He had joined the AMC in 1897 and served as its president in 1906. In 1898, with another AMC activist, Joseph S. Nowell, he had founded the Massachusetts Forestry Association, which became the Massachusetts Forest and Park Association. He was on the Advisory Council of the Society for the Preservation of National Parks, of which Muir was president of the California Branch.[6]

In April 1907, in Fitzwilliam, New Hampshire, Chamberlain had met twenty-eight-year-old Benton MacKaye, and they had sauntered up Mount Monadnock together. MacKaye, who had earned Harvard's first graduate degree in forestry in 1905, was destined to conceive the idea of the Appalachian Trail and to become a founding member of the Wilderness Society in 1935. Their lifelong friendship would provide mutual support for many of their conservation endeavors.[7]

In the summer of 1909, Chamberlain and his son Francis had made a two-month exploration of several of the country's parks and monuments, which included the Sierra Club Outing in July. Along with John Muir and 180 to 220 other participants—their number varied during the month—they had made a circuit from Yosemite to Upper Merced Cañon, Tuolumne Meadows, Grand Cañon of the Tuolumne, Matterhorn Cañon, Rogers Lake, Pleasant Valley, and Hetch Hetchy Valley; on the way some had climbed Clark, Ritter, Dana, Lyell, and Conness mountains. "I appreciated your hospitality of these past four weeks," Chamberlain wrote Muir on the last day, "how keenly I enjoyed the society of you & your fellows, & of your glorious mountains & forests." He was so impressed with Hetch Hetchy that he vowed his support, writing a letter to his newspaper that day and pledging a cash contribution on its behalf.[8]

Back in Boston, Chamberlain had pursued his conservation theme. In October 1909, the *Boston Evening Transcript* featured his "The Saving of Scenery," a sequel to his "Saving England's Scenery," which had appeared in the same paper in July while he was away. In the latter, he payed homage to Charles Eliot, the founder of the Trustees of Public Reservations in Massachusetts.[9] That same month, Houghton Mifflin brought out the new and enlarged edition of Muir's *Our National Parks*, with Gleason's photographs and an appendix of statistical tables that Chamberlain supplied.[10] In December, Chamberlain's long and cogent explanation of the Hetch Hetchy matter appeared in the *Boston Evening Transcript*. Here he discerned that the real meaning of Hetch Hetchy was cheap electricity for San Francisco, not water, which could just as readily be obtained from other sources. Like Muir, whom he did not mention, however, Chamberlain supported roads to Hetch Hetchy, even to Tuolumne Meadows, a myopic ecological view, as it turned out.[11] The following spring Chamberlain's essay on "Scenery as a National Asset" appeared in *The Outlook*. Here he favored stricter laws and more money to adequately protect our great parks, including the Hetch Hetchy Valley, and increased access and accommodations to enable the public to come to know them. The article also included photographs by Gleason, and one by F.P. Clatworthy of John Burroughs and John Muir.[12]

Receiving the support of Chamberlain and Gleason, Muir was encouraged by the prospects for saving his beloved Sierra valley, the one he had first visited in November 1871. He may have recalled that six-day excursion of over forty years earlier, the similarities of Hetch Hetchy and Yosemite, and the snowstorm he encountered upon his return. This he had related to his Boston readers in the *Weekly Transcript* of 25 March 1873, one of his first newspaper appearances. Ah, all that had happened since then to bring him to this place where first he was published.[13]

Muir also must have told his hosts about his recent southern hemisphere travels, for two days later Chamberlain's description of it appeared in the local paper.[14] In the summer of 1919, Gleason would be among the first "tourist party" to complete the John Muir Trail through the High Sierra.[15]

That evening, Muir returned to New York, leaving New England for the last time.[16]

The following week, on Wednesday, 17 April, Muir departed New York, amid headlines on the loss of the *Titanic*. President Taft's loyal aide Archie Butt, having helped some of the estimated 2,224 passengers and crew into the twenty lifeboats, had gone down with the ship. The Cunard Liner *Carpathia* brought the survivors to New York. This disaster was the talk of the parlor and dining cars of Muir's westbound train. On Monday, 22 April, the day after his seventy-fourth birthday, Muir arrived in Los Angeles. Here he saw Helen and her family. By the 27th he was home, after being away just over a year, his last transcontinental journey completed.

Friends and memories, however, kept Muir connected to New England, for the last two and a half years of his life. A letter to "My dear Lover-of-Nature" from a young Boston writer, Eleanor Wilbur Pomeroy, arrived in Martinez in August 1913. She was contemplating a series on "The Playgrounds of American Authors," and asked for Muir's. On her stationery (to be typed later), Muir penciled, "My workshop, playground & prayground & my home is All our glorious planet."[17]

In March 1914, Nelson Evans wrote to remind Muir of an incident that had happened forty-four years earlier. On 3 August 1870, Evans, Muir, and two women from Rockland, Maine, Lucy Hatch and Laura Wood Snow, climbed the Three Brothers from Yosemite Valley. As they approached the highest summit (7,779 feet), a golden eagle took flight. Call it Eagle Peak, Lucy Snow suggested, and Muir agreed. A year later, on 25 July 1871, at the Trinity Church in Boston, Nelson Evans and Laura Snow were married. Their three daughters celebrated their mother, who on the "pioneer trip…with the distinguished John Muir as a guide" named a mountain top. The story delighted Muir, who intended to use it in the next volume of his autobiography, which he never finished.[18]

On Christmas Eve 1914, Bostonians—Annie Fields, the Gleasons and Chamberlains among them—read on the front page of their evening newspaper of New England's white Christmas, a cessation in Europe's war, and John Muir's death in Los Angeles.[19]

# SOURCE ABBREVIATIONS

The following abbreviations of primary and secondary sources are used in the notes.

Ackroyd      Peter Ackroyd. *Dickens*. New York: HarperCollins, 1990.

ECAD      Elizabeth Cary Agassiz Diary, Arthur and Elizabeth Schlesinger Library on the History of Women in America, Cambridge, Massachusetts.

Allen      Gay Wilson Allen. *Waldo Emerson: A Biography*. 1981; New York: Penguin, 1982.

Allen & Gullans      Sue Allen and Charles Gullans. *Decorated Cloth in America: Publishers' Bindings, 1840-1910*. Los Angeles: University of California, 1994.

*ANB*      *American National Biography*. Eds. John A. Garraty and Mark C. Carnes. 24 vols. New York: Oxford University Press, 1999. *Supplement 1*. Eds. Paul Betz and Mark C. Carnes. New York: Oxford University Press, 2002.

*ANW*      *American Nature Writers*. Ed. John Elder. 2 vols. New York: Charles Scribner's, 1996.

Baker      Carlos Baker. *Emerson Among the Eccentrics: A Group Portrait*. New York: Viking, 1996.

*Beatrix*      Jane Brown. *Beatrix: The Gardening Life of Beatrix Jones Farrand, 1872-1959*. New York: Viking, Penguin, 1995.

Benson      Albert Emerson Benson. *History of the Massachusetts Horticultural Society*. Boston: Massachusetts Horticultural Society, 1929.

Brooks      Paul Brooks. *Speaking for Nature: How Literary Naturalists from Henry Thoreau to Rachel Carson Have Shaped America*. Boston: Houghton Mifflin, 1980.

Bunting      Bainbridge Bunting. *Harvard: An Architectural History*. Cambridge: The Belknap Press of Harvard University Press, 1985. Completed and edited by Margaret Henderson Floyd.

Calhoun      Charles C. Calhoun. *Longfellow: A Rediscovered Life*. Boston: Beacon Press, 2004.

Cohen      Michael Cohen. *The Pathless Way: John Muir and American Wilderness*. Madison: University of Wisconsin Press, 1984.

Cohen II      Michael Cohen. *The History of the Sierra Club, 1892-1970*. San Francisco: Sierra Club, 1988.

*CWJ*      *The Correspondence of William James*. Charlottesville and London: University Press of Virginia, 1992-2004. 12 vols. Eds. Ignas K. Skrupskelis and Elizabeth M. Berkeley with the assistance of Wilma Bradbeer.

DWJ      The Diary of William James, Houghton Library, Harvard University, Cambridge, Massachusetts

*DA*      *The Dictionary of Art*. Ed. Jane Turner. London: MacMillan Publishers Limited, 1996. 34 vols.

*DAB*      *Dictionary of American Biography*.

DLB    *Dictionary of Literary Biography.* Detroit: Gale Research.

Volume 35: *Victorian Poets After 1850.* Eds. William E. Fredeman and Ira B. Nadel. 1985.

Volume 189. *American Travel Writers, 1850-1915.* Eds. Donald Ross and James J. Schramer. 1998.

DNB    *Dictionary of National Biography.*

Dear Papa  *Dear Papa: Letters Between John Muir and His Daughter Wanda.* Eds. Jean Hanna Clark and Shirley Sargent. Fresno, California: Panorama West, 1985.

ETE Letters  *The Letters of Ellen Tucker Emerson.* Ed. Edith E.W. Gregg. 2 vols. Kent, Ohio: Kent State University Press, 1982.

LRWE    *The Letters of Ralph Waldo Emerson. Vols. 1-6,* ed. Ralph L. Rusk. Vols. 7-10, Ed. Eleanor M. Tilton. New York: Columbia University Press, 1939-1995.

JMN/RWE  *The Journals and Miscellaneous Notebooks of Ralph Waldo Emerson.* Eds. William H. Gilman, R. H. Orth, et al. 16 vols. Cambridge: Harvard University Press, 1960-1982.

Farrand   "Book of Gardening", 1893-1895, in Beatrix Jones Farrand Collection [Series I: Personal Papers/Folder 8], Environmental Design Archives, College of Environmental Design, University of California, Berkeley. I have made a microfilm of this, which is now available at the archives.

Farrington  Edward I. Farrington. *Twenty-Five Historic Years: How an Exhibition, a Magazine and a Library Brought New Life to a Famous Institution: The History of the Massachusetts Horticultural Society from March, 1929.* Boston: Massachusetts Horticultural Society, 1955.

Fox    Stephen Fox. *John Muir and His Legacy: The American Conservation Movement.* Boston: Little, Brown, 1981.

Stephen Fox, "Massachusetts Contributions to National Forest Conservation," in *Stepping Back to Look Forward: A History of the Massachusetts Forest,* Ed. Charles H. W. Foster, Cambridge: Harvard University, 1998, 257-91.

*The Papers of Benjamin Franklin.* Ed. Leonard W. Labaree. New Haven: Yale University Press, 1959-2001. 36 vols.

Gilder   J. L. and J. B. Gilder, eds. *Authors at Home.* New York: A. Wessels Company, 1902.

Gisel    Bonnie Johanna Gisel, ed. *Kindred and Related Spirits: The Letters of John Muir and Jeanne C. Carr.* Salt Lake City: University of Utah Press, 2001.

Halsey   Francis Whiting Halsey, ed. *American Authors and Their Homes: Personal Descriptions & Interviews.* New York: James Pott & Co., 1901.

Harding   Walter Harding. *The Days of Henry Thoreau.* Knopf, 1965; Princeton: Princeton University Press, 1992.

Harris    John Harris. *Historic Walks in Cambridge.* Chester, Connecticut: Globe Pequot Press, 1986.

HASC    Holt-Atherton Special Collections, University of the Pacific Libraries, Stockton, California, contains John Muir papers and library.

TWHD — Thomas Wentworth Higginson Diary, The Houghton Library, Harvard University, Cambridge, Massachusetts.

*HDTC* — *The Correspondence of Henry David Thoreau*. Eds. Walter Harding and Carl Bode. 1958; Westport, Connecticut: Greenwood Press, 1974.

HHH — *Life, Letters and Diary of Horatio Hollis Hunnewell* (Boston: privately printed, 1906), 3 vols. Edited by his grandson Hollis Horatio Hunnewell.

Howe — M.A. DeWolfe Howe. *Memories of a Hostess: A Chronicle of Eminent Friendships Drawn Chiefly from the Diaries of Mrs. James T. Fields.* Boston: Atlantic Monthly Press, 1922.

Hughes — Edan Milton Hughes. *Artists in California, 1786-1940.* San Francisco: Hughes Publishing Company, 1989. Second edition. The Huntington Library, San Marino, California

*JB* — Clara Barrus. *The Life and Letters of John Burroughs.* 2 vols. 1925; New York: Russell & Russell, 1968.

*JMLJ* — *John Muir's Last Journey: South to the Amazon and East to Africa: Unpublished Journals and Selected Correspondence.* Ed. Michael P. Branch. Washington, D.C.: Island Press/Shearwater Books, 2001.

*JOM* — *John of the Mountains: The Unpublished Journals of John Muir.* Ed. Linnie Marsh Wolfe. 1938. Madison: University of Wisconsin Press, 1979.

Johnson's Certificate — Robert Underwood Johnson, "Certificate of Introduction," JMP, reel 22, frame 0958. Johnson lists fifty-one persons (all men, except two), he claims to have introduced Muir to, plus ten others, who were seen. Though undated it refers to the period of 30 May to 26 June and 22 September to 1 October 1893, when Muir was in New York, New England, and Washington, D.C.

Jones — Holway R. Jones. *John Muir and the Sierra Club: The Battle for Yosemite.* San Francisco: Sierra Club, 1965.

Karson — Robin S. Karson. *Fletcher Steele, Landscape Architect: An Account of the Gardenmaker's Life 1885-1971.* New York: Harry N. Abrams/Sagapress, 1989.

Keyes Diary — John Shepard Keyes Diary, Concord Free Public Library, Concord, Massachusetts.

Kimes — William F. Kimes and Maymie B. Kimes. *John Muir: A Reading Bibliography* (1978; Fresno, California: Panorama West, 1986). References are to pages, not item numbers.

*L&L* — *The Life and Letters of John Muir.* Ed. William Frederic Badè. 2 vols. Boston: Houghton Mifflin, 1924.

*Letters to a Friend* — John Muir. *Letters to a Friend, Written to Mrs. Ezra S. Carr, 1866-1879.* Boston: Houghton Mifflin, 1915. Dunwoody, Georgia: Norman S. Berg, 1973.

*LHWL* — *The Letters of Henry Wadsworth Longfellow.* Ed. Andrew Hilen. 6 vols. Cambridge: The Belknap Press of Harvard University Press, 1966-1982.

LTR                  *The Letters of Theodore Roosevelt.* Eds. Elting E. Morison, John M. Blum, John J. Buckley. 8 vols. Cambridge: Harvard University Press, 1951-1954.

Leyda                Jay Leyda. *The Years and Hours of Emily Dickinson.* New Haven: Yale University Press,1960. 2 vols.

Limbaugh             Ronald H. Limbaugh. *John Muir's "Stickeen" and the Lessons of Nature.* Fairbanks: University of Alaska Press, 1996.

McAleer              John McAleer. *Ralph Waldo Emerson: Days of Encounter.* Boston: Little, Brown, 1984.

Morris               Edmund Morris. *The Rise of Theodore Roosevelt.* New York: Coward, McCann & Geoghegan, 1979.

Morris               Edmund Morris. *Theodore Rex.* New York: Random House, 2001.

Mott                 Frank Luther Mott. *A History of American Magazines.* Cambridge: Harvard University Press, 1939-1968. 5 vols.

JMP

JMJ                  Ronald H. Limbaugh and Kirsten E. Lewis, eds. *The Microfilm Edition of the John Muir Papers, 1858-1957.* Letters are from this source unless otherwise indicated. John Muir's Journal herein is referred to as JMJ. Muir's 1898 journal, not identified in the guide, is at the end of Reel 28. *The Guide and Index to the Microfilm Edition of the John Muir Papers, 1858-1957* (Alexandria, Virginia: Chadwyck-Healey, 1986) edited by Limbaugh and Lewis is indispensable.

                     John Muir. *Rambles of a Botanist among the plants and climates of California.* Los Angeles: Dawson's Book Shop, 1974.

NAW                  *Notable American Women, 1607-1950: A Biographical Dictionary.* Ed. Edward T. James. 3 vols. Cambridge: Belknap Press of Harvard University Press, 1971.

NAW:MP               *Notable American Women, The Modern Period: A Biographical Dictionary.* Eds. Barbara Sicherman and Carol Hurd Green, et al. Cambridge: Belknap Press of Harvard University Press, 1980.

O'Connell            Shaun O'Connell. *Imagining Boston: A Literary Landscape.* Boston: Beacon Press, 1990.

                     Gifford Pinchot. *Breaking New Ground.* 1947; Washington, D.C.: Island Press, 1998.

NYT                  *The New York Times.*

Phillips             Kate Phillips. *Helen Hunt Jackson: A Literary Life.* Berkeley: University of California Press, 2003.

Richardson           Robert D. Richardson Jr. *Emerson: The Mind on Fire.* Berkeley: University of California Press, 1995.

                     Theodore Roosevelt. *An Autobiography.* 1913. New York: Da Capo Press, 1979.

                     Theodore Roosevelt. *Diaries of Boyhood and Youth.* New York: Charles Scribner's, 1928.

| | |
|---|---|
| Roper | Laura Wood Roper. *FLO: A Biography of Frederick Law Olmsted.* Baltimore: Johns Hopkins University Press, 1973. |
| Rusk | Ralph L. Rusk. *The Life of Ralph Waldo Emerson.* New York: Scribner's 1949. |
| Rybczynski | Witold Rybczynski. *A Clearing in the Distance: Frederick Law Olmsted and America in the Nineteenth Century.* New York: Scribner, 1999. |
| Sedgwick | Ellery Sedgwick. *The Atlantic Monthly, 1857-1909: Yankee Humanism at High Tide and Ebb.* Amherst: University of Massachusetts Press, 1994. |
| Simon | Linda Simon. *Genuine Reality: A Life of William James.* New York: Harcourt Brace, 1998. |
| Sutton | S. B. Sutton. *Charles Sprague Sargent and the Arnold Arboretum.* Cambridge: Harvard University Press, 1970. |
| Thompson | Lawrence Thompson. *Young Longfellow (1807-1843).* 1938. New York: Octagon Books, 1969. |
| *Thoreau Log* | *The Thoreau Log: A Documentary Life of Henry David Thoreau, 1817-1862.* Ed. Raymond R. Borst. New York: G.K. Hall, 1992. |
| MLTD | Mabel Loomis Todd Diary, Manuscript and Archives, Yale University Library, New Haven, Connecticut. |
| Tolles | Bryant F. Tolles Jr. *The Grand Resort Hotels of the White Mountains: A Vanishing Architectural Legacy.* Jaffrey, New Hampshire: David R. Godine, 1998. |
| Turner | Frederick Turner. *Rediscovering America: John Muir in His Time and Ours.* New York: VikingPenguin, 1985. |
| Watermans | Laura and Guy Waterman. *Forest and Crag: A History of Hiking, Trail Blazing, and Adventure in the Northeast Mountains.* Boston: Appalachian Mountain Club, 1989. |
| Weinberg | H. Barbara Weinberg. *Childe Hassam: American Impressionist.* New York and New Haven: Metropolitan Museum of Art/Yale University Press, 2004. |
| Whitehill | Walter Muir Whitehill. *Dumbarton Oaks: The History of a Georgetown House and Garden, 1800-1966.* Cambridge: Belknap Press of Harvard University Press, 1967. |
| Wolfe | Linnie Marsh Wolfe. *Son of the Wilderness: The Life of John Muir.* 1945; Madison: University of Wisconsin Press, 1978. |
| Zaitzevsky | Cynthia Zaitzevsky. *Frederick Law Olmsted and the Boston Park System.* Cambridge: Harvard University Press, 1982. |

# NOTES

## PROLOGUE: CONNECTIONS

1. Donald Worster, *A River Running West: The Life of John Wesley Powell* (New York: Oxford University Press, 2001), 434-35, passim. John L. Thomas, "The Major," *Reviews in American History*, September 2001, 380-87, assessed Worster's "revisionist account" thus: though "Powell was not a forerunner of today's environmentalists," he was "one of America's intellectual heroes." Another reviewer of Worster stated that Powell "achieved more than any other government scientist of his time." (David Lowenthal, *Environmental History*, October 2001, 628-29).

2. Wolfe, 116, for date of his arrival. Badè says 27 March, *L&L* I:177. His correspondence, however, supports April: "I arrived in San Francisco in April," Muir to Jeanne Carr, 26 July 1868, near Snelling, Merced Co., California; "I arrived in San Francisco about the first of April," Muir to Catharine [Merrill] et al, 19 July [1868], Hopeton, California. In *A Thousand-Mile Walk to the Gulf* (Houghton Mifflin, 1916), 188, Muir recalled that he "reached San Francisco about the first of April, and remained there only one day, before starting for Yosemite Valley." In his first "Ramble of a Botanist," he says he left San Francisco on 2 April; see Kimes, 4.

3. From Tahoe, Muir took the train north to Redding, from where he walked to the summit of Mt. Shasta. John Muir Journal, First Trip to Mount Shasta, October-November 1874, Reel 24, esp. frames 26-32. Muir's account appeared in the *San Francisco Daily Bulletin*, 2 December 1874, 1; it has been anthologized in *Steep Trails* (Houghton Mifflin, 1918; Sierra Club, 1994) and in *Mountaineering Essays*, Richard F. Fleck, ed. (Salt Lake City: Gibbs M. Smith, 1984; University of Utah Press, 1997).

4. David Haward Bain, *Empire Express: Building the First Transcontinental Railroad* (New York: Viking, 1999), esp. 460, 469, 501.

5. *Mark Twain Letters, Volume 2: 1867-1868*, Harriet Elinor Smith, Richard Bucci, and Lin Salamo, eds. (University of California Press, 1990), 205n1, 208-15, 232n1, 234n2. His return trip was 2 to 29 July.

6. Ackroyd, 1045-47. *LHWL* V:284.

7. *Mark Twain's Letters , Volume 3: 1869*, Victor Fischer, Michael B. Frank, Dahlia Armon, eds., (University of California Press, 1992), 214-18; 386-89.

8. Samuel Bowles, "The Pacific Railroad—Open. How to Go: What to See," *Atlantic* 1869, April, 493-502; May, 617-25; June, 753-62. See George S. Merriam, *The Life and Times of Samuel Bowles* (New York: The Century Company, 1885), II:145-47. Bowles made his first trip West in 1865 by railway from Springfield, Massachusetts, as far as Atchison, Kansas, a Missouri River port, and from there by stage to the Pacific. He returned by steamer, crossing Panama by rail, and continuing by sea to New York (see chapter 2). In 1868, while Muir was exploring California, Bowles spent August in Colorado—"the best month to come"—he believed, not merely as a train-tourist, but as a packer-over-the passes-in-snowstorms kind of journalist. From the apex of the Front Range, Grays Peak (14,270'), Bowles declared "It was the great sight in all our Colorado travel." His adventures recounted first in letters home became *The Parks and Mountains of Colorado: A Summer Vacation in the Switzerland of America, 1868* (Springfield, Massachusetts: Bowles & Co., 1869; University of Oklahoma Press, 1991,

James H. Pickering, ed.), 116 (Grays Peak); 183 (August).

J. D. Whitney, *The Yosemite Guide-book: A Description of the Yosemite Valley and the Adjacent Region of the Sierra Nevada, and of the Big Trees of California* (Geological Survey of California, 1869). Whitney's preface dated 1 May 1869, Cambridge, indicates that Bowles was one of its first readers, enabling him to recommend it in June's *Atlantic*. One of Bowles's closest friends was Maria Whitney, sister of J.D. Whitney (see chapter 3). Richard B. Sewall, *The Life of Emily Dickinson* (1974; Harvard University Press, 1994), 471, 473-74

Wolfe says that Muir read this "soon after coming to the Yosemite" (131). He also took notes on Hetch Hetchy, Tuolumne Meadows, and what is now called the Grand Canyon of the Tuolumne River from Whitney's new, revised and corrected edition (Cambridge: University Press, Welch, Bigelow, 1874); see JMP, Reel 41. Muir's copy, in the HASC, contains his marks and annotations in text and fourteen-item index.

9. John Burroughs, "Spring in Washington: With an Eye to the Birds," *Atlantic*, May 1869, 580-91. *JB* I:95.

10. Letters, Muir to Robert Underwood Johnson, 23 January 1895, Martinez, and Alexander W. Drake to Muir, 4 February 1895, New York.

11.William Least Heat-Moon, *River-Horse: The Logbook of a Boat across America* (Houghton Mifflin, 1999), 281.

12. Letter, Muir to Fay H. Sellers, 3 October 1894, Martinez.

13. Letter, Louie Muir to Muir, 5 September 1893, Martinez.

14. Letter, Wanda Muir to Louie Muir, 7 June 1904, Grand Canyon, Arizona.

15. Letter, Muir to Mary [Muir Hand], 19 December 1893, Martinez.

16. Sarah Orne Jewett, *Letters*, edited by Annie Fields (Houghton Mifflin, 1911), 249. Kay Redfield Jamison, *Exuberance: The Passion for Life* (New York: Knopf, 2004), 14-21, finds Muir to be an exuberant person, a trait of which is "restless energy." I am indebted to Archie Hobson for pointing me to Jamison.

17. Letter, Muir to Helen Muir Funk, 31 March 1911, Martinez. On his pilgrimage to the north, on 8 June 1689, the forty-five-year-old Bashō climbed Mount Gassan (5,577'), where he slept atop in the open air on a bed of leaves and bamboo, Muir-style. Bashō, *The Narrow Road to the Deep North and Other Travel Sketches*, translated by Nobuyuki Yuasa (Penguin, 1966), 125.

18. The length of his Boston stay is not known, possibly a week, which in relation to his other visits seems too long. He was in New Haven for three days.

19. Ronald Limbaugh, "John Muir & His Reading Interests," *The John Muir Newsletter*, Fall 2003, 1, 4-9. I am indebted to professor Patricia Hampl for the ideas of reading as being and listening, which she did not apply to Muir.

20. Letters, Jeanne Carr to Muir, 25 May 1868, Madison, Wisconsin; Muir to Carr, 26 July 1868, near Snelling, California.

21. For the Keiths in New England see Alfred C. Harrison, Jr., *William Keith: The Saint Mary's College Collection* (Moraga: Saint Mary's College of California, 1988), 11 and 21; Brother F. Cornelius, *Keith: Old Master of California* (New York: G.P. Putnam's Sons, 1942), 32, 36, 45-49, 88. Cornelius misidentified Jane Emerson and Margaret Emerson Hutchins as Elizabeth Keith's sisters, and their home as Damariscotta, p. 36. See Benjamin Kendall Emerson, *The Ipswich Emersons*, A.D. 1636-1900 (Boston: Press of David Clapp & Son, 1900), 190. I am grateful to Cindy Murphy for this source. Soon after Elizabeth's birth, her mother died on 3 October 1838 at thirty-two. Her father remarried Mary E. Bright of Newcastle, Maine, where

they resided. The Keiths also painted in New England in 1880.

22. Letter, Muir to [Mr. & Mrs. Henry Fairfield Osborn], 31 January 1912, Near Zanzibar.

23. Letter, Wanda Muir Hanna to Robert Underwood Johnson, 28 January 1915, Martinez.

24. Letter, Muir to Henry Randall, 20 December 1901, Martinez.

## TRIP ONE: 1893
## CHAPTER 1—CONCORD

1. Robert Underwood Johnson, *Remembered Yesterdays* (Little, Brown, 1923), 280.

2. Henry David Thoreau, *Walden*, ed. J. Lyndon Shanley (Princeton University Press, 1971), 193. All further references to *Walden* are to this edition unless otherwise noted; pages are given parenthetically in text.

3. *Boston Sunday Globe*, 11 June 1893, 4. I am ever grateful to Concord naturalist Mary McClintock for opening my eyes to this and other wonders of Walden Woods.

4. Fitchburg Railroad, Hoosac Tunnel Route, *The Official Guide to the Railways* (National Railway Publications, June 1893), 82. The New York Public Library has *The Official Guide* from 1868, except September/October 1898. The Boston & Maine Railroad also served Concord but its schedule does not agree with Muir's and its run was slower.

5. Karl Baedeker, ed., *The United States with an Excursion into Mexico: A Handbook for Travellers—1893* (1893; New York: Da Capo Press, 1971), 112. A brief review of this book appeared in *The New York Times* of 4 June 1893, 19, while Muir was in the city.

　　Later *The New York Times* (19 June 1893, 3) also noted the publication of *Appletons' General Guide to the United States and Canada* (New York: D. Appleton and Company) and *Appleton's Guide Book to Alaska and the Northwest* by Eliza Ruhamah Scidmore, a friend of Muir's and Johnson's and an advocate for wilderness. The former, however, did not recommend a Concord tour, nor mention Concord authors. Appleton's travel guides began publication with *Appleton's Railroad and Steamboat Companion* (1847) and a *United States Guide Book* (1861), according to John Tebbel, *A History of Book Publishing in the United States: Volume I The Creation of an Industry, 1630-1865* (New York: R.R. Bowker, 1972), 288.

　　A popular local guide by George B. Bartlett, *Concord: Historic, Literary and Picturesque* (Boston: Lothrop) published from 1880 to 1895 (Bartlett died in 1896), helped tourists, though probably not Muir. I consulted the 15th edition of 1895.

6. *Concord Enterprise*, 19 April 1893, 1; 4 May 1893,1; 20 July 1893, 4.

7. Letter, John Muir to Louie Muir, 13 June 1893, New York, in *L&L* II:269. Muir quotations hereafter in this chapter are from this letter unless otherwise indicated.

8. Amelia F. Emerson, "John Shepard Keyes," *Memoirs of Members of the Social Circle in Concord* (privately printed, 1940), 5:71-93. Hereafter cited *Social Circle Memoirs*. Percy W. Brown, "Prescott Keyes," *Social Circle Memoirs* (1975) 6:37-48. Prescott Keyes (1858-1943) joined the all-male Social Circle in 1890 and was a devoted member all his life, as was his father, who enrolled in 1846. Leslie Perrin Wilson, " 'Treasure in My Own Mind:' The Diary of Martha Lawrence Prescott, 1843-1836," *The Concord Saunterer*, 2003, 92-152; quote, 137. Two of their children died in infancy.

9. Keyes Diary, 8 June 1893.

10. Johnson, *Remembered Yesterdays*, 326-27.

11. A brief profile of Daniel Chester French appeared in April's *Century* (1893) by W. Lewis

Fraser, 958, as well as French's *The Angel of Death Staying the Hand of the Sculptor*, 846. Margaret French Cresson related her wedding in her *Journey into Fame: The Life of Daniel Chester French* (Harvard University Press, 1947), 256-60.

12. See Michael Richman, Daniel Chester French: *An American Sculptor* (Metropolitan Museum of Art, 1976), 38-47, *Minute Man*; Richman says French made his clay model for the *Minute Man* in the Studio Building, 110 Tremont Street, Boston, from April to September 1873. He completed the statue 30 July 1874 at the same place. This varies with Cresson's account, *Journey into Fame*, 63-80, which I give here, and is supported by Roland Wells Robbins, *The Story of the Minute Man* (New London, New Hampshire: Country Press, 1945). Keyes Diary. Daniel's father, Judge Henry F. French, appears on the Concord Assessors records for the first time in 1867, Joyce Woodman informed me. According to Mary R. Fenn, Old Houses of Concord (*Old Concord Chapter Daughters of the American Revolution*, 1974), Judge French bought the house in 1865.

13. John H. Dryfhout, "The Cornish Colony," *A Circle of Friends: Art Colonies of Cornish and Dublin* (University Art Galleries, University of New Hampshire, 1985), 39. Cresson says two summers but not which ones, *Journey into Fame*, 167. *Concord Enterprise*, 20 July 1893, 1 & 4, and 8 August 1893, 1, for their return to Concord "last week."

14. Selections from William Brewster's journals at the Museum of Comparative Zoology, Harvard University, have been published as *October Farm* (Harvard University Press, 1936) with Daniel Chester French's introduction, and *Concord River* (Harvard University Press, 1937). According to Ludlow Griscom, *The Birds of Concord* (Harvard University Press, 1949), 5-17, Brewster's association with Concord began in 1868 when he came to see French. From April to October 1886 Brewster lived at the Old Manse in Concord. *DAB, ANB*.

15. Henry D. Thoreau, *Journal, Volume 5: 1852-1853*. Patrick F. O'Connell, ed. (Princeton University Press, 1997), 366-67.

16. Nathaniel Hawthorne, *The American Notebooks*. Claude M. Simpson, ed. (Ohio State University Press, 1972), 342-43. Josephine Lazarus, *Century*, April 1893, 923-32.

17. Margaret Sidney, *Old Concord: Her Highways and Byways* (Boston: D. Lothrop, 1888), 63; *Concord Enterprise*, 29 June 1893, 1.

18. ETE Letters 2:174.

19. Johnson, *Remembered Yesterdays*, 327.

20. LRWE 6:155. For an account of their meeting see Stephen Fox, *John Muir and His Legacy*, 3-7.

21. McAleer, 610-13; *Social Circle Memoirs*, 90; Keyes Diary.

22. Nanette Margaret Sexton, *Carleton E. Watkins: Pioneer California Photographer (1829-1916): A Study in the Evolution of Photographic Style During the First Decade of Wet Plate Photography*, Harvard Univ., Ph.D. Dissertation, 1982, 182. Letter, Ralph Waldo Emerson to Thomas Starr King, 7 November 1862, Concord, in The Society of California Pioneers, San Francisco, California. Only a draft portion is included in *LRWE* 5:297-98.

23. Conversation with Peter E. Palmquist, 4 April 2000. Peter Palmquist and Martha A. Sandweiss, *Carleton E. Watkins: Photographer of the American West* (University of New Mexico Press, 1983). See Chronology by Peter E. Palmquist in Douglas R. Nickel, *Carleton Watkins: The Art of Perception* (San Francisco Museum of Modern Art/ Harry N. Abrams, 1999).

24. ETE Letters 2:660. *Concord Enterprise*, 20 April 1893, 5, says that they sailed for Liverpool from New York on the *Teutonic* on 5 April. *Concord Enterprise*, 8 June 1893, 1, for Venice.

Delores Bird Carpenter, ed., *The Life of Lidian Jackson Emerson* by Ellen Tucker Emerson (Michigan State University Press, 1992), 253 n372, says that at Ellen's invitation Helen A. Legate "came to live with her about 1890 and lived on in the Emerson House until her death in 1947[1945]." *The Concord Directory and Guide* (E.H. Smith, 1892) verifies her residence at Emerson's at this time. *Concord Journal*, 31 May 1945, and *Concord Enterprise*, 7 June 1945, give her obituaries. Edith Forbes believed that the friendship of her sister with Helen Legate began in 1889. See her letter quoted in Judith A. Roman, *Annie Adams Fields: The Spirit of Charles Street* (Indiana University Press, 1990), 153-54. I surmise that the "family from New Hampshire," who according to the *Concord Enterprise*, 8 June 1893, had leased Bush for the summer, had not arrived yet.

25. Harding, 431. Thoreau's full journal entry for 23 May 1860 does not mention the wedding. Caroline Ticknor, *May Alcott: A Memoir* (Little, Brown, 1928). In the "Prelude" of *May Alcott*, Daniel Chester French related that his first clay and tools were the gift of May Alcott. Joel Myerson, Daniel Shealy, and Madeleine B. Stern, eds., *The Journals of Louisa May Alcott* (Little, Brown, 1989), 218-19.

26. Johnson, *Remembered Yesterdays*, 327.

27. *Concord Enterprise*, 15 June 1893, 5. *NYT*, 4 June 1893, 19. According to the unidentified reviewer, Sanborn wrote 543 pages, Harris 120.

28. *DAB* for Daniel and Harriet Lothrop; the new *ANB* includes him, omits her. John Tebbel, *A History of Book Publishing in the United States, Volume II: The Expansion of an Industry 1865-1919* (R.R. Bowker, 1975), 275-7, covers D. Lothrop & Co. (which liquidated in January 1894; reincorporated as Lothrop Publishing Company, it went on for another decade without any family members), and its bestseller *Five Little Peppers* (598). Margaret M. Lothrop, *The Wayside: Home of Authors* (New York: American Book Company, 1940) has a chapter on her mother. Margaret Lothrop, who graduated from Smith College, A.B. 1905, and Stanford University, A.M., 1915, taught economics at Stanford from 1915 to 1927; She resided at The Wayside from 1932 to 1965, when it was sold. She died in May 1970, less than a year before The Wayside opened under the auspices of the National Park Service. The Harriett M. Lothrop Family Papers are in the archive of the Minute Man National Historical Park, Concord. Letter, Maria Powers to J. Parker Huber, 15 February 1995, Orchard House, Concord, Massachusetts. *Concord Enterprise*, 22 June 1893, 1, indicated Harriett and Margaret Lothrop's return to Concord the week of 12 June.

29. Her World's Fair visit is taken from Chicago newspaper clippings in Folder 78 of Box 4 of her Manuscript Collection in the Department of Special Collections, George A. Smathers Libraries, University of Florida, Gainesville. An exhibit of D. Lothrop Company was in the Manufactures and Liberal Arts Building of the World's Fair (Folder 66, Box 4, photograph).

30. None of the *Five Little Peppers* series is in the extant Muir library.

31. Letter, John Muir to James Davie Butler, 1 September 1889, Martinez, California, in *L&L* 2:233. Wolfe, 255, for his telling Paddy Grogan stories.

32. Wolfe, 232.

33. Pages are from the 1971 Princeton edition of *Walden*, and for Muir from his 1862 Ticknor and Fields edition in his library at HASC.

34. Henry David Thoreau, *Walden: An Annotated Edition*, Foreword and Notes by Walter Harding (Houghton Mifflin, 1995), 260n4 and 262n7, respectively. Hereafter Harding's commentary is cited parenthetically in text.

35. Lawrence Buell discusses "The Thoreauvian Pilgrimage" and specifically Muir's in his *The*

*Environmental Imagination: Thoreau, Nature Writing and the Formation of American Culture* (Harvard University Press, 1995), 311-38. I am not aware that Muir knew this ancient ritual; he did, however, circle Mt. Shasta in December 1874 and recommend that Helen Hunt Jackson do likewise for her health (Letters, John Muir to Jeanne Carr, 9 December 1874, Sisson's Station, California, and Helen Hunt Jackson, 16 June 1885, Martinez, California, in *L&L* 2: 37-8 and 198-202, respectively).

36. Letter, John Muir to Helen Muir, 9 June 1893, [Brookline, Massachusetts],

37. Henry D. Thoreau, *Journal*, Volume 5:1852-1853. Patrick F. O'Connell, ed. (Princeton University Press, 1997), 79-80.

38. Henry D. Thoreau, *Journal*, Volume 6: 1853. William Rossi and Heather Kirk Thomas, eds. (Princeton University Press, 2000), 191.

39. *The Journal of Henry D. Thoreau*. Bradford Torrey and Francis H. Allen, eds. (Boston: Houghton Mifflin, 1906; New York: Dover, 1962), VI:337.

40. Julie Dapper, *The Alcotts and Orchard House* (Concord: Louisa May Alcott Memorial Assoc., 1993). Thomas Hollis, "Frederick Alcott Pratt," *Social Circle Memoirs*, 58-70. Thomas Blanding, "Thoreau-Alcott 'Yellow House' Chronology [Concord, Massachusetts] n.d.). Diary of Anna (Alcott) Pratt in The Houghton Library, Harvard University - *59M-311(12). I am indebted to Melanie Wisner of The Houghton Library for reporting on this diary. *Concord Enterprise*, 20 July 1893, 4.

41. Keyes Diary.

42. *DAB, ANB*. Harding, *The Days of Henry Thoreau*, 221-22; 259-60; 453-4. Allen French, "Edward Waldo Emerson," *Social Circle Memoirs*, 5:293-311. For wedding, see Keyes Diary, 19 September 1874, and *The Letters of Ellen Tucker Emerson*, 2:150.

43. Keyes Diary, 9 June 1893, for Edward's departure; *Concord Enterprise*, 20 April 1893, 1, for stay in Milton.

44. *The Journals and Miscellaneous Notebooks of Ralph Waldo Emerson*, William H. Gilman, R. H. Orth, eds., et al. (Harvard University Press, 1960-1982), 16:17-18. On the following page of this published journal, John Muir appears in Emerson's list of eight men under the heading "Young America," indicating knowledge of Muir. Could Emerson have possibly read Muir's first published article on his discovery of the rare orchid, *Calypso borealis*, which appeared in the *Boston Recorder* of 21 December 1866? Most scholars believe that their connection came through their mutual friend, Jeanne Carr, whom Emerson met in January 1867 when he gave his second lecture in Madison, Wisconsin (George H. Bresnick, "Ralph Waldo Emerson in Madison...", *Wisconsin Academy Review*, December 1988, 12-20; Bonnie J. Gisel, *Into the Sun: Jeanne C. Carr...* Diss. Drew University 1998, 142-43 (107n). Emerson's first Madison lecture was seven years before on 8 February 1860; the next day he toured the University, where Muir would enroll a year later (Albert J. von Frank, *An Emerson Chronology*, G.K. Hall, 1994, 351.).

45. Edward's "Monadnocks" are in private collections. Alicia Keyes's oil *Monadnock* (1893) is still in the Concord Free Public Library. *Concord Enterprise*, 7 December 1893, 5, for her Court House exhibit. Her oil of *Emerson's Study* (1914) is in the Ralph Waldo Emerson House. According to the *Concord Directory and Guide* for 1892, Alicia M. Keyes (1855-1924) is residing with her parents; however, since there is no mention of her presence this day, I infer that she is absent and place her most likely in Fitzwilliam with her sister Annie. She taught art at Wellesley College (1899-1902) and at the Museum of Fine Arts, Boston (c.1911-1924); neither institution owns any of her paintings.

46. Muir's copy of *The Journal of Henry D. Thoreau*, eds. Bradford Torrey and Francis H. Allen (Boston: Houghton Mifflin,1906) is in HASC. For his text marks and comment see X:459 and 465; and XIV:51-2. His indices appear at back of these two volumes.

47. Keyes Diary, 22 January 1892.

48. The Sheraton Palace Hotel at Market and New Montgomery streets now occupies the former site of the Palace Hotel, which was destroyed by fire in the 1906 earthquake.

49. Marjorie Dakin Arkelian, *Thomas Hill: The Grand View* (Oakland, California: The Oakland Museum, 1980), 33; *Muir Glacier*, Alaska, Fig.21, 35. Muir did not accompany Thomas Hill to Alaska in 1887 as Robert McGrath believed in "New Hampshire Observed: The Art of Edward Hill," *Historical New Hampshire*, Spring/Summer 1989, 32n2.

50. Janice T. Driesbach, *Direct from Nature: The Oil Sketches of Thomas Hill* (Yosemite: Yosemite Assoc., 1997), 79-83.

51. Arkelian, Thomas Hill, 34. Her source is *White Mountain Echo* (Bethlehem, New Hampshire), August 1892 [no day given], a weekly newspaper, which I've searched unsuccessfully for his presence.

52. Arkelian, Thomas Hill, 34-35. *Final Report of the California World's Fair Commission... Chicago 1893* (Sacramento: State Office, 1894), 168.

53. Letter, John Muir to Louie Muir, 29 May 1893, Chicago, in *L&L* 2:261-63. Though Muir specified "four by Hill," the *Final Report of the California World's Fair Commission* (above) lists five; perhaps one—*Muir Glacier?*—had not arrived by the time of Muir's viewing. Muir also mentioned "four by Keith, not his best," while the *Final Report* lists six (169). Muir and Keith might have seen the World's Fair together had Keith not gone on ahead to New York. Though their plan was to see Scotland together, they traveled separately.

54. *Final Report of the California World's Fair Commission*, 170. Edan Milton Hughes, *Artists in California: 1786-1940* (San Francisco: Hughes Publishing, 1989, 2nd ed.), 624-25. Yelland, Hill, and Keith all are in Nancy Dustin Wall Moure, *California Art: 450 Years of Painting & Other Media* ( Los Angeles: Dustin Publications, 1998), see 55 and 42-43, 88-89 and 43-44, respectively, plus their monographs. Kent L. Seavey, compl., *Raymond Dabb Yelland*, 1848-1900 (San Francisco: California Historical Society, [Exhibition] 15 May to 10 July 1964), Catalog.

55. *NYT*, 15 June 1893, 2, c.1. Historian Hubert Howe Bancroft was its premier chronicler in two illustrated volumes, *The Book of the Fair* (Chicago: The Bancroft Company, 1893). See also David F. Burg, *Chicago's White City of 1893* (University Press of Kentucky, 1976). A Chicago Historical Society brochure, "The World's Columbian Exposition: Chicago 1893" (1977) says 25.8 million attended the Fair. Witold Rybczynski, *A Clearing in the Distance: Frederick Law Olmsted and America in the Nineteenth Century* (Scribner, 1999), 385-99.

56. Letters, Muir to Louie Muir, 30 September 1893, Washington, D.C.; Robert Underwood Johnson to Muir, 6 November 1893, New York; Muir to Frank Sellers, 1 January 1894, Martinez (train crash).

57. The Fitchburg Railroad schedule of *The Official Guide* gives Concord departure at 8:22 P.M. and Boston arrival at 9:10. They might have taken another commuter train.

58. "Lakes of Light," *Walden*, 199. "Range of Light," John Muir, "The Treasures of the Yosemite," *Century Magazine*, August 1890, 483-500. Muir wrote this article at Johnson's behest.

59. Mary Oliver, *Winter Hours: Prose, Prose Poems, and Poems* (Houghton Mifflin, 1999), 71.

60. Baker, 502.

61. Letter, Ellen Tucker Emerson to Muir, 7 July 1914, Merced Lake, included with letter of Marion R. Parsons of same date. Ellen T. Emerson, "Through the Tuolumne Cañon," *Sierra Club Bulletin*, January 1915, 258-60, which Muir did not live to read. I assume that Muir did not meet her while he was in Concord. In 1920 Ellen Tucker Emerson married Charles M. Davenport. She died 5 August 1921 at her parents' summer home in Fitzwilliam, New Hampshire. *Concord Enterprise*, 10 August 1921. *The Smith Alumnae Quarterly*, November 1921, 1-4. Emerson House at Smith College commemorates her.

## Trip One: 1893
## Chapter 2—Brookline

1. *L&L* II:264. The Thorndike is on the letterhead of Muir's letter begun 12 June 1893. Sutton, 3-21.

2. *L&L* II:269-70.

3. M. G. Van Rensselaer, "A Suburban Country Place," *Century*, May 1897, 3-17.

4. Jane Brown, Beatrix: *The Gardening Life of Beatrix Jones Farrand*, 1872-1939 (New York: Viking, 1995), 37, opp. 108 (illustration).

5. Letter, Charles Sprague Sargent to Muir, 25 December 1896, Jamaica Plain, Massachusetts. Sutton says fire occurred "on the day after Christmas" (163), while Sargent states in his letter to Muir that it happened in the evening of 15 December. *Boston Evening Transcript*, 3 December 1927, 6:1, for division of estate. Deed, Charles S. Sargent to Alice Sargent, 29 September 1928, with plan of land, shows house on 5.5 acres. Norfolk Registry of Deeds, Dedham, Massachusetts. Application for a Permit for Alterations for 53 Sargent Crossway, 3 November 1947, in Brookline Building Department, proposes removal of roof, second, and third floors, for use as one family dwelling. I am very grateful to James Cotter for his invaluable research into the history of Holm Lea after 1927.

6. Frederick Law Olmsted, autobiographical fragment, in Charles E. Beveridge and David Schuyler, eds., *The Papers of Frederick Law Olmsted, Volume III: Creating Central Park, 1857-1861* (Johns Hopkins University Press, 1983), 40.

7. Roper, 66-76. Charles Capen McLaughlin and Charles E. Beveridge, eds., *The Papers of Frederick Law Olmsted, Volume I: The Formative Years, 1822-1852* (Johns Hopkins University Press, 1977), 9-10, 336-58. He traveled with his brother John Hull Olmsted and their friend Charles Loring Brace. They were on the Continent for a month, returning to London 5 August and leaving for New York 5 October. Only two Olmsted letters from this trip survive, the editors say.

8. Roper, 113-19. Charles E. Beveridge and Charles Capen McLaughlin, eds. *The Papers of Frederick Law Olmsted, Volume II: Slavery and the South, 1852-1857* (Johns Hopkins University Press, 1981), 1-2, 9-11; "Annotated Itineraries of Olmsted's Southern Journeys: 1852-1854," 463-82.

9. Roper, 86-98.

10. Roper, 265-70. Victoria Post Ranney, ed. *The Papers of Frederick Law Olmsted, Volume V: The California Frontier, 1863-1865* (Johns Hopkins University Press, 1990), 20-23, 252-57. Oliver Wolcott Gibbs (1822-1908; *DAB, ANB*) was an ex-officio member with Muir of the 1896 Forestry Commission.

11. *The Papers of Frederick Law Olmsted, Volume V*: 36, 442-43 (Bowles), 488-516 ("Preliminary Report upon the Yosemite and Big Tree Grove"). Roper, 282-88. Witold

Rybczynski, *A Clearing in the Distance: Frederick Law Olmsted and America in the Nineteenth Century* (Scribner, 1999), 256-59. Olmsted served the commission for two years, until his resignation in October 1866. For Bowles, see *DAB, ANB*. David Schuyler and Jane Turner Censer, eds. *The Papers of Frederick Law Olmsted, Volume VI: The Years of Olmsted, Vaux & Company, 1865-1874* (Johns Hopkins University Press, 1992), 60-63.

Samuel Bowles, *Across the Continent: A Summer's Journey to the Rocky Mountains, the Mormons, and the Pacific States, with Speaker Colfax* (Springfield, Massachusetts: Samuel Bowles & Company; New York: Hurd & Houghton, 1865), Letter XXII, The Yosemite Valley and the Big Trees, 223-37. Though this was primarily a description of these two sites, Bowles did support their preservation for the public benefit, and mentioned Olmsted's "laudable and promising effort" to improve access to them, but not his reasons for preserving scenery. He also invited New York to follow California's example and save Niagara Falls and the Adirondacks, "and Maine one of her lakes and its surrounding woods." He did not specify which Maine lake he had in mind, if any—had he been thinking of its largest, Moosehead?—nor was the Down East coast considered, or any of the New England shore. In her diary of 30 January 1867, Annie Fields assessed *Across the Continent* as "intensely interesting & valuable," but marred by "careless writing and careless thinking," quoted in Leyda 2:122.

12. Roper, 450-52; M. G. van Rensselaer, "Frederick Law Olmsted," *Century*, October 1893, 860-67. Letter, Charles Sprague Sargent to Muir, 8 January 1894, says that vol. 5 of the *Silva* was published in October 1893.

13. Witold Rybczynski, *A Clearing in the Distance: Frederick Law Olmsted and America in the Nineteenth Century* (Scribner, 1999), 326, 344-54, 365-68. "The front of the Federal-style farmhouse is rather grand with a two-story-high porch and tall pillars that might recall the plantation architecture of Richardson's Louisiana," Rybczynski describes the Richardson home (344). Whereas Brookline Preservation Commissioner Roger E. Reed classifies it as a West Indian Country House; see Kathleen Howley, "Saving House where Architect Lived, Worked," *Boston Sunday Globe*, 12 December 1999, G1&8. M. A. DeWolfe Howe, ed., *Later Years of the Saturday Club, 1870-1920* (1927; Freeport, New York: Books for Libraries Press, 1968), Charles S. Sargent wrote Olmsted's memoir, 183-87; Charles A. Coolidge wrote Richardson's, 193-200. Both were elected in 1883; Sargent, in 1896. Mariana Griswold van Rensselaer, *Henry Hobson Richardson and His Works* (Boston: Houghton Mifflin, 1888).

14. [Margaret H. Floyd] *Brookline Village Walking Tours* (Brookline Planning Department, 1977), Pill Hill, 16-28. *ANB*. Runkle, however, does not appear in the Cambridge City Directory until 1899; then at 1663 Massachusetts Avenue and at 15 Everett Street in 1901 and 1902. Muir wrote Emerson of Runkle's Yosemite visit, *LRWE* 6:202-04.

15. Sources for Mariana Griswold Van Rensselaer are *DAB, ANB, NAW*. Cynthia D. Kinnard, "Mariana Griswold Van Rensselaer (1851-1934): America's First Professional Woman Art Critic," in Claire Richter Sherman, ed., with Adele M. Holcomb, *Women as Interpreters of the Visual Arts, 1820-1979* (Westport, Connecticut: Greenwood Press, 1981), 181-205 and passim; Cynthia D. Kinnard, "The Life and Works of Mariana Griswold Van Rensselaer, American Art Critic," (Johns Hopkins University, Ph.D. Diss., 1977). For George Griswold (1875-1894) at Harvard and his death, see Kinnard, 28-31.

16. M. G. van Rensselaer, "Fifth Avenue," *Century*, November 1893, 5-18. JMJ, 7[8] November 1898. Moses King, *King's Handbook of New York* (Boston: Moses King, 1893) 2:620-22, photo of the World. Kenneth T. Jackson, ed., *The Encyclopedia of New York City* (Yale University Press/New-York Historical Society, 1995), 1073-74, skyscrapers.

17. M. G. van Rensselaer, "Places in New York," *Century*, February 1897, 501-16; quote, 503.

18. None of Henry James's novels are in Muir's extant library. For births and residences, R.W.B. Lewis, *The Jameses: A Family Narrative* (New York: Farrar, Straus and Giroux, 1991), 45, 58-59. James sold his home in the fall of 1843 and took his family to Europe. The next home he owned—purchased in April 1848—was at 58 West 14th Street, still within walking distance of Washington Square. Here they spent seven years, their longest residence together in one place, according to Lewis. Fred Kaplan, *Henry James: The Imagination of Genius: A Biography* (New York: William Morrow, 1992), consideration of *Washington Square*, 221; his birthplace gone, 494. For Thoreau's visit, see *HDTC*, 101 & 110 and Harding, 149-50. Henry James, *The American Scene* (1907) in *Henry James: Collected Travel Writings: Great Britain and America* (New York: Library of America, 1993), 431, revisiting his birthplace.

19. Henry James, *The American Scene*, 430. Emily Kies Folpe, *It Happened on Washington Square* (Johns Hopkins University Press, 2002), 169-90, for Arch.

20. M. G. van Rensselaer, "Fifth Avenue," *Century*, November 1893, 5-18, with pictures by Childe Hassam, one of them of the Arch; see Folpe, *It Happened on Washington Square*, 144-45. JMJ, 7[8]November 1898. The *DAB*, *ANB*, and *NAW* place her home at 9 West Tenth Street, while the 1898 New York City Directory indicates she lived at 9 West Ninth Street. I am indebted to Emily Kies Folpe for informing me of the loss of Van Rensselaer's home. Letter, Emily Kies Folpe to J. Parker Huber, 5 January [2003], New York.

21. Reviews of *Art Out-of-Doors: Hints on Good Taste in Gardening* (New York: Charles Scribner's Sons, 1893) appeared in *NYT*, 21 May 1893, 19; *Boston Evening Transcript*, 29 May 1893, 6; *The Nation*, 27 July 1893, 71.

22. JMP, 10 September 1903, Shanghai (Reel 29).

23. Letters, Sargent to Muir, 28 October 1895, 13 February and 5 March 1901, Jamaica Plain, Massachusetts; Muir to Sargent, 25 March 1901, Martinez, California.

24. Letters, Houghton Mifflin to Muir, 4 November 1901, Boston; Sargent to Muir, 6 November 1901, Jamaica Plain, Massachusetts; Sargent saw the advance sheets of Muir's book.

25. Letters, Sargent to Muir, 28 May, 13 August, and 17 October 1900, Jamaica Plain. For Sargent-Muir relationship, see also Stephen Fox, "Massachusetts Contributions to National Forest Conservation," 261-69.

26. William Cronon, *Nature's Metropolis: Chicago and the Great West* (New York: Norton, 1991), for an overview, 341-44; and valuable bibliography, 459-60 n1. Paul C. Nagel, "Twice to the Fair," *Chicago History*, Spring 1985, 4-19, for Adams's visits. Henry Adams, *The Education of Henry Adams* (New York: Modern Library, 1931), Introduction by James Truslow Adams, Chapter XXII, Chicago (1893), 331-43, esp. 339-43. *The Education of Henry Adams*, though privately printed in 1907, was not published until 1918, by the Massachusetts Historical Society. Robert Grant, "People Who Did Not Go to the Fair," *Cosmopolitan*, December 1893, 158-64, tells what they missed and speculates on why they did not go, without mentioning names. J. C. Levenson et. al., eds., *The Letters of Henry Adams* (Belknap, Harvard University Press, 1988), IV:103, "a wiser and a gladder man;" for dates, 103-4n1. Patricia O'Toole, *The Five of Hearts: An Intimate Portrait of Henry Adams and His Friends, 1880-1918* (New York: Clarkson Potter, 1990), 90-2, 200-206, passim, for his relationship with Elizabeth Cameron.

Muir and Johnson left Washington on train for Chicago at 11:35 A.M. on 1 October. This time Frank Sellers showed Muir around the Fair. From Chicago Muir went to Portage, Wisconsin, to see his mother and sisters and to the University of Wisconsin in Madison to talk with his former professor James Davie Butler, before returning to Chicago from where he took the Santa Fe home, arriving 16 October. Letters, Muir to Louie Muir, 30 September

1893, Washington [D.C.]; Robert Underwood Johnson, 20 December 1893, Martinez; and Alfred H. Sellers, 31 December 1893, Martinez.

27. For biographical information see *DAB*, *ANB*, *NAW*: *MP*, Jane Brown, *Beatrix: The Gardening Life of Beatrix Jones Farrand, 1872-1959* (New York: Viking, 1995). Brown credits Beatrix's mother's friend, Mariana van Rensselaer, as the inspiration for Farrand's career (Rensselaer at the time was writing *Art Out-of-Doors*, 1893), 26 and 226n29.

Beatrix Jones was not the only woman Sargent nurtured in the profession. See Edmund A. Schofield, "A Life Redeemed: Susan Delano McKelvey and the Arnold Arboretum," *Arnoldia*, Fall 1987, 9-23. Since Mckelvey (1883-1964) was a close friend of Alice Eastwood (1859-1953), the herbarium curator of the California Academy of Sciences of San Francisco, who knew Muir, I presume that during their botanizing of the southwest Muir was mentioned. Eastwood sent Muir an autographed copy of her *A Handbook of the Trees of California* (San Francisco: California Academy of Sciences, 1905) that is at the HASC. Susanna Bryant Dakin, *The Perennial Adventure: A Tribute to Alice Eastwood, 1859-1953* (San Francisco: California Academy of Sciences, 1954).

28. Beatrix Jones Farrand, "Book of Gardening," 1893-1895. Of her time at Chicago's World's Fair, Jones made journal entries for 19 and 26 October, totaling almost five handwritten pages. As she begins with 19 October, she could not have left Boston on that date as Brown states (40). I calculate that her Boston departure was on the 17th, which allowed better than a day's travel. Mary Gray Ward Dorr (c.1820-1901) was a Boston hostess with many connections. Mary Jones, William James, and Josiah Royce (see chapter 3) all visited her at Oldfarm; Brown, *Beatrix*, 27. Oldfarm was removed by the park service, though one of the cottages on the property remains.

29. Charles J. Sander (1847-1938) worked and lived at Holm Lea for fifty-three years, from 1877 until his retirement in 1930(?). He joined the Massachusetts Horticultural Society on 10 April 1897, and from them received four gold medals. *1938 Year Book of the Massachusetts Horticultural Society*, 28; Benson, 495; Farrington, 2, 64-5. In 1929 Sander received the Jackson Dawson Memorial Medal, 191. Sander appears as "Mr. Zander" in Van Rensselaer, "A Suburban Country Place," *Century*, May 1897, 16.

Sheila Connor Geary and B. June Hutchinson, "Mr. Dawson, Plantsman," *Arnoldia*, March/April 1980, 50-75; I am grateful to Karen Madsen for introducing me to this fine essay. Dawson (1841-1916) served the Arboretum from 1873 until his death. From 1886, he lived with his wife Mary McKenna and family at the Arboretum at 1090 Centre Street. "Jackson Dawson—In Memoriam," *Horticulture*, 12 August 1916, 201-3. See Sutton, 65, 180 (photo), 323, 354n21, passim.

30. *Beatrix*, 193, 197-8, Dumbarton Oaks; 200, Arnold Arboretum; 203-16, list of her commissions, 203-16; 189. After the sale of Reef Point, Beatrix bought a Bar Harbor farm for her gardeners the Garlands and there built a cottage where she lived with their care until her death on 27 February 1959. Her last Reef Point Bulletin (17) was her obituary. See Beatrix Farrand, *The Bulletins of Reef Point Gardens* (Bar Harbor, Maine: Island Foundation; Sagaponack, New York: Sagapress, 1997).

In 1927 her husband became director of the Huntington Library that now houses a good collection of Muir's books. She designed the garden for the Director's House.

31. *JMLJ*, 117-18. Walter Muir Whitehill, *Dumbarton Oaks: The History of a Georgetown House and Garden, 1800-1966* (Belknap Press of Harvard University, 1967), 58-70.

TRIP ONE: 1893
CHAPTER 3—CAMBRIDGE

1. Mary Thacher Higginson, *Thomas Wentworth Higginson* (Houghton Mifflin, 1914), 397. Harding, 285. See George Willis Cooke, "Thomas Wentworth Higginson" in Gilder, 149-62, esp. 157-60, for the interior of the Higginson home; also Halsey, 211-20. "His present wife is a niece of Longfellow's first wife," Cooke says (158).

Mary Potter Thacher Higginson (1844-1941) was the niece and namesake of Mary Storer Potter Longfellow, the first wife of Henry Wadsworth Longfellow, who died on 29 November 1835 when the couple was in Rotterdam, Holland. Muir likely saw the portrait of Mary Longfellow in the Higginson house (Halsey, 213-14). Mary Higginson published prose— *Seashore and Prairie* (Boston: James R. Osgood, 1877), where she advocated for wildflowers and birds and related her ascent of Megunticook (1,380') in the Camden Hills of Maine, and *Room for One More* (Lee and Shepard, 1879)—and poetry *Such as They Are* (Boston: Roberts Brothers, 1893) with her husband; *The Playmate Hours* (Houghton Mifflin,1904); *Fugitives* (Portland, Maine: Mosher Press, 1929)—as well as a biography, *Thomas Wentworth Higginson* (Houghton Mifflin, 1914), and *Letters and Journals of Thomas Wentworth Higginson* (Houghton Mifflin, 1921). Her "New Longfellow Letters" *Harper's*, April 1903, 779-86, included some of her aunt's letters as well. *LHWL* 6:147n1, 402n1; 1: 22 (genealogy), 309n1. *Who Was Who in America* I:561. She died on 9 January 1941, almost forty years after her husband; *NYT*, 12 January 1941, 44.

2. Theodora V.W. Ward, "Emily Dickinson and T. W. Higginson," *The Boston Public Library Quarterly*, January 1953, 3-18. Ward also discloses the invalidism of Mary Channing Higginson, the first wife of T. W. Higginson, who died in 1877. Mabel Loomis Todd in her introduction to *Letters of Emily Dickinson* (Boston: Roberts Brothers, 1894) does not mention Higginson. In her introduction to the second edition of *Letters of Emily Dickinson* (New York: Harper and Brothers, 1931), she acknowledges that while Higginson was not involved in the editing of the *Letters*, he "was deeply interested always, and sent me his entire correspondence with Emily, except for a few letters which he thought too personal to print."

Letter, Robert Underwood Johnson to Muir, 4 December 1894, New York.

3. *DAB*; *ANB*. TWHD, 10 June 1893. Mabel Loomis Todd, ed., *Letters of Emily Dickinson* , 2 vols.(Boston: Roberts Brothers, 1894), 2:300-31. Thomas Wentworth Higginson, "Emily Dickinson's Letters," *Atlantic Monthly*, October 1891, 444-56; his visit to her, 452-3. Emily Dickinson, *Poems*, Mabel Loomis Todd and Thomas Wentworth Higginson, eds. (Boston: Roberts Brothers, 1890). Richard B. Sewall, *The Life of Emily Dickinson* (1974; Harvard University Press, 1994), 468. Sewall examines the Higginson-Dickinson relationship through their correspondence and her poetry, 532-76. Joyce Carol Oates believed that Higginson failed to recognize her poetic genius; see her Introduction, *The Essential Dickinson* (Hopewell, New Jersey: Ecco Press, 1996), 5. Residential details are from *The Dickinsons of Amherst* (University Press of New England, 2001), photographs by Jerome Liebling, and essay by Polly Longsworth, "The 'Latitude of Home': Life in the Homestead and the Evergreens," 15-106. For another approach to Emily's wardrobe, see Billy Collins, "Taking Off Emily Dickinson's Clothes," *Picnic, Lightning* (University of Pittsburgh Press, 1998), 74-5.

4. MLTD. Mabel and Millicent Todd had visited Lydia Coonley in Chicago in spring 1890; they left Amherst 12 March and did not return until 15 May. See Polly Longsworth, *Austin and Mabel: The Amherst Affair and Love Letters of Austin Dickinson and Mabel Loomis Todd* (1984; University

of Massachusetts Press, 1999), 346-47 and 361.

5. J. Juan Reid, *Colorado College: The First Century, 1874-1974* (Colorado Springs: Colorado College, 1979), 44, The Summer School ran from 1892 to 1896; 41 & 46, Views of the campus in 1891 and 1894. Frank Herbert Loud (1852-1927), *Who Was Who* I:747, Colorado College website. William Frederick Slocum (1851-1934) served as Colorado College's president for twenty-nine years (1888-1917); see *Who Was Who* I:1134 and Robert D. Loevy, *Colorado College: A Place of Learning, 1874-1999* (Colorado College, 1999), 45-106. *Colorado College Annual Bulletin*, April 1893, 8-9, for faculty.

6. Mabel Loomis Todd, *The Nation*, 5 October 1893, 245-46. On 19 July 1893, Mabel Todd attended Katherine Lee Bates's Summer School class on Chaucer (MLTD).

7. Frank H. Tucker, "A Song Inspired: Katharine Lee Bates and 'America the Beautiful'", *Colorado Heritage*, 3: 1989, 32-42, quotes, 39. Mabel Todd's diary records David's fainting occurred "Just as we started down." Bates later made the "skies" "spacious" and the "plain" "fruited". Lynn Sherr, *America the Beautiful: The Stirring True Story Behind Our Nation's Favorite Song* (New York: Public Affairs, 2001), uses Bates's journal in the Wellesley College Archives, but does not mention the Todds. En route west, Bates stopped briefly in Chicago for the Fair, 1-3 July. Arriving in Colorado Springs on the 5th, she stayed until 1 August. Returning to Chicago, she had three full days at the Fair. See also Dorothy Whittemore Bates Burgess, *Dream and Deed: The Story of Katharine Lee Bates* (University of Oklahoma Press, 1952), 100-03. Both Bates and Coman are in *NAW*; Bates is also in *DAB* and *ANB*. Leland Feitz, *The Antlers: A Quick History of Colorado Springs' Historic Hotel* (Colorado Springs: Little London Press, 1972) shows the hotel Bates stayed in and its successors. A third Antlers Hotel stands today on the same site as the first two.

In August 1895, William James was a lecturer in the Colorado Summer School and, like Katharine Lee Bates and Mabel and David Todd two years before, participated in its Pikes Peak excursion, ascending "by the ignominious method of a cog railroad." While in Colorado Springs, he was the guest of Elizabeth Cass Goddard (1840-1918) at 808 North Cascade Avenue, "a real trump" and "an angelic woman," according to James. James, like the Todds, also dined with William S. Jackson. On 7 August, he ascended Cheyenne Mountain (9,565'), eleven miles southwest of Colorado Springs. "A glorious day," he wrote his wife, "and a very nice easy walk, rather less than going up Chocorua." He went on to to see more of Colorado, crossing the state by train to Grand Junction and staying two nights at the Hotel Colorado in Glenwood Springs at 5,746 feet before returning home. See *CWJ* 8:59-74; 2:355n1, 372-75, and Frederick J. Down Scott, "William James's 1895 Visit to Colorado," *San Jose Studies*, May 1979, 33-40.

8. Lawrence Buell, *Writing for an Endangered World: Literature, Culture, and Environment in the U.S. and Beyond* (Belknap Press of Harvard University Press, 2001), 12. Buell insightfully sees "America the Beautiful" as environmental literature and provocatively compares Muir and Jane Addams, 9-18.

For Enos Mills, see *ANW* II:615-24.

W. H. Rideing, "The Rocky Mountains," in William Cullen Bryant, ed., *Picturesque America* (New York: D. Appleton, 1872 and 1874), II:482-502. Thomas Moran's illustrations of Longs, Grays and Pikes peaks in Colorado accompany Rideing's text. Both volumes of *Picturesque America* are in Muir's library in HASC.

Another source would have been Samuel Bowles, *The Parks and Mountains of Colorado* (see Prologue).

9. Todd, *The Nation*, 5 October 1893, 245. From Polly Longsworth I learned of Mabel Todd's ascent of Fuji.

10. MLTD, 3-6 September 1887. Mabel Loomis Todd and David P. Todd, "An Ascent of Fuji the Peerless," *Century*, August 1892, 483-94.

11. JMJ, 9-10 May 1904. Wolfe, 300. In his letter of 18 December 2001, Richard F. Fleck assured me Muir did not summit Fuji.

12. Mabel Loomis Todd in *The Nation*: "With the Eclipse Expedition to Japan," 1 September 1887, 169; "The Eclipse Expedition in Japan," 22 September 1887, 229-30; "The Ascent of Fuji-San," 13 October 1887, 291-3. Her *Century* article is cited above.

13. Millicent Todd Bingham, *Ancestors' Brocades: The Literary Debut of Emily Dickinson* (New York: Harper & Brothers, 1945), 231, Letters, Todd to Higginson, 23 August 1893; 237, Higginson to Todd, 27 August 1893; 240, Helen Banfield Jackson to Todd, 16 September 1893. This being a book about Emily Dickinson I presume is why Millicent does not mention that the other purpose for their being in Colorado Springs was for her father to lecture in the Summer School. Though Mabel Todd records meeting William Jackson on 24 July 1893 in her diary, she does not indicate anything about Emily Dickinson letters. Todd, *Letters of Emily Dickinson*, II:423-4, shares her "disappointment" in not finding any of Emily's letters in Colorado Springs. In the second edition of *Letters of Emily Dickinson* (Harper & Brothers, 1931), Todd adds in notes the letters of Jackson and his second wife, 412-13.

14. MLTD.

15. Exhibit, "Listening to Nature's Story: The Visual Art of Mabel Loomis Todd," Amherst History Museum, Amherst, Massachusetts, 2 March-6 December 2002. The Robert Frost Trail crosses Mt. Orient. Millicent Todd Bingham, "Rescuing an Island…," *Natural History*, May 1937, 318-28.

16. Paul F. Norton, *Amherst: A Guide to its Architecture* (Amherst Historical Society, 1975), 136, Jackson's east side faced the street; its entrance was on the south side. Kate Phillips, *Helen Hunt Jackson*, 19, 137.

17. Phillips, 144-47. Vivian R. Pollak, "American Women Poets Reading Dickinson: The Example of Helen Hunt Jackson," in Gudrun Grabher, et al, eds., *The Emily Dickinson Handbook* (University of Massachusetts Press, 1998), 323-41.

18. William Shakespeare, *Collected Works, Temple Edition* (London: A. C. Dent, 1894-1896), 36 of the 41 volumes are now back in Muir's home in Martinez, the gift of Mayme Kimes in 2001. Though I've not examined these, they are a fertile field for scholarship. David Blackburn, Chief of Interpretation, the John Muir National Historic Site, says that nearly all the volumes have Muir marginalia (Letter, 20 May 2004). "I am from the fields," Polly Longsworth, "The 'Latitude of Home,'" 40. Judith Farr with Louise Carter, *The Gardens of Emily Dickinson* (Harvard University Press, 2004), 314n5, mountains. Farr shows how central to Dickinson's life and creativity were her outdoor and indoor gardens and the flowers they produced. Dickinson also collected over 400 plants in her herbarium (96). She loved best common wildflowers, yet grew fragrant jasmine in her conservatory. "To shut our eyes is Travel," *The Letters of Emily Dickinson*, eds. Thomas H. Johnson and Theodora Ward (Belknap Press of Harvard University Press, 1958), 482; quoted in Sewall, *The Life of Emily Dickinson*, 613. "Within is so wild a place," Joyce Carol Oates, *The Essential Dickinson*, 4. "[W]ondering hand" and "How dreary," in Thomas H. Johnson, *The Complete Poems of Emily Dickinson* (Boston: Little, Brown, 1974), 153- #323 and 133 - #288, respectively. Alfred Habegger, *My Wars Are Laid Away in Books: The Life of Emily Dickinson* (New York: Random House, 2001), 5-7, errand in the wilderness.

19. Ray Stannard Baker, *Century* series: I. "The Great Southwest," May 1902, 5-15; "The Desert," June 1902, 213-25; "Irrigation," July 1902, 361-73; "The Tragedy of the Range,"

August 1902, 535-45. II: "The Conquest of the Forest," May 1903, 85-97; "The Salmon Fisheries," June 1903, 206-16; "A Place of Marvels: Yellowstone Park as It Now is," August 1903, 481-91; "The Day of the Run," September 1903, 643-55. John Muir, "The Grand Cañon of the Colorado," *Century*, November 1902, 107-16.

20. Letter, S.S. McClure to Muir, 9 April 1901, New York, introduces Baker. Ray Stannard Baker, *American Chronicle* (New York: C. Scribner's Sons, 1945), 141-3, for his time with Muir. "I spent a weekend with him at his home in the Contra Costa hills," Baker recalled. His memoranda book shows him at Muir's Wednesday and Thursday, 16-17 May 1901, perhaps arriving the evening before and departing the morning after (Ray Stannard Baker Papers, Library of Congress, Microfilm Reel 12). Ray Stannard Baker, "John Muir," *The Outlook*, 6 June 1903, 365-77. Baker's profile excited one remembrance by a University of Wisconsin classmate of Muir's, Harvey Reid, whose letter to the editor of *The Outlook* was published 28 November 1903, 763-64.

I've been unable to find Baker's Muir "portrait." I presume it was a photograph, possibly the one that accompanied Baker's *Outlook* article.

21. Though the nine David Grayson books (published by Doubleday, Page between 1907 and 1942) were popular, none appear in Muir's extant library. See Robert C. Bannister, Jr., *Ray Stannard Baker: The Mind and Thought of a Progressive* (Yale University Press, 1966).

22. For Benjamin Kendall Emerson (1843-1932), see *DAB*. Leyda, I:xliv, for Emerson-Dickinson connection. On the Harriman Alaska Expedition, Muir and Emerson served on two committees together (Geology; Geography and Geographic Names). The 1899 trip provided other rich contacts for Muir, such as the three artists with whom Muir along with John Burroughs served on the Committee of Literature and Art: Frederick S. Dellenbaugh (*DAB*), who accompanied John Wesley Powell on his 1871-72 Colorado River trip and authored *A Canyon Voyage: The Narrative of the Second Powell Expedition* (1908; University of Arizona Press, 1984); Louis Agassiz Fuertes (*DAB, ANB*), who at twenty-five was the youngest of the party, a recent Cornell graduate (1897), and a supreme bird painter; and Robert Swain Gifford (*DAB, ANB*), who captured in watercolor the vastness of the Muir Glacier. See William H. Goetzmann and Kay Sloan, *Looking Far North: The Harriman Expedition to Alaska, 1899* (Princeton University Press, 1983), 207-12. Ken Chowder, "North to Alaska," *Smithsonian*, June 2003, 92-101. Thomas Litwin of Smith College, with scientists, artists, and scholars, traced the same territory in 2001, and wrote *The Harriman Alaska Expedition Retraced: A Century of Change* (Rutgers University Press), coming in 2005.

23. Letter, John Muir to Wanda Muir, 14 June 1893, New York, in *Dear Papa*, 36-7. Sewall, *The Life of Emily Dickinson*, 564. Higginson and Todd also attended Emily Dickinson's funeral in Amherst on 19 May 1886. Polly Longsworth, *Austin and Mabel*, 243. Kate Phillips, *Helen Hunt Jackson*, 98-99, 270. *Out-door Papers* is no longer in Muir's extant library. Thoreau read "Snow" and liked it, Mary Thacher Higginson, *Letters and Journals of Thomas Wentworth Higginson*, 114. These four concluding essays in *Out-door Papers* are republished in Howard N. Meyer, ed., *The Magnificent Activist: The Writings of Thomas Wentworth Higginson, 1823-1911* (New York: Da Capo Press, 2000).

24. His election as president is in "Proceedings of the Club" for 14 January 1885, *Appalachia*, July 1885, 170. Thomas Wentworth Higginson, "Footpaths," *Atlantic*, November 1870, 513-22, gives his favorite walking places. [Thomas Wentworth Higginson], "A Day in the Carter Notch," *Putnam's Monthly*, December 1853, 672-78. [Thomas Wentworth Higginson], "Going to Mount Katahdin," *Putnam's Monthly*, September 1856, 242-55; reprinted in *Appalachia*, June 1925, 101-29. See also his Letters and Journals edited by Mary Thacher Higginson, 117-21, and Allen Chamberlain, "When Col. T. W. Higginson was a Guide to Mt.

Ktaadn in 1855 and Now," *Boston Evening Transcript*, 14 July 1923, 5:1&2. Higginson obviously (and Chamberlain too) had read Thoreau's "Ktaadn" that appeared serially in the *Union Magazine of Literature and Art* in 1848. In January 1858, Higginson inquired of Thoreau the feasibility of canoeing from Moosehead Lake in central Maine via the Allagash River to Madawaska at the state's northern border, to which Thoreau replied, relating the details of his 1857 trip in that area, see *HDTC*, 506-08. Higginson told the AMC of the Grand Mulets on 20 July 1880 at the State Normal School, Plymouth, New Hampshire; *Appalachia*, December 1881, 362.

25. Johnson, *Remembered Yesterdays*, 329-332.

26. Muir's copies of Lowell's books are in the Huntington Library, For Thoreau and Lowell see Harding, 392-95, and Walter Harding, ed., *Thoreau: A Century of Criticism* (Dallas, Texas: Southern Methodist University Press, 1954), 44-53, which presents Lowell's review of Thoreau's *Letters to Various Persons* from the *North American Review*, October 1865, 597-608, which Harding calls "probably the most damning analysis of Thoreau that has ever been published." More on Muir and *The Maine Woods* is in chapter 10.

27. Thomas Wentworth Higginson, *Old Cambridge* (New York: The MacMillan Company, 1900), 130; he wrote essays on Longfellow and Lowell, as well as a biography of Longfellow that Houghton Mifflin published in 1902. *LHWL* 4:95, dinner hour. Baker, 285. *LRWE* 4: 366. *Thoreau Log*, 303. For another version of Fanny's death, see Annie Longfellow's story in Calhoun, 216-18. In October 2000, Maymie B. Kimes of Santa Rosa, California, graciously let me examine Muir's copy of Emerson's *Parnassus* (Boston: Houghton, Osgood, 1880).

28. *The Cambridge Chronicle*, 15 April 1894, 4; 29 April 1893, 4; 17 June 1893, 4.

29. Letters, Anita Israel to J. Parker Huber, 25 May and 15 August 2001, Cambridge, Massachusetts. Letter, Alice Longfellow to Edith Longfellow Dana, 23 June 1893, Cambridge, Massachusetts, and "A Visit to the Worlds Fair/Told in/A Diary of Ten Days/June 3 to June 14, 1893" by "Harry Dana" (Actually his account, which begins Saturday, 3 June ends midsentence on Monday, 6 June, making it a diary of four days.); both are in the Archives of the Longfellow National Historic Site, Cambridge, Massachusetts. Edith Longfellow (1853-1915; *NYT*, 22 July 1915,9) and Richard Henry Dana III (1851-1931; *Who Was Who in America*; *NYT*, 17 December 1931, 23), who after graduation from Harvard (1874) and Harvard Law School (1877) was a civil service reformer, tax law expert, and servant to civic organizations such as the New England Conservatory of Music in the 1890s, had four sons and two daughters. Anne Allegra Longfellow (1855-1934; *NYT*, 6 May 1931, 25) and Joseph G. Thorp (1852-1931), who graduated from Harvard (1879) and Harvard Law School (1882) and practiced law in Boston (*NYT*, 6 May 1931, 25), had five children. After playing golf for a year, Joseph Thorp was runner-up in the second US amateur golf championship in Shinnecock Hills, Southampton, Long Island, in July 1896 (*NYT*, 18 July 1896, 6). Ernest W. Longfellow (1845-1921; *DAB*; *NYT*, 25 November 1921, 14) and Harriet Spelman (1848-1937) had no children.

30. Bernice Brown Cronkhite, "'Grave Alice,'" *Radcliffe Quarterly*, November 1965, 11-14. For Longfellow Hall see Bunting, 138(photo)-140.

31. Henry Wadsworth Longfellow: *Poems and Other Writings*. Ed. J. D. McClatchy (Library of America, 2000), 19-20. McClatchy's assessment of Longfellow as "a much better poet than is now supposed," *New York Times Book Review*, 22 October 2000, 39. Editor Hilen on his "frequent walks to Boston," *LHWL* 2:4. He courted Frances Appleton by walking often to her home at 39 Beacon Street, where they were married on 13 July 1843; Thompson, *Young Longfellow*, 255, 267, 335-37 (his most joyous walk ).

32. N.S.B. Gras, *Harvard Co-operative Society Past and Present, 1882-1942* (Harvard University Press, 1942), esp. 35, 57, 94. I am thankful for general manager Allan E. Powell for the loan of this book.

33. TWHD; quotes, 30 June and 30 August 1893.

34. John Clendenning, *The Life and Thought of Josiah Royce* (1985; Vanderbilt University Press, 1999), revised and expanded edition, 12-17. One of their residences before Josiah was born was a small farm near Martinez. Sarah Royce, *A Frontier Lady: Recollections of the Gold Rush and Early California* (1932; University of Nebraska Press, 1977), Ralph Henry Gabriel, ed. H. W. Brands, *The Age of Gold: The California Gold Rush and the New American Dream* (New York: Doubleday, 2002), 133-35, 137-40, 150-52, 168-74, 189-90, 213, 280-81(San Francisco). A map of the Royce Route is between pages 214 and 215.

35. Joseph LeConte, *A Journal of Ramblings through the High Sierra of California by the University Party* (1875; Sierra Club, 1960). Lester D. Stephens, *Joseph LeConte: Gentle Prophet of Evolution* (Louisiana State University Press, 1982), 213, 1893 trip; 298-302, death. William Dallam Armes, ed., *The Autobiography of Joseph LeConte* (New York: D. Appleton, 1903), ix-xiii, death. Muir arrived in Yosemite with his daughters to join the Sierra Club Outing after LeConte's death; Letter, Wanda Muir to Louie Muir, 14 July 1901, Crocker's. Frank Soulé, "Joseph LeConte in the Sierra, *Sierra Club Bulletin*, January 1902, 1-10, for his Yosemite visits. John Muir, "Reminiscences of Joseph LeConte," *The University of California Magazine*, September 1901, 209-13; this whole issue commemorates LeConte. Josiah Royce, "Joseph LeConte," *The International Monthly*, July 1901, 324-34.

36. John Clendenning, *The Life and Thought of Josiah Royce*, 219-20. John Clendenning, ed., *The Letters of Josiah Royce* (University of Chicago Press, 1970), 348-50. Armes, *The Autobiography of Joseph LeConte*, 327. Stephens, in *Joseph LeConte*, 260, says Mrs. LeConte was with him.

37. Clendenning, *The Life and Thought of Josiah Royce*, 168-70, and *The Letters of Josiah Royce*, 25-6; Letters to Johnson and Horace Elisha Scudder, 243-5; 252-69. I have not found Muir's copy of Royce's book on California, which Royce dedicated to his mother.

38. Clendenning, *The Life and Thought of Josiah Royce*, 190, and *The Letters of Josiah Royce*, 313 and note 120. "I have just returned form Chicago," Royce wrote 1 July 1893; "At Chicago I saw the Fair."

39. Telegram, Muir to George A. Plimpton, 9 December 1913, Martinez, California, HASC; Clendenning, *The Letters of Josiah Royce*, 611-12.

40. Simon Schama, *Dead Certainties* (1991; Vintage Books, 1992), 41. St. Botolph, founded in 1880 as a social and literary society for elite men, is still located at 199 Commonwealth Avenue, Boston. According to Adrienne Fried Block in *Amy Beach, Passionate Victorian: The Life and Work of an American Composer, 1867-1944* (New York: Oxford University Press, 1998), 107, Olmsted was a member and women artists exhibited at the club. Joan D. Hedrick, *Harriet Beecher Stowe: A Life* (New York: Oxford University Press, 1994), 289-91, discusses the role of Boston's male clubs.

41. *Garden and Forest*, 15 November 1893, lead editorial. Justin Winsor and John Fiske, *Atlantic*, May 1894, 660-74.

42. *The Historical Register of Harvard University* (Harvard University Press, 1937), 365, and the Quinquennial File, Harvard University Archives.

43. See *ANB*; Helen Lefkowitz Horowitz, *Alma Mater: Design and Experience in the Women's Colleges from Their Nineteenth-Century Beginnings to the 1930s* (1984; University of

Massachusetts Press, 1993), 95-104, 237-47. Dorothy Elia Howells, *A Century to Celebrate: Radcliffe College, 1879-1979* (Radcliffe College, 1978), 1-19. For Fay House, see Bunting, 130-33, photos 131-3. A. W. Longfellow also designed Agassiz House (1904) with Agassiz Theater on the second floor; Boston artist Sarah Wyman Whitman assisted him with the interior, 139. Their moving into their new home in fall 1854 is in Edward Lurie, *Louis Agassiz: A Life in Science* (1960; Johns Hopkins University Press, 1988), 192.

44. Letter, Florence Willard to Muir, 13 March 1913, Cambridge, Massachusetts. For Florence Ryerson (1892-1965), *Biographical Encyclopaedia and Who's Who of the American Theatre*, Walter Rigdon, ed. (New York: Heineman, 1966), 796. See also her folder in the Radcliffe Archives. Letter, Muir to Charles Dwight Willard, 29 December 1912, is in *JMLJ*, 220-21, with Branch's biographical note on Charles Dwight Willard (1860-1914). Letter, Florence Willard to Muir, 26 January 1911, Pasadena, thanking Muir for his gift to replace her lost books. Also see Muir's letter to C.D. Willard, 8 August 1898, Martinez; it was published in Los Angeles *Evening Express* (Kimes, 63).

45. ECAD. Joseph E. Garland, *The North Shore* (Beverly, Massachusetts: Commonwealth Editions, 1998), 5. *L&L* II:292-93. Professor and Mrs. Louis Agassiz, *A Journey in Brazil* (1869; Boston: Ticknor and Fields, 6th edition [1896]; and Boston and New York: Houghton Mifflin, 1909). Both editions are in Muir's library at HASC; both contain Muir's index at the back, the 1909 index being the more extensive, as he prepared to travel to this region in 1911. See Linda S. Bergmann, "Elizabeth Cary Agassiz," in *DLB* 189:12-17.

46. ECAD. Five women were charter members of the Sierra Club, Jones, Appendix A, 170-3.

47. Caroline Hazard, "To Mrs. Agassiz," *The Yosemite and Other Verse* (Houghton Mifflin, 1917), 43.

48. Letter, William James to Charles Eliot, 19 May 1894, Cambridge, Charles W. Eliot Papers, Scrapbook 8, Box 449, Harvard University Archives.

49. Diary of Charles Eliot, 10 June [1893], Frances Loeb Library, Graduate School of Design, Harvard University.

50. President Eliot's home in 1875 is shown in Charles W. Eliot, *Harvard Memories* (Harvard University Press, 1923), 143.

51. Charles W. Eliot Papers, Scrapbook 7, Box 448, Harvard University Archives.

52. Letters, Pelham W. Ames to Muir, 12 February and 3 March 1892, San Francisco. Formal invitation is dated 14 March 1892. *San Francisco Chronicle*, 22 and 23 March 1892, 12 (both).

53. Henry James, *Charles W. Eliot, President of Harvard University, 1869-1909* (Houghton Mifflin, 1930), I:319-21, 343. Samuel Eliot Morison, *The Story of Mount Desert Island* (Boston: Little, Brown, 1960), 47, 51-6. Charles W. Eliot, *Charles Eliot: Landscape Architect* (Houghton Mifflin,1902; University of Massachusetts Press, 1999), xl, 308-15 (Maine coast), 418, 420. Dates are from Charles Eliot's Diary [1893].

54. Bolles does not appear on Johnson's certificate. *DAB, ANB*. William R. Thayer, "Frank Bolles," *Harvard Graduate Magazine*, March 1894, 366-71. Gras, *Harvard Co-operative Society Past and Present, 1882-1942* , 8-9. Although the *DAB* indicates that they had four daughters, as does the *ANB*, the city clerk at Cambridge City Hall has been able to locate only three birth certificates. The name of their fourth child is given in *The Life of Frank Bolles* by Elizabeth Swan Bolles; this manuscript (c.1902) and a typescript thereof by Evelyn Bolles (1962) are in the Harvard University Archives (hereafter *The Life of Frank Bolles*). His office and Eliot's were in 5 University Hall.

For a picture of the Washington Elm with Stephen F. Batchelder's commentary, see Sheila Connor, *New England Natives* (Harvard University Press, 1994), 111.

55. Chocorua House Register, 3 October 1884, Chocorua Public Library, Chocorua, New Hampshire. This register shows nine stays by Bolles from 1884 to 1892, two of them with his wife, and four by William James in this period. Robert L. McGrath, *Gods in Granite: The Art of the White Mountains of New Hampshire* (Syracuse University Press, 2001), 31-53.

56. Frank Bolles, *Land of the Lingering Snow: Chronicles of a Stroller in New England from January to June* (Houghton Mifflin, 1891), 211. Frank Bolles, *At the North of Bearcamp Water: Chronicles of a Stroller in New England from July to December* (Houghton Mifflin, 1893), 159-60. Stephen F. Ells, "From Boston's Hills to Chocorua's Heights: Frank Bolles Wrote from the Land," *Appalachia*, December 2002, 92-112. I am indebted to Stephen Ells for his paper of 25 January 2003 on which this article was based, "Frank Bolles of Chocorua and Cambridge: Writer, Naturalist, and Educator (1856-1894)," his correspondence of 1 February 2003, and for his resurrection of Frank Bolles. I have been unable to locate the journals of Frank Bolles or Lily Bolles for 1893.

57. See Ells, "From Boston's Hills to Chocorua's Heights," 98-100; Charles Foster Batchelder, *An Account of the Nuttall Ornithological Club 1873 to 1919* (Cambridge: Nuttall Ornithological Club, 1937),53-4, 84; for Batchelder (1856-1954), who served as club treasurer for fifty years (1880-1930), 78, 83; also, *Who Was Who in America* 3:55.

58. Unidentified reviewer, "Chocorua in Literature," *Atlantic*, June 1893, 844-48. Frank Bolles's "Individuality in Birds" was in the previous month's issue, *Atlantic*, May 1893, 619-25, and appeared in his *From Blomidon to Smoky and Other Papers* (Houghton Mifflin, 1894), 219-36, which his wife collected after his death.

59. Frank Bolles, *At the North of Bearcamp Water: Chronicles of a Stroller in New England from July to December*, 62. This chapter, "A Night Alone on Chocorua," was published as "Alone on Chocorua at Night" in *Atlantic*, December 1892, 758-64. For all his love of mountains, Bolles did not join the Appalachian Mountain Club. I am indebted to Martha Moore, Archivist, AMC, for checking the Club's Register of Membership.

60. Henry James did visit William at Chocorua in September 1904. Arriving the night of the 2nd, he stayed until the 18th, when the brothers traveled deeper into the White Mountains, stopping in Jackson, New Hampshire, where Henry had another view of the Presidential Range (He had climbed Washington and Lafayette in the summer of 1861; see Leon Edel, *The Life of Henry James: The Untried Years, 1843-1870*, Philadelphia: J. B. Lippincott, 169.). Henry was delighted in Chocorua, according to William, and "in general with the feminine delicacy, charm, elegance, slenderness and sentimentality of Nature in America—especially here in the mountains" (*CWJ* 10:474). Henry then went on to Cambridge, where he walked by Longfellow's and Lowell's, much as Muir had done. Henry captured this time in an essay, "New England: An Autumn Impression," which appeared serially in the *North American Review*, April-June 1905, and as the first chapter in *The American Scene* (30 January 1907), which William enjoyed, especially the Chocorua part. William read the American edition from Harper & Brothers; it was also published by Chapman and Hall in England (*CWJ* 3:337, 342-3,346). For Henry's New England visit, see Fred Kaplan, *Henry James*, 478-87; Leon Edel, *The Life of Henry James: The Master, 1901-1916* (Philadelphia: J. B. Lippincott, 1972), 239-61, 239-42, New Hampshire.

61. Traveling to the White Mountains in the first part of September 1886, James became familiar with the Chocorua country, *CWJ* 6:159-62, 164. Chocorua House Register, 4 September 1886, Chocorua Public Library. On 17 September 1886, James wrote Henry of

his intention to buy land there, *CWJ* 2:51 and n2; On 9 November 1886, James wrote his sister Alice in London that he was buying a place at Chocorua Lake this week for $800, *CWJ* 6:179; Simon, 208. Walk across lake, *CWJ* 6:218; stay at Nickerson's, *CWJ* 6: 218; 403-4 (lunch). James wrote Henry about his five days in Chocorua and later sent him sketch of his property, *CWJ* 2:62, 68-9. Mail, *CWJ* 2:90. Gerry Davies and Mark Smith, *A History of Chocorua Public Library, 1888-1988* (Chocorua Public Library, 1988), 3, 5-7. Intimacy of Keene Valley, *CWJ* 6:587; Simon says that Keene Valley always remained James's favorite retreat, 208; though, according to Ignas K. Skrupskelis, his wife rarely went there with him, *CWJ* 11:xxiv. She did love Chocorua, however, *CWJ* 11:51.

62. *Boston Evening Transcript*, 28 June 1893, 1. Frank Bolles, *From Blomidon to Smoky and Other Papers*, 36. Lily Bolles, "Nova Scotia & Cape Breton" Journal, 25 July-17 August 1893 (pressed flowers within), Tamworth Historical Society, Tamworth, New Hampshire. Had the Bolleses read of Charles Dudley Warner's 1873 trip to Baddeck? It would be interesting to compare their two accounts (see chapter 4).

63. *NYT*, 11 January 1894, 8, obituary. *The Life of Frank Bolles*, 163. Frank Bolles, "From Blomidon to Smoky," "Ingonish, by Land and Sea," "The Home of Glooscap," "August Birds in Cape Breton," *Atlantic*, May, June, July, August, 1894, 592-604, 781-87, 47-56, 158-66, respectively. These articles became the first four chapters of *From Blomidon to Smoky and Other Papers*. *NYT*, 27 October 1894, 3, review. Two days later, the *NYT* reviewed Muir's *The Mountains of California*, 29 October 1894, 3.

64. Between his February 1825 enrollment and his August 1827 graduation, Emerson was absent from Harvard a good deal coping with eye difficulties, teaching, traveling in the South (November 1826-June 1827), and preaching. His famous Divinity School Address was given here on 15 July 1838, when Muir, not quite three months old, was in Scotland.

65. *DAB, ANB*. Edwin Tenney Brewster, *Life and Letters of Josiah Dwight Whitney* (Houghton Mifflin, 1909), 145-46, 355, 357-8. The Northampton Birth Register shows their daughter's name as Lena Goddard. Louisa Goddard Howe was born in Manchester, England.

66. Smith College archivist Nanci A. Young informed me that Maria Whitney (1830-1910) taught at Smith from 1876 to 1880 (Letter, 16 July 2003). She first appeared in the *Cambridge Directory* in 1893; in 1897, she moved to Josiah Whitney's home after his death. See Leyda, I:lxxviii-lxxix, and related entries for her relationship with Emily Dickinson and Samuel Bowels Thomas H. Johnson, ed., *The Letters of Emily Dickinson* contains seventeen letters to Maria Whitney (1877-1885); presumably hers to Dickinson were destroyed, xxiv. *Boston Evening Transcript*, 20 January 1910, 3, 10; *Daily Hampshire Gazette* [Northampton, MA], 20 January 1910, 2, obituaries.

Muir and Maria Whitney also connected through her niece, Katharine Putnam, whom Maria came to California to care for upon the death of Katharine's mother, Elizabeth Whitney Putnam (1822-1863). Samuel Marshall Ilsley, *Katharine Hooker: A Memoir* (Santa Barbara, California: The Schauer Printing Studio, 1935), 16. Though Katharine Hooker (1849-1935) was born in Milwaukee, she lived in Northampton, Massachusetts, until 1853, when she went to California with her mother, her father having gone before in 1849. She married John D. Hooker in 1869 (see chapter 12 n32). She made five trips to Italy (in 1896, 1899, 1903, 1913-1914, and 1922), and wrote *Wayfarers in Italy* (San Francisco: D. P. Elder and Morgan Shepard, 1902), presenting an autographed copy to Muir in June 1907, which is in Muir's library at HASC; it has no Muir index or marks. After Muir's death, her other books appeared: *Byways in Southern Tuscany* (New York: C. Scribner's Sons, 1918), *Through the Heel of Italy* (New York: Rae D. Henkle Co., 1927); and *Farmhouses and Small Provincial Buildings in Southern Italy* (New York: Architectural Book Publishing Co., 1925) with Marian Osgood Hooker and Myron

Hunt. She and Marian Hooker are in *Who Was Who Among North American Authors* (Detroit: Gale Research, 1976), 724.

Maria Whitney's letter of 21 December [1909?], Cambridge, is glued inside Edwin Tenney Brewster, *Life and Letters of Josiah Dwight Whitney* (Houghton Mifflin, 1909) in Muir's library at the HASC. I am grateful to Ronald H. Limbaugh for his discovery of this letter. Muir's twenty-nine item index included six page references to Whitney, two to his death, and two to Mt. Whitney.

67. James Lyman Whitney and William Dwight Whitney are in *DAB* and *ANB*. J. L. Whitney died 25 September 1910; *Boston Evening Transcript*, 26 September 1910, 12, and 27 September 1910, 3.

68. Dennis C. Williams, *God's Wilds: John Muir's Vision of Nature* (Texas A&M University Press, 2002), 92; discussion of Whitney-Muir controversy and Muir's methods of investigation, 70-80. Keith Burich, "Josiah Dwight Whitney, John Muir and Clarence King, and the 'Chasm of the Yosemite,'" in Sally M. Miller, ed., *John Muir in Historical Perspective* (New York: Peter Lang, 1999), 165-84. For Burich, King's "analysis of the Yosemite region was more insightful and, ultimately, more accurate than Muir's" (175). Like Muir, King did not accept Whitney's subsidence hypothesis. Fox, 23-24. Brewster, *Life and Letters of Josiah Dwight Whitney*, 360-61 (quote), 266.

69. F. Allen Burt, *The Story of Mount Washington* (Hanover, New Hampshire: Dartmouth Publications, 1960), 48. Charles T. Jackson and another assistant Eben Baker were also in the Mt. Washington party with Tom Crawford and his seventy-five-year-old father, Abel. Charles T. Jackson, *Final Report on the Geology and Mineralogy of the State of New Hampshire* (Concord, New Hampshire: Carroll and Baker, State Printers, 1844), 27, Jackson's assistants; 49-52, 67-73, reports of Whitney and Williams (called Camels Rump then); 76-78, Lafayette and Washington. Charles T. Jackson, *First Annual Report of the Geology of the State of New Hampshire* (Concord, New Hampshire: Cyrus Barton, State Printer, 1841), 100-03; the Mt. Washington section is the same as in the *Final Report*.

70. For Whitney in Yosemite, see Francis P. Farquhar, ed., *Up and Down California in 1860-1864: Journal of William Henry Brewer* (Yale University Press, 1930), 403-06, 581-2, itinerary. After California, Brewer (1828-1910), who was born in Poughkeepsie, New York, taught at Yale from 1864 to 1903. As members of the 1896 National Forestry Commission and the 1899 Harriman Alaska Expedition, Muir and Brewer came to know each other. Brewer died in November 1910, eight months before Muir came to New Haven (see chapter 16). W.H. Brewer, Sereno Watson, and Asa Gray, *Botany* (Cambridge, MA: John Wilson and Son, University Press, 1880; 2nd rev. ed.), volume I; and volume II by Sereno Watson (Geological Survey of California) are in Muir's library at the HASC; both contain Muir indexes. In his library from Whitney's Geological Survey of California are *Geology. Volume I. Report of Progress and Synopsis of the Field-Work, From 1860 to 1864* (Philadelphia: Caxton Press of Sherman & Co., 1865) with Part II: The Geology of the Sierra Nevada; and S. F. Baird, ed. *Ornithology. Volume I. Land Birds* (Cambridge: University Press: Welch, Bigelow, & Co. 1870) with Muir Index in the latter. Brewer's Diary of the Harriman Alaska Expedition in his papers in the Archives of the Yale University Library, I expect, though I have not consulted it, would reveal something of their relationship. I have not been able to find any correspondence between them. Brewer is in *DAB* and *ANB*.

71. First Ascent: John Muir Journal of Yosemite, Kings Canyon and Mono Trip, 18 September-10 November 1873 (JMP, Reel 24), esp. 128-31; JOM, 172-88, esp. 187; Wolfe, 169-70. Peter Browning, *Place Names of the Sierra Nevada* (Berkeley, California: Wilderness Press, 1986), 236-38. Thirty years later Muir recalled his first ascent as being on 29 October, which is the original

date used in his journal, over which he wrote "21st." See Geo. W. Stewart, "Mt. Whitney," *Mt. Whitney Club Journal*, May 1903, 80-81. Muir was elected a member in the Mt. Whitney Club in 1902-1903, 87. Evidently there were only three issues of the *Mt. Whitney Club Journal*, in May 1902, 1903, and 1904. Returning to Yosemite Valley in mid-November, Muir wrote his sister Sarah, "I have traveled over a thousand miles in this last excursion" (Letter, 14 November 1873). On 16 October, Muir had written Jeanne Carr of his first attempt of Whitney; see Gisel, 225-26 (Letter, 16 October 1873).

72. His second ascent is in Robert Engberg, ed., *John Muir Summering in the Sierra* (University of Wisconsin Press, 1984), 103-12, which reprints his correspondence from the San Francisco *Daily Evening Bulletin*, 24 August 1875. Francis P. Farquhar in "The Story of Mount Whitney," *Sierra Club Bulletin*, February 1929, 39-52, and *History of the Sierra Nevada* (University of California Press, 1965), 173-87, discusses the early ascents of Whitney, including Clarence King's of 19 September 1873, a month before Muir's. Muir's last ascent is in Frederic R. Gunsky, *South of Yosemite: Selected Writings of John Muir* (Berkeley: Wilderness Press, 1988), 103-6. Gunsky says that "Miss Marian Hooker, a grandniece of J. D. Whitney, [who] was seventy-two" accompanied Muir to the top. She did in fact go with Muir to Whitney's summit, though she was just twenty-seven. She was not the first woman to be on top, as indicated in her obituary, Santa Barbara, CA *Morning Press*, 16 February 1968; that honor went to a party of four women on 3 August 1878; see Farquhar, *History of the Sierra Nevada*, 179-80; and account of Anna Mills Johnston, "A Trip to Mt. Whitney in 1878," *Mt. Whitney Club Journal*, May 1902, 1. Marian Osgood Hooker (1875-1968) was a Sierra Club member and a graduate of the University of California, San Francisco, Medical School in May 1910. According to William James she was already studying medicine when he met her in January 1906, *CWJ* 11:140. Letters, Muir to Robert Underwood Johnson, 28 August 1902, Martinez; Marian Hooker to Muir, 7 September 1902, Los Angeles.

## TRIP ONE: 1893

## CHAPTER 4—MANCHESTER-BY-THE-SEA

1. Emerson's walk is mentioned in Stanley Paterson and Carl Seaburg, *Nahant on the Rocks* (Nahant Historical Society, 1991), 90, and in Longfellow's Ms. Journal of 31 August 1851 in the Houghton Library, Harvard University. I am indebted to Professor Albert J. von Frank for his transcription and illumination of this moment. According to Frank, Emerson had come to discuss his *Memoir of Margaret Fuller Ossoli* (1852) with William Wetmore Story (1819-1895; *DAB, ANB*) and his wife Emelyn Bartlett Eldredge Story (1820-1894) both of whom knew Fuller in Italy. Most likely, Emerson was walking to the summer home of Abel Adams in Lynn for the night. This, according to Diane Shephard, was at 39 Ocean Street on Nahant Bay. Adams appeared in the 1851 and 1854 city directories only. In 1856 Boston merchant James Lawrence built a house at this address; this was sold to William T. Hart, president of the New York, New Haven and Hartford Railroad, who lived here when Muir passed. Letters to J. Parker Huber from Albert J. von Frank, Pullman, Washington, 18 October 2001 (postmark) and Diane Shephard, Lynn, Massachusetts, 30 October 2001.

2. Ernest Wadsworth Longfellow, *Random Memories* (Houghton Mifflin, 1922), 16.

3. *LHWL*, 4:508, "The Bells of Lynn"; the original ms. is in the Nahant Public Library, presumably the gift of Alice Longfellow; Letter, Daniel A. deStefano to J. Parker Huber, 21 March 2002. E.W. Longfellow, *Random Memories*, 58, many sails. *LHWL* 4:348-9, Alice's sail. The Longfellow house burned on 18 May 1896, Stanley C. Paterson and Carl G. Seaburg,

*Nahant on the Rocks* (Nahant Historical Society, 1991), 258. For Longfellow's residences before this purchase see the unpublished paper of Douglas Cisney, "Longfellow and Nahant" (2 pages) in the Nahant Historical Society.

Blanche Roosevelt Tucker-Macchetta, *The Home Life of Henry W. Longfellow: Reminiscences of Many Visits at Cambridge and Nahant, During the Years 1880, 1881 and 1882* (New York: G. W. Carlton & Co., 1882), 69-75, passim. The diva Blanche Roosevelt Tucker-Macchetta (1853-1898) arrived by boat at Nahant the morning of 13 July 1880, *LHWL* 6:623. One of Longfellow's last letters, that of 14 March 1882 (*LHWL* 6:780), was to her; it implied that the poet had not read her book, while her introduction indicated that "He reviewed and revised all that was written most thoroughly."

Even Bradford Torrey birded on Nahant; see "A Great Blue Heron," in *The Foot-Path Way* (Houghton Mifflin, 1892), 202.

4. Thoreau related his visit in his *Journal* of 14 January 1858, which Muir read, though he neither marked nor indexed those pages in his copy. ECAD, 10 June 1893.

5. James W. Byrkit, ed., *Charles Lummis: Letters from the Southwest: September 20, 1884 to March 14, 1885* (Tucson: University of Arizona Press, 1989). The last letter is dated 1 March, not 14, 1885. In the Introduction, Byrkit discusses some of the differences in Lummis's letters to Chillicothe and Los Angeles, and in his book; he finds the Chillicothe letters more honest, more revealing of the author, than the Los Angeles ones and the book. "Pike's Peak, Colorado, 5 November 1884," 58-74; Lummis spent the night of 4 November in the U.S. Signal Service Station atop, where snow abounded. La Veta and Middle Creek Pass are in his letter from "Alamosa, Colorado, Tuesday, November 18th, 1884," 96-8. Grand Canyon is at end of his letter from "Peach Springs, Arizona, Tuesday, January 20th, 1885," 255-59. "Los Angeles, California, Sunday February 15th, 1885" for "paradise," etc., 290-93. Charles F. Lummis, *A Tramp Across the Continent* (1892; University of Nebraska Press, 1982), 44-9, Pikes Peak; 76-7, Middle Creek Pass; 242-48, Grand Canyon; 267-70, Cajon Pass to Los Angeles. The March 1892 edition of the Huerfano Park, Colorado, USGS topographical quadrangle shows Lummis's Middle and Wagon creeks, and the old trail he followed over the mountains, a shorter route than that of the Denver and Rio Grande Railroad via La Veta Pass to the north, but this map does not indicate Middle Creek Pass. Mark Thompson, *American Character: The Curious Life of Charles Fletcher Lummis and the Rediscovery of the Southwest* (New York: Arcade Publishing, 2001), says that Lummis went over La Veta Pass (28, 32, 39)—close enough perhaps—and that he missed the Grand Canyon (46), which he did not.

6. Kimes, 117 and 124. Letter, Muir to Charles F. Lummis, 11 June 1895, Martinez; and his reply of 14 June 1895, Los Angeles. Returning Muir's payment of one dollar for a year's subscription, Lummis wrote, "the time has not come when we can take John Muir's money." Elizabeth Pomeroy, *John Muir: A Naturalist in Southern California* (Pasadena, CA: Many Moons Press, 2001), 39-47, selects nine letters from their correspondence, 102-12. *The Masterkey* of July 1945, 127-30, featured nine Muir-to-Lummis letters in the Southwest Museum. There are sixty-seven Muir-Lummis letters in JMP, thirty-seven of them from Muir. While not mentioning Lummis's birthplace, Mark Thompson, in *American Character: The Curious Life of Charles Fletcher Lummis*, states that Muir formed "a close friendship with Lummis," wrote "occasionally for the magazine" (184)—which he did not—and attended social events at El Alisal, signing the guest book (194-6). When telling of Muir's June 1905 visit and his day trip south to San Juan Capistrano with Lummis, Thompson incorrectly identifies one of Muir's daughters as a "railroad engineer" (270). Three Muirs did sign the El Alisal guest book in June 1905, Thomas Andrews, executive director of the Historical Society of Southern California, has verified.

Although Lummis's review of Muir's *Our National Parks* in the March 1902 issue of *Out West* was a paean to the author, not the book, Muir thanked him anyhow (Letter, 18 March 1902, Martinez). Lummis also made several photographs of Muir that he gave him.

Lummis's editorship of *Land of Sunshine* and *Out West* is discussed by Edwin R. Bingham, *Charles F. Lummis: Editor of the Southwest* (San Marino, California: Henry E. Huntington Library, 1955). In two chapters (134-86) Bingham considers the prominent contributors— Lummis was the prime one—and the merits of their prose, poetry, and art. Bingham says that *Out West* stopped appearing regularly in June 1917, and merged in May 1923 with the *Overland Monthly*, which ceased publication in July 1935 (51). Also, Lawrence Clark Powell considers Lummis's editorship as his "classic achievement in Californiana" in *California Classics* (Los Angeles: Ward Ritchie Press, 1971), 292-4 and his life in *Southwest Classics* (1974; University of Arizona Press, 1987), 43-55.

Jane Apostol, *El Alisal: Where History Lingers* (Los Angeles: Historical Society of Southern California, 1994), esp. 41-71. Lummis's photograph of El Alisal in 1905, at the time of Muir's visit, is shown on p. 74.

The new *Writing Los Angeles: A Literary Anthology*, David L. Ulin, ed. (Library of America, 2002) excludes Lummis and Muir, but includes Mary Austin and Helen Hunt Jackson.

7. Robert Underwood Johnson, *Remembered Yesterdays* (Boston: Little, Brown, 1923), 392. For Annie and James Fields see *DAB* and *ANB*. "James T. Fields: The Publisher as Editor," in Sedgwick, 69-111. My discussion is informed by Rita K. Gollin, *Annie Adams Fields: Woman of Letters* (University of Massachusetts Press, 2002).

8. *LHWL* 4:331, 417, 502, for invitations in 1863, 1864, 1865; 5:552-3, 1872.

9. *LHWL* 6:377-8 & 378n1. Longfellow's visit was on 5-7 August 1878. *LHWL* 6:372 and 373n1. His explanation of the poem's factual origin is in his letter of 8 July 1877, 6:281-2. Two weeks after the gale, Longfellow effortlessly composed the ballad as it entered his mind in stanzas, not lines, between midnight of 30 December and sunrise of the next day. Henry Beston, "The Real Wreck of the Hesperus," *The Bookman*, 1925, 304-6, set the record straight: the *Hesperus* did not wreck on Norman's Woe. Elizabeth Stuart Phelps (*Chapters from a Life* [Houghton Mifflin, 1897], 153-7) remembered Longfellow as "one of the gentlest men whom I ever knew" and his coming only once to Gloucester when she showed him Norman's Woe. She boarded then with Clarence and Annie Wonson at the north end of Niles Beach; Longfellow called it "The Sea Shell." Later, in 1880 according to Joseph E. Garland (*The North Shore* [Beverly, MA: Commonwealth Editions, 1998], 132), she built a cottage called "The Old Maids' Paradise" located on the Wonson's land. Apparently this was moved from shore to farm on Grapevine Road in 1888, Joseph E. Garland said (*Chapters from a Life*, 273, implied the early 1890s) in *Eastern Point: A Nautical, Rustical, and Social Chronicle of Gloucester's Outer Shield and Inner Sanctum, 1606-1950* (Peterborough, New Hampshire: William L. Bauhan, Publisher, Noone House, 1971), 155.

10. *LHWL* 6:373. Editor Hilen says that "their correspondence [James T. Fields and Longfellow] does not adequately convey their intimacy.", 5:8-9.

11. *LHWL* 6:507, 3 August 1879; 6:632-33, Longfellow regretted not being able to come to Manchester in the summer of 1880. James Fields's death on 24 April 1881 was "a great shock" to Longfellow, who lost his close friend of almost forty years. The next spring, on 24 March, Longfellow too succumbed.

12. *LHWL* 4:384.

13. Dorothy Becker Neal graciously opened Thunderbolt Hill to me on Sunday afternoon, 5 August 1990, showing the library, James Fields's study (converted to a bathroom), the guest

room, the separate bedrooms of Annie Fields and Sarah Orne Jewett (Gollin says that wherever they stayed, they slept apart, 349n11), and gardens with thirty varieties of chrysanthemums. Dorothy and her husband, Kirke A. Neal (1901-1973), moved from Michigan to Cape Ann to relieve her allergies; they bought the house in 1938 from Annie Fields's nephew Zabdiel Boylston Adams. Dorothy Neal, who was born in 1907 in Detroit, died in 1994.

14. Thoreau, *Journal*, 22-23, 30 September 1858. J. Parker Huber, "Following Thoreau and Other Naturalists," in *Thoreau Among Others: Essays in Honor of Walter Harding*, eds. Rita K. Gollin and James B. Scholes (Geneseo, New York: State University College of Arts and Science at Geneseo, 1983), 40-62, for an account of their venture to Gloucester. The Reverend John Lewis Russell (1808-1873) of Salem became vice president of the Essex Institute when it formed from the merger of the Historical and Natural History societies in 1848; he was a founding member of the latter. Ralph W. Dexter, "The Essex County Natural History Society, 1833-1848" and "Natural History at the Essex Institute, 1848-1898," *Essex Institute Historical Collections*, January 1977, 38-53 and January 1980, 21-33, respectively. Though Russell was professor of Botany and Horticultural Physiology of the Massachusetts Horticultural Society for forty years, its history makes only minimal reference to him at his death; see Benson, 176, and Edmund B. Willson, "Memoir of John Russell Lewis," *Historical Collections of the Essex Institute*, July 1874, 168.

Thoreau had lectured in Gloucester's Town Hall on Wednesday night 20 December 1848. Bradley P. Dean and Ronald Wesley Hoag, "Thoreau's Lectures Before *Walden*: An Annotated Calendar," *Studies in the American Renaissance 1995*, ed. Joel Myerson (University Press of Virginia, 1995), 161-4. Emerson had come to Gloucester and to Manchester numerous times to lecture.

15. Gollin, *Annie Adams Fields*, 66 (dinner). Howe, "With Dickens in America", 135-95. Ackroyd, 1009-1025, Dickens's second American tour ("pedestrian" quote, 1012). Ackroyd says dinner was with the Fieldses only, 1010. *LHWL* 5:187-88, 188n1 passim. The excitement of Dickens and his readings was conveyed in several of Longfellow's letters. Gollin, *Annie Adams Fields*, 65-76, Dickens; 76, quote. J.T. Fields, "Some Memories of Charles Dickens," *Atlantic*, August 1870, 235-45. Her coauthorship of this essay was not recognized, according to Gollin (76). Annie also made selections from her journal for another tribute: Jas. T. Fields, "Our Whispering Gallery," *Atlantic*, August 1871, 222-31. Dickens dominated half of this twelve-part, monthly series that ran for one year only, 1871. A new, short, insightful biography is Jane Smiley, *Charles Dickens* (Lipper/Viking, 2002), a review of which by David Lodge returned Dickens to the *Atlantic* in May 2002 (92-101).

16. Paula Blanchard, *Sarah Orne Jewett: Her World and Her Work* (Addison-Wesley, 1994), 260-4. Robert Underwood Johnson, *Remembered Yesterdays* (Boston: Little, Brown, 1923), 392. Letter, Clarence C. Buell to Muir, 9 March 1892, New York, reporting on his boss Johnson, whom he expected back on 1 June. Gollin, *Annie Adams Fields*, 216 (Manchester), 243-6 (Europe), 270-1 (Johnson), 352n2 (Europe with Johnsons). Annie Fields, ed., *The Letters of Sarah Orne Jewett* (Houghton Mifflin, 1911), 97-100 (Mont Blanc). Letter, Muir to Louie Muir, 16-17 August 1893, Martigny [and Chamonix] and JMJ, August 1893 [undated], p.14-16.

17. *L&L* II:271. John Muir, *Stickeen* (Houghton Mifflin, 1909). Ronald H. Limbaugh in *John Muir's "Stickeen"* relates the evolution of this tale, as told and written. Curiously, its first printed version as written by Emily Swett Parkhurst, eldest daughter of Muir intimates John and Mary Swett, to whom Muir told his story, appeared in *The Youth's Companion* of 13 July 1893; eventually, it was published in the *Century* of September 1897 (Limbaugh, 21-22). Karla Armbruster, "'Good Dog': The Stories We Tell about Our Canine Companions and What

They Mean for Humans and Other Animals," *PLL: Papers on Language & Literature*, Fall 2002, 351-76, esp. 362-68, 372-75, finds Muir's story, contrary to the "classic formula," one exemplary of "a truly caring relationship."

18. Alice Longfellow was no stranger to Maine. She made frequent visits to her aunt and uncle in Portland. In July 1876 she sailed in the yacht *Alice* along the Maine coast (*LHWL* 6:154-55). The next August found her and her sister Annie "in the wild woods of Maine, camping with a party of friends," her father wrote (*LHWL* 6:295). From 27 August to 16 September 1878, she and others vacationed at Caucomgomoc Lake (*LHWL* 6:382-3). This must have been quite an adventure, for it lies in the center of the North Woods between Chesuncook and Allagash lakes. Not even Thoreau's Indian guides took him there. In July 1880 she was at York Beach (*LHWL* 6:619).

19. Blanchard, *Sarah Orne Jewett*, 161-2, 191-2; 270. In 1899 Sarah returned alone to Mouse Island, 312-3. Richard Cary, "More Higginson Letters," *Colby Library Quarterly*, March 1965, 36, 40-41, for his letters to Jewett of 18 and 25 March 1887 and his diary entry of 31 March 1887. Henry Wadsworth Longfellow also had another friend named Sara Jewett (1847-1899), a popular and beautiful actress with whom he corresponded, *LHWL* 6:321 & n1. Sarah shared with Muir the belief in "the spiritual immanence in nature." Blanchard, *Sarah Orne Jewett*, 270.

20. W. D. Howells, "My First Visit to New England," *Literary Friends and Acquaintance*, eds. David F. Hiatt and Edwin H. Cady (Indiana University Press, 1968), 31. Thomas Wortham, et al, eds., *W.D. Howells: Selected Letters, Volume 4: 1892-1901* (Boston:Twayne, 1981), 3, letter of James to Howells, 9 August 1894.

21. *DAB* and *ANB*. Kenneth S. Lynn, *William Dean Howells: An American Life* (New York: Harcourt Brace Jovanovich, 1970), 5-6, 192-4, their homes; 233-35, their summer sojourns; 289-90, 297-8, Winny's health and death. For John Mead Howells (1868-1959) and Mildred Howells (1872-1966) see *Who Was Who* 3:423 and 5:352, respectively. Mildred Howells also edited *Life in Letters of William Dean Howells* (New York: Doubleday, Doran, 1928), 2 v. *The Boston Street Directories* show Howells at 4 Louisburg Square in 1884, at 302 Beacon Street in 1885-1887; not listed in 1888 and 1889; and at 184 Commonwealth Avenue in 1890 and 1891. In light of this and his correspondence, it appears that Edwin H. Cady's statement in the *ANB* that " In truth, Howells hardly ever lived in Boston: only a relatively few months in 1883-1884 and again in 1890-1891..." is incorrect. The new biography of Howells by Susan Goodman and Carl Dawson, expected in May 2005 from the University of California Press, was not available to me at the time of this writing.

Ginette de B. Merrill and George Arms, eds., *If Not Literature: Letters of Elinor Mead Howells* (Ohio State University Press, 1988), discuss the Howellses' penchant for not staying put and Elinor's health. The editors are most impressed with her "vibrancy." They find her a "gifted and charming woman," "not the helpless invalid that all too many accounts present her as being during the greater part of her adult life, especially after Winifred's death." (xxiii, xxxvi, xliii). Robert C. Leitz III, ed., *W.D. Howells:Selected Letters, Volume 3: 1882-1891* (Boston: Twayne, 1980),147-8, states that after Winifred's death, "Elinor, whose health, always fragile, became even more precarious for the rest of her life."

22. Sedgwick, 146. Blanchard, *Sarah Orne Jewett*, 57-67, for early development of her writing. Though "Mr. Bruce" (*Atlantic* 1869, 701-10) was unsigned, the volume contents page identified the author as "A.C. Eliot," Jewett's pseudonym, Blanchard points out. 62. Gollin, *Annie Adams Fields*, 259-61. Gollin posits that Howells may have introduced Fields and Jewett, 347n26. Blanchard suspects their connection came "through James Fields's connections in Portsmouth," 113. *W.D. Howells: Selected Letters, Volume 3: 1882-1891*, 305, Letter to Jewett, 1 February 1891.

23. Johnson, *Remembered Yesterdays*, 354-58. Johnson's certificate indicated that Muir saw Howells, but was not introduced. *The Rise of Silas Lapham* (Boston: Ticknor, 1885) was serialized in eight issues of the *Century* from November 1884 to August 1885. Carl Rollyson, ed., *Critical Survey of Long Fiction* (Salem Press, 2000), 4:1585-87 (quote). Also see George Arms's introduction to *The Rise of Silas Lapham* (New York: Rinehart,1949). This novel—in fact any of Howells's work—is absent from Muir's extant library.

24. *W. D. Howells: Selected Letters, Volume 4: 1892-1901*, 48n2 for their summer itinerary, 50 and notes on 51. "Mr. Howells Sees the Fair," *New York Sun*, 22 October 1893, 9. W. D. Howells, "Letters of an Altrurian Traveller," *Cosmopolitan*, December 1893, 218-32, in an all-Fair issue. *W. D. Howells: Selected Letters, Volume 3: 1882-1891*, 132-34, for their being at Woodland Park Hotel in 1885, from which they moved to Lee's Hotel for rest of their stay, 134-39.

25. W. D. Howells, *Literary Friends and Acquaintance*, eds. David F. Hiatt and Edwin H. Cady (Indiana University Press, 1968). According to editors, the Harvard senior Howells also met was Holmes's son of the same name (1841-1935), who later served on the Supreme Court for thirty years, 324, 44.13-14. Lynn, *William Dean Howells*, 90-102, discusses his first New England visit; 320, quote on *Literary Friends and Acquaintance*.

26. *W. D. Howells: Selected Letters, Volume 5: 1902-1911* (Boston:Twayne, 1985), 3 ("retreated"), 125 (Jewett and Henry James), 133 (heat of summer). The editors say that Howells accompanied James to Berwick to see Jewett, echoing Richard Cary, ed. *Sarah Orne Jewett Letters* (Colby College Press, 1967), 139n2. Blanchard, *Sarah Orne Jewett*, 354, indicates that James made the trip alone. Leon Edel, *The Life of Henry James: The Master, 1901-1916* (Philadelphia: J. B. Lippincott, 1972), 304, implies that James saw them separately without specifying where Jewett was. Odell dates James's departure on 5 July (305); while Howells thought he sailed on the 4th (5:126).

Howells, "My Mark Twain," in *Literary Friends and Acquaintance*, 313-14. Albert Bigelow Paine, *Mark Twain: A Biography* (New York: Harper and Brothers, 1912), 3:1176-78. Henry Nash Smith and William M. Gibson, eds., *Mark Twain-Howells Letters* (Harvard University Press, 1960), 742-48, for their Kittery Point-York Harbor exchanges.

Michael Lee, "William Dean Howells in Kittery Point," *Coast Pilot*, 8 July 1987, 3-6,8. I am grateful to Hope B. Neilson, Director of the Rice Public Library, Kittery, Maine, for sending me this article. Michael Gowell, "Pepperrell Cove," *Cross-Grained & Wily Waters: A Guide to the Piscataqua Maritime Region*, W. Jeffrey Bolster, ed. (Portsmouth, New Hampshire: Peter E. Randall Publisher, 2002), 190-92. Howells's home is now owned by Harvard University.

27. Simon, 230-31; *CWJ* 8:41-2; James wished she also "aspired to the wilderness," as he did.

28. Erica E. Hirshler, *A Studio of Her Own: Women Artists in Boston, 1870-1940* (Boston: MFA Publications, 2001), 34-43, 199; Plate 9 (Thaxter's *An Island Garden*) Plate 10 (Thoreau's *Cape Cod*); *The Book Buyer*, December 1896, 749, reductively considered Watson's "marginal illustrations" the work of an "amateur," and was mute on Whitman's contribution. Whitman's addresses were first, 7 Chestnut Street, and from 1880 until her death in 1904, 77 Mount Vernon Street. See also Nancy Finlay, *Artists of the Book in Boston* (Houghton Library, Harvard College Library, 1985), ix-x, xii, 8-11(*An Island Garden*), 18-19 (Percival Lowell, *Occult Japan or the Way of the Gods*, 1894; with her monogram), 42-3 (*Cape Cod*), 93-4 (Hassam), 106-7 (Watson and Whitman). Sue Allen and Charles Gullans, *Decorated Cloth in America: Publishers' Bindings, 1840-1910* (Los Angeles: University of California, 1994) contains an essay by Gullans in part on Whitman, 55-75, color plates of Whitman, 65-72, and "A Short List of Book Covers Designed by Mrs. Whitman," 97-107.

29. James found Whitman "An extraordinary and indefinable creature!" He told Henry James about Whitman's funeral in his letter of 28 June 1904, *CWJ* 3:272-4. In spring 1903, Whitman executed an oil on canvas portrait of *William James* that is in the Harvard University Art Museums. I was able to date this from the *CWJ* 10: 231, 249, 259, 603.

30. Sarah Wyman Whitman, *Letters* (Cambridge, Mass.: Riverside Press, 1907),v-viii. According to Blanchard, Jewett was not the editor, 352. Of this collection of Whitman letters—written to nineteen persons (identified by name only) and arranged by recipients—Jewett received the most (sixty-four) and Fields the least (one), while William James had ten and Thaxter none. A fuller rendering of Whitman's correspondence with James from 1888 to 1904 is given in the *CWJ*.

At Jewett's initiative, Whitman also designed the interior and windows (including one as a Civil War memorial) for the Fogg Memorial Building of Berwick Academy in South Berwick, Maine—Jewett's alma mater. Blanchard, *Sarah Orne Jewett*, 199-201. Wendy K. Pirsig, "Whitman Sampler," *Preservation*, November/December 2001, 42-7. Whitman would be particularly pleased that her work, demonstrating the value of beautifying the learning environment, has been restored. See also Betty S. Smith, "Inside SPNEA: Sarah de St. Prix Wyman Whitman," *Old-Time New England*, Spring/Summer 1999, 46-64.

31. Blanchard, *Sarah Orne Jewett*, 265. Gollin, *Annie Adams Fields*, 236, 289. According to Gollin, Fields and Jewett were accompanied by the writers Mme. Thèrèse de Solms Blanc, whom they had met in Paris in 1892, and Sarah Chauncey Woolsey of Newport, Rhode Island.

32. A. Growoll, "The Publishers' Exhibits at the World's Columbian Exposition," *The Library Journal*, July 1893, 262-7, esp. 264. "American Publishers' Exhibits at the World's Fair, *The Critic*, 1 July 1893, 7-10 (picture of room, 10). I am indebted to David Hughes for these sources.

33. Sarah Wyman Whitman, *Letters*, 70-1; 101 and 161. *The Boston Evening Transcript*, 29 June 1898, 11. *Revisiting the White City: American Art at the 1893 World's Fair* (Washington, D.C.: National Museum of American Art and National Portrait Gallery, Smithsonian Institution/University Press of New England, 1993), 348.

34. Joseph E. Garland, *The North Shore* (Beverly, Mass.: Commonwealth Editions, 1998), 40-41.

35. For Richard Henry Dana Jr. see *DAB, ANB*, and citations below.

36. *LRWE*, 2:348; McAleer, 69-70.

37. Muir's copy of *Two Years Before the Mast* (Houghton Mifflin, 1895) is in the Huntington Library. Most of Muir's fourteen index items refer to one page only; "Character," however, has twelve page references; one is not legible. I transcribe the index thus:

| | |
|---|---|
| 8 | Sunrise |
| 38 | Albatross |
| 39 | Lost at Sea |
| 44 | Superstition |
| 88 | Character 226. 295 |
| 94 | [?] 276. 300. 318 323, 420, 428, 437 |
| 257 | A dry gale |
| 262 | Grease his[?] yo[semite] |
| 268 | Deer in S[an] F[rancisco] Bay 270 |
| 295 | Home news Auto[biography] |
| 309 | Food flesh etc 415 |
| 324 | Gold |
| 335 | Nuttall [Thomas] |

[3]56    Icebergs 374
453    Yo[semite]

38. For Nuttall (1786-1859) see *DAB, ANB*, and Jeannette E. Graustein, *Thomas Nuttall, Naturalist: Explorations in America, 1808-1841* (Harvard University Press, 1967), esp. 294-317 for the Wyeth expedition to Oregon, which was recorded by ornithologist John Kirk Townsend (1809-1851) in his *Narrative of a Journey across the Rocky Mountains, to the Columbia River, and a Visit to the Sandwich Islands, Chili, &c.* (Philadephia: H. Perkins; Boston: Perkins & Marvin, 1839). For Wyeth and Townsend see *DAB, ANB*. Muir's extant library does not contain any books by Nuttall or Townsend, though he surely knew of Nuttall.

39. D. H. Lawrence, "Dana's 'Two Years Before the Mast'" in *Studies in Classic American Literature* (1922; Garden City, New York: Doubleday & Company, c.1951), 121-42. Lawrence paid homage to Dana for living through and writing about this experience; he praised his description of the voyage home; his book was "a great achievement." After this, however, Lawrence felt the rest of Dana's life was "lifeless." We shall see that this was not entirely true. For another literary assessment, see Robert L. Gale, *Richard Henry Dana, Jr.* (New York: Twayne, 1969), esp. 108-42. Lawrence Clark Powell, *California Classics: The Creative Literature of the Golden State* (Los Angeles: Ward Ritchie Press, 1971), 151-62, believes that *Two Years Before the Mast* "remains the greatest book of maritime California" (153). Powell views Dana's "tragedy was in not having followed the sea" for the rest of his life, as Dana, too, later realized in letters to his wife that Powell cites (160).

40. Muir noted Dana's diet; see "Food flesh" in above index, n37.

41. John Muir, *A Thousand-Mile Walk to the Gulf*, 169-88. Letter, Muir to Jeanne Carr, 26 July 1868, Near Snelling, Merced Co., California. Muir's six-page holograph journal of his 1868 passage from New York to San Francisco (JMP: Reel 23) contained only one date, "March 17th" and focused mostly on Panama. J. Parker Huber, "John Muir's Menu," *Sierra*, November/December 1994, 66-7.

42. Robert F. Lucid, ed., *The Journal of Richard Henry Dana, Jr.* (Belknap Press of Harvard University Press, 1968), 3:841-56 for Panama and California. Galen Clark guided Dana to the Mariposa Grove on 31 August 1859. Dana's time in Yosemite Valley was brief; he arrived late on the first of September, and departed early on the third. Editor Lucid notes that Dana rewrote this journal later, having lost the original, 841. Charles Francis Adams, *Richard Henry Dana: A Biography* (Houghton Mifflin, 1890), II: 178-80; 243, Alps; 248, Longfellow's. Dana never did warm to California. "A noble bay and striking points," he admitted of San Francisco when forced back, "yet I have no wish to see it again." II:190. See Dana's depiction of his return in "Twenty-four Years After," a chapter added to the 1869 and subsequent editions of *Two Years Before the Mast*.

43. *The Journal of Richard Henry Dana, Jr.*, I:364-74. Twenty years later, Dana wrote an account of this venture as a letter to James Fields that became the lead article, "How We Met John Brown," in the *Atlantic Monthly*, July 1871, 1-9. These two versions vary. In the *Atlantic* story, Dana—for dramatic effect, I presume—made it appear that he first found the Browns after he had climbed Marcy and been lost in the woods, thereby omitting an initial meeting four days earlier (23 June) that he recorded in his journal. In the *Atlantic*, John Brown was not present when Dana arrived, but came home some hours later; whereas his journal indicated that Brown was there all along both times. Some journal facts—such as John Brown's being originally from the Berkshires and the Browns' living in a log cabin—he corrected in the later rendition.

44. *The Journal of Richard Henry Dana, Jr.*, 2:445-59.

45. *The Journal of Richard Henry Dana, Jr.*, 2:592-97 and 641-48 for Mt. Washington 1853 and 1854 respectively. Thompson's and Gibb's inns are in Tolles, 55-56, 61-2, 78-9. From 1850 to 1858, Major Joseph L. Gibb managed the first Crawford House, located across the road from Thomas J. Crawford's Notch House.

46. For one of many Manchester visits, see *The Journal of Richard Henry Dana, Jr.*, 2:661.

Dana's son Richard Henry Dana III followed his father through Harvard and its law school. He also sailed around Cape Horn in 1879, landing in San Francisco in February 1880, but returned overland to Cambridge—in all a journey of five months, much shorter than his father's. As seen in the previous chapter, he and his wife Edith Longfellow went abroad for the summer of 1893; otherwise they—at least she and the family—would have been in Manchester. They enjoyed Manchester enough to erect their summer home on one of his grandfather's lots in 1885, and to spend the next thirty summers there, until Edith's death on 22 July 1915. After Dana remarried in 1922, he and his wife, Helen Ford Mumford, preferred to go to Europe every other year and to Bar Harbor or the Berkshires for their other summers, thereby abandoning Manchester and its memory-rich house, which was sold in 1923. See Bliss Perry, *Richard Henry Dana, 1851-1931* (Houghton Mifflin, 1933), 110-15 (Cape Horn voyage), 180 (house), 200-0l (Edith Longfellow's death), 219 (house sale). *NYT*, 22 July 1915, 9, Edith Longfellow's obituary.

47. *DAB, ANB*. Thomas R. Lounsbury, "Biographical Sketch," *The Complete Writings of Charles Dudley Warner* (Hartford, Connecticut: American Publishing Company, 1904), the Backlog Edition, 15:i-xxxviii. It should not be inferred from the ensuing discussion that the Warners' travel was all domestic; in fact, cumulatively, they spent some seven years abroad. J. Bard McNulty, *Older than the Nation: The Story of the Hartford Courant* (Stonington, Connecticut: Pequot Press, 1964), Introduction (n.p.), explains the basis for the *Courant's* claim of being the oldest.

48. Joseph S. Van Why, *Nook Farm* (1962; Hartford, Connecticut: The Stowe-Day Foundation, 1975), ed. Earl A. French, 44-51; map and key, 4-5, photographs of Susan Lee Warner, 50, and their home, 48. *The Complete Writings of Charles Dudley Warner*, photograph of Warner residence, 38. Joseph H. Twichell, "Charles Dudley Warner," Gilder, *Authors at Home*, 325-31. *The Hartford Courant*, 14 January 1921, l-2, obituary of Susan Warner.

49. Charles Dudley Warner, *My Summer in a Garden* (Boston: James R. Osgood, 1871) with "Introductory Letter" of Henry Ward Beecher to James T. Fields. Interestingly, the copy I read at the Neilson Library of Smith College was the gift of Beatrix Farrand (see chapter 2). This is now back in print (New York: Modern Library, 2002) without Beecher's letter, but with an introduction by Allan Gurganus, 53(quote). Warner "uses a wry, cranky humor, drifted over the back fence, to cross-pollinate and humanize his prose Emersonian," as Gurganus characterizes his style (xxxiii). He also says that he found only one photograph of Warner (xix), but there are several portraits of Warner in *The Complete Writings of Charles Dudley Warner*, frontispiece of v. 1 (1897), 2 (1870) 4 (1875) 14(1893) 15 (1899).

*My Summer in a Garden* also initiated a friendship between Warner and Helen Hunt [Jackson], according to Jane Gottschalk, "Charles Dudley Warner and the American Scene 1873-1900," Ph.D. Diss, University of Wisconsin, 1965, 33. She wrote Warner initially on 17 January 1871 and reviewed *My Summer* for *Scribner's*, March 1871, 573-74, at the request of Richard Watson Gilder. Her letters to Warner, itemized by Gottschalk, 376-79, are in the Watkinson Library of Trinity College, Hartford, Connecticut. Her review of Warner's first travel book, *Saunterings* (1872), is in *Scribner's*, July 1872, 377-78. Warner saw her frequently at the Berkeley Hotel in New York (1 December 1883 to 9 March 1884) while she was writing *Ramona*. Charles Dudley Warner, " 'H. H.' in Southern California," *The Complete Writings of*

*Charles Dudley Warner* 14:452-58, and Valerie Sherer Mathes, *Helen Hunt Jackson and Her Indian Reform Legacy* (Austin: University of Texas Press, 1990), 79-80. Kate Phillips, *Helen Hunt Jackson*, 200-01. Since Muir was also a friend of Jackson's (see chapter 13), it is possible Muir learned of Warner through her, even discussed her with Warner.

50. Letter, Muir to Louie Muir, 28 September 1893, New York.

51. Charles Dudley Warner, *Our Italy, Southern California* (New York: Harper & Brothers, 1891). This book is in volume 9 of *The Complete Writings of Charles Dudley Warner;* for Yosemite, 371-80 and Grand Canyon, 401-10.

52. Joseph Hopkins Twichell is in *DAB*. Called "Joe" by Warner and Twain, he was part of the Monday Evening Club with them. Warner's Adirondack essays appeared in the *Atlantic* from January to June 1878, and became *In the Wilderness* (Boston: Houghton, Osgood,1878), which is also in volume 6 of *The Complete Writings of Charles Dudley Warner* and is still in print. See introduction by Alice Wolf Gilborn to *In the Wilderness* (Syracuse University Press, 1990), vii-xx, which draws on in part, Burton P. Twichell, "Mr. and Mrs. Twichell's Early Days in Keene Valley," typescript read before the Keene Valley Historical Society on 3 August 1938, which is in the archives of the Keene Valley Library Association. According to Dorothy Irving of the Keene Valley Library Association, the Warners and Twichells, with Austin C. Dunham, also of Hartford, built a cottage c. 1873-1874 on the Dunham plateau in Keene Valley that still stands (Letters, Dorothy Irving to J. Parker Huber, 17 and 21 December 2002). Warner's story of his summer trip in 1873 to Baddeck, Nova Scotia, with Twichell appeared serially in the *Atlantic* from January through May 1874 and became the book, *Baddeck, and that Sort of Thing* (Boston: J. R. Osgood, 1874); this is volume 1 of *The Complete Writings of Charles Dudley Warner*, with Warner's thank-you to his comrade as the preface. See Gottschalk's discussion, 186-91.

53. Charles Dudley Warner, *On Horseback: A Tour in Virginia, North Carolina, and Tennessee with Notes of Travel in Mexico and California* (Houghton Mifflin, 1889). *On Horseback* is combined with *Being a Boy* in volume 7 of *The Complete Writings of Charles Dudley Warner*. For Thomas R. Lounsbury (1838-1915), see *DAB* and *ANB*. Kent Schwarzkopf, *A History of Mt. Mitchell and the Black Mountains: Exploration, Development, and Preservation* (1985; Raleigh: North Carolina Division of Archives and History, 2000) mentions Big Tom Wilson, particularly in relation to his search in 1857 for the body of Elisha Mitchell, who first determined that the Black Mountains were the highest in the East, but does not mention Warner.

54. Charles Dudley Warner, *Library of the World's Best Literature* (New York: R.S. Peale and J.A. Hill, 1896-1898). Associate editors were Hamilton Wright Mabie, Lucia Gilbert Runkle, and Warner's brother, George Henry Warner. Muir owned two editions of Warner's *Library*: One (New York: J. A. Hill & Co., 1902, 30 volumes) is in the HASC, minus volume 2 (I am grateful for Janene Ford's checking this); the other (New York: The International Society, 1897, Century Edition, 45 volumes) is in the Huntington Library. Only the latter set contains Muir annotations and index. Muir made no commentary on Sarah Orne Jewett in either set. In the 1902 edition see 18:10405-14 for Muir; 14:8269-82 for Jewett (30:278 for a synopsis of *The Country of the Pointed Firs*); 16:9077-83 for Linnaeus. Helen Fiske Jackson was also included: six poems and "A May Day in Albano" from *Bits of Travel* (1872), 14:8057-70, and a synopsis of *Ramona*, 30:550; Phillips, 274.

55. John T. Morse, Jr., *Life and Letters of Oliver Wendell Holmes* (Houghton Mifflin, 1896), II:75-6, gives a typical Beverly Farms birthday. Holmes's life at this time is captured in his letter to Annie Fields that she reprinted in her tribute to Holmes that appeared in the *Century*, February 1895, 505-16, and that became part of her *Authors and Friends*. Since mid-August, Howells had been staying close by in Magnolia, less than three miles east of Manchester-by-

the-Sea, *W. D. Howells: Selected Letters* 4:48-49. Warner had been staying with Thomas Nelson Page and his wife Florence Lathrop Field—they were married 6 June 1893—at Rockledge, York Harbor, Maine (their cottage has since been demolished) from 24 August until 1 September, when he took the train for Manchester-by-the-Sea, arriving in the afternoon. Letters, Charles Dudley Warner to Annie Fields, York Harbor, Maine, 26 and 31 August 1893, Huntington Library. Journal of Annie Fields on Oliver Wendell Holmes, 25 August and 4 September 1893, The Huntington Library. W. D. Howells, "Oliver Wendell Holmes," *Literary Friends and Acquaintance*, ed. David F. Hiatt and Edwin H. Cady (Indiana University Press, 1968), 125-50; of this meeting, 143-45. This essay was first printed in *Harper's*, December 1896, 120-34; "Holmes's Cottage, Beverly Farms" is shown on p.125. Editors say that Holmes's lines are from "The Exile's Secret," in *Songs in Many Keys* (1862), as "The Island Ruin," 327n144.24ff.

56. "The Holmes Breakfast," *The Atlantic Monthly Supplement*, February 1880, 1-24. Phillips, *Helen Hunt Jackson*, 201(Warner), 140-41. Fred Kaplan, *The Singular Mark Twain* (New York: Doubleday, 2003), 356-57. Warner and Twain visited Howells in Belmont.

57. Letter, Charles Dudley Warner to Annie Fields, Hartford, Connecticut, 6 September 1893, The Huntington Library. Annie Fields, *Charles Dudley Warner* (New York: McClure, Phillips, 1904), 164-65, quotes from this letter. Sarah Orne Jewett, "The Hiltons' Holiday," *Century*, September 1893, 772-78; also in *Sarah Orne Jewett: Novels and Stories* (New York: Library of America, 1994), 809-24. Muir may have read this, too. To Willa Cather "The Hiltons' Holiday" was "a little miracle." She remembered that Jewett herself had a "fondness" for it. Willa Cather, *Not Under Forty* (1922, Knopf; University of Nebraska Press, 1988), "Miss Jewett," 81.

58. Lewis Leary, ed., *Mark Twain's Correspondence with Henry Huttleston Rogers, 1893-1909* (University of California Press, 1969), 10-12, for dates and addresses; the introduction provides background on Rogers. Rice introduced Twain to Rogers on Friday, 15 September 1893, at the Murray Hill Hotel, Justin Kaplan says in *Mr. Clemens and Mark Twain: A Biography* (New York: Simon and Schuster, 1966), 320. *Pudd'nhead Wilson* was serialized in the *Century* from December 1893 to June 1894; the American Publishing Company issued it as a book in November 1894. Twain does not mention Muir in his notebooks or correspondence for September 1893; both, as yet unpublished, are in the Mark Twain Papers, Microfilm Reels 62 and 7, respectively, The Mark Twain Project, University of California, Berkeley. *The Love Letters of Mark Twain* edited by Dixon Wecter (New York: Harper & Brothers, 1949), 267-73, give the most details of his life in New York at this time. *NYT*, 22 September 1893, 3, for arrival of the *Campania*. A scan of the *NYT* for the week of 25 September does not reveal anything about Muir or Twain. Fred Kaplan is also silent on Muir. He sees Twain's move to the Players' as more for society than frugality, citing Twain's description of his elegant room, *The Singular Mark Twain*, 479-80. For Paige typesetter, see Fred Kaplan, *The Singular Mark Twain*, 426, 429, 433-41, passim.

59. *Mark Twain's Letters, Volume 1:1853-1866*, Edgar Marquess Branch, et al., eds. (University of California Press, 1988), xxi-xxii, 302, 320. No letters were discovered for eleven months, November 1864 to October 1865. Mark Twain, *Roughing It*, Harriet Elinor Smith and Edgar Marquess Branch, eds. (University of California Press, 1993), 783-93, maps.

60. *Roughing It*, 147-57 (Lake Tahoe); 250-54 (Mono Lake); 254 and 641n254.10-12 (Castle Peak); 385-87 (California landscape). One of Twain's walking excursions was to Yosemite Valley, according to Albert Bigelow Paine, *Mark Twain: A Biography* (New York: Harper and Brothers, 1912), 1:220; the editors of *Roughing It*, however, found no corroborating evidence for this claim, 638n240.16-18. *JOM*, 205-07 (Mono Lake). "The Mono & sagebrush deserts in

gen[eral] are very flowery & gardenlike. We are in the habit of calling all parts of God[']s world desert not fitted for our uses," Muir reflected in his journal of this trip (JMP, Reel 24, Journals: Owens Valley, Yosemite Middle Fork, San Joaquin, c. 7 June-September 1875, 34-35).

61. Frederick Anderson, Lin Salamo, Bernard L. Stein, eds., *Mark Twain's Notebooks & Journals II* (1877-1883), (University of California Press, 1975), 113-15, 140-43, esp. n54 and 59; 153-54, 167 and n17, 172-76. Mark Twain, *A Tramp Abroad* (1880; Oxford University Press, 1996), 355-540, for Twain's humorous version of their ascent of Riffelberg and Gornergrat, and his climb of Mont Blanc by telescope. See Albert Bigelow Paine, *Mark Twain: A Biography*, II:626-32, "Tramping with Twichell;" Fred Kaplan, *The Singular Mark Twain*, 337, for their ten-mile Saturday walks; 345, Switzerland. In September 1885, the Baxters would duplicate the Baedeker recommended climb of Montanvert and later the Rigi-Kulm (see chapter 10). Joseph H. Twichell, "Mark Twain," *Harper's*, May 1896, 816-27 (quote at 824), illustrations by Childe Hassam.

62. *L&L* II:270. Nathan Matthews Jr. is in *DAB* and *ANB*.

63. Journal of Annie Fields on Oliver Wendell Holmes, 16 June 1893, The Huntington Library.

64. Letters, Robert Underwood Johnson to Muir, 4 December 1894, New York; Annie Fields to Muir, December 1894, Boston; Mary Sargent to Robert Underwood Johnson, 8 December [1894?], Holm Lea, Brookline. Responses from the other two were not found.

## TRIP TWO: 1896
## CHAPTER 5—CAMBRIDGE

1. Letter, Muir to Louie Muir, 11 June 1896, Portage [Wisconsin].

2. Letter, Muir to Helen Muir, 19 June 1896, New York.

3. Letters, Muir to Wanda and Helen Muir, 21 June 1896, [Garrison, New York]. For Henry Fairfield Osborn (1857-1935) see *DAB* and *ANB*. For Wing-on-Wing, see John Zukowsky and Robbe Pierce Stimson, *Hudson River Villas* (New York: Rizzoli, 1985), 116-17; an autumnal, aerial view of Castle Rock, as it was also known, is shown here.

4. Millie Stanley, *The Heart of John Muir's World* (Madison, Wisconsin: Prairie Oak Press, 1995), 242. Wolfe, 269-70.

5. Letter, Charles Sprague Sargent to Muir, 30 May 1896, Jamaica Plain, Massachusetts. Letters, Robert Underwood Johnson to Mrs. Muir, 1 and 27 May 1896, New York. Letter, Muir to Johnson, 3 May 1895, Martinez, in *L&L* II:292.

6. The Massachusetts National Lancers are still active. Since 1914 they have reenacted the rides of Paul Revere and William Dawes. Their museum and library is located in Framingham, Massachusetts. I am indebted to Linda B. MacIver of the Boston Public Library for information on them.

7. Letter, James Cotter to J. Parker Huber, 30 March 2000, Millbury, Massachusetts. My gratitude to James Cotter for his translation of this salutation, which appears in Latin in *L&L* II:296 n1.

8. *Boston Daily Globe*, 25 June 1896, 5. See also *Boston Daily Globe, Evening Edition*, 24 June 1896, 1 and 4; *New York Times*, 25 June 1896, 8. There is no journal of Josiah Royce for this date in the Harvard Archives.

9. For Aldrich see *DAB* and *ANB*, Wolfe, 262, and Sedgwick, 161-99. Their connection

seems to be limited to these two meetings.

10. Morris, *Theodore Rex*, 48-58.

11. ECAD, 24 June 1896.

12. *L&L* I:253. A draft of Muir's address appears in his 1896 Journal, which unfortunately does not say anything about his being in New England (JMP, Reel 28).

13. TWHD. Letter, 20 March 2000, Helen Conger, Archivist, Case Western Reserve University, Cleveland, Ohio, to J. Parker Huber.

14. *CWJ* 8:155 and 582. The Calendar gives his first Cape Cod letter of 23 June and his last of 30 June, the latter indicating that he would return that night. His letters, primarily to his wife, reveal the rest of his summer itinerary that took him as far west as Chicago, 8:166-204.

15. *L&L* II:298.

16. Chronology, *Sarah Orne Jewett: Novels & Stories* (New York: Library of America, 1994), 929. Sarah Orne Jewett, "The Country of the Pointed Firs," *Atlantic* 1896, January, 5-18; March, 302-312; July, 75-88; September, 352-66. Possibly Whitman refers to the chapters in July's *Atlantic*, though these were not the last.

17. Betty S. Smith, "Sarah de St. Prix Wyman Whitman," *Old-Time New England*, Spring/Summer 1999, 52 (illustration). *Letters of Sarah Wyman Whitman* (Cambridge, Massachusetts: Riverside Press, 1907), 89-90. For Whitman's unique alphabet, see Charles Gullans, "The New Generation: Sarah Whitman and Frank Hazen," in Allen and Gullans, 64 and 94n23.

18 *CWJ* 8:296 and 3:17. Gollin, *Annie Adams Fields*, 249. JMJ, 11 September 1898. Sarah Hamelin, "Gender, History, and Nature in Sarah Orne Jewett's *Country of the Pointed Firs*," *Maine History*, Spring 2002, 61-80. Three years later, when Sarah Orne Jewett sent Henry James her historical novel *The Tory Lover* (Houghton Mifflin, 1901), he encouraged her to return "to the dear country of the Pointed Firs," as quoted in this chapter's epigraph from *The Letters of Henry James*, IV: 208-9.

## TRIP THREE: 1898
## CHAPTER 6—CAPE COD

1. Letter, Muir to Louie Muir, 13 September 1898, Duluth, Minnesota.

2. JMJ, 12 September 1898.

3. Letter, Muir to Helen Muir, 10 September 1898, Montana.

4. Letter, Muir to Louie Muir, 13 September 1898, Duluth, Minnesota.

5. JMJ, 16 September 1898.

6. Letter, Muir to Wanda Muir, 20 September 1898, Boston.

7. See William A. McKenzie, *Dining Car Line to the Pacific: An Illustrated History of the NP Railway's "Famously Good" Food , with 150 Authentic Recipes* (Minnesota Historical Society Press, 1990); *Great Northern Secrets* (no publisher, no date). Connie Hoffman, secretary of the Great Northern Railway Historical Society, Berkley, Michigan, dates this booklet of dining car recipes to 1932. She has no menus before 1920 in her collection. James E. Vance, Jr., *The North American Railroad: Its Origin, Evolution and Geography* (Johns Hopkins University Press, 1995) and Sarah H. Gordon, *Passage to Union: How Railroads Transformed American Life, 1829-1929* (Chicago: Ivan R. Dee, 1996) offer good overviews.

8. Letter, Muir to Louie Muir, 13 September 1898, Duluth, Minnesota.

9. Though Muir does not identify his steamer, it was most likely one of the three iron ones—*India, China, Japan*—of the Anchor Line of the Erie & Western Transportation Company. Their 1896 brochure gives a flavor of what Muir experienced: "Running water, electric lights and the best of beds in each room....Wide promenade decks extend entirely around the steamer....The Excellence of the Table is an especial feature of this line." And later under "Of Interest to Tourists": "the epicurean who enjoys a fish diet will appreciate the delicious Lake Trout and Whitefish always included in the menu on the steamers of this line." My gratitude to C. Patrick Labadie, Director, Canal Park Marine Museum, U.S. Army Corps of Engineers, Duluth, Minnesota. The menus consulted from this period show little change.

10. For a photograph of the Boston and Providence Railroad Station in Park Square and for information on the construction of South Station see Walter Muir Whitehill, *Boston: A Topographical History* (1959; Harvard University Press, 1975), 102 and 189. Until South Station was completed in 1900, railroads had various terminals.

   This Adams House (1883) closed in 1927 and was demolished in 1931. Calvin Coolidge resided here while serving Massachusetts as lieutenant governor and governor. A former Adams House occupied this site from 1846 to 1883, the successor of the Lamb Tavern. See John Harris, *Historic Walks in Old Boston* (1982; The Globe Pequot Press, 1989), 192-193. A closed Paramount Theatre (built 1932) sat there, two blocks southeast of the Common, on my inspection of 13 September 1995.

11. William M. Canby (1831-1904) discovered a new species of hawthorn in Wilmington, Delaware, in October 1898, which Sargent named *Crataegus Canbyi* in his honor. I cannot verify that Muir and Sargent were with him at the time, though it is likely. For a description of this plant and a biography of Canby, see Charles S. Sargent, *The Silva of North America* (1902; Magnolia, Massachusetts: Peter Smith, 1947), 41-42. A drawing of the plant by Charles Edward Faxon follows on an unnumbered page.

12. Letter, Muir to Charles S. Sargent, 11 May 1898, Martinez. Currently, none of *The Silva of North America* is in Muir's library at HASC or the Huntington Library.

13. Letter, Charles S. Sargent to Muir, 2 June 1898, Jamaica Plain, Massachusetts. Muir reviewed *The Silva of North America* and sent it to Bliss Perry, editor of the *Atlantic Monthly*, 4 Park Street, Boston, on 2 March 1903. Perry replied on 19 March that he was pleased. This lengthy review appeared in the *Atlantic*, July 1903 (9-22), while Muir and Sargent were traveling around the world. See Letter, Muir to Charles S. Sargent, 1 March 1903, Martinez, and chapter 14.

14. Letter, Sargent to Muir, 13 July 1898, Jamaica Plain.

15. Letter, Sargent to Muir, 15 June 1898, Jamaica Plain.

16. In "John Muir and Thoreau's *Cape Cod*," *The Concord Saunterer*, Fall 1997, 135, I mistakenly brought Muir through New Bedford. I am indebted to Susan F. Witzell, a volunteer in the Archives of the Woods Hole Historical Collection and Museum, for showing me the direct Old Colony Line and its schedule (Letter, Susan F. Witzell to J. Parker Huber, 27 May 1998, Woods Hole, Massachusetts).

17. JMJ, 17 September 1898.

18. William B. Bacon and Charles S. Sargent—identified incorrectly as G.S. Sargent—came down by buggy from Barnstable "one summer's day" (the year is not given) and bought property jointly; a toss of the coin decided that Sargent would have the house and Bacon the open point to the south. So relates Winslow Carlton in "Bankers' Row" in Mary Lou Smith, ed., *Woods Hole Reflections* (Woods Hole Historical Collection, 1983), 144, 146. On page 13, an

undated photograph (probably from 1875) shows an earlier form of the Sargent house with carriage house on a treeless lot with stone walls. Today the house cannot be seen from the road. Page 23 offers a view of Little Harbor in 1896. Carlton recounts the same story in "A Stroll Through Woods Hole in the 'Twenties'" in Mary Lou Smith, ed., *The Book of Falmouth* (Falmouth Historical Commission, 1986), 522. The Sargent House is shown as it appeared in 1895 on page 486 (captioned "Abner Davis' inn"); a contemporary view is on page 523.

My query to the Woods Hole Historical Commission led to their discovery that the Charles S. Sargent home had been miscited as that of G.S. Sargent. Letter, J.S. Gaines, Archivist, to J. Parker Huber, 12 January 1995, Woods Hole, Massachusetts.

The house is now known as the Rowe House. The owner when I visited on 15 October 1995 was Mrs. William S. Rowe of Cincinnati, Ohio, who had been here virtually every summer of her life since her birth in 1918. Her great-grandfather was William B. Bacon (1823-1906). Her grandfather was Robert Bacon (1860-1919; see *DAB*, *ANB*), a partner of J.P. Morgan and assistant secretary of state, 1905-1909. Muir and Robert Bacon had Theodore Roosevelt as a mutual friend; Bacon and Roosevelt graduated Harvard in the Class of 1880. On 10 October 1883, Bacon married Martha W. Cowdin (1859-1940). Their daughter, Martha B. Bacon (1890-1967), on 2 June 1914 married George Whitney (1885-1963), a banker and a president of J. P. Morgan and Company. Their daughter, Martha Phyllis Whitney, married William S. Rowe (1916-1988), also a banker (president of the Fifth Third Bank, Cincinnati, Ohio) in 1939. After Robert Bacon died, his widow, Mrs. Rowe's grandmother, bought the Sargent House. Martha Phyllis Rowe died 11 January 2001. *Cincinnati Enquirer*, 14 January 2001, B5, obituary. "The house remains firmly in family hands with two of us owners living in John Muir land," her son, George W. Rowe of San Francisco wrote me on 17 February 2004.

19. Sutton, 20. Sargent's Cape Cod connection came as news to Sutton when we spoke on 29 March 1995.

20. *DAB*, *ANB*, Charles Sprague Sargent; *DAB*, Guy Lowell, reports marriage in April 1898. Thanks to Arnold Arboretum librarians Carol David and Rebecca Anderson for providing the source for dates: Emma Worcester Sargent, *Epes Sargent of Gloucester and his Descendants* (Houghton Mifflin, 1923), 158-60. Molly Sargent, informing Muir of her engagement and marriage, invited him to visit them at 48 West 51st Street in New York; Letter, Mary Sargent to Muir, 25 December [1907], Holm Lea, Brookline; this letter is mislocated in year 1902 of JMP. For Alice in California, see Letter (draft), Muir to Alice Sargent, 27 September [1901], Martinez; Letter, Charles S. Sargent to Muir, 6 November 1901, Jamaica Plain. For some reason, Muir did not accompany her to Yosemite. Alice Sargent (1882-1946), obituaries, *Boston Daily Globe*, 6 February 1946, 10, and *The Chronicle* [Brookline, Massachusetts], 14 February 1946, 12. For Andrew and Charles see Harvard College Class Reports and Bibliographical Files, Harvard University Archives, Cambridge, Massachusetts.

21. *Boston Evening Record*, 29 December 1903, 6.

22. His brother, Charles S. Sargent, who carried his father's name, died 13 February 1959.

23. New York tobacco tycoon John Anderson gave the island and fifty thousand dollars for the school. Edward Lurie, *Louis Agassiz: A Life in Science* (1960; Johns Hopkins University Press, 1988), 380-381. I. Thomas Buckley, *Penikese: Island of Hope* (N. Chatham, Massachusetts: Stony Brook Publishing and Productions, 1997). Letter, Kate N. Daggett to Muir, 19 April 1873, Hot Springs, Arkansas, tells Muir about the school.

24. Letter, Muir to Wanda Muir, 25 August 1893, St. Moritz, Switzerland.

25. *DAB*, *ANB*. Jordan was born on a farm near Gainesville in western New York. David

Starr Jordan, *The Days of a Man* (Yonkers-on-Hudson, New York: World Book Company, 1922), 2 vols. Penikese, I:108-119; marriage, 132—this is the only mention of Susan Bowen in his autobiography. Little is known of Susan Bowen (1844-1885). She attended Mount Holyoke Female Seminary from 1861 until her graduation in 1864; she taught there from 1868 to 1875. See catalogs of Mount Holyoke Female Seminary and biographical notes in Mount Holyoke College Archives, South Hadley, Massachusetts—my gratitude to Archives librarian Patricia J. Albright. Bowen was married in her hometown, Peru, Massachusetts. See also David Starr Jordan, *Science Sketches* (Chicago: A.C.McClurg and Co., 1899), Chapter 5, "Agassiz at Penikese," 133-152.

26. For ouzels see Wolfe,198. *Scribner's Monthly* featured Muir's "The Humming-Bird of the California Water-Falls" in February 1878. For Merrill see Jordan, *The Days of a Man* I:217. For Muir on Merrill see "Words From An Old Friend" in Catharine Merrill, *The Man Shakespeare and Other Essays* (Indianapolis: Bowen-Merrill Company Publishers, 1902), 32-38. The first chapter of this book, pages 1-5, is a "Biographical Notice" of her. Merrill (1824-1900) held the Demia Butler Chair in English Literature at Northwestern Christian University, now Butler University, in Indianapolis, from 1870 to 1883 (See "Endowed Chairs at Butler University," Rare Books and Special Collections, The Irwin Library, Butler University. This I take as the most reliable source, though the above "Biographical Notice" has her at Butler until 1885 and her obituary in *The Indianapolis News*, 30 May 1900, 4 and 11, puts her at Butler in 1873.) See also Katharine Merrill Graydon, *Catharine Merrill: Life and Letters* (Greenfield, Indiana: The Mitchell Company, 1934).

27. Letter, David Starr Jordan to Muir, 10 February 1903, Stanford, California. Jordan even saw the Muir Glacier in Alaska in June 1897 (*Days of a Man* I:578). Jordan might have been on the Alaskan Harriman Expedition in 1899 with Muir, but he declined (*Days of a Man*, II:297). Jordan's tribute to Muir appeared in *Sierra*, January 1916, 7. Jordan was president of Stanford until 1913, then chancellor for three years, and chancellor emeritus until his death in 1931.

28. JMJ, 26 and 27 October 1898.

29. JMJ, 18 September 1898. "I am quite sure that Olmsted never met Muir," editor Charles E. Beveridge wrote me on 24 March 1996. Beveridge added that "Olmsted expressed a desire to do so at a time of controversy at Yosemite." In her letter to me of 21 April 1996, biographer Laura Wood Roper concurs that there was no meeting. For further information see Beveridge's comments in *The Papers of Frederick Law Olmsted, Volume 5, The California Frontier: 1863-1865*, ed. Victoria Post Ranney et al (Johns Hopkins University Press, 1990), 466-69 and 472-73n60; Frederick Law Olmsted to Richard Watson Gilder, 11 July 1889.

There is no recovered correspondence between Muir and Olmsted. While no books by Frederick Law Olmsted are in Muir's library, there is a copy of *The Century Magazine*, October 1893, with an essay on Olmsted by M.G. van Rensselaer, 860-67, which presumably Muir read yet did not mark (see chapter 2). Though Mary Cleveland Olmsted (1830-1921) continued to live at 99 Warren Street until her death, Muir does not mention seeing her. See Elizabeth Stevenson, *Park Maker: A Life of Frederick Law Olmsted* (MacMillan Publishing Co., 1977), 426-27; Laura Wood Roper, *Frederick Law Olmsted*, 58, 474-75, 478. Mary Olmsted's diary that Roper refers to on page 537, notes 28 and 31, has not been located in her papers or those of FLO in the Library of Congress.

30. Letters, Charles S. Sargent to Muir, 26 February 1897, Jamaica Plain, Massachusetts; Walter H. Page to Muir, 4 March 1897, Boston.

31. Letter, Charles S. Sargent to Muir, 22 June 1897, Jamaica Plain, Massachusetts.

32. Letter, Muir to Wanda Muir, 22 September 1898, Cranberry, North Carolina.

33. Letter, Muir to Walter H. Page, 10 January 1902, Martinez; in L&L II:341-43.

34. JMJ, 19 September 1898.

35. Letter, Muir to Louie Muir, 25 September 1898, Cloudland, North Carolina.

36. The railroad came to Sandwich in 1848 and Hyannis in 1854. Henry C. Kittredge, *Cape Cod* (1930; Houghton Mifflin, 1968), 154.

Thoreau kept journals of his Cape Cod tours. Those of 1849 and 1850 were mostly removed from his Journal in preparation for lecturing and publishing—see William Rossi, "Historical Introduction," in *Journal 3: 1848-1851.* eds. Robert Sattelmeyer, Mark R. Patterson, and William Rossi (Princeton University Press, 1990), 484-85, 490. Thus, they were not part of the 1906 edition of the *Journal.* His 5-18 July 1855 record is in the 1906 *Journal,* VII: 432-443; Muir neither marked nor indexed any of these pages.

"The 1857 Excursion" from Thoreau's *Journal* (12-22 June) was not included in *Cape Cod* until 1951, when W.W. Norton published an edition assembled by Dudley C. Lunt—see "Historical Introduction" in *Cape Cod,* ed. Joseph J. Moldenhauer (Princeton University Press, 1988), 295. That Muir read this is indicated by his identifying the same item with a vertical line in the margin of text and in his index of this account: "397 Bobolink song 446", which refers to "A child asked concerning a bobolink, 'What makes he sing so sweet, Mother? Do he eat flowers?'" (20 June 1857; IX:446). Bobolinks are still prevalent on Cape Cod.

For a detailed account of Thoreau's lecture see *Nantucket Inquirer,* 1 January 1855 [2]. On 15 September 1975, I read this paper in the Atheneum on Nantucket, where Thoreau lectured; it was published in *The Thoreau Society Bulletin,* Winter 1984 [1-3] thanks to Don Jordan. Thoreau's lecture trip, never a part of *Cape Cod,* was recorded in his *Journal* (25-29 December 1854), a section Muir read, indexing one item: "97 Persecution, baptists g[ood]", which refers to Thoreau's comment on verses by Peter Folger in Obed Macy's *History of Nantucket* (Boston: Hilliard, Bray, 1835) that God would punish "for the sin of persecution and the like, the banishing and whipping of godly men." Muir must have recalled his father's chastisement of him as a boy—see *The Story of My Boyhood and Youth* (1913; University of Wisconsin Press, 1965), esp. 69. Muir also placed vertical lines beside the last four stanzas by Folger in Thoreau's *Journal* (VII:97-98).

37. Thoreau, *Journal,* 27 June 1856. Muir notes nothing on this date, though he marks (vertical line, four lines) the last paragraph of 26 June 1856. See also Daniel Ricketson, *The History of New Bedford* (New Bedford: privately printed,1858), 125-129. Ricketson, whom Thoreau had been visiting in New Bedford, accompanied him to Naushon. Had Thoreau lived longer, we can imagine his returning to Naushon with Emerson. In his *Journal* Thoreau also mentions seeing Gay Head on Martha's Vineyard "with my glass" (VIII, 393).

38. Thoreau lectured in Massachusetts on Cape Cod on 23 and 30 January 1850 in Concord; 18 February 1850 in South Danvers; 6 December 1850 in Newburyport; and 1 January 1851 in Clinton; as well as in Portland, Maine, on 15 January 1851. See *Thoreau Log,* 162, 163, 174, 176, 177, respectively. For details of these lectures see Bradley P. Dean and Ronald Wesley Hoag, "Thoreau's Lectures Before *Walden*: An Annotated Calendar," *Studies in the American Renaissance 1995,* ed. Joel Myerson (University Press of Virginia, 1995), 127-228.

39. See "Historical Introduction," *Cape Cod* (Princeton), 249.

40. Muir's copy of Thoreau's *Cape Cod* is in the Huntington Library. Date on title page is MDCCCXCVII[1897]; copyrights, 1864 and 1893. The volume contains no inscription nor dates of acquisition or reading. See J. Parker Huber, "John Muir and Thoreau's *Cape Cod,*" *The Concord Saunterer,* Fall 1997, 132-54, for Muir's index to this volume.

41. Muir's copy is in HASC. Again, this copy contains neither inscription nor dates of acquisition or reading. For Muir's purchase of this set, see chapter 17. Muir's index is presented as Appendix B in Huber, "John Muir and Thoreau's *Cape Cod*," *The Concord Saunterer*, Fall 1997, 143-149.

## TRIP THREE: 1898
## CHAPTER 7—BOSTON PARKS AND OTHERS

1. *L&L* II:270.

2. For Sargent's devotion to Parkman, see Sutton, 140. Quote from Henry Dwight Sedgwick, *Francis Parkman* (Houghton Mifflin, 1904) is on page 181 of Walter Muir Whitehill, "Francis Parkman as Horticulturist," *Arnoldia*, May/June 1973. 169-183. Whitehill believed that Parkman was responsible for the selection of Sargent as Parkman's successor as professor of Horticulture at Harvard.

3. Beatrix Jones Farrand, "Book of Gardening," 10 June 1894. The blank space after *Anthericum* indicates her intention to add the species later; it was most likely *Anthericum liliago* L., St. Bernard's Lily. The common names of the others are yellow or flame azalea and great-leaved magnolia. I am indebted to Nathalie Demers and Elizabeth Davidson, librarians of the Massachusetts Horticultural Society, and to Karen Madsen, editor of *Arnoldia* of the Arnold Arboretum for their help in identifying Jones's "Bruno's Lily."

4. Zaitzevsky, 86-91; Jamaica Park Preliminary Plan, 89. Beatrix Jones Farrand, "Book of Gardening," 10 June 1894.

5. Michael Richman, *Daniel Chester French: An American Sculptor* (New York: Metropolitan Museum of Art, 1976), 97-102. Sargent was on the Parkman Memorial committee and wrote the inscription. After its completion, French wrote the project's architect, Henry Bacon, "Even Professor Sargent, who is the most difficult of men, was very much pleased with the structure."

6. In his Journal, Muir dates his first Arnold Arboretum visit 14 October. Later, on 19 October, he realized that he had "lost [a] day somewhere"; in fact, he had made two days with the same date of 12 October. Muir made the correction from that part on, but not in retrospect; hence, I have changed his misdates. Earlier, he had done similarly, but corrected September 20, 21, 22 to 21, 22, 23, respectively.

7. Philip G. Terrie, "William Bartram (1739-1823)" in *ANW*, I:63-74. Helen Gere Cruickshank, ed., *John and William Bartram's America: Selections from the Writings of the Philadelphia Naturalists* (New York: The Devin-Adair Company, 1957), 379-83 for itinerary. Cruickshank followed Bartram's trail. I've not been able to locate Muir's copy of Bartram's *Travels*.

8. C.S. Sargent, "Charles Edward Faxon," *Rhodora*, July 1918, 116-22 (portrait, 116).

9. M.C. Robbins, "A Tree Museum," *The Century Magazine*, April 1893, 867-78, with Harry Fenn drawings.

10. JMJ, 15[16] October 1898.

11. Charles E. Stratton (1846-1932) served as secretary of the Class of 1866 of Harvard College, making his first report in 1872 and his thirtieth and last in 1931; these are in the Boston Public Library and the Harvard University Archives. I am indebted to Linda B. MacIver of the Boston Public Library for calling these to my attention. Stratton paid tribute to Edward Emerson in *The Twenty-ninth Secretary's Report of the Class of 1866 of Harvard*

*College, June 1930* (Boston: privately printed, 1930), 8-13. Michael E. Hennessy, *Four Decades of Massachusetts Politics, 1890-1935* (Norwood Press, 1935), 35-7. *Boston Evening Transcript*, 15 January 1932, 1, obituary. *Who's Who in New England* (1916), 1033. JMJ, 15 [16] October and 26 October 1898.

12. John Algood Pettigrew (1844-1912), *The Boston Globe*, 3 July 1912, 11, with portrait. *The Boston Post*, 4 July 1912, 11. "Loses Mr. Pettigrew," 5 February 1896, newspaper clipping (most likely from the *Milwaukee Journal* or *Milwaukee Sentinel*) in Milwaukee County Historical Society, Milwaukee, Wisconsin, thanks to Steve Daily, Curator, Research Collections. *NYT*, 8 February 1896, 14, refers to him as "James A. Pettinger" in subheading. *Brooklyn Daily Eagle*, 8 November 1896, 5, for the Bostonians' visit to Brooklyn, and 14 December 1896, 6 and 16, for his resignation, thanks to Susan April, Brooklyn Public Library.

13. Zaitzevsky, 65-80, 69 (Olmsted's design of Franklin Park). The Zoo opened in 1913.

14. Rybczynski, 360-64, for how the park has changed and golf in 1890; he reports "120 acres of parkland have been lost." See also, Frederick Law Olmsted, "Notes on the Plan of Franklin Park and Related Matters," *The Papers of Frederick Law Olmsted, Supplementary Series, Vol.I, Writings on Public Parks, Parkways, and Park Systems*, eds. Charles E. Beveridge and Carolyn F. Hoffman (Baltimore: Johns Hopkins University Press, 1997), 460-534, quotes, 483-84. Richard Heath, "Franklin Park, Boston's 'Central' Park," *Arnoldia*, Fall 1988, 29-31.

15. McAleer, 68-9; Allen, 70, 84. Rusk says that the site where the Emersons lived in Roxbury was later included in Franklin Park, 98. Edward Waldo Emerson, *Emerson in Concord* (Houghton Mifflin, 1888) 29, located this farmhouse at what is now Walnut Avenue, near Blue Hill Avenue (which Richardson accepts, 45), which places Emerson just north of the park boundary. See Beveridge and Hoffman, *The Papers of Frederick Law Olmsted, Supplementary Series* 1:480 and 528-29n28 and 29. Olmsted knew William Emerson from Staten Island, the editors say.

16. Edmund S. Morgan, *Benjamin Franklin* (Yale University Press, 2002), 130, 177. An engaging assessment of Morgan's "superficial Franklin" is Alan Taylor, "Poor Richard, Rich Ben," *The New Republic*, 13 January 2003, 29-35. Franklin's Boston birthplace on Milk Street burned in 1810; see *The Papers of Benjamin Franklin* 1:xix and 4. His 1763 New England itinerary is in *The Papers of Benjamin Franklin*, 10:276-79.

17. *The Autobiography of Benjamin Franklin*, eds. Leonard W. Labaree, Ralph L. Ketcham, Helen C. Boatfield and Helene H. Fineman (Yale University Press, 1964), 231-36. *The Papers of Benjamin Franklin*, 6:xxx, Chronology for 1756; 308-09 (itinerary and map); 364-65, Deborah's food; 380-81, quote from letter of Thomas Lloyd. Franklin remained on the frontier until 4 February, when he returned to Bethlehem, and to Philadelphia on the next day. Catherine Drinker Bowen, *The Most Dangerous Man in America: Scenes from the Life of Benjamin Franklin* (Boston: Little, Brown, 1974), 149, mistakenly places Franklin in a hut at his destination on his fiftieth birthday. Elsewhere Bowen notes that "Franklin loved to travel and often said he required it periodically for his health." (112).

18. Letter, Edmund S. Morgan to J. Parker Huber, 23 November 2002, New Haven Connecticut.

19. Bliss Perry, ed., *Little Masterpieces: Benjamin Franklin* (New York: Doubleday & McClure Co., 1901) is in the Muir library of the Huntington Library. This may have been Perry's gift, though there is no inscription to this effect. The *Little Masterpieces* series contained eighteen volumes of British and American authors that also included Abraham Lincoln, Daniel Webster, Washington Irving, and Nathaniel Hawthorne—all edited by Perry. Bliss Perry, *And Gladly Teach*, 137.

D. H. Lawrence's *Studies in Classic American Literature* (1923), professor Gordon S. Wood says, "is the most famous criticism of Franklin ever written," *The New York Review of Books*, 4 December 2003, 22-24. Franklin's darker side, especially his relationship to his wife and children, which contrasted with Muir's devotion to his, is exposed by Claude-Anne Lopez and Eugenia Herbert, *The Private Franklin: The Man and His Family* (1975), Wood says.

20. Quotations in this and following paragraphs, unless otherwise indicated, are from JMJ, 9-10 [8-9] November 1898.

21. For Howard Daniels (1815-1863), see Charles A. Birnbaum and Robin Karson, eds., *Pioneers of American Landscape Design* (McGraw-Hill, 2000), 73-6. Daniels served as superintendent of Druid Hill Park from 1860 to 1863, the year of his death in Baltimore.

22. The next day, 11 November 1898, Muir wrote Reid from Washington to express his regrets at missing him.

When Muir and Reid first met, Reid was teaching at the Case School of Applied Science in Cleveland. Reid (1859-1944), *Who Was Who in America* 2:442. *L&L*, 2:246-8. Muir, *Travels in Alaska*, 286, 312, 315-16. Harry Fielding Reid, "Studies of Muir Glacier, Alaska," *The National Geographic Magazine*, 21 March 1892, 18-55. Reid saw frequent aurorae in August, 53. Reid's map of the Muir Glacier, inserted between pages 52 and 53, shows Muir Camp on the northeast shore of Muir Inlet; it appears more clearly on Reid's map of the "Northern Part of Muir Inlet," PL. 15, between pages 54 and 55. Letter, Reid to Muir, 30 April 1892, Cleveland, Ohio, Reid sent Muir two copies of his report. *NYT*, 19 June 1944, 19, Reid's obituary.

The summer of 1891 Reid spent in the Adirondacks, for the health of his wife's mother, Mary Elizabeth Gittings. In 1892 Reid returned to Alaska. While based at Camp Muir for two months, 7 July to 7 September—"about two days out of three being rainy"—he discovered the Johns Hopkins, Carroll, and Rendu glaciers in Glacier Bay. Harry Fielding Reid, "Glacier Bay and Its Glaciers," *Sixteenth Annual Report of the United States Geological Survey* (Washington: Government Printing Office, 1895), Pt. 1, 421-61. PL LXXXVI is "Map of Glacier Bay, Alaska, Surveyed in 1890 and '92" by Harry Fielding Reid; US Board of Geographic Names designated Reid Inlet, 423n1. Eliza Ruhamah Scidmore, "The Discovery of Glacier Bay, Alaska," *National Geographic*, April 1896, 144-45, with "Sketch Map of Glacier Bay and Muir Glacier" by Harry Fielding Reid.

The finding aid for the Harry Fielding Reid Papers, Special Collections, Milton S. Eisenhower Library, The Johns Hopkins University, credits Reid also with the discovery and naming of the Daniel Gilman Glacier for the then president of Johns Hopkins. The Gilman Glacier of Glacier Bay, however, was named by William Osgood Field Jr. and William S. Cooper, according to Donald J. Orth, *Dictionary of Alaska Place Names* (Washington, D.C.: United States Government Printing Office, 1967), 367. This source also confirms Reid's naming of the glaciers Carroll, 188; Johns Hopkins, 475; and Rendu, 802; and indicates that the members of the 1899 Harriman Alaska Expedition, of whom Muir was one (but not Reid), named the Reid Glacier, which with the Johns Hopkins had emerged as a branch of the Grand Pacific Glacier. See Grove Karl Gilbert, *Glaciers and Glaciation: Harriman Alaska Expedition* (New York: Doubleday, Page, 1904), 20-5, Muir Glacier; 25-33, Reid Glacier. Muir named the Grand Pacific Glacier in 1879. On 16 July 1901, The Mazamas outing, of which Reid himself was a part, named the Reid Glacier on Mount Hood (11,239'), in the Cascade Range of Oregon. Reid was an honorary member of The Mazamas, the Oregon mountain club, founded in 1894 and still active. Jack Grauer, *Mount Hood: A Complete History* (Portland, Oregon: n.p., 1975), 135-36, 289-90. From this source, it is not clear if Reid went to the top of Mount Hood. Harry Fielding Reid, "The Glaciers of Mt. Hood and Mt. Adams,"

*Mazama,* December 1905, 194-200.

Reid and his wife met Muir in June 1893 in New York (Letter, Reid to Muir, 5 December 1898, Baltimore), In summer 1894 Reid spent five weeks in Zermatt, Switzerland, climbing with guides, photographing and measuring glaciers, even playing tennis one day. Though bad weather thwarted his several attempts of the Matterhorn, he reached other surrounding peaks, among them the Dent D'Herens, Point de Zinal, De Tête Blanche (12,218'), and Tête de Valpelline, See his Diary, 21 June-19 August 1894 (which begins aboard ship in Chesapeake Bay and ends in Zermatt) in the Harry Fielding Reid Papers (MS 367), Special Collections, Milton S. Eisenhower Library, The Johns Hopkins University. Here Reid refers to his having been in Zermatt in 1889 and ascending the Dent Blanche (14,295'). A search of his correspondence for this year may reveal more.

Reid was a founding member of the American Alpine Club, attended their first meeting on 1 January 1903 in Washington, D.C., and served on the Council until 1913 and as vice president from 1914 to 1916. Howard Palmer, "Early History of the American Alpine Club," *The American Alpine Journal,* 1944, 169-70. "A Survey of American Ascents in the Alps," *The American Alpine Journal,* 1936, 516, gives Reid's ascents in 1880; his obituary in *The American Alpine Journal,* 1946, 115-17, lists others, among them Mt. Adams (12,276') in southwest Washington on 31 July 1901, and in September 1906 the third highest peak in North America, the snowy volcano Citlaltépetl or Pico de Orizaba (18,405') in eastern Mexico. Rollin T. Chamberlin, "The Ascent of Orizaba," *American Alpine Journal,* 1930, 160-66.

Reid spent the summer of 1905 in the Alps (Dolomites and Engadine), climbing more than studying glaciers, he told Muir. The next July he was in San Francisco as a member of the Earthquake Commission, while Muir was in Adamana, Arizona. Evidently Muir invited him to come with him to the Amazon in 1911, but Reid was off to England and Norway. (Letters, Reid to Muir, 22 December 1905, Baltimore; 12 July 1906, San Francisco; 7 July 1911, Baltimore.)

23. I am grateful to Francis P. O'Neill, Reference Librarian, Maryland Historical Society, for the location of the Mount Vernon House, the Johns Hopkins University in 1898, and the home of Harry Fielding Reid from 1896 until his death in 1944. Letter, O'Neill to J. Parker Huber, 24 January 2003, and comments in mine to him of 3 February 2003. For Gilman see *DAB, ANB,* and John C. French, *A History of the University Founded by Johns Hopkins* (Johns Hopkins University Press, 1946). Gerald Graff, *Professing Literature: An Institutional History* (University of Chicago Press, 1987), 56-59, encapsulates Gilman's accomplishments at Johns Hopkins. Archivist James Stimpert of Johns Hopkins informs me that none of the original campus buildings Muir would have seen are still standing. Letter, James Stimpert to J. Parker Huber, 19 February 2003. Johns Hopkins did not begin to occupy its present campus until 1916. John Glendenning, *Josiah Royce,* discusses his relationship with Gilman, 44-5, 60-73 (Johns Hopkins), 97. Linda Simon, *Genuine Reality: A Life of William James,* 168, 172, 221. *CWJ* 1:298n1; 6: xxix, xxxiii-xxiv (Introduction by Linda Simon), 1-3. James stayed at 132 Madison Street, the home of Mrs. DuBois Egerton; see French, *A History of the University Founded by Johns Hopkins,* 77, 90.

Reid's wife, Edith Gittings Reid (1863?-1954) authored a sympathetic and insightful character study of her friend, *Woodrow Wilson: The Caricature, the Myth and the Man* (London and New York: Oxford University Press, 1934), without discussing conservation or the Hetch Hetchy controversy. Though not a seeker of solace or solitude in nature, Wilson did reveal to her in his letter of 25 February 1902 from Princeton, after a devastating ice storm, that "Ellen [his first wife] and I are worshippers of trees" (62). The editors of *The Papers of Woodrow Wilson* (Princeton University Press, 1970) 8:509n1, dispute her claim as to time of the beginning of her friendship with Wilson. Clearly, though, by early 1896 they were close friends, 9:440; for their relationship, 14:3. For a discussion of Hetch Hetchy, see Roderick Nash, *Wilderness and the American Mind* (1967; Yale University Press, 1982), 161-81; Jones, 82-169.

24. Though Muir does not identify this park, it is presumably Clifton, as the Johns Hopkins Home was sold to the city in 1895 as a public park, and as the park and home are juxtaposed one after the other in Muir's journal. See Kathleen G. Kotarba and W. Edward Leon, eds., *Baltimore City's Designated Landmark List 2002* (Baltimore: Commission for Historical and Architectural Preservation [2002]), #40. Apparently, they missed Federal Hill in southern Baltimore (the city purchased this in 1875), which offered "the best view of the water-front," according to Baedeker.

25. Henry Winthrop Sargent's (see chapter 11n13) consideration of Clifton is in the supplement to the sixth edition of A. J. Downing, *Landscape Gardening and Rural Architecture* (Dover Publications, 1991), 557; also quoted in the following report, 44-45.

For providing the *Final Report, Draft National Register Nomination, Clifton Park* (Bethesda, Maryland: Lampl Associates, September 1997), which informs this description, I am indebted to Myra Brosius, Landscape Architect, Department of Planning, Baltimore. Unlike Druid Hill, Clifton was not professionally designed until the involvement of the Olmsted Brothers in 1904. The plan of the Olmsted Brothers to link Baltimore parks, including Clifton, in imitation of Boston never came to fruition. The report says that "Tall cypress trees, some of which remain today," stood along the lane to the Gardener's Cottage (11).

For Johns Hopkins see *DAB* and *ANB*; French, *A History of the University Founded by Johns Hopkins*, 10-17; Kathryn A. Jacob, "Mr. Johns Hopkins," *Johns Hopkins Magazine*, January 1974, 12-17. The Hopkins home at 18 West Saratoga Street, Jacob indicated, is no longer.

26. JMJ, 9 [10] November 1898.

27. JMJ, 10 [11] November 1898. Letter, Muir to Helen Muir, 11 November 1898, Richmond, Virginia. Though Muir does not say that Stratton and Pettigrew accompanied him to Washington, D.C., I presume that they did, and that from there returned to Boston; they did not join Muir and Sargent on their trip to Florida. John Burroughs, "Spring in Washington: With an Eye to the Birds," *Atlantic*, May 1869, 580-91. This appeared as "Spring at the Capital," in *Wake-Robin* (1871; Houghton Mifflin, 1899), 141 (quote) 144-54, on Rock Creek. Gail Spilsbury, *Rock Creek Park* (Johns Hopkins University Press, 2003). Olmsted "wrote a preamble to an early bill to establish Rock Creek Park," Spilsbury says, 9. The involvement of Frederick Law Olmsted Jr. began in 1900 and culminated in his report of 1918, which she excerpts, 35-43. For Roosevelt's affinity with the creek, see Morris, *Theodore Rex*, 512. Letter, Muir to Robert Underwood Johnson, 3 December 1898, Martinez, for Muir's missing the president and Pinchot. Muir's Washington tour on 30 September 1893 included the White House, a "rather nice dwelling," he wrote Louie that day, "but not at all awfully so." Letter, Muir to Louie Muir, 12 November 1898, Savannah, Georgia, "Have been on the train all night. slept well. It is now 8.30 A. M. Sargent is out for breakfast. I had my coffee 2 h[ou]rs. ago."

28. For their Florida days, see JMJ, 11-20 [12-21] November 1898. On 22 November, Muir corrected his misdating. Letter, Muir to Helen and Wanda, 17 November 1898, Key West, Florida, indicates correct date for his Marquesas excursion, and puts his return time at about 11 p.m.

29. Muir does not mention Audubon's visit in spring 1832. "At Greene and Whitehead Streets is the Audubon House," Mary Durant wrote, though she doubts if Audubon resided there; see Mary Durant and Michael Harwood, *On the Road with John James Audubon* (New York:

Dodd, Mead, 1980), 379-83. Turner identified the Hodgsons; see his valuable note 375-76, and account, 149-54.

30. See Muir's "Cedar Keys" chapter in *A Thousand-Mile Walk to the Gulf*, esp. 123-35, and Badè's Introduction, xxii-xxiv. Letter, Muir to Louie Muir, 21 November 1898, Live Oak, Florida; excerpt in *L&L* 2:315-16. JMJ, 20 [21] November 1898.

31. Letter, Muir to Louie Muir, 21 November 1898, Live Oak, Florida

32. Letter, Muir to Wanda and Helen Muir, Mobile, Alabama, 24 November 1898. For Charles T. Mohr (1824-1901) see *Who Was Who* I:854, *DAB*. On 5 October 1898, Professor Eugene A. Smith, an Alabama Geological Survey colleague of Mohr's, had accompanied them. "Liked very much Dr Mohr," Muir wrote in his journal, "grand benevolent old man of 74. enthusiasm of youth still bright tho health feeble. Prof Smith also. Active simple kind."

   For most of his life Joseph Hinson Mellichamp (1829-1903) was a country doctor in Bluffton, South Carolina, twenty-four miles southwest of Beaufort (in whose woods his father introduced him to plants). He also distinguished himself as a botanist. He contributed "Notes of a South Carolina Naturalist" to *Garden and Forest*, 2 and 9 January 1889, 2-3 and 15-16, respectively, and a letter to the editor describing the largest grapevine he ever saw, 3 April 1895, 139. He read and reread Muir's *Mountains of California*, and "indeed most of what you [Muir] have written." Letter, Mellichamp to Muir, 1 March 1889 [1898], New Orleans, Louisiana. Wilson Parham Gee, *South Carolina Botanists* (University of South Carolina, 1918), 49-52. William H. Canby, *Torreya*, January 1904, 8-10. *New Orleans Times Democrat*, 11 October 1903, 9, obituary. The last two sources differ on the date of death: Canby says 2 October; the newspaper, 3 October.

33. Muir's journal stops on 29 November. Letter, Muir to George A. Kip, 3 December 1898, says he "reached home three days ago," which I interpret to mean 30 November.

34. Letters, J. H. Mellichamp to Muir, 6 and 23 June 1902, San Francisco. His 23 June letter implies that he saw Muir and his family, probably in the city or in Martinez. Letter, J. H. Mellichamp to Muir, 14 January 1903, New Orleans.

35. Letter, J. H. Mellichamp to Muir, 9 August 1903, Bluffton, S.C. Letter, Muir to Louie Muir, 3 October 1903, Darjeeling [Darjiling], India. JMJ, 3 October 1903 (JMP, Reel 29). My gratitude to Ann Elliott of the Bluffton Historical Preservation Society for information on the Mellichamp home and sequoias.

## TRIP THREE: 1898
## CHAPTER 8—VERMONT

1. Letters, Muir to Louie Muir and Robert Underwood Johnson, 17 October 1898, Albany, New York.

2. Letter, Muir to Wanda Muir, 18 October 1898, Burlington, Vermont. This letter is partially printed in *Dear Papa*, 60.

3. JMJ, 18 October 1898. Muir dated this 17 October, later corrected to the 18th when he discovered his error. *Boss* refers to "A smooth and rounded mound, hillock, or other mass of resistant bedrock, usually bare of soil or vegetation," while *roche moutonnée* is "A small elongated protruding knob or hillock of bedrock, so sculptured by a large glacier as to have its long axis in the direction of ice movement," according to the *Glossary of Geology* edited by Robert Bates and Julia A. Jackson (Alexandria, Virginia: American Geological Institute, 1987), 80 and 573, respectively.

4. Letter, John Muir to Wanda Muir, 18 October 1898, Burlington, Vermont.

5. I am indebted to James Cotter and Archie Hobson for this Latin translation. *Catalogue of the University of Vermont and State Agricultural College, Burlington, Vermont, 1898-1899* (Free Press Association, 1898), passim.

6. Ibid., 24.

7. Henry A. Beers, *Four Americans* (Yale University Press, 1919), 67. For Beers, see *DAB*; *Yale Obituary Record;* George W. Pierson, "Teachers and Teaching" in his *Yale College: An Educational History 1871-1921* (Yale University Press, 1952), 282-4; Francis Parsons, *Six Men of Yale* (Yale University Press, 1939), 127-45.

8. Beers, *Four Americans*, 78.

9. Henry A. Beers, *An Outline Sketch of American Literature* (Chautauqua Press, 1887), 144, 147-8.

10. I am indebted to archivist Wilma R. Slaight for finding Emma Condit's notebook in the Archives of Wellesley College, Margaret Clapp Library, Wellesley, Massachusetts. This resulted from my small survey of prominent colleges and universities in the Northeast conducted in 1991. It would be interesting to know if college students were exposed to Thoreau before this date.

11. Syllabi of Hunt and Spaeth are in the Princeton University Archives, Seeley G. Mudd Manuscript Library, Princeton, New Jersey. My gratitude to archivist Ben Primer for showing me these.

12. Sources for UVM are David J. Blow, *Historic Guide to Burlington Neighborhoods* (Chittenden County Historical Society, 1991) and Robert V. Daniels, ed., *The University of Vermont: The First Two Hundred Years* (University Press of New England, 1991).

13. *DAB* and *ANB*; *Howard's Autobiography* (The Baker & Taylor Company, 1907); John A. Carpenter, *Sword and Olive Branch: Oliver Otis Howard* (University of Pittsburgh Press, 1964). For Howard and Muir, see Ronald Eber, "John Muir and the Pioneer Conservationists of the Pacific Northwest," in *John Muir in Historical Perspective*, Sally M. Miller, ed. (New York: Peter Lang, 1999), 185-215 at 188; Howard's review of Muir's lecture, "Glaciers in Alaska," given in Vancouver, Washington, *Morning Oregonian* [Portland], 24 January 1880, 1; Letter, Ronald Eber to J. Parker Huber, 25 October 2004, Salem, Oregon. For Howard's Indian relations, see: O.O. Howard, *My Life and Experiences among Our Hostile Indians* (1907; New York: DaCapo Press, 1972); Dee Brown, *Bury My Heart at Wounded Knee* (Holt, Rinehart & Winston, 1970), 320-330. Robert M. Utley, *Frontier Regulars: The United States Army and the Indian, 1866-1891* (New York: Macmillan, 1973), 296-321, gives a balanced appraisal of both Howard and Joseph; he says they traveled 1,700 miles. See also his assessment in his introduction to Howard's *My Life and Experiences among Our Hostile Indians*, v-xvii. Robert Hamburger, *Two Rooms: The Life of Charles Erskine Scott Wood* (University of Nebraska Press, 1998), 41-58, provides another account of the "epic exodus" of the Nez Perce. Wood was Howard's aide-de-camp. Hamburger does not accent the final e of Perce.

14. See Rayford W. Logan, *Howard University: The First Hundred Years, 1867-1967* (New York University Press, 1969); Walter Dyson, *Howard University: The Capstone of Negro Education, A History, 1867-1940* (The Graduate School: Howard University, 1941).

15. Kevin Dann, "The Prince of Plant Collectors Finds a Home at UVM," *Vermont*, Winter 1986, 7-10. Kevin Dann, *Lewis Creek Lost and Found* (University Press of New England, 2001), 114-34. Dann also discusses Pringle's relationships with Maine botanist Kate Furbish and with his farm's caretaker, Frank Estey.

16. Cyrus G. Pringle Journal, Pringle Herbarium, University of Vermont, Burlington, Vermont (hereafter UVM).

17. Sutton, *Charles Sprague Sargent*, 105-114.

18. Letters, Cyrus Pringle to George E. Davenport, 13 November 1882 (Sutton miscited this letter as Pringle to Gray, 358), 23 November 1882, Charlotte, Vermont, in Gray Herbarium Archives, Harvard University, Cambridge, Massachusetts.

19. Letters, George E. Davenport to Cyrus Pringle, 15 and 27 November 1882, Boston and Medford, Massachusetts, respectively, Pringle Letters, UVM Archives, Burlington, Vermont.

20. Kevin Dann, "The Natural Sciences and George Henry Perkins," in Daniels, UVM, 138-157. Dann believed that Pringle should have been the author of *Flora of Vermont*, not Perkins. The *DAB* is incorrect in saying Perkins came to UVM in Fall 1869.

21. This report is in the Perkins Papers, UVM Archives. It dates his appointment as state geologist to 1 September 1897.

22. Apparently, the Muir Glacier was named in 1880 by Captain L. A. Beardslee, whom Muir told of his discovery. See Kimes, 39-40.

23. John Muir, *Travels in Alaska* (Houghton Mifflin, 1915), 264.

24. Letter, Mary Perkins to her sister, 22 July 1899, Laggan, Alberta, Canada, in Perkins Papers, UVM Archives. This gives date of their Victoria departure; it also tells why she destroyed her letters: because of "some allusion to family or private matters."

25. See *JOM* for his journey's end, 419-21; his visit to Muir Glacier, 384-5. Frank Buske, "John Muir's Alaska Experience," *The Pacific Historian*, Summer/Fall 1985,113-23.

26. Letter, Mary Perkins to Henry F. Perkins, 5 August 1899, Sitka, Alaska, in Perkins Papers, UVM Archives. W. Osgood Field, "The Fairweather Range," *Appalachia*, December 1926, 460-72; 468 for ice in Muir Inlet.

27. E. Ruhamah Scidmore, *Alaska Its Southern Coast and the Sitkan Archipelago* (Boston: D. Lothrop, 1885), 135.

28. Letter, E.R. Scidmore to John Muir, 27 December 1885, Washington, D.C. Six more of her letters are in the JMP. Muir's copy of her *Alaska* is in HASC.

29. These letters have been published by Robert Engberg and Bruce Merrell, eds., *Letters from Alaska: John Muir* (University of Wisconsin Press, 1993).

30. Eliza Ruhamah Scidmore, "The Discovery of Glacier Bay, Alaska," *National Geographic*, April 1896, 144. On Scidmore, see *DAB, ANB*.

31. T. D. Seymour Bassett, "President Matthew Buckham and The University of Vermont," in Daniels, *UVM*, 116, on Olmsted. Robin W. Winks, *Frederick Billings: A Life* (Oxford University Press, 1991), 303-04, Billings Library; 130, 168, 276-78. Winks does not give details of his Yosemite trips.

32. T. D. Seymour Bassett, "The George Perkins Marsh Papers," *Dartmouth College Library Bulletin*, November 1969, 9-14; and preface of the Printed Catalogue of the George P. Marsh Library in Bailey/Howe Library, UVM. Winks, *Frederick Billings*, 276 and 286, Muir; 274-92, Billings's conservation ethic. James Davie Butler, one of Muir's teachers at the University of Wisconsin and a life-long friend, also influenced Billings. In 1869, Billings purchased the boyhood home of George Perkins Marsh and 260 acres; he expanded the land, managed its forest, planted white pines and Norway spruces, created carriage roads on Mount Tom, and operated a model farm, Winks, 297-99. This is now the Marsh-Billings-Rockefeller National Historic Park. Still displayed in the mansion are Bierstadt's *Cathedral Rocks, Yosemite* (1870)

and William Keith's *Mount Hood from Sandy River* (n.d.) from the Billingses's art collection; see Robert L. McGrath, *Special History Study: Art and the American Conservation Movement* (Boston: National Park Service, 2001), 82-83 and 100-101, respectively.

33. Winks, *Frederick Billings*, 275, calls *Man and Nature* "the first American book on ecology." Wolfe, 83; Edmund A. Schofield, "John Muir's Yankee Friends and Mentors: The New England Connection," *The Pacific Historian*, Summer/Fall 1985, 65-89, esp. 66-71; Cohen, *The Pathless Way*, 9-11, Ezra Carr introduced Muir to Marsh's *Man and Nature*; 20-22, the differences of Marsh and Muir on Man's place in nature; 191, Marsh's influence on Muir's thinking about Sierran forests. Robert Merideth, *The Environmentalist's Bookshelf: A Guide to the Best Books* (New York: G. K. Hall, 1993), includes Marsh's *Man and Nature* along with Thoreau's *Walden*, Emerson's *Nature*, and Muir's *My First Summer in the Sierra, Our National Parks, The Yosemite*, and *The Story of My Boyhood and Youth*.

On Marsh, see *DAB*; *ANB*; David Lowenthal, *George Perkins Marsh: Versatile Vermonter* (Columbia University Press, 1958); David Lowenthal, *George Perkins Marsh: Prophet of Conservation* (University of Washington Press, 2000), 302, classic; 304, 352-53 for Sargent, who corresponded with Marsh and paid tribute to him in the *Nation*, 17 August 1882, 136; 415-19, for discussion of Thoreau and Muir. "Muir keenly admired Marsh," Lowenthal believed, "drawing extensively on *Man and Nature* to secure Sierra soils and forests as watershed protection for Yosemite. I cannot locate Muir's copy of *Man and Nature*, which Wolfe saw and said Muir "copiously marked" (83).

34. Lowenthall, *Marsh* (2000), 4, view from Mount Tom; 26-27, Green and White Mountains; 254-57, Alps. Marsh would have been interested in Muir's "Living Glaciers of California" and "The New Sequoia Forests of California" in *Harper's Monthly*, November 1875 and 1878, respectively. Marsh's letters contain his writings on glaciers, Lowethal said in conversation on 31 May 2004.

35. Howard H. Peckham, *The Making of the University of Michigan 1817-1967* (University of Michigan Press, 1967), 69.

36. Charles T. Morrissey, *Vermont: A Bicentennial History* (New York: W. W. Norton, 1981), 73.

37. Bradford B. Van Diver, *Roadside Geology of Vermont and New Hampshire* (Missoula, Montana: Mountain Press, 1987), 46-8 and 133-4. Elizabeth H. Thompson and Eric R. Sorenson, *Wetland, Woodland, Wildland: A Guide to the Natural Communities of Vermont* (University Press of New England, 2000), 14-16, 25-6.

38. Mona Van Duyn, "Three Valentines to the Wide World" (1959) in her *If It Be Not I: Collected Poems, 1959-1982* (New York: Alfred A. Knopf, 1993), 4.

39. Charles Scribner's Sons of New York published *The Rough Riders* on 20 May 1899; *NYT*, 20 May 1899, Saturday Review, 331. Morris, *The Rise of Theodore Roosevelt*, 683-84.

40. Walter Teller, *Joshua Slocum* (Rutgers University Press, 1971), 156-7; 59-61; 76 (quote). Muir may have read Slocum in the *Century*, which serialized his book from September 1899 to March 1900, when it was published by the Century Company. See Thomas Philbrick, "Introduction" to Joshua Slocum, *Sailing Alone Around the World* (Penguin Books, 1999), xxviii-xxxi. Also, Bert Bender, "Joshua Slocum: Reality of Solitude," *ATQ* (*The American Transcendental Quarterly*), March 1992, 59-71. Ann Spencer, *Alone at Sea: The Adventures of Joshua Slocum* (Buffalo, New York: Firefly Books, 1999). Though Slocum made San Francisco home port in the 1860s and 1870s, he was mostly at sea.

41. Letter, Muir to Wanda Muir,18 October 1898, Burlington, Vermont.

42. Charles Haight Farnham, *A Life of Francis Parkman* (1900; Boston: Little, Brown, 1902)

is in Muir's Library along with Parkman's works in HASC. Quote, 12-14, 1901 ed.

43. Mason Wade, ed., *The Journals of Francis Parkman* (Harper & Brothers, 1947), I:61. UVM students were introduced to Parkman in Henry A. Beers, *An Outline Sketch of American Literature*, 192-93.

44. Simon Schama, *Dead Certainties* (1991; Vintage Books, 1992), 50.

45. Farnham, *Francis Parkman*, 196.

46. Farnham, *Francis Parkman*, 197. Muir's concept of wilderness is discussed by Max Oelschlaeger, *The Idea of Wilderness* (Yale University Press, 1991), 172-204.

47. Henry D. Thoreau, *A Yankee in Canada* (1866; Harvest House, 1961), 18, 44.

48. HDTC, 299; Joseph J. Moldenhauer explained its publication history, as well as the reason for Thoreau's delay in Burlington in "Thoreau, Hawthorne, and the "Seven-Mile Panorama," *ESQ*, 4th Quarter 1998, 266-67 n2 and 249.

49. Muir's copy of Henry D. Thoreau, *Excursions and Poems* (Boston: Houghton Mifflin, 1906), Volume V of *The Writings of Henry David Thoreau* is in HASC.

50. Francis Parkman, *Montcalm and Wolfe* (1884; Collier Books, 1962), 497.

51. John Muir, *The Yosemite* (1912; University of Wisconsin Press, 1986), 14. Muir had camped at Niagara in September 1864 (Wolfe, 93).

52. Francis Parkman, *A Half-Century of Conflict* (1892; Collier Books, 1962), 67.

53. Watermans, 355.

54. Muir did not say where he stayed; nor is the inn's register for then available. Logic, however, dictated this choice.

55. Noel Grove, "Greenways: Paths to the Future," *National Geographic*, June 1990, 77-99.

56. Edwin L. Bigelow, *Stowe, Vermont* (Stowe Historical Society, 1964), 158.

57. *Letters to a Friend*, 177; Gisel, 258.

58. John Muir, *The Cruise of the Corwin* (1917; Sierra Club Books, 1993), 94-96, 99, 215 (plant list).

59. For Emerson's Mansfield experience, see Joel Porte, ed., *Emerson in His Journals* (Harvard University Press, 1982), 551-53. Emerson's letter of 24 August 1868 to his brother William identifies George Bartlett as son of Dr. Josiah Bartlett of Concord "a colorful figure, a strolling player and director of amateur theatricals" (*LRWE* 6:30).

John A. Wriston, *Vermont Inns & Taverns: Pre-Revolution to 1925: An Illustrated and Annotated Checklist* (Rutland, Vermont: Academy Books, 1991), 548, says of Prouty's Hotel in Underhill Center that Emerson was "once a guest according to oral tradition;" This now can be confirmed by Emerson himself. Prouty's Hotel, now apartments, still stands on Main Street.

60. For his account of their meeting, see John Muir, *Our National Parks* (Houghton Mifflin, 1901), 131-36.

61. Letter, Muir to Helen Muir, 11 November 1898, Richmond, Virginia.

62. What I have learned of Smith comes from the U.S. Census for Stowe, Lamoille County, Vermont, and the birth-death-marriage records of the Town Clerk's Office, Stowe, Vermont. I am indebted to Patricia Haslam of Stowe, a certified genealogical record searcher, for her help.

63. Letter, D.R. Smith to Muir, 19 December 1898, Stowe, Vermont. I am assuming that this is the book Muir sent. It is not identified, and though I wished it to be still in Stowe, I have not been able to find it.

64. *Dear Papa*, 61-2.

65. C.G. Pringle, "Reminiscences of Botanical Rambles in Vermont," *Bulletin of the Torrey Botanical Club*, 29 July 1897, 350-57. His first visit to Mansfield was on 15 June 1876.

66. The New England Botanical Club has two specimens of *Isoetes echinospora* collected by Mann from Mansfield, botanist Ray Angelo informed me (Letter, 6 November 1993). Neither are dated, alas. A former NEBC herbarium curator and author of *A Flora of Concord* (The Museum of Comparative Zoology, Harvard University, 1974), Richard J. Eaton speculated in a specimen annotation that Mann collected *I. echinospora* between 1862 and 1864. Eaton also gave a short biography of Mann in his *A Flora of Concord*, 34-5.

    For Mann and Thoreau see Walter Harding, "Thoreau's Minnesota Journey: Two Documents," *Thoreau Society Bulletin* (1962) number 16; Harding, *The Days of Henry Thoreau*, 444-451. Profiles of Mann are in *Bulletin of the Essex Institute* (Salem, Massachusetts), February 1869, 25-31; *The Proceedings of the American Academy of Arts and Sciences*, 8 June 1869, 129-131; A. Hunter Dupree, "Thoreau as Scientist: American Science in the 1850s," in Edmund A. Schofield and Robert C. Baron, eds., *Thoreau's World and Ours: A Natural Legacy* (Golden, Colorado: North American Press, 1993), 42-7.

67. On 28 July 1842, Parkman walked from Burlington to Underhill to North Cambridge. The next day, he walked through the Lamoille River valley, passing Jeffersonville to Johnson, from where he went by stage north to Troy. See *The Journals of Francis Parkman* I:61-3.

68. Clare Dunn Johnson, *"I see by the Paper...": An Informal History of St. Johnsbury* (The Cowles Press, 1978), 40, 70, 145; and Wriston, *Vermont Inns & Taverns*, 479-82. I am assuming that this is the hotel where Muir dined because of its proximity to the railroad station. As the hour of his arrival is noon, it is likely that he would have eaten before exploring the town. St. Johnsbury House (1850) on Main Street, now a senior center, is also a possibility, though a longer walk from the depot.

69. *Dear Papa*, 28. Occasionally, Muir telegraphed. See Letter, Muir to Louie Muir, 30 September 1898, Knoxville, Tennessee. AT&T opened New York-San Francisco telecommunications on 25 January 1915. See John Brooks, *Telephone: The First Hundred Years* (Harper & Row, 1975), 139. Harold Wood, "John Muir's Telephone Number," *The John Muir Newsletter*, Winter 2001/02, 8.

70. Van Diver, *Roadside Geology of Vermont and New Hampshire*, 107.

71. *DAB*; *ANB* has Erastus Fairbanks only. *Fairbanks Standard, 1830-1980: 150 Years* (Fairbanks Weighing Division, n.d. [1980?]).

72. Letter, Ben Mosley, Park Ranger, John Muir National Historic Site, Martinez, California, 14 November 1993. He related that Helen Muir in her diary mentioned going to the fruit packing houses to be weighed.

73. Norman R. Atwood, "Two Walks in St. Johnsbury, A Victorian Village" (typescript available from chamber of commerce, n.d.) is helpful, as is his *Walk to Noteworthy Buildings of St. Johnsbury* (Bicentennial St. Johnsbury House Foundation, n.d.).

74. Emily Hiestand, *Green the Witch-Hazel Wood* (Saint Paul, Minnesota: Graywolf Press, 1989), 7, from "This is Something Simple."

75. Gordon Hendricks, "Bierstadt's *The Domes of the Yosemite*," *The American Art Journal*, Fall 1971, 23-31; Nancy K. Anderson and Linda S. Ferber, *Albert Bierstadt: Art & Enterprise* (The Brooklyn Museum/Hudson Hills Press, 1990), 90-91, offers a color plate of this painting and discussion by Anderson and Mark Twain.

76. Letter, Nancy K. Anderson, Associate Curator, American & British Paintings, National

Gallery of Art, Washington, D.C., to J. Parker Huber, 28 September 1992. "It seems quite likely that Muir and Bierstadt would have met but I have not yet seen a document that would confirm such a meeting." They did meet later, however, in June or September 1893, most likely in
New York. As this was their introduction, according to Johnson's certificate, I assume it was
their first meeting, and that, therefore, they did not meet in Yosemite, as I speculate here.

77. Hendricks, "Bierstadt's *The Domes of the Yosemite*," 31.

## TRIP THREE: 1898
## CHAPTER 9—NEW HAMPSHIRE

1. JMJ, 20 October 1898. Pondicherry NWR, *Appalachia*, June 2001, 143-44. "Pondicherry
Named Important Bird Area," *Appalachia*, December 2003, 151.

2. According to the *OED*, muir is a variant of *moor*, an open landscape feature filled with heath
vegetation.

3. John Muir, "The Grand Cañon of the Colorado," *The Century Magazine*, November 1902,
107-116. Muir worked on this essay during the first half of 1902. In January of that year, he
visited the Grand Canyon to see it in winter. On 9 July, he finished the article and sent it to
Robert Underwood Johnson at the *Century*. It was reprinted in *Steep Trails* (1918).

4. M.F. Sweetser, *The White Mountains: A Handbook for Travellers* (15th edition; Houghton
Mifflin, 1896), gives the season for the Fabyan House as 20 June to 1 October (158), for the
Crawford House "opens about June 1st" with no closing date (148). M.F. Sweetser, *Chisholm's
White Mountain Guide-Book* (Chisholm Bros., 1898) refers only to a hotel season of July and
August. King's *Handbook of the United States 1896* (reissued by Benjamin Blom, 1972) for which
Sweetser wrote the text, while not naming particular establishments, states, "The favorite season
is July, August and September, though June and October are also included in the pleasure-time.
Many hundreds of farmers' houses are kept open for boarders..." (546). Nor does Karl
Baedeker, *The United States...A Handbook for Travellers, 1893* (Da Capo Press, 1971) indicate
when these hotels close. Moses Foster Sweetser (1848-1897) modeled his guidebooks after the
German Baedekers. His *White Mountain Guide Book* and numerous others establish him as the
preeminent American travel guide writer in the late nineteenth century. See David Tatham,
"Moses Foster Sweetser's *Views in the White Mountains*," *Historical New Hampshire*, Summer/Fall
1981, 119-148. Oscar Fay Adams, *A Dictionary of American Authors* (Houghton Mifflin, 1897),
369, lists his other guides. Muir is also in this *Dictionary*, as well as Emerson, Hawthorne,
Thoreau, and other friends of Muir's, Helen Hunt Jackson, Sarah Orne Jewett, and Asa Gray.
No guidebooks of the White Mountains are in Muir's extant library.

5. Both volumes of William Cullen Bryant's *Picturesque America* are in Muir's library, HASC.
They are without Muir holograph. Harry Fenn (1845-1911), a founder of the American
Watercolor Society, also illustrated seventeen of the other thirty-four articles in this volume,
ranging from Florida to Maine, as well as seven (one was with J.D. Woodward)—all on New
York places, except Mt. Mansfield, Vermont—of the thirty-one articles of the second volume.
Susan Nichols Carter (1835-1896) was head of the art school of Cooper Union for the
Advancement of Science and Art in New York City (*Boston Evening Transcript*, 11 August
1896, 5; *The Critic*, 15 August 1896, 110). Michael P. Branch, "William Cullen Bryant: The
Nature Poet as Environmental Journalist," *ATQ*, September 1998, 179-98, illuminates
Bryant's contribution to conservaton in his advocacy of forests, urban parks, and native plants.

   Charles H. Hitchcock, *The Geology of New Hampshire* (Concord: E. A. Jenks, state printer,
1874-1878), 3 volumes and atlas. Especially germane was "The Distribution of Plants in

New Hampshire," I:381-415, with map of "The Distribution of Trees in New Hampshire" opp. 382, and "Scenographical Geology," I: 586-635. Apparently, Moses Woolson, then living in Concord, New Hampshire, facilitated this gift to Muir. See his letters to Muir of 19 October 1878 and 14 February 1880. Muir's copy is missing from his extant library. For Hitchcock (1836-1919) see *DAB* and *ANB*; Watermans, 137-44 (Moosilauke and Washington), 168-75 (survey), 191 (first AMC councillor of topography). His father, Edward Hitchcock (1793-1864), a professor at and president of Amherst College, authored *Elementary Anatomy and Physiology* (1862) and *Elementary Geology* (1840), books familiar to Muir.

6. Charles Sprague Sargent, "Charles Edward Faxon," *Rhodora*, July 1918, 116-22. George G. Kennedy, "Edwin Faxon," *Rhodora*, June 1900, 107-11. Alpine Bluet, *Houstonia caerulea* L., var. *Faxonorum*, is in Stuart K. Harris, *Mountain Flowers of New England* (Appalachian Mountain Club, 1964), 125.

7. C.H. Merrill is in George E. McAvoy, *And Then There Was One: A History of the Hotels of the Summit and the West Side of Mt. Washington* (The Crawford Press, 1988), 45 and passim. McAvoy states "Mr. Merrill had built a cottage for artists which was used by Cole, of the famous Hudson River School of Painters, among others." Since Thomas Cole died in 1844, this is not true.

8. Jane Roy Brown, "A Mountain Vision: AMC's Highland Center Opens in Crawford Notch," *AMC Outdoors Magazine*, October 2003, 19-21. *Full of Facts and Sentiment: The Art of Frank H. Shapleigh* (Concord: New Hampshire Historical Society, 1982), exhibition catalog by James and Donna-Belle Garvin with essays by Charles O. Vogel and David Tatham. This contains only one of Shapleigh's Sierra studies, that of El Capitan, 60. His studio is shown on page 8. Letters, Muir to Jeanne Carr, Yosemite, 29 July [1870] in Gisel, 114-16, and C.L. W[aterston] to Carr, 10 July 1871, Boston, in Gisel, 144-45. For Shapleigh exhibit at 79 Studio Building, *Boston Evening Transcript*, 19 May 1871 [2]. Also exhibited in Boston in May 1871 was the *View of the Great Yosemite Falls* of Henry Cheever Pratt, who also was in the valley in June 1870, at the same time with Shapleigh and the Waterstons. This was shown at Pratt's studio at 8 Bromfield Street. See *Boston Evening Transcript*, 18 May 1871[1]. Alice Doan Hodgson, "Henry Cheever Pratt (1830-1880)," *Antiques*, November 1872, 842-47.

Anna Waterston (1812-1899) was the youngest daughter of Eliza Morton and Josiah Quincy; her father was mayor of Boston (1823-1827) and president of Harvard (1829-1845; *DAB, ANB*). Beverly Wilson Palmer, ed., *A Woman's Wit and Whimsey: The 1833 Diary of Anna Cabot Lowell Quincy* (Boston: Northeastern University Press, 2003), Introduction, 3-14; appendix C, 149-55, is Anna Quincy's tribute to Jane Austen from the *Atlantic*, February 1863, 235-40, a contribution Annie Fields suggested, Rita K. Gollin, *Annie Adams Fields: Woman of Letters* (University of Massachusetts Press, 2002), 37, 323n19.

R. C. Waterston is in *Appleton's Cyclopaedia of American Biography*. J.P. Quincy, "Memoir of Rev. R. C. Waterston," *Massachusetts Historical Society Proceedings*, October 1893, 292-302. Harriette Knight Smith, *The History of the Lowell Institute* (Boston, New York, London: Lamson, Wolffe, 1898), 68, indicates that he gave twelve lectures, while the *Boston Evening Transcript*, 27 January 1871 [2] states six. They were well attended, despite the severe winter and another concomitant California talk by Marshall P. Wilder, which the *Transcript* published on 9 February 1871 [4]; Wilder said that he did not visit Yosemite. On Wednesday eve, 15 February 1871, Waterson's subject was the "Forests and the Yo-semite Valley." Kimes, 143, for Boston Society of Natural History meeting. Clark's Letter (undated) is in the *Boston Society of Natural History Proceedings*, 15 January 1873, 259-61. See also Rev. Robert C. Waterston, *Letter from San Francisco, Cal., to the Massachusetts Historical Society* (Cambridge: John Wilson and Son, 1870). This letter of 29 August 1870, read at the 8 October 1870 meeting of the Massachusetts Historical Society and reprinted from its proceedings, tells of Waterston's visits to the missions of San Francisco, San Jose, and Santa Clara, as well as to the Mariposa Grove. I am indebted to Linda B. MacIver of the Boston Public Library for this find.

It is interesting to speculate who was with Shapleigh when he painted Hetch Hetchy. As Muir's first exploration of that valley did not occur until November 1871, I presume that Muir did not guide him there.

9. For Shapleigh on Mt. Washington, *Among the Clouds*, 17 August 1898, [1] and [4]. John Paul and Emily Selinger succeeded Shapleigh at the Crawford House studio in 1894; they returned each season until his death in 1909. Charles and Gloria Vogel, "Jean Paul and Emily Selinger," *Historical New Hampshire,* Summer 1979, 125-42. Charles O. Vogel, "The Artists-In-Residence at the White Mountain Hotels," *Historical New Hampshire*, Spring/Summer 1995, 81-94.

10. Letter, Muir to Wanda Muir, 28 October 1898, New York.

11. Thomas Crawford's, called the Notch House, located west of Saco Lake at the north end of Crawford Notch, called Gateway of the Notch, was built in 1828 and burned in 1854. Tom was forced to sell to Joseph L. Gibb when he overinvested in the creation of a new inn nearby, Crawford House, which Gibb completed. The Crawford House, destroyed in April 1859 and resurrected in sixty days, occupied this site until 20 November 1977, when the new building also succumbed to fire. I am indebted to historian Randall H. Bennett of the Bethel Historical Society, Maine (personal conversation 29 April 1996). See his *White Mountains* (Arcadia, 1994), 24, 45; F. Allen Burt, *The Story of Mount Washington* (Dartmouth Publications, 1960),41, 69-70; Bryant F. Tolles Jr., *The Grand Resort Hotels of the White Mountains* (Boston: David R. Godine, 1998), 55-60. David Emerson, *White Mountain Hotels* (Arcadia, 1996), 20, 27.

Thomas Crawford's famous Notch House is shown in Thomas Cole's famous oil, *The Notch of the White Mountains (Crawford Notch)*, 1839, National Gallery of Art, Washington, D.C. Cole (1801-1844) first came to the White Mountains in 1827 and walked through the Notch in 1828. See Catherine H. Campbell, "Two's Company: The Diaries of Thomas Cole and Henry Cheever Pratt on Their Walk through Crawford Notch, 1828," *Historical New Hampshire*, Winter 1978, 309-33; and her "The Gate of the Notch", *Historical New Hampshire*, Summer 1978, 91-122; and Theodore E. Stebbins Jr., "Thomas Cole at Crawford Notch," *National Gallery of Art: Report and Studies in the History of Art*, 1968, 133-145. Cole sketched this scene on his last visit in July of 1839 (Louis Legrand Noble, *The Life and Works of Thomas Cole*, 1853; Harvard University Press, 1964; Elliot S.Vessell, ed., 204). Why his painting makes the season autumn is not clear. He missed Thoreau by two months. Thoreau knew Cole's work, however; see Robert D. Richardson Jr., *Henry Thoreau: A Life of the Mind* (University of California Press, 1986), 51.

12. *The Writings of Henry David Thoreau: Journal 1* edited by Bradford Torrey (Houghton Mifflin, 1906), 1-13 September 1839, in HASC. Muir owned three copies of *A Week on the Concord and Merrimack Rivers*: Ticknor and Fields, 1868; Houghton Mifflin, 1897; Houghton Mifflin, 1906 (volume 1 of *The Writings of Henry David Thoreau*)—all are in HASC. Muir read the 1868 and 1906 editions, as his marginalia and indices verify. Nowhere, however, does he highlight Mt. Washington/White Mountains. His 1868 index cites "201 on mtn top", referring to Thoreau's sunrise experience atop Saddleback Mountain (now Greylock) in northwest Massachusetts in July 1844, an account of which he gives in the Tuesday chapter of *A Week* (Princeton edition, 189). His 1906 index offers "Mtns" on pages 171 and 189, designating Monadnock and Peterboro Hills, which Thoreau sees from Concord Cliffs (actu-

ally on p.170), with no other holograph for the rest of the poem; and Hoosack Mountain, from where Thoreau views his journey west through the village of North Adams and up Saddleback (PE,180). Fifty-four years later, on 17 September 1898, Muir's train tunneled through Hoosack Mountain on its way to Boston. His spelling of Hoosack is the same as Thoreau's, though now the "k" has been dropped.

Muir most likely did not read the 1897 edition of *A Week*. At least his pencil is limited to one comment in the margin of the first page. Here he responds to Thoreau's speculation that the Musketaquid (Concord) may be as old a river as the Nile: "No. *JM* A comparatively young river al[t]hough some of the highest tributaries of of [sic] the Nile heading [?] on gls? [glaciers] may be younger."

13. Thomas Starr King, *The White Hills: Their Legends, Landscape, and Poetry* (Boston: Crosby, Nichols, Lee and Company, 1860) is not in Muir's library. In 1911 Allen H. Bent called this "a classic of English literature" and "still the best book about the White Mountains" in his *A Bibliography of the White Mountains* (1911, Appalachian Mountain Club; New Hampshire Publishing Co., 1971, ed. E. J. Hanrahan), x, 2. See Burt, *The Story of Mount Washington*, 51. King Ravine on Mt. Adams also celebrates the author-preacher, who explored this cirque in 1857. *DAB* and *ANB*.

14. *The Writings of Henry David Thoreau: Journal 11* (Houghton Mifflin, 1906), 1-19 July 1858. Muir's copy is in HASC. For the entire volume he marks twenty passages in text, and indexes ten items on twelve pages; he makes no comments in text.

15. *LRWE*1:275-281. Emerson identified their lodging only as Crawford's. Based on his mention of Thomas Crawford in his journal, I presume he stayed at Thomas Crawford's, ten years before Thoreau. *JMN* 3:16. Itineraries are in Albert J. von Frank, *An Emerson Chronology* (G.K. Hall, 1994), 41-42.

16. Richardson, 23-28. His chapter on her is excellent. Emerson read her intently, filling 870 manuscript pages with her, which have yet to be published. *The Selected Letters of Mary Moody Emerson* have been edited by Nancy Craig Simmons (The University of Georgia Press, 1993) and Phyllis Cole has written her biography, *Mary Moody Emerson and the Origins of Transcendentalism: A Family History* (Oxford University Press, 1998).

17. Ethan Allan Crawford (1792-1846) was the legendary "Giant of the Mountains." In 1817, he married his cousin Lucy Howe (1793?-1869) whose *History of the White Mountains* was printed in Portland, Maine, in 1846, 1883, and 1886; then edited by Stearns Morse (Dartmouth Publications, 1966) including some of Lucy's 1860 manuscript; his introduction gives details. Curiously, Lucy does not mention Emerson's visit. This inn, opened in 1818, transferred management in 1837—the Crawfords going to Guildhall, Vermont, where Lucy was born—expanded and renamed Mount Washington House under Horace Fabyan, burned in 1853. The Crawfords returned in 1843 to run another inn a mile from their old one until Ethan's death in 1846.

18. *JMN* 4: 27-30, 228-229. Richardson, 125. McAleer, 122. Rusk, 161-162. Frank, *An Emerson Chronology*, 72. Cole, *Mary Moody Emerson*, 218.

19. Watermans, 41 and 43 discussion; 42, map. *LRWE* 3:337-338. The cog railway displaced the upper portion of the original CP2.

20. *JMN*7:232-236. Frank, *An Emerson Chronology*, 146. *LRWE* 2:220-222. Richardson, 324.

21. *JMN* 16:195-196 (itinerary and expenses); Edward W. Emerson and Waldo Emerson Forbes, *Journals of Ralph Waldo Emerson* (Houghton Mifflin, 1909-1914), 10:327-328; Edward embellishes his father's account. *LRWE* 6:131. Frank, *An Emerson Chronology*, 465. Rusk, 445.

This Crawford's, the third Emerson stayed in, neither that of Thomas nor Ethan Allen

Crawford, was the one rebuilt in 1859 by Joseph Gibb, located at north end of Crawford Notch until its demise. See note 11 above.

22. For Muir's account of their meeting, see John Muir, *Our National Parks* (Houghton Mifflin, 1901), 131-136. Emerson may well have discussed Vermont's Mt. Mansfield too, which, three years earlier on 13 August 1868, he and his daughter Ellen climbed (see chapter 8).

23. *LRWE* 6:277. *ETE Letters* 2:176-179. Ellen does not mention staying at Crawford's. Frank accepts her itinerary, *An Emerson Chronology*, 504. Since Ellen's letter was written 2 July from Plymouth, Emerson's 7 July after their trip was over, I prefer his account and put them at Crawford's. The hotel register in the New Hampshire Historical Society, furthermore, confirms their arrival at tea time on Monday 5 July, and their stay in rooms 79 and 80.

24. Thomas Woodson, L. Neal Smith, Norman Holmes Pearson, eds., *Nathaniel Hawthorne: The Letters 1813-1843* (Ohio State University Press, 1984), 226-227 (*The Centenary Edition of the Works of Nathaniel Hawthorne*, v.15.). The editors mistakenly lodge him at Thomas Crawford's Notch House. Hawthorne's being at Ethan Allen Crawford's put him six miles, not the "three miles" of the editors, from the Willey House. The register of Ethan Allen Crawford's, in the Dartmouth College Library, Special Collections, does not contain Hawthorne's name. Hawthorne's letter of 16 September 1832 is from Burlington, Vermont; thus, Muir has reversed Hawthorne's journey, coming from Burlington to the White Mountains.

25. John F. Sears, *Sacred Places: American Tourist Attractions in the Nineteenth Century* (Oxford University Press, 1989), chapter 4, "The Making of an American Tourist Attraction: The Willey House in the White Mountains," 72-86.

26. This edition is in the HASC. Volumes 5, 23, and 24 are missing.

27. Limbaugh, 45, 47, 154-159.

28. Letter, Muir to Wanda, Helen, Louie, 18 October 1898, Burlington, Vermont. Muir did not cross the *t*s in *Swett* and placed a double hyphen in *hereabouts*.

29. John Swett, *Public Education in California: Its Origin and Development, with Personal Reminiscences of Half a Century* (New York: American Book Company, 1911), 38, 63, 80, 284, 292. This book, without Muir markings and index, is in Muir's library at the HASC; its inscription, "To John Muir, my most intimate personal friend for more than thirty years," is dated 30 April 1913, less than four months before Swett's death on 22 August 1913. I am indebted to Janene Ford for checking this for me.

30. John Swett (1830-1913) is in *DAB* and *ANB*. His educational career dominates the biographies of William G. Carr, *John Swett: The Biography of an Educational Pioneer* (Santa Ana, California: Fine Arts Press, 1933) and Nicholas C. Polos, *John Swett: California's Frontier Schoolmaster* (Washington, D.C.: University Press of America, 1978). See also Nicholas C. Polos, "The Educational Philosophy of John Swett and John Muir," *The Pacific Historian*, 1982 (26, No. 1), 58-69. Carr incorrectly places Reed's Ferry in Massachusetts, 33. Swett's summary of positions held is in *Public Education in California*, 6.

31. Carr, *John Swett*, 134-38; he misdates this venture as occurring in 1874. Robert Engberg, ed., *John Muir Summering in the Sierra* (University of Wisconsin Press, 1984), 73-90. *JOM*, 201-09. *Public Education in California*, 199-200, 235, 310, children; 231-33, Muir. Swett indicated that they had six children, while I account for only five. For Muir's McChesney and Swett residencies, see Gisel, 234-39, 266, 268.

Joseph B. McChesney (1832-1912), who was born in Brunswick, New York (east of Troy) and came to California in 1858, lived with his wife Sarah S. Jewett, a native of Vermont, and their children, Clara Taggart, Mary Alice, and George Jewett, at Franklin near Eighteenth, the Oakland city directory of 1874 indicates. *The Bay of San Francisco, The Metropolis of the Pacific Coast and Its Suburban Cities: A History* (Chicago: Lewis Publishing Co., 1892), II:198-99.

32. Swett, *Public Education in California*, 274, 277, 300-01. Carr, *John Swett*, 167-68. *Among the Clouds*, 8 September 1898, front page, indicates that Swett was a late arrival at the Summit House on Wednesday, 7 September; French is not listed with him.

## TRIP THREE: 1898
## CHAPTER 10—MAINE

1. Nathan Goold, *A Memorial of William and Nabby T. Goold of Windham, Maine* (Portland: The Thurston Print, 1898). William (1809-1890); Nabby (1816-1897); their children and their birthdays are given on page 5. Nathan Goold's most notable work was *Portland in the Past* (Portland: B. Thurston, 1886). Interestingly, this National Register application was made solely on the basis of Abba Woolson's father, despite the fact that she gained a wider reputation than he.

2. For Abba Woolson, see *DAB, NAW, Who Was Who in America*. Obituaries, *Portland Evening Express & Advertiser*, 7 February 1921, 11; *Boston Evening Transcript*, 7 February 1921, 20. Nathan Gould, "Moses Woolson, The Old-Time Teacher," *Portland Sunday Times*, 11 March 1906, 12. Before coming to Portland, Moses Woolson (1821-1896) had been principal of Chesterfield, New Hampshire, academy and principal of the first Brattleboro, Vermont, high school and of the Bangor, Maine, high school. In Cincinnati, Ohio (1862-1865), he taught at the Woodward High School, and she, at Mt. Auburn School for Girls. He attended Dartmouth College for one year, 1839-1840. Colby College conferred an "honorary" degree upon him in 1847 (centennial edition of the college catalog—thanks to Pat Burdick, Special Collections Librarian).

3. Letters, Abba G. Woolson to Muir, 4 February 1872 and 21 March 1872, Boston (quotes are from the latter). These are her first letters to Muir in the JMP. Abba Woolson, "Spring, As Seen from a City Window," *Browsing Among Books, and Other Essays* (Boston: Roberts Brothers, 1881), 168-88. She refers to Thoreau, 12-13.

Her copy of *Walden* (Boston: Ticknor and Fields, 1862) is in Muir's library at HASC; see discussion of it in chapter 1. It contains her signature and the date of acquisition, "Sept. 1863," on top of title page and Muir's marginalia and index. An interesting question is whether the margin dots are his or hers.

4. Letter, Abba G. Woolson to Muir, 23 March 1873, Boston. John Muir, "Hetch Hetchy Valley," *Boston Weekly Transcript*, 25 March 1873, 2; reprinted in Muir, *Rambles of a Botanist*, 29-39. Abba Goold Woolson, *Woman in American Society* (Boston: Roberts Brothers, 1873) with an endorsement by John G. Whittier; quotes in order of appearance: 208, 165, 155, 206. Though she indicated sending this book to Muir, it is not among those in his library today.

5. Her copy of Thoreau's *Excursions* (Boston: Ticknor and Fields, 1863), a first edition, is in Muir's library at HASC. It contains her signature and Muir's with "Yosemite Valley" under Muir's on a blank page at the front and Muir's index at the back.

Over thirty years later, Muir refreshed his memory of "Walking" when the new edition of *The Writings of Henry David Thoreau V: Excursions and Poems* (Houghton Mifflin, 1906) arrived in Martinez sometime in early 1908. It is still in Muir's library at the HASC. Muir's marks appear in the margins of twelve pages of the essay; he indexes "'Walking' v.g.[very good]."

Lewis Hyde, ed. *The Essays of Henry D. Thoreau* (New York: North Point Press, 2002), 338, says this is a false etymology; its origin is still unclear. For stimulating commentary on "Walking," see Alan D. Hodder, *Thoreau's Ecstatic Witness* (Yale University Press, 2001) 286-91. Hodder relates this sauntering of the foot to Thoreau's wish for "a true sauntering of the eye." William Rossi, ed., *Wild Apples and Other Natural History Essays* by Henry D. Thoreau (University of Georgia Press, 2002), Introduction, xvi-xviii. For Muir's practice see, Arthur W. Ewart, "Spiritual Sauntering," *Sierra*, July/August 1986, 48-51.

The other possible source Thoreau cites is "*sans terre*, without land or a home, which, therefore, in the good sense, will mean, having no particular home, but equally at home everywhere." This meaning Muir did not relate to others, at least not Palmer.

Albert W. Palmer, *The Mountain Trail and Its Message* (Chicago: The Pilgrim Press, 1911), signed by the author, is in Muir's library at HASC; Muir neither marked nor indexed this short sermon. A new edition (Fresno, CA: Sixth Street Press, 1997) with introduction and commentary by Charles Palmer Fisk and epilogue by Holly Van Houten contains Palmer's journal of the July 1908 Sierra Club Outing with Muir, 13-18; Muir's letter of 9 November 1908, thanking Palmer for his photographs, 19; and, from the earlier edition, "A Parable of Sauntering," 41-43. I am grateful to Sarah Rabkin for introducing me to this. Palmer's second daughter finished his autobiography. Margaret Palmer Taylor, ed., *Albert W. Palmer: A Life Extended* (Athens, Ohio: Lawhead Press, 1968), which contains only what is said about Muir in *The Mountain Trail*. and omits the 8 July 1908 entry. Albert W. Palmer (1879-1954), *Who Was Who* III:661.

6. Letter, Abba G. Woolson to Muir, 4 February 1872, Boston. *LRWE* IX:125-26. Emerson included five Ingelow poems in *Parnassus*. She was also in Edmund Clarence Stedman, ed., *A Victorian Anthology, 1837-1895* (Houghton Mifflin, 1895), as well as on the front page of the *Boston Evening Transcript*, 8 July 1870. Emma M. Converse panegyrized Jean Ingelow in *The Aldine*, April 1871, 67-68. A Portsmouth, New Hampshire, ship was named for her, "for no poet has sung of the sea more sweetly than she." On 17 April 1871, the *Jean Ingelow* began its maiden voyage from Boston, taking a cargo of ice to Calcutta. Ray Brighton, *Tall Ships of the Piscataqua* (Portsmouth, New Hampshire: The Portsmouth Marine Society, 1989), 301-08. *Boston Evening Transcript*, 28 February 1871 [2]. Jean Ingelow, *The High Tide on the Coast of Lincolnshire 1571* (Boston: Roberts Brothers, 1883) was richly illustrated by eleven artists; Childe Hassam provided seven drawings.

Muir's copies of Ingelow's *Poems* and *The Monitions of the Unseen* are in his library at the HASC. Neither book contains Muir markings. The latter is inscribed "John Muir from Mrs. M[oses]. W[oolson]. 1872" in pale ink on dark brown paper. Indicative perhaps of the sustained interest in Ingelow, at least by Louie Muir, was the 1904 Christmas gift of *The Poetical Works of Jean Ingelow* (New York: Thomas Y. Crowell, 1894) to Louie Muir from her sister-in-law, Sarah M. Galloway, which is in the Muir library in the Huntington Library; it contains no Muir marginalia or index.

For Ingelow, see *DNB*; *DLB*, 35:105-10; Maureen Peters, *Jean Ingelow: Victorian Poetess* (Ipswich, U.K.: Boydell Press, 1972). Unlike Woolson, according to Peters, Ingelow was not a rebel; she "never felt constricted in her crinoline." (53) Like Emily Dickinson, she stayed single at home, believing "more was to be done by abiding in one place and by growing in it than by constantly uprooting oneself." (91) Though later in life, to escape London's fog, she wintered in Cannes, France. In common with Tennyson, her friend, Ingelow's "aesthetic faculties [were] stirred by wind and dyke, field and fen." (92) Peters prints two of her letters (undated) to Longfellow, 69-70; one of his to her is in *LHWL* V:33.

7. Letter, Abba G. Woolson to Muir, 27 September 1874, Concord, New Hampshire. Abba Goold Woolson, ed., *Dress-Reform: A Series of Lectures Delivered in Boston, on Dress as it*

*Affects the Health of Women* (Boston: Roberts Brothers, 1874). Woolson argued for both health and beauty in costume. Woolson was chair of the dress reform committee of the New England Women's Club; see Julia A. Sprague, *History of the New England Women's Club from 1868 to 1893* (Boston: Lee and Shepard, 1894), 19-20. This also includes Woolson's poetic sendup on the Club Tea, 61-65, and an impressive roster of club speakers and topics, 87-99.

8. Letter, Abba G. Woolson to Muir, 28 February 1876, Concord, New Hampshire. Her photograph is in JMP, Fiche 31, Item #1802.

9. Letters, Moses Woolson to Muir, 19 October 1878 and 14 February 1880, Concord, New Hampshire. I am still searching for Muir's letters to the Woolsons and for her Yosemite lecture. Muir's Alaska writing appeared in the San Francisco *Daily Evening Bulletin* in 1879 and 1880.

10. *Portland Evening Express*, 20 October 1898, 1, 2, 3.

11. Kirk F. Mohney, "The Eastern and Western Promenades," in Theo H.B.M. Holtwijk and Earle G. Shettleworth, Jr., eds. *Bold Vision: The Development of the Parks of Portland, Maine* (Greater Portland Landmarks/Phoenix Publishing, 1999), 36-50.

12. Herbert Adams, "Deering Oaks," in *Bold Vision* supra, 74-93. James P. Baxter, "The Story of Portland," *New England Magazine*, November 1895, 349-70.

13. Martin Dibner, ed., *Portland* (Greater Portland Landmarks, 1972), 180-8l, and *Portland City Guide* (Forest City Printing Company, 1940), 271, for Baxter home.

14. Diary of James Phinney Baxter, 2-17 September 1885, Baxter Memorial Library, Gorham, Maine. I am indebted to reference librarian Joanne Gordon for pointing this out to me. Edward Whymper, *Chamonix and the Range of Mont Blanc, A Guide* (London: John Murray, 1896), 99-102 and 112. Whymper remarks on the various spellings of Montanvert.

15. Diary of James Phinney Baxter, 31 May-4 June, 19-21 October 1898. Baxter also received two honorary degrees from Bowdoin, a Master of Arts in 1881 and a Doctor of Letters in 1904, Kathy Petersen, Archives Assistant at Bowdoin College, informed me in her letter of 11 December 2003. *American Antiquarian Society Proceedings*, October 1921, 262-63; this obituary indicates that Baxter became a member of the Council in 1897, and served to his death. *The New England Historical and Genealogical Register*, July 1921, 163-75, esp. 163 for dates of his tenure. *Portland Evening Express*, 21 October 1898, 2.

16. Diary of James Phinney Baxter, 20-24 June, 28 September, and 27-30 October 1898. Neil Rolde, *The Baxters of Maine: Downeast Visionaries* (Gardiner, Maine: Tilbury House, 1997), 64-69. Rolde believes that Muir influenced Percy, 233, and that Percy learned about preservation from the Hetch Hetchy controversy, 239. J. Parker Huber, *The Wildest Country: A Guide to Thoreau's Maine* (Boston: Appalachian Mountain Club, 1981), 148-49. John W. Hakola, *Legacy of a Lifetime: The Story of Baxter State Park* (Woolwich, Maine: TBW Books, 1981), "Percival Proctor Baxter Biographical Essay," 281-95. Hakola says that in the summer of 1898, Percy Baxter studied in the Portland law firm of Libby, Robinson and Turner (284), which closed in 1915.

17. Edward Allen, *The Wadsworth-Longfellow House*, Portland, Maine (Maine Historical Society, 1995). *Longfellow's Portland and Portland's Longfellow* (Maine Historical Society, 1987), essays by Joyce Butler and Daniel Aaron. Thompson, *Young Longfellow*, 9-22.

18. JMJ, 21 October 1898.

19. Letter, Muir to Wanda Muir, 28 October 1898, New York. The version of this letter in *Dear Papa*, 61-63, omits most of his Maine journey.

20. JMJ, 21 October 1898.

21. For Thoreau's journeys, see Huber, *The Wildest Country*. For railroads, Emma J. True, ed., *History of Greenville* (Augusta, Maine: The Augusta Press, 1936), 14. Actually, the depot was in West Cove (renamed Greenville Junction in 1900), 1.5 miles west of Greenville.

22. Richard F. Fleck, *Henry Thoreau and John Muir Among the Indians* (Hamden, CT: Archon Books, 1985), 37. Edmund R. Schofield, "John Muir's Yankee Friends and Mentors: The New England Connection," *The Pacific Historian*, Summer/Fall 1985, 69, 85. Wolfe, 79.

23. Muir's copy of *The Maine Woods* is in his library, HASC. For easy reference, I have used the more accessible Henry D. Thoreau, *The Maine Woods*, ed. Joseph J. Moldenhauer (Princeton University Press, 1972), 3. In 1893, the United States Geographic Board adopted Katahdin as the acceptable spelling; Edward S. C. Smith and Myron H. Avery, *An Annotated Bibliography of Katahdin* (Washington, D.C.: The Appalachian Trail Conference, 1950), 1n1.

24. Huber, *The Wildest Country*, 107-11.

25. William Wingate Sewall, *Bill Sewall's Story of T.R.* (New York: Harper & Brothers, 1919), 6-8. Sewall remembered incorrectly that all Roosevelt's visits occurred in the fall and that he lost his shoe on their trip to the Munsungun Lakes—in the Catasacoka Stream—not coming to Katahdin, as Roosevelt clearly states happened in his diary for 26 August 1879.

26. Diary of Theodore Roosevelt, 26 August-2 September 1879, Theodore Roosevelt Papers, Library of Congress (Microfilm #429). This gives few place names, yet it is possible to approximate his route. I assume he ascended from the Great Basin, for the Keep Path to the south was in disuse then. His camp, also, was at the "head" of Katahdin Lake, rather than the foot, from where the Keep Path ran. Carleton Putnam, *Theodore Roosevelt. Volume I: The Formative Years, 1858-1886* (New York: Charles Scribner's Sons, 1958), 153-64. John W. Hakola, *Legacy of a Lifetime: The Story of Baxter State Park*, 33-34, believed that Roosevelt used the Lang-Jones Trail between Wassataquoik Stream and Katahdin Lake. Charles E. Hamlin, "Routes to Ktaadn," *Appalachia*, December 1881, 306-31. Hamlin gives the condition of the route from the East in 1879, the year of T. R.'s climb, 324, and indicates that only eight visitors, exclusive of guides, came that way that year, including Hamlin, 331. From Hunt's on the East Branch there was a logging road that crossed Wassataquoik Stream twice before reaching Katahdin Lake, a distance of twelve miles. It was from Katahdin Lake that Marcus R. Keep in June 1848 made the first path to the mountain via Avalanche Brook to the East Slide. Keep took C. H. Hitchcock this way in 1861. Twenty years later, in 1881, Keep returned to Katahdin with Hamlin, this time to the Great Basin. By 1879 Keep's way had been "obstructed" by lumbering. Myron H. Avery, "The Keep Path and Its Successors: The History of Katahdin from the East and North," *Appalachia*, December 1928, 132-47, esp. 135-41.

27. "Except when hunting I never did any mountaineering save for a couple of conventional trips up the Matterhorn and the Jungfrau on one occasion when I was in Switzerland," Roosevelt said in his *Autobiography*, 33. Roosevelt, "could never resist the highest peak in any neighborhood, in any weather," Morris writes, and gives some of the other hills he had climbed in *The Rise of Theodore Roosevelt*, 737-41. For French-Swiss itinerary, see T. R.'s *Diaries of Boyhood and Youth*, 38-49, 59; Morris, 52; Putnam, *Theodore Roosevelt*, 58. *Letters from Theodore Roosevelt to Anna Roosevelt Cowles*, 1870-1918 (New York: Charles Scribner's Sons, 1924), 45-47 (Mount Pilatus and the Matterhorn). T. R.'s record was insufficient for admission to the Alpine Club; so they made him an honorary member in 1887; "A Survey of American Ascents in the Alps," *The American Alpine Journal*, 1936, 517.

28. For T. R. in Adirondacks and Whites in 1871, see his *Diaries of Boyhood and Youth*, 241-60, and Putnam, *Theodore Roosevelt*, 73-74. Putnam believed the Adirondacks provided T.R.'s first wilderness experience.

29. According to the *Diary of Theodore Roosevelt* (Library of Congress), 20 July- 6 August 1880, Newport is the only mountain T.R. climbed, though Morris says he scaled mountains (130). Putnam, Theodore Roosevelt, 200-01, limits his ascents to one.

30. Diary of Theodore Roosevelt (Library of Congress; Microfilm #430), 25 May-6 August 1881 (their whole time abroad is from 12 May to 2 October 1881). Morris, *The Rise of Theodore Roosevelt*, 145-49. Putnam, *Theodore Roosevelt*, 231-33. *LTR*, 1:49-50. Karl Baedeker, *Switzerland...Handbook for Travellers* (Leipzig: Karl Baedeker, 1899, 18th edition, and 1909, 23rd edition), maps, itineraries, elevations. David Starr Jordan, "An Ascent of the Matterhorn," *Science Sketches* (Chicago: A. C. McClurg, 1899), 232-55. Jordan's party of eleven included five guides. Their moment atop, Jordan wrote, "was as cold as midwinter. The north wind whistled and howled, so that we dared not rise to our feet, and the snow fell thick and fast."

31. For T. R.'s journey from Marcy to Buffalo, see Morris, *Theodore Rex*, 3-11.

32. *The Maine Woods* (1972), 59-61, 63-65, 70-71. Muir makes four indices to *The Maine Woods* (1868), each on its own unnumbered end page of the book. I refer to these in order as I-1 (32 items), I-2 (31 items), I-3 (no pages; 3 dates and 8 items), and I-4 (7 items in pencil on brown end paper). I infer that each index corresponds to a reading of *The Maine Woods*. All quotations in this paragraph are are in index 1.

Muir also read the 1906 edition of *The Maine Woods*, volume 3 of *The Writings of Henry David Thoreau* from Houghton Mifflin. His copy is in his library in HASC. For more on Muir's reading of these editions of *The Maine Woods*, see J. Parker Huber, "John Muir and Thoreau's Maine," *The Concord Saunterer*, Fall 1995, 105-18. Here (110) I was unaware that Muir's "Canada West" in 1870 referred to Ontario. I am indebted to Stan Hutchinson of Sierra Madre, California, for pointing this out to me (Letter, 3 June 1997).

33. Lewis Hyde, *The Essays of Henry D. Thoreau*, 330. *The Oxford English Dictionary* gives only two illustrative quotations, Hyde says, Thoreau's and one of Emerson. Maxine Kumin, "The Unhandselled Globe: With Thoreau in Darkest Maine," *Harper's*, July 1986, 63-65, does not define the word. John Muir, "Hetch Hetchy Valley," *Boston Weekly Transcript*, 25 March 1873, 2; reprinted in Muir, *Rambles of a Botanist*, 29-39; see 34 and 38.

34. The Bangor and Aroostook Railroad baggage car transported deer, moose, and caribou killed by hunters in the 1890s. Jerry Angier and Herb Cleaves, *Bangor and Aroostook: The Maine Railroad* (Littleton, Massachusetts: Flying Yankee Enterprises, 1986), 23.

35. Though Attean Lake Lodge officially opened in 1900, their brochure says, Brad Holden, the current owner, whose grandfather ran the lodge, indicated that there were cabins on the island accommodating guests before that. No written history of the lodge exists, but he has material on its early years (conversation,19 September 2003).

36. As far as I know, Muir never wrote about moose, though he surely must have seen them in Alaska, Ontario, and Yellowstone National Park.

37. Among other options, this one appears the most direct, does not recover ground he had already seen, such as the route south through Crawford Notch to Rochester or Portland, and offers the most exposure to the Merrimack River, which he was with long enough to comment on.

## TRIP THREE: 1898
## CHAPTER 11—WELLESLEY

1. *Road Map of the Boston District...*", Geo. H. Walker & Co., Boston, Massachusetts, 1898 edition, Harvard Map Collection. Letter, Muir to Wanda Muir, 28 October 1898, New York.

David Arnold, "Inside the Country Club," *The Boston Globe Magazine*, 19 September 1999, 15 passim. When golf was introduced here in 1892, sheep kept the greens trim. The Ryder Cup is now played here.

2. These stations are shown in Elizabeth M. Hinchliffe, *Five Pounds Currency, Three Pounds of Corn: Wellesley's Centennial Story* (Town of Wellesley, Mass., 1981), 52-3. Wellesley Hills Station is described in Jeffrey Karl Ochsner, *H. H. Richardson: Complete Architectural Works* (MIT Press, 1982), 400-01; Sargent's role, 242. Wellesley Square and Wellesley Farms were posthumous Richardson works, Professor James F. O'Gorman informed me, "actually erected during tenure of Sleepley, Rutan & Coolidge." See James F. O'Gorman, *Living Architecture: A Biography of H. H. Richardson* (Simon & Schuster, 1997).

3. Sutton, 64, 134-36. Zaitzevsky, 175 and 245n38 identifies the architect.

4. HHH, *Diary*, records the many visits of these two men, Sargent sometimes bringing his wife Mary (Minnie) and at least once their daughter Alice; see 2:116 for sleigh ride of 2 January 1881. Benson, 180, 203, 363, 507-08, and passim.

5. JMJ, 23 October 1898. All Muir quotes are from this source unless otherwise indicated.

6. M.F. Sweetser, *Chisholm's White Mountain Guide-book* (Portland, Maine: Chisholm Brothers, 1898), 67. HHH, *Diary*, 1:222 and 2:270-1. In all Hunnewell spent nine seasons in Bethlehem from 1891 to 1901; he also vacationed in the White Mountains in 1880, 1881, and 1883, definitely staying at Maplewood in 1881 and probably the other two times as well. Bryant F. Tolles, Jr., *Summer Cottages in the White Mountains: The Architecture of Leisure and Recreation, 1870-1930* (University Press of New England, 2000), 106-08 (Maplewood) and 113-15, 272n20 (Sayer).

7. Kate Phillips, *Helen Hunt Jackson*, 151-54. H.H., "Mountain Life," *The New York Evening Post*, 18 October 1865, 1.

8. She may have read both of these accounts earlier. Thoreau's "Ktaadn" essay was published in the *Union Magazine of Literature and Art* of July 1848. Winthrop's "Life in the Open Air" ran in the *Atlantic* of 1862: August, 203-11 with Emerson's "Thoreau," 239-49; September, 293-303; November, 527-33, preceded by Thoreau's "Wild Apples," 513-26; and December, 678-94.

9. H.H., "In the White Mountains," *New York Independent*, 13 September 1866, 2. Charles H. Hitchcock, *The Geology of New Hampshire* (Concord: E.A. Jenks, state printer, 1874-1878) 1:620, placed the spire of Katahdin at 150 miles, and "with a glass...the ocean steamers in Casco bay" could be seen. The accompanying atlas offers a splendid panoramic view from Mount Washington. W. H. Pickering, "Distant Points from Mt. Washington," *Appalachia*, March 1877, 86-90, indicates that Katahdin at 163 miles distant was not visible. This is confirmed by Brent E. Scudder, *Scudder's White Mountain Viewing Guide* (Littleton, NH: Bondcliff Books, 2000), 83, 225.

10. Phillips, 155. H.H., "A Second Celestial Railroad," *New York Independent*, 13 October 1870, 1.

11. H.H., "A Sermon Among the Mountains," *New York Independent*, 21 September 1871, 1. H.H., "Mount Washington in September," *New York Independent*, 28 September 1871, 1.

12. HHH, *Diary*, 2:226-29.

13. A. J. Downing, *Landscape Gardening and Rural Architecture* (Dover Publications, 1991), 442-45. This reprint of the sixth edition (1859) that Henry Sargent edited and supplemented for his close friend Downing, who died in 1852, was originally published in 1841 under a long title that begins, *A Treatise on the Theory and Practice of Landscape Gardening*, George B.

314 A WANDERER ALL MY DAYS

Tatum explained in the introduction. Herein are engravings of "Wellesley" and its French parterre and Italian garden; Downing's appreciation of Brookline (40) and description of "Wellesley." For Downing see *DAB* and *ANB*; Henry Winthrop Sargent, *DAB*.

14. See "The Young Gardener" in Dumas Malone, *Jefferson and His Time: The Sage of Monticello* (Little, Brown, 1981) 6:43-54.

15. Albert Fein, "A Garden for the Public: H. H. Hunnewell's Rhododendron Show," *Horticulture*, July 1978, 53-55.

16. Charles Sprague Sargent, "The Pinetum at Wellesley in 1905," HHH, 3:167-78. Sargent questioned the value of such displays in rural America. Alan Emmet, *So Fine a Prospect: Historic New England Gardens* (University Press of New England, 1996), 84-100, is a helpful resource.

A marvelous picture of the Italian Topiary Garden is in: Richard Cheek, *Land of the Commonwealth: A Portrait of the Conserved Landscapes of Massachusetts* (Trustees of Reservations/University of Massachusetts Press, 2000), 30-1. Other Muir destinations are also photographed.

Allyson M. Hayward, "Private Pleasures...Derived from Tradition," Independent Thesis Project, The Radcliffe Seminars, Radcliffe College, May 1997, 1:33, is a valuable resource for the Hunnewell Estates Historic District.

17. [Charles Sprague Sargent] "The Terrace Garden at Wellesley," *Garden and Forest*, 27 February 1889, 2:98-9, and 103, illustration. Fein, "A Garden for the Public," 54. Sutton, 131-33, for an overview of the magazine. Roper, *FLO*, 404-5, 415. Sargent wrote a total of 367 articles for *Garden and Forest*, according to Alfred Rehder, "Charles Sprague Sargent," *Journal of the Arnold Arboretum*, viii, 1927, 68-87 at 75 and 81.

18. Char Miller, "A High-Grade Paper: Garden and Forest and Nineteenth-Century American Forestry," *Arnoldia*, v.60, no. 2, 2000, 19-22. (This issue of *Arnoldia* and the next are devoted to *Garden and Forest*, with articles, illustrations, even ads from the originals.) According to Saul E. Zalesch in *ANB*, Mariana Griswold Van Rensselaer wrote more than fifty articles for *Garden and Forest*. L.H. Bailey's twenty-one articles on The Columbian Exposition began 31 May and ended 1 November 1893. Gifford Pinchot had eleven articles in the magazine, "among his first important publications," according to Stephen Fox, "Massachusetts Contributions to National Forest Conservation," 266 and 289n17. His subjects were: "The Sihlwald," 30 July, 6 and 13 August 1890, 374, 386, 397-8; "Forest Policy Abroad," 7, 14, and 21 January 1891, 8-9, 21-2, 34-5; "Forestry for the Farmer," 2 March 1892, 104-5; "The Need of Forest Schools in America," 24 July 1895, 298; and "Forest Protection," 26 February, 4 and 18 March 1896, 87-8, 99, and 118-19.

19. Horatio H. Hunnewell, *Garden and Forest*, 23 April 1890, 3:201-02, "Hardy Rhododendrons"; 25 May 1892, 5:250-51; 24 May 1893, 6:228-29; 22 May 1895, 8:209 (quote); 3 June 1896, 9:229.

20. Henry Sargent Hunnewell, *Garden and Forest*, 3 June 1896, 9:229 (quote); 24 June 1896, 9:257-58, roses; 28 April 1897, 10:168, red cedars; T.D. Hatfield, 8 July 1896, 9:278-9. For Henry Sargent Hunnewell and The Cedars, see Hayward, "Private Pleasures," I:95-160. It's likely Muir met him, for in his letter to Wanda Muir of 28 October 1898, he says that he saw Hunnewell's sons.

21. Beatrix Jones, *Garden and Forest*, "Nature's Landscape-gardening in Maine", 6 September 1893, 6:378-79; "Bridge over the Kent at Levens Hall", 15 January 1896, 9:22, fig. 25; "The Garden in Relation to the House," 7 April 1897, 10:132-2. Jane Brown, *Beatrix*, 56, believes the second of these articles to be her first published work, while the former clearly is unless it is

considered as a letter to the editor. For Brown's commentary on the third piece see p.65-66.

22. HHH, *Diary*, 2:205 & 250-51. In these entries, the editor identifies "Jones" as "[Beatrice]" in the first and just "[B.]" in the second.

23. HHH, *Diary*, 2:191, Stiles visited on 26 June 1894. [Charles Sprague Sargent], "William A. Stiles," *Garden and Forest*, 13 October 1897, 10:399-400. Phyllis Andersen, "'Master of a Felicitous English Style': William Augustus Stiles, Editor of *Garden and Forest*," *Arnoldia*, v.60, no.2, 2000, 39-43. Sargent reported Stiles's death to Muir in his letter of 11 October 1897. Pinchot drew "much wisdom and encouragement" from Stiles; *Breaking New Ground*, 33.

24. "A Mountain Meadow," *Garden and Forest*, 3 July 1889, 2:314. The ad is in *Arnoldia*, v.60, no. 2, 2000, 36. The advertising sections of *Garden and Forest* were removed from the copies I saw at the W.E.B. Du Bois Library of the University of Massachusetts at Amherst; Phyllis Andersen says that this was common practice when libraries had the periodical bound (*Arnoldia*, v.60, no.2, 2000, 39). Sargent had been in Japan from August to early November of 1892; Sutton, 202-06. Sargent's articles were collected into *Forest Flora of Japan* (Houghton Mifflin, 1894).

*L&L* II:270. Muir wrote Louie that he dined with "Styles, of the 'Forest and Stream'" among others. Since I cannot locate a "Styles" as editor of *Forest and Stream: A Weekly Journal of the Rod and Gun* of New York, of which George Bird Grinnell was editor, I presume that Muir meant Stiles of *Garden and Forest*. Johnson introduced W. A. Stiles to Muir; see Johnson's Certificate.

25. Letters, L.H. Bailey to Muir, 10 July [1901], Berkeley, California; Muir to Louie Muir, 20 July 1901, Tuolumne Meadows; Muir to C. Hart Merriam, 15 August 1901, Martinez; Bailey to Muir, 23 August 1901, 10 September 1901, 15 November 1901, Ithaca, New York. I have not been able to locate Muir's letters to Bailey. Bailey was editor of *Country Life* for its first year only (*Public Libraries*, June 1909, 213); the magazine ended in 1942 (Mott, 4:338).

26. Letters, Muir to Mrs. [Helen Lukens] Jones, 22 February 1901, Martinez; Helen Lukens Jones to Muir, 8 March 1901, Pasadena, California.

27. Liberty Hyde Bailey, *The Holy Earth* (1915; Ithaca, New York: New York State College of Agriculture and Life Sciences, 1980), 26, 86-88 (Muir), 90, 14. Like Muir, Bailey did not consider limits to growth, nor did he foresee the downside of road expansion. Accessibility, he believed, would increase the value of the earth's "physical wealth" and "wonderful scenery" (40). Someone should compare Bailey's praise of the forests with Muir's and his of the apple—"a thing of exquisite beauty" (69-72)—with Thoreau's "Wild Apples." Peter Schmidt, *Back to Nature: The Arcadian Myth in Urban America* (1969; Johns Hopkins University Press, 1990), xxii-xxv.

28. *L&L* II:265. The most likely dates for their meeting are Sunday or Monday, 4 or 5 June 1893. Harold K. Steen informed me that he found no Pinchot diary for June 1893 in the Library of Congress, only notes (Letter, 17 October 2002). Char Miller, *Gifford Pinchot and the Making of Modern Environmentalism* (Washington, DC: Island Press, 2001), 125-6. Professor Miller erroneously places Muir and Pinchot together in the Adirondacks in October 1892, when Muir was in fact in California. On Saturday, 24 September, Muir was at the newly formed Sierra Club in San Francisco, and he expected to attend a meeting of its Board of Directors that was called for the following Saturday, 1 October 1892; Letters of William D. Arms of University of California, Berkeley, to Muir of 25 and 29 September 1892. There is only one Muir letter in the JMP for the month of October 1892.

Interestingly though, Pinchot did come to know a John Muir in the Adirondacks. At the behest of Dr. W. Seward Webb to evaluate his woodlands, Ne-Ha-Sa-Ne Park, in 1892, Pinchot spent four days surveying Webb's wilds on horseback and foot with various guides. On Monday afternoon, 3 October, he went to Sand and Rock lakes with John Muir, and apparently stayed the night in his "shanty," enjoying "some capital young venison." One wonders if Pinchot ever told Muir of his Adirondack namesake. See Gifford Pinchot, Diary, 30 September-4 October 1892, Library of Congress.

In 1889, W. Seward Webb and a party of eleven made a transcontinental railroad trip. In the luxury of four private cars with a staff of nurses, maids, cooks, servants, porters, and detectives, they traveled for two months. Leaving New York City in early April, they returned to the Webb summer home in Shelburne, Vermont, on 10 June. Their itinerary included Wawona, where they stayed at Clark's, the Mariposa Grove of sequoias, and two nights in Yosemite Valley (25-27 April). Webb's belief that the valley was formed by volcanic activity showed his unawareness of Muir's glacial origin theory. Even later, when they sailed the Alaska coast and anchored off the Muir Glacier (23-24 May)—some of the group going ashore and walking over the ice—there is no mention of Muir. Webb's statement that "The waters in this region are totally unexplored" again reveals his ignorance of Muir's Alaska research. In fact, neither Galen Clark nor Muir appear anywhere in Webb's account.

See William Seward Webb, *California and Alaska and over the Canadian Pacific Railway* (New York: G.P. Putnam's Sons, 1891), 81-102, Mariposa and Yosemite Valley; 232-4, Muir Glacier (photo b/w 234 and 235). Webb's book is not in Muir's extant library. A notice for an "Edition de Luxe" of this book indicates the inclusion of an etching of the Muir Glacier by R. Swain Gifford (unnumbered page before frontispiece). Though arrivals and departures are dated throughout, the starting date is omitted. When passing Mount Shasta in northern California (4 May), Webb quoted on pages 133-34 from Clarence King's *Mountaineering in the Sierra Nevada* (Boston: James R. Osgood, 1872), 231-2.

29. Letter, Gifford Pinchot to Muir, 8 April 1894, New York City. Gifford Pinchot, *Biltmore Forest* (Chicago: Riverside Press, 1893) is missing from Muir's Library. Pinchot wanted Muir to come to his family home, Grey Towers, in Milford, Pennsylvania, overlooking the Delaware River. Letters, Gifford Pinchot to Muir, 13 September 1893, Milford, Pennsylvania, and 23 May 1894, New York. Muir did not visit Grey Towers in 1893, nor at any other time that I can determine.

30. Gifford Pinchot, Diary, 10-11 May 1891, Library of Congress. Harold K. Steen, *The Conservation Diaries of Gifford Pinchot* (Durham, North Carolina: The Forest History Society, 2001), 42-47. Gifford Pinchot, *Breaking New Ground* (1947; Washington, D.C.: Island Press, 1998), 44-45. Char Miller, *Gifford Pinchot*, 1-4. Miller also says that Pinchot learned of Muir from his parents. Clark appears in Pinchot's diary and autobiography, not in Steen's or Miller's accounts. According to Shirley Sargent, *Galen Clark: Yosemite Guardian* (Sierra Club, 1964), "Clark appointed Cunningham sub-guardian of the Mariposa Grove in 1878" (130n5).

31. Letter, Muir to Robert Underwood Johnson, 13 May 1891, Martinez.

32. Charles Dormon Robinson (1847-1933) is in Hughes, *Artists in California*, 473, which indicates he was born in Monmouth, Maine, and that after his 1880 Yosemite initiation, he "spent 24 summers there;" whereas *Who Was Who in America*, 1:1044, indicates that Vermont was his birthplace and that he "Spent 19 seasons in Yosemite and high Sierras." Kent L. Seavey, *Charles Dorman Robinson* (San Francisco: California Historical Society, 1965), exhibition catalog of 250 copies, contains a four-page biography. Spellings of his middle name are Dorman and Dormon; I have used the latter adopted by *Artists in California*.

33. Marjorie Dakin Arkelian and George W. Neubert, *George Inness Landscapes: His Signature Years 1884-1894* (Oakland, CA: The Oakland Museum, 1974) reveals the Keith-Inness

California relationship. Alfred C. Harrison,Jr., *William Keith: The Saint Mary's College Collection* (Moraga, CA: Hearst Art Gallery, Saint Mary's College of California, 1988), 33-36, 40. Brother Cornelius, *Keith: Old Master of California* (New York: G.P. Putnam's Sons, 1942), 213-24, 544, for Inness and Muir. On 30 May 1893, William and Mary Keith saw the Innesses at their home in Montclair, New Jersey, and again upon their return from France in mid-July (257-58, 261). C. D. Robinson, "A Revival of Art Interest in California," *The Overland Monthly*, June 1891, 649-52. Robinson also praised Keith's work in this review.

34. Letter, Muir to Robert Underwood Johnson, 2 July 1891, Martinez. Muir related this trip in greater detail in his journal, especially the mule episode of 11 June; see JMJ, 30 May-13 June 1891, JMP, Reel 28; portions also in *JOM*, 322-33, which interweaves passages from his *Century* article.

John Muir, "A Rival of the Yosemite. The Cañon of the South Fork of King's River, California," *Century*, November 1891, 77-97 (The article uses the possessive for Kings in title and text). Nine of the article's twenty-one pages contain Robinson pictures; pages 78 and 79 are maps. Text is included, except the conclusion, in "The Need of Another Great National Park," in Frederic R. Gunsky, *South of Yosemite: Selected Writings of John Muir* (1968; Berkeley, CA: Wilderness Press, 1988), 83-103. Gunsky reads "goods" as "grub," which makes sense too, though I stick with my transcription; their loss was more than food. Muir and Robinson did have a guide, who struggled with them to rescue their mule from the current. For Robinson's version of their trip, see Norman L. Wilson and Lucinda M. Woodward, "C.D. Robinson and John Muir in the Kings River Canyon," in Sally M. Miller, ed., *John Muir in Historical Perspective* (New York: Peter Lang, 1999), 83-95. For creation of Kings River National Park, see Fox, *John Muir*, 212-17.

35. JMJ, 16 July 1896 (JMP, Reel 28). Steen, *The Conservation Diaries of Gifford Pinchot*, 73.

36. This paragraph and the preceding one draw on JMJ, 20-21 July 1896, "weary & feverish;" 28-30 September 1896, Grand Canyon; *JOM*, 356-64; Pinchot, *Breaking New Ground*, 100-104; Steen, *The Conservation Diaries of Gifford Pinchot*, 73-75; Letters, Pinchot to Muir, 23 July 1896, Missoula, Montana; Muir to Louie Muir, 21 September 1896, Los Angeles, and 2 October 1896, Flagstaff, Arizona

37. Wolfe, 275-76. Miller, *Gifford Pinchot*, 119-25. Steen, *The Conservation Diaries of Gifford Pinchot*, 83. The Rainier Grand Hotel has been replaced by an office building, Darlene E. Hamilton of the Seattle Public Library informed me.

38. Steen, *The Conservation Diaries of Gifford Pinchot*, 88-90. Miller, *Gifford Pinchot*, 138. JMJ, 17 September-24 November 1898. Their differences about wilderness emerged over the Commission report—Muir and Sargent wanted to save the trees and protect them with the US Army; Pinchot, who from the start was upset with Sargent's unprofessional approach to the forest survey, wanted the reserves open to development and closed to military involvement.

39. Gifford Pinchot, Diary, 8-12 August 1899, Library of Congress. Steen, *The Conservation Diaries of Gifford Pinchot*, 97. Pinchot, *Breaking New Ground*, 170-71.

40. Morris, *Theodore Rex*, 514-18. Pinchot, *Breaking New Ground*, 344-55, does not mention Muir or Sargent. Pinchot and Johnson differ on the origin of the Conference; Johnson took credit for the idea. Not being personally invited—an official invitation was sent to the *Century*—Johnson decided not to attend. His boss Gilder, however, thought it wise for the *Century* "in whose office the Conference had its origin" (Johnson's words) to be represented and ordered him to Washington. Johnson cited other forest experts besides Muir and Sargent who were not included. Johnson also blamed Pinchot for the extinction of the Hetch Hetchy

Valley. Johnson, *Remembered Yesterdays*, 300-07. Roderick Nash, *Wilderness and the American Mind* (1967; Yale University Press, 1982), 139-40. Miller, *Gifford Pinchot*, 143-44. Muir's absence from the event "symbolized the final wedge between his views and those of Gifford Pinchot," Michael Cohen II, 181. *Sierra Club Bulletin*, January 1906, 55, for Pinchot's election as an honorary vice-president, a postion he held until 1912, Caitlin Lewis informed me.

41. Jean Glasscock, ed. *Wellesley College 1875-1975: A Century of Women* (Wellesley College, 1975); The Great Fire, 339-350.

42. *Calendar of Wellesley College. 1898-99*. (Boston: Frank Wood, Printer, 1898), 5-11, 74. Abbe Carter Goodloe, "Undergraduate Life at Wellesley," *Scribner's Magazine*, May 1898, 515-538. "Float-Day at Wellesley," *The Boston Sunday Globe*, 11 June 1893, 8.

43. See *DAB* and *ANB* for Henry Durant. Glasscock, *Wellesley College*, passim. Harvard president Charles William Eliot in his inaugural address for Caroline Hazard and Bryn Mawr president M. Carey Thomas at her luncheon talk gave different views of women's education; see Helen Lefkowitz Horowitz, "The Great Debate," *Harvard Magazine*, November-December 1999, 56-7.

44. Goodloe, "Undergraduate Life at Wellesley," 532.

45. Susan M. Taylor, "A Woodland Garden," *Michael Singer and Michael McKinnell: A Collaboration* (Davis Museum and Cultural Center, Wellesley College, n.d.), 2. Discussions with Michael Singer of Wilmington, Vermont, on 24 November 2000.

46. HHH, *Diary*, 2:230-31. Hunnewell dated his entry "Oct. 24" and headed it "John Muir". I am indebted to Francis W. Hunnewell of Dover, Massachusetts, for a copy of the holograph diary of his great-great-grandfather, the substance of which compares favorably with the published version.

47. Though Hunnewell's *Diary* reveals several winter trips to Florida (see 1872, 1875, 1882, 1883, 1887), St. Louis, Missouri, reached on his southern journey of 28 January to 15 March 1881 was evidently his farthest west.

48. Letter, Muir to Wanda Muir, 28 October 1898, New York.

49. HHH, *Diary*, 2:232 (snowstorm and return to Boston); 2:270-1 ("mountain air"); 2:253-4 (ninetieth birthday).

## TRIP THREE: 1898
## CHAPTER 12—BOSTON AND CAMBRIDGE

1. Alumni and obituary records, Archives, Williams College, Williamstown, Massachusetts. Gibbs lived from 23 December 1850 to 6 December 1925. *The Boston Evening Transcript*, 8 December 1925, 9, obituary, and II:[2] commemoration by F[erris]. G[reenslet]. Before moving to Newtonville in 1892, Gibbs lived in Cambridge, at 280 Pearl Street, until 1892 (*Cambridge Directory*).

2. Torrey was more famous then than now, alas. Contemporary American regional anthologies of nature writing keep him alive. Richard Rankin, ed., *North Carolina Nature Writing* (Winston-Salem, North Carolina: John F. Blair, 1996) includes a selection from *A World of Green Hills*, 86-95 (as well as three pages of Muir's *A Thousand-Mile Walk to the Gulf*, 60-63), as does *The Height of Our Mountains: Nature Writing from Virginia's Blue Ridge Mountains and Shenandoah Valley*, eds. Michael P. Branch and Daniel J. Philippon (Johns Hopkins University Press, 1998), 200-04. See *DAB*; Kingsbury Badger, "Bradford Torrey: New England Nature Writer," *The New England Quarterly*, v. 18, 1945, 234-46; Paul Brooks, *Speaking for Nature*, 139-41.

3. Whitman also had done the cover of Torrey's earlier book, *A Rambler's Lease* (Houghton Mifflin,1889), which he sent to Celia Thaxter in November 1889 and to Sarah Orne Jewett in January 1890; see Titus, *By this Wing*, 37 and 39, in n5 below. Torrey's other two books published in Thaxter's lifetime—*Birds in the Bush* (Houghton Mifflin, 1888) and *The Foot-Path Way* (Houghton Mifflin, 1892)—were also gifts to her inscribed by the author; see Titus, *By this Wing*, 69-70; Dorothy M. Vaughan, "Celia Thaxter's Library," *Colby Library Quarterly*, December 1964, 542. Thaxter read Torrey's essays in the *Atlantic* before they were combined into books.

4. *Youth's Companion* contained thirty-nine Thaxter poems, twenty Torrey pieces, and none by Muir. *Index to the Youth's Companion, 1871-1929*, Richard Cutts, ed., (Metuchen, New Jersey: Scarecrow Press, 1972), 933-34, 956.

5. A. F. and R. L. [Annie Fields and Rose Lamb], eds., *Letters of Celia Thaxter* (Houghton Mifflin, 1895), 185. This volume contains a dozen of her letters to Bradford Torrey. Review in the *Nation*, 8 August 1895, 105. Donna Marion Titus, ed., *By This Wing: Letters by Celia Thaxter to Bradford Torrey about Birds at the Isles of Shoals, 1888 to 1894* (Manchester, New Hampshire: J. Palmer Publisher, 1999) offers forty-five Thaxter-to-Torrey letters and one from Torrey to Sarah Orne Jewett. Titus includes those from the Fields and Lamb edition, giving the full text in those cases where it had been elided. According to Norma H. Mandel, who is at work on a biography of Thaxter, Torrey and Thaxter never met; see her "Celia's Friends" in Sharon Paiva Stephan, *One Woman's Work: The Visual Art of Celia Laighton Thaxter* (Portsmouth, New Hampshire: Portsmouth Athenaeum, 2001), 52. Annie Fields called attention to the "delightful correspondence" between Thaxter and Torrey in her eulogy of Thaxter that appeared in *Atlantic*, February 1895, 254-66; this was reprinted in Annie Fields, *Authors and Friends* (Houghton Mifflin, 1897), 6th edition, 229-62. A year after Torrey received Thaxter's letter of 7 December 1888, he quoted its beginning in his essay "December Out-of-Doors" in *Atlantic*, December 1889, 752-61 (letter, 756); this piece was included in his *The Foot-Path Way* (Houghton Mifflin, 1892).

6. Susan G. Larkin, "Hassam in New England, 1889-1918," in H. Barbara Weinberg, *Childe Hassam: American Impressionist* (Metropolitan Museum of Art/Yale University Press, 2004) 118-177 (118-145, for Thaxter and Isles of Shoals). "The definitve study of Hassam on Appledore," Larkin says (174n9) is David Park Curry, *Childe Hassam: An Island Garden Revisited* (W.W. Norton/Denver Art Museum, 1990). Ann Edwards Boutelle, " 'A Crescent that Shall Orb into a Sun': The Art and Friendship of Celia Thaxter and Childe Hassam," *Over Here*, Winter 1997, 115-38. Boutelle insightfully explores their floral conversation in *An Island Garden*, and finds their relationship "deep and loving" and mutually significant. Sara A. Hubbard praised both the gardener and the painter of *An Island Garden* in *The Dial*, 1 June 1894, 333-35. The *Atlantic* reviewer, September 1894, 412-13, while critical of Hassam, said very little about the text. *Boston Evening Transcript*, 23 March 1894, 6, notice of publication on the following day; 5 May 1894, 7, unsigned review.

On 17 October 1898, Hassam (1859-1935) celebrated his thirty-nineth birthday; he and his wife of fourteen years, Maud Doane, lived in the Rembrandt at 152 West Fifty-seventh Street, two blocks south of Central Park, having moved to New York from Boston at the end of 1889. At the 1893 Chicago World's Columbian Exposition, Hassam exhibited five oils and five watercolors. Though engaged in Exposition-related projects in Chicago in late 1892 and early 1893, even painting the *Horticulture Building*, he apparently left before the opening on May Day. There is the possibility that Muir may have seen some of his work there. See H. Barbara Weinberg, "Hassam's Travels, 1892-1914," 178-182 (377, for his entrees) in Weinberg, *Childe Hassam*.

Though not known as a painter of mountains, Hassam executed a number of alpine scenes, primarily in the Northwest. On his visits in 1904 and 1908 to his patron Charles Erskine Scott Wood, in Portland, Oregon, he produced watercolors of Mount Hood, and an oil of Steens Mountain in the state's southeast desert, *Golden Afternoon*, according to Weinberg, 188-89 and 331(fig. 336), who relied on Margaret Bullock, Associate Curator of American Art, Portland Museum of Art. Bullock is curator of the Hassam Exhibition, 11 December 2004-6 March 2005, and author of its catalog, *Childe Hassam: Impressionist in the West* (Portland Art Museum, 2004), which shows two works of Mounts Adams and St. Helens in southwest Washington (40-41), as well as four of his of Mount Hood (32, 58, 61, 98). Hassam also painted Mount Jefferson, southeast of Portland, Oregon, Bullock wrote me, 11 August 2004. In New England and New York, he produced *White Mountains, Poland Springs*, 1917 (Fogg Art Museum), mentioned in Weinberg 266n43; the oil *Looking over Frenchman's Bay at Green Mountain*, 1896 (Pennsylvania Academy of Fine Arts) shown in Pamela J. Belanger, *Inventing Acadia: Artists and Tourists at Mount Desert* (Farnsworth Art Museum/University Press of New England, 1999), 10, fig. 1; and in 1915, the Hudson River watercolors *Back of the Fishkill Mountains, Mount Beacon in Spring*, and *Mount Beacon in Winter* in Weinberg, 371, 390, *Back of the Fishkill Mountains*, fig. 345 in Weinberg, 336. For more of Hassam's mountains, we await his catalogue raisonné.

Muir knew C. E. S. Wood. Coming East on 9 September 1898, Muir met him in Portland, where they discussed Wood's recent Glacier Bay trip. Wood had been in Glacier Bay in 1877 and wrote "Among the Thlinkits in Alaska," *Century*, July 1882, 323-39, an article that Muir likely read. Letter, Muir to Louie Muir, 13 September 1898, Duluth, Minnesota, and JMJ 9 September 1898. Robert Hamburger, *Two Rooms: The Life of Charles Erskine Scott Wood* (University of Nebraska Press, 1998) gives a brief, unflattering portait of Hassam (142), but does not mention Muir. Nor is Muir part of Erskine Wood's recollections of his father, *Life of Charles Erskine Scott Wood* (by the author, 1978). Likely, Muir's Portland lectures in January 1880 attracted Wood, Wood having been aide-de-camp to General O. O. Howard (see chapter 8n13).

Vera Norwood, *Made from This Earth: American Women and Nature* (Chapel Hill: University of North Carolina Press, 1993), 102. See also Vera Norwood, "Celia Thaxter, " *ANW* II:905-17; *NAW*; and *ANB*, S1.

7. Ina D. Coolbrith, *The Singer of the Sea: In Memory of Celia Thaxter* ([San Francisco]: The Century Club of California, December 1894). In March 1897 in Berkeley, she lectured on Celia Thaxter, 231. Letter, Ina Coolbrith to Muir, 19 November 1894, Oakland [California]. Alison Hawthorne Deming, *Poetry of the American West: A Columbia Anthology* (Columbia University Press, 1996), includes two of Coolbrith's poems, "Longing" and "The Captive of the White City", 46-51. My discussion relies on the fine biography by Josephine DeWitt Rhodehamel and Raymund Francis Wood, *Ina Coolbrith: Librarian and Laureate of California* (Brigham Young University Press, 1973), who relate the circumstances of her resignation. For her relationship with Muir and her verse about him, 132-35. She is also in the *DAB*, *ANB*, and *NAW*.

At least one child, Isadora Duncan, could not wait for the school day to end, so she could go to Oakland's public library and be with Ina Coolbrith. Isadora's father, Joseph Duncan, was the first to publish Ina Coolbrith. Peter Kruth, *Isadora: A Sensational Life* (Boston: Little, Brown, 2001),10, 19.

8. Rhodehamel and Wood, *Ina Coolbrith*, 3-7.

9. Rhodehamel and Wood, *Ina Coolbrith*, 179-82. *Songs from the Golden Gate* also included her sonnet "The Art of William Keith.", 115 [Each title has a period at the end.]

10. Rhodehamel and Wood, *Ina Coolbrith*, 224-30. To alleviate painful rheumatism, she lived in New York City from 1919 to 1923, with interludes in San Francisco, 333-45; for her residences, 500. The San Francisco earthquake of 18 April 1906 destroyed her Russian Hill home, library, letters, and Keith paintings, 255-61 (Some of her correspondence with Stedman and Charles Warren Stoddard was recovered.). She died on 29 February 1928 in Berkeley.

11. Bradford Torrey, "June in Franconia," in *The Foot-Path Way* (Houghton Mifflin, 1892), 1-35, esp. 18-19 (thrushes) and 31 (places). He recounts his first and second ascents of Lafayette of 11 June 1890 (?) and 19 and 28 June 1891 (?), the latter less so, and mentions his three ascents of Cannon. See also Bradford Torrey, *Footing It in Franconia* (Houghton Mifflin, 1901), where he refers to two autumn ascents of Lafayette, 23; he says it has been twenty years since he started going up and down Bald Mountain, 137; and relates "A Visit to Mount Agassiz."

12. Bradford Torrey, "In the White Mountains," *Birds in the Bush* (Houghton Mifflin, 1885), 77-102.

13. Bradford Torrey, "Five Days on Mount Mansfield," *The Foot-Path Way* (Houghton Mifflin, 1892), 90-110. Possibly Sarah Wyman Whitman drew the narrow vertical black image on the center of the green front cover—a branch of a fir tree with four upright cones and multiple leaves; the author's name on the spine is in her hand. A brief review appeared in *Atlantic*, December 1892, 842-3.

14. Bradford Torrey first appears in the *Santa Barbara City Directory* of 1911-12 at 1404 de la Vina Street, the Hotel Upham; by the next year he had moved across the street to a cottage on the property of H. G. Crane.

15. Muir's journal of this Sierra Club Outing (JMP, reel 30) focuses on flowers, trees, and places, not people; at the end, however, appears a list of names—participants, I presume— one of whom is Torrey. Torrey stayed in Yosemite Valley until about 6 July. If he had joined the Outing, I suspect that he would have said so and related more about Muir, and that Muir would have remembered him. As it happens Muir in 1913 recalled their meeting in Boston in 1898 and only once in Yosemite "a few months before his death." Letter, Muir to John G. Taylor, 7 June 1913, Martinez.

16. *JB* I:330; II:146-7.

17. Taylor knew Muir from the University of Wisconsin, where Taylor received three degrees in 1868, 1869, and 1872. After graduating from Chicago Theological Seminary in 1872, Taylor became a minister of the Congregational Church in Santa Cruz, California, and later in Arlington Heights, Massachusetts. See Reuben Gold Thwaites, *University of Wisconsin* (University of Wisconsin Press, 1900), 778. Taylor was also a friend of Bradford Torrey. Letter, Herbert Gleason to Muir, 21 October 1912, Boston.

    *A Florida Sketch-book* (Cambridge: Riverside Press, 1895) is the only book by Torrey in Muir's library; it contains neither inscription nor Muir annotations. I have not found Muir's copy of Torrey's *Field-Days in California*, a review of which appeared in the *Sierra Club Bulletin*, June 1913, 121.

18. *Who Was Who in America*, VI:22; *New York Times*, 25 October 1953, 5, obituary. After Robert, the Allens had three daughters: Elizabeth, born 24 November 1903; Lucy, 3 November 1904; and Frances, 4 February 1907 (Record of Birth, Registry Division, Boston). Charles Foster Batchelder, *An Account of the Nuttall Ornithological Club 1873 to 1919* (Cambridge: Nuttall Ornithological Club, 1937), Allen: 59, 60, 77, 81; Torrey: 52, 53, 104.

19. For women nature writers in the *Atlantic*, Lawrence Buell, *The Environmental Imagination: Thoreau, Nature Writing, and the Formation of American Culture* (Harvard University Press,

1995) 44-5.

Letter, Olive Thorne Miller to Muir, 22 October 1894, Brooklyn, New York. She mentions her plan to call on him when in San Francisco, where she expects to be in March 1895. Though I find no mention of their meeting in March 1895 or on 12 June 1902 in Muir's correspondence, the latter visit is reported in her diary ("California 1902"), now in the Manuscript Division of the Library of Congress. I am indebted to Senior Archivist Bradley E. Gernand for bringing this to my attention.

Olive Thorne Miller was a pseudonym for Harriet Mann Miller. For Miller see *DAB* and *ANB*; Florence Merriam Bailey, *The Auk*, April 1919, 163-69; Paul Brooks, *Speaking for Nature*, 165-70; and Henry C. Tracy, *American Naturists* (New York: E.P. Putnam & Co., 1930), 116-129. Miller and Mary Austin are the only women Tracy included with Muir, Thoreau, Burroughs and other men. He feels that her *With the Birds in Maine* (1904) belongs with *Walden, Wake-Robin*, and *Steep Trails*. Modern anthologies such as *The Norton Book of Nature Writing* (1990) and its successor *Nature Writing: The Tradition in English* (2002), both edited by Robert Finch and John Elder, as well as *ANW*, omit her. *At Home on this Earth: Two Centuries of U.S. Women's Nature Writing*, edited by Lorraine Anderson and Thomas S. Edwards (University Press of New England, 2002), reprints two chapters of Miller's *A Bird-Lover in the West* (1894).

Muir made no index, and only sparsely marked the margins of *A Bird-Lover in the West*, now in HASC. Reviews appeared in *The Nation*, 10 May 1894, 347, and *The Dial*, 1 June 1894, 334. It was published the same day as Celia Thaxter's *An Island Garden*, and the same year as Muir's *The Mountains of California*.

20. Letters, Irene Grosvenor Wheelock, 24 May 1902, to Muir, Grand Hotel, San Francisco, California; Wheelock, 16 September 1903, to Muir, Evanston, Illinois; Muir, 24 September 1905, to Wheelock, Martinez. Since Muir's copy of Irene Grosvenor Wheelock, *Birds of California* (Chicago: A.C. McClurg & Co., 1904) in the Huntington Library has neither her inscription nor his annotations, I wonder if this is the copy she sent him. Irene Grosvenor Wheelock was elected a director of the Illinois Audubon Society in 1906. She was joined by her husband Harry B. Wheelock the following year, and they served until their resignations in 1908. She was then elected a vice-president, an office she held to at least 1914. I am indebted to Shirlee A. Fraley of the Illinois Audubon Society for her search of their minutes from their inception in 1897 until the death of Irene Grosvenor Wheelock in 1927.

21. Though Muir spelled "Rodgers" with a *d* in his journal and did not use his first name, his addition "of illustrating department" confirms his identity. Before this phrase is an undeciphered word, perhaps "famous."

For Rogers, see *ANB, DA*; *Who Was Who in America* III:738; Joseph Blumenthal, *Bruce Rogers: A Life in Letters, 1870-1957* (Austin: W. Thomas Taylor, 1989), esp. 1-26. Georgia Mansbridge, *Bruce Rogers: American Typographer* (New York: The Typophiles, 1997), 1-17. Anne (Annie) Embree Baker is in *The Officers and Alumni of Purdue University, 1875-1896*, 26. *NYT*, 30 December 1931, 19, obituary. Elizabeth Rogers (1901-1924).

Rogers also designed Emerson's *Compensation* (1903), *Success* (1912), and *Records of a Lifelong Friendship, 1807-1882, Ralph Waldo Emerson and William Henry Furness* (1910). Joel Myerson, *Ralph Waldo Emerson: A Descriptive Bibliography* (University of Pittsburgh Press, 1982), A 10.56, A 31.14, and A 53. This reference does not mention Rogers's work on the *Journals*, A52.I.1. Frederic Warde, *Bruce Rogers: Designer of Books* (Harvard University Press, 1926), 51-75, lists books designed by Rogers, with an index to authors, but does not include Emerson's *Journals*.

22. *Boston Evening Transcript*, 13 July 1904, 18. Allen contributed a nature column to this

paper; here he compares Thoreau and Muir.

23. I cannot locate Rogers's residence in October 1898; he is not listed in Boston, Cambridge, Brookline, or Belmont directories.

24. Harris, *Historic Walks in Cambridge*, 254-5; JMJ; Jeannette E. Graustein, *Thomas Nuttall, Naturalist: Explorations in America, 1808-1841* (Harvard University Press, 1967), 182. *Boston Sunday Globe*, 4 October 1998, G1 and 4. The Gray house, on the National Register of Historic Places, was sold in September 1999.

25. Arthur M. Schlesinger Jr., *A Life in the Twentieth Century: Innocent Beginnings, 1917-1950* (Houghton Mifflin, 2000), 35.

26. Jane Loring Gray, ed. *The Letters of Asa Gray*. (Houghton Mifflin, 1893), 2 vols. Muir marked passages and added his own index to his copy that is in HASC. Letter, Muir to Charles Sprague Sargent, 31 December 1893, Martinez, for quote.

27. Clendenning, *The Letters of Josiah Royce*, 379-80.

28. *CWJ* 8:444.

29. William James, "Talks to Teachers on Psychology," *Atlantic* 1899, February, 155-62; March, 320-29; April, 510-17; May, 617-26. As Muir was also writing for the *Atlantic*—his Yosemite articles appeared in the November and December 1898 and August 1899 issues— it is likely that he at least was aware of James's presence in the periodical.

30. The primary source for James's itinerary is his letters to his brother Henry, *CWJ* 3:38-42, and to his wife Alice and others, *CWJ* 8:402-37. His companion was Charles Montague Bakewell (1867-1957), *CWJ* 8:638. The editors find "some of his most detailed descriptions of nature" contained in his letters to Alice. Secondary treatments are Frederick J. Down Scott, "William James' 1898 Visit to California," *San Jose Studies*, February 1977, 7-22, and Allan Shields, "William James Visits Yosemite in 1898," *Yosemite Association*, Summer 2001, 6-9. The latter, for which I am indebted to Sarah Rabkin, identifies James's route in the Sierra. For "my completest union," see Scott, 21 and Simon, 282.

31. *CWJ* 8: 408 and 435 (James met both Joseph LeConte and his son Joseph Nisbet LeConte); 427-8 (Stanford). Scott, "William James' 1898 Visit to California", 17, and Frederick J. Down Scott, "William James and Stanford University, 1898-1905", *San Jose Studies*, February 1975, 9-23.

32. The primary sources for James in California in 1906 are his diary and correspondence.
    Letter, Muir to Helen Muir, 16 May 1910, Grand Canyon, Arizona. *JMLJ*, 21n32. Professor Branch also includes Muir's correspondence with Katharine Hooker in 1911-1912 in *JMLJ*. For her, see chapter 3 n66. John D. Hooker (1838-1911) was born in Hinsdale, New Hampshire, and attended Williams College in 1860-1861 before moving to California, where he engaged in manufacturing of steel pipe and established J. D. Hooker Co. He was also president of Western Union Oil Co. and Baker Iron Works. *Who Was Who* I:584, *National Cyclopedia of American Biography* 22:210-11 (photo), and Williams College catalog.

33. DWJ, January-May 1906. Frederick J. Down Scott, "William James & Stanford University: 1906," *San Jose Studies*, May 1975, 28-43. Gay Wilson Allen, *William James: A Biography* (New York: Viking Press, 1967), 450-56. Allen implies that gout prevented James's being in San Francisco to meet Alice, while Scott puts him in the city but not at the station for his wife. His diary and correspondence confirm that he had gout; the former indicates his inability— he was still on crutches—to come to meet Alice's train. Simon, 333-42. *CWJ* 3:311-13; 11:xxiv-xxv, 133-216.
    Katharine Hooker also visited the Jameses at Stanford on Friday 13 April (DWJ).

According to Samuel Marshall Ilsley, *Katharine Hooker: A Memoir* (Santa Barbara, California: Schauer Printing Studio, 1935), 31-36, Katharine Hooker cared for her father in San Francisco during the earthquake.

34. In 1930 Ansel Adams built a home next to his parents on the same (south) side of 24th Avenue. About 1960 these houses were conjoined. Since 1970, Barbara and Peter Winkelstein, to whom I am grateful for this information, have lived there.

35. Ansel Adams with Mary Street Alinder, *Ansel Adams: An Autobiography* (Boston: Little, Brown, 1985), 4-8, Adams family house photo, 5. Mary Street Alinder, *Ansel Adams: A Biography* (Henry Holt, 1996), 1-6. Jonathan Spaulding, *Ansel Adams and the American Landscape: A Biography* (University of California Press, 1995), 11-12, and Nancy Newhall, *Ansel Adams: The Eloquent Light: His Photographs and the Classic Biography* (Millerton, New York: Aperture, 1963; revised edition, 1980), 26. In these accounts of Spaulding and Newhall, Ansel hits his head on the pavement and brick path, respectively. Ric Burns, *American Experience, Ansel Adams: A Documentary Film* (PBS premiere, 21 April 2002), and review by Ron Wertheimer, *NYT,* 20 April 2002, A19 and 27.

According to Alinder and Spaulding, the primary influence on Charles Adams and his son was Emerson, not Thoreau, who is not even mentioned. As for Muir, Alinder says that "Ansel never saw him as a mentor and did not even read his work until he was about eighteen." (29) She adds two years to the ages of Ansel and Muir when the latter died in 1914 (28). While Spaulding emphasizes their similar responses to wilderness, he does not give examples of Muir's influence (50-1). James R. Guthrie stresses the "special affinity" between Adams and Thoreau as well as Emerson in "Ansel Adams: Transcendental Eye," in Alexander Lee Nyerges, *In Praise of Nature: Ansel Adams and Photographers of the American West* (Dayton: Ohio: Dayton Art Institute, 1999), 182-94.

The most recent study—Anne Hammond, *Ansel Adams: Divine Performance* (Yale University Press, 2002), 58—indicates that James M. Hutchings's *In the Heart of the Sierras* (1886) "fired Adams with the determination to see Yosemite in 1916," not Muir's *The Mountains of California.* Two books of Ansel Adams show the impact of Muir: *Sierra Nevada: The John Muir Trail* (Berkeley, CA: Archetype Press, 1938) published in the centennial year of Muir's birth and *Yosemite and the Sierra Nevada* (Houghton Mifflin, 1948) with Muir's text edited by Charlotte Mauk (47-8 and 111). Regarding the production of the latter, Hammond says that Adams's correspondence revealed "a comprehensive knowledge of Muir's writings," 171n8. Adams also had an early interest in William James's writings, Hammond explains, 7, 148n25.

The Muir books in Adams's library, that Hammond kindly identified for me, show the photographer's absorption of the mountaineer. In addition to W. F. Badè, *The Life and Letters of John Muir* (1924) and L.M. Wolfe, *Son of the Wilderness* (New York: Alfred A. Knopf, 1945\*), Adams's collection contained *The Mountains of California* (New York: The Century Co., 1894\*), *Our National Parks* (1901\*), *Stickeen* (1909\*), *My First Summer in the Sierra* (1911\* two copies), *The Yosemite* (1912\*), *Story of My Boyhood and Youth* (1913\*), *Travels in Alaska* (1915\*), *Letters to a Friend* (1915\*), and *Notes on My Journeying in California's Northern Mountains* (n.d.)—all publshed by Houghton Mifflin unless otherwise indicated; a first edition is identified with an asterisk—along with L. M. Wolfe, ed., *John of the Mountains: The Unpublished Journals of John Muir* (1938), and the first and sixth volumes of the Sierra Edition of *The Writings of John Muir.* Hammond also pointed out that the *Sierra Club Bulletin,* especially when Adams was first associated with the club, from 1919 to the early 1930s, was rich with writings by and about Muir. Letter, Anne Hammond to J. Parker Huber, 19 August 2002, Iffley, Oxford, England.

36. William James, "On Some Mental Effects of the Earthquake," *Youth's Companion*, 7 June 1906, 283-84; reprinted in William James, *Essays in Psychology* (Harvard University Press, 1983), 330-38, Keith, 337. James drew on his letters of 22 April 1906 to Henry James and to Miss Frances R. Morse for this article. DWJ, May 1906.

37. According to Alfred C. Harrison, Jr., *William Keith: The Saint Mary's College Collection* (Moraga, California: Saint Mary's College, 1988), 44, "Keith's studio with 2,000 paintings in it burned to the ground." "How Artists Came out of the Disaster," *San Francisco Chronicle*, 14 May 1906, 10, identifies one of the good Samaritans as Keith's friend and critic, the Rev. Joseph Worcester, who rescued twenty-six pictures from Keith's studio at 424 Pine Street and took them to his home on Russian Hill. Louis J. Stellmann, "Local Artists Reestablishing Their Colony," *San Francisco Chronicle*, 30 June 1907, 5. In recalling his actions of the previous April, Keith remembered his work in "the Sutter-street place" instead of Pine Street. Charles Keeler, *San Francisco Through Earthquake and Fire* (San Francisco: Paul Elder & Co., 1906), 50, for Keith. A plaque now marks the site of Keith's Berkeley home, Susan Dinkelspiel Cerny, *Berkeley Landmarks: An Illustrated Guide to Berkeley, California's Architectural Heritage* (Berkeley Architectural Heritage Association, 2001), 158. Philip L. Fradkin's *The Great Earthquake and Firestorms of 1906: How San Francisco Nearly Destroyed Itself*, expected in April 2005 from the University of California Press, is awaited for his insights.

38. *JOM*, 433-36. Robert Burns (1759-1796).

39. JMJ, 2 August 1905, golden eagles, JMP, reel 30. Muir's Petrified Forest journal is scant: 30 July-2 August and 24 September 1905 (fourteen pages; mostly partial entries); 22 July-1 August and 27-29 October (Calistoga, California) 1906 (three pages and six lines); and 14-22 February and 8 April 1909 (two pages and seven lines).

40. Letter, Muir to Helen Muir, 2 May 1906, Martinez. This is Muir's first letter from home; It is not clear when he arrived in Martinez. There is little chance, however, that he was in Berkeley on Thursday, 26 April, the night the Jameses stayed with the Howisons. For George H. Howison see *DAB, ANB*.

41. Letter, Muir to Helen and Wanda Muir, 13 May 1906, Martinez, of Keith. Letter, Muir to Helen and Wanda Muir, 3 June 1906, Martinez. Mary-Ellen Jones, "Spokesman for a Vanished Era," *Bancroftiana*, August 1936, 10-11. Hughes, 301, for Louise Keeler. Charles Keeler, *The Simple Home* (Salt Lake City: Peregrine Smith, 1979), a reprint of the first edition (San Francisco: Paul Elder, 1904) with an introduction by Dimitri Shipounoff and photographs of the Keeler home and of others of similar style. The Keelers lived in this home from 1895 to 1907. After Louise died on 5 February 1907 at age thirty-five, Charles Keeler and family moved to his mother-in-law's at 2727 Dwight Way. Keeler also designed and built a cottage studio on El Camino Real in Claremont Hills, Berkeley (1907); see photos opposite pages xxxiii (exterior) and xlv (interior). After the 1923 Berkeley fire destroyed many wooden homes, Maybeck replaced the Keelers's shingles with stucco, and made other interior and exterior changes for the new owners. Charles died on 31 July 1937, at age sixty-five.

Leslie Mandelson Freudenheim and Elisabeth Sussman, *Building with Nature: Roots of the San Francisco Bay Region Tradition* (Santa Barbara and Salt Lake City: Peregrine Smith, 1974), discusses "Bernard Maybeck and Charles Keeler: Development of the Simple Home," 42-53, with exterior and interior illustrations of the Keeler house and studio, and the role of the Hillside Club, which Keeler founded in 1898, in Berkeley's environment, 55-75; the Faculty Club is shown on p. 82. See also Cerny, *Berkeley Landmarks*, 246, "Charles Keeler House & Studio"; 239 (photo of Keith, Keeler, and Muir in Berkeley Hills, 1909); 233, John Muir School (1915), 2955 Claremont Avenue, is not far from Keeler's Claremont Hills studio. A color photograph of Keeler's 1902 studio in Richard Sexton, *The Cottage Book* (San

Francisco: Chronicle Books, 1989), 88, shows its steep gables with tall brick chimney.

42. Wilson N. Stewart and Gar W. Rothwell, *Paleobotany and the Evolution of Plants* (1983; New York: Cambridge University Press, 1993), *Sigillaria*, 145 (illustration), ff; *Lepidodendron*, 127 (illustration), ff. My thanks to Petrified Forest National Park. Paul Russell Cutright, *Theodore Roosevelt: The Making of a Conservationist* (University of Illinois Press, 1985), 225-6.

43. Letter, Muir to Helen Muir, 10 June 1906, Martinez, relates his Stanford visit. "Founder's Day" in Scott, "William James & Stanford University: 1906," 32. "Stanford's Ideal Destiny," in William James, *Essays, Comments, and Reviews* (Harvard University Press, 1987), 102-6. Professor Anderson (1851-1933) also delivered an address with James on 9 March. In the spring of 1895 Anderson bicycled to Martinez to see Muir; Letters, Melville Best Anderson to Muir, 30 May 1895, Leland Stanford Junior University, and Muir to Anderson, 23 June 1895, Martinez; Anderson to Muir, 25 June 1895, for his itinerary after being with Muir. *Who Was Who in America* I:24. Professor Rolfe (1858-1945), who was born in Dorchester, Massachusetts, and educated at Amherst College, offered to obtain paleobotany books from Harvard and the Library of Congress for Muir, who declined, pleading enough to read already. Letters, Rolfe to Muir, 5 July 1906, Stanford University; Muir to Charles Keeler, 12 July 1906, Adamana, Arizona. *Who Was Who in America* IV:807. *Amherst College Biographical Record.* Although William James recorded his contacts in his diary for 1906, he does not mention Muir.

44. Muir to Helen Muir, 17 June 1906, Martinez, for expected dates of departure and arrival. Wanda Muir to Muir, 9 July 1906, Crocker's Station, Sequoia, California, for their itinerary.

45. Had the Adirondack Mountain Club and the Harvard Mountain Club been in existence—they were founded in 1922 and 1925, respectively—James might have joined them.

46. *CWJ* 7: 188-9, 193-4, 196. William James, "A Charming North Carolina Resort (1891)," in *Essays, Comments, and Reviews* , 133-5. James wrote this in Chocorua, New Hampshire, the end of August; it appeared in the *New York Evening Post*, 3 September 1891. Jennifer Bauer Wilson, *Roan Mountain: A Passage of Time* (Winston-Salem, North Carolina: John F. Blair, 1991) for Cloudland, Johnson City and Cranberry Railroad, Cloudland and Roan Mountain Station, 88-92, passim. For Hugh MacRae (1865-1951), see William S. Powell, ed., *Dictionary of North Carolina Biography* (University of North Carolina Press, 1991), 4:191-2.
James returned to North Carolina on 13 June 1894 accompanied by Charles Atkinson. Staying in Blowing Rock, they endured heat, drought, and frosted rhododendron blossoms. In Linville, they climbed Grandfather Mountain on Friday the 22nd—the only ascent he noted—before leaving Cranberry on Saturday the 23rd for Cambridge. *CWJ* 7: 516-20.

47. Sargent too had been in the mountains of the Carolinas, in 1886, in search of *Shortia galacifolia*, the same plant that had brought Asa Gray to Roan and Grandfather mountains in 1841. Ashton Chapman, "The Search for the 'Lost' Shortia," *Audubon*, May/June 1956, 113-15, 127.

48. Letter, Muir to Louie Muir, 25 September 1898, Cloudland, North Carolina. JMJ, 24 September 1898.

49. Letter, Muir to Helen Muir, 26 September 1898, Lenoir, North Carolina. A page and a half of Muir's journal contains his drawing, "From Grandfather Looking W[est]." He skipped ahead to make this sketch, for the other half page relates the events of 6 October. He also collected an aster and sand myrtle from Grandfather Mountain, and pressed these into *The Balsam Groves of the Grandfather Mountain: A Tale of the Western North Carolina Mountains* by Shepherd M. Dugger (Banner Elk, North Carolina: Shepherd M. Dugger, 1892), along with seventeen other plants. He also wrote in this book (which is in Muir's

library at the HASC; the plant specimens are now saved separately) the name of the plant and its location in six instances, and in five instances just the location, Roan Mountain. No other Muir comments appear, not even his usual index. It is inscribed "With Compliments of Linville Imp Co., H.P.K.", apparently the gift of Harlan P. Kelsey of the Linville Improvement Company. For Shepherd M. Dugger (1854-1938) see William S. Powell, ed., *Dictionary of North Carolina Biography* (University of North Carolina Press, 1986), 2:115, and Leslie Banner Cottingham and Carol Lowe Timblin, *The Bard of Ottaray: The Life, Letters and Documents of Shepherd Monroe Dugger* (Banner Elk, North Carolina: Puddingstone Press, 1979).

50. Melville B. Anderson, "The Conversation of John Muir," *The American Museum Journal*, March 1915, 119. Linnie Marsh Wolfe also related this anecdote, quoting from Anderson, as I have, but changing his "man" to "mon" and putting from "Come" to the end in quotations, *Son of the Wilderness*, 277-8.

When I arrived at Grandfather Mountain in late September 1994, there was no memory of Muir to be found. Highway signs celebrated the botanical explorations of Andre Michaux in 1794 and Asa Gray in 1842, but no one knew of Muir's presence, not even the owner of Grandfather Mountain, Hugh Morton.

A tall, handsome, generous aristocrat, Morton was born in Wilmington, North Carolina, in 1923. Since childhood continual summer visits have nurtured his intimacy with his mountain. Only World War II separated them. "I went over as a still photographer," he spoke of his service. "Then I learned that one of the movie people had been taken out of action."

"Morton, you look like a movie man," his captain assessed him.

"I do, Sir?" Morton, equivocal, shivered.

"Yes, you do." The captain assured him.

"From that point on I was a movie man," Morton smiled.

Until the Japanese wounded him on Luzon in the Philippines. He recovered and went on to climb and photograph mountains all over the world—Cook in New Zealand, Matterhorn in Switzerland, McKinley in Alaska. Now surgery on both knees keeps him on level ground. A devoted conservationist, he put Grandfather Mountain in an International Biosphere Reserve and served on the Board of Directors of North Carolina's Environmental Defense Fund. Each summer, he hosts the Highland Games and Scottish Clans.

At the death of his maternal grandfather, Hugh MacRae, in 1951, Morton inherited the mountain. I asked Morton if MacRae might have met Muir in September 1898, as he had James seven years earlier. "I don't recall any reference by him to John Muir," he said, "It could have happened." The Hugh MacRae Papers in the Special Collections Library of Duke University reveal no evidence of their meeting, nor MacRae's whereabouts in late September 1898. Thank you to William R. Erwin, Jr., Senior Reference Librarian, for checking this.

Morton and I discussed possible routes for Muir. Coming from the west, Muir likely passed through Linville and came up the hill, now Route 221, to the entrance, from where a carriage road ascended Grandfather Mountain as far as Cliffside. A path, overgrown in 1994, led from Cliffside to Linville Peak (5,280 feet), the first of several peaks on this ridge. To reach the highest, Calloway (5,964 feet), Muir would have followed Grandfather Mountain Trail for 2.3 miles over MacRae (5,939 feet) and Attic Window (5,949 feet) peaks—a challenging path, up several steep faces (which now have ladders), requiring at least two hours one way. Morton doubted that Muir had time in his day, which also included travel from Roan to Blowing Rock (about 38 miles), to attain the summit.

I am grateful to Hugh Morton for his introduction to Grandfather Mountain and for his allowing me to camp at 4,200 feet on 29 and 30 September 1994, where on the first night a black bear visited me.

51. JMJ, 26 September 1898.

52. JMJ, 27-29 September 1898. Letters, Cathleen Baldwin, Biltmore Estate, Asheville, North Carolina, to J. Parker Huber, 14 and 27 October 1994 and 3 February 1995, convey copy of Guest Book, whereabouts of the Vanderbilts, and Muir books in the Vanderbilt Library. *Guest Guide, Biltmore Estate, Centennial 1895-1995*. I am grateful to William A. V. Cecil for his free admission to the Biltmore Estate on 2 October 1994. George W. Vanderbilt (1862-1914) is in *DAB* and *ANB*, S.1.

53. *CWJ* 10:224-7, 230 passim. Letter, Muir to Louie Muir, 30 September 1898, Knoxville, Tennessee.

54. Letters, Muir to Walter Page, 9 May 1905, Martinez, California; Water Page to Muir, 21 December 1905, Englewood, New Jersey—his belated thank-you.

   In 1899 Page joined the new publishing house of Doubleday, Page and Company in New York. The next year he founded *The World's Work*, of which he was editor until 1913. *DAB*, *ANB*. B. J. Hendrick, *The Life and Letters of Walter H. Page* (New York: Doubleday, Page, 1922-1925), 3 volumes. B. J. Hendrick, *The Training of an American: The Earlier Life and Letters of Walter H. Page, 1855-1913* (Houghton Mifflin, 1928) contains four of his letters to Muir, 305-307. Walter H. Page, *A Publisher's Confession* (Doubleday, Page, 1923) does not mention Muir. Ellen B. Ballou, *The Building of the House: Houghton Mifflin's Formative Years* (Houghton Mifflin, 1970), 457, views Muir in the *Atlantic* as "[o]ne of Page's singular triumphs."

55. JMJ, 27 October 1898. *A Thousand-Mile Walk to the Gulf*, 186. Letter, Muir to Louie Muir, 1 June 1893, New York. T. Mitchell Prudden, "Some Records of the Ice Age About New York," *Harper's*, September 1894, 593-600, with pictures of glacial features in Central Park, 593, 595, and 597, appeared the year after Muir was in Central Park and may have been read by Muir.

## TRIP THREE: 1898
## CHAPTER 13—THE BERKSHIRES

1. JMJ, 29 October 1898.

2. *L&L* II:265. Robert Underwood Johnson in *Remembered Yesterdays* (Little, Brown, 1923), 88, described Gilder. Arthur John, *The Best Years of the Century: Richard Watson Gilder, Scribner's Monthly, and The Century Magazine, 1870-1909* (University of Illinois Press, 1981). *DAB* and *ANB*.

3. I made my reconnaissance on 18 June 1989. The Berkshire Scenic Railway moved to Lenox and no longer comes to Lee. It is rumored that Lee's railroad station was the creation of New York architect and Gilder friend Stanford White, but I cannot substantiate this. It is not on the "List of Works of McKim, Mead and White" in Charles Moore, *The Life and Times of Charles Follen McKim* (Houghton Mifflin, 1929), 338-48. Perhaps the builder Thomas Heaphy was the architect too.

4. Helena de Kay Gilder (1846-1916) is in Peter Hastings Falk, ed., *Who Was Who in American Art* (Sound View Press, 1985), 232. Winslow Homer painted her portrait in 1871-1872, when they had studios in the Tenth Street Studio Building In New York. They were close friends, if not intimate, at this time. See Nicolai Cikovski, Jr. and Franklin Kelly, *Winslow Homer* (National Gallery of Art and Yale University Press, 1995), 122-23; Elizabeth Johns, *Winslow Homer: The Nature of Observation* (University of California Press, 2002), 66-67, 81. In 1897, her younger brother, the poet and art critic, Charles de Kay (1848-1935) returned from three

years as U. S. consul-general in Berlin; see *National Cyclopedia of American Biography* (New York: James T. White, 1897), 9:206 and *Who Was Who in America* I:311.

Helen Maria Fiske Hunt Jackson may have the longest name in the *DAB*; shortened to Helen Hunt Jackson in *ANB*. Ruth Odell, *Helen Hunt Jackson* (H.H.) (New York: D. Appleton-Century, 1939), 86, "Midway"; 113, Gilders. Kate Phillips, *Helen Hunt Jackson*, 124-26, and *JMN* 16:104-05, for meetings with Emerson and his praise of her poetry. Biographers of Emerson do not mention Jackson. Much of her oeuvre is still in print: *Poems, Ramona, A Century of Dishonor, Saxe Holm's Stories, Mercy Philbrick's Choice, Zeph.*

5. Fifteen of Jackson's sixteen California essays appeared in the *New York Independent* from 20 June to 28 November 1872; the final one, "My Day in the Wilderness," was in *Scribner's* of August 1873; these became the first part of her *Bits of Travel at Home* (Boston: Roberts Brothers, 1878). See Ruth Odell, *Helen Hunt Jackson (H.H.)* (New York: D. Appleton-Century, 1939), 120-28, California; 261-63, bibliography; Phillips, 164-68. How long Jackson spent in Yosemite Valley is not clear. Odell says she spent ten days, 126. I figure from her narrative at least nine days, counting the days of arrival and departure, but use Jackson's own declaration of eight days. John L. Murphy (1824?-1894), who never married, spent summers at his cabin on Tenaya Lake, where he served travelers, and winters in Mariposa. Murphy Creek is named for him. I am indebted to Linda Eade of the Yosemite Research Library, Yosemite, California, for information on him.

6. Helen Jackson, "A Burns Pilgrimage," *Glimpses of Three Coasts* (Boston: Roberts Brothers, 1886), 153-74. From Dumfries, Muir went north to Stirling and "through the Trossachs, to Oban[.] Thence to Edinburgh by Glasgow & next morning sailed from Leith to Norway." Letter, Muir to Dear Cousins, 8 August 1893, London.

7. *L&L* II: 197 & 200.

8. *L&L* II:202-3. Letters, Muir to Louie Muir, Alameda, California [11 August 1885] and Sissons Station, California [12 August 1885]. Bonnie Johanna Gisel, "'Go to the Mountains!'—Helen Hunt Jackson," *The John Muir Newsletter*, Winter 2002/03, 1, 5-10. Gisel dates Muir's attempted visit on 11 August; however, since his letter written at 5:30 A.M. on 11 August refers to his having been already to Jackson's, I use the previous day. Had Muir gained access, he would have found Jackson incommunicable. Kate Phillips says that Jackson was "seldom conscious" after 8 August, *Helen Hunt Jackson*, 273.

9. *JOM*, 368; JMJ, 29 October 1898. Letter, Lawrence Campbell to J. Parker Huber, 24 August 1989 [postmark], New York. Campbell died 30 June 1998 before completing his history of the Art Students League of New York. Marchal E. Landgren, *Years of Art: The Story of the Art Students League of New York* (New York: Robert M. McBride, 1940), 24. For the Manhattan Gilder residences see Maria Hornor Lansdale, "Life-Work and Homes of Richard Watson Gilder," *Century*, March 1911, 716-733. In fall 1909, they were intending to move to 24 Gramercy Park, which he and others had built, when he died. *DAB* and Marylin Bender, "Gramercy Park…" *New York Times*, 14 July 1968, 56. Helena Gilder died there on 28 May 1916, *New York Times*, 29 May 1916, 11. Carole Klein, *Gramercy Park: An American Bloomsbury* (Houghton Mifflin, 1987), 164-69, is also helpful.

10. *The Berkshire Hills: A WPA Guide* (1939; Northeastern University Press, 1987), 198.

11. Rosamond Gilder, ed., *Letters of Richard Watson Gilder* (Houghton Mifflin, 1916), 329.

12. Allan Nevins, *Grover Cleveland* (New York: Dodd, Mead, 1933), 311.

13. Richard Watson Gilder, *Grover Cleveland: A Record of Friendship* (The Century Company, 1910), 61. Cleveland arrived in Tyringham 3 July and left 12 September 1901 (he also stopped there on 26 June). Here he heard of the assassination of President William McKinley in Buffalo on 6 September 1901. He made no record of his Tyringham time. His diary, also on

microfilm, is in the Cleveland Papers in the Library of Congress. As far as I know Muir and Cleveland never met, nor can I find any correspondence between them. The latest biography, H. Paul Jeffers, *An Honest President: The Life and Presidencies of Grover Cleveland* (William Morrow, 2000), for "a general readership," does not discuss Tyringham.

14. Then at Four Brooks Farm, these quest books are now in the Gilder Papers, Rare Books and Manuscripts Division of the New York Public Library.

15. JMJ, 29 October 1898. Though Muir does not mention them by name, it is clear who they are by the process of elimination and from Dorothea Gilder's *Diary*, 1898-99, which I read at Four Brooks Farm. On 1 November she recorded the return of her father and mother and Francesca and Rosamond to their Manhattan home. Muir's journal puts them back in New York at 7:00 p.m. that Tuesday (He misdates this as 31 October; see also *L&L* II:312). If Muir's supper with Johnson that night included the Gilders, they may not have seen Dorothea until the next day.

Rosamond Gilder (1891-1986), who never married, lived in her mother's home at 24 Gramercy Park; she is in *ANB*, *Current Biography*, November 1945, 18-19, and the *1986 Current Biography Yearbook*, 633. Dorothea (1882-1920) married Dallas D. K. McGrew at 24 Gramercy Park, *New York Times*, 20 May 1916,11. Francesca (1888-1985) married Walter Walker Palmer (1882-1950) on 12 October 1922. He died while raking leaves at Four Brooks Farm, 28 October 1950, *New York Times*, 29 October 1950, 92. "He was one of the best loved, most distinguished, and most valuable members of the Harvard Medical Alumni Association," concluded the *Harvard Medical Alumni Bulletin*, January 1951, 58-9. See also *Amherst College Biographical Record, Class of 1905*, 358-59, and *Who Was Who in America* III:663. Rodman de Kay Gilder (1877-1953) is in *Harvard College Class of 1899: Twenty-Fifth Anniversary Report* (privately printed, University Press, Cambridge, 1924), 266-67, and *Fiftieth Anniversary Report of The Harvard Class of 1899* (privately printed, Cambridge, 1949), 329-31. George de Kay Gilder (1885-1931) is in *Harvard College Class of 1908: Twenty-Fifth Anniversary Report* (privately printed, Cosmos Press, Cambridge, 1933). I am indebted to Barclay Feather, Milton Academy archivist, for verifying his attendance there from 1897 to 1904.

16. JMJ, 29 October 1898.

17. R.L. Bates and J.A. Jackson, eds. *Glossary of Geology* (third edition; American Geological Institute, 1987), 129, defines *cobble*: "A term used in the NE U.S. for a rounded hill of moderate elevation." The most famous example is Bartholomew's Cobble, southwest of Tyringham in Ashley Falls, also owned by the Trustees of Reservations. *A Guide to the Properties of the Trustees of Reservations* (Beverly, Massachusetts: Trustees of Reservations, 1991), 14-15, 31. Christopher J. Lenney, *Sightseeking: Clues to the Landscape History of New England* (University Press of New England, 2003), 64-66, says "Cob(b) is a widespread English dialect word for the summit of a hill. He finds "twenty or so" cobbles between the Hudson and Connecticut rivers. Though my geologist friend Sherman M. Clebnik does not teach this term to his undergraduates at Eastern Connecticut State University, I rather fancy it.

18. JMJ, 29 October 1898.

19. *Poems and Inscriptons* (The Century Co., 1901), 10-16, "A Letter from the Farm." Gilder's inscribed copy is in Muir's Library at HASC; Muir indexed this poem and three others. This poem also appeared in *The Poems of Richard Watson Gilder* (Houghton Mifflin, 1908), 288-291, with some punctuation changes.

20. Letters, Richard Watson Gilder to Muir, 2 November 1899, New York, and Muir to Gilder, 14 November 1899, Martinez.

21. James D. Hart, ed., *The Oxford Companion to American Literature* (fifth edition, Oxford University Press, 1983), 281. This also includes Muir, 514-15. Richard Watson Gilder, *The New Day: A Poem in Songs and Sonnets* (The Century Company, 1885, 1887), fourth edition, is in Muir's Library at HASC. Helena de Kay Gilder drew fifteen illustrations to accompany text.

22. The authority on Cecilia Beaux (1855-1942) is Tara L. Tappert, formerly Curatorial Assistant, Painting and Sculpture, National Portrait Gallery (NPG), Smithsonian Institution, Washington, D.C. She wrote her dissertation on Beaux in the American Studies Program of George Washington University and "Cecilia Beaux: A Career as a Portraitist," *Women's Studies*, 1988, 389-411. She curated NPG's Beaux exhibit (6 October 1995-28 January 1996) and wrote the catalog *Cecilia Beaux and the Art of Portraiture* (Smithsonian Institution, 1995). This shows Dorothea and Francesca (1898), pl. 15, p. 54-5, Richard Watson Gilder (1902-1903), pl.23, p.88-9, and *Les derniers jours d'enfance*, pl. 1, p.12-13. Beaux also painted a portrait of the grieving widow Helena de Kay Gilder in 19ll, see 108-09.

Beaux taught at the Pennsylvania Academy for twenty years, 1895-1915. In 1905, she built "Green Alley" on Eastern Point in Gloucester, Massachusetts, which still serves as a private residence, and lived there from May to December, the rest of the year in New York. Hildegarde Hawthorne describes Green Alley in "A Garden of the Heart," *Century*, August 1910, 581-87. Her niece Catherine Drinker Bowen gives insight into Beaux's character in *Family Portrait* (Little, Brown, 1970).

23. Cecilia Beaux, *Background with Figures: Autobiography of Cecilia Beaux* (Houghton Mifflin, 1930), 208-10, 217-18.

24. For George F. Gilder (1939-) see *Current Biography Yearbook 1981*, 166-69; *Contemporary Authors*, NRS (2002) 102:222-26.

25. Eloise Myers, *Tyringham: A Hinterland Settlement* (1963; Hinterland Press, 1989), 79-89. Cornelia Brooke Gilder, *Views of the Valley: Tyringham, 1739-1989* (Hop Brook Community Club, 1989), 134-39. The Historic District Inventory in the History Room of the Tyringham Library was also helpful. Catalogs of garden seeds raised and sold by the United Society, Hancock.

26. *ETE Letters* I:74. Baker, 352.

27. Henry D. Thoreau, *Journal, Volume 1: 1837-1844* (Princeton University Press, 1981), 277, 3 March 1841. Thoreau uses a variant spelling of "batchelor's" that Elizabeth H. Witherell kindly let me see in his own handwriting.

28. Letter, Mark Twain to Richard Watson Gilder, 7 June 1904, in Albert Bigelow Paine, *Mark Twain* (1912; Chelsea House, 1980), III:1221. Clara's 1903 visit is in Herbert F. Smith, *Richard Watson Gilder* (Twayne, 1970), 124.

29. Splendid photographs of Gilder and Twain appeared on the front page of *Berkshire Resort Topics*, 13 August 1904, and of Twain and Prosper on page two.

30. *DAB* and *ANB*. Alan and Mary Simpson with Ralph Connor, *Jean Webster: Storyteller* (Poughkeepsie, New York: Tymor Associates, 1984) is in the Tyringham and Smith College libraries. The Clarence White photograph is the frontispiece of her biography. White also did Richard Watson Gilder's portrait; see Peter C. Bunnell, *Clarence H. White: The Reverence for Beauty* (Athens, Ohio: Ohio University Gallery of Fine Art, 1986), 67 and 79 (Though dated c.1912, this would have been taken earlier since Gilder died in 1909).

31. George W. E. Russell, coll., *Letters of Matthew Arnold* (MacMillan, 1895), II:398.

32. Letter, Muir to Helen Muir, 31 August 1893, London, for Muir's visit to Kew. [Author

unknown] *Royal Gardens, Kew: Official Guide to the Royal Botanic Gardens and Arboretum* (Her Majesty's Stationery Office, 1885). Muir also saw them in London's parks. A. D. Webster, *London Trees* (London: Swarthmore Press, 1920), 53-8. I am indebted to Couig Brough, Enquiries Librarian of Kew Gardens, for these references. Forester Oscar P. Stone told me that I would have to be a "dendrologist with book in hand" to know the difference between the American and English elms. Both varieties, Stone said, succumbed to Dutch Elm disease. Thomas J. Campanella, "Henry David Thoreau and the Yankee Elm," *Arnoldia* 61 (No.2, 2001), 26-31.

33. *New York Times*, Sunday, 30 October 1898, front page.

34. Letter, Muir to Helen Muir, 1 November 1898, Tyringham. Muir misdated this letter, for on 1 November he was in New York. Part of this letter is in *L&L* II:312, where the addressee is given incorrectly as Wanda Muir.

35. Letter, Robert Underwood Johnson to Muir, 12 October 1895, Stockbridge, Massachusetts. As Johnson also alerted Muir to two articles, "Bryant and the Berkshire Hills" by Arthur Lawrence and "Reminiscences of Literary Berkshire" by Henry Dwight Sedgwick in the *Century* for July and August 1895, 368-75 and 552-68, respectively, Muir already had some background on this region.

The Choate library at Naumkeag comprises over two thousand volumes, but none of them are by Muir.

36. Henry C. Sturges, comp., *Chronologies of the Life and Writings of William Cullen Bryant* (1903; Burt Franklin, 1968), 1xviii, indicates that "Monument Mountain" was published 15 September 1824. *The Poetical Works of William Cullen Bryant* (D. Appleton, 1913), 63-66, contains the poem. Claude M. Simpson, ed., *Nathaniel Hawthorne: The American Notebooks* (Ohio State University Press, 1972), 295.

Asher B. Durand's *Monument Mountain, Berkshires*, c.1855-1860, is in the Detroit Institute of Arts, Detroit, Michigan. His *Scene among the Berkshire Hills*, 1872, is in the New Jersey State Museum, Trenton. These are in David B. Lawall, *Asher B. Durand: A Documentary Catalogue of the Narrative and Landscape Paintings* (Garland Publishing, 1978), fig. 151, cat. 287, p. 149 and fig. 158, cat. 299, p. 162, respectively; and in Maureen Johnson Hickey and William T. Oedel, *A Return to Arcadia: Nineteenth Century Berkshire County Landscapes* (Pittsfield, Massachusetts: Berkshire Museum, 1990), fig.9, p. 43 and cat. 26, p. 37. 51, respectively. See also John Durand, *The Life and Times of A. B. Durand* (C. Scribner's Sons, 1894), 178, 184.

37. As quoted in Karson, 283.

38. *L&L* II:314.

39. For the Gilders in London, see Edward Sandford Martin, *The Life of Joseph Hodges Choate* (Charles Scribner's Sons, 1927), 116. President McKinley visited Naumkeag in September 1897. Muir's letters home of 8 and 12 June 1903 give his time in London.

40. JMJ, 31 October [1 November] 1898; Muir dates two days 31 October. Wolfe, 97. Letter, Muir to Jeanne Carr, 21 January 1866, in *Letters to a Friend*, 4.

41. On 28 January 1926, fire also destroyed the Tyringham rake shop. See Eloise Stedman Myers, "The Lowly Rake," *The Chronicle of the Early American Industries Association*, June 1957, 15-16, 19-20.

42. JMJ, 31 October 1898. Richmond Pearson Hobson, "The Sinking of the 'Merrimack'," *Century*, Part I: December 1898, 265-83; Part II: January 1899, 427-450, Part III: February 1899, 580-604; Part IV: March 1899, 752-779 (Beaux sketch, 753). *The Sinking of the Merrimack* (The Century Company, 1899). Review, *New York Times*, 22 April 1899, 260. *DAB, ANB* for Hobson.

43. Letter, Muir to John Burroughs, 14 December 1909. John Burroughs signed the Four Brooks Farm guest book on 9 August 1905 when he attended an afternoon tea there after the library dedication.

44. *Berkshire Eagle*, 30 November 1999, B2., Clark, and 26 July 1995, B, n.p., Palmer.

## TRIP FOUR: 1903
## CHAPTER 14—BOSTON

1. *L&L* II:409.

2. Fox, 125-26. *NYT*, 16, 17, 18, 19 May 1903, 2, 3, 1, 1, respectively. Morris, *Theodore Rex*, 32, 214-35, esp. 229-31. This, Roosevelt's first visit west of the Pacific slope, was part of his eight-week western tour by private train; the last car of six, *Elysian*, was the chief executive's and spared no luxury. No women were on board. In Yosemite, he ate "T-bones and broilers," Morris says, 237. The most detailed account of their visit, Morris says (651n230[1]), is William F. Kimes, "With Theodore Roosevelt and John Muir in Yosemite," in Westerners Los Angeles Corral, *Brand Book Fourteen* (Los Angeles, 1974), 189-204, 243(notes).

3. Interview with Edmund Morris on NPR, 27 November 2001, 7:40 A.M. EST.

4. Letter, Muir to Louie Muir, 25 May 1903, Brookline, Massachusetts.

5. Allen, 9. McAleer, 11-14.

6. Len Gougeon, "Emerson at 100," *Emerson Society Papers*, Spring 2003, 1, 6-7. *Boston Evening Transcript*, 23 May 1903, 4. The Society of American Authors, who gathered in the Astor Gallery of the Waldorf in Manhattan for dinner, also honored Emerson; see *New York Times*, 25 and 26 May 1903, 9 and 5, respectively.

7. "The Emerson Celebrations," *The Outlook*, 6 June 1903, 303. *Boston Globe*, 25 May 1903, 3 (Morning), Van Ness. *Boston Evening Transcript*, 25 May 1903, 3, gave a summary of the sermons.

8. Charles W. Eliot, "Emerson as Seer," *Atlantic*, June 1903, 844-55. Eliot's talk, *Boston Globe* (Morning), 25 May 1903, 3. See Len Gougeon, "Looking Backwards: Emerson in 1903," *Nineteenth-Century Prose*, Spring/Fall 2003, 50-73, for how Emerson appeared in the press, particularly Eliot's conservative view of Emerson.

9. Hamilton Wright Mabie, "Ralph Waldo Emerson in 1903," *Harper's*, May 1903, 903-8, and "Concord and Emerson," *The Outlook*, 2 May 1903, 18-29. "Our Inheritance in Emerson," *Century*, May 1903, 156-58. Thomas Wentworth Higginson, "The Personality of Emerson," *The Outlook*, 23 May 1903, 221-27; "Emerson as a Reformer," *Boston Daily Advertiser*, 23 May 1903, 9, 16; and "The Emerson Centenary," *Success*, May 1903, 288-89. William Dean Howells, "Impressions of Emerson," *Harper's Weekly Magazine*, 16 May 1903, 784; for Howells in Cambridge and Boston, see O'Connell, 74-91.

"The single most important part of Emerson's education was that provided by his aunt Mary Moody Emerson," says Robert D. Richardson Jr. in *Emerson: The Mind on Fire* (University of California Press, 1995), 23-8. Richardson cites her teaching "the necessity of doing what you are afraid to do" on p. 27. His discussion relied on the "incomparable knowledge of the subject" of Phyllis Cole, who has since published *Mary Moody Emerson and the Origins of Transcendentalism: A Family History* (Oxford University Press, 1998).

10. Concord, Massachusetts, Social Circle, *The Centenary of the Birth of Ralph Waldo Emerson* (Cambridge: Riverside Press, 1903). *Concord Enterprise*, 27 May 1903, 1 and 5 (An Emerson Edition of two pages of quotations was part of this paper for 20 May). TWHD, 25 May

1903. As of 13 May 1903, James had not begun writing his Emerson talk, though he had been reading Emerson, *CWJ* 10:244, 247. *Evening Boston Globe*, 25 May 1903, 5. *Boston Evening Transcript*, 25 May 1903, 1-2, reported the morning and afternoon exercises in Concord and reprinted the speeches of Senator Hoar, Samuel Hoar, Thomas Wentworth Higginson, and William James, but not that of Charles Eliot Norton. James's address is reprinted in William James, *Writings 1902-1910* (New York: Library of America, 1988), 1119-1125. Hugo Münsterberg, "Emerson the Philosopher," *Boston Evening Transcript*, 23 May 1903, 20. Münsterberg was the first of five speakers in Harvard's tribute, *Boston Evening Transcript*, 16 May 1903, 32. Keyes Diary, 25-27 May 1903.

Apparently, the cornerstone for Emerson Hall that was to be laid on 25 May was delayed; construction did not begin until the following spring. The dedication occurred on 27 December 1905, with Edward Waldo Emerson speaking on "Emerson and Scholars." His address is in the *Harvard Graduates Magazine*, 1905-1906, 383-91. See *Boston Globe*, 28 December 1905, and various news clippings in the Harvard University Archives (HUB 1361.2). William James was present, and the American Philosophical Association and the American Psychological Association held their annual meetings at Harvard then, *CWJ* 11:129.

11. Baker, 417-19.

12. Bliss Perry, *Park-Street Papers* (Houghton Mifflin, 1908), 4-5. "Suitings" refers to fabrics for making suits. *Saturday Review of Books and Art, New York Times*, 23 May 1903, 348, 352, and 353. The ad for "Books Published Today" on page 352 reverses "Addresses and Lectures" in the title of volume one.

13. *LRWE* 10:67-8. Fox, 6-7; Fox says that this is the first time Muir read Emerson's essays. Muir's copy of volume one of *The Prose Works of Ralph Waldo Emerson* (Boston: Fields, Osgood, 1870) is in the Beinecke Rare Book and Manuscript Library of Yale University. Muir's extensive index in the back, his commentary and marks of passages in the margins provide much grist for scholars. Muir turned to this book for his writing; see Limbaugh, 151 passim. John Muir, "The Forests of Yosemite Park," *Atlantic Monthly*, April 1900, 493-507, for his meeting of Emerson. A review of the Centenary Edition of Emerson appeared in "Books of the Day" of *Boston Evening Transcript*, 27 May 1903, 20.

14. Ellen B. Ballou, *The Building of the House: Houghton Mifflin's Formative Years* (Houghton Mifflin, 1970), 488. My discussion of Bliss Perry relies on his memoir, *And Gladly Teach: Reminiscences* (Houghton Mifflin, 1935), especially his chapter on "The Atlantic Monthly," 176 (Muir), 186 (Emerson and Thoreau), 188-92 (Whitman); and Ellery Sedgwick, *A History of the Atlantic Monthly, 1857-1909: Yankee Humanism at High Tide and Ebb* (University of Massachusetts Press, 1994), 274-318. When Perry came in spring 1902 to lecture at the University of California, he missed Muir (letter, Bliss Perry to Muir, 18 September 1902, Boston; *And Gladly Teach*, 226.). He served as president of both clubs. *DAB*.

15. William L. Howarth, "Editing Thoreau's Journal: A Brief History of the 1906 Text," an undated typescript based on his partial transcription of the Houghton Mifflin letter books, 1903-1906, in the Houghton Library, Harvard University. "General Introduction," to *The Writings of Henry D. Thoreau, Journal, Volume 1: 1837-1844.* Edited by John C. Broderick, Elizabeth Hall Witherell, William L. Howarth, Robert Sattelmeyer, and Thomas Blanding (Princeton University Press, 1981), 585-9l. Bradford Torrey, "Introduction," to *The Writings of Henry David Thoreau* (Houghton Mifflin, 1906),VII: xix-Ii (Journal v.1). Muir's copy is in HASC.

16. Amelia Forbes Thomas, ed. *The Letters and Journals of Waldo Emerson Forbes* (Philadelphia: Dorrance, 1977), 153, 208, 275, 277, 305. These contain disappointingly little

about their editing of Emerson's journals. Waldo Emerson Forbes married his cousin Ellen Forbes of Milton, Massachusetts, on 20 January 1910; they had three children. He died 17 June 1917 at age thirty-eight. *Harvard College Class of 1902: Twenty-Fifth Anniversary Report, 1902-1927* (Cambridge: The University Press, 1927), 230-33.

17. Bliss Perry, *Emerson Today* (1931; Archon Books, 1969), 9, 104, 133 (quotes), passim.

18. *Emerson Centenary Services Program* in Joel Myerson, Introduction to the AMS Edition of *The Complete Works of Ralph Waldo Emerson* (New York: AMS Press, 1979), I:n.p. This includes the contract of 9 March 1903. *Boston Evening Transcript*, 25 May 1903, 9, gives names of dignitaries at Eliot's talk.

19. For *Silva*, see chapter 6. For California issue, letters, Bliss Perry to Muir, 18 September 1902, 6 January and 4 February 1903, Boston; Muir to Perry, 25 January 1903, Martinez. Perry midwifed Mary Austin's *Atlantic* articles into her first book *The Land of Little Rain* (Houghton Mifflin, 1903).

20. For assessments of *Thomas Hart Benton* and *Gouverneur Morris* see Morris, *The Rise of Theodore Roosevelt*, 331-35 and 378-81, respectively. Roosevelt's chapters 7-11 of *Morris*, Morris states, "are the best stretch of pure biography he ever wrote." Both books are reprinted consecutively in the National Edition of Theodore Roosevelt's *Works* edited by Hermann Hagedorn (Scribner's, 1926), 7: 1-233; 235-470. Ballou, *The Building of the House*, 539-42, for T. R. visit.

21. *Boston Globe*, 25 May 1903, 9.

22. Perry, *And Gladly Teach*, 176.

23. Letter, Muir to Louie Muir, 25 May 1903, Brookline, Massachusetts.

24. *CWJ* 10:251-52, to Frances Rollins Morse, 26 May [1903]; *CWJ* 3:234, to Henry James, 3 May 1903. *CWJ* 3:xxvii, Robert Dawidoff's discussion. Further musing, "Emerson 1905," *The Works of William James: Manuscript Essays and Notes*, ed. Frederick H. Burkhardt et al. (Harvard University Press, 1988).

25. *Boston Evening Transcript*, 27 May 1903, 1.

26. *NYT*, 21 May 1903, 2, for his surgery. John Muir, *Edward Henry Harriman* (Point Reyes, California: Coastal Parks Association, 1978), Foreword by W. Averell Harriman, passim. See Kimes 86, 129, and 133 for its publication history. Rudy Abramson, *Spanning the Century: The Life of W. Averell Harriman, 1891-1986* (New York: William Morrow, 1992), 67-70, Harriman Expedition; 679, Muir's biography of Harriman. I am indebted to Arthur M. Schlesinger Jr., himself a friend of Averell Harriman, for the latter reference. Professor Cohen sees a "fine distinction at best" between Harriman's philosophy of philanthropy and that of nature's destroyers; see Cohen, 334-35,

27. Letter, Muir to A. H. Sellers, 11 April 1900, Martinez, California.

28. Letter, Muir to Louie Muir, 29 May 1903, New York. *NYT*, 29 May 1903, 6. "At the Hotels"; The *Celtic* sailed at 7:30 a.m. Muir to Helen Muir, 11 June 1903, London, with ship's log. Morris, *Theodore Rex*, 236; 240-41.

## TRIP FIVE: 1911 AND 1912
## CHAPTER 15—BOSTON

1. Letter, Muir to Katharine Hooker, 24 May 1911, New York. See *JMLJ* for his journal of his journey to South America and Africa and for his time before and after this trip.

2. Richard F. Fleck, "A Note on John Muir and AMC," *Appalachia*, 15 June 1995, 181-82. Fleck's dates of 10 and 11 May 1911 are incorrect; Muir was in Washington, D.C. then. *Sunday Herald*, Boston, 21 May 1911, 8.

3. *Appalachia*, May 1899, 117. Letter, John Ritchie, Jr. to Muir, 1 February 1899, Boston. Ritchie was the AMC corresponding secretary. For example, Theodore S. Solomons, "The Grand Cañon of the Tuolumne," *Appalachia*, November 1896, 164-79, tells of Muir's being the first to travel through the canyon and shows a picture of the Muir Gorge, which was named for him in 1894. Muir, however, never wrote for this periodical, but was remembered in it: LeRoy Jeffers, "John Muir: An Appreciation," *Appalachia*, June 1919, 390-93. Jeffers, a librarian at the New York Public Library, member of the Sierra and American Alpine clubs, mountain climber, and conservationist, reviewed Muir books; see *Appalachia*, June 1915, 286-91; December 1915, 398-405; June 1916, 185-86. He died in an airplane accident near Wawona, California, 25 July 1926, at age forty-six; *Appalachia*, December 1926, 540-41.

4. Actually, it was the AMC's second meeting that voted to admit women as members; Watermans, 191.

5. *Boston Evening Transcript*, 10 May 1911,1, 2, 4,5; 12 May 1911, 1, funeral.

6. "Honors to John Muir," *Appalachia*, July 1911, 283-84; this misdates his talk as 21 April. That day Muir was eastward bound in a private car of William Herrin, a vice president of the Southern Pacific Railroad, having left Martinez at 9:30 p.m. on 20 April. John Ritchie, Jr., "John Muir Talks...," *Boston Evening Transcript*, 24 May 1911, 31.

7. For Badè's Hetch Hetchy talk, see *Boston Evening Transcript*, 8 January 1909, 14. *Appalachia*, July 1909, 95-96, mention. Badè continued to speak and write on behalf of Hetch Hetchy; see [William F. Badè], "Ignorant Vandalism," *The Independent*, 28 July 1910, 201-02; author is identified by letters of July and August 1910 in JMP. Badè knew the Sierra Nevada; see *Appalachia*, December 1915, 393. Francis P. Farquhar, "In Memoriam," *Appalachia*, June 1937, 414-15.

8. *JMLJ*, 8, 20, 28. Kimes, 88, 90.

## TRIP FIVE: 1911 AND 1912
## CHAPTER 16—NEW HAVEN

1. According to the New York City directory there were two Manhattan hotels then, at 201 East 34th Street and 19 East 42nd Street.

There were four women among the forty-five initial members in 1902: Fay Fuller and Mrs. Robert E. Peary of Washington, D.C.; Annie S. Peck of Providence, Rhode Island; and Mrs. Fanny Bullock Workman of London, England. Peck and Workman had substantial climbing records; Muir was recognized for his "Mountain and glacial studies in California and Alaska," not his ascents. See *American Alpine Club Constitution, Bylaws and Members* (American Alpine Club, 1902). Brief biography of Muir in *American Alpine Club Annals*, v.6, 1946-1947, 104-107. Alden Sampson, "A Talk by John Muir," *Sierra Club Bulletin*, v. XII, no.1, 1924, 43-46. This misquotes Muir as saying that Edward Emerson came with his father to Yosemite. Howard Palmer, "Early History of the American Alpine Club," *American Alpine Journal*, 1944, 163-96; Muir at 169, 176-77, 196.

H. P., "In Memoriam: Harrington Putnam, 1851-1937," *American Alpine Journal*, 1938, 203-6; According to this, Putnam was also a member of the AMC and Sierra Club, and served as president of the Fresh Air Club, an elite community of walkers based in New York. *Who Was Who in America*, I:1002.

Gifford Pinchot Diary, 17 June 1911, Library of Congress

2. William Lyon Phelps, *Autobiography with Letters* (Oxford University Press, 1939), 354-75. Diary of William Lyon Phelps, 19 June 1911, in Huron City Museums, Port Austin, Michigan.

3. JMJ 4[5] November 1898.

4. *L&L* II:365-66.

5. *NYT*, 20 and 21 June 1911, 10 and 7. Phelps Diary, 20 June 1911.

6. Letter, Muir to Mrs. [Charlotte] Kellogg, 4 February 1911, Los Angeles.

7. JB II:144-46. *JMLJ*, 25, Muir's photo.

8. Phelps, *Autobiography*, "Second Sabbatical," 514-21.

9. Phelps, *Autobiography*, xviii.

10. Letter, Muir to Helen Muir, 18 July 1908, Funston Camp.

11. Phelps, *Autobiography*, 494. Fox, *John Muir*, 134-36.

12. Phelps, *Autobiography*, 145.

13. Letters, Muir to William Kent, 14 January and 6 February 1908, Martinez. See Roderick Nash, *Wilderness and the American Mind* (1967; Yale University Press, 1973), 172-180, for Kent's gift and his later role in the Hetch Hetchy controversy when he represented California in Congress.

14. Letter, William Kent to Muir, 16 October 1908, Kentfield, Marin Co. [California].

15. Letters, Helen Muir to Muir, 21 and 27 August 1908, Daggett, California. In the latter, Helen enclosed "three snapshots" of her father with the Van Dykes; John, she said, left "about a week ago." Muir's copy of John C. Van Dyke's *The Desert: Further Studies in Natural Appearances* (Charles Scribner's Sons, 1901) is in HASC; it contains Muir's marks in margins and in the back his index of seventeen items, of which "color" most fascinated him. *The Autobiography of John C. Van Dyke: A Personal Narrative of American Life, 1861-1931*, edited by Peter Wild (University of Utah Press, 1993), 167-8, refers to their meeting without dating it (247n4). Professor Wild implies that Muir had read *The Desert* by this time, therefore by August 1908. See also Peter Wild, "John Muir and the Desert Connection," *John Muir Newsletter*, Spring 1995, 2 and 6. Wild believes "That Van Dyke's famous book [*The Desert*] is largely make-believe," in "John C. Van Dyke" in *ANW* II:951-62 (958, quote).

16. *L&L* II:365-6. For Woodbridge and Woolsey Halls see *Buildings and Grounds of Yale University* (Yale University Press, 1979).

17. *NYT*, 21 June 1911, 7. *New Haven Evening Register*, 21 June 1911, 4. Letter, Anson Phelps Stokes, Jr., to Josiah Royce, 18 May 1911, Archives, Yale University Library. Julia Bristol, who was born on 5 February 1854 in Lockport, New York, married Eugene Bristol, treasurer of the Union Trust Company of New Haven, on 18 July 1903; she lived in this New Haven residence from her marriage until her death on 13 March 1943. (Arnold Guyot Dana Scrapbook, 60: 47-49, in the New Haven Colony Historical Society).

18. Letter, Secretary, Yale University [Anson Phelps Stokes, Jr.], to Muir, 13 May 1911, New Haven. On 18 April Secretary Stokes wrote Muir (and Royce) to inform him that the Yale Corporation had voted on 17 April to confer the degree on him.

19. *NYT*, 6 October 1909, 5; 7 October 1909, 3; 8 October 1909, 3; 9 October 1909, 5; 10

October 1909, 9, and "Galen Clark", 12 (This says Clark was born in Dublin, New Hampshire, in 1812. According to Shirley Sargent, *Galen Clark: Yosemite Guardian* (Sierra Club, 1964), 15, he was born near Shipton, Quebec, Canada, in 1814, and moved to Dublin in 1819.); 17 October 1909, Picture Section [4]. Letter, Muir to Mrs. [J. D.] Hooker and Marian, Martinez, 20 October 1909, for "the merriest man" quote. Muir's voting for Taft is in Wolfe, 337. Taft kept his wife informed by letters and telegrams, which are in the William Howard Taft Papers, Library of Congress, of which there is a Microfilm Edition. Judith Icke Anderson, *William Howard Taft: An Intimate History* (Norton, 1981) also informed my discussion of Taft. Henry F. Pringle in his biography, *The Life and Times of William Howard Taft* (New York: Farrar & Rinehart, 1939), omitted Muir and Yosemite. Lastly, do not miss Edmund Morris's descriptions of "Big Bill" Taft in *Theodore Rex*; for examples, "once he got under way, he had the ponderous momentum of an elephant" (308); and in another activity, Morris likens Taft to "a beached whale" (313). Taft preferred golf to politics, 534-35. Don Van Natta, Jr., *First Off the Tee: Presidential Hackers, Duffers, and Cheaters From Taft to Bush* (New York: PublicAffairs, 2003), 16, 117-33, assesses Taft's golf game as "atrocious." Yet he was the first presidential golfer, and a devoted one.

20. *New Haven Evening Register*, 22 June 1911, 1, 4, and 9, includes statements on honorary degree recipients and Taft's speech. *NYT* puts Taft's departure at 10:30.

21. Phelps Diary, 21 and 22 June 1911. In 1843, Sarah Porter (1813-1900) started Miss Porter's School in the village of her birth, Farmington, Connecticut, eight miles southwest of Hartford. Her brother Noah Porter, who at this time was pastor of the Second Congregational Church in Springfield, Massachsuetts, served as president of Yale (1871-1886) for three of Phelps's undergraduate years. See *DAB*, *ANB*, and *The Handbook of Private Schools* (Boston: Porter Sargent Publishers, 2001), 86-7, 1246. According to archivist Shirley Langhauser, Miss Porter's School did not hold formal commencement exercises in 1911. Had Phelps been in Farmington, Connecticut, he would have detrained in Hartford, not Springfield, twenty-three miles farther north. Since there was not another school of this name in Springfield at this time, it seems apparent that some kind of ceremony honoring the 1911 graduates was created in Springfield.

22. Letter, Muir to William Colby, 1 July 1911 [Garrison, New York].

23. Wolfe, 328.

24. *L&L* II:366-7. Henry Fairfield Osborn, "John Muir," *Sierra Club Bulletin*, January 1927, 29-32. Osborn included this tribute almost verbatim (omitting his naming of the cabin where Muir worked in Muir's honor) in Henry Fairfield Osborn, *Impressions of Great Naturalists: Reminiscences of Darwin, Huxley, Balfour, Cope and Others* (New York: Charles Scribner's Sons, 1924), 201-02. Osborn remembered Muir's coming on Friday, 21[23] June.

## TRIP FIVE: 1911 AND 1912

## CHAPTER 17—BOSTON

1. *NYT*, 4 April 1912, 13. For the Burroughs-Barrus relationship, see Edward J. Renehan, Jr., *John Burroughs: An American Naturalist* (Post Mills, Vermont: Chelsea Green Publishing, 1992), 216-20, who believed they had an affair. For commentary on this see review essay of David Schuyler, "Coming Home with John Burroughs," *New York History*, Winter 2003, 88-102, esp. 99-100.

2. *JB* II:408.

3. Possibly they conferred at the AMC, a suite of rooms on the tenth floor of the Tremont Building. The AMC moved to 5 Joy Street, which is still its home, in December 1922; John Ritchie, "Fifty Years of Progress," *Appalachia*, February 1926, 345. Gleason joined the AMC in 1901; *Appalachia*, May 1902, 121. Harding, 13. Letter, Allen Chamberlain to Frank Allen, Pigeon Cove, Massachusetts [undated, though text dates it to 1936, possibly 1937], Francis Allen Papers, Henley Library, Thoreau Institute, Lincoln, Massachusetts. For role of AMC, Chamberlain, and Gleason regarding Hetch Hetchy, see Jones, 101, 119-20, illustration 61.

4. Dale R. Schwie, "Herbert W. Gleason: A Photographer's Journey to Thoreau's World," *The Concord Saunterer*, 1999, 150-65. Letter, Herbert Gleason to Muir, 18 December 1907, Boston. This revises the account of Richard F. Fleck in *Henry Thoreau and John Muir among the Indians* (Archon Books, 1985), 24.

5. I await Dale R. Schwie's biography of Gleason for his travels in Alaska. Letters, Muir to Gleason, 7 May and 10 June 1912, Martinez; H.W. Gleason to Muir, 23 June 1914 [Boston] and 12 October [1914], San Francisco, for lectures and intended visit to Muir on 15 October. *Berkeley Daily Gazette*, 9 and 10 October 1914, lecture; this also identifies Gleason as a member of the Sierra Club.

6. Stephen Fox, "Massachusetts Contributions to National Forest Conservation," 272-73. *Who Was Who in America* III:147. Marjorie Hurd, *Appalachia*, December 1945, 522-23.

7. Larry Anderson, *Benton MacKaye: Conservationist, Planner, and Creator of the Appalachian Trail* (Johns Hopkins University Press, 2002), 56-7, 45, passim. Fox, *John Muir*, 210-12.

8. "Report of the Outing Committee, 1909 Outing," *Sierra Club Bulletin*, January 1910, 189. Muir's journal and July letters to Helen tell about this excursion. I cannot locate this Outing's roster of participants. Letter, Allen Chamberlain to John Muir, Hotel Stewart, San Francisco, Sunday [1 August 1909].

9. Allen Chamberlain, "Saving England's Scenery" and "The Saving of Scenery," *Boston Evening Transcript*, 7 July 1909, 17; 23 October 1909, 3:3.

10. Letters, Houghton Mifflin Company to John Muir, 22 May and 12 July, 1909, Boston, and John Muir's responses of 4 June and 12 August 1909.

11. Allen Chamberlain, "Nation Versus City," *Boston Evening Transcript*, 8 December 1909, 21. Michael Cohen, *History of the Sierra Club*, 25.

12. Allen Chamberlain, "Scenery as a National Asset," *The Outlook*, 28 May 1910, 157-69, mentions his participation with Muir in the 1909 Sierra Club Outing. Chamberlain's writings made books later: *Vacation Tramps in New England Highlands* (Houghton Mifflin, 1919), which begins with a Muir quote; *Beacon Hill: Its Ancient Pastures and Early Mansions* (Houghton Mifflin, 1925), *The Annals of the Grand Monadnock* (1936; Concord, New Hampshire: Society for the Protection of New Hampshire Forests, 1975), and *Pigeon Cove: Its Early Settlers and Their Farms* (1940; Rockport, Massachusetts: Sandy Bay Historical Society and Museums, 1999).

13. *Boston Weekly Transcript*, 25 March 1873, 2; the article is dated March 1872. Reprinted in Muir, *Rambles of a Botanist*, 29-39. In the introduction William F. Kimes says that this is Muir's fourth newspaper column. Kimes's dating of this ramble in the fall of 1872 is incorrect, as he himself knew; see Kimes, 6, and Wolfe, 156. One of his readers was Abba Woolson (see chapter 10). Muir's first publication was in the Boston *Recorder*, 21 December 1866, 1, according to Kimes, 1.

14. Allen Chamberlain, "John Muir's Tree Pilgrimage," *Boston Evening Transcript*, 13 April 1912, 3:3. I am indebted to Michael P. Branch for his location of this article; see *JMLJ*, 274-

75.

15. Herbert W. Gleason, "The John Muir Trail," *Appalachia*, November 1920, 36 and plates XII-XVII of six photographs on unnumbered pages.

16. Letter, Muir to Mr. and Mrs. [Edward T.] Parsons, 12 April 1912, New York.

17. Letter, Eleanor Wilbur Pomeroy to Muir, 1 August 1913, Boston.

18. Letters, Nelson F. Evans to Muir, 10 March and 13 June 1914, Philadelphia, and Muir to Evans, 4 April 1914, Martinez.

19. *Boston Evening Transcript*, 24 December 1914, 1. Twelve days later, Annie Fields died at her Charles Street home; *Boston Evening Transcript*, 5 January 1915, 1.

# Appreciations

*My thanksgiving is perpetual.*
—Thoreau to H.G.O. Blake,
6 December 1856

My rambles on the John Muir Trail over the supernal crest of the Sierra Nevada—in 1982 with Kirk Sinclair, co-teacher of a Muir seminar, and again in 1986 with British artist Tony Foster—prompted this question: Did Muir climb any mountains in the Northeast? Little did I know then that the inquiry into that simple question would lead to this book.

This journey began in the depths of New England winter. On the cold morning of 8 March 1989, I called the Tyringham Public Library, in the Berkshires of western Massachusetts, and reached the post office. Postmistress Irma Clark told me that the library had no phone, and that she served both places. I asked about Four Brooks Farm. Yes indeed, she knew its location and its owner, Gilder Palmer. "When he comes in for his mail today, I'll tell him you called," her merry voice rang off. My then accompanying Tony Foster while he painted in the Grand Canyon for the month of April delayed my arrival in Tyringham. So it was not until 24 May that I met Irma Clark and Gilder Palmer in Tyringham. Gilly, as he is called, graciously showed me his home, where John Muir had stayed in late October 1898.

From there, John Muir led me deeper into New England, to its landscapes—urban, rural, wild—and its people, mostly literary folks of the late nineteenth and early twentieth centuries. Along the way, my appreciation of my homeland blossomed. (Though born in Philadelphia, I was baptized in the salt water of Lynn, Massachusetts, in the summer of 1942. After living in Pennsylvania, Ohio, and Michigan, I came to New England in June 1972, and stayed.) Muir's association with a place deepened my experience of it. His past presence awakened my senses to what is there now. Much of the country, I found, still throbs with his spirit, and with that of the many connections Muir made there—with Thoreau and Emerson, and with Annie Fields and Sarah Orne Jewett, for instance.

Much of my time learning about Muir was spent inside—inside libraries; and inside books, letters, diaries, microfilm, the internet—searching for John Muir, his outer and inner life, his quotidian rounds, his relationships. Some of this felt empty; there was the absence of conversation with my subject and his friends, a longing for all that they could have revealed had we talked. Other moments were pregnant with the thrill of discovery. Reading in Muir's journal of his ascent of Mt. Mansfield in Vermont, for example, gave me the answer to my initial question.

I regret not knowing more about the women in Muir's life, including his wife. Two New Englanders, Elizabeth Keith and Abba Woolson, fascinated me and called for much more attention. The wives of the two men closest to Muir in the Northeast—Charles Sprague Sargent's Mary Robeson and Robert Underwood Johnson's Katharine McMahon—and of those of the other famous men he encountered, such as Thomas Wentworth Higginson's Mary Thacher and Richard Watson Gilder's Helena de Kay, invited further research. On the other hand, thank God for the "scholars [who] have worked to recover the reputations of many forgotten women writers," as Kate Phillips says at p. 32 in her splendid new biography of Helen Hunt Jackson, which has done just that. Rita K. Gollin has superbly achieved this, too, for Annie Adams Fields, as have Paula Blanchard for Sarah Orne Jewett and Bonnie Johanna Gisel for Jeanne C. Carr. It remains to be accomplished for other women.

I am grateful that Muir lived and cared enough for the natural and human worlds to honor, protect, and write about them. In fact, that passionate caring strikes me as his driving, defining characteristic, the one responsible for drawing me to him, and to this humble project. "Love was the well-spring of all his work," Edward Hoagland wrote in introducing the Modern Library's new edition of Muir's *Travels in Alaska.* "[W]hat a loving man Muir was," Professor Michael P. Branch exclaimed in his introduction to *John Muir's Last Journey.* And in response to one of the chapters in this book, singer-dancer-artist Elizabeth Starling of Prescott, Arizona, wrote to me on 12 July 2001: "I know how close to your heart John Muir's life experiences have been. And I get the feeling that your writing about him is an act of prayer." Indeed it is. For Muir's joy and rhapsody, his friendships, his love, I am deeply indebted.

This journey was made more joyous by the many wonderful people I met along the way, who have contributed to this study. *The Concord Saunterer* published "John Muir in Thoreau's Maine," Fall 1995, pp. 104-18; "John Muir and Thoreau's Cape Cod," Fall 1997, pp. 132-54; "Eight Hours: John Muir in Concord," 2000, pp. 102-25; and "John Muir and the Emerson Centennial," 2003, pp. 38-49, which, revised, have become chapters 10, 6, 1, and 14, respectively, of this book. I am grateful to *The Concord Saunterer* editors Ronald Wesley Hoag and Richard J. Schneider for their improvement of my work. "Intimacies of a New England Trip: John Muir's 1898 Excursion" appeared in *The John Muir Newletter,* Fall 1997, pp. 1, 3-5, under the editorship of Sally M. Miller. The late T.D. Seymour Bassett commented astutely on an earlier version of the Vermont chapter in 1993. Janene Ford of the Muir Archive at the University of the Pacific provided invaluable service over the years. Jennifer Irion drew the maps and created the cover in her Westminster West, Vermont, studio. Sarah Rabkin of Soquel, California, has ably read and edited the text, which enabled my rewriting with her insights for inspiration. The final editing was done by Archie Hobson of New Rochelle, New York. No one could have had finer editors. I accept full responsibility for any errors that remain. I am also grateful to Archie Hobson for having edited *The Cambridge Gazetteer of the United States and Canada: A Dictionary of Places* (Cambridge University Press, 1995), an indispensable treasure. Robert France of Green Frigate Press made the manuscript a book. Always eager to learn more, I would appreciate receiving your comments, additions, corrections at P.O. Box 360, Brattleboro, Vermont 05302.

In addition I wish to thank the following individuals and institutions for their generous and invaluable help with this study. My apologies for any omissions.

Nancy K. Anderson, Associate Curator, American and British Paintings, National Gallery of Art, Washington, D.C.

Ray Angelo, Cambridge, Massachusetts

The Bancroft Library, University of California, Berkeley, California—Bonnie Hardwick, Susan Snyder, Jessica Lemieux

David S. Barrington, Professor of Botany, University of Vermont, Burlington, Vermont

Betty Barto, Windham Historical Society, Windham, Maine

T. D. Seymour Bassett, Shelburne, Vermont

Randall H. Bennett, Bethel Historical Society, Bethel, Maine

Larry Berkson, Pittsfield Historical Society, Pittsfield, New Hampshire

David Blackburn, Chief of Interpretation, John Muir National Historic Site, Martinez, California

David J. Blow, Archivist, University of Vermont, Burlington, Vermont

Kathleen Brewster, Santa Barbara Historical Society, California

Brooks Memorial Library, Brattleboro, Vermont—Jennifer Ansart, Jerry Carbone, Rebecca Davis, Catherine Galvin, Therese Marcy, Richard Shuldiner, Jeanne Walsh, Debbie Tewksbury

Couig Brough, Enquiries Librarian, Royal Botanic Gardens, Kew, Richmond, Surrey, England

Sylvia Kennick Brown, Archives, Williams College, Williamstown, Massachusetts

Jean Cargill, Gray Herbarium Archives, The Botany Libraries of Harvard University, Cambridge, Massachusetts

William A.V. Cecil and Cathleen Baldwin, Biltmore Estate, Asheville, NorthCarolina

Sherman M. Clebnik, Professor of Earth and Physical Science, Eastern Connecticut State University, Willimantic, Connecticut

Jonathan Cobb, Executive Editor, Shearwater Books/Island Press, Tarrytown, New York

Constance J. Cooper, Manuscript Librarian, The Historical Society of Delaware, Wilmington, Delaware

Concord Free Public Library, Concord, Massachusetts—Marcia Moss, Joyce Woodman, Leslie Wilson

William Copeley, Librarian, Tuck Library, New Hampshire Historical Society, Concord, New Hampshire

James Cotter, Millbury, Massachusetts

Peter Crane, Mount Washington Observatory, North Conway, New Hampshire

Mary F. Daniels, Librarian, Special Collections, Frances Loeb Library, Graduate School of Design, Harvard University, Cambridge, Massachusetts

Kevin Dann, Woodstock, Vermont

Daniel A. deStefano, Director, Nahant Public Library, Nahant, Massachusetts

Nathalie Demers and Elizabeth Davidson, Librarians, Massachusetts Horticultural Society, Wellesley, Massachusetts

A. Hunter Dupree, Professor of History, Emeritus, Brown University, Providence, Rhode Island

Mary Durda, Wellesley Free Library, Wellesley, Massachusetts

Linda Eade, Yosemite Research Library, Yosemite, California

Ann Elliott, Bluffton Historical Preservation Society, Bluffton, South Carolina

Leslie Emmington, The Berkeley Architectural Heritage Association, Berkeley, California

Richard F. Fleck, Denver, Colorado

Albert J. von Frank, Washington State University, Pullman, Washington

Bradley E. Gernand, Senior Archivist, Manuscript Reading Room, The Library of Congress, Washington, D.C.

Bonnie Johanna Gisel, Curator, LeConte Lodge, Yosemite Valley, California (Summer 2004)

Joanne Gordon, Baxter Memorial Library, Gorham, Maine

Sharon Greule, Peru Library, Peru, Massachusetts

Susan Haas, The Society of California Pioneers, San Francisco, California

Harvard University Archives, Cambridge, Massachusetts—Brian A. Sullivan, Reference Archivist, and associates

Patricia Haslam, Genealogist, Stowe, Vermont

Beth Hinchliffe, Wellesley, Massachusetts

The Houghton Library, Harvard University, Cambridge, Massachusetts—Melanie Wisner, Jennie Rathbun

Janet R. Houghton, Curator, Marsh-Billings-Rockefeller National Historical Park, Woodstock, Vermont

Patti L. Houghton, Rauner Special Collections Library, Dartmouth College, Hanover, New Hampshire

David Hughes, Colgate University Libraries, Hamilton, New York

Francis W. Hunnewell, Dover, Massachusetts

The Huntington Library, San Marino, California—Alison Dinicola, Cathy Cherbosque, Alan Jutzi, Lisa Ann Libby, Lenora Shull

Stan Hutchinson, Sierra Madre, California

Lewis Hyde, Cambridge, Massachusetts

Dorothy Irving, Archivist, Keene Valley Library Association, Keene Valley, New York

Anita Israel, Archives, Longfellow National Historic Site, Cambridge, Massachusetts

Ronald Dale Karr, Branch Line Press, Pepperell, Massachusetts

Tevis Kimball and Kate Boyle, Special Collections, The Jones Library, Amherst, Massachusetts

Maymie B. Kimes, Santa Rosa, California

Kathy Kraft, Radcliffe Archives, Cambridge, Massachusetts

Caitlin Lewis, William E. Colby Memorial Library, Sierra Club, San Francisco, California

Ronald H. Limbaugh, Stockton, California

Linda B. MacIver, Reference Librarian, Social Sciences Department, Boston Public Library, Boston, Massachusetts

Karen Madsen, Editor, *Arnoldia*, The Arnold Arboretum of Harvard University, Jamaica Plain, Massachusetts

Mary McClintock, Concord, Massachusetts

Carrie L. McDade, Reference Specialist, Environmental Design Archives, College of Environmental Design, University of California, Berkeley, California.

Mary Anne McMillen, Director, Records Library, National Geographic Society, Washington, D.C.

Joseph J. Moldenhauer, Austin, Texas

Daryl Morrison, Head, and Janene E. Ford, Assistant Archivist, Holt-Atherton Department of Special Collections, University of the Pacific Libraries, Stockton, California

Hugh Morton, Linville, North Carolina

Kelly Murphy, Research Archivist, Starsmore Center for Local History, Colorado Springs Pioneers Musuem, Colorado Springs, Colorado

Clifford L. Muse Jr., Archivist, Howard University, Washington, D.C.

Hope B. Neilson, Director, Rice Public Library, Kittery, Maine

Laurel Nilsen, Wellesley Historical Society, Wellesley, Massachusetts

Peter E. Palmquist, Arcata, California

Allan E. Powell, Harvard Cooperative Society, Cambridge, Massachusetts

Maria Powers, Orchard House, Concord, Massachusetts

Ben Primer, Archivist, Princeton University, Princeton, New Jersey

Esther Proctor, Manchester Historical Society, Manchester-By-The-Sea, Massachusetts

Robert D. Richardson Jr., Hillsborough, North Carolina

Dean M. Rogers, Archives and Special Collections, Vassar College Libraries, Poughkeepsie, New York

Arthur and Elizabeth Schlesinger Library on the History of Women in America, Cambridge, Massachusetts—Wendy Thomas and Kendra Van Cleave

Calantha D. Sears, The Nahant Historical Society, Nahant, Massachusetts

Diane Shephard, Archivist/Librarian, Lynn Museum, Lynn, Massachusetts

Frances Skelton, Reference Librarian, The Whitney Library, New Haven Colony Historical Society, New Haven, Connecticut

Wilma R. Slaight, Archivist, Wellesley College, Wellesley, Massachusetts

Nadia S. Smith, Special Collections Librarian, University of Vermont, Burlington, Vermont

Amy Stempler, The University Archives, The George Washington University, Washington, D.C.

Oscar P. Stone, Marlboro, Vermont

Carla M. Summers, Department of Special Collections, George A. Smathers Libraries, University of Florida, Gainesville, Florida

Tara Leigh Tappert, Washington, D.C.

Judy Throm, Reference Services, Archives of American Art, Washington, D.C.

Robert Young, Archivist, Ernst Mayr Library, Museum of Comparative Zoology, Harvard University, Cambridge, Massachusetts

Cindy Todd, Bangor Public Library, Bangor, Maine

Mary White, Librarian, Marlboro College, Marlboro, Vermont

Richard E. Winslow III, Rye, New Hampshire

Elizabeth Hall Witherell, Editor-in-Chief, *The Writings of Henry D. Thoreau*, Founders Memorial Library, Northern Illinois University, DeKalb, Illinois

Yale University Library, Manuscripts and Archives, New Haven, Connecticut—Tom Hyry and Diane E. Kaplan

Peggy Zeigler, Library Volunteer, North Baker Research Library, California Historical Society, San Francisco, California

# PERMISSIONS

My great gratitude to the following sources for permission to quote from their materials.

## LIBRARIES, ASSOCIATIONS, INDIVIDUALS

The Baxter Memorial Library for the diary of James Phinney Baxter.

The Botany Libraries, Harvard University, for the letter of Cyrus Pringle to George E. Davenport of 13 November 1882.

The Library of Congress for the diary of Theodore Roosevelt and the diary of Gifford Pinchot.

Ralph Waldo Emerson Memorial Association for *The Letters of Ellen Tucker Emerson*, edited by Edith E.W. Gregg (1982).

The Houghton Library, Harvard University, for the diary of Thomas Wentworth Higginson (bMS AM 1162).

The Huntington Library for the letter of Charles Dudley Warner to Annie Adams Fields of 6 September 1893 (FI 4311).

Seeley G. Mudd Library, Princeton University, for the 1898 American literature syllabus of Professor Theodore Whitefield Hunt and the 1921 "Literary History of American Ideals" of Professor J. Duncan Spaeth.

John Muir Papers, Holt-Atherton Special Collections, University of the Pacific Libraries. Copyright 1984 Muir-Hanna Trust.

Joel Myerson for *The Journals of Louisa May Alcott* (Little Brown, 1989).

The Schlesinger Library, Harvard University, for the diary of Elizabeth Cary Agassiz.

The University of Vermont, Bailey/Howe Library, Special Collections, for Perkins Papers; and the Department of Botany and Agricultural Biochemistry, for Cyrus G. Pringle diary.

Wellesley College Archives for the notebook of Emma Condit.

## PUBLISHERS

Columbia University Press for *Poetry of the American West: A Columbia Anthology* by Alison Hawthorne Deming (1996) and *The Letters of Ralph Waldo Emerson*, eds. Ralph L. Rusk, vols. 1-6, and Eleanor M. Tilton, vols, 7-10 (1939-1995).

Cornell University Cooperative Extension for *The Holy Earth* by Liberty Hyde Bailey (1980).

Forest History Society for *The Conservation Diaries of Gifford Pinchot*, ed. Harold K. Steen (2001).

Houghton Mifflin for *The Life and Letters of John Muir* by W. F. Badè, *Winter Hours* by Mary Oliver (1999), and *River-Horse: The Logbook of a Boat across America* by William Least Heat-Moon (1999).

Indiana University Press for W. D. Howells, *Literary Friends and Acquaintance* eds. David F. Hiatt and Edwin H. Cady (1968).

Island Press for *Breaking New Ground* by Gifford Pinchot (1998).

Ohio State University Press for *Nathaniel Hawthorne: The Letters 1813-1843*, eds. Thomas Woodson, L. Neal Smith, Norman Holmes Pearson (1984), and *Nathaniel Hawthorne, The American Notebooks*, ed. Claude M. Simpson (1972).

Texas A&M University Press, *God's Wilds: John Muir's Vision of Nature* by Dennis C. Williams (2002).

The Thoreau Society for my articles in *The Concord Saunterer*.

University of California Press for *Helen Hunt Jackson: A Literary Life* by Kate Phillips (2003), *Mark Twain's Letters, Volume 2: 1867-1868*, eds. Harriet Elinor Smith, Richard Bucci, Lin Salamo, *Mark Twain's Letters, Volume 3:1869*, eds. Victor Fisher, Michael B. Frank, and Dahlia Armon, *Roughing It* by Mark Twain, eds. Harriet Elinor Smith, Edgar Marquess Branch (1993), *Mark Twain's Notebooks & Journals II (1877-1883)*, eds. Frederick Anderson, Lin Salamo, Bernard L. Stein (1975).

University of Washington Press for *George Perkins Marsh: Prophet of Conservation* by David Lowenthal (2000).

# INDEX

Exhaustively researched and deftly edited by Robert Lawrence France (Associate Professor, Harvard University Graduate School of Design, Cambridge, Massachusetts), *Profitably Soaked: Thoreau's Engagement With Water* compiles quotations by Henry David Thoreau from all of his many works, and arranged them under the headings 'Adventure,' 'Joy,' 'Contact,' and 'Contemplation.' Dwelling in particular on water as a medium that Thoreau used to immerse himself in nature and live life to the fullest, *Profitably Soaked* is an expressive and thoughtful collection that reveals a shining window into the life of a great writer and thinker. *Profitably Soaked* is a welcome and innovative contribution to Thoreau Studies reference collections and supplemental reading lists.

*Midwest Book Review*

As Robert France shows us in this exhilarating and thought-provoking book, Thoreau's visionary transcendentalism has its boots deep in the mud of experience; and it is this embodied vision that makes him so significant a seer for our dissociated times. Thoreau's deceptively gentle style belies a profound radicalism that invites us to cast off from our islands of imposed intellectual order and to immerse ourselves fully in nature's vitality and variety, inspiring us toward a fuller engagement with the natural world.

David Kidner, professor at Nottingham Trent University and author of *Nature and Psyche: Radical Environmentalism and the Politics of Subjectivity*

Thoreau knew that water can change the focus of the spirit. Thankfully, Robert France has perfectly captured and consolidated the Master's timeless work to bring Thoreau's essence alive. This handy volume can be opened and read at random while visiting Mother Earth's lifeblood, when we find the opportunity to connect with water, and be a part of its moments, whether it be a pond, river, or ocean. It is a collection of quotations that may offer surprise at the precise appropriateness of the casually chosen quotation. A reading from *Profitably Soaked* in the presence of water can spark a spiritual epiphany in ourselves, such as those that Thoreau himself sought and described with such commitment.

John Middendorf, professional river guide, international big wall climber, and equipment designer

Again I am impressed with how alive Thoreau was—and after one hundred and forty years—still is. How still and focused he could be. How much of his communion, recreation and travel involved being with ponds, lakes, rivers, and the ocean. How often wet he was! How in love with the world he was. And I thank Professor France's stimulating presentation, *Profitably Soaked*, for this gift.

J. Parker Huber, author of *The Wildest County: A Guide to Thoreau's Maine*

In terms of intervention, what knowledge, per chance would Thoreau have us bring to a cycle of culturally conditioned experience and the actions that arise from such conditioned states? And what knowledge would we descendents of Thoreau, the contemporary lovers of land and water, have to bring to the conscious construction of our sensibilities? My guess is that Thoreau would emphatically suggest knowledge born out of bodily experience with the natural world. In the present compilation of quotations, Thoreau charges us to walk, listen, look, and immerse ourselves. This is how we know. It is only with experience, with sincere immersion in the sensible world, that our bodies begin to know—and thus to inform our every step.

Laura Sewall, professor at Prescott College and author of *Sight and Sensibility. The Ecopsychology of Perception*

One would expect that an inveterate pondside dweller such as Henry Thoreau would have something to say about water. But who would have thought that he could be so ecstatic about the subject. And so eloquent. A fine assembly of Thoreau's thoughts.

John Hanson Mitchell, editor of *Sanctuary Magazine* and author of *Walking Towards Walden: A Pilgrimage in Search of Place*